20 00

69183

WATERGATE

WATER GATE

The Corruption and Fall of Richard Nixon

FRED EMERY

JONATHAN CAPE
LONDON

First published 1994

1 3 5 7 9 10 8 6 4 2

First published in the United Kingdom in 1994 by Jonathan Cape
Random House, 20 Vauxhall Bridge Road, London SW1V 2SA

Random House Australia (Pty) Limited
20 Alfred Street, Milsons Point, Sydney,
New South Wales 2061, Australia

Random House New Zealand Limited
18 Poland Road, Glenfield,
Auckland 10, New Zealand

Random House South Africa (Pty) Limited
PO Box 337, Bergvlei, South Africa

Random House UK Limited Reg. No. 954009

A CIP catalogue record for this book
is available from the British Library

ISBN 0-224-03694-7

Printed in Great Britain by Clays Ltd, St. Ives PLC

To Marianne

Contents

Acknowledgments

The idea of retelling the Watergate story for a new generation originated with the fall of another leader, Margaret Thatcher. It was while making a BBC-TV *Panorama* program in 1990 about the crisis that ousted the British prime minister that Phil Craig, a brilliant young producer, listening to my Watergate stories, said, "We have to tell it again." For his generation of thirty-somethings, Watergate loomed important, but as distant as the Napoleonic Wars.

Craig, who has now moved on to bigger things, took the idea to Brian Lapping Associates, which took it to the BBC and to the Discovery Channel. Viewers will now judge whether the series Lapping Associates has made for the twentieth anniversary of Richard Nixon's fall can repeat the success of its award-winning *The Second Russian Revolution.* I am indebted to Brian Lapping for his encouragement to write a fresh history of Watergate based on my own personal experience and research.

I was privileged as a foreign correspondent to come straight from reporting the Vietnam and Cambodia fighting to Washington and then spend seven years there, which included the bulk of the Nixon presidency. I owed the position to two outstanding foreign editors of *The Times* of London, Iverach McDonald and E. C. Hodgkin. The newspaper's editor, William Rees-Mogg, though at times alarmed by my Nixon coverage, still graciously maintained me in the post. At the time it was the best story a reporter could have.

Re-interviewing twenty years on, the moment I most cherish came in a long debriefing with H. R. Haldeman a few months before he died in 1993. In a passage not retained for the TV series he was explaining his long-held line that what he had been involved in was "political containment" of the scandal to the Watergate break-in alone, not a criminal cover-up of all the administration's offenses. He suddenly suggested my expression betrayed some skepticism. I tried explaining the difficulty I had with his distinction. He smiled and said winningly that it was a "concept I've never gotten across to anybody, including even my wife, who says 'I just don't understand what you're saying.' " He added: "My wife felt definitely that I had to be convicted . . . that I was better off not being pardoned . . . and I now believe she was right." This was not the Haldeman of the stereotype, and it was fine tribute to Jo, his wife of forty-four years.

Encouragement for the book came from a number of friends. From Johnnie Apple and David Brinkley I reached Ashbel Green of Knopf. Debbie Owen gave me sage advice and Peter Osnos, publisher of Times Books, had the courage to decide the book was a "go." En route I had a boost when John Tusa read the first couple of chapters; and Marianne Emery, my life's support, was ever wonderful in demanding the next chapter. She lived Watergate twice over.

I was blessed with Chuck Elliott of Jonathan Cape in London. As an editor he can have few peers: unfailingly encouraging, gifted with lucidity, and, as all who know him agree, a man of rare calm and quiet humor, a perfect foil to my (at times) frenetic approach.

People who have helped with the book at key stages are: Sarah Hume, a former BBC producer in Washington, D.C.; the expert staffs of the National Archives, both in the capital and at the Nixon Project in Alexandria, Virginia, in particular, Scott Parham; Jackie Andrews, Lisa Gartside, and Lisa Soverall at Brian Lapping Associates. I ask British readers to be forbearing with the American spellings used for publishing expediency: I have insisted on avoiding Americanisms incomprehensible outside the United States. All the conclusions and mistakes are my own.

Woodsyre, London
1994

Introduction

Watergate is a compelling story of botched government that in two years went from the implausible to the unthinkable—the first resignation in history of a U.S. president. If it was a self-destruct tragedy for Richard Nixon, for the American people it was a drawn-out ordeal that tested the robustness of democratic processes. Despite some alarms, institutions held steady, law was upheld, and a chastened republic survived.

Modern leaders have had their terms of office involuntarily terminated in a number of ways. In the Communist party of the former Soviet Union, Nikita Khrushchev was simply replaced by a secret politburo vote; in its dog days, Mikhail Gorbachev was deposed in a coup, restored, then found that the entity for which he was president, the USSR, had itself been dissolved, and he was left officeless. Equally firmly, British Prime Minister Margaret Thatcher, who had never lost a vote in Parliament and had won three elections, was, when her party feared she might lose the fourth, "persuaded" to step down—in what she has since reviled as an act of "treachery" by Cabinet colleagues.

In the United States, no living president had involuntarily given up office until the thirty-seventh president, Richard Nixon. He resigned two and a half years short of completing his second term rather than risk being removed from office by a congressional vote for impeachment.

Myth would have it that what Nixon's men did was no worse than their predecessors, except that they were caught. Or that Nixon, admittedly a difficult character, fell victim to the vicious partisanship of the opposition Democrats who controlled Congress. Like all myth, there is a core of truth. But the greater truth is that no president, least of all as powerful a man as Nixon, faces impeachment for purely partisan reasons or for misconduct on the level of bugging opponents. It was a pattern of malfeasance by him and his men that led to the damning—and bipartisan—vote in Congress. Had it not been for the defection of Republicans and pro-Nixon conservatives, he would have survived.

Watergate, the name of a luxury apartment-office complex by the banks of the Potomac River in Washington, D.C., came in the early 1970s to symbolize such an all-encompassing presidential scandal that, twenty years on, it has gone not just into the language but into many languages. The suffix "-gate" now routinely connotes government cover-up and almost invariably the corruption of power. But this, notwithstanding Iran-, Iraq-, and now Whitewater-, is still the mother of all "gates."

When five men hired by Nixon's election committee and equipped with electronic bugging devices were caught red-handed by police in the Democratic Party headquarters at the Watergate on June 17, 1972, it might have been only a "third-rate burglary attempt." But it was also the tip of an iceberg of lawless abuses of office on which the Nixon presidency was to founder.

Nixon felt trapped and therefore tried to cover up. He dared not turn on those involved because they were either close to him or had earlier been involved in secret illegal schemes done at his direction. To have risked unraveling the whole scandal, he and his men feared, might cost him reelection later that year. Ironically, the cover-up was probably unnecessary; the opposition candidate had so little support that Nixon, fresh from foreign policy triumphs, could probably have made a clean breast of Watergate and still been reelected. But Nixon, while claiming to have dared greatly, did not dare in small things. One of his own associates and speechwriters, William Safire, was even harder on him: "Those who invested their lives in the causes he shared will never forget that Nixon failed, not while daring greatly, but while lying meanly."

To protect himself and his closest lieutenants, the president ran a conspiracy in which his oath and his office were abused and justice obstructed. Two years later, he was found out, squealed on by accomplices, and most thoroughly convicted by the tapes of his own conversations, recorded secretly for his own use.

In the extraordinarily tense climate of war and superpower crises, Richard Nixon was a bold and far-thinking president. He ended America's role in the Vietnam War, reopened American relationships with China, laid the foundations for detente with Russia, and planted the seeds for a Middle East settlement. All of that heightens the tragedy of self-infliction that this complex man, so effective and visionary in high policy, should have as his epitaph: Watergate.

Cast of Characters

Spiro T. Agnew: vice president (1969–73); resigned after pleading nolo contendere (no contest) to a tax evasion charge.

Howard Baker: senator (R-TN); vice-chairman of the Senate Watergate Committee.

Alfred C. Baldwin: bugging lookout at the Watergate break-in who turned state's evidence.

Bernard L. Barker: leader of Cuban American teams for break-ins; served twelve months in jail.

Alexander P. Butterfield: deputy to H. R. (Bob) Haldeman (1969–73); first disclosed Nixon's taping system.

J. Fred Buzhardt, Jr.: Nixon's Watergate counsel.

John J. Caulfield: White House investigator (1969–72); author of the Sandwedge political intelligence plan.

Dwight L. Chapin: Nixon's appointments secretary (1969–73); served eight months in jail.

Charles W. Colson: special White House counsel (1970–73); served seven months in jail.

Archibald Cox: first Watergate special prosecutor.

Samuel Dash: chief counsel to the Senate Watergate Committee.

John W. Dean III: counsel to the president (1970–73); served four months in jail.

John Doar: special counsel to the House Judiciary Committee's impeachment inquiry.

John D. Ehrlichman: chief domestic policy adviser to the president (1969–73); served eighteen months in jail.

Sam J. Ervin: senator (D-NC); chairman of the Senate Watergate Committee.

Gerald R. Ford: House Republican minority leader; vice president; president who pardoned Nixon.

Leonard C. Garment: White House adviser (1969–74).

Virgilio R. Gonzalez: lockpick of the Watergate break-in; served fifteen months in jail.

L. Patrick Gray III: acting director of the FBI (1972–73), resigned; burned documents from E. Howard Hunt's safe.

Alexander M. Haig: White House chief of staff (1973–74).

H. R. (Bob) Haldeman: White House chief of staff (1969–73); served eighteen months in jail.

E. Howard Hunt, Jr.: longtime CIA clandestine officer; White House consultant; White House Plumber; member of the Fielding and Watergate break-in teams; served thirty-three months in jail.

Leon Jaworski: second Watergate special prosecutor.

Herbert W. Kalmbach: Nixon's personal lawyer; raised hush money; served six months in jail.

Henry A. Kissinger: national security adviser (1969–73); secretary of state (1973–77).

Richard G. Kleindienst: attorney general (1972–73); received a suspended one-month jail sentence.

Egil (Bud) Krogh, Jr.: deputy to John Ehrlichman; White House Plumber; served four and a half months in jail.

Frederick C. LaRue: chief adviser to John Mitchell; served five and a half months in jail.

G. Gordon Liddy: White House Plumber; counsel to reelection committee; led the Fielding and Watergate break-ins; served fifty-two months in jail.

James W. McCord, Jr.: longtime CIA security officer; bugging man; left tape on the door in the Watergate break-in; wrote a letter implicating higher-ups; served four months in jail.

Jeb Stuart Magruder: deputy director of the 1972 reelection campaign; served seven months in jail.

Robert C. Mardian: assistant attorney general (1969–72); his conviction at the main Watergate trial was later quashed.

Eugenio Rolando Martinez: CIA anti-Castro boat captain; member of the Fielding and Watergate break-in teams; served fifteen months in jail.

John N. Mitchell: attorney general (1969–72); director of the 1972 reelection campaign; served nineteen months in jail.

Richard M. Nixon: president (1969–74); resigned from office and accepted a pardon.

Lawrence F. O'Brien: chairman, Democratic National Committee.

Paul L. O'Brien: lawyer for the reelection committee.

Kenneth W. Parkinson: lawyer for the reelection committee; acquitted at the main Watergate trial.

Henry E. Petersen: assistant attorney general in charge of prosecutions.

Herbert L. (Bart) Porter: assistant to Jeb Stuart Magruder; served thirty days in jail.

Elliot L. Richardson: attorney general (1973); appointed Archibald Cox as Watergate special prosecutor; resigned when ordered to fire him.

Peter W. Rodino, Jr.: congressman (D-NJ); chairman of the House Judiciary Committee.

Donald H. Segretti: Nixon campaign dirty trickster and saboteur; served four and a half months in jail.

Earl J. Silbert: assistant U.S. attorney; prosecuted the first Watergate case and trial.

John J. Sirica: chief judge, U.S. District Court for the District of Columbia; presided over the Watergate break-in and cover-up trials and Nixon tapes litigation.

Hugh W. Sloan, Jr.: treasurer of the reelection committee.

Maurice H. Stans: secretary of commerce (1969–72); finance chairman of the reelection committee; fined $150,000.

Gordon C. Strachan: H. R. (Bob) Haldeman's liaison to the reelection committee; charges during the main Watergate trial were dismissed.

Frank A. Sturgis: member of the Watergate break-in team; served thirteen months in jail.

Anthony T. Ulasewicz: ex-NYPD; private eye for the White House; made hush money drops; sentenced to one year's unsupervised probation for failing to declare expenses for income tax.

Rose Mary Woods: secretary to President Nixon; said she "must have" erased part of eighteen and a half minutes from a tape.

David R. Young: aide to Henry Kissinger (1969–71); White House Plumber; granted immunity from prosecution in return for prosecution testimony in the Fielding break-in trial.

Ronald L. Ziegler: Nixon press secretary (1969–74).

WATERGATE

CHAPTER 1

Breakthrough and Break-in

The contrast between what was happening in Moscow that Sunday, May 28, 1972, and what was happening in Washington was extraordinary. In Moscow, Richard Nixon was nearing the climax of the first-ever summit to be held there between American and Soviet presidents. Five thousand miles away in Washington, the first of several illegal entries into the Democratic National Committee (DNC) headquarters in the Watergate complex was taking place.

Nixon was preparing to make a television speech to the Soviet people, a speech he would later reckon to be one of the best he ever made.[1] It was to be high-minded and inspiring, an attack on the fear that he believed had poisoned the relations between the United States and the Soviet Union and which made the world a dangerous place.

> Through all the pages of history, through all the centuries, the world's peoples have struggled to be free from fear, whether fear of the elements or hunger, or fear of their own rulers, or fear of their neighbors in other countries. And yet time and again people have vanquished the source of one fear only to fall prey to another. Let our goal now be a world without fear . . .

Back home, however, the president's election managers had fallen prey to another fear, one in the end as irrational and dangerous as it could be. For despite Nixon's high standing, they—like Nixon himself—were obsessed with fear of losing, the fear of not having as much dirt on political opponents as they might have on you. The president had imbued his staff with a determination to do whatever it took to win. This came to mean an insatiable need for political intelligence, sabotage, smearing, and bugging.

This urge to do down his political enemies, along with Nixon's vision in policy making, were the dominant traits of this most perplexing politician. They were never more in evidence than in the middle of this, his third and last campaign for the presidency, more such campaigns than any other man since World War II.

In 1972, the last year of Nixon's first term, he was well prepared to run for a second. His political position seemed unassailable. The Moscow triumph was only the latest. He had started the year with a bang, confounding the Democrats, who had been ceaselessly pressing him to negotiate an end to the Vietnam nightmare, by revealing in January that he had been secretly talking to the Communist side for years. Then in February, completely upstaging the first primary elections, came his highly publicized summit with Chairman Mao in Beijing.

Now Nixon had pulled off the summit double with Moscow. This had looked against the odds because only two weeks before his Kremlin arrival, Nixon had boldly countered a renewed Communist offensive in Vietnam with an action the Joint Chiefs of Staff had been urging for years. He ordered the mining of Haiphong, the North's main port, and the bombing of hitherto off-limits targets in Hanoi. Some Soviet merchant sailors were reported casualties, and few thought the Kremlin would stand idly by.

But the Soviet leaders, not wishing to take second place to China in the superpower triangle, neither reacted nor cancelled the rendezvous; so the White House had "its mining and bombing and summit too," in the words of Henry Kissinger, Nixon's national security adviser. In the face of alarmist comment, even worries over World War III, Nixon was exultant and, typically, instructed his staff to see that all the doomsayers among politicians and commentators ate their words.[2]

Despite the blitz on Hanoi, he had reduced the number of American troops in Vietnam from the half million he had inherited on taking office to some fifty thousand. In the Cold War, he believed he had made great progress in engaging the Soviet leaders in what he called a structure for peace, slowing the nuclear arms race with the Strategic Arms Limitation Treaty (SALT) talks—which were to produce the first SALT treaty during this Moscow visit.

Nixon, in short, was at the height of his powers. His achievements made all the more ironic what was being done on his behalf back home in Washington.

Bugging was hardly an invention of the Republicans or the Nixon campaign team. The Kennedys and Lyndon Johnson had resorted to it. They had both used, and abused, the legitimate functions of the Federal Bureau of Investigation and the Central Intelligence Agency. Lawful, court-authorized, telephone tapping and other electronic eavesdropping were carried out, mainly against organized crime, by the FBI; the FBI also had, still has, a lawful counterintelligence function against foreign espionage within the confines of the United States. By law, the CIA was prohibited from engaging in domestic (as opposed to foreign) intelligence activity. What marked out Nixon's people was that, when they were thwarted by the FBI and CIA, they decided to act themselves.

Most Americans accepted that there was such a thing as political espionage, just as commercial and foreign espionage existed. But most people believed that their own affairs were safely protected by the Bill of Rights, which—like England's common law—guaranteed them freedom from unlawful search and seizure.

Most, but not all. Shortly after Nixon's image disappeared from the television screens, a group of men in Washington finally completed a very frustrating Memorial Day weekend. Starting on the previous Friday, they had made not one but three attempts to gain entry to the Democratic headquarters in the Watergate building. It would have been hilarious had it not been so sinister. They had failed in their first attempt on Friday to get past what they thought was an alarm. They were thwarted in their second attempt next day by not having the right lockpicking tools. Finally, on the Sunday Nixon was speaking in Moscow, having sent the locksmith back to Miami on a day round-trip, they got the door wrenched open, and went in.

One member of the gang was actually caught. Felipe De Diego, a former U.S. Army intelligence officer, was intercepted inside the Watergate complex by a security guard but simply told to leave the premises.[3] The others, ordered to continue regardless, photographed documents and planted a couple of listening devices inside telephones. They left undetected and a few days later were making plans for the next target.

Two of the men were employees of the Nixon campaign organization known as the Committee to Re-Elect the President (CRP). The six others were paid with CRP funds.

On June 6, the man virtually certain to be Nixon's rival in the November election all but clinched the Democratic presidential nomination by winning the California primary. He was ultraliberal Senator George McGovern, the opponent Nixon had least expected and most wanted because he seemed easiest to beat. McGovern's campaign headquarters on Capitol Hill was next on the list for the Nixon campaign's bugging. Entry day was set for June 17, 1972, but there was a snag. The Watergate bugging had been unsatisfactory. One of the bugs did not seem to be working. Before penetrating McGovern's offices, the break-in gang was ordered to go back into the Watergate.

Information and money. These two indispensable political commodities were immediately pinpointed by Richard Nixon—with the election victory barely savored in 1968—as cardinal to his reelection four years later. Even before Nixon's first inauguration, the instructions to White House chief of staff Bob Haldeman were meticulous. In a memo inadvertently released by the National Archives over Nixon's objection, he wrote that he wanted a huge buildup of funds during his first year. It stated: "Funds should now be collected to take care of our deficit and transition expenses from those who failed to contribute before the election . . ."[4]

In fact, rather than a deficit, Nixon carried away a secret surplus from the 1968 campaign. But even so the ominous note in that memo about "those who failed to contribute" did not go unheeded by Nixon's collectors. And the difference from what his predecessors had done was Nixon's secrecy; there was to be a private fund for secret political purposes. The Nixon men were to run up huge amounts by methods close to extortion. This approach, as we shall see later in the story, contributed mightily to Watergate and to the abuses associated with its initial cover-up.

Political intelligence was regarded as crucial. "I decided that we must begin immediately keeping track of everything the leading Democrats did," Nixon wrote. "Information would be our first line of defense."[5] And if possible, attack. Ever since his first congressional campaign in 1946, Nixon had had the reputation for indulging in smears while self-righteously denying any such thing. Very early in his first term, Nixon told John Ehrlichman, his other trusted top staff man, that the White House needed a "private eye," someone outside government channels who could get them dirt.[6]

Ehrlichman engaged a former New York City policeman, John Caulfield, known to Nixon as part of his security detail in the presidential campaigns. But Caulfield suggested that from inside the White House he supervise the detective, a former police colleague named Anthony Ulasewicz. To ensure that this connection was at one remove from the White House, Tony was to be paid through the president's personal lawyer, Herbert Kalmbach, but out of the secret political funds.

One of Ulasewicz's first tasks in July 1969 was to monitor events after Chappaquiddick. When Senator Edward Kennedy drove his car off the bridge there and Mary Jo Kopechne drowned, Nixon had a live interest in seeing a feared potential rival for 1972 damaged beyond repair in the scandal. Ulasewicz spent weeks around the investigation posing as a news reporter. From these small beginnings of political nosiness, the White House do-it-yourself taste for investigation was to develop into a habit and an obsession.

It could never be said of Richard Nixon that he wanted merely to be president; unlike some of his successors, he had clear ideas of what he wanted to achieve. He wanted to roll back what he saw as the permissive influences of the sixties, and on some issues, like welfare reform, he was before his time. Abroad, rejecting fashionable defeatism, he sought a recasting of America's influence amid a new balance of superpowers.

Yet the hair's breadth margin by which he had gained office in 1968 seemed to have affected his hold on it; for him, winning by 1 percent was not enough. Having felt the opposition's breath down his neck, he wanted revenge. Nixon seemed driven by the need to win overwhelmingly and unchallengeably next time.

The seeds of Richard Nixon's insecurities lie deep within his character, but they must also have been born in large part from the truly amazing seesaws of his political career. Most men are happy to contest one presidential campaign; some are lucky enough to succeed twice, in reelection. Nixon, unique in his generation, was a candidate in five presidential campaigns. In the first two he was elected vice president and served the classic heartbeat away under Eisenhower. In the next two, with an eight-year gap separating them, he was the Republican presidential nominee, losing the first time to John Kennedy by a mere 113,000 votes.

The abiding suspicion that Democratic vote fraud in Illinois and Texas had stolen that election led Nixon to a special fear and hatred for the Kennedys. At the time Nixon resisted the temptation to challenge the 1960 result. He later wrote, "I vowed that I would never again enter an election at a disadvantage by being vulnerable to them—or anyone —on the level of political tactics."[7] For a fighter who needed lessons from no one in political skulduggery and manipulation, that was a declaration of all-out political war.

Yet as voters went to the polls in 1968, Nixon was made frantic by the Democrats' tactics in support of their candidate, Vice President Hubert Humphrey. The president, Lyndon Johnson, suddenly announced a bombing halt in Vietnam and the opening of negotiations. On election night, Nixon had to wait into the next morning to be certain he had defeated Humphrey. Still, as he told his relieved supporters, "It sure beats losing."

It was one of the most phenomenal comebacks in American political history, but there was a problem. Nixon was the first president in 120 years to take office with both houses of Congress controlled by the opposition. As many of his closest associates later noted, Nixon never seemed to have accepted that he had finally won. Indeed, from the outset of his presidency in 1969, Richard Nixon seemed obsessed with the fear of being a one-term president.

"Without the Vietnam War there would have been no Watergate,"[8] says Bob Haldeman, who went to prison for it. Certainly, the Vietnam War Nixon inherited from the Democrats had to be his first order of business. It brought him his worst problems and brought out his worst responses.

Nixon had barely been in office a month when he was confronted with a test of his mettle. He had persisted in Johnson's bombing halt over North Vietnam, with the associated "understanding" that there would be no major attacks by the other side on cities. Yet in February, the Communists launched an offensive in the south. United States ground strength in Vietnam was then at its peak at 549,000 men. But there was another figure that had prime significance for the American public: By early March, in three successive weeks the toll of American soldiers killed in action was running near record levels: 351, 453, 336. And, of course, uncounted Vietnamese.

Nixon's options in ending the war as he had promised were limited. The joint chiefs could offer him only more of the same. Military escalation had been discredited under Johnson, and was opposed by an extraordinarily vigorous antiwar movement. The Democratic Congress was rapidly detaching itself from responsibility for American involvement.

Nixon chose to be bold and different. He ordered B-52s to bomb not Vietnam but Vietnamese Communist (Vietcong) bases inside neighboring Cambodia. Cambodia was officially neutral but its neutrality had long been violated by the Vietcong who used these "sanctuaries" to launch attacks in South Vietnam without fear of serious retaliation. Most important, and characteristic of Nixon, the new bombing operation was begun in secret, partly to avoid arousing what Henry Kissinger later called "the dormant beast of public protest" and partly to test key diplomatic reactions.[9]

There were none. The enemy being bombed kept it secret. So did the ruler of Cambodia, then Prince Norodom Sihanouk. And even more impressive diplomatically, there was complete silence on the issue in Moscow and Beijing. Nixon and Kissinger, who had never officially informed Congress, could hardly believe their luck.

It could not last, of course. Washington is a competitive place for the news media, especially in the first days of a new administration. And in a bursting forth of leaks about the Nixon policy-makers' innermost thinking, March and April stories about bombing of Cambodian targets were followed by the full story of the "unprotested" secret B-52 bombing of Cambodia, leaked onto the front page of *The New York Times* on May 9. It was attributed, like so much in those days, to Nixon administration sources. The president and Kissinger were enraged.

Nixon's response was typical and, as it turned out, fateful. He turned to two men to throttle at birth what he believed was a conspiracy to undermine his new administration from within. The first was John Mitchell; the second J. Edgar Hoover, director of the FBI.

Mitchell was a man Nixon counted as "[his] most trusted friend and adviser" whose counsel he wanted "not just on legal matters but on the whole range of presidential decision making." Nixon appointed him attorney general, but so powerful was Mitchell that he came to be regarded in that first term as deputy president. Mitchell had spent years and made millions as a lawyer specializing in municipal bond launches, that arcane mechanism by which American cities and local authorities bring their funding issues to market. His work and contacts gave Mitchell unique insights into state and city politics, especially in the Republican Party.

Mitchell and Nixon became New York lawyers around the same time in 1963. According to an associate in New York, they were attracted to each other because they were both new boys and outsiders in typically East Coast law firms. Their friendship prospered and eventually their firms merged into Nixon Rose Mudge Guthrie and Mitchell. Mitchell was all bluff pipe-smoking taciturnity, but if Nixon seemed to others to be in awe of his partner, Mitchell showed unwavering devotion to Nixon. Mitchell was the boss of Nixon's 1968 campaign and the first man to call Nixon "Mr. President," a moment that Nixon says affected him deeply.[10]

Two days after he assumed office, Nixon, coming from lunch with his new attorney general, told the writer Theodore White that he had instructed Mitchell to control wiretapping with an iron hand; Nixon wanted "no climate of fear in this country, no wiretapping scare."[11] Oddly, Nixon makes no mention of this in his own memoirs. He goes on at length, in a different context, with claims about how much more wiretapping previous administrations, above all the hated Kennedys, had conducted than he did. It is difficult, therefore, to judge how sincere the remark was—for the sentiment did not last long. What is certain is that in that spring of 1969, when Nixon turned to his attorney general for advice on what to do about leaks, Mitchell said call in the FBI.

Enter John Edgar Hoover, legendary and feared director of the FBI. Hoover had served under eight presidents. He had cut his teeth catching spies in the United States who were working for the Germans during the First World War. Hoover was in charge not only of the investigation of federal crimes but also of counterintelligence inside the United States. His unofficial brief, it was assumed, included keeping up-to-date intelligence on politicians. The dirt was lodged in his secret office files, which, to Nixon's chagrin, eluded his grasp when Hoover's loyal secretaries swiftly removed and destroyed them at his death in 1972.

Over his long career, Hoover amassed considerable political clout in Congress. At the age of seventy-six, he was past his best, yet nobody dared seek his resignation. Nixon always claimed that he had a great relationship with "Edgar," meeting frequently with him socially and relying on him for the kind of conservative hard-line support he craved, but rarely received from others. Hoover's support was something Nixon acknowledged inheriting from his predecessor.

The month before he assumed office, Nixon had been warned by Lyndon Johnson that "leaks can kill you." Moreover, Nixon quoted LBJ as saying, "If it hadn't been for Edgar Hoover, I couldn't have carried out my responsibilities as Commander-in-Chief. Period. Dick, you will come to depend on Edgar. He is a pillar of strength in a city of weak men. You will rely on him time and time again to maintain security. He's the only man you can put your complete trust in."[12]

Summoned to the Oval Office with Mitchell, his nominal superior, Hoover told Nixon that the FBI could conduct background checks on the leak suspects, have them tailed, or tap their phones; but phone tapping was the only effective way to nail down who the leakers were. Dr. Kissinger was asked to join them and suggest the names of some of his officials who had access to the secrets being leaked.

Ever since that time Kissinger has sought to justify the tapping while minimizing his role in the selection of staff and close friends among those to be tapped. One insider account says Kissinger agreed to wiretapping even before the leaks began.[13] But certainly the day the secret Cambodia bombing story broke Kissinger was on the phone instantly to Hoover, and he called him back three more times before the day was out.[14]

By 5 P.M. Hoover was back with a rundown of likely culprits; there was much talk of anti-Nixon people and Democrat holdovers in the Pentagon. But most fingers, Hoover's memo recalls, pointed at one of Kissinger's own men, Morton Halperin, chief of his National Security Council planning group. Kissinger responded, according to the memo, that "they will destroy whoever did this if they can find him, no matter where he is."[15]

Not long before, Hoover had objected on security grounds to a number of Kissinger's appointments, among them Halperin. At thirty-one, Halperin was an assistant professor at Harvard and had served in the State Department in the Johnson administration. Kissinger overruled the objections. Hoover, however, must have been primed, for within an hour of talking to Kissinger on May 9, the tap was working on Halperin's home phone, and stayed there until mid-1971, a forerunner of political bugging pure and simple.

This first tap was thus already working when Kissinger's military assistant, Colonel Alexander Haig, went on Saturday, May 10, to FBI headquarters with Halperin's name and the names of three others on the initial target list. At the outset it was Kissinger and Haig who inspected the FBI summaries. Kissinger was said to have been shaken by some of the things he read. "It is clear," he told William C. Sullivan, then number-two man at the FBI, "that I don't have anybody in my office I can trust, except Colonel Haig."[16]

At the same time Kissinger ordered others on his staff to keep a close watch on the Colonel. Haig, it has been written, used to monitor Kissinger's phone calls without telling him, on a so-called dead-key extension.[17]

For the first twelve months, summaries of the conversations that took place on the phones bugged by the FBI—thirty-seven in all—were supplied by Sullivan to Kissinger; letters explaining tapped material were also sent by Hoover directly to Nixon. Suddenly in May 1970, the president cut Kissinger out and had the wiretap summaries delivered instead to Chief of Staff Haldeman, with some going to John Ehrlichman, until the wiretapping finally ended in February 1971.

In all, FBI taps were placed on the phones of thirteen U.S. officials working at the White House and State and Defense departments and on one foreign and three American reporters. Although he later denied authorizing them, Mitchell was found to have signed the requisite forms in each instance, though he did not bother to review them every ninety days as the law required. There was no attempt to secure a court order for them and they were operated, apparently at Hoover's suggestion, "outside channels." That is to say, the records were not kept in the routinely authorized wiretap files at the FBI, its so-called Electronic Surveillance Index. This was important in maintaining deniability. American judicial practice requires that any defendant in a court case inquiring whether his telephone had been tapped is entitled to be so informed if there is relevance to his case. The files are searched and any potentially incriminating or exculpatory material must be revealed to the court by the authorities. In this case, with the phone tap files sequestered "outside channels," any such request could be answered with a denial that taps existed. And such false denials were eventually knowingly made. The "Kissinger taps," as they became popularly known, to Kissinger's fury, were the administration's first dirty little secret.

The upshot of the early leaks and taps episode was twofold. First, it eased the administration's slide into illegality. By repeatedly asserting the pretext of "national security," it made resorting to bugging seem respectable. In a bizarre episode, the White House even had the president's brother, Donald Nixon, tapped. The ostensible reason was to protect the businessman-brother from being contacted by suspected unsavory characters "who might be attempting to embarrass the President."[18]

Second, the leaks themselves led to even tighter secrecy in policy making and to what some later described as paranoia. Indeed, members of Kissinger's National Security Council staff, like his personal assistant, David Young, have recently disclosed how this episode caused all but a very few of their number to be excluded from policy making. The others were reduced to watching the comings and goings of limousines before racing down from the Executive Office Building to the White House West Wing on a pretext to try to find out what was going on.[19]

The paranoia, as Nixon himself admitted, was heightened that first year by the administration's sense of siege. Nixon certainly could never hope to satisfy the antiwar movement. Indeed, his new policy of "Vietnamization"—withdrawing American forces and transferring the military effort to the supposedly strengthening South Vietnamese—together with his newly enunciated "Nixon Doctrine" of supplying only the arms and not the men to allies in need aroused, rather than mollified, the protesters.

That autumn of 1969 they staged some massive demonstrations, calling for yet more rapid withdrawal and an end to the Vietnam fighting. It was clear that Nixon was to be given very little breathing space. Nixon's response was to acknowledge at a press conference on September 26 that there was opposition to the Vietnam War on campuses and in the nation at large and that he expected demonstrations. He then added: "However, under no circumstances will I be affected whatever by it."

Nixon was actually intending his remarks for the leaders in Hanoi with whom—although no one knew—he had just opened secret negotiations and to whom he had also given a November 1 ultimatum. They were to agree to a settlement or face a renewed military onslaught. The North Vietnamese continued to send messages of encouragement to what they saw as the "broad and powerful offensive" of the peace movement. Nixon, believing the protests had destroyed what little possibility might have existed for ending the war in 1969, decided to appeal to a broader audience. The result was the the now-renowned "silent majority" speech of November 3, 1969. It was wrestled through twelve drafts; it came out as a surprise both for what it said about Vietnam and for its appeal on the home front.

The United States, Nixon said, would continue fighting in Vietnam until the Communists agreed to negotiate an "honorable settlement" or until the South could stand alone. Demonstrations would not affect policy. He believed his plan would succeed. "If it does succeed, what the critics say now won't matter. If it does not succeed anything I say then won't matter. . . . And tonight—to you, the great silent majority of my fellow Americans—I ask for your support. . . . Let us be united against defeat. Because let us understand: North Vietnam cannot defeat or humiliate the United States. Only Americans can do that."

It was vintage Nixon. He remembered it long afterward as one of the great moments of his presidency, a rare speech that actually influenced history, he claimed. It struck a resonant chord. As if awakened, middle America's support for their president flowed in a tide of phone calls and in telegrams, even if later it was proven some of the response was orchestrated by Nixon's own White House staff.

Appealing to the silent majority made a better end to 1969 than the president had dared hope. It seemed to confirm to Nixon that he had won the election over again; that his view was the majority's and the opposition's the minority. The president's favorable rating in a Gallup poll in late November soared to 68 percent, the highest since his assuming office. It also cheered up Nixon that he had just taken onto his staff Charles Colson, a Republican from Massachusetts, an ex-Marine who loved hardball politics. The two came to spend hours together discussing political grievances and possible counterattacks, and Colson rapidly gained a reputation for both power and playing to Nixon's darker side.

Colson was to be the White House liaison with special interest groups, such as organized labor and white ethnic Americans. But Colson was a one-man presidential special interest group, as Nixon later explained in his memoirs. "His instinct for the political jugular and his ability to get things done made him a lightning rod for my own frustrations at the timidity of most Republicans in responding to attacks from the Democrats and the media. When I complained to Colson I felt confident that something would be done, and I was rarely disappointed."[20]

But even a new political hatchet man was not much use for the travails Nixon faced in 1970, with midterm elections in November. Despite the support of the "silent majority," he had made no progress over Vietnam. Nixon knew that with the Communists' refusing to negotiate, his policy of unilateral troop withdrawals carried huge risks. The public expected the withdrawals to increase continually but that prospect caused fears among the military that they could be courting disaster on the ground.

Nixon himself was furious that the Democrats, who had taken the United States into Vietnam in the first place, were now not only failing to support him but were also making political capital out of his inability to extricate the country from the morass. And the president fretted over the antiwar protesters. He wanted the law enforcement agencies to come up with proof not just of subversion, but of foreign Communist financing. It must be there, he insisted, and it exasperated him to contemplate what he saw as the inactivity and incompetence of the counterintelligence agencies.

A series of February 1970 memos traces the intensity of the president's concern. Haldeman pressed his own assistant, Larry Higby: "Find out quickly for me from someone what the Subversive Activities Control Board does. . . . See if it would be within their appropriate area of authority to investigate the Chicago Seven and the Black Panthers and these other related conspiracy groups to find out whether they are involved in subversive activities and specifically what their funding sources are. . . . I've got to get a report to the President on it."

In fact, the board was dormant. Two weeks later Haldeman sent an "eyes only" follow-up to Egil (Bud) Krogh, a young staffer then working under John Ehrlichman. Acknowledging receipt of a Krogh memo, Haldeman urged additional digging on "revolutionary groups' " financial support, singling out student groups. The memo notes that "many of the sources are not determined" and suggests a better rundown on sources and amounts given. There was no mistaking the president's determination to unmask and deal with those Americans he had assured the silent majority were the only ones who could humiliate and defeat America. "I think the country is ready for some outspoken confrontations on this issue . . ."[21] Nixon said in a memo to Haldeman.

The opportunity was about to present itself, though in a way no one could have foreseen. A coup in Phnom Penh overthrew Sihanouk, who ended up in Beijing. Sihanouk aligned himself with the Vietnamese Communist forces, and all of a sudden the North Vietnamese were the dominant force in Cambodia.

Nixon sensed quicker than most Americans that the stakes for his Vietnam policy were enormous. The Vietnamese Communists were seen to be in a position to turn Cambodia into one giant sanctuary for their war in the South. Vietnamization and the policy of an "orderly retreat" (as Kissinger much later called it) would look hopeless.

Nixon took six tense weeks to reach his decision, repeatedly viewing the movie *Patton,* which glorified the Second World War tank commander, for inspiration. In the interim he announced that 150,000 more Americans would be withdrawn from South Vietnam over the coming year, stating audaciously that "we finally have in sight the just peace we have sought."

But then came a different announcement and it was momentous. The public was initially to see only the first move, a feint: South Vietnam's army (ARVN) launched "incursions" into Cambodia's sanctuaries, with U.S. air support. Still, the outcry in the United States was instantaneous. Nixon was widening the war. Demonstrations were immediately declared.

The president plunged forward. On April 30, 1970, having overruled the objections of his secretaries of state and defense, and having noted that Kissinger was "leaning against" his decision, the president took TV prime time to broadcast he was also sending American combat forces into Cambodia to "clean out the sanctuaries." Nixon clothed his actions in near apocalyptic rhetoric and undoubtedly fanned the flames of protest. "I would rather be a one-term president," he said, "and do what I believe is right than be a two-term president at the cost of seeing America become a second-rate power and to see this nation accept the first defeat in its proud 190-year history."

In fact, Nixon made what he had done seem more cataclysmic than it was. He was certainly widening the war and defying parts of American opinion, yet he was not invading North Vietnam and not taking on the other superpowers. What was basically only a tactical military operation was now linked by Nixon to both his party's fate in the midterm elections and his own in the still-distant presidential contest. It suggests how desperately close Nixon thought he was to "losing" the Vietnam War and the presidency.

The reaction in the United States was a convulsion, part fury, part numbing dismay, with very little cheering. Here was a president supposedly winding the war down by widening it and justifying it with pseudo-Churchillian flights of defiance. In the week that followed there was uproar. A Cabinet member, Interior Secretary Walter Hickel, protested publicly and three of Kissinger's staff resigned, including Anthony Lake (who is now Clinton's Kissinger). And around the country the campuses erupted. Some 450 colleges shut down or went on strike as riots raged with serious acts of violence.

Then there was tragedy.

On May 4, the Ohio governor called out the national guard to keep order at Kent State University after days of disorder and some damage; in a volley of rifle fire from the nervous undisciplined guardsmen, four students were killed and nine others wounded. Two were also shot dead and twelve wounded by police at Jackson State University in Mississippi, but they went almost overlooked in the paroxysm after the dramatic pictures from Kent State. Nixon, who had himself been under enormous strain, sent out his press secretary to state defensively that the killings "should remind us all once again that when dissent turns to violence it invites tragedy."

The outraged reaction to Kent State made people largely forget the Cambodian operation and turn on each other. In New York City, a student demonstration in the financial district was met with violence when construction workers in hard hats waded into them with clubs and tools. In Washington, government employees conducted office sit-ins. That weekend a national day of protest had been called and tens of thousands were converging on the capital. The White House was itself in a state of siege, blockaded protectively behind a ring of ninety buses.

Something had to give. Nixon decided, on May 8, the Friday before the weekend protest, to hold a news conference in TV prime time, even at the risk of making things worse. He announced a surprise eight-week limit to the Cambodian incursion by American forces—a clear cave-in—and then tried, however awkwardly, to reach out to the students. Asked what he thought they were trying to say, Nixon ventured: "They are trying to say that they want peace. They are trying to say they want to stop the killing. They are trying to say they want to end the draft. They are trying to say that we ought to get out of Vietnam. *I agree with everything they are trying to accomplish*. . . . You can be sure that everything I stand for is what they want." (Emphasis added.)

Did he mean it? It hardly mattered. The president's credibility was at a nadir. Kissinger wrote afterward that Nixon was deeply wounded by the hatred of the protesters and that he would have given a great deal to gain their affection, the way the envied Kennedys had done. For Kissinger, Nixon had reached a point of exhaustion that caused his advisers deep concern, and what happened next was "only the tip of the psychological iceberg." Nixon recalls saying to a Kissinger made disconsolate by attacks from his former Harvard friends, "Henry, remember Lot's wife. Never turn back. Don't waste time rehashing things."[22]

Nixon's daily diary records that after his 10 P.M. news conference he got on the phone, as was his wont, but that he was agitated and uneasy. It has gone into history as a sleepless night, but in his own memo at the National Archives Nixon wrote that he "slept soundly" between 2:15 and 4 A.M. In fact, his log of phone calls shows he was awake and talking again by 3:15.

He could see knots of students gathering for the demonstrations on the Ellipse between the White House and the Washington Monument. To his Spanish-born valet, Manolo, appearing with coffee, he said that the Lincoln Memorial at night was the most beautiful sight in Washington, and he asked him if he'd ever seen it. Manolo said no, so Nixon said, "Let's get dressed and go." What ensued was one of the more remarkable episodes of Nixon's presidency.[23]

"Searchlight on the lawn" were the first words heard in the White House command post by duty staff man Egil Krogh. "Searchlight" was Nixon's code name, and Krogh, having confirmed that Nixon was leaving the White House before dawn with a tiny Secret Service detail, had to wake up his boss at home. Ehrlichman, who was rarely at a loss for a pithy phrase, said, "Go render assistance."

Krogh caught up with Nixon at the Lincoln Memorial, showing Manolo the flood-lit massive seated statue and moving down the steps to talk to an amazed group of some eight or so students that grew to fifty. Krogh said they seemed traumatized. Twenty years later some of those who heard him still marvel at it. Some thought he was a Nixon impersonator. Some said he was white faced and mumbling.

After perhaps forty-five minutes, with the dawn now breaking, Nixon ordered that they drive to the Capitol as the tour for Manolo continued. They found a duty clerk to unlock the House chamber, and Nixon had Manolo sit in the speaker's chair, urging him to make a speech while the president led the party in applause. Nixon then chatted with three black cleaning women, one of whom asked him to sign her Bible.

To close off this curious escapade, Nixon wanted to walk back to the

White House, but it was impossible. The buses blocked off all access. What idiot put all these buses here? he shouted at the hapless Krogh. Krogh knew. He had organized the bus blockade himself. They drove back.

When reporters finally caught up with the story, the coverage was dominated by students who told them the president had talked to them about football and travel. Nixon was furious. He gave an off-the-record account to a reporter from the Washington *Star*. It too failed to counter the students' versions.[24] He dictated, for his closest staff, a long memo about the encounter. Its keynote was that he deliberately chose not to have a dialogue with the young people on the war but that he was trying "to lift them a bit out of the miserable intellectual wasteland in which they now wander aimlessly around." He had been trying to communicate on "qualities of spirit, emotion, of the depth and mystery of life which the whole visit really was all about" and urged them not to let their opposition to his policies turn into hatred for their country.

The same day Nixon sent another memo to Haldeman about media coverage. He complained that he was the first president to come into office "with the opposition of the major communications powers" and that ever since, with only a few exceptions, he had been heavily opposed not just editorially, but also by slanted reporting. "You might say that this is really a time for soul searching on the part of the press to see whether it is they who are out of tune with the people rather than the President."[25]

This was more like the real Nixon. Lesser men might have been overwhelmed by the Cambodia–Kent State crisis. But it was typical of Nixon that when he had his back to the wall he was the toughest of opponents. Within three weeks of Kent State he was even welcoming to the White House, under Colson's tutelage, the leaders of the "hard hat" demonstrators who had attacked students. Looking back now it can be seen that the worst was over: In Nixon's purely politico-military terms, the Cambodia operation was a success, and after Kent State, the student protest movement was never as strong again. But Nixon had decided that it was time to wage secret war on his domestic dissenters.

CHAPTER 2

"Dirty Tricks"

It was Nixon's misfortune that just when he perceived the greatest need for counterintelligence on the most radical of antiwar and revolutionary groups, his great hero J. Edgar Hoover was being difficult. Instead of doing the president's bidding and feeding his beliefs that the Black Panthers and the Weathermen were being funded and trained by North Korea and North Vietnam, or Algeria and Cuba, Hoover chose in early 1970 to cut off the FBI's contacts with the other intelligence agencies.

Why this reluctance, when Hoover had so recently installed the Kissinger wiretaps, has never been properly explained. It has been put down to Hoover, now elderly and sensing retirement, wishing to preserve his beloved FBI's reputation—and his own—from political damage. Perhaps Hoover didn't want once again to arouse congressional interest in the FBI. (In 1966 Hoover had, in the face of a congressional investigation, summarily canceled all FBI break-ins—so-called black bag jobs—and canceled as well the planting of room bugs since they, too, required "surreptitious entry.")

With the internal "war of the FBI succession" beginning, Hoover was inordinately concerned about invasions of his territory and infringement of his own prerogatives by would-be successors. He cut off contacts with the CIA when they refused to tell him the name of an FBI officer who had cooperated with them without his authorization. He punished FBI agents if he caught them circumventing his restrictions. Hoover cherished his access to the White House, but he and Nixon were soon to be at cross purposes.

Hoover's recalcitrance had unsettled the Johnson administration, which, among other irregularities, had initiated a program of infiltrating protest groups with U.S. Army intelligence agents. The problem of radical violence was certainly real. The Black Panthers had since their inception in the mid-1960s urged murders and bombing; in Nixon's first year they engaged in shoot-outs with the police. The Weathermen were an offshoot of the Students for a Democratic Society (SDS), and they, too, began a campaign of bombings, sometimes blowing themselves up. As with all such tiny groups, advance intelligence was not easily come by. The surprise was not that Nixon wanted action; it was that he was resisted.

The president was already dissatisfied with the CIA. Although the CIA was banned by its founding charter, the 1947 national security law, from domestic spying functions, it had repeatedly and, of course, secretly broken that law in responding to presidential bidding with a large-scale program of spying on radical domestic organizations. But CIA Director Richard Helms was regarded by Nixon as an eastern establishment elitist, and it worsened their relationship when Helms could not produce the proof Nixon craved that campus radicals above all others were financed by foreign Communists.

This intelligence deadlock seemed miraculously, if momentarily, broken by the diligence of the first of a line of ambitious young men Bob Haldeman empowered in the Nixon White House. Tom Charles Huston had been national chairman of the archconservative Young Americans for Freedom and had been known to Nixon since the presidential campaign. He was a libertarian, extraordinarily articulate, and initially was assigned to the speechwriters team. But Huston also had a background in army intelligence and with the revival of the antiwar protest was, via the art of the sedulous memo, trying to get his masters interested in campus violence.[1]

His first appeal to their instincts in early 1969 was to suggest using the tax investigators of the Internal Revenue Service against radical organizations in probing their tax-exempt status. Huston, despite meeting twice, he said, "at the direction of the President," with the IRS commissioner, could not make the bureaucracy dance to Nixon's tune. And a year later Huston was complaining to Haldeman that "the truth is we don't have any reliable political friends at IRS whom we can trust, and as I suggested a year ago, we won't be in control of the government and in a position of leverage until such time as we have complete and total control of the top three slots at IRS."[2]

In mid-1970, Huston propounded the view that the greatest danger to internal security was not so much the actions of a violent handful as the response, in a climate of fear, of those who demanded repression. So Huston, claiming a principled position, argued for secretly mobilizing the state's own repressive resources to ensure the situation did not get out of hand.

It was what the president wanted to hear. Huston effectively proposed untying the hands of the intelligence agencies while quietly ignoring the Constitution. And who better—like Kissinger with foreign policy—to coordinate this new intelligence coup at the White House than the twenty-nine-year-old staff director, as Huston proposed he be designated?

On June 5—a month after Kent State—the president called a meeting of all his intelligence chiefs: Hoover; Helms; General Donald V. Bennett of the Pentagon's Defense Intelligence Agency; and Admiral Noel Gayler of the supersecret communications monitor, the National Security Agency. Haldeman, Ehrlichman, Huston, and Bob Finch were also present—Finch was one of Nixon's old line political confidants.[3]

In his memoirs, Nixon says very little about this meeting. He claims he wanted to know what the problems were in intelligence gathering; others recall a blistering dressing-down. They were overstaffed, they weren't getting the story, they were spending too much money. He wanted a report submitted jointly by this ad hoc committee with—a neat bureaucratic trick—Hoover to act as chairman.[4]

It was a trick because Nixon appointed Huston staff director. Huston immediately convened a subordinate working group composed of deputies from the intelligence agencies. Deputizing for Hoover, and thus effectively chairman, was Hoover's number-two man, William Sullivan, formerly head of the FBI's domestic intelligence. Sullivan, who had often complained of Hoover's restrictions, had been point man for the Kissinger taps and was very much regarded as the "White House man" at the FBI.

Even before the group's first meeting, Huston moved quickly to test the levers of his new function. In a June 8 memo he asked Haldeman to ensure that anything Kissinger received from CIA, DIA, NSA, or the military services relating to "foreign activities of American revolutionary leaders" now be passed on to him for coordination with the FBI and other strictly domestic collection sources. He said under current practice that "CIA input goes to Henry while the FBI contribution comes to me—and never do the twain meet."[5]

The next day at the first meeting of the working group, Huston told the impassive intelligence professionals that the president wanted them to recognize that "everything is valid, everything is possible." Their report did not disappoint the president when it was delivered a few weeks later. The point to remember is that the Huston plan was first approved by the heads of all three agencies—CIA, DIA, and NSA. As Richard Helms claimed later, "You don't say no to a president even if you don't intend to implement it." The odd man out was Hoover. The FBI director had footnoted his personal objections, mainly, it seems, out of worry over possible press disclosure.

The forty-three-page report opened with an analysis of the current threat. It suggested that the new left had a potential for serious domestic strife. It differentiated between supposed terrorist groups and those that merely indulged in rhetoric. At the time, Huston listed 776 bombing and arson attacks in the United States in the previous eighteen months.[6] Nixon in his memoirs estimated the total for the same period to be 40,000, by adding in without differentiation attempted bombings and bomb threats and hoaxes. Even without the exaggeration, the threat was real: Forty-three people had been killed.

The report examined available counterintelligence techniques, the restrictions on them, and the pros and cons of lifting them. Hoover's objections were central. He said he did not mind the NSA increasing its monitoring of overseas telecommunications (in fact, it sucked up everything). But the FBI director was against increased bugging, the resumption of black bag jobs, and domestic mail opening, as well as any increase in recruitment of campus informants.

Huston sent a separate memorandum to the president calmly discounting Hoover's objections. He recommended that the president go ahead and select all the options for the maximum relaxation of restraint, all the above and more. His memo, speaking of surreptitious entries, noted particularly:

> Use of this technique is clearly illegal; it amounts to burglary. It is also highly risky and could result in great embarrassment if exposed. However, it is also the most fruitful tool and can produce the type of intelligence which cannot be obtained in any other fashion.[7]

It was a "however" the paladins at Nixon's court could not seem to get out of their minds. Certainly, the president liked what Huston had written even though the young aide had noted that problems remained to be worked out "since Mr. Hoover is fearful of any mechanism which might jeopardize his autonomy." Nixon obviously believed these problems surmountable; typically he thought, as he wrote later, that Hoover was afraid that if he agreed to go along, the other agencies might undercut him by leaking word of his cooperation.[8]

One week later on July 14, Haldeman notified Huston that apart from vetoing an increase in military intelligence involvement, the president had bought his plan. Huston was to coordinate a permanent new interagency group as its new staff director. He should prepare a formal "decision memorandum" notifying all the intelligence bosses. This was Nixon's routine if somewhat pointless precaution to keep the president's signature off the document. Huston promptly issued the memo. The Huston plan was to go into force on August 1.[9]

The duty is clear on the part of elected government to act to protect life, ensure domestic tranquillity, and guard national security. But in resorting to methods beyond the law, the Nixon men fell into a classic trap: They failed to distinguish between what would be broadly accepted in a democracy as necessity in pursuit of the common good and what would be abhorrent as abuse when perverted for party interest.

The blur in the Nixon men's minds between enemies of the state and political opponents of their administration was instantly illustrated.

Even before the paperwork was authorized, the impatient Huston was supplying Haldeman with a ready target: The Brookings Institution, the liberal think tank in Washington, to which a number of Johnson and Kennedy administration officials had repaired to write critical analyses and hold seminars on Vietnam and other policies.

Toward the end of a long memo to Haldeman dated July 18, Huston remarked, "We really want to start playing the game tough." He suggested Haldeman might again consider his suggestion of some months ago of "going into the Brookings after the classified material which they have stashed over there." There were a number of ways it could be handled and risks in all of them, of course, "but there are also risks in allowing this government-in-exile to grow increasingly arrogant by the day."[10]

There it was. More than a year ahead of Charles Colson and two years ahead of Watergate. Charles Colson has been rightly blamed for many Nixon White House schemes. Until today he has been singled out for his hair-raising suggestion to firebomb The Brookings Institution in order, at Nixon's behest, to cover a White House–sponsored burglary to steal its papers—an option overruled in July 1971. But Huston was casing the joint a year before, a fact established in that astonishing paper trail of fantasy illegalities filed away by the methodical Haldeman and now to be found in the National Archives.

But even as Huston reached out to satisfy the president, he had reached too far. What followed was an illustration of the ability of great institutions like Hoover to frustrate presidential will. Despite Nixon's belief that bugging and break-ins and the rest were justified by the violence being unleashed and his later pious assertion they would not be used to threaten legitimate dissent, Hoover made use of the ultimate Nixon deterrent. He went to John Mitchell.

The attorney general, chief enforcer of the law and order Nixon was claiming to deliver, apparently now heard for the first time the extension of the secret police power being proposed without his advice. Hoover appealed the president's judgment; the danger of exposure was too great to justify the risks. He might, some have speculated, have raised his own hints of counteraction if the Huston plan went ahead. Certainly, the Nixonites were ever vigilant at the prospect of being blackmailed, and they often worried about Hoover.

Mitchell went back to the president and told him he agreed with Hoover. Nixon wrote later that he realized that if Hoover did not cooperate the plan was dead. He claimed he worried that Hoover might resign in protest. On July 28, before the plan could be implemented, Nixon withdrew his approval, or so he claimed.

With awful irony, a few days later, a research scientist on the Madison campus of the University of Wisconsin was killed in a bomb blast at his laboratory. The Weathermen claimed responsibility. Had black bag jobs and bugs been used to prevent such atrocities few would have complained, but it was the bureaucratic and institutional infighting that held center stage.

Huston was instructed to recover the incriminating memos from the agency chiefs to ensure the paper trail would disappear. But by 1970, the photocopier was already outflanking the shredder and copies of the Huston plan were left in files like time bombs. They erupted three years later.

Huston frantically lobbied for a reversal of the reversal. In a memo to Haldeman on August 5 he wrote: "At some point Hoover has to be told who is President. He has become totally unreasonable. . . . All of us are going to look damn silly in the eyes of Helms, Gayler, Bennett, and the military chiefs if Hoover can unilaterally reverse a presidential decision. . . ." Huston railed on, touching one of Nixon's most sensitive nerves and grievances: "For 18 months we have watched people in this government ignore the President's orders, take actions to embarrass him, promote themselves at his expense and generally make the job more difficult. It makes me fighting mad."[11]

Alas poor Huston. He was relieved of his intelligence overlordship. He had one final claim on this history, delivering himself in early 1971 of what looks like the embryo White House "enemies list." Just as he had been among the first to try bending the Internal Revenue Service to Nixon's will, just as he had been ahead of the pack in pushing for surreptitious entries, so in a January 25, 1971 memo he supplied a list, by groups, of the unfriendly—"it would be easier to list our friends and assume those not listed were otherwise," he scoffed.[12] By midyear, Colson and John Dean were to expand the enemies list to hundreds.

Huston's legacy lived on in a way he could not have anticipated. A lot of people in government knew the president had backed away from a showdown with Hoover, but it was also widely known by insiders that for a month and a half the president had lobbied for the Huston plan. And that together with four of his intelligence chiefs, Nixon had *formally approved* the extension of buggings and break-ins. The seeds planted the previous year with private eye investigations, illegal bugs, and domestic wiretapping were beginning to exfoliate into strange growths and make further development seem logical. The president wanted this development; some of the official organs of the state were frustrating his wishes. The wish was father to the thought. If they won't do it, why not us?

When in the following year the next peril presented itself, the urge for the White House to take over and run some police functions itself was irresistible.

In the wake of the Huston plan fiasco, Nixon made changes among his senior staff in the hope of asserting presidential control over the bureaucracy that flouted him. With an eye both on the midterm elections due in November and the presidential contest in 1972, he named John Ehrlichman to be his new domestic policy chief.

This had one immediate effect that was pregnant with risk: He needed a successor for Ehrlichman as White House counsel even while he intended downgrading the job. Bob Haldeman sifted the list for likely young men. Ehrlichman's deputy, Egil Krogh, recommended a friend of his, an associate deputy attorney general at the Justice Department. John Mitchell said yes, he was good but too good for the lowly job the president had in mind. But an overpowering nexus was forming.

Haldeman had the young man fly to California and spirited by military helicopter to San Clemente, the so-called Western White House. After half an hour and a brief introduction to the president, John Wesley Dean III had the job. Aged thirty-one, having practiced law for six months, "I entertained a reverie about what a big shot I would be as counsel to the President."[13]

Haldeman dispensed with the usual background checks since Dean came so well recommended. Had Haldeman stuck with routine he might have avoided a lot of grief. Dean had left his first private law job in a dispute; his senior partners had discovered that he had an interest in a TV station license that the firm itself was pursuing. They separated, as they say, with accusations of conflict of interest flying.

Dean was another young man on the make. He rapidly built his office into the White House's law firm, making himself useful in conflict of interest problems for the staff and in sorting out Mr. and Mrs. Nixon's wills. Haldeman also made him responsible for monitoring demonstration violence (a specialty Dean had pursued with verve while at the Justice Department), and he leaped to do Haldeman's bidding in pursuing political intelligence. From Ehrlichman he took over command of the private eye operation run by John Caulfield with Tony Ulasewicz; they came with the job, he was told. And Dean promptly picked up where Huston had left off in seeking to use the IRS to help friends and hurt enemies.

Indeed, one of the first memos addressed to Dean from Haldeman's office concerns both the IRS and no less a figure than Howard Hughes. The industrialist billionaire, lately turned recluse, had had many entanglements with the Nixon family, and his name was to recur repeatedly and tantalizingly in the events to come. Its very mention rang alarm bells at the White House. The EYES ONLY memo to Dean on August 10, 1970 instructed the newcomer to see whether the IRS could be persuaded to "replace" its staff lawyer, who was too aggressively pursuing the recipient of a possible Hughes payoff of $140,000. Referring to one of the president's brothers, it noted: "As you probably remember there was a Hughes/Don Nixon loan controversy years ago, and the prosecution of this case could reopen that entire issue which could be very damaging politically."[14]

Dean's response has disappeared, but shortly thereafter Hughes cropped up again in a political context. Haldeman was advised that Nixon's old bugbear, Lawrence O'Brien, was on the board of an international consulting firm and ought to be challenged. (O'Brien, who used to sit in the same office in John Kennedy's White House now occupied by Ehrlichman, had become chairman of the Democratic National Committee, then revving up for the midterm elections.) The memo to Haldeman urged, "Can't we raise a big fuss about this? . . .

demand to know what fees he'll be getting . . . we could have a little fun and keep O'Brien on the defensive."[15]

Those might have been the first innocent shots fired in Nixon's war on O'Brien. Within weeks the president had discovered that, in fact, O'Brien's new lobbying firm had Howard Hughes as one of its clients, and that made his antennae twitch. Nixon's own entanglements with Hughes had not ended with the Hughes/Don Nixon loans that had plagued both his 1960 presidential campaign and the 1962 bid to become governor of California. (It was alleged the loans were in return for Vice President Nixon's 1956 intervention to secure tax exempt status for a Hughes medical institute.)

As president, Nixon also had a Hughes secret. He had received illegal campaign contributions from Howard Hughes concerns *after* the 1968 election that had gone into a secret fund. For the first two years of Nixon's term, Hughes had backed both horses. While supporting Nixon, Hughes had on retainer a lobbyist to the Democrat-controlled Congress, O'Brien. The prospect of O'Brien's stumbling across Hughes's illicit donations while he was, as Democratic national chairman, in Hughes's pay, made O'Brien a double fascination and danger —and an ideal target for Nixon's emerging offensive/defensive intelligence capability.

The oncoming midterm election that November understandably heightened Nixon's worries about his political vulnerability. He had dared hope at one stage that he might exploit and benefit from the so-called social issue with traditional Democrats being drawn over to the Republicans out of fear of crime, drugs, and school busing. He had high hopes, too, for his so-called southern strategy, which was aimed crudely at adding to the Republican vote the 13 percent George Wallace had secured as a third party candidate in 1968. The president spoke at times of building a new majority with Senate candidates like Congressman George Bush. His eye was particularly on the Senate, where he had ambitions of a seven-seat gain to crack the Democrats' hold.

But the polls turned against Nixon. He decided to reverse his deliberate aloofness and plunge into the campaigning, visiting twenty-two states where he thought Republican Senate candidates had a chance. In the face of demonstrations, he was extraordinarily combative. There was a lot of ugliness wherever Nixon went.

All these efforts failed. On election day, the Republicans lost nine House seats and eleven state houses; in the Senate races, George Bush lost in Texas to Lloyd Bentsen, and the Republicans, though they made two gains, still fell well short of securing the control that alone would have given credibility to the Nixon claim of a new majority.

The political consensus, with the Republicans having shown poorly in the populous states, was that Nixon was in bad shape for 1972. The risks of being a one-term president were real indeed. The Nixon inner circle held conclaves as to how they might reverse the trend. Conclusion: The president must become less partisan and more presidential. And so Nixon duly presented himself for a joint interview with four network newsmen, saying, "I am now going to wear my hat as President of the United States."

That, however, was for public consumption. Significantly, the man who was telling Nixon what he wanted to hear at this time and who had been promoted to his inner circle was Charles (Chuck) Colson. Of Swedish extraction, the Scandinavian genius for consensus had long been hammered out of his genes. He was a political bruiser. Colson had been a Protestant on the wrong side of the tracks in Roman Catholic Boston. He had served in the marines but kept a Green Beret motto on his wall: "If you've got 'em by the balls, the hearts and minds will follow." He had worked hard to qualify as a lawyer and was a Massachusetts Republican, an effective one, too. In 1960, when John Kennedy destroyed Nixon's first bid for the White House, Chuck Colson had helped elect Republican Senator Leverett Saltonstall.

Colson was not downcast by the midterm elections, and his memo on the subject was balm for Nixon's wounds. "The results, had you not campaigned, would have been far worse and you would have taken the full blame which would have hurt in 1972," he wrote. His analysis for the rest was perceptive and candid about the economic issue's hurting badly. On the precise reason for Bush's losing Texas, Colson noted that the candidate refused to let Colson's men use derogatory information about Bentsen. He stated that Bush probably lost because he ignored the "social issue" and tried to be more "liberal." Next to this in Nixon's handwriting: "probably true."[16]

If 1971 was a nonelection year, for Nixon there was no such thing as a nonpolitical year. His memoirs make this plain:

> As each day brought the election closer, and as the competition heightened, the need for action and information became irresistible. . . . I ended up keeping the pressure on the people around me to get organized, to get tough, and to get information about what the other side was doing. Sometimes I ordered a tail on a front-running Democrat, sometimes I urged that department and agency files be checked for any indications of suspicious or illegal activities involving prominent Democrats. I told my staff that we should come up with the kind of imaginative dirty tricks that our Democratic opponents used against us and others so effectively in previous campaigns.[17]

Nixon later wrote that the first months of 1971 were "the lowest point" of his first term. The problems seemed intractable, with unemployment at 6 percent, its highest since 1961, and the dollar at its lowest point since 1949. There was the continuing Vietnam deadlock, which included the perennial spring crisis. This time there was a near debacle in Laos when, with U.S. air support, South Vietnamese units muddled a much touted attempt to "cut" the so-called Ho Chi Minh Trail down which the North Vietnamese brought their supplies to the South. Nixon later wrote of his concern that he might not even be renominated in 1972, let alone reelected.

Yet his mood was aggressive. The secret agenda was buzzing. The president now wanted dirt on Lawrence O'Brien and Hughes. Flying back from the New Year's break at San Clemente, he dictated a memo for Haldeman.

> It would seem that the time is approaching when L. O'Brien is held accountable for his retainer with Hughes. Bebe has some information on this although it is, of course, not solid, but there is no question that one of Hughes' people did have O'Brien on a very heavy retainer for "services rendered" in the past. Perhaps Colson should make a check on this.

Haldeman wrote on the memo ". . . Dean, let's try Dean."[18]

Nixon was referring here to his close friend Charles G. "Bebe"

Rebozo, a Miami banker who was at the time secretly managing one hundred thousand dollars of Hughes contributions to Nixon's campaign. A big news story at this time concerned the upheaval in the Hughes empire. The billionaire had sacked his top manager, Robert Maheu, and replaced him with a team of Mormon businessmen. The effect this produced in Washington was a change of Hughes "ambassadors" to the federal government. Lawrence O'Brien was out and a Nixon appointee in the Department of Transportation, Robert Bennett, son of a Utah senator, was to get the Hughes lobbyist job.

Nixon hated and feared O'Brien. To Nixon he represented the worst of Kennedy's political fixers. His abiding nightmare, in spite of the massive setback of the drowning in the summer of 1969 at Chappaquiddick, was that O'Brien would somehow rebuild Teddy Kennedy to be his opponent for the presidency in 1972. O'Brien's predictably partisan statements seemed to incense Nixon more than the statements of most Democrats. He complained long afterward that O'Brien had virtually accused him of killing the four students shot at Kent State.

Charles Colson saw O'Brien as the most shrewd and effective operator the Democratic Party had—"the one pro we took seriously." He admits discussing with Nixon that "if we could get something on him that might discredit him, that would be wonderful." They eyed the "vulnerability" of his Hughes connections.[19]

Their gambit against O'Brien involved publicizing his retainer from Hughes and showing—if possible—that it had not been reported as income for tax purposes. Given the president's own Hughes imbroglios, it proved to be an impossible risky business, and, after involving Colson, Dean, and even Nixon's close friend Bebe Rebozo, in the end fizzled out. Nixon did order an IRS audit, but it cleared O'Brien, goading the Nixon team into an obsession with finding other dirt on him.[20]

O'Brien's replacement, Robert Bennett, had left DOT to take over the Mullen Company, a public relations firm in Washington. This was the firm where, with the sponsoring help of CIA Director Helms, E. Howard Hunt had been placed since he formally retired from the agency in May 1970 after twenty-seven years' service. So Hunt, who was an old chum of Colson's, and Bennett, deemed a Colson ally, were now working together.

The association was more than coincidence. Out of the Mullen public relations firm—which also gave cover to CIA operatives working in Amsterdam, Stockholm, Singapore, and Mexico City—Hunt, in Colson's words, was already working on special assignments of a very sensitive nature for the White House. Bennett was also being used on "outside projects" paid for by funds channeled through the White House. Colson thought Hunt important enough in January 1971 to request that he and his wife, Dorothy (also a sometime CIA officer but then secretary to the Spanish ambassador in Washington), be invited to the after-banquet White House reception for Don Juan Carlos, the future king of Spain. Six months before Hunt was finally put on the White House payroll, Colson wrote, "It is very important politically that we let him know he is in the family." It was one of the many curious webs being spun out of the White House that year.

Another was the first of the tails Nixon admits he ordered on a front-running Democrat. On December 15, 1970—much earlier than was established by the Senate Watergate Committee—came the first of a series of intelligence reports from a source, code-named Chapman's Friend. They were sent to the White House by a journalist covering the embryonic campaign of Democratic front-runner Senator Edmund Muskie. A lot of the paper generated at the Nixon White House was dour reading; this was very funny. Chapman's Friend passed on inside information about unprofessionalism in the Muskie camp and the way labor union leaders distrust him; how Chapman's Friend himself answers the Muskie office phone for important would-be Democratic helpers and even plants suggestions with top columnists like Stewart Alsop. Heaven knows how true it all was, but the journalist's usefulness to the Nixon campaign apparently warranted a one-thousand-dollar monthly retainer.

Then in February 1971, Nixon embarked on perhaps the most momentous reversal of office policy to affect him personally. He claims it was done because LBJ sent word that he was finding it far easier to write his memoirs from a complete record. So, having ordered LBJ's White House taping mechanisms ripped out when he assumed office, Nixon now fatefully ordered that virtually *all* his conversations be tape-recorded. The Secret Service's technical division, whose job included "sweeping" the president's offices against bugging, was ordered to do the installation. Its chief was Alfred Wong. It was supersecret. In the beginning only Haldeman, the Secret Service, and Alexander Butterfield, the man who managed the president's paper flow under Haldeman, knew about it.

The system eventually consisted of a network of seven stations, mostly using noise-actuated recorders. In the beginning, five microphones were implanted in the president's Oval Office desk and two more on either side of the fireplace; two were placed in the Cabinet room near the President's chair. Two months later, four more microphones were installed in Nixon's hideaway office in the Executive Office Building next to the White House—three in the desk and one in the kneewell. The president's two office telephones and one in the Lincoln sitting room were also wired; and in May 1972, the president's study at Aspen Lodge in the Camp David retreat was hooked up. Altogether, more than five thousand hours of conversations were taped, of which only about sixty hours have been publicly released, the latest in May 1993.

In his memoirs Nixon circumspectly explains his thinking. The record produced, he claimed, would be useful to the extent he might feel vulnerable to revisionist theories—whether from within or outside his administration. He noted this was particularly so given that the issues were as controversial and "the personalities so volatile." Nixon was protecting himself against his own people and intended to use the tapes even more extensively than LBJ did as an aid in writing his own memoirs. (In this connection, it should be noted that to date he is, in fact, the only author to have access to all the tapes.)[21]

What Nixon tape-recorded is different in terms of comprehensiveness from anything that had been done in the White House before. He makes much of the fact that his predecessors recorded conversations, and Franklin Roosevelt seems to have begun the practice. Despite initial indignant denials, the John F. Kennedy Memorial Library in Cambridge, Massachusetts, has admitted having forty hours of tapes that JFK made secretly. Johnson's tape system, which recorded conversations with Robert Kennedy among others, was not automatic; it had to be manually operated. Nixon's system was automatic and all pervasive, except for Key Biscayne in Florida and San Clemente in California, which for some reason were left unequipped. It was never intended that the system be disclosed; indeed, despite a leak-prone administration, for more than two years almost no one knew about it.*

Another doom-laden decision was made that spring of 1971. It was to set up a campaign organization. Ultimately called the Committee to Re-Elect the President, it was known as CRP in the official abbreviation, forever "CREEP" to the watching world. It was to be separate from the Republican Party's national committee and located outside the White House, although its offices were just across the street. Nixon had decided that his campaign chairman, in 1972, would again be John Mitchell. Mitchell would eventually resign as attorney general and move into 1701 Pennsylvania Avenue. The building already conveniently housed the Washington office of the old Nixon-Mitchell New York law practice; the CRP offices would be on another floor. In the interim, Haldeman sent one of his young men across from the White House to run it. CRP's first director was Jeb Stuart Magruder, aged thirty-one.

Magruder was from New York before landing in Southern California; he had moved around several corporations, developing a taste for campaign politics and by 1968 was running a cosmetics firm. Haldeman recruited him for the office of White House communications director, where he swiftly went to work devising ways to get back at Nixon's media critics. Magruder was another master of the memo and eager to please the stern Haldeman. Indeed, he was said to be afraid of him.

That spring turned sour for the White House because of novel pressure from the antiwar protesters. For the first time, veterans of the fighting, the Vietnam Veterans Against the War, put in an appearance, led by a young former officer named John F. Kerry, now senator from

* At this point in 1971, Nixon thought that his secret was intact. But in his sympathetic biography, *Nixon: A Life* (p. 497), Jonathan Aitken reveals that British Foreign Secretary (and former prime minister) Alec Douglas-Home discovered it. According to Aitken, Home was expounding the detail of some British position on Middle East policy in the Oval Office when he noted that neither Nixon nor, more important, Henry Kissinger was taking any notes. Home discreetly asked the British ambassador, Lord Cromer, whether Nixon had the Oval Office taped. Cromer asked the embassy man from MI6 to check with his CIA contacts, who "owned up . . . and kept wanting to know how we'd found out." Since the CIA at the time was not supposed to be in on Nixon's secret, it is possible the British tipped them off.[22]

Massachusetts. They all received huge TV coverage when they went up to Capitol Hill and threw their medals over a wall.

Then on May Day, student protesters undertook to shut down Washington. There were extraordinary scenes. They announced plans to close the bridges across the Potomac and to conduct guerrilla theater in downtown streets. In fact, although Nixon mobilized military forces, it was the D.C. police who carted off tens of thousands for detention in the main stadium, sweeping up reporters among them. But Nixon was not relying on regular forces alone. An Oval Office tape of this period reveals an unpleasant exchange. Haldeman says that Colson is getting the Teamsters Union to send "their eight thugs," and Nixon observes, "they've got guys who'll go in and knock their heads off."

> *Haldeman:* We can deal with the Teamsters. And they, you know—
> *Nixon:* Yeah.
> *Haldeman:* —it's the regular strikebusters-types and all that and they [tape noise] types and this and then they're gonna beat the shit out of some of these people, and, and hope they really hurt 'em. You know, I mean go in with some real—and smash some noses.[23]

Nixon got little credit for having kept the government and the capital open for business. For the first time he fell behind Senator Edmund Muskie, then the leader for the Democratic presidential nomination, in the polls. Nixon responded with a round of press and TV interviews with the few friendly correspondents he could muster, but it was clear to him that he had little support in the media.

The reasons went back decades. Except for a brief period in the midsixties when a "new Nixon" was setting gingerly about his comeback, Nixon's relations with the press had been based largely on mutual disrespect. There were clear ideological problems. The bulk of reporters were opposed to Nixon's right-wing brand of often vindictive politics. Nixon let his contempt and his self-pity show, as in his famous 1962 farewell when, after losing the election for governor of California, he told reporters, "You won't have Nixon to kick around anymore." It was effectively a hate-hate relationship.[24]

In the wake of the White House correspondents' annual dinner that spring, his anger spilled over in a memo to Haldeman. Nixon was furious at his staff for arranging him to be present when the awards were made, all, he claimed, "to way out left wingers . . . while the drunken audience laughed in derision. . . . What I want everyone to realize is that as we approach the election we are in a fight to the death for the big prize. Ninety-five percent of the members of the Washington press corps are unalterably opposed to us because of their intellectual and philosophical background. Some of them will smirk and pander to us for the purpose of getting a story but we must remember that they are just waiting for the chance to stick the knife in deep and to twist it. . . . We simply have to start growing up and being just as tough, ruthless and unfeeling as they are; otherwise, they will sink us without trace."[25]

Within weeks the president and the press would come to grips in unprecedented fashion. First came a day that was clearly one of the happiest in the president's life—the wedding in the White House garden, seen live on television by fifty-nine million people, of his elder daughter, Tricia, to Edward Cox, Jr. The president was filmed dancing with his wife, Pat, a rare carefree moment of a happy head of the First Family.

The next day, Sunday, June 13, 1971, the president picked up his *New York Times*. There, next to the picture of the daughter and father with the story of the wedding, was a strangely headlined three-column story: VIETNAM ARCHIVE: PENTAGON STUDY TRACES 3 DECADES OF GROWING U.S. INVOLVEMENT.[26]

The Pentagon Papers had been leaked. It was an act that in the eyes of the Nixon administration would represent the ultimate antiwar protest, tantamount to treason, an act requiring the severest of countermeasures.

CHAPTER 3

The Pentagon Papers

The Pentagon Papers uproar began quietly enough. There was little stir on the talk shows that Sunday even though Melvin Laird, the defense secretary, appearing on one was primed with a temporizing answer. (On weekend duty to report to London, I remember phoning the home of an official in the State Department's East Asia Bureau for reaction that afternoon. He apologized; he had not yet got around to reading *The New York Times.*)

Nixon's initial public reactions were relaxed, sensing an opportunity, not a disaster. And no wonder: The keynote of this first installment of a forty-seven-volume in-house Pentagon study of U.S. Vietnam involvement, commissioned by Robert McNamara when he was secretary of defense, documented the evident deception by Lyndon Johnson about his Vietnam intentions during 1964, when he was running for president against Barry Goldwater. To Nixon, infuriated at the way the Democrats blamed him for failing to end "their" war, this was political manna. All his political instincts, and those of Colson, welcomed the chance to exploit these revelations against the Democrats. It seemed nicely timed for the 1972 elections.

Nixon was still telling Republican leaders this as late as the following Tuesday. By then, however, things were getting out of hand. The first day's leak of three pages of stories and three more pages of documents had turned into a flood. It included full texts of previously coded cables to and from the U.S. Embassy in Saigon, an obvious security breach, which White House officials said could give away actual codes. Upset, Defense Secretary Laird confirmed what *The New York Times* had coyly not included in its scoop—that the documents carried the classification TOP SECRET SENSITIVE—and said he was "highly disturbed" by the disclosure. Laird stated that he had asked the Justice Department to determine who had "violated the law concerning national security."

The government had clearly been caught off base. Also on Tuesday, Secretary of State William Rogers reported that he was getting complaints from foreign countries about this washing of dirty linen—Canada and Australia, for instance, had not looked too good in the Pentagon Papers disclosure of their role as intermediaries in Vietnam diplomacy. The same day the attorney general sent the FBI into action, and the government went to court to stop *The New York Times* from further disclosures—with Nixon characteristically issuing a ban on all White House staff interviews to that newspaper.[1] By evening a federal district judge in New York had granted the government a restraining order against the *Times*. It was temporary pending the government's application for a permanent injunction, but the government jumped to an appeals court and won a stay. Nixon's war with the press erupted.

It was a swift and frantic struggle, which Nixon took personally. He later wrote that *The New York Times* decision to publish, without so much as a single check with government, was "clearly the product of the paper's antiwar policy." He felt strongly that he had a legitimate case: It was for the government, not newspapers, to decide what secrets must remain secret.[2]

But the country's leading newspapers joined in defense of their constitutional rights to a free press and their right to sell. No sooner was one newspaper restrained in the courts than a different one began printing yet another segment of what—despite Haldeman's written decree they should be known as the "Kennedy-Johnson Papers"—were now universally dubbed the Pentagon Papers.[3]

The Washington Post was next. Here the judge ruled against the government, which then appealed but lost its attempt to prevent publication. The federal appeals courts were now at odds, too. *The Boston Globe* took up the baton; it was also restrained by a federal judge. Then the *Chicago Sun Times* began releasing State Department memoranda concerning U.S. collusion in the 1963 coup that overthrew South Vietnamese President Ngo Dinh Diem and ended in his assassination.

In all, twelve newspapers got involved in publishing secret Vietnam policy papers and one Democratic senator, Mike Gravel, started reading the Pentagon papers into the Congressional Record. There was an immense hullabaloo. Former President Johnson weighed in with fury, telling the White House, so Nixon wrote, that the newspapers were trying to "re-execute" him.[4]

The case went rapidly to the Supreme Court. By that time at least the White House's code-breaking scare had been demolished—although no one enlightened the public. The head of the National Security Agency, Admiral Noel Gayler, briefed Solicitor General Erwin Griswold just before he was to argue the government's case in the highest court. The admiral laughed at the idea that the newspapers, by printing the plain text of previously enciphered cables, might help code breakers. "That has not been true since about 1935," he said, explaining the principle of one-time codes, changed for each cable. With that, Griswold felt that about half the government's case went out the window.[5]

In the end Griswold made it clear that the government was mostly concerned with preventing publication of only a handful of potentially damaging documents—and he filed a "special appendix," itself secret, of material that if disclosed would "cause grave danger to national security." On June 30, four days after hearing oral argument, the Supreme Court delivered a 6–3 rebuff to the government. The justices dismissed even the argument set out by Griswold that publication might hinder the ending of the Vietnam War, among other secret negotiations.

In fact, the Supreme Court majority was not the ringing defense of absolute press freedom newspaper people have fondly claimed. Only three associate justices, including Hugo Black, utterly rejected the idea of injunctions; "every moment's continuance of the injunctions against these newspapers amounts to a flagrant indefensible and continuing violation of the First Amendment of the Constitution," Black thundered. Three other associate justices held there could be prior restraint, but not in these cases. Faithful Chief Justice Warren Burger, appointed by Nixon, was among the dissenters, arguing there ought to have been more time to enable the court to find out whether a serious threat to national security was involved.

That certainly seemed true. The lower courts were "blind" in that they judged without seeing the documents the newspapers had in their possession. In fact, Griswold only discovered in 1991 that neither *The New York Times* nor anyone else had possession of the four Pentagon Papers volumes the government was most concerned about—those dealing with the Vietnam negotiations options. Griswold has said that if the government had known this in time, it would not have pursued the court action against the newspapers.[6]

A few days later Griswold and his wife had a rare invitation to a White House lunch. In the receiving line Griswold shook Nixon's hand, saying:

> "Well, Mr. President, we did not do so well in the Pentagon papers case." The result left a vivid impression on me. The President froze, and seemed to glare, saying nothing. It was, to me, a wholly unnatural sort of reaction. I said nothing more and quickly moved on. I had of course underestimated the importance of the case to the President . . .

Griswold was dropped by the Nixon administration after the 1972 election. His successor was Robert Bork.

What escaped notice in the general press euphoria was that the Supreme Court's decision lifted only the prior restraint on publication. Nothing stopped the government from prosecuting those responsible for leaking the Pentagon Papers.

The chief perpetrator was rapidly disclosed to have been one Daniel Ellsberg, a former hawk who had worked in Vietnam on the CIA-run "pacification" program in the 1960s, before returning home disillusioned. Ellsberg, by then an MIT research associate, had also actually worked for Henry Kissinger both at Harvard and in the White House at the outset of the Nixon administration. This made his action especially treacherous, in the view of the national security adviser.

Most recently, while working at the Rand Corporation, the think tank that conducted many top secret defense studies, Ellsberg, who enjoyed high security clearances, had systematically organized the photocopying of the Pentagon papers over many months, allegedly beginning as early as 1969. Ellsberg went into hiding when the FBI called, but on June 23 turned up on the CBS-TV evening news and in justification claimed that "Americans bear major responsibility . . . for every death in combat in Indochina in the last twenty-five years and that's one to two million people." In subsequent interviews Ellsberg said he was against the executive branch and was convinced that Nixon intended to escalate the war; he called for increased public opposition to force a complete U.S. withdrawal from Vietnam.

Nixon was by now furious. The initial thought of political advantage was jettisoned, at least for the moment. Now it was obvious that further disclosures could damage Nixon, not just his predecessors. On June 22, the Senate, partly upset over Nixon's refusal to provide Congress with copies of the Pentagon Papers, for the first time voted for a unilateral withdrawal from Indochina, regardless of the consequences. For the first time, too, a Gallup poll recorded a majority favoring an end to the war, "even at the risk of eventual Communist takeover."

Nixon's immediate concern was twofold: "getting" Ellsberg was imperative to deter any other would-be leakers and face them with trial and imprisonment, and foreign countries needed rapid reassurance that the United States could keep its secrets.

The public did not know it but Nixon was one month away from sending Henry Kissinger on his secret mission to Beijing to pave the way for the historic opening to China, which ended more than twenty years of U.S. nonrecognition. And Kissinger was also in the throes of his still-secret negotiations with the North Vietnamese while nuclear weapons negotiations with the Soviet Union were at a critical point. In these circumstances Nixon needed no one to inflame his anger. So much could be imperiled through government inaction in the face of this most spectacular leak of its secrets.

But inflamed he certainly was, and by Kissinger. At a meeting on Thursday, June 17, with Haldeman and Ehrlichman, Kissinger was, by the chief of staff's account, at his most portentous. In his own memoirs Kissinger wrote: "Our nightmare at that moment was that Peking might conclude our government was too unsteady, too harassed, and too insecure to be a useful partner. The massive hemorrhage of state secrets was bound to raise doubts about our reliability in the minds of other governments, friend and foe, and indeed about the stability of our political system." In those last words apocalypse was pending.[7]

Haldeman's book *The Ends of Power* states that Kissinger really knew how to get to Nixon. "It shows you're a weakling, Mr. President. . . . The fact that some idiot can publish all the diplomatic secrets of this country on his own is damaging to your image, as far as the Soviets are concerned, and it could destroy your ability to conduct foreign policy. . . ." Haldeman recalled that Henry had a problem because Ellsberg had been one of his boys. "As I remember, it ended with charges against Ellsberg by Kissinger that in my opinion go beyond belief. Ellsberg, according to Henry, had weird sexual habits, used drugs, and enjoyed helicopter flights in which he would take potshots at the Vietnamese below. . . . By the end of the meeting Nixon was as angry as his foreign affairs chief. The thought that an alleged weirdo was blatantly challenging the President infuriated him far more than it might, let's say, if Ellsberg had been one of those gray-faced civil servants. . . ."[8]

Neither Kissinger nor Nixon knew what they were facing in Ellsberg, but they had some real worries. They had been advised by the FBI that the Soviet Embassy received a set of the papers. They also believed that Ellsberg had access to the secret list of U.S. strategic nuclear targets. Nixon wanted action. He set it going in a number of parallel channels that showed his determination, this time, to destroy an opponent. These channels became so fantastically interlinked that each must be examined in detail.

First was the decision to get Ellsberg through the criminal justice system. In Los Angeles, near the Santa Monica headquarters of the Rand Corporation, a federal grand jury was swiftly empaneled and quickly began questioning Ellsberg's alleged coconspirators. On June 24, Anthony J. Russo, also of the Rand Corporation, appeared under subpoena but refused to testify on the grounds he might incriminate himself. Then on June 28, Ellsberg, who had been evading the FBI, surrendered in Boston to federal authorities. To a cheering crowd outside the courthouse, he admitted being the leaker and announced that, before turning to the press, more than a year earlier he had given the Pentagon Papers to Senate Foreign Relations Committee Chairman Senator J. William Fulbright. (Fulbright, a Nixon "enemy," had not, in fact, made use of them. This disclosure was calculated to infuriate Nixon.)

The same day the grand jury in Los Angeles indicted Ellsberg on charges of unauthorized possession of national defense information and theft of government property. The federal prosecution was placed under the control of Robert Mardian, a right-wing assistant attorney general. If the prosecutors could prove a conspiracy to get the Pentagon Papers into the hands of foreign intelligence or foreign governments, then they could ask for a maximum sentence of ten years. As it happened, however much the Nixon men were attracted by the idea of a Communist conspiracy, the charge of supplying foreigners was not retained in the superseding indictment later that year.

Once the criminal prosecution process gets under way, certain strict rules apply, especially regarding defendants' rights. In view of this, it is astonishing that the lawyers in Nixon's supposed law and order administration thought they could get away with what they attempted. For almost immediately, the Ellsberg case began to run afoul of earlier Nixon White House secrets necessitating a cover-up. Covering up was to become a habit.

On July 2, Mardian officially asked the FBI for any wiretap information regarding Ellsberg; this was a routine action to ensure the prosecutors knew what they might have to disclose to the defense. On July 9, Mardian made a similar request regarding Morton Halperin, the former Kissinger aide who turned out to be one of the authors, during the Johnson administration, of the Pentagon Papers study. The FBI checked what it called its indices and formally reported back that there was nothing in the wiretap files on either man. This was narrowly correct as far as the official indices were concerned, but in fact was a big lie. As we have seen, the 1969–71 Kissinger taps were conducted by the FBI outside channels, and the logs and files of the taps that were sent to the president, Kissinger, and Haldeman were kept in a special FBI file not included in the indices.[9]

In fact the tap on Morton Halperin's phone had picked up Ellsberg on no fewer than fifteen occasions, sometimes when he was a guest at Halperin's home. Apparently, nothing was said that had the remotest bearing on the Pentagon Papers leak. So on the face of it, the government had nothing to lose in being prepared to confirm that Ellsberg's phone had been tapped—nothing except its need to protect a program of wiretapping it wished to deny.

Secretly, Nixon's aides were alive to the possibility the Kissinger taps might reveal something further. On July 6 in a taped discussion with the President, Haldeman suggested that the summaries of these wiretaps, by now discontinued, be gone over again by the FBI to see if they were made more meaningful by Ellsberg's action.[10]

An Ehrlichman note of a conversation with the president reveals that there was definite concern in the Nixon entourage about the Kissinger taps and the Ellsberg grand jury, concern and then relief. On July 10, Ehrlichman wrote: "Re: grand jury—dont worry re tapes on discovery—re WHs' [White House]."

"Discovery" is the legal term for the procedure under which both prosecutors and defense counsel obtain relevant evidence from each other in a case prior to trial. The Nixon men, by withholding the evidence of the wiretapped Ellsberg conversations, were embarking on a course to thwart that process, which, if discovered, could risk a miscarriage of justice against Ellsberg. What had happened to ease that "worry re tapes" and make them confident they were not endangering their all-important case against Ellsberg?

The answer was nothing less than another extraordinary development in the FBI's internal war. The man who was guarding the Kissinger tap files, William Sullivan, the assistant director in charge of domestic espionage and the FBI officer regarded as the Nixon administration's friend, had become increasingly at odds with Hoover over antisubversion policy and tactics. Sullivan was about to be forced into retirement. Around this time he paid a call on Robert Mardian and offered to turn over the Kissinger tap files. The reason Sullivan gave was sensational.

According to Mardian's account to the FBI two years later, Sullivan said that "Mr. Hoover had used wiretap information to blackmail other presidents of the United States and he [Sullivan] was afraid that he could blackmail Mr. Nixon with this information. Mr. Sullivan reiterated his request of Mr. Mardian to personally contact the president of the United States and pass along Mr. Sullivan's information and request."[11] Mardian, saying this was the first he had heard of the Kissinger taps, reported this information to Mitchell who, he said, told him "he would handle it."

Mardian got the tap summaries, which were delivered to him by another FBI assistant director in a beat-up olive satchel bearing Sullivan's initials. Mardian put them in his safe, notified the White House, and later (perhaps as late as October, according to a White House tape)[12] was advised to take the material to Kissinger and Haig. Mardian went to the White House, and subsequently claimed to have delivered it in the end to Nixon himself.

Nixon's memoirs fail to confirm his personal receipt of the Kissinger taps material but they do speak of the Hoover blackmail issue. The president did not believe, he says, that Hoover would use the taps as blackmail "to retain his position" or that Hoover would ever disclose "national security wiretaps." Why, then, would Nixon go to such extraordinary lengths to have the material removed from Hoover's control at the FBI? Nixon's version is that he could not permit the wiretap reports to "fall into the hands of someone like Ellsberg," and so he approved their transfer to Ehrlichman's custody at the White House. There they remained, secretly—despite a search ordered that October by an enraged Hoover, according to John Mitchell—until their disclosure two years later wrought judicial and political havoc right in the middle of the unfolding Watergate scandal.[13]

Nixon's problems with Hoover would not go away. The director was being prickly over the FBI investigation of Ellsberg. The father of Ellsberg's second wife, it developed, was a horse-racing buddy of Hoover, and in opposition to White House wishes the director had forbidden FBI agents to interview him. They did so anyway, but Hoover's recalcitrance made Nixon angry. As the president put it: "If the FBI was not going to pursue the case, then we would have to do it ourselves."[14]

The first thing Nixon wanted done, "ourselves," it seems, was a black bag job at the opposition think tank, The Brookings Institution in Washington. The idea of going in had been knocking around at the White House, as we have seen, for at least a year, since Huston suggested it to Haldeman. Nixon's memoirs recall his outrage on hearing that a secret report on the 1968 bombing halt he believed had nearly cost him the election had been taken from the Pentagon to Brookings but could not be obtained by the Nixon men. "When I was told that it was still at Brookings, I was furious and frustrated. . . . I could not accept that we had lost so much control over the workings of the government we had been elected to run—I saw absolutely no reason for that report to be at Brookings, and I said I wanted it back right now *even if it meant having to get it surreptitiously* [emphasis added]."[15]

Charles Colson was ever obliging and suggested an ingenious scheme. Under District of Columbia federal regulations, FBI agents would be permitted to accompany firemen in the event of a fire alarm at Brookings. The FBI men could then "acquire" the documents Nixon was after. But the plan, given to Jack Caulfield, the former policeman working for John Dean, fell through. Caulfield didn't like the sound of firebombing Brookings. Nor did Dean, who got Ehrlichman to "turn it off" on grounds of risk. Colson maintains it was never really serious, but Nixon's memoirs make clear where the idea came from.[16]

All this was happening at the very time Nixon was demanding maximum action from his lieutenants, not only against Ellsberg but against all his enemies in what he called the "countergovernment," and inside the government, too. As Colson recalled in 1974, "The president, speaking to Haldeman and me, said in effect 'I don't give a damn how it is done, do whatever has to be done to stop these leaks and prevent further unauthorized disclosures; I don't want to be told why it can't be done. . . . I don't want excuses, I want results, I want it done, whatever the cost.' "[17]

"You're going to be my Lord High Executioner from now on," Haldeman says Nixon told him—and Colson noted the same remark.[18] Haldeman was ordered to confront personally every cabinet member and agency head, "brutally chew them out and threaten them with extinction if they didn't stop all leaks in the future."[19]

First, however, Nixon wanted to get to the bottom of the Ellsberg affair. He wanted Ellsberg, his motives and his message, discredited. Above all he wanted the Kennedys, who had "started" Vietnam and with whom Ellsberg identified, smeared; and if ahead of the 1972 election this could damage the last of the line, Teddy Kennedy, so much the better.

Colson was quite ready to set about discrediting Ellsberg—"he is a natural villain to the extent he can be painted evil"—as well as prosecuting him. Beyond that he wanted thought given to "the subtle ways in which we can keep the Democratic party in a constant state of civil warfare."[20]

Haldeman's action paper of June 15 had expressed the need for someone at the White House to handle the "whole situation," which typically was seen in PR terms. By June 22, the Chief of Staff's strategy memo, echoing his master's voice, read, "The key now is to poison the Democratic well." By the end of the month Haldeman and Ehrlichman had asked Colson to recommend someone to research the Pentagon Papers, with a view to exploiting them politically.[21]

So at this stage there were at least three operations running: the overt prosecution of Ellsberg, the end-all-leaks-or-else by Haldeman, and Colson's scheme to dig for more dirt on Ellsberg and the Democrats.

Colson's operation was first in the field. He came up with seven possible candidates to run it, one of them, Patrick Buchanan, was then a Nixon speechwriter. Buchanan forcefully responded that he was not the man for the job and perceptively concluded that while a permanent discrediting of Ellsberg and associates might be good for the country, it "would not it seems to me be particularly helpful to the President politically."[22] Colson decided to try one of his favorites, the former CIA man E. Howard Hunt.

Colson had taken the precaution of tape recording the sounding-out phone conversation he had with Hunt on July 1:

Colson: Let me ask you this, Howard, this question. Do you think with the right resources employed that this thing could be turned into a major public case against Ellsberg and coconspirators?

Hunt: Yes, I do, but you've established a qualification here that I don't know whether it can be met.

Colson: What's that?

Hunt: Well, with the proper resources.

Colson: Well, I think the resources are there.
Hunt: Well, I would say so absolutely.
Colson: The . . . your answer would be we should go down the line to nail the guy cold?
Hunt: Go down the line to nail the guy cold, yes . . . I want to see the guy hung if it can be done to the advantage of the administration.[23]

With that commitment established, the next day Colson urged Haldeman to meet Hunt. His memo noted that he had forgotten to say that Hunt was the CIA "mastermind" of the Bay of Pigs. Colson well knew that once more nailing Kennedy for the disastrous 1961 Bay of Pigs invasion of Cuba was a pet Nixon project. It was to recur again and again even during Watergate. By July 6, Colson was suggesting that Ehrlichman meet Hunt, "to assure yourself the kind of man we're getting." Hunt is "dying to get with it and will drop everything if we ask him to." Ehrlichman sent that note on to Haldeman.[24]

It is not clear if Ehrlichman and Haldeman realized the kind of man they were getting. Hunt had had an amazing career as a covert intelligence officer and as a prolific thriller writer, and it is trite to say these fantasy worlds must have merged. His retirement from the CIA suggests he was past his best and going no higher, yet since he had "retired" before, it is difficult, as with all spies, to be sure. He had seen a lot of action. He volunteered straight from college for navy duty before Pearl Harbor. He claims to have been a *Life* magazine war correspondent. Then he joined the precursor of the CIA, the Office of Strategic Services, and served behind the lines in China. After the war Hunt tried Hollywood screenwriting and had a spell as Ambassador Averell Harriman's spokesman in Paris in the economic cooperation administration, known as the Marshall Plan.

From 1949 on he fought in the Cold War. He served in the CIA in Vienna, Mexico City, Tokyo, Uruguay, and Madrid; he planned covert operations in the Balkans and Guatemala; and he was on the planning staff for the April 1961 attempted invasion of Cuba at the Bay of Pigs—with which Nixon, as vice president until January 1961, had been closely involved. Hunt was not the Bay of Pigs mastermind Colson promoted, but had been principally concerned with organizing the politics and public relations of an exile group that was supposed to fly in and pronounce itself a Cuban "provisional government." Hunt became a legend to a group of Cuban exiles under the code name Eduardo.

Hunt later described his capabilities: "I was trained in the techniques of physical and electronic surveillance, photography, document forgery and surreptitious entries into guarded premises for photography and installation of electronic devices. I participated in and had the responsibility for a number of such entries, and I had knowledge of many others. To put it unmistakably, I was an intelligence officer—a spy for the Government of the United States."[25] It all sounded impressive.

On July 7, Colson took Hunt to see Ehrlichman. Colson later said he had to have Ehrlichman's authority to hire Hunt. Ehrlichman said he thought Hunt was already on the job. And, indeed, July 6 is the starting date in Hunt's White House employment records, though the date might have been inserted when the file began a month later. At a hundred dollars a day Hunt was taken on as a part-time consultant to the president, although a handwritten line has been drawn through the words "to the President." The first two and a half weeks he worked every day.

Hunt later testified that from the beginning he was asked by Colson to collect derogatory information about Ellsberg. But it is clear that his primary task as self-styled "White House resident expert on the origins of the Vietnam War"[26] was to get dirt on the Kennedys. Indeed, that first task seems to have been domestic rather than foreign. The same day he was introduced to him, Ehrlichman phoned the CIA to request assistance for Hunt at the president's behest.

According to General Robert Cushman, then deputy CIA director, Ehrlichman called to say that Hunt would be coming to see him "and would I lend him a hand?" Ehrlichman originally denied making any such call but now admits doing so. "You should consider he has pretty much carte blanche" was what Cushman's secretary recording the conversation quotes Ehrlichman as saying.[27]

With a presidential introduction, Hunt was off and running. Within days he was interviewing at the White House over drinks a top CIA Vietnam hand, Lucien Conein. His task was to obtain the inside story of the Kennedy administration's involvement in the 1963 overthrow of South Vietnamese President Ngo Dinh Diem. Not for the last time, Hunt botched matters. The tape recorder placed under the couch cushion for the interview failed to work because Colson sat on it. The next day Hunt attempted to recoup by phone.

Hunt's next task was to try getting more dirt on Teddy Kennedy over Chappaquiddick. He had been tipped off by his colleague at the Mullen Company, Robert Bennett, that a source in New England had new information. Hunt later said Colson told him to go ahead, providing his connection with the White House was not revealed—a recurring concern among Nixon's top men as they launched these investigations.

To conduct the New England interview, Hunt felt he needed a disguise and aliases. So he picked up Ehrlichman's introduction and on July 22 drove out to CIA headquarters at Langley, Virginia, to meet General Cushman, asking that his staff assistant leave the room. The CIA deputy director agreed, and instantly set his hidden tape recorders running—an interesting precaution given Ehrlichman's earlier call. The transcript has Hunt saying he was on a "highly sensitive" White House mission to "elicit information from an individual whose ideology we aren't entirely sure of." He wanted alias documentation, a fake driver's license for checking in under a false name at a hotel, what he called "pocket litter," as well as a disguise for "a one-time op—in and out."

Cushman replied, "I don't see why we can't." Hunt asked that it be ready the next day and given to him at a CIA safe house so that he could stay clear of headquarters at Langley. He wanted it for the weekend of July 24. Hunt used Ehrlichman's name and for good measure gave Colson's office as the White House number where he could be reached. Hunt could not restrain himself from boasting to Cushman of his twelve-hour working days at the White House and telling him that the one thing that had really electrified Nixon's men was the Pentagon Papers.[28]

The next day, in two visits to a CIA safe house off Wisconsin Avenue near the Washington National Cathedral, Hunt, under the code name Edward, met one of the CIA's technical services experts. Hunt was given a toupee, often later described as a "red wig"; a pair of spectacles, which, though thick looking, provided clear vision; and a speech-altering device to give him a lisp and a gait-altering device to make him limp. The pocket litter included a driver's license, Social Security card, and various other cards made out in the name of Edward Joseph

Warren; it was close to one of Hunt's old professional aliases, Edward J. Hamilton.[29]

It all seemed extraordinarily elaborate for a meeting in Providence, Rhode Island, with a federal civil servant who said he had worked for the Kennedys in a previous campaign. The man, as it turned out, was willing to talk of womanizing and swinging parties but when Chappaquiddick came up, he begged off because Hunt would not identify his "principals."[30] Yet this incident gave Hunt an opening with CIA clandestine services and put him in a position to be useful for Nixon's next big idea.

On July 2, John Ehrlichman says he was ordered by Nixon, with Haldeman present, to recruit someone for the White House to take full responsibility for the Ellsberg case and to take charge of the investigation of the conspiracy.[31]

The timing is crucial. It was three days after Ehrlichman received John Mitchell's call about Hoover's foot-dragging over Ellsberg's father-in-law. Time now for the White House to "do it ourselves." This was what Ehrlichman called the "genesis" of the decision to form a White House Special Investigations Unit, later known as the Plumbers.

Staffing the unit took place simultaneously with some extraordinary foreign policy developments. On July 9, on the very day Kissinger in Pakistan shook off reporters and secretly flew to Beijing, Nixon and Ehrlichman at San Clemente decided on David Young to head part of the new unit. Young was at the time working as assistant on Kissinger's national security council staff. A youthful New York lawyer sent by Kissinger's patron, Nelson Rockefeller, Young was summoned to San Clemente and on July 14 told he was being detached to work on the new top secret project.

The next day, July 15, Kissinger returned from China and Nixon proudly announced the epic turnabout in U.S. relations with the third superpower. Although Nixon sternly warned everyone, from White House staff to congressional leaders, not to say so publicly, it was clear that his opening to China had disconcerted Hanoi. Here were North Vietnam's two sponsors, the Soviet Union and China, agreeing to meet their enemy while the Indochina fighting raged on.

That evening, in a rare exception to his policy of not socializing with his staff, Nixon took Kissinger, Haldeman, and Ehrlichman to a celebration dinner at Perino's, then a posh restaurant in Los Angeles. Ehrlichman slyly recalls Nixon and Kissinger pretentiously selecting a rare Bordeaux and then leaving the President's navy aide to haggle the bill down from six hundred dollars a bottle. But even amid the celebrations of this diplomatic coup, the Pentagon Papers affair intruded.[32]

On the short journey back from the restaurant by helicopter, Kissinger objected to the loss of Young from his staff. Nixon overruled him; Young was to stay on the new special project. Haldeman saw it later as an Ehrlichman "stroke of Machiavellian genius" to involve a Kissinger man; he noted that all too often Kissinger ignited a fuse and then stood off swearing he knew nothing about it or had even been against it.[33]

Two days later, July 17, Ehrlichman added his own man to the team: Egil Krogh, his young former law partner who had become his assistant director on the domestic council. Krogh, who had been so awestruck by Nixon's dawn foray to the Lincoln Memorial the previous spring, now returned to San Clemente from a visit to Vietnam, where he had been on an antinarcotics mission. Krogh was put in overall charge of the Special Investigations Unit, but it was intended to be part-time while Young served as the staff director.

Ehrlichman said he told Krogh and Young of the president's sense of urgency and that they must be prepared to work directly with the president, at his option, or through himself. They were to return immediately to Washington to decide how to stimulate the various government units to plug future leaks and how to move the Justice Department's Ellsberg conspiracy investigation to an early and successful conclusion. Krogh remembered only the Ellsberg focus. He later testified that one reason for undertaking "an independent investigation, centralized among White House staff," was Hoover's relationship with Ellsberg's father-in-law.

Even before Krogh and Young got back to Washington, someone else had already thought of what was to become their big idea—prying information out of Daniel Ellsberg's psychiatrist. On July 20, FBI agents went to the Beverly Hills office of Dr. Lewis Fielding, an expert in psychoanalysis, and sought to interview him about his patient of the past two years. Fielding declined and told the FBI agents they would hear from his lawyer. On July 26, the lawyers confirmed Fielding's refusal.[34]

In Washington, where Young was diligently making the rounds of top government officials demanding to know what they were doing about the Pentagon Papers affair, he made what he considered a fascinating discovery. "The CIA was not then conducting and had not conducted an examination or study on Ellsberg's personality," he reported. It was suggested that he inquire at the Department of Justice.*[35]

It is clear from Young's memos that week that his initial task involved far more than plugging leaks. It also included coordinating congressional hearings favorable to the administration and taking over from the Justice Department's Robert Mardian the overall job of developing leads in the Ellsberg case. Many of the high-level meetings were in Ehrlichman's presence. John Mitchell specifically insisted that Ehrlichman take responsibility if the Department of Justice was to be subordinate.[36]

Krogh was also busy that first week. One of his most important actions was to recruit a man he had known at the Treasury Department who had recently been transferred to the White House staff. This man, like Krogh, had worked in combating drug smuggling and gun control. He also had experience as an FBI agent, which seemed to Krogh to be an asset to the Special Investigations Unit. His name was G. Gordon Liddy.

Liddy, an exceptionally articulate man with rambunctious right-wing views, a Roman Catholic who had taken a law degree at a Jesuit college, led something of a charmed life in the Nixon administration. He had also had a colorful career. When he could not get into a war, he had joined the FBI, convinced it was an elite corps. During his five years he had come to the attention of Director Hoover.

After leaving the FBI, in the 1960s Liddy became a controversial assistant district attorney in Poughkeepsie, up the Hudson from New York City. He was fascinated by guns and an absolute opponent of gun control; indeed, he was a gun freak before the term existed. Once, at a

* The point is of importance. In the Watergate story the idea of getting a CIA psychological study, or profile, of Ellsberg has always been attributed to Hunt—who on this date was yet to join the Krogh-Young operation. In fact, the idea seems to have been Young's.

trial he was prosecuting, he fired a pistol to make his point—mercifully it was a blank. In 1968, he contested the Republican congressional primary against Hamilton Fish, Jr., scion of a famous family who had the support of the party establishment. Liddy beat Fish in Dutchess County but lost districtwide by a whisker, 51–49 percent. Because Liddy eventually refrained from supporting the then emerging Conservative faction and was active in the local Nixon-Agnew presidential campaign (in which Liddy felt he was serving John Mitchell), he had to be rewarded.

With the Republicans in the White House, he was introduced to his job at the Treasury Department via the good offices of then congressional minority leader Gerald Ford. But bureaucratic infighting did not suit Liddy; finally the assistant treasury secretary got rid of him. Liddy transferred to the White House under Mitchell's aegis to be involved in policy on "narcotics, bombing and guns." One of his close colleagues at the Justice Department later admiringly said of Liddy, "He was a knight looking for a liege lord to serve."[37] He found two of them in Mitchell and Nixon.

Liddy always considered himself Mitchell's man. And although he was the sole Watergate participant to honor a vow of silence on the whole affair—until the statute of limitations expired in 1980—when he did talk he came up with some plausible if startling notions. One was that the Special Investigations Unit was, in fact, a focus for the main power centers of the administration: Krogh and Young he saw as Ehrlichman's and Kissinger's men, respectively; himself as Mitchell's appointee; and the fourth man, soon to come on board, E. Howard Hunt, as Colson's nominee. There is a certain symmetry to it.[38]

Hunt was rapidly proposed to Krogh as soon as Colson was aware of the new unit's existence. Colson later claimed assigning Hunt was Ehrlichman's idea. In any case, Colson had already given Hunt the task of picking out the areas of the Pentagon Papers "where we might be able to expose the Harrimans, the Warnkes, the Cliffords, the Vances, the MacGeorge Bundys and McNamaras." He went on, "Each of the prospective Democratic opponents next year can be vulnerable if we can tie them or their advisers into gross misjudgments committed during this period." Indeed, Colson wanted to tie them to the "enemy camp" and depict the president as rescuing the nation from their subversion. Colson said "Leddy [*sic*] is an excellent man" but suggested that Hunt take the lead on discrediting the Democrats—without involving Young—and that Ehrlichman and he sort out some administrative points. Evidently, Colson wanted his fingers in the Plumbers—and the president was kept aware of his memo.[39]

Hunt, who had his own little office on the third floor of the Executive Office Building, was taken to the top security offices of the new unit in room 16 on the ground floor. The unit already had a secretary, Kathleen Chenow, assigned to Young; a special alarm system; a three-way combination safe; and a big bulletin board detailing the group's ongoing projects. A bit later there was a simple sign outside; when Young told his mother-in-law his new job was stopping leaks in government, she is supposed to have remarked: "We have a carpenter in the family, how nice to have a plumber." The sign said PLUMBERS, and they were immortalized.

Inside, Liddy's first self-assigned task had been to give the unit's paperwork a special stamp to indicate its supersecurity. He said it was an acronym: "Our *o*rganization had been *d*irected to *e*liminate *s*ubversion of the *s*ecrets of the *a*dministration"[40]: ODESSA. Its connection with the Nazi war criminal escape group (Liddy in his book misspells it and calls it a "German Veterans organization") seems to have eluded the White House. It was dropped after a month because Ehrlichman thought it too obvious. No one has accused Liddy of admiring the Nazi creed, but he had an inordinate admiration for Nazi paraphernalia, their songs and marches, their political organization. He even had a Leni Riefenstahl film of a Hitler Nuremberg rally shown at the White House.

At the time the two younger men seemed to have been impressed with the ex-CIA ex-FBI credentials of their operatives. Young, meanwhile, had equipped room 16 with a massive KYX scrambler telephone, the size of a safe, which he used principally for his conversations with the CIA and the Pentagon, while Hunt had requested an unusual direct-dial outside line that avoided the White House switchboard.

The outside line in room 16 was used mainly by Hunt to receive calls from his contacts. It was paid for by the White House yet billed via the home address of the Plumbers secretary, Kathy Chenow. The arrangement was to turn out to be too clever by far a year later when Watergate broke.

The Plumbers had barely time to settle down in room 16, when on July 23 another major newspaper leak convulsed the administration. Again it was *The New York Times*. This time the scoop was nothing less than the U.S. "fallback" position in the SALT negotiations with the Soviet Union. Kissinger was again beside himself and Nixon responded by ordering Krogh to give lie-detector tests to practically everyone in the bureaucracy, immediately. Dealing for the first time face-to-face with the president, Krogh was given to understand that he must stop at nothing.

The next week Nixon's men all came back to Ellsberg with a bump. The refusal of Ellsberg's psychiatrist, Dr. Fielding, to be interviewed by the FBI inspired the Plumbers to focus on getting a psychological profile of Ellsberg using their own resources. Young remembered from his days on Kissinger's staff that the CIA had done such a profile on Fidel Castro, among others. Hunt chimed in to say it was child's play for the CIA. By July 27, Young's memo to Ehrlichman reported they had already requested the CIA to deliver a complete profile on Ellsberg.

In fact, the CIA chiefs claim they were not happy when Young phoned with the request. Young was told that a CIA profile of Castro was one thing, but a profile on a U.S. citizen "who was involved in a legal sense with the U.S. government" was another.[41] Young would have to obtain Director Helms's approval.

In spite of Young's use of Ehrlichman's name, Helms balked. The CIA was in no position to write a profile on Ellsberg, on whom it had no information; it would be too difficult. Young pleaded with him; the CIA was the only agency capable of undertaking it, using, he now added, information Young's unit would supply. Young again said how important Ehrlichman, and Kissinger as well, said the profile was. Helms responded, with great reluctance, "All right, let's go ahead and try it." One of the CIA's psychiatrists was instructed to do what he could with the "sparse material," but Helms insisted he be shown the result before it was handed to the Plumbers.[42]

For Young and Krogh, here was the CIA foot-dragging, just like the FBI. They arranged for Ehrlichman to meet Helms and drafted a presidential letter to Hoover. The FBI director promptly wrote back on August 3 that he had passed to Krogh "all information acquired to date," including individual reports of interviews with seventeen persons who were named in an attachment. Hoover wrote to Krogh that the president had asked that a comprehensive background paper on Ellsberg "be sent to you."[43] That looked impressive on paper, but the Plumbers had learned that Hoover was still not making the Ellsberg case an all-out bureau special investigation in the FBI's tradition of mass deployment of agents.

Until this moment, arguably, no crimes had been committed. The White House was certainly sailing very close to the wind in failing to disclose the Ellsberg wiretap material, but it could still have done so with plausible explanations for the delay. And certainly the emerging Colson-Hunt conspiracy to smear Ellsberg in press articles and congressional hearings was at the verge of obstructing justice. Still, had the Plumbers held back from the next step, they, and Nixon, might have gotten away with it.

But Krogh and Young (with presidential direction to stop at nothing in their minds) and two tough-seeming operatives in their office were ready for "do-it-ourselves" action. Liddy claims the credit for suggesting to Hunt that "a bag job was in order"—that they ought to "go in" to Dr. Fielding's office to get whatever information was there on Ellsberg's motives in leaking the Pentagon Papers from his psychoanalysis sessions. Liddy, according to Krogh, said that "entry operations" by the FBI in national security cases took place while he was in the bureau; he had done them himself. Hunt piped up to say (also according to Krogh) that the CIA undertook such entries in sensitive operations overseas, though not often. He then mentioned that he had some former CIA associates who were available.

Hunt later asserted that he had asked why the FBI couldn't do it. Liddy supposedly replied that some five years earlier, Hoover had halted surreptitious entry operations and disbanded the trained cadres. Hunt then asked why the Secret Service couldn't do it. "Either Liddy or Krogh responded that the Secret Service did not have the full confidence of the White House for a matter as sensitive as this." He and

Liddy, said Hunt, finally told Krogh that if the go-ahead was given, the entry operation could be accomplished. But Hunt got the impression that Krogh could not make the decision himself.[44]

On July 28, Hunt sent a memo to Colson. Entitled "Neutralization of Ellsberg," it set out a "skeletal operations plan" to pull together all overt and covert derogatory information. The aim was to determine "how to destroy his public image and credibility." It proposed such items as interviewing Ellsberg's first wife as well as his Saigon contacts, including a restaurant owner's "mistress whom Ellsberg coveted." It wanted the "full holdings on Ellsberg" from all the intelligence and counterintelligence agencies. And it included this direct proposal: "Obtain Ellsberg's files from his psychiatric analyst." This is the first written evidence of a proposal to "obtain" what Dr. Fielding had, as Hunt knew, already refused even to discuss with the FBI.[45]

Colson says he sent the memo to Krogh; Krogh and Young replied on August 3 that "we will look into the other suggestions which Hunt made."[46] Colson also talked to Ehrlichman. But since criminality was now on the agenda, it is not surprising that memories of what happened next are sharply at variance.

Both Krogh and Young say they went to Ehrlichman sometime in early August; Krogh states it was on August 5. Krogh remembers telling Ehrlichman that to gain access to the Ellsberg psychiatric records "something other than the regular agencies through the FBI or through the ongoing agencies would have to be undertaken." Ehrlichman was told that "we did have individuals in the unit and individuals available who had had professional experience in this kind of investigation." Young remembers that "Ehrlichman simply listened and, in effect, said 'let's think about it.' He did not say 'good' or 'bad' or approve or disapprove. It was simply a let's think about it type of reaction."[47]

On August 11, the CIA delivered to Young the reluctantly promised psychological profile of Ellsberg. It came with a covering note: "I know that you appreciate that however this is used, the Agency should not become involved." The CIA's so-called indirect personality assessment was one and a half single-spaced sheets. It stated that brilliant though Ellsberg was, he might have suffered a midlife crisis by failing to achieve the prominence and success he expected and desired. "It may well have been an intensified need to achieve significance that impelled him to release the Pentagon Papers." The psychiatrist quickly added: "There is no suggestion that subject saw anything treasonous in his act. Rather he seemed to be responding to what he deemed a higher order of patriotism."

This was hardly what the White House had ordered. That same day Krogh and Young sent a memo to Ehrlichman, reviewing progress in not one but two grand jury investigations (and incidentally disclosing further wiretaps were under way). At item two they came to the crunch: They considered the CIA profile "disappointing and very superficial." They would meet with the head CIA psychiatrist (which they did the next day) to impress on him the depth and detail they expected and would supply him with further information. The memo went on:

> In this connection we would recommend that a covert operation be undertaken to examine all the medical files still held by Ellsberg's psychoanalyst covering the two-year period in which he was undergoing analysis.

In the middle of the memo in the "Approve" box was a signed handwritten *E,* plus the notation "if done under your assurance that it is not traceable."

All of the preceding paragraph—concerning the profile, the covert operation, and Ehrlichman's approval—was missing from the copy of the document provided by the White House to the House Judiciary Committee impeachment investigation. But it had survived in the files of those to whom Ehrlichman had sent it back with his approval.

For twenty years Ehrlichman has maintained that while he approved the "covert operation" he never knew (until afterward) that it would involve a break-in. He testified that the Plumbers could have gained access to two years' worth of files through another doctor or a nurse.[48] Many years later a Nixon tape disclosed Ehrlichman's saying that his authorization "could be read to be that they walked in when the nurse wasn't looking and they flipped through the file"—a subtle difference from his testimony.[49] In denying that he talked about a break-in beforehand, Ehrlichman has accused Young of fabricating his account of the early August discussions to get himself off scot-free. Ehrlichman insists that those August meetings with Krogh and Young were confined to discussing Hunt and Liddy doing "some first-party investigations."

Ehrlichman testified that he had told the president of Krogh's plans, of the change to a "do-it-yourself approach, and the president approved." Ehrlichman stated that the president "responded that Krogh should of course do whatever he considered necessary to get to the bottom of the matter—to learn what Ellsberg's motives and potential further harmful action might be." Ehrlichman insisted it "was well within the president's mandate" to have "the investigation include a covert attempt to learn what Ellsberg may have disclosed to Dr. Fielding."[50]

Since giving that testimony, Ehrlichman has concluded that it was Colson who intervened to get Nixon's direct approval for a break-in. Nixon's memoirs admit nothing but give away a great deal:

> I do not believe I was told about the break-in at the time but it is clear that it was at least in part an outgrowth of my sense of urgency about discrediting what Ellsberg had done and finding out what he might do next. Given the temper of those times and the peril I perceived, I cannot say that had I been informed of it beforehand, I would have automatically considered it unprecedented, unwarranted or unthinkable.

It is clear that Krogh and Young correctly interpreted Nixon's wishes in deciding to go ahead.

Certainly, the Plumbers were in no doubt of what and who they needed to pull off an undetected burglary. Hunt, who had told Krogh that he had associates from his time in the CIA, turned again to a group of Cuban exiles with whom he had been involved in the Bay of Pigs disaster.

The ground for this was already laid. Earlier in 1971, before he was formally on the White House payroll, Hunt had been in Miami where he got back in touch with an old comrade, Bernard Barker. Barker, an American born in Havana, was a Batista-era policeman who had been stationed in England during World War II in the U.S. Army Air Force as part of a bomber crew and had been shot down over Germany and made a POW. Now he was established in Miami in the more mundane world of his own small real estate practice. Barker had been Hunt's liaison in the Bay of Pigs venture. The next day Barker took Hunt to the tenth anniversary ceremony of the veterans of the Anti-Castro 2506th Brigade. Hunt was gratified to be warmly recognized when introduced by his undercover name of Eduardo. Then they went to lunch in Miami's Little Havana district.

Barker was enchanted. As he later explained his motivation in following Hunt's orders: "Eduardo represents the liberation of Cuba, the anti-Communist symbol. It represents the government of the United States in one form, in its covert form."[51] He assumed, from the old CIA days, that "something was up" and so did others Barker invited to lunch. One was Rolando Martinez, another Bay of Pigs veteran who, in the ensuing years, took part in the CIA-funded anti-Castro sabotage campaign as a legendary boat captain piloting more than three hundred missions into Cuba. Martinez was still on a CIA retainer although officially retired.

What was up? Colson, who as early as 1970 had been using Hunt on sensitive missions for the White House, points out that Hunt was obviously prerecruiting.

> Hunt's visit to Barker was, pure and simple, a get-ready-for-action call . . . but there wasn't any action anticipated. Not then. The Pentagon Papers hadn't been published. The Plumbers were months away.[52]

Around August 15, Hunt traveled to Miami to recruit Barker and friends for the Plumbers. He told Barker he was working for something in "national security which was above CIA and FBI." They had "an entry operation" to perform on the West Coast against a traitor who was passing secrets to a foreign power. Would Barker get some good men?[53]

Barker would indeed. Already the Cubans had imagined or were led to believe that there might be a quid pro quo: If they helped a new national security mission, maybe Eduardo could get his president to take action against Castro's Cuba. Martinez felt the same. Here was Hunt in contact for the second time that year.

Barker arranged for Martinez and for his fellow real estate man Felipe

De Diego, another Bay of Pigs veteran and former U.S. Army intelligence officer, to be on standby. They would get their orders when the mission was launched.[54]

Without much more than perfunctory government checks on the names Hunt supplied, Krogh and Young okayed the recruitment of the Cubans. But first Hunt and Liddy had to case Dr. Fielding's office and apartment in Beverly Hills, California, performing what they called a feasibility and vulnerability study. They had to persuade Krogh and Young that they could meet the Ehrlichman criterion that the operation be "not traceable."

It meant another trip to a CIA safe house. This time the CIA technicians were disconcerted when Hunt introduced an outsider, Liddy, using the alias "Leonard." Yet they accepted the assumed White House authorization and Liddy, too, got a disguise, fake identification, and a special camera concealed in a tobacco pouch.

With the aliases "Edward Warren" and "George Leonard" but with their trip paid for by a government travel voucher, the two men flew to Los Angeles and stayed at the Beverly Hilton, which conveniently had a view of Dr. Fielding's office.

On August 26, they made a reconnaissance. Wearing disguises they took photos of the doctor's office from all angles, with Liddy in the foreground posing as if he were a tourist. They included the parking space marked DR. FIELDING as well as the doctor's car license plate; they did the same at Fielding's apartment building with Liddy going inside to check the apartment's precise location.

That night they entered the office building and were spotted by the Hispanic cleaning woman. Hunt, in Spanish, told her that he and Liddy were doctors who had to leave an urgent message for Dr. Fielding. She obliged by opening his office door, and while Hunt engaged her in small talk, Liddy slipped in, firing away with the tobacco pouch camera. He saw locked filing cabinets but reckoned they could be defeated easily with a torsion bar and lockpick. As he came out he took a close-up of the office door lock while Hunt tipped the cleaning woman. By Liddy's own account he was no longer wearing his disguise, so would have been in theory traceable.[55]

The two Plumbers continued watching the building "for several hours" and were surprised that the cleaning woman, when she departed at midnight, left the front and rear building doors unlocked. Hunt telephoned the CIA technician requesting he meet their flight at Washington's Dulles Airport next morning. He was to collect their film and develop it—and keep photocopies for the CIA.

Within hours General Cushman was on the telephone to Ehrlichman complaining that Hunt was getting out of hand. Instead of his simple "one-time in-out op," he was now demanding the CIA assign him his own former secretary, New York telephone links, and even credit cards. He was becoming a pain in the ass. The CIA was cutting off technical assistance to Hunt, he said. Ehrlichman, according to Cushman's note to CIA Director Helms, said he would "restrain" Hunt. "Good" scrawled Helms at the bottom, but his relief was premature.

Undaunted, Hunt and Liddy showed their pictures to Krogh and Young, and told them the bag job was feasible. The proposal was typed up for the meticulous Krogh, who wanted a specified budget. Krogh later recalled being shown a sketch plan and pictures of Fielding's office, with the inevitable psychiatrist's couch. Liddy said the tobacco-pouch camera had not functioned too well, but Young remembered seeing clear 3 x 5 prints of both the interiors and exteriors, including those with Liddy standing in them. Young stated later that he had been surprised and troubled to realize Hunt and Liddy had managed to get inside by talking to the cleaning woman. The possibility that Hunt and Liddy might have blown their cover led to a change of plan.

The next day, according to Liddy, Krogh came back saying they "had a 'go,' " except that Hunt and Liddy were not to take part in the actual entry, to ensure that the operation not be traceable to the White House. Liddy subsequently claimed that this restriction "killed it as far as I was concerned" but he fell in with Hunt's idea of having the Cubans do it.[56]

By now the operation to get at Dr. Fielding's files had a bureaucratic momentum of its own. Indeed, it was part of a wider scheme of discrediting the Democrats as well as Ellsberg. On August 26, the day before Hunt and Liddy returned from their scouting mission, a wide-ranging memo Young sent to Ehrlichman stated:

> If the present Hunt/Liddy Project #1 is successful, it will be absolutely essential to have an overall game plan developed for its use in conjunction with the congressional investigation.

Young remarks that in an earlier discussion that week Colson said he would take care of the "press planting." Young, wanting "to orchestrate this whole operation," recommends that Ehrlichman prod Colson to be specific. On August 27, Ehrlichman tied himself for the second time in writing to Hunt/Liddy Project #1. "On the assumption that the proposed undertaking by Hunt and Liddy would be carried out and would be successful" in producing materials, he instructed Colson to provide a game plan by the following Wednesday on how they should be used.[57]

Hunt selected the Labor Day weekend as giving them the longest period of quiet and sent word for the Cubans to meet them in Los Angeles. In preparation Hunt had brought a large suitcase into the White House. Kathy Chenow, seeing it, was amazed. So were Krogh and Young, but as Liddy explains:

> . . . after the reconnaissance, but prior to the break-in, Mr. Hunt appeared with a chest of equipment, rope ladders, crowbars or pry-bars, all kinds of equipment. . . . Essentially burglary tools, if you will . . . and I said, "Well, how are we going to get this stuff in there?" And what I was told was that one of the men would, or more of the men, would pose as delivery persons, put on uniforms, and that's actually what happened. They went, they persuaded this Spanish-speaking people, that—with whom, of course, they could converse fluently—that they needed to place this package inside Dr. Fielding's office. So when they broke in the equipment was waiting for them.[58]

Before the action could begin, the Plumbers needed money. There were the airfares, the hotels, more equipment, and payments of a hundred dollars a day to compensate the Cubans, according to Hunt. Krogh needed five thousand dollars for the budget but worried about keeping the cash untraceable. Colson says Ehrlichman asked him to provide the cash, but Ehrlichman denies it. Krogh says he asked Colson for it.

In any event, Colson was used to putting political contributions to use. He called up a public relations friend who occasionally handled White House advertising and asked him for a favor. The friend obliged. Colson later had the money returned to him from part of a milk lobby political contribution made to a sham body called People United for a Good Government Committee.

On September 1, the friend was told by Colson to deliver the cash to Krogh's office. Krogh rushed around to Hunt and Liddy, who were impatient to catch their plane. Krogh was anxious to the last. "For God's sake, don't get caught," Liddy quoted him as saying, together with the demand that he be called the instant the operation was over. They agreed that Krogh's code name would be Wally Fear.

Hunt and Liddy stayed overnight in Chicago, where they bought chain-store walkie-talkies and more cameras to replace the one supplied by the CIA. On Friday, September 2, they flew on for their California rendezvous. Liddy, meeting the Cubans for the first time, was impressed. They were "fine men."[59] Now the entry team was at last informed of its mission, but not until the Cubans were inside Fielding's office were they told to look for the "traitor" Ellsberg's files and photograph them.

On the evening of September 3, the first part of the plan worked well. Barker and De Diego, dressed as deliverymen, arrived with the impressively labeled suitcase containing yet more equipment. It was rather late, around 11 P.M., according to a male cleaner they met. Noting their Cuban accents, the cleaner accepted the case for Dr. Fielding, and they were allowed to enter the office and leave it. On the way out, they set the latch to unlocked so that they could return once the cleaner had departed.

Alas for such brilliant plans. The cleaner discovered the latch and promptly locked both office and building doors. Finding their way barred and with no plan B, the Cubans consulted Liddy, who was in the parking area outside. Hunt was keeping an eye on Fielding's apartment to make sure the psychiatrist did not return to his office. Liddy authorized the men to break a ground-floor window hidden behind shrubbery and to go up to the second-floor office. He would cover for them. He later wrote that although he was expressly forbidden to participate, he had been prepared to draw a knife if necessary to protect "my men."

Hunt arrived, reporting that Fielding's car was gone, and he wanted the Cubans out. Liddy claims he counseled calm and radioed the team for a progress report. There was no response. Hunt tried. Silence. Hunt wanted to go in, but while he and Liddy argued the Cubans emerged from behind the shrubbery and they all dispersed.

Back at the hotel, Barker explained that they had had to force Fielding's supposedly unlocked office door, and, with the break-in no longer covert, decided to wreck the offices and scatter a box of vitamin pills to make it look like a druggie's burglary. It had pained Barker to vandalize someone's office, he said later.

They had recovered their suitcase of tools and brought out the doctor's mail (which Hunt immediately dumped down a rubbish chute). They had photographed the damage. They had taken Polaroid pictures of the filing cabinets' contents so that, in theory, they would know later how to replace the files to make them look undisturbed. This was, of course, pointless since they had had to wrench open the filing cabinets. And they had not found any Ellsberg files.

Hunt, according to Liddy, was unbelieving. "Are you sure?" he asked Barker. Liddy noted that "we were quite disappointed." Still, no one had been caught. This, with Hunt's having cooled some champagne in advance, was deemed cause enough for celebration. Liddy telephoned Krogh at his Virginia suburban home to confirm that "Odessa special project #1" had at least ended without arrests.[60]

Unfazed by the outcome, Liddy and Hunt speculated that perhaps Fielding had taken the Ellsberg file to his apartment as an inactive case. After sending the Cubans back to Miami, Hunt and Liddy again reconnoitered Fielding's apartment, with Liddy taking the hazardous step of photographing the doctor's front-door lock and closely inspecting his patio for an escape route.

Hunt and Liddy flew home with a proposal for a second mission to go into Fielding's apartment in search of the Ellsberg files. Hunt's first action on reporting in to the White House was to see Colson, he testified. Producing the Cubans' Polaroid pictures, Hunt told him, "I have something here I would like to show you in connection with my activity last weekend." Hunt says Colson passed him, went into his inner office, and closed the door, saying, "I don't want to hear anything about them."

Hunt and Liddy next showed the pictures to Young and Krogh, who later claimed to have been appalled. Krogh particularly was distressed.

"Covert" to him meant no evidence of a break-in. Yet here were Hunt and Liddy showing pictures of a shambles. But police, they maintained, would attribute it to some form of a "drug ripoff raid" and that while it looked bad it was probably better than anything else. (They were correct in that assumption for nearly two years.)[61]

Despite their expressed shock, both Krogh and Young were prepared to go to Ehrlichman with a proposal for a second crack at Fielding's files. They knew where the authority lay.

According to Young, Krogh also showed the pictures to Ehrlichman. Krogh said that when he went to Ehrlichman and explained what had happened and told him of the proposal for another break-in, Ehrlichman was dismayed. "He was not saying at that point that the whole operation was far in excess, but I did get the clear impression that what had been done was excessive, and beyond what he thought he had approved," Krogh reported.[62]

Ehrlichman maintains that this was the first he had heard of the operation's going beyond an "investigation" to a break-in. He says he gave Krogh "instructions that the thing should be terminated, discontinued, finalized, stopped."[63]

By his own account, Ehrlichman did not tell the president about the break-in until after Watergate, nearly a year later, but he did tell Colson. Colson was ordered to forget the memo ordering him to have a game plan to exploit the material; the attempt to get Ellsberg's psychiatric records had failed. He was not to discuss Hunt and Liddy operations with anyone. Colson got the impression from Ehrlichman that there had been a break-in and that the highly secret classification had been ordered by the president. Colson was a man from whom the president had no secrets.[64]

Ehrlichman protested too much perhaps. Break-ins might be out, for the moment. Yet "I certainly wasn't in any position to blow the investigation by calling the police or anything of that kind. We were in the middle of a national security investigation. . . . It was, at least in my evaluation, terribly important to the national security that we keep going with the investigation."[65]

And keep going they did. Despite all the supposed shock and dismay, Ehrlichman and Krogh did not relieve Hunt and Liddy of their functions; the two men were not even reprimanded. They were free to continue their White House special projects. Against Ellsberg they were unrelenting. Liddy devised a scheme to make an ass of Ellsberg at a public dinner by putting LSD into his soup—it was called off. And Liddy and Hunt, along with Young, persisted with the CIA psychological profile of Ellsberg. In November they at last got something more interesting. This time the eight-page analysis asserted that Ellsberg was motivated by aggression against his father, the president, and even his analyst.[66]

It is not clear to what use the CIA profile was put, but Colson was at work trying to discredit Ellsberg publicly. In late August, Hunt had drafted an article about Ellsberg's leading defense counsel who had already made a name for himself as a defender in various causes célèbres on the left and whose daughter had even been involved in the Weather Underground. Hunt's article brought all this together. The intention was to smear Ellsberg by association. The material was given by Colson to journalists in Washington, an action for which he was later to go to jail, having pleaded guilty to infringing Ellsberg's civil rights to a fair trial.[67]

Nixon's yearning to smear the Democrats over Kennedy's handling of Vietnam led Colson and Hunt to focus on the 1963 assassination of South Vietnam's President Ngo Dinh Diem, which preceded Kennedy's own assassination by a month. Diem, a strong president, but a devoted Roman Catholic in a largely Buddhist country, had been murdered by his own soldiers after the generals' coup that overthrew him. That the United States colluded with the coup is accepted history, as is the fact that this bloody episode dragged the Americans even deeper into the Vietnam quagmire. But Nixon wanted more. He wanted proof that the Kennedys had personally conspired in the assassination of a Roman Catholic president. That would not only remind the public who got the United States into Vietnam but it would also presumably disgust American Catholic voters in the presidential contest the following year. It was arguably legitimate politics, if the proof existed.[68]

Accordingly, preceded by Young's formal requests, Hunt and Liddy were sent to plumb the secret Defense and State department files of the 1963 period. Eventually, Hunt reported to Colson that the closer he got to the key dates, the thinner the files became. From his own reading,

Hunt said he was convinced the United States had colluded in the assassination, but there was no actual proof.

At that, Nixon went public. At a September 16 news conference in answer to a question about whether the United States ought not to use its leverage in Vietnam, Nixon answered that if what was suggested was "that the United States should use its leverage now to overthrow [President Nguyen Van] Thieu, I would remind all concerned that the way we got into Vietnam was through overthrowing Diem, and the complicity in the murder of Diem." There was no great public outcry to this though specialists in and out of government wondered where the information had come from. There was nothing to support it in the files. Not yet, that is.

Two days later, on September 18, 1971, the president, meeting with Mitchell, Haldeman, and Ehrlichman, worked on a follow-up to Nixon's initial accusation. Ehrlichman's notes have Nixon saying that the Diem assassination was the best way to get at Teddy Kennedy and Edmund Muskie through the Democratic elder statesman Averell Harriman, who held office in 1963. The president wanted friendly Republican senators to pick up his news conference statement and demand in particular that Lucien Conein—Hunt's recent contact—be released from his silence as a former CIA man. Krogh should be told that Nixon wanted the entire Diem file by the following Friday. The president must be kept out of it, it was noted, but Ehrlichman was to use Liddy and Hunt among others. And while they were at it, Nixon wanted the CIA to hand over the full secret Bay of Pigs file for his inspection, "or else." "Let CIA take a whipping on this," Ehrlichman's notes of the meeting read.[69]

But ten days later, there was a key change of plan. Even as Nixon prepared to meet CIA chief Helms to insist that the reluctant director turn over the full Bay of Pigs file, Ehrlichman made a note about the other subject: "CIA—wait on Diem—Life Mag release."[70]

What had happened was that Hunt was fabricating State Department cables to "prove" U.S. involvement in the Diem assassination, intending to plant them in *Life* magazine. Hunt asserts it was Colson's idea to invent the "missing cables" (though Colson later denied knowing about them). Using White House and State Department typewriters, plus—an old 1963 date stamp—Kathy Chenow, the Plumbers' secretary, remembers being asked to find one—and a razor blade to slice up photocopies, Hunt's talent as a writer produced plausible versions.

One cable purported to be from the U.S. Embassy in Saigon requesting instructions in case Diem and his brother Ngo Dinh Nhu were to request asylum either of the embassy or of U.S. Army Vietnam Commander General Paul Harkins. The other cable was the purported reply from the State Department seeking to implicate the Kennedy White House in Diem's assassination. It read: "At highest level meeting today decision reluctantly made that neither you nor General Harkins should intervene in behalf of Diem or Nhu in event they seek asylum."[71]

Not only did no such cable exist, but the Pentagon Papers suggested the opposite. They included a transcript of an admittedly bleak telephone conversation between President Diem and the U.S. ambassador, Henry Cabot Lodge, in which he said, "If I can do anything for your physical safety, please telephone me." So the new "cable" provided by Hunt was dynamite.

Hunt says he warned Colson that his work, though impressive, could not survive sophisticated technical evaluation. Colson was not put off. He tipped off *Life* journalist William Lambert, one of the magazine's key investigative reporters. On September 24, Colson sent a memo to Ehrlichman saying if Lambert was granted access to "certain documents which have not been published," *Life* would make it a major exposé and cover story. (It was after this that Ehrlichman noted, "CIA—wait on Diem—Life Mag release."[72]) Colson noted that Hunt would run the entire operation from his home or his outside office.

Hunt showed the cables to Lambert without disclosing their forgery. The journalist was delighted but naturally wanted to photograph them. Hunt allowed him to make verbatim notes but demurred at photography. He said clearance was needed; in reality, he feared discovery. Lambert was never able to satisfy his editors of the cable's authenticity, so the story was still hanging when *Life* ceased publication at the end of 1972.

But Hunt's counterfeit was not wasted. His old CIA colleague Lucien Conein was to appear in an NBC-TV program, "White Paper: Vietnam Hindsight," scheduled for December 1971. Hunt showed Conein the forged cables; he was astonished. "Funny the things you don't know when you're working in the field," he told Hunt. When the program was broadcast, *The New York Times* reviewed it, saying that Conein "leaves the viewer with little doubt about the extent of United States implication" in Diem's death. Ironically, the reviewer was Neil Sheehan, the very reporter to whom Ellsberg leaked the Pentagon Papers.[73]

The wider implications of these acts, directly connected as they were with the White House, were very serious. Nixon's men, claiming that they were attempting to forestall worse, had taken direct steps to interfere illegally in a high-profile criminal prosecution. They had set up without statutory or congressional oversight a secret police squad in the Plumbers. They were using forgery to provide dirt on their political opponents when they could not find evidence to support their smears, and they were doing none of it very competently. Most important, they had acquired a taste for corruption and convinced themselves that it was what the boss wanted. The next, still more dangerous, moves were increasingly inevitable.

CHAPTER 4

From SANDWEDGE to GEMSTONE

Nixon's "I don't care how it's done" attitude in pursuing Ellsberg and the Democrats rapidly permeated his staff's approach to political intelligence. Not that they needed much encouraging. Nixon men, in and out of the White House, had been gearing up for months for the 1972 reelection of the president. Some of the dirty tricks schemes were set running independently of each other. Virtually all the plans contained illegalities. What was missing at the start was coordination.

The earliest model for what matured at Watergate was dreamed up by Jack Caulfield, the gumshoe operative John Dean inherited from Ehrlichman. Caulfield had been languishing somewhat; there was little call for his services in the Plumbers. In the summer of 1971, he got in first with a plan to equip the Nixon election campaign with a fully fledged "offensive intelligence-defensive security" operation. Its code name was Operation SANDWEDGE.

Caulfield proposed running the operation under the cover of a new security firm in the private sector, which would service Republican corporate clients alone. It would be funded by their "contributions," as well as by any genuine fees picked up, with the aim of being "untraceable to any part of the Administration." An added spin-off was that the espionage services to the Nixon campaign would be provided free.

This idea was not as far-fetched as it sounded. Ehrlichman had originally wanted Caulfield hidden as a private eye in the private sector when he was first taken on in 1969; it was Caulfield who then insisted being in-house at the White House. Now he sensed lusher pickings outside, especially if the White House would embrace what he called this large and sensitive undertaking.

On the defensive side, Caulfield proposed a security operation to protect what was then called the Committee for the Reelection of President Nixon and to prevent disruption of the Republican convention. Under the rubric "offensive," Caulfield had grander things in mind. He proposed a clandestine New York-based operation to:

- supervise penetration of the Democratic presidential nominee's entourage and headquarters with undercover personnel;
- have a "black bag capability (discuss privately)";
- conduct surveillance of Democratic primaries, convention, and meetings;
- develop a derogatory information investigative capability worldwide; and
- meet "any other offensive requirement deemed advisable."[1]

Caulfield later claimed an innocent intention behind his use of the term "black bag." But as we have seen, it is an FBI/CIA euphemism for illegal entry, usually to plant bugging devices. As such the term was accepted by Republicans. Caulfield himself had already taken part in two White House–ordered phone taps—one on columnist Joseph Kraft, the other on the president's brother Donald, which he was assigned to monitor. And Caulfield requested fifteen thousand dollars for electronic surveillance equipment in an attachment to the plan he submitted to presidential counsel John Dean.

After discussing the idea of a private security agency with Myles Ambrose, then commissioner for customs, Caulfield proposed himself as one of three SANDWEDGE principals. Another would be Joe Woods, then a part-time commissioner in Cook County, Illinois, formerly of the FBI and, most significantly, the brother of the president's secretary, Rose Mary Woods. The third would be Mike Vernon Acree, deputy commissioner of the IRS. Acree, who, as Caulfield noted, was a Nixon loyalist (who has "so proved it to me personally on a number of occasions"), would be assigned "IRS information input," among other things.[2]

Caulfield's trusted operative, Tony Ulasewicz, would be assigned to run the New York operation in "extreme clandestine fashion." Gordon Liddy also claimed to have been approached by Caulfield "a number of times" to join in what he claimed was a "half-million dollar" operation. But Liddy said he was not interested in joining Caulfield.[3] It was because SANDWEDGE was ultimately replaced by the Liddy Watergate plan that the idea that the White House rejected it has gained currency. In fact, the Nixon men, though disinclined to give Caulfield a leadership role, embraced SANDWEDGE readily.

Haldeman was particularly interested. Having sent one of his White House lieutenants, Jeb Magruder, to run CRP earlier that spring, Nixon's chief of staff insisted on being informed of all the campaign minutiae, political intelligence especially. After all, Nixon was the ultimate campaign manager. As Haldeman's personal eyes and ears at CRP another of his White House recruits was dispatched, a loyal and eager young lawyer named Gordon Strachan.

Strachan kept up a stream of "general political matters memos" to Haldeman, several of which survived the immediate post-Watergate shredding. One dated July 1, 1971 reported initial high-level approval for SANDWEDGE: "Ehrlichman and I believe it would be a good idea, but that it should be set up by Herb Kalmbach. John Dean would be the control point for all intelligence and in particular would supervise Caulfield's activities."[4]

Herbert Kalmbach, the president's personal attorney, now to "set up" SANDWEDGE, had been paying, out of leftover campaign funds, for the salary and investigative assignments of Tony Ulasewicz. Ulasewicz got his assignments through Caulfield, who worked at the White House for John Dean. So Dean's central position at the intersection of White House thinking on political intelligence was clear enough.

Early in September, Dean decided that CRP acting director Magruder should be briefed about the intelligence assets SANDWEDGE would bring to the campaign, and he introduced him to Caulfield over lunch at the White House. Magruder took his lead from the president's men: If they wanted SANDWEDGE, he would buy it.

But the follow-up did not satisfy the White House. By September 18,

Strachan was asking Haldeman whether "intelligence shouldn't receive a greater allocation of time and resources than it is receiving now." A handwritten *H* is at the box "Yes more resources"; underneath it is scrawled "develop recs as to what"—i.e., recommend something.[5]

Strachan turned up the heat. He noted to Haldeman that campaign staff were complaining that John Mitchell, then still attorney general but due to take command of CRP the following spring, was not making the important early decisions. Among areas Strachan listed where task force planning studies were completed and decisions needed were "Sandwedge and other covert activities." On October 7, Haldeman agreed that a meeting with Mitchell be arranged for October 28.[6]

In the meantime, Kalmbach was reported saying that at Mitchell's direction he had transferred "$50,000 to Caulfield for Sandwedge." Kalmbach also transferred the responsibility to pay Ulasewicz's salary to Caulfield. But memos complaining about the lack of movement on what Strachan called "covert complicated intelligence" continued to pass among Strachan, Dean, and Larry Higby, known at the White House as Haldeman's Haldeman.[7]

All these memoranda indicate clearly that pressure for action, for a development into something bigger than Caulfield's schemes was coming directly from Haldeman's White House entourage. In the later quarrel over just where Watergate started, there is documentary support here for the case advanced by both Mitchell and Magruder that the White House not only started the push but also intensified it.

For the October 28 meeting with Mitchell, Strachan's so-called talking paper of points for Haldeman to raise directly in discussions with the attorney general included: "Intelligence: Sandwedge has received an initial 50, but are we really developing the capability needed? John Dean reports that nothing is happening right now. Should his involvement be expanded to something more than mere White House contact . . . or Kalmbach become more involved?" And on the key question of funding, Haldeman was to ask Mitchell: "From the campaign funds I need $800,000—300 for surveillance, 300 for polls, and 200 for miscellaneous. Will you direct?" Here is the first documented beginning of a budget for surveillance and a Haldeman fund that within a year would plague first him and then the whole Nixon White House.[8]

By this time, according to Dean, it was plain that the lead role in

SANDWEDGE Caulfield had fancied for himself was not finding favor with either Haldeman or Mitchell. Dean hadn't the heart to tell him. While SANDWEDGE was still pending, however, Caulfield had helped recruit a man whose role was to be of the greatest moment.

James McCord was a retired senior CIA officer who had his own small security firm. Caulfield, on the basis of his prospective SANDWEDGE remit, needed someone to protect both the Republican National Committee and CRP from bugging. McCord came recommended by the Secret Service officer who protected the president's own offices from bugs. CRP initially engaged McCord part time, but he went full time on January 1, 1972.

Caulfield had a last fling at impressing Mitchell. With the fifty thousand dollars in hand from Kalmbach, he dispatched Ulasewicz to New Hampshire, where California Republican Congressman Paul "Pete" McCloskey was campaigning for the upcoming primary election. McCloskey, running on an antiwar ticket, was no more than a nuisance, but he had the effrontery, though a Republican, to call for Nixon's impeachment! Ulasewicz interviewed McCloskey campaign staff, posing as a newsman as he had after Chappaquiddick. As late as December, Caulfield described his activities as a "Sandwedge-engineered penetration."

Clearly, SANDWEDGE was a long time dying. On January 12, Dean sent Mitchell a memo stating that "Sandwedge will be in need of refunding at the end of the month." This suggested that the fifty thousand dollars intended to carry Ulasewicz through to the end of the campaign had been quickly exhausted. Mitchell claims he then, for once, said enough—even though Ulasewicz would still be needed.[9]

Caulfield had by now decided to reduce his ambitions and humbly seek a campaign job as a scheduling aide with Mitchell. He had a meeting with the attorney general on November 24, and when he came out he saw another man waiting to go in. It was Gordon Liddy. Caulfield later reflected, not without justification, that Liddy was going to "steal" his SANDWEDGE ideas.

Mitchell, in putting off Caulfield until this date, had told Dean that he saw the principal problem in campaign intelligence as one of convention security. By this he meant dealing with thousands of antiwar demonstrators, who were expected to try to disrupt the Republican convention then planned for San Diego. Mitchell wanted a lawyer and intelligence expert in charge, not a former policeman like Caulfield. Magruder and Strachan told Dean that this new recruit would serve as CRP general counsel and also direct intelligence gathering. Dean had recently traveled the country with David Young, interviewing prospective Supreme Court candidates. He asked Egil Krogh whether he could spare Young for the job. Krogh refused but had another name—with the caveat that his own boss, Ehrlichman, first had to approve the transfer. It was Gordon Liddy.

Since the fiasco of the September break-in at Dr. Fielding's office, Liddy had not been discouraged, nor, he noted, had the White House. He had been busy with Hunt devising schemes to get at Ellsberg. And once again Nixon's and Colson's demand to recover secret government documents from The Brookings Institution was revived. Caulfield and Dean might have thought they had the firebombing turned off, but Liddy wrote that it appealed to him *because* it had been turned down.

Together with Hunt, Liddy developed a plan to buy a fire engine similar to those used in Washington, D.C., dress the Cubans in firemen's gear, and firebomb Brookings "at night so as not to endanger lives needlessly." The bogus firemen would respond first, raid the Brookings documents vault, and get away in the confusion of other fire engines' arriving. This time the White House "no" was swift. "Too expensive. The White House wouldn't spring for a fire engine," quoth Liddy.[10]

Early in October, Krogh gave Liddy his most sensitive assignment to date. The president wanted advice on what to do about Hoover, his recalcitrant FBI director. Liddy was to consult his sources in the FBI and report back.

What Ehrlichman called the internal war of the FBI had heated up. As Mitchell put it, Hoover was "tearing the place" up and has "Gestapo all over the place" searching for the FBI's secret Kissinger wiretap files. Mitchell wanted Ehrlichman to take over the material, which, as we have seen, had been spirited to his assistant attorney general, Robert Mardian, by the now-ousted assistant FBI director, William Sullivan.[11]

Sullivan had told Mardian that Hoover intended blackmailing Nixon over the tapes. Now, said Mitchell, Hoover has virtually cut off Mardian from the FBI and "is getting senile actually." The president responded that "he should get the hell out of there.[12] When Hoover died the following May, Nixon claimed that he had resisted pressures to get rid of him.

Liddy took a couple of weeks investigating and doubtless consulted the disgruntled Sullivan. And just as a series of newspaper and magazine articles was emerging about the breakdown of relations between the FBI and other intelligence agencies, Liddy produced his report.

After analysis of Hoover's golden years, Liddy chronicled the fall. Significantly, he noted that Hoover had "threatened the President" and warned of the likelihood of Hoover's making good on this threat, whatever it was. He also raised the possible imminent disclosure by Sullivan of Hoover's abuses, such as using an FBI supervisor to run Hoover's stock and tax matters, the painting of his house by FBI services, and more. Liddy perceptively weighed the political advantages of the president removing Hoover before the election next year—and before the Ellsberg trial, which was also scheduled for 1972. Finally, Liddy came straight out with the recommendation that it would be best for the nation, the president, and the FBI if Hoover retired before 1971 was out.

Within three days, the president had read Liddy's memo and commended it to Ehrlichman. There was no question now that Nixon knew who Liddy was: "Smart isn't he? . . . must be as conservative as hell."[13] According to Liddy, Ehrlichman called him to say that the president had sent the memo back "with A+s all over it." So when Krogh suggested Liddy to Dean as the man CRP was looking for, the ground was well prepared.

The meeting at which Dean made his pitch to Liddy has been variously reported. Liddy's account is at variance with Dean's, and Krogh's is at variance with both. Liddy says Dean opened by saying, "Gordon, it may be necessary for you and Jack [Caulfield] to go in the closet for a while." Apparently, this meant go undercover. Dean, says Liddy, explained they needed "an absolutely first-class intelligence operation," something better than SANDWEDGE, "much more complete and sophisticated than that." Liddy replied it would be expensive. Dean responded, "How's half a million for openers?" To which Liddy—reflecting on the fact that they had used the entire SANDWEDGE budget to start up—replied it would probably take another half million before they were finished. The million-dollar budget was in place.[14] Dean denies any such money talk, and Krogh cannot recollect any discussions at all of Liddy's intelligence role.

Dean asked for Liddy's reaction to the job offer. Liddy reports that he said that he was ready for illegal action in the coming "war" to reelect the president, but was not going into action on the say-so of some White House junior. He wanted Krogh to get Ehrlichman's endorsement and Dean to get Mitchell's; if both agreed, "then I'm your man."[15]

Dean says Krogh informed him that Ehrlichman approved and that he called Mitchell to say that Krogh, with Ehrlichman's sanction, recommended Liddy. Liddy says Krogh told him both Ehrlichman and Mitchell agreed that he become "general counsel for the '72 campaign . . . and you'd be right there to run the intelligence operation." Liddy goes on to say that Krogh advised him not to do it for less than thirty thousand dollars a year, which meant an increase in his White House salary.[16] The record shows that, on Krogh's recommendation but against Jeb Magruder's initial objection, Haldeman made an exception to his iron rule that no White House staffer cross Pennsylvania Avenue to get a higher salary at CRP—and authorized the raise.

That Krogh claims not to remember any discussion of the intelligence function is odd in view of his knowledge of Liddy's former activities. Yet Liddy's role in botching the Fielding "covert operation" evidently set some alarm bells ringing. What Krogh says he does now recall is cautioning Magruder:

> I do remember having a conversation with Jeb Magruder at one point, and I'm not sure whether this was right then or maybe a week later or two, after Gordon Liddy had gone to the Committee to Re-Elect, and basically said to Jeb, "Be very careful here, you know, watch him very closely." Because I was concerned that some things might take place that would be extremely damaging.[17]

As for Ehrlichman, he has always denied knowing that Liddy (whom he carried on his section of the White House payroll up to this move) had left the White House to go to CRP until after the Watergate break-in seven months later. The record shows that Mitchell, while still attorney general, interviewed Liddy in late November; by Liddy's account the conversation never got to intelligence at all. Mitchell gave him the job.

So Liddy had presidential admiration, Attorney General Mitchell's confirmation, and Bob Haldeman's salary raise. Moreover, he had been recommended by Krogh, who knew what he had done at the Fielding break-in and who spoke for Ehrlichman. Liddy was now loose inside the president's election campaign. On December 6, 1971, he started work and lost no time in telling the good news to fellow Plumber Howard Hunt.

Nixon's wider anxieties about his own electability had, toward the end of 1971, begun to be eased by policy successes. In the middle of his secret fury over Ellsberg, he had followed up his China breakthrough with a stunning turnabout in economic policy. On August 15, Nixon announced he was imposing wage and price controls for ninety days, slapped a 10 percent surcharge on imports, and, in a reform still with us twenty years on, abolished the convertibility of the dollar into gold, effectively beginning the regime of floating currencies. Although these actions became known abroad as the "Nixon shocks," at home there was a public approval for what seemed the sudden smack of firm leadership. His own poll ratings rose again, even if they remained neck and neck with his Democratic challengers.

Abroad, there were surprises, too. A landmark agreement to reduce East-West tensions was announced for Berlin. This was followed on October 12 by news of a breakthrough in the SALT talks with the Soviet Union and plans for a Moscow summit the upcoming spring. December saw a frantic round of summitry with the western allies. All this made it look as if Nixon were going to be campaigning for reelection more in Beijing and Moscow than in New Hampshire and other primaries.

Then in December 1971, another leaks and secrets crisis almost unhinged the Nixon White House. It arose in the midst of the war India launched against Pakistan, which resulted in the creation of Bangladesh. Nixon and Kissinger, although publicly neutral, were secretly engaged in a "tilt to Pakistan" policy to ensure that India did not pursue the conflict beyond the liberation of Bangladesh. In the middle of tense diplomatic exchanges with the Soviet Union—occasioning the first use by Nixon of the hot line with Moscow—and movements of the U.S. fleet into the Indian Ocean, minutes of top secret government crisis management meetings leaked and were published by columnist Jack Anderson. The tilt to Pakistan that Kissinger was insisting on was out of the bag.[18]

That was publicly embarrassing, but not much more. But because so very few officials at the heart of government were privy to the documents, the White House was again exercised by the threat it saw to national security. What ensued was sensational and kept from the public for nearly two more years. But its impact in mid-December 1971 was an implosion.

Young and Krogh of the Plumbers were put on the case. Almost immediately, Rear Admiral Robert O. Welander, who had dictated one of the leaked papers, reported that he suspected his secretarial assistant, Navy Yeoman Charles Radford, to be the leaker, because, he claimed, few others could have seen it. Welander served as liaison between the Joint Chiefs of Staff at the Pentagon and Kissinger's National Security Council staff. The yeoman—a naval petty officer with clerical duties—was confronted and put under stern grilling and polygraph tests at the Pentagon. He admitted meeting Jack Anderson but denied giving the papers to him.

Eventually he broke down and wept and asked permission to telephone Welander. The admiral told him he had to tell the truth. Radford then delivered an even greater shock to those grilling him. He revealed that for a couple of years he had been systematically filching secret documents from the National Security Council and passing them, not to Anderson, as Welander presumed, but via his superiors, Welander and his predecessor, to the Chairman of the Joint Chiefs of staff, Admiral Thomas Moorer. Radford had traveled abroad as secretarial assistant to Alexander Haig, and, on Haig's recommendation, to Henry Kissinger. He had been with Kissinger on the July mission that led to the opening of China. He had been in Kissinger's briefcase and "burn bags" to get copies of documents. He had sent back a copy of the Kissinger cable to Nixon relating his conversation with Chinese Premier Chou En-lai—arguably one of the most secret of all Nixon administration documents. It was all done on the orders of his superiors; they told him repeatedly what a good job he had done.

In consternation, Young took the news to Ehrlichman, who was appalled. Other investigators' suspicions that they might be confronting a thriller-type military coup plot might have been overheated, but it was deeply troubling. Certainly, Admiral Moorer, whose liaison officer Welander was, was supposed to be on the highest security circulation list; and in any case, Moorer had potential access to all Kissinger's secret traffic. Much later it was revealed that Moorer had given Kissinger supersecret naval Task Force 157 communications for his sensitive diplomacy that cut out all other government departments, including the CIA.[19] Still, for the country's top military to have a line into rifled colleagues' briefcases and burn bags seemed worse than ungentlemanly; it looked like a military spy ring.

Ehrlichman and Young confronted Welander and tape-recorded what he had to say. Welander essentially confirmed the story, suggesting that Haig, then Kissinger's military assistant on the NSC staff, ought to be interviewed. Haig, not knowing that Ehrlichman had Welander on tape, was at first dismissive. Then he and Kissinger were invited to listen.[20]

Kissinger ordered the JCS liaison office immediately closed. He subsequently wrote that he was beside himself and stormed in to see the president. Young asked Krogh to order wiretaps. He refused, but Ehrlichman, hinting he had Liddy's help, requested them done.[21] Again outside channels, the FBI installed three more taps under Mitchell's proforma authorization.

On December 22, Nixon had Mitchell, Ehrlichman, Young, and Haldeman in to "review the whole case."[22] It was decided the attorney general would talk to Admiral Moorer. According to Krogh, Mitchell threatened Moorer with jail. Moorer always maintained he had no idea that the materials coming to him were improperly obtained.

Nixon told Ehrlichman he would "prosec[ute] Yeoman, Admiral [presumably Admiral Welander]" as well as Jack Anderson but only after the 1972 election.[23] The president, who was irritated by secret threats to resign from Kissinger, told his national security adviser that he might drop Moorer, but worried about publicly washing the military's dirty linen in the middle of the Vietnam fighting. In the end the president did nothing. He even reappointed Moorer a few months later to a second two-year tour as chairman of the Joint Chiefs of Staff. Defense Secretary Melvin Laird overruled recommendations for courts-martial. Welander was given a ship command while Radford was simply posted far away to a training job in Oregon.

Nothing interfered with the rise of then Brigadier General Alexander Haig, either. Young, who clearly believed the Welander reference to Haig was suspicious and ought to have been explored, wrote that Haig was the joint chiefs' man close to Nixon and that even in the Kissinger taps, Haig's constituency was the Pentagon.[24]

If nothing else, the whole episode increased the atmosphere of paranoia and mistrust in the White House. Against most of the evidence, Nixon chose to argue that the leak to Anderson had a political basis and was a more serious offense than the military spying on the White House. And from that Kissinger had drawn a distinctive if tortuous conclusion, offering it as a basis for the kind of actions that derailed the administration: "While this would not excuse the transgressions constituting the body of Watergate, it might partially explain their origin and thus mitigate the judgment."[25]

David Young wrote afterward that the shock of such upheavals as the Moorer-Radford affair led to even more drastic secrecy. Even fewer people participated in policy making. By the end, he said that those in the know on Vietnam were, with Nixon, down to seven people, none of them in the Cabinet.[26]

Amid this turbulence one man sensed the opportunity handed to him to do whatever it took to defend Richard Nixon from overthrow. Looking back in a book written in 1980 after eight years of silence, Gordon Liddy wrote that, like a gunner using "battle override" on the fire control switch, he was ready to risk blowing the entire system in order to destroy the Democrats. "To permit the thought, spirit, lifestyle, and ideas of the Sixties movement to achieve power and become the official way of life of the United States was a thought as offensive to me as was the thought of surrender to a Japanese soldier in 1945."[27]

In this mood Liddy drew up his plans. "I knew exactly what had to be done and why, and I was under no illusion about its legality. Although spies in the enemy camp and electronic surveillance were nothing new in American presidential politics, we were going to go far beyond that. As far as I was concerned anything went."[28]

Liddy, by Hunt's account, called on him in room 16 in a state of excitement over how big the CRP intelligence operation was to be. He mentioned Dean's telling of the half million dollars start-up. He said the Republicans did not want their convention marred by the police-demonstrator clashes the Democrats endured in 1968 in Chicago. But he said the attorney general was not averse to causing trouble for the Democratic convention in Miami Beach. That was where he needed the Cubans; would Hunt help? "I can't think of any reason not to" was Hunt's reply. Not long afterward one of Colson's White House assistants phoned CRP offices to tell Magruder that since they were engaged in intelligence they would "find Mr. Hunt very valuable." Magruder said Liddy would employ him. Now the two Plumbers were loose at the heart of Nixon's campaign.[29]

Liddy's account of this is that Dean and Magruder told him to prepare detailed plans for presentation to Mitchell. Magruder, who was already finding Liddy a difficult customer, particularly noted that Mitchell had to okay the million-dollar budget Liddy was mentioning. In the meantime, he was being funded with cash by Magruder's young assistant, Herbert (Bart) Porter. Magruder infuriated Liddy by introducing him at a senior CRP staff meeting as general counsel and then going on to say, "Gordon will also be in charge of dirty tricks." Magruder's version is that he called him "supersleuth." Liddy claims he rebuked Magruder for compromising his cover and asked Dean to have him "zip Magruder's lip."[30] The Magruder-Liddy relationship spelled trouble, but the White House antennae were also in battle override mode—oblivious.

Although Liddy had formally left Krogh's Plumbers, he kept his White House pass. And he and Hunt continued plotting in room 16, with Hunt noting that Liddy kept all the paperwork separate from Young's operation, securely locked in his third-floor White House office safe. The outline plan for their operation included planting operatives on Democrats' staffs; making surreptitious entries to plant electronic bugs and photograph documents such as donor lists and position papers; exploiting sexual weaknesses among Nixon's challengers; and promoting ill feeling among Democratic candidates.

Hunt was given the main recruiting task. He promptly got in touch with old CIA acquaintances and also telephoned the CIA's official placement service asking for résumés of retirees like himself. Hunt spoke to one CIA veteran of Guatemala days, and at Hunt's instigation, Bernard Barker got in touch with another CIA pensioner living in Florida who, when told of plans to bug and kidnap, turned the offer down. Barker's Cuban-exile team was also put on standby. One of them, Martinez, who was still on a CIA retainer, notified his CIA case officer. Hunt's renewed activity with former CIA "assets" in early 1972, after his high-level on-off relationships through the Plumbers the previous fall, can hardly have gone unnoticed at CIA headquarters.

Liddy wrote that as they flew around that January, he and Hunt traveled first class and stayed at the best hotels and entertained potential recruits at the finest restaurants. Liddy's point was that anyone recruited must believe that money was no object if they were to take the risks "under believable assurance of complete support in the event of trouble."[31]

Liddy also chose another sensational way to demonstrate unbreakable commitments to his recruits. For years in the 1960s, he said in his book *Will,* as a ritual of "building my willpower," he tested himself by burning himself deliberately. So as not to harm his gun hand, he scorched his left hand and forearm, progressing from cigarettes through matches to candles. By 1967, his will had hardened sufficiently for the flames to begin leaving permanent scars. Then he made a mistake; he burned the second joint of his index finger so badly it needed surgical attention and a year's worth of special exercise. For Liddy, this was proof he could take it:

> Since my will was now so strong I could endure a long, deep flesh-charring burn without a flicker of expression I wasn't concerned. I thought I'd gone as far as I reasonably could and saw no need to try to go further.[32]

In Los Angeles, however, Liddy found himself attempting to recruit a secretary, to be planted as a spy inside the camp of a Democratic candidate to copy the files. Had he succeeded this could have been Ehrlichman's ideal covert operation. Liddy has described how the enterprise backfired when he tried to convince her that no one would ever find out:

> She said, "Well, they can make anybody talk." And I said, "Well, generally speaking that's true but nobody can make me talk." She said, "I believe that." I noticed she was a smoker. . . . I said "just hold out your cigarette lighter and turn it on," and she did and I held my left palm over it—because I would never damage my gun hand—and looked in her eyes. And she realized it was burning me and my ability to do that frightened her. The poor woman was terrified. And she suddenly recalled that she was to be married to a Swiss airline pilot in September and therefore couldn't do the job.[33]

Liddy, despite his bandaged hand, had better luck on a trip to Miami with Hunt. They interviewed a dozen men gathered by Barker for Liddy's planned "counter-demonstrator and anti-riot squad." One of them spread out his hands like talons and said of Liddy *"El halcón"*—Barker said it was "the birds other birds fear" and Falcon became Liddy's code name. Liddy liked that.[34] He was less impressed with the dark-haired Hispanic prostitutes Hunt and Barker kept lining up for the sex-and-tell sessions Liddy intended proposing for the Democratic convention. Liddy preferred blondes and thought the Democrats would, too. Two women were retained.

On January 5, Nixon formally announced his own candidacy in the New Hampshire primary. Despite McCloskey, he faced no serious contest for the Republican nomination, so the White House and CRP had the luxury of focusing on the Democrats rather than on their own party.

Their "attack" strategy was straightforward: Derail the front-running Edmund Muskie, divide the Democrats, watch out for a late run by Teddy Kennedy, and try in whatever way possible to get the weakest Democrat nominated. Patrick Buchanan, the young speechwriter who had Nixon's ear on political tactics, had been articulating the strategy throughout 1971. Now on January 11, Buchanan recommended to Haldeman that Republican resources on the ground be used against

Muskie. He suggested that the Republican organization in Florida drum up support for George Wallace, the Alabama governor then running strongly as spoiler in the Democratic primaries. Dispatch resources as well into New Hampshire, Buchanan urged. The objective was "cutting Muskie's lead in the Granite State and insuring his defeat in the Sunshine State. Methinks the fellow who achieves that will be doing the President as much good as anyone else this election year." It was prophetic stuff.[35]

Foul play was about to dominate the agenda. On January 27, in his office in the Department of Justice, John Mitchell, the chief law officer of the United States, convened a meeting with the president's counsel, John Dean, and Gordon Liddy, his campaign committee general counsel. Lawyers all, they were about to make outlaws of themselves, taking down with them the one non-lawyer in attendance, Mitchell's caretaker at CRP, Jeb Magruder.

Magruder's office staff was to remember that appointment. The staffers had to rush at the last minute to ensure there was an easel on hand for Liddy's charts. These elaborate affairs, prepared at Hunt and Liddy's request by CIA graphic artists, illustrated each proposed facet of Liddy's intelligence plan, now code-named by Hunt Operation GEMSTONE.

Liddy set up his charts and before the pipe-smoking stone-faced Mitchell began his presentation. It was to last some thirty minutes. Liddy claims he prefaced his chart show with the explanation that the proposed intelligence service was what had been requested by John Dean, and off he went. Liddy can be spellbinding in his intensity and articulation: It must have been a command performance.

He started with DIAMOND. This was his plan to counter antiwar demonstrations at the Republican convention, at that time still scheduled for San Diego. Liddy contended the site was indefensible, so DIAMOND would kidnap the demonstration leaders before trouble occurred, drug them, spirit them over the nearby border to Mexico, and hold them until after the convention was over. These sudden disappearances Liddy labeled *Nacht und Nebel*—the night and fog of Nazi storm-trooper tactics. The charts listed Liddy operatives as a Special Action Group, an SS euphemism for death squad.

By Liddy's account, John Mitchell interrupted to doubt whether such a team could operate the way Liddy proposed. Liddy wrote later that he grew impatient at the complete lack of support he was getting from Dean and Magruder, who sat silently gazing at the attorney general.

Liddy reckoned Mitchell, a World War II naval officer, would get the message if he translated his special action group back into its original. "An *Einsatzgruppe,* General," he claims he said, giving the hard G for "General," an abbreviation of the AG's title often used in its English form. Liddy went on to explain that his men included professional killers who had, as Hunt had told him in Miami, accounted for twenty-two men between them, "including two hanged from a beam in a garage."[36] To Mitchell's question of where he would find such men, Liddy said they were from organized crime, and they did not come cheap. Mitchell commented, "Let's not contribute any more than we have to to the coffers of organized crime."[37]

Liddy said he did not know whether Mitchell was being sarcastic or objecting to the budget, so, mindful of Dean's and Magruder's silence, he plowed on. RUBY was to infiltrate spies into Democrat campaigns, including the nominee's. COAL was a program to furnish money clandestinely to the campaign of black New York Congresswoman Shirley Chisholm [the first woman ever to announce for president]; Liddy says Mitchell ruled that out, saying that Nelson Rockefeller [then governor of New York] was "already taking care of that."[38] Then came EMERALD. This was for a "chase plane" to pursue the Democratic nominee's airliner and buses and bug their radio communications. QUARTZ was to intercept microwave telephone traffic.

Liddy explained he already had an option to lease a houseboat in Miami Beach to which prostitutes in SAPPHIRE would lure top Democrats, and CRYSTAL, a communications center, would eavesdrop their pillow talk. Mitchell listened impassively as Liddy wound on with this phantasmagoria.

And so to the buggings. OPAL I–IV were four black bag jobs designed to place microphone surveillance as well as TOPAZ document photography teams in Muskie and McGovern headquarters in Washington, a Miami Beach hotel for the convention, and one reserve target of opportunity Mitchell might wish to designate. Mitchell kept sucking his pipe when Liddy looked at him inquiringly

There were two disruption operations: GARNET for outrageous demonstrations "supporting" Democratic candidates and TURQUOISE, which called for a Cuban commando team to sabotage the Democrats' convention hall air-conditioning system during the worst of the midsummer heat.

Liddy closed with the spending flow chart, showing high initial outlays on equipment purchases, then the total budget: $1 million. There was silence. Dean later claimed that when he caught the attorney general's eye, Mitchell winked. Mitchell, he said, told Liddy it "was not quite what he had in mind."[39] Magruder claimed he was appalled. Mitchell insisted that he told Liddy that CRP was most interested in information gathering and protection against demonstrators—hardly a put-down. He said later, "I should have thrown Liddy out of the window."[40]

Liddy remembers that Mitchell made much of filling and relighting his pipe and then said, "Gordon, a million dollars is a hell of lot of money, much more than we had in mind. I'd like you to go back and come back with something more realistic." And he told Liddy to burn the charts, personally. That evening Liddy did so in his main fireplace at home; such incineration of evidence was to become a favored tactic of those involved in Watergate.[41]

But, as Liddy wrote, the fire burned in his eyes as he left Mitchell's office. He said he was furious with both Magruder and Dean, who he felt had misled him over the million-dollar budget. Magruder was solicitous; he suggested cutting out the most expensive stuff. Dean, too, suggested cutting back. After they had dropped Dean off at the White House, Liddy claims Magruder suggested that if half a million had been suggested for openers he ought now to cut the million-dollar budget in half.

So by all except Mitchell's testimony, nothing was turned off, only scaled down. The outlandish illegalities of GEMSTONE might have been expected to provoke consternation from a man so close to the president, even were he not the nation's principal law officer. But for men like Mitchell and Liddy, who certainly knew of the military spying on the White House, it was perhaps spy or be spied on.

The next afternoon Mitchell had a meeting with the president and Haldeman. There is nothing in Haldeman's notes to suggest that GEMSTONE was raised; it need not have been at this stage. However, Magruder claimed he had faithfully told his White House liaison, Gordon Strachan, what was afoot, so that Haldeman could be kept abreast of developments. Strachan denied learning anything of GEMSTONE until two months later. These disagreements will probably never be resolved.

Hunt reported Liddy coming back dejected from the Mitchell meeting. Hunt, Liddy says, was annoyed by the absence of a decision and worried that his people on standby would lose confidence. Hunt remembered that he suggested cutting back on electronic surveillance on cost grounds. Liddy, he said, replied that Mitchell still wanted it. They went to work on a half-million-dollar plan.

By now James McCord, the new CRP security coordinator, was in on the proceedings. According to him, Liddy soon regained his cockiness, reporting a few days later that Dean was saying things "looked good" but "some means would have to be found for deniability for Mr. Mitchell" and that funding would have to be untraceable.[42] McCord said he was asked whether he would be willing to join an operation to bug Democratic headquarters at the Watergate if it was approved. Impressed by Liddy's Mitchell connections, but without worrying about jeopardizing his own deniability, McCord agreed.

In a recent interview, his first in almost twenty years, McCord says he "took the color of legality" from all that he heard from Liddy—and Caulfield—about high-level authority, including Mitchell, Dean, Magruder, Colson, and, he assumed, the president. He was wrong, but he had not realized it until too late.[43]

Out went Liddy's chase plane, however, and the microwave communications interception and the air-conditioning sabotage. He dropped the houseboat, but kept the hookers. The number of bugging targets was reduced. The charts also were replaced with standard sheets of paper plus a flowchart produced by Liddy's wife, Fran—as good, he said, as that the CIA produced originally.

Within a week, Liddy had GEMSTONE's proposed budget down to half a million dollars, and a second meeting was arranged in the attorney general's office for February 4, at 4 P.M. The same group was invited to attend. Dean was late—but, according to Liddy, did arrive in time to hear that GEMSTONE II still contained the kidnappings of demonstrators, the buggings, and the plants in Democratic campaign offices.

The participants' versions begin diverging seriously after this second meeting. Most damagingly, Magruder specifically recalls bugging targets being discussed, including Lawrence O'Brien's office at the Democratic National Committee at the Watergate. Mitchell, Magruder said, also suggested an additional target, Hank Greenspun, a Las Vegas newspaper publisher who allegedly had materials damaging to Senator Muskie in his safe. But Liddy's version, as we saw, is that targets were proposed at the first meeting.

There is also argument over what John Dean reports he said, a remark that was afterward to become famous. Dean says he interrupted the meeting:

> Mr. Mitchell, I felt, was being put on the spot. The only polite way I thought I could end the discussions was to inject that these discussions could not go on in the office of the Attorney General of the United States and that the meeting should terminate immediately.

Liddy's version is crucially different, suggesting Dean was merely pursuing deniability for Mitchell. He quotes Dean as saying: "Sir, I don't think a decision on a matter of this kind should came [*sic*] from the Attorney General's office. I think he should get it from somewhere else—completely unofficial channels."[44] Liddy says Mitchell simply said "I agree." What no one denies is that Mitchell did not give approval for the plan at this meeting. He simply told Liddy he'd have to think about it and would let him know.

Liddy was again furious. He now told Magruder what Hunt had told him earlier. "His people" would want out. "I want a fucking decision and I want it fast." Magruder said that Dean had a point but he'd follow through on it, and "get you a decision."[45]

Mitchell testified he was aghast after this second meeting, but if so, his dismay was never communicated. Mitchell's deputy, Magruder, said that this time not only did he pass on information for Haldeman through Strachan but he also gave Strachan the mini-charts Liddy presented, including the budget documents and bugging targets. Further, he claimed, Strachan—either after the first or this second meeting —got back to him, saying, "Whatever decision Mr. Mitchell made was acceptable to the White House on this matter."[46]

Haldeman was also informed more directly. Shortly after the meeting, Dean testified, he went to Nixon's chief of staff, having told Liddy that he would never again discuss the matter with him and "if any such plan were approved I did not want to know."[47]

Dean said he told Haldeman of the Liddy plan, and exclaimed that it was "incredible, unnecessary, and unwise." CRP needed "an ability to deal with demonstrators" but it did not need bugging, mugging, prostitutes, and kidnappers. No one at the White House should have anything further to do with it, he recommended. Haldeman agreed that Dean should have no further dealings with it.[48]

This was hardly heroic. Dean was simply stating that the White House should sever its connection, not that the plan be dropped. For more than a year, while Dean and Haldeman were still in cahoots, Haldeman accepted that he had been told this by Dean; he even told the president so, according to a White House tape. The issue is of exceptional importance because it showed that Haldeman had pre-knowledge of the Watergate break-in planning.

By the time Haldeman came to testify about it, Dean was an outcast. Dean had, in his view, ratted on the president and on Haldeman himself. Haldeman could no longer recollect Dean coming to see him. Dean had said it to him so many times he had accepted it, but now he could not remember.

Did it happen? It is the only direct testimony that Haldeman knew of GEMSTONE so early. Recent claims that the Dean-Haldeman meeting could not have happened on February 4 because Haldeman was not in Washington are wrong. True, the writing in Haldeman's desk diary says that he was in Key Biscayne, the president's sun spot outside Miami. But Haldeman's own notes prove he stayed behind in Washington holding meetings, phoning the president in Key Biscayne. As late as 6:28 P.M. on February 4, Nixon's official daily diary records that "the President talked long distance with Mr. Haldeman in Washington DC." Only the next day did Haldeman join him.[49]

After the February meeting Liddy was indeed kept waiting for a decision on GEMSTONE II, but he was not inactive. He kept hearing of other Republican spying schemes and immediately suspected a Democrat agent provocateur. The reports coming in from Nixon-Agnew offices in a number of states all told of a young man dressed in Ivy League fashion wearing wire-rimmed glasses. He was soliciting help in running "countercampaign" activities. Liddy dispatched an all-points bulletin only to hear from Magruder to relax; the young man had been hired by Haldeman and was following orders. When Liddy complained, he was told to take over the young agent.

In the tragedy of Watergate, Donald Segretti might be classed as light relief. He had first been contacted by the White House in 1971, when Strachan, Buchanan, and others, including Dwight Chapin, a young man Haldeman had selected to be the president's appointments secretary, discussed the need for a "non-Colson dirty tricks operation." Chapin, who had been at the University of Southern California with Segretti and Strachan, proposed to Haldeman that he be used as their "political prankster" to disrupt Democratic campaigns. Haldeman with Strachan arranged for Segretti to be paid, again out of leftover campaign funds by Herbert Kalmbach. He was offered sixteen thousand dollars a year plus expenses. Segretti began recruiting some of his friends. Chapin was his secret contact man.[50]

The Segretti dirty tricks campaign has often been dismissed as of little consequence. But it was more than childish pranks, hilarious though some were made to seem in retrospect—like bogus offers of mass free lunches and false bulk orders of pizza and liquor to Muskie fund-raisers. It was a considerable political destabilizing operation in its own right, and it wrought a lot of petty havoc that caused the Democrats bitterness when they suspected each other. Haldeman insisted he gave instructions that there be no illegal acts; inevitably there were.

Many Republicans were complaining to Magruder of the problems Segretti was causing by the time Liddy contacted him. Segretti had been active in sixteen states holding Democratic primaries and contacted at least eighty people in his efforts to set up an organization. He was especially active in the states holding the first two primary elections, New Hampshire and Florida, where he made his most successful distribution of false campaign literature. Segretti and his men distributed three-hundred Day-Glo posters that read HELP MUSKIE IN BUSSING MORE CHILDREN NOW—a hugely unpopular position in Florida at that time. At a Governor Wallace rally they distributed printed cards that read on one side IF YOU LIKED HITLER YOU'LL LOVE WALLACE and on the reverse VOTE MUSKIE.

While Segretti pursued his dirty tricks, Liddy discovered still more CRP spying operations set running without his knowledge, this time by Magruder himself. Some of these, though small scale, were among the more productive political intelligence schemes the Nixon men launched for the 1972 campaign.

The various operations were now all to come in from the cold and be put under Liddy's umbrella. The first, beginning in September 1971, was a plant in the Muskie campaign, eventually known as RUBY I. Paid for out of CRP funds, a taxi driver volunteered part-time services driving for the Muskie office in Washington. Soon, he was ferrying correspondence, speech drafts, even floor plans between the candidate's Senate and campaign offices. His handler photographed the "take" and it was analyzed on a viewer at CRP offices by Magruder's assistant, Bart Porter. Mitchell later admitted seeing some of the material; some of it was retyped and anonymously leaked to columnists to damage Muskie; and a lot of it was circulated to the White House. The operation continued for eight months, until Muskie withdrew from the race. It cost about eight thousand dollars.

Magruder's "pranks" ran under a Marine Corps code name, SEDAN CHAIR I. It was no great shakes as an operation designed to harry the Democrats campaign advance men. Bart Porter later testified it was supposed to rob motorcades of car keys, schedule fake meetings, or steal shoes in hotels that had been put out for cleaning (then still a service in the U.S.) Despite a fair amount spent, the pickings were meager.

In contrast, SEDAN CHAIR II, who was more a plant than a prankster, was a success that even Nixon became aware of. Again through Porter but using unidentified post boxes to place the operation at one remove from CRP, Michael McMinoway of Louisville, Kentucky, was recruited to infiltrate several Democratic campaigns. After Muskie dropped out, McMinoway was transferred to the McGovern campaign. His intelligence reports were passed by Magruder up the paper chain to John Mitchell and Gordon Strachan. Believing them to be wiretap reports, Strachan attached them to his political matters memos to Haldeman. Nixon, talking to Haldeman about the McGovern camp only days before the Watergate break-in, asked, "Did our guy give us a report?"[51]

Liddy later wrote that the fact that the SEDAN CHAIR missions were turned over to him by Magruder made him believe that eventually there would be approval for GEMSTONE. But it was a long time coming.

In that frenetically busy February, Liddy and Hunt had also been ordered by Magruder to proceed with a plan to target Hank Greenspun, the Las Vegas newspaper publisher.

The plan was for a covert entry operation shared between CRP and the Howard Hughes organization headquartered in Las Vegas. Both had an interest in materials supposedly in Greenspun's safe. Liddy and Hunt say that despite repeated meetings, the plan was finally aborted by the Hughes side. But later in 1972, Greenspun reported that someone had tried to get into his safe. Nixon, well aware of the Hughes connection, was later told by Ehrlichman that Hunt's team had actually "busted the safe."[52] Whether they did or not, what the White House was after in the first place has never been made clear. It no doubt had to do in part with Hughes's dubious financial dealings with Nixon's brother Donald—and possibly with Nixon himself; in part with efforts by Hughes lieutenants to discredit the Hughes "memoirs" hoax by author Clifford Irving; and also in part by Greenspun's rumored possession of anti-Muskie material.

James McCord said that Liddy told him he had visited Las Vegas to "case" the job. Unhappily, according to both Liddy and Hunt, the whole thing fell through when the Hughes organization declined to supply the promised getaway plane. The upshot of the bizarre mission has often been overlooked: More and more people were becoming aware of the White House–connected capacity and eagerness for covert entries.

Greenspun was let off lightly by Liddy compared with what he had in store for journalist Jack Anderson: Liddy admits in his book *Will* to offering to assassinate the columnist. He justified it on the grounds that an Anderson article had, so he believed, cost the life of a CIA agent overseas. Liddy's grimly simple explanation is that he would kill anyone if ordered to do so by a legitimate authority and if he was satisfied the killing was a "rational response" to the problem.[53]

By Liddy's account it was not an idle plan. He and Hunt had lunch in late March with Dr. Edward Gunn, a CIA expert in neutralizing drugs that might be used against American agents. All agree that no names were discussed. The target was identified, said Gunn, only as someone of Scandinavian descent. Gunn, interviewed eight years before Liddy broke his silence, said Hunt and Liddy asked only for "something that would get him out of the way, make him look foolish." He insisted murder had never been discussed and that he had advised only that alcohol was the best method to make someone look foolish in public.[54]

Liddy, whatever else he has been accused of, has not been accused of lying. He laid out a much more chilling account. When they got off the subject of drugs and on to murder, he said Gunn suggested arranging a car crash with CIA techniques. But they settled, said Liddy, on making Anderson "a fatal victim of the notorious Washington street crime rate." Liddy says he gave Gunn a hundred-dollar bill from CRP intelligence funds as a fee for his services.[55]

Afterward, says Liddy, he and Hunt talked about having "the assassination of Jack Anderson carried out by Cubans already recruited by the intelligence arm of the Committee to Re-elect the President." When Hunt said his "principal" (which Liddy assumed to be Colson) might not agree, Liddy said to tell him "if necessary I'll do it."[56] Liddy still says that the killing had been called off as "too severe a sanction."[57]

Liddy says he made a second suggestion to eliminate Anderson, this time only in jest as a way of scaring Magruder, whose relationship with Liddy was becoming increasingly stormy. It so unsettled Magruder that he actually visited the columnist to apologize, according to Anderson—an astonishing breach of CRP's security.

Magruder even felt the wrath of a Liddy threat against himself. He had complained to Liddy about a legal brief he, as counsel, had drafted on primary election laws. In the lobby in front of colleagues, Magruder remonstrated with him and imprudently leaned on Liddy's shoulder. "Jeb," Liddy said, "if you don't take your arm off my shoulder, I'm going to tear it off and beat you to death with it." Liddy claims he later heard Magruder telling people he was threatening to kill him.[58]

At last shaken to excess, Magruder decided to get rid of Liddy. And it was perhaps another missed opportunity by the Nixon men that they did not heed him. Fred LaRue, Mitchell's chief adviser, argued that Liddy's departure could destroy the infant intelligence-gathering operation. Then, after Liddy appealed to Dean, word came back from Krogh and Dean and Strachan that Magruder should put aside his personal feelings. "Liddy's a Hitler," Strachan said, "but at least he's our Hitler."[59]

Liddy stayed in charge of political intelligence but moved downstairs, out of Magruder's immediate orbit, to become counsel to the separate finance committee of CRP. This was Nixon's war chest, and Maurice Stans had recently arrived to run it, having resigned from the Cabinet as commerce secretary. Stans's treasurer was another former White House aide close to Haldeman and Chapin by the name of Hugh Sloan. Liddy helped Sloan with the legal side and they got on well.

It was while waiting for approval for GEMSTONE and to hear whether they should kill Jack Anderson that Liddy, so he writes, decided he'd like to meet Hunt's "principal." Specifically, he wanted to do something about the continuing lack of a decision on GEMSTONE. He was also keen to secure a good job in the second Nixon administration. Charles Colson he saw as a man after his own heart.

This was now the second time GEMSTONE had been introduced into the White House. Dean claimed Haldeman had agreed with him after February 4 that the White House not be further involved. But Colson represented a different White House power center and one equally close to the president.

Liddy's version is that he told Hunt he would ask Colson to "get us a decision on GEMSTONE." Hunt obliged with the appointment and, after introducing the two men, withdrew to the rear of Colson's grand EOB office. Liddy claims he told Colson he hoped he'd be working with him in the future because their approaches were similar, and "I used that to lead into the problem of a decision about GEMSTONE."[60] But Colson cut him off, saying, "All you need is a decision, right?" He phoned Magruder. According to Liddy, Colson said:

> Gordon Liddy tells me he can't get a decision out of you people on his intelligence program. I don't want to get into a debate of the merits; it just seems to me that after all this time somebody ought to be able to make a decision. Let's get on it.[61]

Liddy says that is all there was to it. Hunt's version has one key difference: that only after the meeting as they left together did he realize Liddy had broached GEMSTONE with Colson and that he was slightly irritated at the maneuver. Still, Liddy told him, "I think I may have done us some good."[62] Hunt later testified that he knew from a January meeting with Colson that he was already aware of Liddy's overall plan—even if he did not know that Watergate was a prospective target for bugging.

Across Pennsylvania Avenue at CRP, Magruder was impressed by the call from Colson. He was already being pushed by Haldeman via Strachan for better intelligence information. He had also recently been overruled by Haldeman in a dispute with Colson.[63] Now here was Colson again. According to Magruder, Colson told him "to get off the stick and get the Liddy project approved so we can get the information from O'Brien."[64] That implies Colson knew of plans to get information from Lawrence O'Brien's Watergate office. Colson, of course, was already part of the 1971 plan to exploit any dirt concerning O'Brien. But he has always denied ever knowing anything about breaking in at Watergate although he has admitted that Mitchell told him his men had a bugging capability.

Colson's version is that he called Magruder and asked him to listen to the Hunt-Liddy plan—an odd way to put it because, of course, Magruder by this time was well versed in the plan. Colson also insists that when Hunt offered to tell him the details he refused to listen.

Another potential witness to Colson's call was Fred LaRue. Magruder said he was in the room; Mitchell later testified that LaRue told him he was in the room when Colson called. LaRue, who was otherwise to be a devastating witness in Watergate affairs, said he could not remember.

A Colson aide also followed up with Magruder and what happened next suggests that the Colson call had its effect. Magruder, says Liddy, discussed with him and approved a further scaling down of the GEMSTONE budget to $250,000. Magruder says he sent a copy of the

GEMSTONE III plan to Strachan for transmission to Haldeman, which Strachan denies receiving. Magruder then traveled to Key Biscayne for a meeting with Mitchell and LaRue. This was the clincher.

The third meeting about GEMSTONE was on March 30. Mitchell was on holiday at Key Biscayne in a house owned by Bebe Rebozo, that was adjacent to the presidential residence. Having just resigned from the Justice Department, he had not had much time to devote to the details of the Nixon campaign. Since his nominal appointment on March 1 as CRP chairman, Mitchell and the White House had been embroiled in a huge congressional and press hullabaloo over a reported secret campaign contribution by the International Telephone and Telegraph Corporation (ITT). The affair was taken by Nixon's people as a dire threat to the president's reelection, and they later claimed it made them take their eye off the ball at the key moment.

The cause of the trouble was, once again, Jack Anderson. On February 28, Colson sounded the alarm to all the top Nixon men. He attached an advance copy of a "Jack Anderson stiletto" to appear the next day.[65] The syndicated column claimed that ITT's four-hundred-thousand-dollar contribution to the San Diego Republican convention was a secret quid pro quo for the Nixon Administration's favorable treatment of the conglomerate in a 1971 antitrust suit. Anderson quoted a memo claiming as much by an ITT lobbyist in Washington: Mrs. Dita Beard.

There was a furor. Lawrence O'Brien, Democratic National Committee chairman, was especially effective in denouncing the appearances of corruption, and he infuriated the White House further. Mitchell had been attorney general at the time of the antitrust suit, but had assigned it to his deputy, Richard Kleindienst. Kleindienst, who had just been through sticky nomination hearings as Mitchell's successor, demanded that they be reopened to clear his name. That, as Nixon admitted later, was a mistake. It fueled the flames.

In the meantime, Colson—again dispatching Hunt with his CIA-supplied wig and disguise as a secret intermediary, this time to Mrs. Beard, now in a hospital in Denver—turned the White House and the administration upside down in trying to massage political and press reaction. At the end of it all, there was such confusion that the Congress and the press tired of the affair. Kleindienst was eventually confirmed by the Senate as attorney general.

A White House tape subsequently revealed that the president himself had angrily telephoned Kleindienst in 1971 to order the antitrust suit against ITT be dropped and the Justice Department officials pursuing it fired. Kleindienst, who, like Mitchell, would end up convicted, although let off with a suspended sentence, acquiesced to the extent of deferring the government's appeal to the Supreme Court. Mitchell had then persuaded the president to back off, saying, "There are other ways of working this out."[66] A couple of months later an out-of-court settlement reversed the government's whole approach to divestiture. Significantly, ITT kept its prize acquisition.

In many ways, the manner in which Nixon and his men handled the ITT affair was a dress rehearsal for Watergate. Documents were shredded; many witnesses perjured themselves; the White House affected to know nothing, assuming that press interest would eventually die down. Initially, in both ITT and Watergate, that actually happened. The second time around matters turned out somewhat differently.

Nixon, who had just returned from his historic summit in Beijing, was furious when the ITT story broke. His convention-financing arrangements were being impugned, and he was determined to get back at the Democrats. He ordered Haldeman to find out where *their* convention funds were coming from, which resulted in a huge public fuss over AT&T (American Telephone & Telegraph) that appeared to have forgiven 1968 Democrat campaign debts.

The main public outcome of the ITT furor was that the Republican convention was transferred from San Diego to Miami Beach. The secret result was that Lawrence O'Brien became an even more important target for the Nixonites' revenge.

When Magruder arrived at Key Biscayne, he had Liddy's $250,000 scaled-down GEMSTONE III proposal in his briefcase. It was one of thirty-odd items requiring decisions from Mitchell. Fred LaRue told

Magruder to come back the next day, March 30, took the briefcase, and prioritized the papers. The Liddy GEMSTONE project he left until last. When Magruder returned, they went through the items, carrying on through lunch. The disagreements, eventually absolute, concerned what happened next.

Magruder said no one was enthusiastic about GEMSTONE; they discussed it for some twenty minutes and then Mitchell, he said, approved it, providing for an initial entry into the Democratic National Committee offices at Watergate, and, as more funds became available, entries into the Democratic nominee's headquarters in Washington and his convention hotel, the Fontainebleau, in Miami Beach. This was close to the OPAL scheme of GEMSTONE I. Later Magruder elaborated on his version and said that at this meeting he had also told Mitchell of the pressure for political intelligence from Haldeman via Strachan and Colson, and that the president wanted it. At that Mitchell was supposed to have replied: "Okay, if they say do it, go ahead." In his book Magruder wrote that after starting at $1 million they were reluctant to send Liddy away with nothing. So Mitchell "signed off on it in the sense of saying 'OK let's give him a quarter of a million dollars and let's see what he can come up with.' "[67]

Mitchell has always been adamant that he said no such thing. His first testimony, like his last, was that he had wearily told Magruder, "We don't need this, I'm tired of hearing it, let's not discuss it any farther."[68] The third man present, LaRue, neither agreed with Magruder's version nor with Mitchell's, and that in the end was highly damaging to Mitchell.

LaRue said that Mitchell asked him what he thought of GEMSTONE. LaRue has always testified that he then said it was not worth the risk—amoral, but a nice professional political judgment. Mitchell had replied, LaRue said, "Well, this is not something we will have to decide on at this meeting."[69]

After the Key Biscayne meeting, Magruder promptly telephoned Gordon Strachan and told him of Mitchell's decisions, including his okay of GEMSTONE. It is only at this stage, Strachan later insisted, that he first heard of Liddy's plan. Strachan's follow-up memo was quickly on its way to Haldeman. He recalled that one of the thirty items he listed stated:

> Magruder reports that 1701 [CRP] now has a sophisticated political intelligence gathering system with a budget of 300.

The original "political matters memo No. 18" came back to Strachan, so he testified, with Haldeman's check mark against the Liddy plan paragraph, indicating that the chief of staff had read it.[70]

Haldeman got a call from Mitchell the next business day back in Washington, April 4, asking for a meeting; he was to see the president, too. Strachan, who was listening in, testified that Mitchell said "Well, we had better get together and talk about some matters."[71] Straightaway, Strachan prepared Haldeman his usual "talking paper for John Mitchell." When Strachan testified, he did so in the belief that the talking paper no longer existed; Haldeman had ordered that it be shredded, along with other incriminating material, in the wake of the Watergate break-in. By a miracle, a copy survived and was only recently discovered in another section of Haldeman's all-too-voluminous files.[72]

Dated April 4, 1972, the four pages that have survived list, on the first page, number two out of fifteen items:

> *Intelligence*—Gordon Liddy's intelligence operation proposal ($300) has been approved. Now you may want to cover with Mitchell who will be privy to the information. The current system is Magruder and Reisner. (Magruder's administrative assistant.) Now that Liddy will begin receiving this political intelligence information, you may want to cover with Mitchell, who should be charged with the responsibility of translating the intelligence into an appropriate political response. If it is to be Colson, you may want to lay the groundwork with Mitchell now. Mitchell may suggest Buchana[n], who enjoys that role.

Signally, this is clearly a new Liddy plan; it went beyond things like SEDAN CHAIR II, which Strachan had already passed on to Haldeman. Revving up top aides to exploit it can only mean, in the context of the buzz word "sophisticated" used in the earlier memo, that it was wiretapping, electronic surveillance. Magruder and Mitchell knew; so did LaRue. The White House men will never admit it, of course. It ties them to preknowledge, which they have always denied.

In Strachan's memo the Liddy budget appears here increased by an unexplained fifth to three hundred thousand dollars. Strachan said he used to drop the extra zeros because they were always dealing with such large sums. More important, Strachan is moving Haldeman's focus on the project forward from the approval stage to deciding who should be politically exploiting the intelligence product.

On account of the post-Watergate file cleaning, the paper trail ends here, and subsequent testimony is contradictory. Strachan testified that it was Haldeman's practice where a matter had not been discussed to indicate that it ought to be raised again. When this talking paper came back from Haldeman, Strachan says "in this case it was not raised again, indicating that he would have covered the subject." Haldeman's recollection failed when he testified. He got the "political matters memo" but did not "recall" seeing the Liddy item. And while he did not deny receiving Strachan's talking paper, he could not recall having seen it—even though the Liddy plan item was second on the list.[73] Nor did Mitchell. They both testified that a CRP intelligence plan was not discussed at this April 4 meeting.

Had Mitchell truly disapproved of Liddy's plan or even deferred a decision, he would surely have countermanded what was about to happen. The record shows he had an opportunity to do so but did not. For almost immediately Mitchell was asked to authorize Liddy's suddenly large requests for money. Instead of saying "What the hell is that for?" Mitchell assented.

And Haldeman certainly knew there was a Liddy plan. For this fact one need not rely on the disputed word in February of John Dean or on the Strachan memos. After the April 5 Democratic primary election in Wisconsin, when Senator Muskie was effectively knocked out of the campaign and replaced as front-runner by Senator George McGovern, Haldeman called Strachan into his office and told him to inform Liddy to transfer whatever intelligence capability Liddy had for Muskie to McGovern. Haldeman had a particular interest in discovering the connection between McGovern and Teddy Kennedy. Strachan passed on the command to Liddy. GEMSTONE was now properly launched.

CHAPTER 5

The Money Trail

By the time Magruder gave the go for GEMSTONE, the political landscape had altered dramatically in Nixon's favor. Voters in Democratic primary elections were fulfilling the Nixonites' wildest dreams. Muskie had won the New Hampshire primary—but not by enough, so the media deemed—and McGovern, the candidate the Nixon men thought the easiest to beat, was credited with the momentum. In Florida, George Wallace, running against school busing, won the Democratic primary, with Muskie nowhere. Then the day after the April 4 meeting between Nixon and Mitchell, McGovern again upset Muskie by winning the Wisconsin primary, thereby effectively becoming the Democratic front-runner.

Nixon at this stage insisted on seeing McGovern as a stalking horse for the feared Teddy Kennedy. The last of the Kennedy brothers, though a noncandidate, was holding back from the muddled fray of the primaries in order somehow to be acclaimed and given the nomination at the convention. So Nixon believed. He told Haldeman the White House should make a "big effort to smoke Teddy out." And the president wanted Mitchell to "be sure we have a McGov plant to see how close the K. alliance is." Here, as early as April 5, was a president deeply involved in campaign intelligence. It was shortly afterward that Haldeman told Strachan to order Liddy to switch his capability from Muskie to McGovern.[1]

On April 27, Muskie withdrew, leaving McGovern, Hubert Humphrey, and Wallace to fight it out. Nixon wanted to tilt the result. "Get out fake polls showing [McGovern] doing well in trial heats,"[2] Nixon suggested to Colson, even while announcing his second diplomatic coup, the Moscow summit. If ever a campaign had less need of illegal and hazardous intelligence operations against its opposition at that point it was Nixon's.

But now at CRP headquarters, despite a faltering start, the operation seemed unstoppable. From the Key Biscayne meeting Magruder told his administrative assistant, Robert Reisner, to telephone Liddy. "Tell him it's approved. Tell him we want to get going in the next two weeks." Reisner did so, without, he says, knowing what it meant. It was Magruder's signal to Liddy that the GEMSTONE buggings were a go.[3]

In spite of a brief renewal of the Magruder-Liddy squabbling—during which (according to Reisner) Liddy said they had left it too late, and Magruder claims nonchalantly to have left the decision to go ahead to Liddy[4]—Hunt was given the "good news" by Liddy. There would be more money than the "initial" $250,000; additional projects could be approved on an individual basis. Hunt reactivated the Cuban Americans.[5]

Now Mitchell's time of decision arrived: Call off or reconfirm Liddy's project. Liddy showed Hugh Sloan, treasurer of the Finance Committee to Re-Elect the President, a piece of paper with his budget of $250,000. Sloan saw only the figure and heard Liddy announce that he would soon be drawing substantial cash payments, the first of them $83,000. Sloan checked with Magruder, who confirmed the amounts but said he wanted to clear each disbursement personally. Sloan balked. He was used to dealing with large cash amounts but this $83,000 "was totally out of line with anything we had done before." He went to see his boss, Maurice Stans, and asked that he reconfirm Magruder's authority. Stans said he would check with Mitchell.

Stans came back and, according to Sloan, told him that Mitchell okayed Magruder's spending authority. Sloan testified that when he questioned the purpose of such high spending, Stans had told him, "I do not want to know and you do not want to know." Sloan said that later he found that comment to be highly significant. At the time he had taken it to mean only that Stans had lost the argument about controlling the campaign's spending; he said that the cash funding was in "a runaway situation."[6]

Stans confirmed the exchange, but placed his remark entirely in the context of frustration with spending. He and his men, he said, had no part in spending decisions; he had never even known there was a budget for intelligence. He recalled telling Sloan, "I don't know what's going on in this campaign, and I don't think you ought to try to know." But what had Stans asked Mitchell? He later testified, damagingly for Mitchell, that they had the following exchange:

> "Sloan tells me that Gordon Liddy wants a substantial amount of money. What's it all about?"
>
> And John Mitchell's reply was "I don't know. He will have to ask Magruder because Magruder is in charge of the campaign and he directs the spending."
>
> I said, "Do you mean, John, that if Magruder tells Sloan to pay these amounts or any amounts to Gordon Liddy that he should do so?" And he said, "That's right."[7]

Mitchell, in his version, tried making capital of the fact that Stans had not mentioned any specific figure. He disagreed with Stans's claim to have mentioned "a substantial amount." He insisted he had merely been assenting to Magruder's continuing authority to approve Liddy expenditures. But Mitchell could never explain the core contradiction: Why, if he had just told Magruder at their March 30 Key Biscayne meeting, that the $250,000 Liddy plan was rejected, would he a few days later affirm to an inquiring Stans—the chief of the money operation—Magruder's authority to pay "any amounts" to Liddy?

In any case, with Mitchell's say-so both the political and finance chiefs of Nixon's campaign were giving Liddy unquestioning assent. Stans said Liddy got the money around April 6, a very significant date. On April 7, the new Federal Election Campaign Act came into force. From that date the old days of anonymity were over; campaign contributions and expenditures would henceforth have to be declared and contributors identified.

In practice, under the old law, the suitably named Corrupt Practices

Act of 1925, contributions to nominated candidates actually running for election had to be identified, but those to people not yet formally nominated did not. This meant that fund-raising and expenditures for candidates in primaries and nominating conventions escaped any kind of reporting. The new law eliminated that distinction.

The 1972 election was, therefore, a last-chance saloon, and offered an enormous opportunity and complication. Nixon, like the Democratic hopefuls, was still only a candidate for nomination, not the nominee. Those wishing to preserve the anonymity of their contribution—or cover up the way the contribution had been extorted or offered as a bribe—had to get the money in, or at least promise it, before midnight on April 6. For Nixon's campaign, particularly where traditional big-money Democratic contributors wished to hide the fact they were backing both horses, it meant a cascade of cash.

From the outset, Nixon was determined to line up contributions all through his first term. He had no intention of risking reelection for lack of funds. From 1968 some $1.6 million was left over; it was used as a secret political fund. And fresh "early money," either cash or pledges, kept on coming in, with, until April 7, no need to report it. (Nixon's campaign finally raised and spent what was then the record sum of $60 million against McGovern's $40 million.)

Before April 7, some key dispositions of the cash on hand had already been made. Haldeman, as we saw, had asked for his own "set aside" of $800,000—"300 for surveillance, 300 for polls, and 200 for miscellaneous." In fact, Liddy got $250,000–$300,000; Herbert Kalmbach kept back $250,000 for "miscellaneous"; and Haldeman had $350,000 placed "for polls" in a fund under secret White House control.

The saga of "the 350," as it became known, was extraordinary. The cash, mostly in hundred-dollar bills (CRP had some rare thousand-dollar bills on hand at the time, too), was stashed in a briefcase in Sloan's office. Sometime in early April, Gordon Strachan collected it and took it to the White House. Because Haldeman did not want it in his safe, Strachan was told to find a trusted outsider to keep it.

Strachan asked Alexander Butterfield, deputy to Haldeman, if he knew anyone. Butterfield took the 350 out of the White House in his car to the Key Bridge Marriott Hotel just across the Potomac in Virginia. There he met an old friend who ran a management consultancy and who had agreed to be the "front" for the cash, making it available on White House demand. The friend put it in a safe-deposit box in an Arlington, Virginia, bank, where it waited to play a key role in Watergate.

By the April 7 deadline, Nixon had raised $20-odd million. Some $1.8 million was in handy cash, stashed in safes and deposit boxes in and outside CRP offices. And more was pouring in, legal and illegal. Hugh Sloan later recalled dealing with $6 million personally over one two-day period. Contributors either flew to CRP offices in Washington with the money, securities, or checks or Sloan sent out a small flying team to pick them up. Sloan testified they had so much to do that they ignored places where only $50,000 was waiting. The finance committee was a madhouse, one secretary said.

Some of the unreported money came in after April 7. As long as it had been promised beforehand, it was deemed by Nixon's men to have beaten the deadline. When in doubt the FCRP consulted its counsel, who was also part of the traveling team of collectors, Gordon Liddy.

One category of contributions could be especially troublesome. Under the old law as well as the new, corporate contributions were illegal. But if they came in—unreported—before April 7, who would find out? So the reasoning went, and it helped justify the heavy squeeze the Nixon campaign put on potential corporate donors. When it all came out in the post-Watergate wash, Nixon's campaign was found to have accepted $749,000 in corporate contributions (plus $632,000 more from milk producers pursuing a controversial 1971 price support increase). Democrats were not blameless, either, but their presidential contenders got only $40,000 in corporate contributions and $200,000 from milk producers.[8]

One man had a special talent for convincing corporate donors to come through. Herbert Kalmbach, the president's personal attorney, was Nixon's chief fund-raiser until Stans took over in the spring of 1972. Kalmbach has appeared in our story only as a paymaster for Nixon's private eyes, but that was small potatoes compared with his feats of fund-raising.

Kalmbach's proximity to the president was obviously his special power. His great skill was in inviting prospective donors to recognize their interests—particularly if they were big companies in trouble with the government or seeking new regulatory rulings.

He also did well with people who saw themselves as potential ambassadors. Both parties have always appointed top contributors as ambassadors, but in Nixon's case, it was to excess.[9] Thirteen of those named after 1972 contributed $706,000 among them to his campaign. Sometimes, of course, the payoffs did not pay off. There are two documented cases of men who got Nixon appointments to small embassies and who then contributed $100,000 more for the 1972 campaign on the explicit understanding that they would be upgraded to European embassies. They weren't.[10]

With such a quantity of legal and illegal funds sloshing around the Nixon campaign finance committee, it is easy to see why Hunt's idea that money is the cheapest commodity could hardly fail to make an impression on Liddy. His talents inevitably found an outlet. Liddy claimed to have devised for Stans a scheme under which campaign donors of stocks and shares that had greatly appreciated could avoid the tax consequences while FCRP got the benefit of the capital gain. Liddy said he personally set up a welter of phony committees to accept and "lose" a contribution from the Howard Hughes organization. And rushing around the country as a collector, he was for a while too busy for intelligence operations. "I had no time for Gemstone," he later wrote.[11]

In his capacity as FCRP counsel, Liddy had legal responsibility for advice on handling of dubious money. Two contributions—one an illegal U.S. corporate contribution laundered in Mexico; the other from a noted Humphrey supporter named Dwayne Andreas, who wished to remain anonymous—were to lead to disastrous Liddy decisions. To conceal the provenance of the checks, totaling $114,000, Liddy undertook to convert them to cash. Instead of going openly to CRP's bank, Liddy took the checks to Hunt and asked if he could help. Indeed, said Hunt. His answer, as always, was to turn to his Cuban American network.

Bernard Barker obliged, paying the checks into his own bank account in exchange for cash. Liddy returned the proceeds in hundred-dollar bills to Sloan at FCRP—less twenty-five hundred dollars in unexplained expenses. The perfect money laundering, it would seem. Except that U.S. banks had by then begun the practice of recording the banknote numbers of large cash withdrawals. The bills went into Sloan's safe to be disbursed to Liddy a few weeks later. Unwittingly, Liddy had connected a little money chain to hang himself with.

Liddy now also tightened another careless knot. Because of time pressure imposed by Magruder, he said, Liddy turned for bugging expertise not to an outsider—from whom all in the Nixon campaign could be distanced and deniability maintained—but to the man closest at hand: James McCord. CRP's own security chief was engaged for GEMSTONE's first targets—the bugging of the Democrats.

In choosing McCord as part of the entry team, Liddy broke one of the basic rules of espionage. He was directly exposing to arrest an identifiable member of the Nixon campaign team. He was also picking a man who had some complex elements in his background.

McCord, apart from Second World War service in the U.S. Army Air Force, had spent his entire career in the secret world; he had been an FBI man for three years and then between 1950 and 1971 in the CIA. He personally acknowledged, among all his classified work, only his "security" duties. He apparently dealt with background security checks as well as technical and physical security. McCord regarded Al Wong, the Secret Service's technical chief, as his counterpart at the White House. Wong had, of course, recommended McCord for the Republicans' job when Caulfield approached him the previous September.

While working as both Republican National Committee and CRP full-time security coordinator, McCord also kept his own security consultancy going. After taking early retirement from the CIA in February 1971 at forty-eight, he had set up the firm. He employed part-time investigators. There have been suggestions that McCord knew Hunt earlier than either man has admitted and that McCord had been involved in the CIA's controversial and undoubtedly illegal domestic spying operations. McCord, although in 1993 he broke his near twenty-year silence on Watergate, claimed to the author he knew nothing about the allegations of being involved in other buggings.[12]

For a man with CIA counterbugging expertise, McCord behaved very much like an amateur. Instead of checking with former colleagues when it came time to equip himself at CRP, he went, he says, through the

Yellow Pages to find suppliers. Drugstores and small radio shops were his technical resources in the bugging that was now planned. Nor did McCord display any open concern about the fact that as a known employee of Republican organizations, he was about to engage in illegal activities. Indeed, he says his rationale, since he was working for John Mitchell, was that the former attorney general had presidential authority to order wiretapping. McCord's major new accusation, when he broke silence in 1993, was that Jack Caulfield told him John Dean had assured him the Watergate break-in was going ahead. McCord's explanation for not stating this twenty years ago nor recording it in his contemporary notes, is that he had more pressing revelations to make.[13] Dean, as we have seen, has always maintained he heard nothing more about GEMSTONE after the February meeting. McCord maintains that hearing of Dean's okay was another reason he assumed presidential authority for what he was doing. The only personal precaution McCord admitted to taking at the time was pecuniary. He accepted $2,000 a month extra from Liddy in danger money, plus $2,000 per job. Billing it as "overhead" of $12,000 in expenses he later supplied to the Ervin Committee, McCord charged for four months and two entry jobs.

On April 12, Liddy gave the bulk of the $83,000 he had drawn from Sloan to McCord for equipment purchases. His instructions to McCord, he said, were to obtain as quickly as possible a supersophisticated transmitter of a kind they had discussed earlier. The estimate Liddy says McCord gave for this custom-built listening device was $30,000. In fact, no item of that magnitude ever showed up in McCord's equipment purchases and McCord now says he has no recollection of that amount. McCord says now he persuaded Liddy to drop the idea of a room bug—because, unlike phone bugs powered by the line current, its batteries would soon run out.[14]

In the rushed weeks following approval for GEMSTONE, each of its three Washington principals had other tasks to perform in addition to the main planning. McCord, besides spending $40,000 on equipment, was given the job of providing extra security for the Mitchells. As attorney general, the CRP chairman had previously enjoyed official protection. Now McCord helped out, escorting the Mitchells' young daughter to school, checking the Mitchells' apartment—coincidentally located in the Watergate complex—for bugging, and vetting drivers.

McCord decided he needed help. Through the FBI placement service for former employees, he got in touch with Alfred Baldwin in Connecticut. Baldwin was ex-FBI and out of a job. He joined McCord as a tryout security guard for Mrs. Martha Mitchell on a campaign speaking tour. McCord got Fred LaRue's approval for the hiring and LaRue equipped Baldwin with a pistol. Apparently, Baldwin was found wanting by Martha, not an easy employer, but McCord found other work for him monitoring possible threats to CRP offices and personnel from antiwar demonstrators then again gathering in Washington. This was pending more permanent employment. Baldwin did not have to wait long.

Hunt, who was also being paid extra salary and three thousand dollars per entry by Liddy, had helped switch capability from Muskie to McGovern, per Haldeman's instructions. This consisted of shifting Thomas Gregory, a young Mormon student from the University of Utah, from the Muskie campaign organization, which he had infiltrated, to McGovern's Washington headquarters. He was soon funneling details back, including the office layout.[15]

Before GEMSTONE could move ahead, there were more diversions. On May 2, J. Edgar Hoover, whose resignation Nixon had sought but dared not ask for, was found dead on the floor near his bed, an apparent victim of a heart attack. There had never been another FBI director; now Nixon had an unprecedented opportunity.

That same day he attended the swearing in of his "own man," General Vernon Walters, to be deputy director of the CIA, Nixon dispatched another military henchman to the FBI. L. Patrick Gray was a former submarine commander who had worked with Nixon when he was vice president as well as in the 1960 and 1968 presidential campaigns. Since 1969, Gray had had a number of top jobs, ending up at the Justice Department as deputy attorney general designate. The president, though he had earlier worried that Gray would be seen as a "Nixon stooge," now appointed him acting FBI director.[16]

Gray arrived at Hoover's office that afternoon under orders to secure the famous secret files Hoover was supposed to have amassed. The Nixon men could hardly wait "to find out what's there, who controls it —where skeletons are."[17] It seemed legitimate political booty; by comparison anything overheard at the DNC or found in Hank Greenspun's safe was tittle-tattle.

Acting Attorney General Kleindienst had ordered Hoover's office to be sealed, but by the time Gray arrived it was already too late. The crown jewels had been spirited away. Hoover's loyal staff denied secret files existed; Gray left frustrated and empty-handed and the Nixonites were furious at being thwarted.[18] While few of them mourned the director's death, his lying in state was the occasion for a Liddy operation, supposedly devoted to preventing an antiwar demonstration being held on the Capitol steps from disturbing Hoover's catafalque.

This specific rationale for the operation comes from Hunt; it is equally possible that the antiwar demonstration, regardless of Hoover, was the target of Nixon's fury. After all, Ellsberg was listed among those attending. In any case, Hunt was asked to bring in the Cuban Americans, who flew north to do their duty.

They jeered at the demonstration. They claimed they cut the wire to the microphones or the amplifiers, punched a few demonstrators, and one of them was briefly arrested then let go. The melee was barely noticed in the newspapers. All in all an expensive excursion, although Liddy says he got money over and above the GEMSTONE budget.

From Liddy's standpoint, one of the things accomplished was that the expedition gave him the chance to show his Cuban Americans what he had planned for them. They recall being shown McGovern's headquarters on Capitol Hill and then being driven past the Watergate building. "That's our next target," Liddy said.[19]

There was one more diversion before Watergate, and it involved another extraordinarily cynical Nixon manipulation. On May 15, George Wallace was shot and badly wounded while campaigning in the Maryland primary; his assailant, Arthur Bremer, was immediately seized and arrested. At the time Wallace totaled more primary votes than any other Democrat and was second only to George McGovern in convention delegates. But the assassination attempt effectively removed Wallace from the campaign, and thereby settled the 1972 election. Nixon now knew for certain he would not be threatened by a Wallace third-party candidacy as in 1968.

There is still dispute about what Hunt and his principal, Colson, were up to on this occasion. Hunt's story was that Colson first asked him to break into Bremer's rented rooms in Milwaukee in search of incriminating materials, then called it off. As early as 1975, however, the suspicion was in print that Colson had asked Hunt to "plant" literature in the apartment to link Bremer to the Democrats.[20] In 1980, Liddy confirmed this, saying Hunt told him the planted documentation was to link Bremer to the radical left.

In 1988, the origin of the plant idea moved from Colson to the Oval Office. In a National Archives oral history interview, Colson was asked whether it was Nixon who suggested making the plant. He said he could not remember, but agreed that if it was on the tapes it must be true.[21] Colson has elaborated further:

> Nixon expressed a fear that this guy [Bremer] might be a right-wing zealot or a Nixon supporter and that the blame would then come upon Nixon. We sat there for a couple of hours talking. Early in the conversation Nixon said, "Get over to the FBI and find out what they know."
>
> I picked up a phone from the president's office, so it's on the tapes, and got hold of Mark Felt and said, "What do we know?" and Felt said, "We know nothing; we've got the name and address of the fellow. We're sending agents out to his apartment right now . . . "
>
> Nixon's having a cocktail, he's sitting there with his feet back, we're waiting for the FBI to call. As happened hundreds of times under those circumstances, he would say, "Wouldn't it be great if . . . oh, wouldn't it be great if they had left-wing propaganda in that apartment?" And in the course of conversation back and forth he said, "Too bad we couldn't get somebody there to plant it. Maybe could find out what was behind this." I excused myself, went out, called Howard Hunt . . . [22]

Colson sought to make light of it, saying that it was simply an example of Nixon's political fantasies, "the sort of thing he was always doing." Colson's handwritten notes of his meetings that night with the president show that the version of Bremer's being left wing and with left-wing literature in his apartment was "our story," which the Associated Press was already running. Colson, telephoning from the president's own EOB office, also tried to sell Mark Felt, deputy FBI director, "our story": "I told him we had heard rumors that there were political motivations to the killing [*sic*], to wit: Bremer had ties with Kennedy or McGovern political operatives, that obviously there could be a conspiracy."[23]

This enterprise—to seek falsely to link the name of the leading Democratic candidate to a would-be political assassin—came to nothing, but not for want of trying. After Colson called Hunt, they learned the Bremer lodgings had been sealed by the FBI.

The Wallace episode can only have confirmed Hunt and Liddy in their belief that the continuous pressure for illegal entries and political smears had the highest White House sanction.

On May 22, Nixon arrived in Moscow for his summit with the Kremlin leadership. On the same day back in Washington, the Liddy team gathered to prepare for what was to be the first break-in at Watergate, OPAL.

Liddy's first OPAL target had been McGovern headquarters on Capitol Hill. Politically, it made the most sense in that McGovern now appeared to be the likely Democratic nominee. Thomas Gregory, their McGovern plant, attended the briefing; so did the rest of the team, including the Cuban Americans. Gregory had supplied the headquarters layout and arranged a tour of the office for McCord, who posed as an out-of-town uncle. McCord reckoned the bugs could be planted within five minutes. The plan was to have Gregory be the last one to leave work in the evening and admit McCord. That plan fell through, however, and Gregory became jittery. Hunt revived the plan that had worked with the Fielding break-in—making a fake delivery. McCord would deliver a typewriter and while inside the offices plant listening devices. Again the plan aborted when the McGovern campaign deployed security men.

By now Liddy was planning a full-scale break-in at McGovern's headquarters to coincide with his OPAL entry into the Watergate. On a May 25 reconnoiter with some of the team, Liddy decided there was too much illumination from two clusters of floodlights at the rear of the McGovern offices. With his Walther *Luftpistole*—which is no child's air pistol but a silent murderous weapon—he shot out the bulbs. His partner in this bizarre venture was Frank Sturgis, a recent recruit to the Miami team.

Magruder later testified that Liddy reported this shootout to him while he was having a meeting with Gordon Strachan. He claimed both had been very concerned because they had understood from Liddy that neither he nor anyone would participate in activities that could in any way be connected to CRP. But neither Magruder nor Strachan did anything about it.

In the eight weeks that had elapsed since GEMSTONE was supposedly approved by Mitchell, the DNC offices at Watergate had become the prime target. This displeased Liddy; he had planned the DNC for later, when it became headquarters for the Democrats' presidential candidate. But according to Liddy, out of the blue he got orders from Magruder himself at the end of April. Could they tap the phones and put a bug in Lawrence O'Brien's office? "We want to know whatever's said in his office, just as if it were here; what goes on in this office."

Magruder added that he also wanted the entry team to photograph whatever it could find. Liddy reckoned that Magruder was acting on orders, and there was no doubting his new urgency. "Get in there as soon as you can, Gordon; it's important," Liddy quotes him as saying.

Liddy was unsettled over the time it was taking McCord to get all his bugging equipment together and startled to hear that he was waiting for Federal Communications Commission approval for the frequencies his transceivers would be using ("like registering a gun you're going to use in a holdup," in Liddy's opinion.)[24]

That week of May 22, Liddy also had the Cuban Americans familiarize themselves with the target. One night, because of the "excellent cover" given by a large transport exhibition in Washington, he simply had the whole gang sign the security register of the Watergate office building reception before going up to the sixth floor to inspect the DNC front doors. Hunt, he said, took a soft-clay impression of the lock.

McCord, meanwhile, had rented a room for Al Baldwin at the Howard Johnson Motor Inn opposite the Watergate. Having returned from a vacation, Baldwin was then told he would be working over the Memorial Day weekend. He was fascinated to see all the apparatus and tape recorders that had appeared in his absence in room 419.

Baldwin later testified, three times, that on that first evening, of May

26, McCord let Baldwin put headphones on and listen to a telephone conversation. This was before any bugs had yet been installed by the team at the DNC, and it poses the question of just who else McCord might have been bugging. One book suggests it was a call girl operation.[25]

Baldwin remembers McCord being visited in room 419 that evening by men he later recognized as Hunt and Liddy. McCord tried using aliases but got muddled. Also characteristic of the sloppy security for such a high-risk operation, the room was booked in the name of McCord's firm, and Baldwin made many long-distance phone calls home to his parents. It was all to be very easily traceable.

McCord told Baldwin that they would be going into the offices across the street later that night. Baldwin, armed with a walkie-talkie, was to act as lookout. In fact, room 419 was not an ideal observation post; it was at least one floor lower than the DNC offices, which were recessed behind a terrace. Even so, Baldwin claims he did see McCord inside the DNC that evening, which is yet one more oddity in a story growing curiouser and curiouser. McCord is here reported inside the DNC two days before the bugging team managed to get in, after immense difficulty. McCord now says Baldwin has got it wrong.

Liddy's account shows no sign he knew what McCord was doing either. He, Hunt, and the Cuban Americans had that day moved across town into two rooms in the Watergate Hotel, which is adjacent to the office building. On hand were the Ellsberg psychiatrist's break-in team of Barker, Martinez, and De Diego plus three more of Barker's associates: Virgilio Gonzalez, a locksmith who worked for the Missing Key Company in Miami; Reinaldo Pico; and Frank Sturgis. Sturgis was not a Cuban American but a U.S. citizen and blowhard soldier of fortune who had fought in Cuba and had had many other escapades.

The break-in team all used aliases, but the booking for their "board meeting" dinner that evening in the hotel's Continental Room had been made on the stationery of a Miami firm that included Barker among its directors. Again, this was easily traceable.

The dinner was cover for their entry. The Continental Room, though run by the hotel, was actually in the basement of the Watergate office building. It opened into a corridor linking the Continental Room to the office stairwell. With the dinner over and the waiters well tipped and dismissed, team members could walk up to the sixth floor to the DNC offices, pick the locks, and gain entry undetected. At least that was the plan.

Why it failed at the first attempt is a matter of much dispute. Hunt's original version had the dinner party dispersing at 10 P.M., with Hunt and Gonzalez staying behind. At 10:30 P.M. a guard said the two would have to vacate the Continental Room, but when the lights were turned off they hid in a closet. They heard the guard lock the other exit door. They were waiting for a signal from the lookout that the last person working had left the DNC offices. The plan was for them to go through the corridor door to the stairwell beyond. The deadline was 11 P.M., because the alarm on the corridor was to be activated then. (Hunt noted that McCord was supposed to have "defeated" the alarm but had not done so.)

Eleven o'clock passed and Hunt and Gonzalez were stuck. The corridor door was now, they assumed, alarmed and Gonzalez was unable to pick the lock of the other door. The operation was called off and they spent the night in the closet. Liddy, who had left the Continental Room earlier, went off with other members of the team to try McGovern's headquarters. They were also thwarted there.

This version of what happened has been effectively challenged by James Hougan's book, *Secret Agenda,* in which he points out the many anomalies. First, no guard was on duty before midnight; second, the guard who did then check the Continental Room reported in his rounds book:

> Contineal roam [*sic*] open
> Having meeting cont
> Room close at 2:10AM

Hougan's third item is the clincher: There was *no* alarm on the door of the Continental Room or the corridor, according to the Watergate maintenance supervisor, Royce Lea.[26]

Liddy, writing many years later but before Hougan's revelations, evidently believed what Hunt had told him. He had after all left the dinner to go back to the command post. Why he was misled by both Hunt and McCord at the time—who stated they had seen the alarm—

is a mystery. What emerges in Liddy's book is his annoyance with McCord, his habit of "always slipping away . . . he hated to stay in one place very long . . . sometimes he would just loiter in the shadows, on the sidelines, so to speak, trying hard not to be noticed. I wasn't sure whether this was the product of long clandestine-induced caution or a lack of nerve."[27]

The next night, Saturday, they tried again, and failed again in even more ludicrous circumstances. According to Liddy, the burglars simply signed in under aliases with the security guard at the Watergate office reception desk, as they had done a few days before, took the elevator to the eighth floor, and walked down the stairwell to the sixth floor where the DNC's offices were. This brazen tactic unsettled Martinez, who was left with the impression they must be part of an inside job. Except they again did not get in. Gonzalez couldn't pick the lock.

Liddy, waiting at the command post in one of the hotel rooms, was unbelieving when the burglars all trooped in disconsolate. Fearful that they might have damaged the DNC door lock, he and two others went back yet again signing at the front desk. Satisfied that the lock would not give them away, Liddy ordered the night's efforts ended, but not before sending Gonzalez—over Hunt's protests—to Miami to get the right tools. Liddy had decided they would go in again Sunday night, come what may. "I had no intention of going back to Magruder on Monday morning to tell him that I'd failed."[28]

On Sunday night they got into the Watergate at garage level and taped the basement stairwell door open—a rather simple McCord stratagem that might have worked the first time. Once on the sixth floor, Gonzalez now used a pressure wrench to twist the lock on the stairwell rear door to the DNC and they were in.

McCord worked dismantling telephones near the terrace windows with Gonzalez in attendance. Barker and Martinez started photographing documents while Sturgis, Pico, and De Diego served as corridor lookouts. At one point, De Diego was confronted by a guard and escorted out of the building. But the guard did not call the police.

McCord said he placed one phone bug, a tiny radio transmitter, in a terrace-side office later identified as that used by Spencer Oliver, chairman of the association of Democratic state chairmen. A second bug went on a phone in a terrace office facing Virginia Avenue on "an extension of a call director [a subswitchboard] that was identified as Mr. O'Brien's." In his book, McCord added the detail that this call director carrying O'Brien's lines was in "an adjoining room" to the first phone that he had bugged. (Contrary to frequent statements, the bug was not on Larry O'Brien's own phone; his office was far away on the opposite side of the complex and, McCord now claims, locked.)[29] McCord further claimed that he tested both bugs to see that they were working. Certainly both had line-of-sight transmission to the listening post across the avenue at Howard Johnson's.

McCord says he finished his wiring in about fifteen minutes but that the photographic team had finished sooner. He urged them to go, but they stayed together. Five minutes later, all descended the stairwell, removing sticky tapes from the door-latches as they went. Liddy, said McCord, was elated with the success.

Liddy was, too. Barker brought back two rolls of 36-exposure 35mm film plus Polaroid pictures to show that desks had been returned to order. Liddy congratulated them and "we had a small victory celebration in the command post." There was some disagreement about the speed with which the operation was concluded, with Hunt complaining about how few photos had been taken. Barker, after only an hour inside, blames the early completion on McCord: "I guess he didn't want to hang around."[30] But Liddy took the films, saying, according to Hunt, that he would have McCord arrange for their printing. On Monday morning, Liddy could show Magruder the Polaroid snaps of inside the DNC.

Nixon, home from Moscow in triumph, immediately plunged into the thick of campaign planning. He was later to claim that only after Moscow did he really concentrate on reelection politics; but in truth they were never far from his mind. On June 6, McGovern won the California primary and would now almost certainly be the Democratic presidential candidate. He was the choice the Nixon camp had hardly dare hope for.

They promptly targeted McGovern as the extremist, intending the election to be a replay of the rout the Republican "extremist" Barry Goldwater had suffered in 1964. A detailed assault book drawn up by Patrick Buchanan for the president conveyed the flavor: Buchanan referred to McGovern as an SOB and said the book contained enough statements, positions, and votes "not only to defeat the South Dakota Radical—but to have him indicted by a grand jury." Nixon himself wanted intelligence, asking Haldeman whether "our guy" in the McGovern camp had furnished a report.[31]

At this point, Nixon really had turned the tables on his opponents. The combined effects of the failure of prominent Democrats like Muskie and Humphrey, the success of Nixon's summit diplomacy in Beijing and Moscow, plus some of the most decisive action of the Vietnam War had put him in a commanding position in the opinion polls. On June 12, assuming the semiparalyzed Wallace would not run, Gallup gave Nixon a 53–34 percent lead over McGovern. The election seemed unlosable unless the Nixon camp threw it away.

At the DNC offices in the Watergate, key staffers were leaving to prepare their Miami Beach convention, even as the bugging of their phones began. The day after the first break-in, Baldwin and McCord moved up three floors at the Howard Johnson to room 723. From there they had a far better view, directly across and looking slightly down into the DNC terrace offices. According to Baldwin, he now began regular eavesdropping of phone calls that would exceed two hundred before the next three weeks were out and typed up summaries, rather than making handwritten notes, for McCord to edit. McCord, however, claims the transmissions were so low-powered that it took two days to find them on his sophisticated sixty-five-hundred-dollar receiver. From one of the two bugs there was not a peep.

Liddy says he was impatient for results. McCord again invited him to the listening post, demonstrating with the equipment the difficulty he was having capturing anything at all from the "O'Brien bug." Liddy was surprised that tape recorders were not being used and when McCord explained that the resistances were mismatched, Liddy suggested recording the calls over a loudspeaker through a microphone. McCord claimed that such a course would breach security; Baldwin was using headphones. In any case, McCord said, there was no need for recorders; the log showed that much of what was coming over was of no intelligence value and was being edited out. "I told him I wanted it all; that I'd do any editing," retorted Liddy. That was on June 1.

By all accounts it was very lackadaisical surveillance. While at the White House, Nixon's noise-activated recorders were capturing every word, here at the listening post keeping track of calls depended on a lone eavesdropper. When Baldwin was out for whatever reason—and he took most of his meals outside the room—there was no listening at all. Had the second bug been working, how he would have listened to both simultaneously has never been explained. And two hundred calls over twenty days is less than it sounds for a busy office.

Liddy said that when he read the badly typed logs he realized he couldn't send them to John Mitchell: The telephone being tapped was used by a number of different people, none of them O'Brien. The next day's "take" was as bad. On June 5, to satisfy Magruder, Liddy dictated from the logs to his secretary, Sally Harmony. She later boasted to the Senate committee that she could "keep a secret" and eight times typed up the "take" onto special GEMSTONE stationery Liddy ordered. It was all shredded after Watergate, but stationery samples survived at the printers. Each sheet carried the warning that EXPLOITATION MAY COMPROMISE SOURCE AND TERMINATE FLOW OF INFORMATION. This warning, according to Liddy, was to stop the likes of Magruder inadvertently tipping off the Democrats by using the material. In the event, Magruder did pass on at least two items. One was that CRP official Harry Flemming had been intercepted telephoning Spencer Oliver. This momentarily caused consternation at CRP but it turned out that they were both members of a group called Young American Political Leaders. The other item that Magruder raised with Fred LaRue involved some senior Democrats setting up sexual liaisons.

Titillating though this might be, Liddy knew it was not what his $250,000 budget was for. He was under the impression that the second, and so far nontransmitting, bug was the sophisticated listening device that McCord had expected to pay $30,000 for. Rather than wait for his principals to tell him to correct the defective bug, Liddy was already contemplating going back into the Watergate.

McCord now says that apart from fixing the defective bug, his particular reason for wanting to go back into the DNC concerned demonstration intelligence. He had been told the Vietnam Veterans Against the War were planning sabotage of the Republican convention, and he had learned one of their representatives had a desk at the DNC. He intended rifling it.[32]

Liddy gave his meager product to Magruder in a double-lined envelope for delivery to Mitchell, explaining the difficulties. The next day, June 9, Magruder called Liddy in to say the contents were hardly worth the risk and expense. Could the defective bug be made to work? Liddy said they were targeting McGovern headquarters for June 17, but as for the DNC, there was no problem in "requiring my wireman to get things working properly; it could be a quick in and out job with McCord and only two others." Magruder said he would get back to him.[33]

Magruder replied on Monday, June 12, but with new emphasis on photography rather than bugging. Liddy's account reads:

> "*Here's* what I [Magruder] want to know." He swung his left arm back behind him and brought it forward forcefully as he said, "I want to know what O'Brien's got right here!" At the word *here* he slapped the lower part of his desk with his left palm, hard. "Take all the men, all the cameras you need. *That's* what I want to know!"

Liddy said Magruder was referring to the place in his desk where he kept his dirt on the Democrats. And Liddy concluded: *"The purpose of the second Watergate break-in was to find out what O'Brien had of a derogatory nature about us, not for us to get something on* him [Liddy's italics] . . . "[34]

That was Liddy's great conclusion, written in 1980. Get their dirt on us, not find dirt on them. Just what that dirt might be has spawned more than one theory, including an alleged connection between a federal prosecution of a call-girl operation and its links to White House and congressional personalities. Hard evidence of the link to Watergate is lacking.[35]

Magruder's own version of how the second break-in came about has undergone numerous challenges. He never accepted the initiating role

Liddy attributed to him. Indeed, in his Senate testimony he later answered no when asked if he knew "this" operation would take place. On the other hand, he admitted knowing, as he stated in that same testimony, that "Liddy indicated there was [a] problem with one wiretap and one was not placed in a proper phone and he would correct these matters and hopefully get the information that was requested."[36]

Magruder placed that remark by Liddy at a meeting in mid-June with John Mitchell. If true, it was highly damaging to Mitchell, of course. Magruder said he had taken the GEMSTONE materials to that meeting with Mitchell and that a duplicate set had already been put in "Mr. Mitchell's file," as was office routine with all papers, according to Magruder's administrative assistant, Robert Reisner.[37]

Magruder said he and Mitchell reviewed the GEMSTONE files, and Mitchell called Liddy to his office and indicated his dissatisfaction. Mitchell indicated that "it was worthless and not worth the money he had been paid for it." It was then, Magruder testified, that Liddy responded that he would "correct matters."

Mitchell, when he testified later, denounced Magruder's story as "a palpable damnable lie." When Liddy broke silence in his book *Will,* he claimed that on June 15 he had told Mitchell at a meeting, "The problem we have will be corrected this weekend, sir." But Liddy makes no mention of being chided by Mitchell over the wiretaps. Indeed, although Liddy claims that he placed on Mitchell's desk a thick envelope containing the accumulated wiretap logs, Liddy is specific that Mitchell gave no verbal acknowledgments. When Liddy slipped the envelope on his desk, saying, "That's for you, General," Mitchell just nodded his head slowly.

Only when Liddy persisted in telling Mitchell of another creative idea for the Democratic convention did the CRP boss react. A group of zonked-out hippies, paid by Liddy, were going to swarm into McGovern's suite when he held a press conference, and then conduct a mass pee-in on the carpet. Everyone laughed, Liddy said, except Mitchell, who was to succeed McGovern in the same hotel suite at the Republican convention. He roared: "Goddamn it, Liddy, that's where I'm staying." Another Liddy idea was dropped.

Mitchell himself denied any such foreknowledge of bugging. Yet at another meeting about three days before the final Watergate break-in,

Charles Colson recalls a damning discussion with Mitchell about Dwayne Andreas, the Humphrey backer who had also contributed to the Nixon campaign. "Tell me what room Andreas is staying in and I'll tell you what he's saying," Mitchell said. Colson took this as Mitchell acknowledging the Nixon campaign's bugging capability. (It is, of course, also proof of Colson's own foreknowledge, pre-Watergate).[38]

Magruder claimed he was also communicating the GEMSTONE materials to Gordon Strachan, his liaison with Haldeman at the White House. Because of their sensitivity, however, Strachan had to come to Magruder's office to inspect them.

Liddy reports more direct contact, which he could have done without. Strachan summoned him to the White House to complain, like Magruder, that the "submissions" from the electronic surveillance were unsatisfactory. Liddy says he repeated what he had told Mitchell of the technical problem with the bug; and "that we intend to correct it by going back in shortly."[39] Now, according to Liddy, Magruder, Mitchell and Haldeman's man all had been notified of the imminent return mission to Watergate. Needless to say, Haldeman and Strachan subsequently denied any such knowledge.

Hunt was dismayed by the prospect of a return to Watergate. Liddy says that after protesting, he accepted it like a professional. Hunt's version is that, hearing it first on June 14, he urged Liddy to go back and argue against it, twice, and that Liddy did so. But when Liddy returned claiming "the Big Man [Mitchell] says he wants the operation," Hunt acquiesced, reluctantly.[40] Liddy says he explained to Hunt that this time McCord was merely to be a "hitchhiker," correcting only his bugs. The main task was to be a photo mission: "They want everything in the files," he told Hunt, who was incredulous.

Discrepancies among versions abound. Liddy later wrote that they were bringing up the men from Miami anyway for the McGovern mission, so going back into Watergate was just an extra. But Hunt's version is the opposite: that only when he agreed to call up the Cubans on two days' notice for Watergate did Liddy say "and while the boys are here we might as well have another try at the McGovern offices."

Theoretically, Hunt was in charge of the photography; McCord, the bugs. Yet Hunt, as we saw, said Liddy gave the two rolls of exposed film from the first mission to McCord. Hunt's account goes on to state that a week later Liddy, saying McCord's photographic man was out of town, asked Hunt if Barker could handle it. Liddy's version treats the photographs as simply part of Hunt's mission, which it was.

Hunt flew to Miami especially for the day and had Barker collect the film. Processing the 8×10 prints was rushed to catch Hunt's late-afternoon plane back to Washington. Hunt noted in surprise that the envelope bore the address of a Rich's Camera Shop in Miami; but he assumed the developer was a trusted Barker associate who would not talk.

The glossy blowups of Democratic Party documents showed gloved hands holding them down and a shag rug in the background. Since such a rug could be found in the Howard Johnson's but not in the DNC offices, questions arose. Had the film been switched? Or had some of the documents simply been photographed, unbeknownst to Hunt and Liddy, back in McCord's room? McCord today expresses ignorance. Liddy said the photos were in the envelope he put on Mitchell's desk. Magruder remembered seeing them; Reisner and Sally Harmony caught sight of them, too. They were shredded later and so remain another mystery.

McCord's version of being told to go back into Watergate has him taking it in stride. His main discrepancy from the others is the room bug; only now, he states, was he ordered by Liddy to install in O'Brien's office the sophisticated room listening device capable of monitoring all conversation. This was in addition to correcting the malfunctioning phone bug. Yet today he claims he talked Liddy out of the room bug altogether.

McCord had Baldwin make what he called a "pretext" visit to the DNC during office hours to establish, he says, O'Brien's whereabouts. Baldwin explained its purpose was to pinpoint the location of O'Brien's office. Knowing from his eavesdropping that Spencer Oliver was out of town, Baldwin, pretending to be a nephew of a sometime senior Democrat, asked the receptionist if he could meet Oliver. Instead, he got the secretary, Maxie Wells (on whose calls he had also been eavesdropping), and she gave him a tour of the office. Baldwin located O'Brien's office and Miss Wells obligingly gave him O'Brien's private number in Miami Beach, where he was preparing for the Democratic convention ten days hence.

With the information from Baldwin's casing and the number of filing cabinets he reported, Liddy said he ordered the Cubans to bring up fifty rolls of film for the photography mission, which would give them a capacity for eighteen hundred pages. Liddy reckoned the combined OPAL (black bag job) and TOPAZ (photography) mission would take up to four hours between guard inspection rounds. Again Hunt was startled by the load they were putting on the men from Miami with two missions the same weekend. Hunt says McCord expressed misgivings: "I kind of wish we didn't have to do this again."[41]

On June 16, Hunt met with McCord and Thomas Gregory, the student plant, to settle the final details of the entry into McGovern's headquarters. Gregory surprised them by saying he wanted out: "This is getting too deep for me." They might be better off without him. McCord remarked that the last time he had met Gregory inside the McGovern offices "I noticed he was sweating. I don't think he was cut out to be an agent." Liddy commented that the loss of Gregory was not considered fatal to the operation. Nobody seemed concerned that Gregory knew a great deal and that he had explained why he wanted out to the man who introduced him to Hunt, Robert Bennett, boss of the Mullen Company.[42]

Another danger to the operation, a man who certainly sensed something was up, was none other than columnist Jack Anderson. He bumped into the Miami contingent as they arrived at Washington's National Airport on June 16. Anderson greeted Sturgis, about whom he had written several stories, and Sturgis said they were in town on private business. He introduced two of his companions while the others hung back. As Anderson flew off, he "made a mental note to find out what Sturgis was up to"; there might be a story in it.[43]

The men from Miami picked up rental cars and drove straight to the Watergate Hotel, where they checked in under aliases—Barker and Martinez in room 214; Sturgis and Gonzalez in 314. They phoned Hunt, who made sure they had brought all the film requested, plus a second camera, and arranged to meet them later that evening.

McCord rejoined Baldwin at the Howard Johnson listening post in late afternoon and, according to both men, they worked testing bugging devices. McCord tested one on the hotel room phone, and wired another into a smoke alarm. Baldwin was sent out to buy some flashlight batteries but failed to find speaker wire, which was also on the shopping list; McCord went out to get it himself. He left the inexpert Baldwin—who had a phone tap log still in his typewriter—to solder the batteries in series for what McCord said was a "spare device." Within seconds Baldwin had melted the whole lot uselessly together.

Liddy, telling his wife not to wait up late, drove his distinctive Buick-powered green Jeep (four-wheel-drives were a rarity then) into Washington for the Watergate rendezvous. Jumping a yellow light he was pulled over by a policeman, but released with a verbal warning. He parked outside the Watergate Hotel, positioned for a quick getaway.

Hunt was already in room 214 with the Cuban Americans. Liddy found them practicing with their cameras and in good spirits, even though two of the guards from the earlier mission, including De Diego who had been briefly caught, had been left at home. Liddy distributed the cash—one hundred dollars for each man to have on him to bribe with if caught. All their other possessions, including the "pay" to make up for lost time at work, they were told to leave behind in a briefcase in Hunt's custody. Hunt provided McCord and Sturgis with bogus identification earlier supplied to him by the CIA, and Liddy handed over his George Leonard documentation he had used for the break-in at Ellsberg's psychiatrist's.

McCord had arrived to say the DNC was still occupied by someone working late (in fact, it was a volunteer using the Democrats' WATS line to make free phone calls to his friends around the country). McCord had this time brought six walkie-talkies, but two had dead batteries, a detail that struck Liddy as unprofessional. Still, with the entry team reduced in size, they had enough—one for the command post of Hunt and Liddy, one for the listening post with Baldwin, one for McCord, and one for Barker as photography team leader.

McCord as usual remembers it differently. He says that when he went to the hotel room he was alone with the Cubans reviewing the plans and that Hunt and Liddy kept coming in to hurry them up. The impression, McCord said, was that "both were anxious to get the operation over with."[44]

But after many comings and goings and meals and snacks and chance meetings between team members and film stars like Burt Lancaster and Alain Delon, who happened to be staying at the hotel, it was not until

12:45 A.M. that McCord alerted Liddy and Hunt that the DNC was at last dark. The second Watergate break-in could begin.

McCord told them that he had taped open the B-2 garage-level door latch leading to the stairwell. He had done this, like the last time, by signing in at the Watergate office reception, taking the elevator to the eighth floor, and walking down the stairs to the DNC sixth-floor offices. He had taped the sixth-, eighth- and ninth-floor stairwell doors as well as the door he exited by at garage level. All this was to give rapid escape possibilities in case they were discovered, or so McCord claimed. He says he volunteered to do this after Hunt nervously declined.

What happened next is, as usual, another hugely disputed imbroglio. According to Liddy, it was 1 A.M. before McCord joined them at the hotel. The delay went unexplained, but then the team quickly and silently left on the mission, "everyone wished each other luck."[45]

Within a few minutes, in Liddy's version, McCord, Martinez, and Barker were back. McCord reported that the tape he had put across the garage-level lock was gone. They had left Gonzalez, protected by the burly Sturgis, to pick another door lock while the others returned to give Liddy the options: abort or press on.

In Liddy's version, Hunt wished to abort; he argued that it must have been a guard who removed the tape. McCord, whom Liddy took aside for a quiet professional chat, was for going on; he argued that the presence of mailbags suggested that a postman had removed the tape, according to Liddy. The two Cubans stood ready to do whatever was decided, Liddy wrote, although Barker said he was against going ahead.

Hunt's account is totally at odds with Liddy's. Hunt says McCord told them he had already *re*taped the door lock when he arrived at the command post hotel room the first time. Although he protested, Liddy made the decision, saying, "McCord wants to go, Howard."

McCord's version is that he did not even attend the session reporting the removal of the tape; that was left to Barker and one unidentified member of the team while Gonzalez and another tackled the door. McCord wrote that he awaited the decision in the room at the Howard Johnson Motor Inn until he received a phone call from Hunt telling him the operation was to proceed and that Gonzalez had already picked the lock and was inside.

It is impossible to reconcile such discrepancies that are not, in the end, very important. Liddy admits to making the decision to go ahead, so perhaps his version of how the decision was made—if not on the details of what happened inside Watergate—is credible. He explained his thinking: With the men inside, they were well covered. The DNC was in darkness and Baldwin, across Virginia Avenue as lookout, could alert them of any flashlight used by a guard making the rounds. Baldwin would radio them the instant any police car drove up. Liddy clipped a portable antenna to the command post sliding window in the Watergate Hotel room and attached it for better reception to his walkie-talkie. He sat down and waited with Hunt.

But having decided to take the risk and proceed with the break-in, who redoubled the hazard by deciding to retape the locks? "I'd no idea McCord was going to retape the locks," Liddy wrote in *Will.* Twenty years ago McCord maintained that he did not do it. When asked during Senate hearings who did, McCord answered, "I don't know." He was reexamined, and then explained that his answer related to the *second* door taping that night. McCord said when he went back into the Watergate at garage level, he found the door already retaped. Barker said that Sturgis did it and that McCord was supposed to remove it when he came in a little later. McCord claimed that as he went up the stairs, where he could hear his colleagues struggling again to force the lock on the DNC's rear stairwell door, he did remove tapes as he went. Martinez later said he specifically asked McCord if he had removed the telltale retaping of the garage-level door. Martinez said he assured him he had.[46]

In fact, despite McCord's assurance, several pieces of tape had unaccountably been left in place, including the one that mattered. No wonder McCord called his slim volume *A Piece of Tape.* It was that piece of tape that unstuck everything, and everyone.[47]

The man who discovered, and removed, the first tape on the garage-level door had been the private security guard, Frank Wills, a young black man who had been on duty during the first, undetected break-in. He came on shift at midnight to work until 8 A.M. and his first task was to check the basement doors for tampering. On finding that several doors had been taped to stay unlocked, he decided to phone a superior for advice. He left a message with an answering service and was promptly called back. Wills was told to check to see if other doors had been taped and to call back in fifteen minutes. Had Wills called the police at this stage, probably none of the burglars would have been caught.

In the interim, instead of checking other doors for tape, Wills chatted with the young volunteer who was at last leaving the DNC offices. The two of them decided to get some take-out food at Howard Johnson's.

When Wills returned, he attended to his burger, french fries, and milk shake, and another hour passed during which time the entry team and McCord had slipped into the building. Only after eating did Wills decide to check the other doors, but for some reason went back to the garage level again. When he discovered the new tape, he left it in place and discussed what to do with a fellow guard who watched over a section of the Federal Reserve Board offices on the eighth floor. His colleague advised calling the police, but Wills once again checked back with his superior and finally called the police at 1:47 A.M.

At this point, the break-in gang, having failed once more to pick the lock, was beginning a final struggle to remove the DNC rear door from its hinges altogether. According to McCord, as they worked "the concrete stairwell echoed like a cave."[48]

Liddy's confidence that any arriving police cars would be spotted by the lookout, who would alert the burglars in a timely enough fashion to make their escape proved itself misplaced.

When the call went out for a car to respond to a suspected burglary at the Watergate, the nearest regular police cruiser replied that it was low on gas. The dispatcher then asked, "Any TAC unit car in the area?" (TAC was a tactical unit of officers in civilian clothes using an unmarked car.) TAC 3 carried Sergeant Paul Leeper, commander of the Second District's "casual clothes squad," and Officers John Barrett and Carl Shoffler. They were a minute and a half away from Watergate when they responded, and at 1:52 A.M. they drew up outside the office building and went in. Across the avenue, Baldwin noted that it was a "beautiful night." He watched the car arrive but said he did not really pay attention. Leeper later claimed the use of an unmarked car ensured their success, since "we got five minutes on Baldwin."[49]

Inside, Wills and the oddly attired policemen—they looked like hippies—could not quite understand each other. So Wills took them down to the garage level to show them the door that had been retaped with light-colored masking tape along the edge, preventing the lock from engaging. They found three other doors taped there. Wills told the police—which they knew already from their own crime sheets—that there had been burglary attempts reported recently at the Watergate, on the eighth and sixth floors. The police sent Wills back to the reception area to watch the elevators. They made for the eighth floor, walking up a separate stairwell from that taken by McCord and the team.

Hearing footsteps coming up an adjacent stairwell, McCord claims he suggested to Barker that they leave. But the men were now lifting the door off its hinges; they were about to get in. Someone made the catastrophic decision to have Barker turn off their static-emitting walkie-talkie, apparently as a precaution against noise. The second element of a radio alert in Liddy's fail-safe system had just closed down.

The policemen, reaching the eighth floor, discovered the stairwell doors taped open. They checked the Federal Reserve Board office doors, found nothing untoward, and put all the lights on. Baldwin, without having been instructed what call signs to use, said he radioed something like, "Base One to any unit, do you read me?" A voice came back, "What have you got?" Baldwin said he answered: "The lights just went on on the entire eighth floor." The voice answered, "We know about that, that is the two o'clock guard check." According to Liddy, his was the voice, and it was shortly after 2 A.M. Liddy said he also got on his radio to the team with call sign Two. "One to Two, did you read that?" There was no answer.

The police tackled a different stairwell. Officer Barrett was sent to the ninth floor while Leeper and Shoffler went down. The seventh-floor door was locked. They continued to the sixth, found the same tape keeping the doors open, and called Barrett to join them. Officer Shoffler later testified that it had not even been necessary for the burglars to tape the door from the floor to the stairwell to get out—it opened from that side without a key. The tape served simply as another telltale sign to the police.

Inside the DNC the team had been moving toward its tasks: Gonzalez to open the glass door to O'Brien's suite, McCord accompanying Barker to the file area. Sturgis and Martinez were on guard at the door. McCord says he picked up some college press credential forms for the Democratic convention. Then, hearing from Gonzalez that O'Brien's suite was open, they all moved back there. No sooner had they entered the suite than Sturgis arrived saying somebody was coming. A light went on and they heard shouts of "Come out, police!" The team's exit was barred; they had no alternative but to crouch down, hoping not to be seen.

Meanwhile, Baldwin both saw and was seen. Standing on the balcony of room 723 of Howard Johnson's, he noticed lights flickering on the sixth floor and then saw two men go onto the DNC terrace. One had a university windbreaker on; the other, wearing a cutdown army jacket, had long blond hair. Baldwin was looking at Leeper and Shoffler, and Shoffler had his gun out. Shoffler later testified seeing Baldwin watching them and saying to Leeper, "Do you think that guy's going to call the police?"

Baldwin was calling Liddy. "Base One to Unit One, are our people in suits or are they dressed casually?" And the call came back: "Our people are dressed in suits. Why?" Baldwin: "You have some trouble because there are some individuals out here who are dressed casually and have got their gun out." The person at the other end, Baldwin said, went a little bit frantic. It was Liddy, commanding the team to respond: "One to Two, are you reading this? Come in, that's an order."[50]

McCord has said that were the police search less thorough, they might have escaped detection. But the police searched each cubicle in the DNC in turn. Officer Barrett was the first to spot an arm move behind the glass and shouted, "Hold it. Come out." Sergeant Leeper, who had also drawn his revolver, jumped onto a desk, looked over the partition, and saw five men. They were raising their hands, which he remembered were covered with blue rubber gloves. Some were trying to remove the gloves.

At this point, Liddy says, came the first and last transmission, a whisper, from the entry team: "They got us." Baldwin heard McCord's voice asking, "Are you Metropolitan police?"

Leeper said they ordered the men out from behind the desks and lined them up facing the wall. Barrett frisked four of them and laid their possessions on top of the desks; Shoffler likewise frisked Martinez. McCord said the officers were edgy; Sturgis called out they had nothing to fear because they were unarmed. (None of the officers then or at the trial or at Senate hearings made any mention of gunplay or scuffles.) Leeper later said, "They were probably five of the easiest lockups I have ever had."

Baldwin kept up a fascinated commentary from across the street as police cars began arriving. Liddy and Hunt soon broke off listening and frantically began packing. Hunt, according to Liddy, suddenly said, "We've gotta get out fast. I just remembered Macho's [Barker] got this room key." At that recollection, in the middle of disaster, whatever discipline they had seems to have cracked. The police would hardly come immediately; indeed, they took another twelve hours to obtain search warrants and raid the rooms.

In panic, however, Hunt and Liddy left an amazing haul of easily traceable material behind in room 214. More was in room 314, the key to which was also seized from the break-in team. This blunder wrecked whatever strategy they had for maintaining deniability. They crammed extra electronic gear into McCord's briefcase, Hunt compressed the portable antenna and slid it down his trouser leg, and after a last command to Baldwin to wait until Hunt came across to him, Hunt and Liddy hobbled out past the drowsy desk clerk.

They came out onto Virginia Avenue half a block from a group of police cars with lights flashing, got into Hunt's car, and drove a short way toward Liddy's Jeep. Liddy asked Hunt if he had the ten thousand dollars they had put aside for an emergency. Hunt said he was on his way to collect it. Hunt's version is that he told Liddy to go home and get himself an alibi. Liddy said good night and that he would be in touch later that morning.

Liddy recalled one further detail: Before parting he told Hunt to get in touch with "Caddy" and use the money. Douglas Caddy was a lawyer who had worked at Mullen with Hunt. Liddy said they had him in mind for emergency use.

This sudden reversal of roles, with Hunt taking charge when Liddy, the boss, departed the field of action at its most crucial hour has never been explained by either man. And, in fact, what both did and failed to do was to have devastating consequences.

With Liddy gone, Hunt did a U-turn and parked two blocks from the motel, "within pistol range of the police cars." He went up to Baldwin's room. As Baldwin described it to the Senate committee, Hunt crouched behind a table and asked "What is going on? What is going on?" Baldwin reported that the police were leading McCord and another of the group out of the Watergate, and he told Hunt, "Come on and see." Hunt replied, "I have got to use the bathroom." When Hunt came back, Baldwin said, he called a lawyer. He dialed a local call, and Baldwin said he heard Hunt discussing money, bail, and bonds.

Baldwin and Hunt conflict in their accounts of what then took place. Baldwin said Hunt told him to load McCord's van with the listening post equipment and drive to McCord's house in suburban Maryland. Hunt insists it was Baldwin who asked if that is where he should go and Hunt told him, "That's the last place to go. I don't care if you drive the van into the river, just get the stuff out of here." Hunt then ran off down the hall with Baldwin shouting plaintively, "Does this mean I don't get to go to Miami?"[51]

Baldwin drove the van to McCord's home in Rockville, outside Washington. It was loaded, he said, with the duplicate set of the GEMSTONE file, that day's log of the bugged phone calls, and all the gear. He then had a distraught Mrs. McCord drive him back to Howard Johnson's to pick up his own car, and proceeded through the dawn to his mother's house in Connecticut.

As the famous Senate committee was to state, the Watergate break-in was over; the cover-up had begun.

CHAPTER 6

The Lost Weekend

The Watergate affair had a slow windup that Saturday, June 17. The police were puzzled by the quality of the men in suits they had arrested; no ordinary burglars they. The men gave only their aliases and declined to give addresses. Some senior officers thought they might be jewel thieves; some very rich people lived and were burgled in the Watergate apartments. But that was soon ruled out. The little black devices with wires protruding that had been found in McCord's bag, especially the one that looked like a smoke alarm, might be bomb detonators, other officers thought. All except McCord had between two hundred dollars and eight hundred dollars cash on them in hundred-dollar bills, with serial numbers intriguingly close in sequence. The suspects were asked whether they wished to call a lawyer and declined. The police called in an assistant U.S. attorney, and sensing this was a federal crime, they called in the FBI, too.

From the Plumbers to the first undetected Watergate break-in, Hunt and Liddy had come to regard success as not getting caught. Now they were in a particularly catastrophic situation because of McCord's arrest; whatever alias he had given would soon be cracked. His fingerprints were on file with the FBI. McCord's link to Nixon as a full-time employee of his election campaign committee could not remain secret for more than a few hours. The only hope was to get McCord's release ordered discreetly through the power structure. This had to be accomplished within minutes rather than hours, before the investigation involved too many people. Yet Liddy slept and Hunt seemed paralyzed.

There might even have been no need to get Liddy's principals out of bed. Magruder, Mitchell, and their top CRP entourage were in Los Angeles on a California campaign weekend. For them it was barely 11:45 P.M. when Liddy and Hunt fled the Watergate as their team was led away by the police. Nevertheless, by his account, Liddy felt he could not disturb Magruder in California. It is a weak argument and suggests that whatever confidence Hunt and the hapless Cuban Americans had in their principals, Liddy did not share it.

Liddy wrote in *Will* that it was about 3 A.M. (midnight California time) when he slipped into bed. His wife stirred and asked if anything was wrong. Liddy replied, "There was trouble. Some people got caught. I'll probably be going to jail." If Liddy's wife made any further inquiry, he did not record it. They both went to sleep.

Hunt, meanwhile, having sent Baldwin into headlong flight, was feeling doom-laden. He watched the last of the five being loaded into the paddy wagon outside the Watergate. "It seemed so damned final, I thought, as I walked to my car." Nonetheless, Hunt went first to his White House office, where he stuffed the case containing McCord's extra electronic gear into his safe, along with address books, notebooks, and other items. From this same safe in room 338, his third-floor EOB office, Hunt also removed the ten thousand dollars in contingency money Liddy had given him from CRP funds. Hunt also claimed that he called the lawyer Douglas Caddy from here.

Hunt then went to his office at the Mullen Company opposite CRP. There he signed in using the name of an associate because, he said, he did not want any lasting record of his movements. Hunt claims that all he did here was phone Barker's wife in Miami, informing her of the arrests and telling her to use a pay phone to call Caddy. The poor woman was upset but quickly focused on what had to be done.

Next Hunt drove to Caddy's apartment and related what had happened. Caddy was a very right-wing young man, according to Hunt's associate Robert Bennett. He, too, had worked for Mullen but Bennett arranged Caddy's transfer to the law firm where he was now working. Hunt handed over eighty-five hundred dollars of the contingency money and asked Caddy to get down to the police station to arrange bail for the team. "I want them out of jail and out of town before dawn," Hunt said.

Caddy was uncertain and apprehensive. He knew nothing of criminal law and proceeded to wake up the more senior partners of his law firm. They were neither amused nor impressed with Caddy's involvement in the case, but one of them engaged another lawyer, Joseph Rafferty, who soon called back. Caddy said he would dress and be ready to leave with Rafferty. Hunt says that by now he reckoned that Liddy would have called one of his principals and that if the bail effort failed, then perhaps one of the White House or Justice Department eminences would call the D.C. police chief to arrange the men's release. Confident, Hunt wrote, that Liddy would ring sometime before noon to say the men had been released without their names having been discovered, Hunt went home and took a sleeping pill. "For now there was nothing to do but sleep."[1]

In his book, Hunt omitted to mention, as Liddy (and the first trial record) recalls, that he first woke Liddy up with a 5 A.M. phone call. Liddy was irritated; Hunt was asking his opinion about hiring Caddy and his fee. He put Caddy on the line. Liddy states that he asked Caddy to represent both himself and Hunt as prospective codefendants—that made their relationship legally privileged. He confirmed the instruction to get the men bailed out. Liddy guessed it might take ten thousand dollars each; since 10 percent might be required paid in cash, there was money enough on hand. With that Liddy went back to sleep.

The next thing to surprise the police and increase their suspicion was the arrival early that morning at the Second District station house of Caddy, then Rafferty. The lawyers stated they were representing the five men whose aliases Hunt had given them. But the police knew that none of the five had availed themselves of the offer to call a lawyer. Who had sent them? Caddy and Rafferty would not say. A deadlock ensued, but the men arrested were impressed. The appearance, unbidden, of lawyers, meant, as one of them said later, that "whoever my backers were" they were looking after us.

The lost hours while Liddy and Hunt slept had allowed the FBI to get under way. Big federal bodies, like supertankers, once up to speed are difficult to slow down and too big to hide. Although reluctant to pass up his children's Little League baseball practice that Saturday morning, Angelo Lano, of the FBI's Washington field office, went in to

D.C. police headquarters. Shown the devices from McCord's bag, Lano suspected they were electronic bugs but sent them to the FBI's labs, which quickly confirmed it. Lano immediately had the assistant U.S. attorney prosecuting the case add suspected bugging to the search warrant they were obtaining for rooms 214 and 314 of the Watergate Hotel.

As Liddy ought to have known from his own vaunted FBI expertise, that Saturday morning, far sooner than he had imagined, fingerprints had revealed all the men's true identities. "Frank Carter" turned out to be Bernard Barker; "Jene Valdez" was Eugenio Rolando Martinez; "Raoul Godoy," Virgilio Gonzalez. Two of those arrested carried fake CIA identification: "Edward J. Hamilton" (one of Hunt's old aliases) and "Joseph di Alberto" were the same man, Frank Sturgis, and "Edward Martin" was McCord, who also carried Hunt's alternative "Edward Warren."

All of these investigative points had been made, as detectives say, with many more hot leads humming when Liddy at last set about alerting his principals. His most important task, he later wrote, was to "get the facts to John Mitchell as quickly as possible."[2] At 7 A.M. he drove to a gas station near his home and called the White House switchboard to locate Magruder. Told that he was with Mitchell in California, Liddy realized it was now 4 A.M. their time, and again he decided not to disturb them.

Instead, he drove to CRP offices and began shredding the GEMSTONE files and anything else that might prove incriminating. He chose to use the office's small high-security machine, and it was slow work. Before he was through, Liddy would shred hotel soap wrappers he had collected from his travels and even stacks of hundred-dollar bills, surplus from GEMSTONE funds. Liddy said he had to be careful as the morning wore on and more CRP employees came in. But then Liddy broke his own code of secrecy.

In the hallway he met the man who had queried Magruder's disbursements of so much cash, FCRP treasurer Hugh Sloan. "Our boys got caught last night. It was my mistake and I used someone from here, something I told them I'd never do." Liddy gestured toward the shredder: "I don't know how much longer I'm going to be able to keep this job."[3]

Sloan later recalled he had only been going to say "good morning."

He said Liddy was in a hurry and thought he was talking of some campaign mistake, the sort of thing that causes people to lose their jobs all the time. It was later that day, when he heard the news of the break-in, that the significance sank in.

Liddy's statement, almost exactly corroborated by Sloan, probably indicates his true state of mind. It again suggests a panicky awareness that there was little chance of springing the men from jail. Liddy realized he needed a lawyer; despite having hired Caddy that morning on the phone, Liddy decided to call Peter Maroulis, his old law associate from Poughkeepsie, New York, and ask him to fly down. Others at CRP remember seeing Liddy that morning; Robert Odle, director of administration, showed him how to work the other, bigger shredder. Liddy, concerned about the possibility of press inquiries, went upstairs to find the deputy CRP press spokesman, Powell Moore, and again breaching the need to know principle, told him of the arrests and that they had to keep McCord's true identity secret. Moore had disturbing news for Liddy—Mitchell, he said, was scheduled to hold a news conference in California at 3 P.M. Washington time. Liddy now at last realized he had to get word to California, and on a secure phone.

Liddy had kept his White House pass. He crossed Pennsylvania Avenue and went to the Situation Room in the basement of the West Wing. The man who had just botched the bugging of the opposition party headquarters was now inside the White House supersecret communications center. Liddy, who loved gadgetry, placed a scrambler call through the White House switchboard to Magruder. The exact timing of this call and what happened subsequently are matters of great dispute. One thing is certain: They were to connect the Watergate cover-up to the highest level of the president's campaign.

Magruder's earliest revised version, once he started coming clean with the prosecutors the following April, fixed the Liddy call at 9 A.M. California time; then, correcting himself, he said 8 A.M. Liddy's version is 8:30 A.M. The relative earliness, as we shall see, is what complicates much that follows.

Liddy's terse message to Magruder was that he had to get to a secure phone; the Situation Room staff told him the nearest KYX scrambler phone was at El Segundo Air Force Base, ten miles from Magruder's Beverly Hills hotel. Magruder protested. Liddy claimed he told him: "Get your ass to a secure phone and call me, or I guarantee by noon Mitchell will be building you a new one," and he hung up. Magruder's version is that Liddy told him straight out that McCord had been arrested inside the Watergate—an unlikely event in view of Liddy's insistence on a secure and unbuggable phone. Liddy maintains he said nothing about McCord at that point.[4]

Magruder received Liddy's call when a waiter brought a telephone to his breakfast table. He and his wife, and much of the rest of the top CRP entourage and their wives (the LaRues, Mardians, and Porters), were at breakfast in the hotel's Polo Lounge. Magruder turned to Mitchell's right-hand man, Fred LaRue, saying that something confidential had come up. LaRue suggested that the pay phone in the hall outside was as secure as any. Damagingly for Magruder, LaRue later testified that he remembered him saying "last night was the night they were due to go back in the Watergate."

Magruder called Liddy back from the pay phone. Liddy knew he was not using a scrambler but nevertheless laid the story out for him, saying that he did not know how long McCord's alias could hold up. Liddy's book quoted Magruder as responding with horror: "You used *McCord*? Why, Gordon? *Why?* That's the question I'm going to be asked."[5]

Magruder remembered telling Liddy furiously, "You were supposed to keep this operation removed from us. Have you lost your mind?" Liddy, according to Magruder, replied that McCord was the only one he could get to handle the electronics, saying, "You didn't give me enough time." Magruder reflected: "I couldn't believe it—Liddy was blaming his fiasco on me."

Liddy's version claims that he accepted the responsibility and said that it was no time for recriminations. Magruder states that he calmed down and listened as Liddy told him, "Don't worry. My men will never talk." But McCord was the real disaster, Magruder saw. He said he told Liddy he had to talk to Mitchell. Liddy was concerned about embarrassing questions at Mitchell's press conference. His version, characteristically contemptuous of Magruder, says that he cut Magruder off: "Get working on that statement. I'll tell you about it later. Now move."

To Magruder, shattered by the news but not wishing to spoil the wives' planning for the big Hollywood fund-raiser they were attending that night, "breakfast seemed to drag on forever." Only when they left the Polo Lounge did he take LaRue aside and tell him they had to talk.

Although there are disputes over timing, Magruder and LaRue went to the wing of the hotel that the CRP party had taken over and asked to borrow the room of Mitchell's bodyguard. Magruder filled LaRue in, moaning, "Why didn't I fire that idiot Liddy when I had the chance?" LaRue, quick to the point as always, said he had to tell Mitchell. He went across the corridor and got Mitchell out of a meeting with top Republicans: "That's incredible" LaRue said Mitchell exclaimed when told of McCord's arrest.

They called in Magruder and Robert Mardian, who had been brought by Mitchell to CRP from the Department of Justice, was also on hand. At this point, again discrepancies blur the account. Those involved still say it was "damage control"; not yet a cover-up. But it would eventually be termed a conspiracy to obstruct justice and to this day no one is eager to claim responsibility for setting the conspiracy in motion.

Magruder, when he decided in 1973 to tell all to the prosecutors, first said that Mardian, on Mitchell's instructions, phoned Powell Moore at the CRP office in Washington and told him to have Attorney General Kleindienst get McCord released before his identity was discovered. At his next interview with the prosecutors, however, Magruder stated that at Mitchell's suggestion it was *Liddy* whom Mardian called, telling him to get to Kleindienst. This was the version Magruder later gave in Senate testimony. By the time he was a prosecution witness at the trial at which Mitchell and Mardian were convicted, Magruder had added this key detail: that it was Liddy in the second, secure, phone conversation who first suggested the idea of getting in touch with Kleindienst.[6] Mitchell and Mardian always denied any part in it whatsoever.

Liddy's book makes no mention of his suggesting the contact with Kleindienst. Hunt's book *Undercover*, as we saw, has him fantasizing earlier that morning that Liddy would have informed one of his principals and perhaps Kleindienst could call the D.C. police chief. But Hunt was out of this picture, literally so, having taken his sleeping pill.

Magruder produced yet another version: "Someone" had done it. Before his appearance as a trial witness and years before Liddy's book *Will* was published, Magruder's own book, *An American Life,* crucially blurred the precise genesis of the idea of calling Kleindienst. Here it is only "someone suggested" and, significantly for what was to happen over the next few days, "someone" recalled McCord had once worked for the CIA. That could be the excuse—say he was working on a special mission. "After all *we* were the government."[7]

So "one of us suggested" that Mitchell call Kleindienst. Magruder said Mitchell deemed that inappropriate and suggested Mardian. Mardian in this Magruder version telephoned Kleindienst's home and found him out playing golf. Magruder continued that "we" then suggested that he call Liddy. But these two did not get along. "It was agreed" Mardian should call Liddy, but from a pay phone, not the phone in Mitchell's suite; so Mardian went to a pay phone. This was the story in Magruder's book.

Seven years later, when Liddy published his account, the story hardened: "It was Magruder." Liddy received the call at CRP where he had gone back to talk to Powell Moore. Magruder had a message for Liddy from Mitchell: Find Kleindienst and say "John sent you" and ask him to get McCord out of jail, say "it's a personal request from John." Another direct witness who confirms Liddy's version was Magruder's assistant, Robert Reisner. At around noon Washington time, Magruder phoned Reisner, who tracked Liddy down in Moore's office to take Magruder's call.[8]

The telephone company record shows that a call was made from Mitchell's suite to CRP at 9:48 A.M. California time, 12:48 P.M. in Washington. That helped convict Mardian at the trial. Liddy at the time was keeping his silence until the statute of limitations ran out.

Mardian has always protested his innocence and claims now that John Dean, the president's counsel—at that moment on a government junket to Manila—initiated the idea of calling Kleindienst. Mardian also believes Magruder has relented, based on a quoted interview with him in a recent book, *Silent Coup.* However, Magruder continues to maintain it was Mardian.[9] Liddy is adamant that it was Magruder. LaRue, while failing to corroborate the details of Magruder's account, agrees that Mitchell asked someone—Magruder or Mardian—to tell

Liddy to contact Kleindienst, who in turn, said LaRue, was to contact the D.C. police chief. But LaRue said this was only for Kleindienst to get back to them with information, not to spring the men from jail.

Liddy asked Powell Moore, who had come to CRP from the Justice Department, where he would be likely to find Kleindienst. (Mardian could have told him; he was to have been Kleindienst's partner at a member-guest golf tournament but had canceled due to the California trip. This argues against Mardian's making the call to Liddy.) But whoever initiated the instruction, what mattered was whether it was acted upon. Liddy says he believed the attempt to approach Kleindienst would only make matters worse but an order from Mitchell was not to be disobeyed. Moore, said Liddy, was dismayed when he explained why they had to find the attorney general, but he, too, followed orders. He phoned around and discovered that Kleindienst was at Burning Tree Golf & Country Club, an exclusive Maryland retreat where even presidents may not be photographed on the course. Moore drove Liddy there.

Kleindienst, who had been confirmed as attorney general just the previous Monday, had already been interrupted once that morning. As he was leaving for the golf course, he had been telephoned by the assistant attorney general in charge of the criminal division, Henry Petersen, to be told about the Watergate arrests. Obviously, the D.C. police had very early on sensed that their political masters must be alerted.

After the eighteen holes, Kleindienst was having luncheon with his partners when his eye was caught by someone violently gesturing at him. It was Liddy, with Powell Moore. Kleindienst left his guests and Liddy told him he had a personal message from Mitchell. They went to a little room off the locker area where Kleindienst remembers President Eisenhower used to play cards after a round on the course.

Liddy says they sat down facing each other, with Moore standing to Liddy's left. He asked Kleindienst whether he had heard of the Watergate arrests. Kleindienst said Petersen had called, and asked, "What about it?" Liddy said he spilled the lot—that he was running the operation, that the men would keep their mouths shut, that McCord was on the regular CRP payroll under his true name. "Jesus Christ," interjected Kleindienst, in Liddy's version.

Kleindienst interrupted to ask Liddy if he had received his message directly from Mitchell. Liddy said that although it came through Magruder, it was "a personal request from John" to get McCord out of jail before he was found out.[10]

Liddy said Kleindienst looked stunned, and Moore was shaking his head from side to side. Liddy said, "I know. There's no way you can even try to do it without it getting out. Then what happens to you?" Liddy went on:

> Kleindienst exploded. "*Me?* Fuck what happens to *me*! What happens to the *President* if I try a fool thing like that? It's the goddamnedest thing I ever heard of."

According to Liddy, Kleindienst exclaimed, "What the fuck did you people think you were doing in there?" When Liddy started to explain, Kleindienst waved him off. Then he told Liddy, "You tell whoever it was that John Mitchell knows me well enough to call himself if he has anything more like that to say to me. And tell them I can't do it—*won't* do it. For the President's sake I'm going to handle this like any other case." Liddy says they shook hands and left.

This account was not known until Liddy published *Will* in 1980. Today, Kleindienst asserts that Liddy's version essentially corroborates his own, which is surprising in itself. Kleindienst, the highest law officer in the United States at the time, hears the full Watergate story from a perpetrator, refuses to cooperate—on political, not law enforcement, grounds—and then shakes Liddy's hand! Moreover, because Kleindienst turned a blind eye, Liddy's role was to remain unknown to the FBI and prosecutor for several more weeks, and Magruder went unchallenged by Kleindienst until he turned state's witness ten months later.[11]

Clearly, Kleindienst was discomfited by Liddy's approach. He now says he passed on what Liddy told him to Petersen, who agreed that the whole business was "crazy and ridiculous."[12] But the information on Mitchell's role did not reach the investigators. All in all, Kleindienst must be accounted fortunate. Indeed, Petersen told Kleindienst a few days later, "Boss, if we get out of this thing without going to jail, we're going to be lucky."

Liddy says that he was very impressed by Kleindienst's commitment to the president, that it jibed with his own determination to keep silent at all costs. After lunch that Saturday, it was in any case too late for anything to be done about freeing McCord. Police and the FBI with their new search warrants went to the rooms the team had used at the Watergate Hotel. Lano, the FBI man in charge, had some hopes of finding the "sixth" man, who he believed had tipped off Caddy. Nobody was there but clues were in abundance. The investigators recovered another forty-six hundred dollars in hundred-dollar bills in sequential serial numbers, which they sent off to have traced through the Federal Reserve, the United States' central bank system. They recovered the briefcase into which the men had put their true identification documents and personal possessions. Hunt had supposedly been in charge of it, but had left it behind in his panic to escape.

There was more: an address book belonging to Barker and an address file belonging to Martinez. In Barker's address book they found the notation "WH HH" and a telephone number. More blatant, the Martinez index read "H Hunt WH" and the same number. In a drawer was a stamped envelope addressed to the Lakewood Country Club in Maryland, containing a check for $6.36. It was signed "E. Howard Hunt."

The FBI had made their sixth man. A quick check of the FBI's famous indices revealed that Hunt had been routinely vetted by the FBI for his White House job, and that he had been in the CIA. A telephone call established that the number found in the address book was in the White House. The FBI White House liaison checked with the Secret Service. Yes, Hunt was a White House consultant. An FBI man was soon on his way to Hunt's house on Witches Island in suburban Maryland. Within twelve hours of the break-in, the investigators had Watergate linked to the White House, even before they linked it to the Nixon campaign.

That Saturday the president was relaxing in the warm waters of the Bahamas during a post-Moscow summit rest. He confided to his diary that the extra day of fresh air and exercise that weekend had given him "a bigger lift than I had realized was possible." He felt "frankly more sharp and more eager to get work done."[13]

Nixon had flown on Friday to the private islet home of his friend Robert Abplanalp, the millionaire inventor-manufacturer of part of the aerosol valve. On Saturday morning, seven hours after the arrests, Nixon telephoned from Walker's Cay to Bob Haldeman, who was in Key Biscayne. (Mitchell's wife, Martha, claimed that Haldeman or Ehrlichman—she mixed the names—had telephoned her husband at about this time, dawn in California, to notify him of the arrests, but no corroboration has ever been found.) There is nothing in Haldeman's note of the short call with Nixon to indicate that Watergate was discussed. And there is no other notation in the president's official diary of any other Nixon-Haldeman calls that day, nor to anyone else. Haldeman maintained he only heard about the Watergate break-in through news agency reporting later that afternoon.*

In *The Ends of Power*, Haldeman recalls that he and his assistant Larry Higby were sunning themselves on Key Biscayne in the late afternoon. "Hey look," Higby said, "Old Whaleboat." It was the White House code name for Ron Ziegler, the president's press secretary. In bathing trunks, Ziegler walked along the beach trailing a long white roll of paper.

Ziegler was reading news agency copy reporting that five men had been caught breaking into the DNC offices with electronic equipment. To Haldeman, the item was jarring but ludicrous. He had nothing against bugging, but it "couldn't be our people" because there was nothing worthwhile in the DNC; "useful political information" could be found only in the candidates' offices. Then another thought struck him: "They've caught Chuck Colson." Higby said the same: "I bet they're Colson's gunners." Haldeman says it was a chilling thought. If Colson was involved it could very well have been one of his projects for the president.

Should they inform the president? Haldeman reasoned that Ehrlichman had the duty in Washington; he would have called already had any real problem surfaced. So by Haldeman's account, they did nothing to

* In a recent book, Abplanalp is quoted as saying that he was with Nixon when he heard about Watergate and that Nixon was very surprised and angry at such stupidity. According to the president's daily diary and helicopter manifests, Abplanalp was with Nixon only that Saturday; he did not accompany Nixon and his other friend Bebe Rebozo to Key Biscayne when Nixon flew back on Sunday, which is when Nixon has always insisted he first learned about Watergate.[14]

"worry the President"; indeed they did nothing more that day apart from going out to eat stone crabs. Haldeman says he got no call from Ehrlichman.

That evening Ehrlichman was, however, being brought into play. He remembers the westering sun on his porch in suburban Virginia when a Secret Service man at the White House telephoned. The police had found Hunt's check and the address books with his White House phone number among the effects of the burglars arrested. (Alexander Butterfield of the White House, reached by the FBI, confirmed that Hunt had been a White House consultant on "highly sensitive confidential matters," but claimed it had been nine months previously.[15] Jack Caulfield, Dean's private eye, had received the same tip-off from the Secret Service.)

Ehrlichman, like Haldeman, immediately thought of Colson, his proximity to the president, and the fact that there were only 150 days to the election. Ehrlichman telephoned Colson, who, he said, assured him that Hunt no longer had any connection with the White House. Colson, according to Ehrlichman, said he did not know why Hunt still had a White House phone. Ehrlichman claimed he phoned Ziegler in Key Biscayne and told of his talks both with the Secret Service and Colson. But what Ehrlichman has never explained is that he had special reason to fear the mention of Hunt in this affair. It was not just Hunt's connection to the White House and Colson. Ehrlichman would know in a flash, as very few did, that Hunt and the Cubans were the same crew that had carried out the Ellsberg break-in in which Ehrlichman was involved. If that break-in by the Plumbers was unraveled, it might also lead to the covered-up Moorer-Radford scandal. Here was reason enough, on day one of Watergate, for Ehrlichman to concentrate on Hunt, or at least to worry about him above all else.

Ehrlichman would have been even more worried had he learned what had been happening in D.C. Superior Court late that afternoon. Just prior to the burglars' arraignment on charges of attempted interception of communications, a D.C. police officer recognized McCord as someone he had met when visiting CRP offices for security purposes. He quickly told his police colleagues of McCord's connection with

Nixon's campaign and the Republican National Committee. Now the police and the FBI realized they had a burgeoning political case on their hands; there was no way bail would be set low as if for common burglars.[16]

At the hearing before Judge James A. Belsen, Earl Silbert, the prosecuting assistant U.S. attorney, opposed bail. The suspects had originally given false names and possessed $2,400 in cash on their persons; $3,500 more had been found in their hotel rooms. They were engaged in clandestine work. Bail was eventually set at $50,000 for the four Miami men and $30,000 for McCord.

When the judge asked the men their occupations, one answered "anti-Communist." The others nodded. McCord replied that he was a security consultant, retired from government service. A reporter caught the exchange:

> "Where in government?" asked the Judge.
> "CIA," McCord whispered.
> The Judge flinched slightly.
> Holy shit, [Bob] Woodward said half aloud, the CIA.[17]

Woodward was then a local *Washington Post* reporter called unwillingly into Saturday duty who, through persistent joint reporting of Watergate with a colleague, Carl Bernstein, was to win a Pulitzer Prize for their newspaper. This Saturday, however, he simply contributed his tidbit, one of eight staffers filing for a story published under the byline of Alfred Lewis, their police reporter, who got the first police tip on the story.

The *Post* editors put the bizarre story on Sunday's front page, but no one had stumbled onto McCord's connection with CRP. The CIA was checking on McCord, however. CIA Director Richard Helms was notified that Saturday evening that both McCord and Hunt were involved. Helms now says that this same evening he telephoned Acting FBI Director L. Patrick Gray to advise him to investigate connections with John Ehrlichman. In FBI records there is no record of this call, but it suggests Helms was pointing Gray toward the Plumbers' activities at a very early stage.[18] At that same time, Henry Petersen formally asked the

FBI to request the CIA to list which of those arrested were actively employed by the agency. Just as formally, the CIA misinformed the FBI. It told them that Martinez had no connection with the CIA when he was, in fact, the only one of those arrested actually on a CIA cash retainer.[19]

The men arrested had not made bond. In his book, McCord described how they were sent off to a D.C. jail—an overcrowded "100 year old prison, dank and reminiscent of the European dungeons of a century ago."

At the Watergate the police were wrapping up the evidence. Oddly, though both the FBI and the telephone company "swept" the DNC offices for bugs, they did not find any in the phones.

In California, Mitchell's press conference went off without questions about the break-in. Magruder had managed to draft a statement disowning McCord as a precaution, but he was still frantic, knowing that Kleindienst had refused to have McCord released. Magruder and the CRP party had also learned from Washington of the cash found on the men arrested. They hoped, he wrote, that it might prove to have come from the Democrats; they retained a suspicion that McCord was a double agent. But they also worried, rightly, that it would turn out to be CRP's own cash. Mardian remembers hearing a conversation about money that day:

> Mitchell asked Magruder point-blank, "How much money did you give Liddy?" And Magruder replied "eighty thousand dollars." Mitchell was aghast. He said "eighty thousand dollars?" and before he finished the sentence, Magruder said, "But you—authorized two hundred thousand dollars." Mitchell's reply was "Yes, but the campaign hasn't started yet."[20]

It was another of the rare instances in which Mitchell indirectly admitted approving Liddy's budget, something he always denied.

Magruder, hearing that Liddy was still shredding away, realized that his own files contained dangerous material. He phoned Robert Reisner at home and asked him to get back to CRP's office. There, after watching the evening news, Reisner and Robert Odle talked to Magruder in a conference call. Reisner was told to remove certain sensitive files from Magruder's desk and take them home; when his briefcase was full, he shared the chore with Odle. And it was Odle, apparently not curious enough to look at what he got, who took the GEMSTONE file of wiretap logs. It stayed in his closet over the weekend.

In the Bahamas the president dined early with his friends before watching a movie, *The Notorious Landlady*. Across the continent, Magruder and the CRP delegation prepared for that evening's party. It was at the Bel Air home of Taft Schreiber, then vice president of the Music Corporation of America. This was an important political event meant to demonstrate that big show business personalities were on the president's side. Even by White House standards. Magruder wrote, it was a lavish affair. But Watergate had rather spoiled the fun.[21]

Later, after the reception, Magruder says, there was a discussion about Watergate in Mitchell's suite, with LaRue and the others. Mitchell wanted Mardian to fly back on Sunday to "direct the cover-up." Magruder was not aware that Liddy had called Mardian urgently asking that someone in authority other than Magruder be sent back. Magruder wrote:

> At some point that Saturday morning I realized that this was not just hard-nosed politics, this was a crime that could destroy us all. The cover-up, thus, was immediate and automatic; no one ever considered that there would *not* be a cover-up. It seemed inconceivable that with our political power we could not erase this mistake we had made.[22]

That is what Hunt, back in Washington, wanted to believe, too. In his CIA career he had been used to sophisticated backup, of quiet cover-ups, and no questions asked. As Watergate's longest day came to an end, Hunt was astonished that the team was still in jail. He had been shaken when the FBI agents called at his house. He confirmed only that it was his check and that he worked part time at the White House. He rang Liddy, "as his attorney," who told him to tell the FBI when they returned that on advice of counsel he had nothing to say.[23]

All else having failed, that was about the only tactic left. Stonewall it.

On Sunday morning, the president helicoptered back to the U.S. mainland and to his Key Biscayne residence, accompanied by his close friend Bebe Rebozo. It was midday, he picked up a *Miami Herald*. The main story was about his Vietnam withdrawals, headlined GROUND COMBAT ROLE NEARS END FOR U.S. In the middle of the front page a smaller story caught his eye: MIAMIANS HELD IN D.C. TRY TO BUG DEMO HEADQUARTERS. In his memoirs Nixon wrote: "It sounded preposterous; Cubans in surgical gloves bugging the DNC! I dismissed it as some sort of prank."[24]

This is how Nixon would have us believe he first heard about and reacted to the break-in. He notes he made a call to Haldeman, but says nothing about Watergate. He mentions a call to Colson about his concern "that the media would be sympathetic to McGovern." And Nixon quotes his next day's personal diary to show that it was only on Monday evening that he got the "disturbing news from Bob Haldeman" that the break-in "involved someone who is on the [CRP] payroll."

Can this be true? Nixon, in his 1990 introduction to the paperback edition of *RN*, likes to say that "no one has ever questioned a fact" in his memoirs but this, the moment the cover-up began at the White House, looks questionable. Certainly, it makes liars of his own closest aides. For it is not what Colson remembers, nor Haldeman. First Colson's version of a Sunday morning Nixon call:

> I thought it was utterly preposterous, so did Nixon, when he called me he said, "No one in our operation could be this stupid, could they?" and I said, "I don't believe so." I said, "I know nothing about it; it's the dumbest thing I've heard of." He said, "Of all places, the Democratic National Committee. Why did they break in?" He said, "I was so mad when I heard that this morning," he said "I smashed an ashtray down." He said, "It can't be that any of our people were that dumb." And that was the initial reaction of Richard Nixon.[25]

If Nixon had smashed an ashtray in anger that morning, he apparently did not tell Haldeman. But they did discuss Watergate, even though the president's memoirs show no trace of it. At midday, the president had an eighteen-minute telephone conversation with the chief of staff. Haldeman later wrote that his suspicion of Colson's—and, therefore, Nixon's—involvement dissolved completely. The president sounded amused rather than concerned. Nixon scoffed at anyone wanting to go into the DNC. "Nothing but crap in there. The real stuff is in the candidates' headquarters," Haldeman quoted Nixon saying. "Track down Magruder," Nixon instructed.[26] But why call Magruder if he still knew nothing about the CRP connection? The answer is that Nixon well knew who, under Mitchell, was in charge of the whole range of CRP functions, both aboveboard and below.

Indeed, it was odd that Haldeman himself had not yet ridden herd on Magruder. Haldeman's aide, Gordon Strachan, had been trying to get hold of Magruder all Saturday but failed, although Magruder claimed they spoke. Haldeman now roused Magruder at the Beverly Hills Hotel early Sunday morning. Haldeman subsequently wrote that Magruder was nervous and did not tell him the full story of his own involvement (though he mentioned Liddy was the ringleader). Magruder also told him that the statement they were putting out in Mitchell's name "was accurate as far as it went to my knowledge." In fact, by Haldeman's own account in *The Ends of Power,* he knew the statement could not be accurate: Magruder told him, he states, that McCord was "our security man at CRP," working for Liddy.[27]

A better and contemporary record of their crucial Sunday conversation survived and has only recently become available. It was found in out-of-date order at the National Archives by an expert researcher, either misfiled or deliberately hidden. It indicates clearly that Haldeman was informed that "the real problem is whether anything is traceable to Liddy," and that "2 to 3 others were implicated," with an allusion to Hunt. And it demonstrates that the statement being put out with Haldeman's approval was certainly inaccurate—"get it as confused as possible" was the line. The record is Haldeman's own handwritten note of his call to Magruder.*

* 6/18
Mag[ruder]
AP t[a]lk[e]d to [CRP spokesman] Shumway—
ident.[ified] McCord
we plan:
rel.[ease] st[ateme]nt as soon as conn[ection] uncovered
"just l[ea]rned man ident[ified] as employ[ed] by comm.[ittee] has a
priv[ate] sec.[urity] agency—empl[oyed] to instal syst[em]
has # of clients

While Nixon's memoirs would have us believe he learned only on Monday evening of the connection between the break-in and CRP, it is inconceivable that Haldeman kept it from him for another thirty-six hours after his conversation with Magruder. Haldeman's Sunday note also indicates that he called Ehrlichman and then Colson, who gave him the further hair-raising news that Hunt, although off the White House payroll from the previous April, still had an office and files in the White House.

And Haldeman in his book stated he did speak to the president after these calls. Haldeman had learned from Ehrlichman about Hunt's check being found and of Ehrlichman's own call to Colson on Saturday. Haldeman said Ehrlichman confided that "if brother Colson is involved

---

not op[erating] in our behalf or w[ith] our consent
have our own sec[urity] prob[lem]s—not as dram[atic]
but of serious nature to us
dont know if related
no place for this—w[ill] not permit or condone"

real prob[lem]—whether anything traceable to Liddy
he says no—but not too confid.[ent]
t[hin]k[ing] of getting Mard[ian] back—keep eye on Liddy

was AP story re our leak
have Chapman report that McG[overn] writer
said they have lines into 1701
Th[in]k X will be OK—but concerned re Liddy
[be]cause of his lack of j[ud]g[me]nt + reliability
have heard 2–3 others implicated
The cash was DNC's not ours
If there was—w[ou]ld have come from Duke [Hugh Sloan]

p2
w[ill] refer to the AP article
& the Chap[man] report
idea—to get it as confused as poss[ible]—
& keep up idea of McCord's other empl[oyme]nt

E[hrlichman] th[in]ks st[ateme]nt is OK—get out fast

Cols[on] one was on payroll until Apr[il] 1 (Hunt)
did l[ea]v[e] office & files . . .

(In plain language, an enterprising Associated Press reporter had started the ball rolling, identifying McCord from campaign spending reports listing him as CRP security chief, confirming it with CRP spokesman DeVan Shumway. "Chapman's friend," the White House "plant," was even supposed to be reporting on a McGovern "plant" at CRP.)

in this little jamboree we're in for a lot of problems." Haldeman's account of his call with Colson has the Nixon hatchet man groveling. " 'You gotta believe me Bob. It wasn't me. Tell the President that. I know he'll be worried . . .' He frothed on till I hung up."

Haldeman, knowing about both Liddy and Hunt, was certainly worried but claims that he relaxed again when he talked to the president. Colson's name apparently never occurred to Nixon, even when Haldeman mentioned Hunt. "It has to be some crazies over at CRP, Bob. . . . The American people will see it for what it is: a political prank, hell, they can't take a break-in at the DNC seriously." Nixon wanted to get on with presidential business; Haldeman had the extraordinary news from Colson that McGovern was not going to get the support of the head of the big union federation, the AFL-CIO.

Still, Haldeman's book notes, what an effort that cool amused façade must have cost the president. It was not until years later that he learned that Nixon had been "frantically telephoning Colson himself" and throwing ashtrays across the room.

Nixon had, in fact, twice telephoned Colson on Sunday—the first time for half an hour at 3 P.M., the second time for nine minutes at 6:39 P.M.—just when *NBC Nightly News* had finished a rather challenging report on Watergate. The telephone calls from the Key Biscayne White House (like those from San Clemente) were not covered by Nixon's taping system.

What happened as a result of the Haldeman-Magruder call was a crisis change of plan in California. Haldeman, saying the president did not trust Mardian, ordered Magruder back to Washington instead; it was so urgent that when Magruder and his wife could not book a commercial connection from Chicago, LaRue had them charter an executive jet. Before he left, Magruder said Mitchell told him to get in touch with John Dean.

The Mitchell party moved on to another Southern California political reception at Newport Beach, the very heart of Nixon country and home of Herbert Kalmbach. And here LaRue had a meeting at the Newporter Inn with Acting FBI Director Gray. They discussed Watergate, LaRue recently disclosed, and arranged to be in touch once back in Washington. Given the secret pressure that was about to hit the FBI, this surely was a potent encounter.[28]

Whatever the White House was up to in secret, to "get it as confused as possible" in public did not work immediately. The press pounced on McCord's CRP connection. As Sunday duty man for *The Times* of London, I did myself. Mitchell's statement referring to McCord's other employment was a transparent diversion and *The Times* Monday headline on the lower front page—NIXON CAMPAIGN MAN HELD FOR 'BUGGING DEMOCRATS'—was perfectly accurate. I claim no prescience. Most of the media got the beginning right.

The next phase got so confused, however, that almost everyone became bored with the Watergate story. The break-in was dismissed as a "caper." Newspapers and television networks swallowed the line—as the White House intended—that it was all got up by the Cuban Americans. The Liddy connection was kept from the public for more than a month.

That Sunday, Liddy met his lawyer, Peter Maroulis, who flew his own light plane down from New York State. Liddy told him that he expected to be indicted but intended remaining silent. To Maroulis he told the whole story, and Maroulis agreed to represent him. The most hopeful prospect, so far as Watergate was concerned, was that "I could stop the thing with me," Liddy said. While for himself, "the best we'd be able to do was play for error" by the trial judge. That and stonewalling remained defense tactics for another nine months.

If Liddy told Hunt this, Hunt did not record it. Hunt's account is of the world falling apart. "I could no longer conceal from myself that the episode was assuming alarming proportions," he wrote. Caddy told Hunt that his law partners were upset at his involvement in the case, and Hunt agreed he should withdraw. Hunt claims Liddy never reported to him about Kleindienst's refusal to intervene; had he done so, Hunt might have acted differently rather than continue to hope for White House help once the Nixon team returned to Washington. When the FBI called on him a second time, Hunt explained that his lawyer had advised him not to talk and that his lawyer's name was Liddy![29]

The FBI and prosecutors that Sunday were making the first of their huge gaffes. Despite holding McCord, establishing his CRP connection, and discovering in Philadelphia that he had purchased bugging equipment, the FBI and prosecutors made no move to obtain a search warrant for his home. Had they done so they would have discovered his van and all its contents still intact. They never did get around to it. Later the prosecutor and FBI inspectors made an extraordinary claim that there was no probable cause to support a warrant.[30]

Not that the FBI investigation was stalled. Someone had recognized McCord's picture in the paper and reported to investigators that they had seen him in the Howard Johnson cafeteria. Within hours the FBI had acquired and pored over the Howard Johnson room records and telephone calls. But instead of giving McCord the full treatment, it was Baldwin they went after. The lookout and bug monitor had made many calls home and the FBI quickly got on his trail.

Everyone else in the affair seemed to have forgotten Baldwin. Hunt, who had told him to flee, apparently did not get in touch. McCord was in jail. Yet on this Sunday, according to Baldwin himself, he met two lawyers in Connecticut, Robert Mirto and John Cassidento. Baldwin still states that they unsuccessfully tried getting in touch with CRP to see what was being done about getting him a lawyer.[31] Cassidento, who later became a Democrat-appointed judge and is now dead, found more interest in Baldwin's story elsewhere. He did not tell the U.S. authorities, but Lawrence O'Brien, the DNC chairman, instead.

That very Sunday, O'Brien had publicly demanded an investigation be launched into the break-in at his headquarters. He issued a statement saying it "raised the ugliest question about the integrity of the political process that I have encountered in a quarter century of political activity." Now, according to Baldwin, Cassidento had put the Democrats in the picture.[32] It seems possible that at this stage the hated O'Brien might have known as much as Nixon, possibly more.

One man who claims he still knew very little as the day after Watergate drew to an end was John Dean, returning from his junket to the Philippines. When he landed on Sunday morning in San Francisco, intending to pause in his long journey, he phoned his deputy, Fred Fielding, who told him about the break-in and suggested that he had better get back fast. Dean wrote that he met Fielding briefly that night, since they lived close to each other. Fielding told him about the Hunt check, and Dean, like his White House colleagues, said he immediately thought of Colson. "My God, one of Colson's crazy schemes has finally backfired."[33] Too late to do anything else and exhausted, Dean went to bed. Apparently, he was unaware that, so Ehrlichman wrote, it had been agreed with Haldeman that they would turn the case over to the White House counsel on Monday.

That day Jack Nicklaus won the U.S. Open golf championship, and Nixon's last recorded phone call of the day was to phone the champion in Monterey, California, to congratulate him. Before making an early night of it, Nixon read the last chapters of Churchill's World War II history, the final volume entitled *Triumph and Tragedy*.

CHAPTER 7

Instant Cover-up

Nixon had contemplated returning to Washington on Sunday night, but Hurricane Agnes passed close by, promising a miserably bumpy flight. So he waited a day. It is tempting to say that had Nixon returned and taken charge that Monday at the White House he might have taken the bumps but avoided his political hurricane. But there is nothing in the record to suggest he would have done anything other than encourage his aides to act the way they did, which was to proceed with the cover-up.

Nixon says Watergate was still the furthest thing from his mind. Yet that morning, Nixon's mouthpiece, Ron Ziegler, who never spoke without checking with the boss, uttered to the traveling White House press corps in Key Biscayne the first of his memorable Watergate phrases: "a third-rate burglary attempt" not worth dignifying with further comment. This unconcern was a sham. Nixon tapes released in 1993 fill in more of the picture of accelerating anxiety. Quickly, several presidential meetings a day were taken up with plotting how to contain the scandal.

That first Monday, when he met with Haldeman at noon, Nixon was already scheming a thrust against the Democrats. The president wanted Colson to go through his opponents' attacks and "collect the worst smear stuff on Nixon for a speech—have a counterattack available to challenge them." And to bolster CRP (and perhaps sideline Magruder), Nixon instructed Haldeman to talk to Mitchell about having a new executive officer so the campaign director would be free for decision making.[1]

In Washington, although most White House people were too busy with Watergate to notice, Mitchell and Nixon suffered a serious legal reversal. The Supreme Court that Monday handed down a unanimous ruling: Government electronic bugging of U.S. citizens in internal security cases must be first authorized by a court-ordered warrant. It was a tremendous blow to the Nixon-Mitchell doctrine that the president had "inherent power" to bug at will, as they had claimed in January 1971 in the so-called Keith case. The FBI rushed to remove the last eight warrantless buggings in the Kissinger taps series, including those on Yeoman Radford's telephone. But if a tremor passed through Ehrlichman's office, where he secretly stored the FBI files from the earlier taps, it was not recorded.

Across the road at CRP headquarters, Magruder, having flown back from the West Coast ahead of Mitchell's party, was in early. He immediately began the double life that continued until the following April, trying to reassure CRP staff while living the lie, as he put it. Magruder's first and most critical encounter was with Hugh Sloan. The FCRP treasurer immediately confirmed Magruder's worst fears: The money found on the burglars was cash he had given to Liddy and could probably be traced. Sloan's candor was eventually to disturb, if not upset, Magruder's cover story.

Magruder called in Liddy. It was apparently their first meeting since the Saturday calls and the failed mission to Kleindienst. They despised each other; Magruder's later account relished the occasion: "James Bond had been exposed as a bumbling clown." He quoted Liddy, "I goofed."[2]

Magruder, who had just recovered the GEMSTONE and other "sensitive" files, which his aides, Reisner and Odle, had taken home for the weekend, was now assured by Liddy that the destruction of evidence was well advanced. McCord's office had been cleared out by his wife and staff on Sunday; Liddy himself had worked the shredders overtime. Magruder phoned Strachan at the White House; Strachan had routinely been given copies of all Magruder's files for Haldeman, except the

GEMSTONE bugging log. But Strachan still thought SEDAN CHAIR II reports also came from bugging, and those had been passed on to Haldeman. Strachan, like Liddy, assured Magruder there would be no problem with the files; he had been frantically weeding and shredding them from Sunday on.

Magruder suggested that Liddy talk to John Dean. Dean's phones were soon off the hook. Caulfield was first, reporting his tip from the Secret Service of McCord's arrest. Magruder called, then Ehrlichman. Dean called Colson; Strachan called. Dean called Kleindienst. Bases were quickly being touched, but it was already more than fifty hours since the arrests. Apart from destroying evidence, nothing really had been done.

Dean confirms that Magruder asked him to see Liddy. He claims that he first checked with Ehrlichman, who told him to go ahead—and that he then reported back Liddy's involvement. This is something Ehrlichman vehemently denies. Had he learned of Liddy's participation, Ehrlichman states that he would immediately have turned his suspicion to Mitchell instead of Colson.[3]

Some of the key versions are wildly at variance about this first Monday of Watergate, which was crucial in all that followed in the White House cover-up. Ehrlichman's supposed ignorance of Liddy's involvement requires one to assume that Haldeman had not passed on Magruder's critical Sunday disclosure of the "real problem—whether anything traceable to Liddy" and that Ehrlichman, when he heard on Saturday that Hunt and the Cubans were involved, did not immediately suspect it was Liddy's Plumbers up to their old tricks.

Dean and Liddy met and their accounts of the encounter, which was dramatic, accord surprisingly closely. Liddy was pleased to be seeing again the man who had recruited him for the intelligence job. Dean, he felt, was the logical choice to serve as White House "damage control action officer," as he put it. Now they would get some decisions and get their men out on bail. From Liddy's point of view, it was time to unload the full story, not just of Watergate but also the whole catalog of the Plumbers' exploits, on the assumption that in telling Dean he was telling the president.

Liddy, who still had his White House pass, tells in his book *Will* how he was intercepted in the corridor of the Executive Office Building by Dean, who said, "Let's go for a walk." They went down 17th Street, past the Corcoran Gallery, and sat on a park bench. Liddy confessed, "I was commanding the aircraft carrier when it hit the reef." Dean, said Liddy, cut in to ask exactly who in the White House knew that they planned going into Watergate. Liddy replied that Gordon Strachan did; he might not have known the exact day, but Liddy had told him that they would correct the defective bug.

Colson? Not unless Hunt told him and Liddy did not believe he had. Liddy continued that if the White House was worried about who gave the order, it was not Strachan; it was Magruder. "If anybody was pushing Magruder from the White House, you'll have to ask him." Dean, he said, asked whether Magruder authorized using McCord. Liddy admitted that this was his own mistake. Magruder never knew about McCord.

Dean rose to go but Liddy wanted him to have the full story. His men would never talk but he wanted Dean to know what they were in a position to tell if they had to. There was the Ellsberg break-in (which Dean claimed he already knew about from the White House grapevine). But when Dean was told the same Cubans were involved, his composure wilted. Liddy, proud of his men, reassured Dean:

> "They won't talk. But I think it's imperative we get them bailed out. That D.C. jail's a hellhole, especially in summer, and they expect it. They were promised that kind of support."

Liddy has never revealed who made that promise. What kind of support? Liddy told Dean: "The usual in this line of work. Bail, attorneys' fees, families taken care of . . . " Dean, says Liddy, confidently answered, "That goes without saying. Everyone'll be taken care of."

This, the promise of support that would rapidly become "hush money," is the single largest discrepancy between Liddy's and Dean's versions of their meeting. In his book, *Blind Ambition,* Dean wrote that he said the opposite: "I can't do anything about that and I think you can understand why . . . " Liddy insists that his account is correct. No matter who is right about what was said, what actually happened, as we shall see, is that Dean was very rapidly involved in setting up hush money payments and has never denied it.

Liddy was not done. He realized that what he had told Dean could cost Nixon the election, and Dean's face looked troubled. Liddy knew *he* would keep silence, but how could Dean and those above him be sure? It occurred to him, Liddy wrote, that those who seriously considered drugging Ellsberg and killing Jack Anderson might wish to assassinate him. As Liddy put it in his book, he regarded being terminated in this way as "reasonable." The bungled break-in was his fault. But so far as he knew he was the only person "available to the White House for a domestic sanctioned killing." They could not turn to the CIA without handing its director, Richard Helms, "the keys to the kingdom" (whatever that meant). And Liddy did not want some amateur endangering his family with a shotgun blast through the window.

As they walked back, Liddy said, "If someone wants to shoot me . . . just tell me what corner to stand on." Dean, startled, replied, "I don't think we've gotten *there* yet, Gordon."

From phantasmagoria to practicalities, Liddy now had expert advice for Dean from his time as an agent. To keep on top of the FBI's investigation and, more important, to know where it was heading, he must ensure he got the agents' raw reports—not the summaries their bosses later passed on. What Dean needed were the Airtels and forms FD302; if Dean could obtain those, he would know what informants had told agents in interviews and what the FBI in Washington was instructing its officers elsewhere to follow up.

Liddy said that Dean asked after Hunt and, told he was lying low, suggested that Liddy tell him he would be better off out of the country, sooner rather than later.

Finally, Dean told Liddy it would not be a good idea for them to talk again. "Someone from 1701" would get in touch, Dean said mysteriously; he would identify himself. Dean was now switching from one foot to the other in his nervousness to get away, and Liddy said he apologized for the way things had turned out. "Sure is a mess," said Dean, and Liddy says he saluted him as he went back to his office at 1701 Pennsylvania Avenue, CRP headquarters, to call Hunt.

Hunt had been one of the earliest into the White House that Monday. His office had not been entered, he noted, and his safe was still in place. He looked for Colson—which, considering that the FBI had visited Hunt twice over the weekend, was madness—but he was not yet in. Colson's secretary was surprised to see him; she must have been even more surprised when he asked her to tell Colson, "That safe of mine upstairs is loaded."[4] Then he left the White House for the last time.

Liddy found Hunt at his Mullen Company office, opposite CRP, and arranged a street rendezvous with him one block west on 18th Street. It was just after noon, Liddy said. Hunt did not favor the idea of leaving the country like a fugitive, not even joining his wife and children, then on vacation in England. But when Liddy indicated that the idea came from the White House and that he should depart that day, Hunt consented. He asked only that Liddy find him a lawyer.

Back at CRP, Liddy confirmed that his secretary was shredding her notebooks and tried to get back to what he called his committee legal work. The phone rang; it was Dean. "Gordon, that message to Hunt. Cancel it." When Liddy protested that it might be too late, Dean replied: "Ehrlichman says cancel it."[5]

Hunt was at home when Liddy reached him; Hunt's confidence in the White House was not heightened by this about-face. Hunt told Liddy he had business in New York and would go there first, and he left town. There remains a fierce dispute about the orders to Hunt. Ehrlichman still insists it was Dean who initiated it and he, Ehrlichman, who reversed it at an afternoon meeting with Colson present.[6] Dean says the opposite. Colson's version was that *he* told Dean to call off Hunt's flight—with Ehrlichman not even in the room.

Up to this point Hunt's connection with the burglars had not become public. Before he left that evening for New York, however, a reporter telephoned him at his Mullen Company office put through via the White House switchboard. It was Bob Woodward who had traced him, asking why his name and phone number were in two address books belonging to the men arrested at the Watergate. "Good God," Woodward says Hunt replied, "in view that the matter is under adjudication, I have no comment" and slammed down the phone. That same afternoon, Robert Bennett, Hunt's employer, had told Woodward of Hunt's CIA ties. It was certainly news to Woodward and another tasty link in the story he was breaking in next morning's *Washington Post*.[7]

Ehrlichman was waiting to be briefed by Dean on what he had found out. Besides Liddy, Dean had now talked to Strachan, who assured him that he had consulted Haldeman and that he had shredded all the problem files—including, he thought, wiretap logs. Hugh Sloan phoned to tell Dean about the large cash bundles handed to Liddy and expressed his worry that his fingerprints might be detected. It seemed to Dean that Liddy was "a real beggar's crossroads," leading to disaster in all directions: "Through Magruder up to Mitchell; through Strachan up to Haldeman and the President; through Krogh up to Ehrlichman and the President."[8]

Versions again part company here. Dean stated that he told Ehrlichman everything, including his own presence at the first two GEMSTONE planning meetings for which he was ready to resign.[9] However, he withheld one key detail: what Liddy had said about Strachan's prior knowledge of the break-in. It was too gruesome, he wrote. He would leave that to Haldeman. He told Ehrlichman that Colson wanted the three of them to meet. Ehrlichman agreed, but he had to send a "Care package off to Florida"—his report to the presidential party still at Key Biscayne.[10]

Ehrlichman's account touches on none of this, only on the later meeting with Colson and Dean. But that meeting was momentous enough, quite apart from the business over Hunt leaving the country. Ehrlichman wanted Hunt's status established. Was he or was he not still on the White House payroll? An administrative aide was summoned with the records. The last payments to Hunt had been in March, but they still carried him on the books and Hunt still had an office and safe in room 338.

Ehrlichman provided the White House communications office with an obfuscatory holding answer for the press. Dean meanwhile was told to take custody of the contents of Hunt's safe. Even though Hunt claimed to have provided Colson's office with the combination, a team had to be ordered up from the General Services Administration to drill it open. Dean assigned his assistant to supervise.

Mitchell, leaving his wife in California, had flown back to Washington with LaRue and Mardian. He found time to call Haldeman in Key Biscayne, but apparently not the president. The only record of the call is in Nixon's diary: "Mitchell has told Bob on the phone enigmatically not to get involved in it."[11]

Mitchell then called a meeting in his Watergate apartment—Magruder and Dean joining Mardian and LaRue. Magruder had just taken a call from a furious Martha Mitchell, who wanted to know why they were firing McCord. He had worked for her and ferried her daughter to school. He couldn't have done anything wrong. Magruder did his best to placate her.

Magruder's account of what ought to have been a crisis management meeting makes it sound like a wake. Mitchell's men and Dean were sitting and drinking and talking in bitter, despondent voices. They had lost control of events, and Magruder says he could see "a long evening of booze and self-pity shaping up." He was happy to receive a call from the vice president's office inviting him to make up a tennis foursome later that evening. Before he left he had a final question for Mitchell: What should he do with the GEMSTONE file he had brought in his briefcase? "Maybe you should have a little fire at your house tonight," he says Mitchell replied.[12]

Mitchell later vehemently denied saying any such thing, but LaRue inconveniently remembered having heard it. That night, Magruder kept the GEMSTONE file at the side of the tennis court. It did not take him long to realize that he had been invited so that Vice President Agnew could ask him what was going on. Told by Magruder that it was a CRP operation that screwed up, the vice president frowned, saying, "I don't think we should discuss it again."

At the meeting in Mitchell's apartment, Dean says, Mitchell reported that he had telephoned the president (although there is no record of one that Monday). "He was taking it much better than I thought he would. Hell, he tried to cheer me up," Dean quoted Mitchell as saying. At this stage, Dean remarks, he was sure that Mitchell had "criminal responsibility" for the Watergate operation. Any such revelation, however, would be a death blow to the president's reelection chances. Martha called from California; she was hysterical. According to some accounts she had to be sedated because she kept telephoning United Press International White House reporter Helen Thomas to claim that her husband was involved in Watergate. Dean made his excuses and left the meeting. One decision had been made; LaRue and Mardian, the latter as CRP counsel, were to take over dealing with Liddy from Dean.

Meanwhile, although no one had yet done anything about getting the arrested men out on bail, McCord was able to telephone his wife. She had already arranged for further items to be removed from his CRP office (including an inscribed photo of CIA director Helms). Now she told her husband that she had received a bomb threat. From the jail McCord advised his wife to burn his papers—implausibly, so he wrote later, to prevent a possible bomb setting fire to his house. Mrs. McCord obeyed. Helped by McCord's former secretary and her husband, a one-time top FBI man and CIA contact named Lee Pennington, Mrs. McCord dispatched the GEMSTONE flimsies and other documentation in a roaring fire in the fireplace. There was so much smoke that the sitting room had to be repainted. McCord now claims this was caused by burning CRP's typewriter ribbons. (Not far away, Magruder returned home from tennis. His wife was in bed. He, too, went to his fireplace. He looked at the GEMSTONE file, which he said was four or five inches thick, meaning hundreds of pages. He had to feed the flames slowly. Magruder's wife woke up. "Jeb, what would we tell the firemen if you burned the house down in June?" "It's all right," Magruder replied. "It's just some papers I have to get rid of.")[13]

The FBI might well have been expected to secure this evidence. After all, it knew McCord was CRP's man as early as Saturday, yet by Monday, agents had still not visited CRP's offices. The bureau, however, was making headway elsewhere. The seized banknotes were tracked from the Bureau of Printing and Engraving to the Federal Reserve in Atlanta, which issued them to a bank in Miami. The FBI also discovered McCord's giveaway application to the FCC for licensed frequencies for his bugs.

As a result of its own investigation into Hunt, on Monday the FBI made a request to interview Colson. That request was now pending with senior FBI officials who were awaiting the return of their boss, L. Patrick Gray, from the West Coast and of the president from Florida. The FBI's top echelon prepared memos summarizing the investigation for both Haldeman and Kleindienst.

But the FBI men were dazzled, and understandably distracted, by the extraordinary connections of all those involved. Here was Baldwin, like McCord, with FBI links, while Hunt and McCord were retired CIA. There was a profusion of still more CIA connections among the Cuban Americans.[14] Angelo Lano, heading the FBI team, remarked, "What is this? CIA people, FBI people, you know, what is going on here, who's hiring all these people and why?"[15]

Lano's boss, Robert Kunkel, in charge of the Washington field office, went further. His theory, which he put in a memo to superiors, was that the Watergate break-in "was in furtherance of the White House efforts to locate and identify 'leaks.'" Without realizing it, Kunkel had stumbled on the link to the Plumbers, but it was never explored. Kunkel was later demoted to St. Louis; he died in 1992.[16]

The FBI belief that it had run into a CIA operation at the Watergate suggests how easy it would have been, with a modest amount of advance planning, to quash the whole investigation at the outset by getting the burglars out of police hands. All that would have been needed was a trusted Nixon man at the CIA to make the timely phone call. Liddy and Hunt had seemed incapable, however, of ensuring that this was organized in advance.

Nixon at last left the Florida sunshine and headed back to Washington. On board the *Spirit of '76,* the Air Force One of its day, between calls to Saigon and other distractions, the president talked with Haldeman about Watergate. Haldeman marveled at Nixon's serenity.[17]

On Tuesday, June 20, with the president and Haldeman back in town, the more structured phase of the cover-up began. The drift of three days had to stop. As if to emphasize the urgency, Hunt's White House link to Colson was bannered in that morning's *Washington Post.*

At 9 A.M. while the president spent an hour in the Oval Office, above his head in Ehrlichman's office the first top White House Watergate meeting was about to begin. It seems to have been called in a hurry, judging from Haldeman's telephone messages. The routine political meeting had been canceled. When Haldeman got in to work, he found a phone message from Ehrlichman inviting him to join his meeting with Mitchell and Attorney General Kleindienst. A further message from Haldeman's assistant Higby suggested that John Dean be included: "Somebody should keep track of all the elements of this thing and Dean is probably the best . . . " Haldeman later wrote that he never quite knew how Dean took over from Ehrlichman; here was the answer, in his own staff.[18]

All accounts make it seem to have been a falsely cheerful session, with the president's top men circling each other warily. Haldeman recalled how much better Mitchell looked and was reassured when Mitchell insisted he hadn't approved the Watergate break-in. Ehrlichman describes it as a matter-of-fact session to decide who should handle what. Kleindienst's reported presence, however, indicates clearly their need to get on top of the criminal investigation of the break-in.* The day before, Kleindienst had received a briefing from the FBI. Kleindienst, Ehrlichman wrote, stated that Colson was guiltless and that he saw no White House involvement. But evidently the attorney general did not tell them about the approach by Liddy at Burning Tree golf club.

Dean's account was most sardonic. He wrote in *Blind Ambition* that the White House faction did not trust the Justice Department faction, and no one wanted to acknowledge how serious the problem might be. Dean himself—considering how much he knew and had told Ehrlichman—hardly said a word. It was, Dean said, the first round of *internal* stonewalling.

But important steps to further the cover-up by fixing the officials in charge of prosecutions were taken immediately. Dean says he and Kleindienst went to the attorney general's office. Dean had served at Justice under Kleindienst before moving to the White House to become the president's counsel, and at this stage Kleindienst liked and trusted Dean. What occurred next, however, is a matter of total dispute.

According to Dean, the attorney general exploded. He told Dean of his encounter with Liddy at the golf club; Dean says he assumed Kleindienst had not mentioned it earlier for fear of implicating Mitchell and Liddy. Kleindienst, said Dean, told him that if Mitchell was in

* Kleindienst later (in 1985) claimed not to have been at the meeting.[19] But his presence was noted by Ehrlichman, Haldeman and Dean.

trouble, "I'll resign before I'll prosecute him." Dean, deciding to confide in him, said he was afraid that the affair could lead to the president and that could mean that he might not be reelected. At this Kleindienst called in Henry Petersen, assistant attorney general in overall charge of criminal prosecutions, who delivered a report on the first days of the Watergate investigation.

Kleindienst's version of this meeting is totally self-exculpatory. He later testified before the Senate Watergate Committee that he and Petersen wanted Dean to know of their "apprehension and the grave seriousness with which we received the news." They wanted Dean, as counsel to the president, to understand that the Department of Justice and FBI would be compelled to launch "a full-scale intensive thorough investigation," even though it went to the heart of the political system. And the president should be told.

Kleindienst said that Dean volunteered to do this; indeed, said that he had been delegated by the president to report back on the investigation. Petersen added to this in his own Senate testimony that he wanted to urge the president "to instruct the Attorney General publicly to run an all out investigation and let the devil take the hindmost." It sounded great, but it didn't happen.

When Kleindienst left the two alone, Dean's version is that he told Petersen, "I don't think the White House can stand a wide-open investigation . . . there are all kinds of things that could blow up in our face." Dean feared it could lead directly to the president. Petersen, Dean says, reassuringly explained that he had advised Earl Silbert, the assistant U.S. attorney prosecuting the case, that "he's investigating a break-in . . . he knows better than to wander off beyond his authority . . . "

When Petersen later testified, he said he could not recall Dean saying anything about "leading to the President" or about the White House being unable to withstand a wide-open investigation. He admitted, however, they had agreed that there ought not be a general probe of the White House in an election year. And Petersen said he gave assurance there would be "no fishing expedition."

Peterson also suggested to Dean that he urge the president to move quickly to cut his losses. Dean agreed. Petersen's willingness to limit the prosecutor's authority to the break-in itself was just what they wanted. It was the key to containing the scandal; that must be the cover-up strategy. It was critical to keep the investigation from stumbling into other areas.

Just how critical Dean realized when he got back to his office. Boxes had been delivered; the contents of Howard Hunt's safe. Dean's assistant, Fred Fielding, fetched surgical gloves—no fingerprints wanted—from the White House physicians' office across the hall, and they sifted through the contents. As Hunt had said, the safe was loaded. In addition to McCord's leftover bugs, there were:

- a .25 caliber revolver, with a clip of ammunition;
- a folder containing papers on Ellsberg, including the two CIA-produced psychological profiles;
- a folder containing material on Edward Kennedy, and Hunt's Chappaquiddick interviews;
- a pile of copies of State Department cables, including the two on Diem fabricated by Hunt, plus a memo to Colson regarding Hunt's attempts to interest *Life* journalist Lambert in them;
- two clothbound notebooks and an address book.[20]

Clearly, the political stuff was dynamite. It was also evidence. For the moment, they decided to turn the diplomatic cable copies over to David Young, co-chief of the Plumbers. Dean put the Watergate bugging equipment and the gun in a closet; but the sensitive files, with the fake Diem cables, he put into his safe. Then he made an appointment to see Ehrlichman.

That morning Ehrlichman had gone straight from his office to his first meeting with Nixon since Watergate. Haldeman, who was not there, would have us believe that there was no Watergate discussion; in his memoirs Nixon mentions only that their talk was about school busing and "other domestic issues." No tape of the conversation has been released. Ehrlichman had realized—as he claims Nixon had too—that Hunt and some of the same Cubans had been involved in the previous year's Plumbers break-in. But Ehrlichman remembers that Watergate *was* discussed. In the midst of talking about amendments to a higher education bill, Ehrlichman says that Nixon spoke of the unfairness of the Watergate accusations. That morning Nixon had underlined on his staff's daily press summary the outpouring of dismay among Democrats in Congress. "We've reduced the number of wiretaps by fifty percent in this administration," he quoted Nixon saying in a familiar refrain.

In an apparent reference to the Supreme Court's ruling prohibiting warrantless wiretapping, Nixon remarked that "our primary interest is in the foreign contacts made by domestic subversive groups." The president seemed to be trying out a line, rehearsing, as he so often did, statements he wanted put out to the press: "As the President said a year and a half ago it is the policy of this administration to use taps sparingly . . . " Ehrlichman says he waited for Nixon to close the circle between the two topics, "but that was all he said about Watergate."[21]

While Ehrlichman was with the president, Haldeman saw Gordon Strachan for the first time since Watergate. Strachan, terrified of Haldeman's reaction, found him smiling. He showed his boss what was left in the files he'd been shredding; it was the famous "political matters memo" number 18 of April 4, which mentioned approval for Liddy's sophisticated $300,000 intelligence plan. Strachan said, "This is what can be imputed to you through me, your agent." Haldeman read the memo's attachment referring to SEDAN CHAIR II. "I should have been reading these. These are quite interesting," Haldeman commented. Then: "Make sure our files are clean." This account is from Strachan; Haldeman claims not to recall the exchange.[22]

At the time, Haldeman, like Strachan, believed that SEDAN CHAIR reports were the product of wiretapping. It is plausible, therefore, that Haldeman would have shared with the president Strachan's link to the bugging. Immediately after talking to Strachan, Haldeman went to the president's hideaway office. But we shall never know what they said to each other. The tape of this meeting is the one with the notorious eighteen-and-a-half-minute gap on it. When the existence of the erasure was revealed in November 1973, it was a fatal blow to Nixon's credibility. Nixon later cited Haldeman's notes as evidence that the talk dealt only with public relations. Yet Haldeman's book *The Ends of Power* makes clear that his notes were not exhaustive but devoted to actions to be assigned or executed. Haldeman goes on to reconstruct what *might* have been said since the president was, as he admits himself in his memoirs, worried that Colson "might have gone too far." The key parts of Haldeman's reconstruction of the conversation are:

Nixon: Colson can talk about the president, if he cracks. You know I was on Colson's tail for months to nail Larry O'Brien on the Hughes deal. Colson told me he was going to get the information I wanted one way or the other. And that was O'Brien's office they were bugging, wasn't it? Colson's boy, Hunt, Christ!
Haldeman: Still Magruder didn't even mention Colson.
Nixon: He will.
Haldeman: Why?
Nixon: Colson called him and got the whole operation started. Right from the goddamn White House. With Hunt and Liddy sitting in his lap. I just hope the FBI doesn't check the office log and put it together with that Hunt and Liddy meeting in Colson's office . . ."[23]

Haldeman remembered that they discussed Colson's professions of innocence and then went on to discuss counterattacking. The action—"PR offensive to top this"—[i.e., overcome the break-in] is, in fact, mentioned in Haldeman's notes.

Nixon, naturally, would not accept such an incriminating version. But it carries a verisimilitude that only Haldeman after all his hours of presidential conversation could give it. Haldeman knew what Nixon had been urging against O'Brien for years. But Nixon claims in his memoirs that a second conversation with Haldeman that afternoon—the tape of which survived—provides a better idea what the first contained.

"It has always been my habit," Nixon writes in his memoirs, "to discuss problems a number of times often in almost the same terms and usually with the same people." (No wonder Haldeman wrote he often had to sit through long periods of "rambling discussions and recitation of gripes . . . ")

Haldeman's notes of the morning meeting show that Nixon was worried about his own hideaway office being bugged: "Be sure EOB office is thoroughly checked re bugs at all times." As for the counterattack, it should be for "diversion." Nixon wanted the "libertarians challenged"—"do they justify Watergate less than stealing Pentagon Papers?"[24] Nixon asked. It was the double standard Nixon was always complaining about, as if the Republicans could never keep up with the wrongs done to them by the other side.

By the time of the afternoon meeting, there had been an important development. Lawrence O'Brien formally launched the Democrats' civil suit for $1 million damages against CRP. Already there were hints at O'Brien's news conference of the inside information he had received from Baldwin's lawyers. "How many other attempts have there been and just who was involved?" O'Brien asked rhetorically. Reporters were told, unattributably by Democrats, that the suspects might have been involved in an earlier break-in on May 28—all information that at that stage could only have come from Baldwin.[25]

What most worried the president about the suit, as we shall see, was the legal discovery process. O'Brien's lawyers could now call as witnesses and take sworn depositions from almost the entire CRP and White House staffs. Nixon was alarmed and desperate to work out arrangements to delay the depositions.[26]

The tape of the June 20 afternoon meeting was released for public listening only in 1993, although Nixon alone had access to it for his memoirs. It begins with Nixon asking Haldeman, "You got anything further on the Mitchell operation?" This question, not found in Nixon's memoirs, suggests that Nixon had already decided, with some accuracy, whose responsibility Watergate was. Despite the lack of clear audibility —no transcripts have been provided by the National Archives—the tape leaves no doubt that Nixon knew his campaign was conducting political espionage.

Nixon: I think I told you, I contacted Colson [unintelligible].
Haldeman: I think [last night?] we all knew that there were some . . .
Nixon: . . . intelligence [unintelligible] . . .
Haldeman: Yes, some activities.
Nixon: [Unintelligible].
Haldeman: [Unintelligible] I don't think Chuck knew specifically that, you know, this project was under way or that these people were involved.
Nixon: He did [unintelligible] . . .[27]

In his memoirs Nixon was less forthright in admitting the extent of Colson's knowledge. "I said I thought he had, but then I said that was just second-guessing him." The tape is less clear. For the record, this newly released tape stands as the earliest recorded Nixon post-Watergate conversation. It was made three days before the so-called smoking gun tape, which eventually left Nixon with his final choice: resign or be impeached.

The two men's conversation is replete with potentially incriminating knowledge of what had happened at the Watergate, at the time some of it unknown even to the FBI. The account in Nixon's memoirs makes omissions, but for the rest broadly reflects the conversation, although he did reorder the sequence in which things were said.

According to the memoirs, Haldeman said he thought Mitchell had not known about the break-in plan. Nixon says he thought Mitchell was surprised and anyway "too goddamned [unintelligible]" to be involved; "smart" was the word supplied in the memoirs.

That thought is picked up by Haldeman's reply. He describes those involved (not just those who were caught, as Nixon's memoirs have it): "These guys apparently were a pretty competent bunch of people. They were doing other things [unintelligible]"—an implied reference to more than campaign activities.

On the tape Haldeman explained the intricacies of the two Watergate missions, the bugs and the photography:

> *Haldeman:* They had a three-channel transmitter in there and then two of the channels went out [unintelligible].
> *Nixon:* Really?
> *Haldeman:* . . . they could only get pictures of the stuff . . .

Haldeman adds details that he got from Dean or Colson, details which at this stage the FBI did not know:

> *Haldeman:* He was across the street in the Howard Johnson Hotel, the direct line of sight room, observing from across the street, and that was the room in which they had the receiving equipment for the bugs they put in there.

Another aside not in Nixon's memoirs but on the tape:

> *Nixon:* It's fortunately, it's fortunately a bizarre story.
> *Haldeman:* Yeah.
> *Nixon:* Don't you think so?
> *Haldeman:* It's bizarreness almost helps to discredit it.

Nixon's memoirs also neglect to note that McCord, contrary to the statement Mitchell put out, was on a permanent or regular monthly retainer from both CRP and the Republican National Committee.

Although Liddy had told Dean the men would stay silent, Haldeman reported an emerging cover story. McCord, far from being totally silent, was reported by the FBI on Saturday to have "denied anyone put him up to the job and that all participants decided on doing [the] job themselves."[28] Haldeman now told Nixon, "McCord, I guess, will say he was working with the Cubans . . . for their own political reasons." This is what Nixon wanted to hear.

According to the tape, Haldeman went on to discuss with Nixon having Hunt, whose involvements with Colson the president well understands, "disappear to a Latin American country"—we could un-disappear him if we want to." There was a question whether it had been bad for Hunt to leave the country—Haldeman's reference to the previous day's on-off orders—but "the original thought was probably good."

Haldeman reminds Nixon that Hunt was with the Cubans in the Bay of Pigs invasion—something Nixon has already heard from Colson. And although Haldeman cannot quite explain how McCord fits in with Hunt, Nixon is already interested in possibly involving "the Cuban community." As Nixon's memoirs explained: "A Cuban explanation" would conceal CRP's involvement, and it would undercut the Democrats by emphasizing McGovern's naïve policy toward Castro.

Indeed, on the tape Haldeman suggests (half jokingly, the memoirs insist) a way out. They should just plead guilty and say they were spying on the Democrats to save the nation from McGovern. "They were going in to get this because they were scared to death that, that a crazy man was going to become President and sell the U.S. out to the Communists." Comments Nixon: "Very nice touch."

That same afternoon, Nixon had a talk with Colson. A tape of this has been in the public domain since 1988, and from its content it is plain that Nixon and Colson had already spoken on the telephone about Watergate many times before this meeting. Colson, though furious at having his name dragged into the papers through Hunt, cheerfully tells Nixon the fuss "will be less than ITT." Nixon, saying he doesn't want his staff "to get in a tizzy," suggests a cynical public response:

> *Nixon:* A lot of people think you ought to wiretap.
> *Colson:* Well they, I'm sure most people . . .
> *Nixon:* . . . knew why the hell we're doing it, and they probably figure they're doing it to us, which they are.

Nixon, again revealing deep knowledge of the developing strategy, raises the "real question" of what will happen "if we are going to have this funny guy take credit." (Nixon's memoirs said he meant McCord but that Colson thought he meant Hunt. In fact, the transcript is not clear; it could have been Liddy.) Nixon then comments, oddly, "If we didn't know better [we] would have thought it was deliberately botched."

"Of course," Nixon tells Colson, "we are just going to leave this where it is, with the Cubans . . ." Colson tells the president that he would love to make a deposition in the Democrats' civil suit: "I'm not —because nobody, everybody's completely out of it." The president demurs: "I don't think you should . . . you're an inside man."

That afternoon Mitchell's men LaRue and Mardian were also at last moving to get their end of the cover-up organized. Mardian wanted to borrow LaRue's apartment to hold a meeting with Liddy and he invited LaRue along. It was also in the Watergate complex. Liddy took this to mean that they were the new damage control action officers Dean had spoken of. Liddy characteristically asked them to leave a radio playing while they talked, to inhibit eavesdropping.

Liddy already knew Mardian from his time as assistant attorney general and thought him an explosive character. Mardian said he was now CRP's in-house attorney and whatever Liddy said was protected by attorney-client privilege. To the horrified Mardian and LaRue, Liddy now again unloaded. To the two Watergate burglaries, he added all the Plumbers exploits, plus Hunt's ITT mission for Colson with Dita Beard, using CIA disguises. Mardian later testified that Liddy had told them that all their missions had been "on the express authority of the President of the United States with the assistance of the CIA."[29]

Liddy in *Will* later wrote that Mardian could not hear enough about the CIA and all its connections to the Cuban Americans. And, very significantly, Liddy mentioned that "commitments had been made." Indeed, Liddy told them, only the day before John Dean had assured him that the men would be receiving all the usual family support and legal fees. They should be bailed out of the D.C. lockup.

Neither LaRue nor Mardian remembers Liddy saying that it was Dean who had made "commitments"; instead they insist that they never found out who had. Liddy, said Mardian, had passed on a message from Hunt that CRP ought to post bail for the men. Mardian later, at the Senate committee hearings, gave a graphic account of this meeting. He said he was shocked and half-disbelieving. Liddy had, he said, spelled out that the second Watergate entry was at Magruder's insistence, and they were "operating under a budget approved by Mitchell and the White House."

Mardian said he was worried about Liddy's being traced and suggested he ought to give himself up. But Liddy had maintained there was nothing traceable, no fingerprints, and the men would never talk. (In fact, Liddy's alias had been immediately penetrated through reservations at the Watergate Hotel. The same alias and White House telephone number had been found in Martinez's address list and were about to be identified by the FBI.)

Finally, Mardian said, Liddy told them how Hunt was "like a god in the Cuban community of Miami as a result of the Bay of Pigs"; extremely well connected, even to wealthy people there. Mardian claimed he advised Liddy to tell Hunt to look to the Miami community for bail since it was unlikely Mitchell would agree to use CRP funds. LaRue, however, remembers no doubts about payoffs. "I told Gordon, I said 'Gordon, if the commitments were made I'm sure they will be kept.' " Mitchell and he just knew, he said, those commitments had to be kept.[30]

Mardian and LaRue then went to Mitchell's apartment in the Watergate and briefed him on what Mitchell called "the White House horrors." According to Mitchell, the president's closest friend, neither then nor later did he ever mention them to Nixon. He would have us believe they had to be kept from him for fear the president would turn on all those involved, and so precipitate the loss of his own reelection. This was difficult reasoning to accept at the time. In light of what we have learned that Nixon did know, it is harder to accept now.

It was around the time of this meeting in Mitchell's apartment that the president's daily dairy recorded his first telephone call to Mitchell since the break-in. There is no tape. The call was from a White House residence phone, one of those not part of Nixon's taping system. Nixon's own personal diary records:

> I also talked to John Mitchell late in the day and tried to cheer him up a bit. He is terribly chagrined that the activities of anybody attached to his committee should have been handled in such a manner and he said that he only regretted that he had not policed all of the people more effectively . . . in his own organization.[31]

Nixon had also told Mitchell not to worry and that the White House "may be able to keep things under control." On that same evening of June 20, Nixon made a call to Haldeman.[32] He had a new idea for handling Watergate. Had it come, via Mitchell, from Mardian's fascination with the Cubans' CIA connections and the Miami community? Nixon claimed he got it from his afternoon talks with Colson and Haldeman.

In any case, Haldeman gave it great significance. In this call, according to Haldeman, Nixon himself initiated the idea of raising funds for the Watergate burglars in an indirect manner. Even more surprising, he indirectly suggested the idea of involving the CIA in the Watergate investigation—three days before it happened.

Where this idea came from has never properly been explored but it was probably Hunt's connection. Faced with his own notes of the conversation, Haldeman confirmed it in a recent interview.[33] Nixon, in his memoirs, confirmed only the first part of the plan, that "if the Cuban explanation for the break-in caught on, I would call Rebozo and have him get the anti-McGovern Cubans in Miami to start a public bail fund for their arrested countrymen . . ."

What Nixon omitted in his memoirs was any reference to having Haldeman talk to Ehrlichman. Haldeman's note has the president telling him cryptically to "talk to E[hrlichman] the whole group all tied to the Bay of Pigs; anti-Communist common bond." In his book *The Ends of Power,* Haldeman elaborated, quoting Nixon as adding: "Ehrlichman will know what I mean." When Haldeman passed on the president's message Ehrlichman referred sardonically to tackling CIA headquarters: "Our brothers from Langley? He's suggesting I twist or break a few arms." Ehrlichman told Haldeman that—unlike his fencing in the fall of 1971 with CIA Director Helms—this time he wanted to do nothing about it. But three days later, he would fatefully take it up.

Haldeman's points are doubly damaging. First, that the president himself laid the groundwork for paying the burglars from a fund to be organized by his friend Bebe Rebozo—just at the time Mitchell was hearing from Mardian of the demand for "commitments"—and that the president initiated the idea of linking the CIA, Hunt, and the Bay of Pigs to the break-in investigation, and kept returning to it, as newly released tapes show, for the rest of the week.

The president, from his afternoon discussion, knew that Hunt had become a fugitive. In fact, the FBI had lost Hunt and was about to lose Liddy. Hunt was staying with an old CIA friend in Los Angeles, having decamped from New York. Liddy, informed by Robert Bennett that Hunt wanted an attorney and some money, decided to join him the next day. Both were now lying low.

On Wednesday, June 21, the cover-up suddenly moved to take on what would be its final shape. The first priority, as Nixon put it in his memoirs, was "getting to the FBI." Although they had been advised, presumably by Kleindienst, not to tackle the FBI head-on, "Mitchell said today that we've got to." John Dean, as we shall see, made sure he was not thwarted.

Newly released Nixon tapes indicate that Ehrlichman came up with a possible positive strategy. It was devised, Haldeman tells the president, first thing that morning "to see if there's something we can do other than just sitting here and watching it drop on us bit by bit."[34]

The Ehrlichman scenario Haldeman unveiled to the president was something they knew to be made of whole cloth. It was that Liddy had pulled off Watergate as his own idea. Liddy would confess, saying "I thought it would be a good move, it would build me up" in CRP's operations. Haldeman says of Liddy that "apparently he is a little bit nuts . . . the beauty of the Liddy scenario is that all the guys think he is the top guy." Once the story was out the Nixon campaign would "ask for compassion—this is a poor misguided kid who read too many comic books."

Nixon says he is for Ehrlichman's plan. Its advantage was obvious: It meant that the investigation need not go above Liddy to Magruder and from him to Mitchell, and on up to the president. If there were guilty pleas, there need not be any trial. It would also, Nixon thought, cut off the DNC civil suit and its fishing expedition in all the other areas he feared would be uncovered.

The problem with the Ehrlichman scenario was Mitchell. If it involved him, Nixon said, then he did not wish to proceed. Here Haldeman was no longer reassuring. Ehrlichman was afraid that Mitchell might be involved. When Haldeman had asked him, almost directly, whether he was, Mitchell had not given a clear denial. "I'm not really sure—he obviously knew something. I'm not sure how much," Haldeman said. Nixon's chief of staff also reported that Mitchell was "a little bit afraid because of Liddy's instability—he says he'll do it, but what exactly will he do?"

Haldeman said the attractiveness of this scenario "is that you establish an admission of guilt at a low level, rather than just a presumption, instead of imply guilt at the highest level, which I tell you, they're trying very hard to; I tell you, the press . . ." Nixon reacted both with realism and cynicism. "Anything as bizarre as this and interesting would be a national story." But he ventures, "The country doesn't give a shit about bugging . . . the country expects us to bug, political parties do it all the time, companies do it."

The priorities are clear: "The main concern is to keep the White House out of it . . ." Nixon lightly toys with a new idea: "I could take an affidavit today to say that I know nothing about it." Haldeman demurs, "This is not an issue which rubs off on you. Keep the President out of this . . ." Then Nixon interjects, "We've got to talk to Gray."

The acting FBI director had no sooner returned from his West Coast trip and to his office this Wednesday than Dean was telephoning him. Gray has never admitted discussing Watergate with Helms on the Saturday when the CIA director claims he suggested to focus on Ehrlichman; but FBI records confirm his contact with "Mitchell's man" (LaRue) on Sunday night at the Newporter Inn. Gray had been kept in touch by headquarters about the main lines developing.[35]

Gray, ever pliant in Nixon's service and ever ready to jump to White House orders, stated he had no qualms about telling Dean everything because he assumed Dean was speaking for the president. Indeed, he later testified that Ehrlichman had telephoned him that morning to say that Dean was handling Watergate and that Gray should deal directly with him.

By 11:30, Dean was in Gray's office, and the acting director promptly set about doing Dean's bidding. Gray immediately put a hold on distributing FBI leads to the prosecutor and ordered that FBI interviews of White House staff be delayed. This was despite high-level FBI worries, taken up with him by his top officers as soon as he returned, that the FBI's reputation was at stake.

Dean, as the president's counsel, had gone through proper channels first. Taking Liddy's advice, he had asked Kleindienst whether he could have the raw reports from the FBI investigation, only, of course, to keep up with the details. Kleindienst claimed he said no, but that Dean could have summaries orally. If the president wanted to see a particular file, Kleindienst said he would take it in personally, sit down with the president, "let him look at it and then bring it back." That was not exactly what Dean had in mind.[36]

Kleindienst was nominally Gray's boss, but Dean decided to go behind the attorney general's back and have his way with Gray. Their illicit relationship was already established. Gray earlier in the year had secretly extracted from the FBI and handed to Dean the original of the notorious Dita Beard ITT memo. This Wednesday there were three telephone calls, including a tip from Gray of the FBI's intention to interview Colson. Dean and Colson rehearsed what he would say the next day. Gray also told Dean that the FBI had not yet traced the origin of the banknotes found on those arrested, and Dean passed that information on to Haldeman.

There was one serious loose end. Neither Dean nor Gray apparently knew what was happening to Al Baldwin. Since Sunday, the bugging and lookout man had been trying to find out what help he could expect from CRP. A CRP lawyer flew from Washington to West Haven,

Connecticut. He wanted to know, according to Baldwin's lawyer, Robert Mirto, whether Baldwin could implicate Mitchell and others. Mirto has recently stated that when he and his partner, John Cassidento, talked to the man from CRP, "We told him that we thought Al had a lot of circumstantial evidence connecting Mitchell, but he was only concerned about admissible evidence, whether or not they could convict Mitchell. Once he realized that most of what Al knew was inadmissible, then he cut us loose . . ."[37]

Baldwin was concerned at what he took to be CRP threats to "follow the scenario." "My lawyers came out and brought me into the office and said there is a lot we have to do here. 'They are not going to acknowledge you even exist. They are disowning you. They have no concern for you. They are not going to supply a lawyer for you as long as you can't identify Mitchell or you can't identify anyone else from the White House. They don't care about you,' " he was told repeatedly.[38]

With that, Baldwin's lawyers decided to tell the FBI that their man was ready to talk. The U.S. attorney prosecuting the Watergate case was about to get his first insider witness.

A faraway event occurred that Wednesday that no one realized might have much significance. The longtime chairman of the House of Representatives Judiciary Committee, Emmanuel Celler, unexpectedly lost his New York district Democratic primary election to an unknown insurgent, Elizabeth Holtzman. It was a very momentous loss. Celler, an old chum of Nixon's, was the last person who could be imagined presiding over an impeachment hearing. Now he was on his way out. Nobody discussed it in this context. Impeachment vexed the president and Colson as a topic on this day only because of a *New York Times* ad urging it. The prospect was simply too remote to be real.

Despite the initial flurry of publicity over the break-in, by Thursday, June 22, the Watergate affair was already sliding down the news agenda. A good illustration was Nixon's first news conference following the break-in. To the first question Nixon repeated—despite all his fears over Colson—what Ziegler had stated at the outset:

Nixon: . . . As Mr. Ziegler has stated, the White House has had no involvement whatever in this particular incident. As far as the matter now is concerned, it is under investigation, as it should be by the proper legal authorities, by the District of Columbia police, and by the FBI. I will not comment on those matters, particularly since possible criminal charges are involved.

Amazingly, there was not a single follow-up question from the White House press corps. Watergate was a bizarre and confusing episode, and it seemed removed from the run-of-the-mill administration policy stories. Anyway, the Democrats' infighting against McGovern continuing up to the convention seemed more pressing.

In a tape released to the public only last year, Haldeman and Nixon had this exchange:

Haldeman: . . . the great thing about it is that the whole thing is so totally fucked up so badly done that nobody believes—
Nixon: —that we could have done it.
Haldeman: That's right. It's beyond comprehension . . . the thing we forget is that we know too much and that we read too much into other things that people can't read.[39]

Yet the panic button was close to being hit. The money given to Liddy was becoming a desperate problem—all the money, not just the cash found on the burglars. In that same taped conversation with Nixon, Haldeman told the president "at this point it would be good to get Liddy out of the country. We can wait and see if we want to bring him back." At this point, with Liddy's involvement still unknown to the FBI, the president was going along with a proposal that he become a fugitive.

If the Ehrlichman scenario of Liddy as the fall guy was going to work, Magruder at CRP had to have a way of explaining the money given to him. And how much *had* been given? Magruder kept asking Sloan, CRP's treasurer. Sloan said he could not tell him yet; part of the problem was that pre-April 7 accounts had been shredded.

Magruder and Sloan did not get on well. Magruder caustically commented to Sloan that as treasurer he could well be personally responsible for the disbursements to Liddy under the new campaign finance laws. It was in this context he openly suggested to Sloan that to protect himself he might, in regard to the true amount given to Liddy, have to be prepared to perjure himself.

Magruder suggested the total given to Liddy should be in the range of up to $80,000. Sloan knew that this figure was wrong because Magruder himself had authorized the single $83,000 payment for starters. That was much too low, he told Magruder, and he had no intention of perjuring himself. According to Magruder's book, Magruder had replied, "You might have to." Sloan seethed. Knowing that Liddy had told him on Saturday about CRP's "boys" getting caught, he suspected Magruder was deep in Watergate. Being told to perjure oneself was itself proof of his superiors' criminality, and Sloan was not about to help Magruder.

That same morning, as Sloan was discussing the money with Fred LaRue, Sloan's secretary told him two FBI agents were waiting to see him. LaRue advised seeing Mitchell first. When he did, Mitchell uttered another of the aphorisms that will always be associated with Watergate. Sloan later testified to the Watergate committee:

> I was essentially asking for guidance. The campaign literally at this point was falling apart before your eyes. Nobody was coming up with any answers as to what was really going on. I had some very strong concerns about where all of this money had gone. I essentially asked for guidance, at which point he [Mitchell] told me, "When the going gets tough, the tough get going."

Finding this unhelpful, Sloan went to meet the FBI agents with some foreboding. But all they wanted to ask him was whether Baldwin had been on CRP's payroll.

That Thursday, Sloan was invited to a party on board the presidential yacht. He sought out some of his former White House colleagues and told them guardedly that they ought to do something to get on top of a dangerous situation at CRP. Somewhat mystified, Dwight Chapin, the president's appointments secretary, agreed to talk to him, and it was also arranged for Sloan to meet Ehrlichman. Sloan was clearly a loose cannon on the White House deck.

Colson, with Dean in attendance, was that afternoon the first high official to be interviewed by the FBI. The agents asked if they could be taken upstairs to Hunt's office to see if he had left any clues. Dean, they remembered, affected surprise that Hunt had an office (this was two days after Dean had supervised the opening of Hunt's safe). Dean said he would have to check and get back to them. The FBI, having no search warrant for an office in the inner sanctum of the White House, could hardly insist.

Gray quickly informed Dean afterward that Colson had "passed" his FBI interview with no problems. But Gray had a disturbing message for Dean about the banknotes. Only that morning, Haldeman had been giving the president Dean's report of the previous day—"good news" is the description in the Nixon memoirs—that the burglars' new hundred-dollar bills had not been traced. This might have been optimistic, but it was accurate. The FBI had traced the burglars' banknotes to the bank to which they had been issued, which happened to be Bernard Barker's bank in Miami. But as banks did not record to whom the notes were paid out, the cash evidence pointing to Barker was purely circumstantial.

Gray was to disturb this comforting state of affairs, however. He reported to Dean that the FBI had just found out that checks totaling $114,000 had been passed through Barker's account. Four were cashier's checks from a Mexican bank paid to Manuel Ogarrio; the other was a check signed by Kenneth Dahlberg. Gray was mystified but, alerted by Dean, Mitchell and Stans knew the answer: These were the Nixon campaign contribution checks Liddy had laundered for Sloan the previous April.

Dean knew from Magruder that the burglars' cash had come from CRP. What was alarming was not simply that the anonymous and illegal contributions from the Texas big shots, via Mexico, and from Dwayne Andreas, via CRP fund-raiser Dahlberg, would now be uncovered. Much more dangerous was that these checks would be traced to CRP and the burglars linked directly to the campaign coffers. It would become a great deal harder now to pretend that Liddy and Co. were off on a lark of their own.

Gray had yet more for Dean. He said that even as they spoke, the FBI had ordered its Mexico City "legat," the FBI agent stationed as "legal attaché" at the U.S. Embassy under diplomatic cover, to interview the Mexican who had signed the checks. And Gray wanted to pass on to Dean the theory that had bubbled up from Angelo Lano the previous Monday: that Watergate was somehow a CIA operation. Gray said that that afternoon he had telephoned CIA Director Helms, who had told him the CIA was not involved. But Gray wondered whether this Mexican connection was not, after all, a "CIA money chain."

According to Dean, Gray had worked out a reason for Helms's denial:

> . . . they couldn't get the CIA to face up to it because obviously it was a domestic activity the CIA had no business doing, but that was his leading theory.

Dean was transfixed. He saw both the danger and the opportunity. He told Gray to hold on; he would have word from his superiors the next day.

Dean rushed to tell Mitchell. Mitchell later vigorously denied having such a conversation,[40] but he certainly learned about the checks from Dean. First thing next morning, he was arranging for CRP finance chief Maurice Stans to have fund-raiser Dahlberg fly immediately from Minnesota to discuss the check.

Dean insists to this day that he discussed Gray's news with Mitchell and that the two of them hatched the next stage of the plan. Gray was proving a Nixon trusty. Why not have him meet the other Nixon favorite, the recently appointed CIA deputy director, General Vernon Walters? He, rather than the difficult Helms, could confirm Gray's worries and make sure that the FBI stayed clear of this possible CIA operation in Mexico. It would head the FBI off at the pass and restrict the scope of the investigation to the five men arrested.

Dean telephoned Haldeman first thing the next morning, June 23. Haldeman listened intently. The news on the money front was upsetting. Haldeman saw the urgency of acting fast. The Oval Office tape recorders were whirring as Haldeman went in to see Nixon. It would be two more years and two months before the public would read what they had said. But when they did, everyone recognized that this recorded conversation was the smoking gun of Watergate. It undid all Nixon's avowals of innocence and ignorance.

Haldeman explains what has been happening. Despite having installed Gray as acting director, the FBI was not merely unresponsive; it was that worst of all Nixon sins, "not under control."

> *Haldeman:* Now on the investigation, you know the Democratic break-in thing, we're back in the problem area because the FBI is not under control, because Gray doesn't exactly know how to control it and they have, their investigation is now leading into some productive areas, because they have been able to trace the money, not through the money itself but through the bank sources, the banker. And, and it goes in some directions we don't want it to go . . . Mitchell came up with yesterday, and John Dean analyzed very carefully last night and concludes, concurs now with Mitchell's recommendation that the only way to solve this, and we're set up beautifully to do it, . . . that the way to handle this now is for us to have Walters call Pat Gray and just say, "Stay to hell out of this. This business here we don't want you to go any farther . . ."[41]

Nixon asks and is told the money is traceable to CRP and that the FBI will get the names today. The president's not untypical response is that those who donated should simply lie to the FBI and say they were approached by the Cubans for it. Haldeman counters that that will mean the cover-up will be relying on more and more people; taking the CIA route means "they'll stop." Nixon briskly says, "Right, fine."

"The proposal," Haldeman says, is for him and Ehrlichman to call in Helms and Walters. Nixon again says, "Right, fine." The president ponders how to approach the prickly Helms, and says, "Well, we protected Helms from one hell of a lot of things." Then Nixon rehearses what they would say to Helms:

> *Nixon:* Of course, this Hunt, that will uncover a lot of things. You open that scab, there's a hell of a lot of things and we just feel that it would be very detrimental to have this go any further. This involves these Cubans, Hunt, and a lot of hanky-panky that we have nothing to do with ourselves.

Nixon then immediately returns to one of the issues that had gnawed at him all week: Did Mitchell know about this? Haldeman replies: "I think so. I don't think he knew the details but he knew." Nixon erupts when he hears about the check laundering. He suggests that Mitchell could not have known how the money would be handled, and asks, "Who was the asshole that did, is it Liddy, is that the fellow? He must be a little nuts?" "He is," answers Haldeman, having suggested it earlier. He explains that Liddy was under great pressure to get more information. "Pressure from Mitchell?" asks Nixon. "Apparently," Haldeman responds. "All right, fine, I understand it all. We won't second-guess Mitchell and the rest. Thank God it was not Colson."

Haldeman has news (from Gray via Dean) of the FBI's interview with Nixon's special counsel:

> *Haldeman:* . . . After their interrogation of Colson yesterday, they concluded it was not the White House, but are now convinced it is a CIA thing, so the CIA turnoff would—
> *Nixon:* Well, not sure of their analysis. I'm not going to get that involved. I'm [unintelligible].
> *Haldeman:* No, sir, we don't want you to.
> *Nixon:* You call them in.
> *Haldeman:* Good deal.
> *Nixon:* Play it tough. That's the way they play it and that's the way we are going to play it.[42]

The conversation lasted more than an hour and a half and ranged wide. A later mention of Mitchell once again sparks the idea Nixon has been mentioning all week and which he now wants put to Helms:

> *Nixon:* Say, "Look, the problem is that this will open the whole Bay of Pigs thing, and the president just feels that, without going into details,"—don't, don't lie to them to the extent to say there is no involvement, but just say this is a comedy of errors, without getting into it, "the president believes that it is going to open the whole Bay of Pigs thing again . . . and that they should call the FBI in and [unintelligible] don't go any further in this case, period!"

There was much much more in this long conversation about the conventions, about the Nixon women, and how the helicopters spoiled their hairdos. Nixon points out that his daughters have been treated rudely, especially at nonpolitical arts events. "The arts, you know, they're Jews, they're left wing. In other words, stay away." It was unbuttoned Nixon.

At just past 1 P.M. when the two top CIA men had arrived to see Ehrlichman, Haldeman has a last run-through of the scenario:

> *Nixon:* " . . . it's likely to blow the whole Bay of Pigs thing, which we think would be very unfortunate for the CIA and for the country at this time, and for American foreign policy, and he better just tough it and lay it on them." Isn't that what you—
>
> *Haldeman:* Yeah, that's, that's the basis we'll do it on and just leave it at that.
>
> *Nixon:* I don't want them to get any ideas we're doing it because our concern is political.
>
> *Haldeman:* Right.
>
> *Nixon:* And at the same time I wouldn't tell them it's not political.
>
> *Haldeman:* Right.

So, as Haldeman later noted, Nixon himself moved the whole sordid venture from the Dean-Mitchell ploy onto his beloved higher ground of national security.[43]

By 2:20 P.M., Haldeman was back with Nixon, having met with Helms and Walters in Ehrlichman's office. "No problem," he reported. Curiously, Haldeman did not tell Nixon of Helms's reaction, which was explosive. Before the meeting, according to his book, Haldeman had gone into Ehrlichman's office and said, "Guess what? It's Bay of Pigs time again." Ehrlichman replied, "This time you're going to push the red button, not me."

When Helms arrived, according to Haldeman, the CIA director surprised them by telling them of Gray's phone call, and how he had made clear to the FBI man that the CIA was not involved in Watergate. Haldeman countered with the president's warning that the Bay of Pigs might be blown. Haldeman's account goes on:

> Turmoil in the room, Helms gripping the arms of the chair leaning forward and shouting, "The Bay of Pigs had nothing to do with this. I have no concern about the Bay of Pigs."[44]

Haldeman, shocked, writes that nonetheless the atmosphere changed. The president's tactic had worked. Now Helms raised no objection to Walters going to Gray. Ehrlichman's version of the meeting is similar, except that he claims to have gone into the meeting cold, with no idea of what the plan was.[45]

Still, as Haldeman told Nixon, there was no problem. Nixon wrote in his memoirs with unconscious irony:

> It seemed that our intervention had worked easily. As far as I was concerned, this was the end of our worries about Watergate.

The previous evening Dean had told Gray that he would get back to him; he now notified him that Walters was coming to see him. He called a second time just before Walters's arrival to stiffen Gray's nerve. Walters, after leaving the White House, had been told by Helms to remind the FBI of their joint agreement that they must notify each other when they ran afoul of each other's operations. Walters says Helms told him to suggest—crucially—that the investigation not go beyond the five arrested. Helms later disputed giving this instruction, but a Helms memo to Walters a few days later made the CIA's request to the FBI unmistakable:

> We still adhere to the request that they confine themselves to the personalities already arrested or directly under suspicion and that they desist from expanding this investigation into other areas which may well, eventually, run afoul of our operations.[46]

Walters did the dirty deed. Gray followed through. He instructed the FBI to hold off temporarily from interviewing Ogarrio in Mexico City and to stay away from Dahlberg. The FBI was allowed to keep pushing at the periphery of the banking transactions, but not to interview the only leads who could take the money trail back to CRP.

Twenty years later, Helms would have us believe that there are things presidents know that even the CIA doesn't know. Anyway, a president's wish cannot simply be flouted, so he went along. Walters did, too, and it worked. The FBI interviews with Ogarrio and Dahlberg were stalled for another ten to fourteen days. By that time, the heat was off, and the cover-up well and truly launched.

That same Friday McCord, released on bail, went home. He was astonished to find all his equipment still sitting in the van and promptly set about "disappearing" it.

That day, too, Hugh Sloan got his White House interviews. Dwight Chapin, his old friend, thought he was overwrought about the money and suggested a vacation. Sloan then got in to see Ehrlichman, immediately after Helms and Walters left. Ehrlichman was not amused to hear about the vast amount of money paid to Liddy by Magruder. He sharply suggested to Sloan that, if asked questions, he might have to claim "executive privilege"—meaning that he could decline to answer because his work was protected by the secrecy of the president's privilege.

Also that Friday, a federal grand jury of twenty-three ordinary citizens of the District of Columbia, which had been empaneled on June 5, began its secret hearing of testimony in a new criminal case. It was the break-in and bugging at the Watergate.

Finally, Agnes—the hurricane that had kept Nixon in Florida—struck Washington with full force. The Potomac hit record flood levels, National Airport was closed, and John Dean in Alexandria, Virginia, had to sandbag his home against the rising tide. With hindsight, the omen was unmistakable.

CHAPTER 8

Payoffs and Perjury

By the end of the first week of Watergate, the co-conspirators, including the president, had already committed most of the offenses with which they were later charged. In the second week, two more crimes were approaching commission: payoffs and perjury. They were the two ingredients crucial to sustaining the cover-up.

To keep the defendants quiet and willing to accept jail sentences, large cash sums were needed and promises of clemency. As early as June 30, presidential pardons for the burglars were discussed; on a newly released tape Nixon tells Haldeman, "I'll pardon the bastards" (not Liddy alone as his memoirs have it).[1] The cash was to come from secret campaign donations to elect the head of the government's executive branch—the very branch responsible for prosecuting the offenders receiving the payoffs.

And, of course, there was a constant need for lies—perjury—to keep the case from going any higher than Liddy. That they almost got away with it, at least for nine months, says little about their skill as liars and not much more about the gullibility of the FBI and the prosecutors. There was more to Watergate than that. The Nixon administration, from the president down, skillfully used and abused not only the powers but also the continuing presumption of office. There was a growing certainty, in the summer of 1972, that Nixon would be in office for four more years—and that ensured the investigation was safely contained.

By late August, Nixon and Agnew, having been through a virtual coronation at the Republican convention, were so far ahead of McGovern—who had been forced to replace his running mate—that campaigning seemed almost superfluous. The prospect of certain reelection emboldened the president's men and intimidated their pursuers. Certainly, Nixon's mighty lead in the polls ensured that nobody, not the prosecutors, not the top brass at the FBI, not even in the crunch some key Democratic congressmen (and not the media, with a few honorable exceptions) were going to push an investigation aggressively.

It helped that from the start Pat Gray gave John Dean the inside track of the FBI investigation. It helped that Henry Petersen not only chimed in with Dean but also made doubly sure everyone realized that it was an election year. There were to be no fishing expeditions for evidence beyond the break-in itself. It also helped that the Nixon campaign coffers were so overflowing with dirty funds that there was hush money in abundance. Payoffs would eventually reach nearly half a million dollars.

Given the daring of some of the White House ploys to abuse the FBI and the CIA, it is amazing that there was only a trickle of leaks dealing with quite insubstantial matters. The essential elements of the cover-up and the president's involvement in it remained solidly secret.

What leaks there were, initially, ranged from the farcical to the insidious. One reaching *Time* magazine reporters suggested that Gray had met with Mitchell when in California and that on returning home he had ordered the investigation wrapped up in twenty-four hours. Gray flatly denied it and *Time* toned down the item. Gray was so upset that he lined up all twenty-seven agents from the Washington field office, berated them, and demanded that the guilty man step forward. No one moved and the leaker was never found.

Gray, of course, had reason to be nervous. He had, in fact, met Mitchell's man Fred LaRue in California; he was already slowing down the investigation and keeping secret from his own men his incessant contacts with Dean. That second weekend Gray directed that all the FBI paperwork on the investigation be sent to his home, including all the teletype messages between offices and headquarters. He began passing on the contents to Dean, eventually handing over bundles of the documents themselves. The White House not only learned what the

FBI had done, but it was also informed what it planned to do. Witnesses who asked to be interviewed by the FBI away from either White House or CRP lawyers found themselves afterward confronted with demands to know why they were secretly talking.

Gray's career officers that second week got so fed up with his stalling that they demanded a statement in writing from the CIA telling them not to pursue the investigation of the Mexican and Dahlberg checks. Gray arranged a meeting with Helms, told Dean, then found Ehrlichman on the line to say peremptorily that Gray's appointment with Helms was canceled. The White House wanted meetings confined to "their" CIA man, Deputy Director Walters.

Gray was deep in the woods. On June 28, Ehrlichman and Dean decided to call him to the White House; there was the awkward matter of the contents of Howard Hunt's safe. Dean had taken a week to hand over the safe's less controversial contents to FBI agents, but among the items still held back were two envelopes containing the fake Diem cables and Hunt's Chappaquiddick interviews. Ehrlichman—according to Dean's later Senate testimony—had suggested that Dean deep-six the material by tossing it into the Potomac River on his way home across the bridge; Dean said Fred Fielding advised him not to, and he declined. Instead, Dean suggested handing what he termed the "political dynamite" to Gray, and Ehrlichman agreed. If ever asked, they could say that everything in the safe had been handed "to the FBI."

They told Gray that the contents of the envelopes were not Watergate related. Gray heard that they were political dynamite, that they "should not see the light of day." They never did. Gray kept them for six months, in Washington and at his home in Connecticut. He flicked through them, he later testified to the Senate, before deciding to burn them with the Christmas trash. He later testified that he thought he was following the president's bidding as expressed by his top adviser and his counsel. When it was disclosed the following April that the top man at the FBI had himself destroyed evidence, the revelation sank Gray, damaged Ehrlichman, and tarnished the FBI's reputation for a decade.

Evidence linking the president and Haldeman to this transfer of evidence to Gray—if not its destruction—surfaced in 1993 in newly released tapes. Nixon's memoirs carried only a glancing reference to the incident. The tape is a thirteen-minute discussion of a June 30 story on the contents of Hunt's office leaked to the now-defunct evening newspaper the Washington *Daily News*. The story is about the gun, wiretapping equipment, and a map of the DNC offices. It was the first public statement of Hunt's link to the break-in itself. Nixon is irritated. Haldeman assures him that other contents of Hunt's safe were "handled at supposedly a very high level—discreetly."[2]

Dean failed to pull off an equally gross trick with General Walters over the hush money.[3] CRP, pretending the break-in was a private caper of Liddy's, of course could not pay family support and lawyers' fees to the burglars openly. Dean's plan—based, he claimed, on an idea Mardian discussed with Mitchell—was to get the CIA to pay. Dean telephoned Walters, Walters checked him out with Ehrlichman—and was told, he said, "he's in charge of the whole matter"—and then on three successive days went down to the White House to hear the ever more desperate pleas from the president's young counsel.

At the first meeting, Walters insists he told Dean there was no CIA involvement and that he was prepared to resign before he did anything to implicate the CIA.[4] At the second meeting, Walter's memo has Dean complaining that the men arrested are "wobbling." He asked Walters if the CIA could use "covert action funds" to provide bail (the four from Miami were still in jail) and pay their salaries. Walters said he replied that that could only be done upon direction at the highest level (meaning the president). The CIA's funds also had to be accounted for. Involving the agency would transform what was now a medium-size conventional explosive into a multimegaton bomb.

Walters's later Senate testimony was that he realized at this point that "something improper was being explored." He and Helms agreed that memos for the record should be written. At the third meeting, Dean asked Walters if he had any suggestions to stop the FBI investigation going beyond the five arrested. Walters tried explaining that they had got it wrong in imagining he, as their appointee, could fix it for them; as deputy CIA director he was not in the CIA chain of command and had no independent authority. He warned that if it leaked that the agency was involving itself, it "could be electorally mortal."

What Walters *did* suggest to Dean was that they explore the Cuban caper aspect—the Cubans had a plausible anti-Castro motive. "This might be costly," Walters wrote in his memo. "But it would be plausible. Dean said he agreed that this was the best tack to take but it might cost half a million dollars." Neither Walters nor Helms, of course, informed the FBI about this White House approach for payments to defendants. Spies don't talk; they write memos for the files.

Having drawn a blank as far as CIA "unvouchered funds" were concerned, Dean was told by Mitchell that the White House ought to take the strain. Mitchell never forgot that the White House had sent Liddy to him in the first place and that Haldeman had pushed for political intelligence. With Haldeman's and Ehrlichman's assent, Dean turned for cash to the original Nixon fund-raiser, Herbert Kalmbach. Now the president's personal lawyer, Kalmbach was drawn into the cover-up by the president's official lawyer.

Kalmbach was doomed. On the same day Walters turned him down for the third time, Dean phoned Kalmbach in Newport Beach and summoned him from California on "a very important assignment." Kalmbach took the overnight flight, checked into his hotel, phoned Dean, and plunged, trustingly, he said in his later testimony, deep into Watergate.

Dean took Kalmbach for another walk in the park, this time in Lafayette Square opposite the White House. He laid out the secret fund-raising and payoff mission "we" wished undertaken—the "we" that Kalmbach was to say he took to be Haldeman and Ehrlichman and Dean on behalf of Nixon.

Kalmbach said he had tried suggesting a different route, a public defense fund, maybe the defendants' mortgaging their homes until a fund-raising committee was set up. But Dean had insisted this might be "misinterpreted." They needed fifty thousand dollars to one hundred thousand dollars and absolute secrecy was a must so as not to jeopardize Nixon's reelection. Dean or LaRue would give instructions who was to be paid and how much. Dean suggested that Kalmbach use as bag man the New York ex-cop whose salary he had been paying for the past three years, Tony Ulasewicz.

Kalmbach checked with no one. He trusted Dean. Oddly, given that Mitchell and Mardian claimed they did not wish CRP funds used,

Kalmbach's first port of call was Maurice Stans. Despite the fact that Stans, as FCRP chairman, was nervous about the Mexican and Dahlberg checks and the money handed out to Liddy, when Kalmbach phoned him on June 30 he came straight around with a package of $75,100 cash in hundred-dollar bills. Again it was trust among friends and no receipts. Kalmbach told Stans he could not tell him what the White House wanted the money for, and Stans asked no questions. The extraordinary Keystone Kops saga of the money drops now unfolded.

Ulasewicz, arriving in Kalmbach's hotel room from New York, said he warned the lawyer that large amounts of money always surfaced in the end and could lead to blackmail. Kalmbach apparently assured him that his principals insisted everything would be all right. They agreed, as precaution against bugging, that they would communicate only by pay phones using cash. Ulasewicz would be known by the code name Mr. Rivers. Since he had no briefcase, Ulasewicz wrapped the cash in a hotel laundry bag—henceforth they called the funds "laundry."

Kalmbach, consulting Dean and LaRue (who kept the cash in his filing cabinet), ordered Ulasewicz to make his first payment the following week. It was $25,000 for Douglas Caddy, the lawyer who had turned up at the police station at Hunt's request. But Caddy would not play; he refused to accept the cash. Kalmbach, instructed by Dean and LaRue, then approached Paul O'Brien, one of the lawyers retained by CRP. He, too, refused.[5]

The hush money operation was off to as decidedly bad a start as the rest of Watergate. Only in mid-July was the first successful contact made. Hunt's new lawyer, William Bittman, accepted a bizarre delivery of $25,000 in an envelope left on a ledge in the downstairs lobby of the prestigious firm of Hogan and Hartson. Ulasewicz, informed of the color of Bittman's suit, watched as the lawyer stepped out of the elevator and went over to pick up the package. Ulasewicz arranged a similar drop with Liddy at National Airport, where the cash was in a luggage locker.

As a form of "cut-out," Ulasewicz ended up dealing with Mrs. Hunt (code name the "Writer's Wife"). She provided him with a five-month "budget" for all seven men involved. It totaled $450,000. As an indication the scheme was working, Colson received a note mentioning "the overwhelming importance of re-electing the President, and you may be confident that I will do all that is required of me toward that end." It was from Hunt himself.[6]

John Dean had his hands full at this time with another overriding priority: prevent the investigation from uncovering the Plumbers. While it is arguable that Nixon's election might not have been thrown off course had the president dared make a rapid apology for the Watergate break-in, including dismissal of Mitchell and Magruder, it is less likely that he could have survived disclosure of everything the Plumbers had been up to. Certainly, Nixon himself did not think so. Hunt, he notes in his memoirs, had been involved in a number of worrisome "political things" with Colson—Kennedy and Chappaquiddick, the fake Diem cables, the ITT caper, and finally the idea of planting McGovern literature on the Wallace gunman.

Dean was busy making sure that there were no disclosures from the two men who, like Ehrlichman, must have put two and two together as soon as they heard Hunt and the Cubans were involved. These were the Plumbers codirectors, Egil Krogh and David Young. Krogh was driving through the Midwest when he heard the news of Watergate and promptly telephoned John Dean. (Krogh would later commit perjury about Hunt and Liddy's travels to California.) Young, having just received part of the contents of Hunt's safe from Dean, now had something more worrying to report back.

The FBI had traced the Plumbers secret phone number, which they found in the two address books seized at the burglars' Watergate Hotel room. Hunt thought he had used tradecraft to make it "untraceable" by having the phone billed at her home address to Young's secretary at the Plumbers office, Kathleen Chenow.

The FBI, Young told Dean, now wanted to interview her. Informed that she was on vacation in England, the FBI was preparing to have its agent at the London embassy track her down when Dean intervened with Gray. Dean said that national security was involved. And the obliging Gray ordered the Chenow interview held up. In haste, Dean dispatched his deputy, Fred Fielding, to find her and bring her back to Washington, first class.

Coached by Dean, Miss Chenow successfully avoided telling the FBI anything of value. The Plumbers were intact; whereupon she was allowed—at White House expense—to resume her vacation in England.

The FBI had finally, and laboriously, discovered Liddy. Agents had been frenetically pursuing anyone they could find under the name George Leonard, the name found in the Watergate Hotel register. On June 26, the FBI finally got from the D.C. police the seized burglars' address books. There in Martinez's list under "Howard Hunt" was the notation "George," with a phone number. It was also Chenow's. But in Barker's book, "George" was listed under another number. They rang it and a secretary at CRP answered that this was Gordon Liddy's office. So much for his untraceability.

Two FBI agents turned up at CRP on June 28. Liddy kept them waiting. When he did appear he declined to answer questions and, characteristically, as a former FBI man, offered to write up the agents' report for them.

The next step was inevitable. It was CRP's policy that its employees were required to show cooperation with law enforcement officers. LaRue told Liddy it was the end of the road. Stans told him gently that he could resign or be dismissed; hearing that dismissal included severance pay, Liddy chose that. The news was not to surface for nearly a month.

If the tough, like Liddy, were getting going, it was still a bombshell when the public was told on Saturday, July 1, that the toughest of them all, John Mitchell, was resigning from CRP for family reasons. The true reason, as has become even clearer from recently released tapes, was that Nixon and Haldeman realized Mitchell would most likely become the target of both the investigation and the media. Mitchell was too close to Nixon for comfort. He had to be taken out of the firing line and—although Nixon protests often that this is not so—eventually made the fall guy. The day Liddy was fired Haldeman told Nixon of Mitchell, "We've got a lid on it and it may not stay on it and his getting out may just be a good way out. Ultimately it goes to him."[7]

The family reason was Mitchell's wife, Martha. She had become one of the dour Nixon administration's real characters. A vivacious southern belle, she was famous for speaking her mind. She was in demand on the talk shows and at Republican fund-raisers. Privately, she caused torment in the Mitchell household, because of her worsening mental state. Haldeman wrote that Mitchell worried she might throw herself off her Watergate apartment balcony and that he often rushed home from meetings to be with her. Nixon rather callously remarked in his memoirs that one day he had asked his friend Bebe Rebozo why Mitchell put up with her. Rebozo quoted Mitchell: " 'Because I love her.' " Now, with Watergate, there was talk of suicide.

Martha had certainly not had an easy time after being left behind by Mitchell in California a week earlier. While she was telephoning the press, her security man, at Fred LaRue's instruction, had wrenched her phone out of the wall. She had then reportedly pushed her hand through a plate glass door and was sedated and secretly hospitalized under the watchful eye of Herbert Kalmbach. Once free from the hospital, she had been on the phone again to the press with allegations she was a "political prisoner," that she knew all about Watergate and threatened to leave her husband if he didn't quit politics.

During the second week of Watergate, Mitchell visited her at the Westchester Country Club outside New York City. Only once, stated Nixon in his memoirs, did Mitchell ever break down and confide to Haldeman: "You and the President don't realize how much time I have to spend keeping her on an even keel—or how much it's affected my ability to run the campaign." Later, in his dictated diary, Nixon observed that Mitchell had been distracted and obsessed with his Martha problems, and so had not properly watched over CRP. "Without Martha," Nixon claimed provocatively, "I am sure the Watergate thing would never have happened."[8]

Now his campaign was to be without Mitchell, at least without Mitchell out front. "We can still make use of him; he's indispensable in Missouri," Haldeman tells Nixon in a conversation that makes quite plain their exploitation of the Martha pretext. "We should encourage him to do it. It's a beautiful opportunity . . . kind of like the Duke of Windsor giving up his throne for the woman he loves . . . "[9]

Until now only the tape of the final Nixon lunch with Mitchell on June 30 has been publicly available and in a heavily censored form with the portions relating to Martha cut out by Judge Sirica who vetted it for privilege claims. But even the sanitized transcript makes clear both the president's determination to reduce the risk by getting Mitchell out and at the same time clothe Mitchell's resignation in "human terms."

Nixon: . . . if there is something that does come out, we hope nothing will, it may not, but there's always the risk.

Haldeman: As of now there's no problem there, 'cause as of any moment in the future there is every single potential problem.

Nixon: Nope, I'd cut the loss fast. I'd cut it fast. If we're going to do it I'd cut it fast . . . if you put it in human terms I think the story is positive rather than negative, because as I said I was preparing the answer for that press conference—I just wrote it out, as I usually do, the ones that I think are sensitive. And I know but by golly [unintelligible] a hell of a lot of people'll like that answer. They will. And if it made anybody else that asked any other question on it look like a savage son of a bitch, which I thoroughly intend them to look like . . .

[Tape's second segment]:

Mitchell: . . . expect to resolve the Westchester Country [Club] problem with all the sympathy in the world.

Nixon: That's great.

Mitchell: [Unintelligible].

Haldeman: With you taking this move, which people won't expect you to do, will be a surprise.

Nixon: No, if it is a surprise—otherwise, you're right, it will be tied right to Watergate. It won't lighten me. If you wait too long . . .[10]

It would be harsh to say there was no political sympathy at all for the Mitchells at this development, but the news was greeted at the time with great skepticism. Certainly, Mitchell continued to be involved in campaign decisions. But with former Congressman Clark MacGregor taking over as CRP chairman and freeing Mitchell from day-to-day chores, he did have more time to devote to the Watergate cover-up. And he stayed physically at the center of things, moving a little down the corridor at 1701 to his conveniently located law partnership offices.

Inside the Oval Office, worry and anger increased. Nixon was exasperated by the newspaper story about Hunt's safe. He thought the FBI had been turned off by Walters's seeing Gray the week before. Now, after his lunch with Mitchell, Haldeman—in a tape released only in 1993—

tells him that Gray "doesn't know how to turn the Department of Justice off . . . the U.S. attorney and the criminal division are both pushing the bureau."

To this Nixon responds with the same stratagem that failed at Burning Tree golf club:

> *Nixon:* I'm not at all sure if Mitchell shouldn't call Kleindienst and Gray and say . . . to halt investigation.[11]

Obstruction of justice could hardly be more explicit, more incriminating even than the so-called smoking gun. The tape was of the last White House conversation before Nixon flew to California for most of the next three weeks. It remains unestablished whether any step was taken to use the president's leverage to bully Kleindienst into betraying his oath of office. But there is no doubt what the conversation says about the mood and manner of the president and his men.

The contrast between public face and private plotting was further pointed up that afternoon on the same tape, when Nixon first assured Clark MacGregor that the White House and CRP had nothing to do with Watergate, and then, with MacGregor barely out the door, immediately resumed discussing the cover-up with Haldeman. The chief of staff now brings Nixon up to date on Ehrlichman's scenario of having Liddy falsely claim to have acted independently of CRP. Nixon remains convinced, however, of the "need to keep the scenario involved with the Cuban plot."

The reason, as this newly released tape shows, is to keep the investigation away from the Plumbers. Despite Nixon's insistence that he did not learn of the Fielding break-in until the following year, when Haldeman tells him, "Hunt's tied to Krogh. Liddy's tied to Krogh. They are all tied to Ehrlichman . . . tied into Dave Young," the president expostulates:

> *Nixon:* You mean the Pentagon Papers? What the hell's the matter with that?
>
> *Haldeman:* It's an investigation, the process. Just the process they used.
>
> *Nixon:* Well, that will be all right.

Is Haldeman referring to the process Hunt and Liddy used in their Pentagon Papers investigation—a reference to the Fielding break-in? It must never be forgotten that Haldeman and Nixon knew that the tape was rolling and the ear cannot verify what meaningful looks pass when certain odd words are exchanged between them.[12]

At the FBI, Gray was now facing a near mutiny from his top officers, who were unwilling to accept the delays he was imposing on interviews, both about the checks with Dahlberg and Ogarrio, and the mystery phone with Chenow. Dean, as we have seen, took care of the last item. Dahlberg, meanwhile, had been squared away by Mitchell after his flying visit to CRP headquarters to confer with Stans. Nixon was promptly told the truth: that the money behind the Dahlberg check had come from Humphrey backer Dwayne Andreas and that Dahlberg had concocted a cover story. But still Gray was hanging back from interviewing him. Walters's original warning to Gray—that FBI interviews could imperil a CIA operation—had been all too effective.

The number two at the FBI, Mark Felt, now insisted that Gray must tell the CIA that the Ogarrio and Dahlberg interviews would go ahead unless the CIA put in writing its national security objections. Gray agreed to approach Walters.[13]

As he had told Dean in not dissimilar circumstances, Walters could not oblige with the written justification; but on July 6, he and Gray got together to talk over the situation. Walters brought with him a memo setting out the CIA contacts of the men arrested and those suspected. A follow-up memo listed the aliases given to Hunt and Liddy the previous autumn. (Gray never passed these on to his agents.) But as for a written statement saying that the FBI investigation would jeopardize CIA activities in Mexico, no dice. In fact, Walters's memo said the opposite—that Ogarrio "had not had any operational contacts with this agency"; that the last recorded CIA contact with Dahlberg was eleven years previously.

Walters said that he decided to be frank with Gray. He told him now of his meeting with two senior White House assistants and about seeing Dean. Gray seemed disturbed, Walters said, and agreed "that we could not allow our agencies to be used in a way that would be detrimental to their integrity."

In Walters's memo for the record—revealed ten months later—he says he did not believe that a letter requesting the FBI to lay off on spurious grounds "would serve the President." Indeed, he says he told Gray that he would write such a letter "only on direction of the President and only after explaining to him how dangerous I thought such an action would be to him and that if I were really pushed I would be prepared to resign."

According to Walters's memo, the meeting concluded with similar brave talk, both Nixon's choice appointees outdoing the other in vows not to be pushed around by middle-level White House men. Gray's recollections, in testimony before the Senate committee, differed somewhat—he said he could not remember Walters disclosing that "he had been instructed to bring a false report to me"—but that was a year later, and Gray did not make memos for the record. Gray did recall one more significant detail, however. He said Walters suggested that the president be contacted.

After Walters left, Gray decided the president should be told, but typically could not bring himself to ring him. That morning he telephoned Clark MacGregor in San Clemente at 7:55 California time. He asked that he tell the president that Gray and Walters believed that White House people were being careless in their use of the FBI and CIA and they "were wounding the President." In his Senate testimony, MacGregor, curiously, swears he did nothing about the call.

But thirty-seven minutes later, Nixon phoned Gray. The president congratulated the FBI on the termination of a hijacking in San Francisco, and Gray claimed he saw his chance:

> Mr. President, there is something I want to speak to you about.
>
> Dick Walters and I feel that people on your staff are trying to mortally wound you by using the CIA and FBI and by confusing the question of CIA interest in or not in people the FBI wishes to interview.
>
> I have just talked to Clark MacGregor and asked him to speak to you about this.

There was a slight pause, Gray went on, and the president replied, "Pat, you just continue to conduct your aggressive and thorough investigation."

Nixon asked no questions, Gray stated, nor did he hear anything further from either Nixon or MacGregor. He later told Walters of the call and asked if he had heard any feedback. Walters had received a call from the president but not on Watergate. In other words, nothing came of Gray's call. Gray concluded, "Walters and I had been alarmists."

As usual, however, Walters made a memo for the record of what Gray told him about his conversation with Nixon and it differed signally from Gray's recollection. Nixon had apparently been aware that Walters had met Gray again and asked Gray what Walters was recommending. In his memo, Walters wrote:

> Gray replied that the case could not be covered up and it would lead quite high and he felt the President should get rid of the people that were involved. Any attempt to involve the FBI and the CIA in this case could only prove a mortal wound (he used my words) and would achieve nothing. . . . Later that day Gray talked to Dean and relayed the conversation to him . . . Dean had said "okay."

Nixon, in his memoirs, echoes Gray. He accepts that Gray told him of the "mortal blow" of White House or CRP people trying to cover up and that he responded by telling Gray to proceed "with his full investigation." There is no mention, however, of "using the CIA." In his diary, Nixon blandly reflected his hope to bring the investigation "to a conclusion without too much rubbing off on the Presidency before the election. . . . In this instance how we handle it may make the difference as to how we come out."[14]

Right at the end of his presidency, when the Gray and Walters versions were public knowledge, Nixon tried to claim that this was the point at which his role in the cover-up ended! He drafted—but did not issue—a statement saying: "This clearly demonstrated that when I was informed that there was no national security objection to a full investigation by the FBI, I did not hesitate to order the investigation to proceed without regard to any political or other considerations."[15] As we have seen, and shall see, this was far from the truth.

With the president in California was John Ehrlichman, who had the lead duty because Haldeman was on vacation. Ehrlichman's note of what happened after Gray's call reads:

> re call to Gray. P says McG[regor] not discreet mcG never talk to P re Watergate . . . don't raise hell with Gray & Walters—take heat wont be that bad.

Nixon's order was not pushing for an all-out investigation, but simply ordering a lighter touch with Gray and Walters. Within a couple of days, he was rehearsing a new PR line. "We must get out to the press the enthusiastic nature of the investigation," Ehrlichman has Nixon saying. "Can't appear to cover up, no whiff of cover up." And with nary a backward glance at Gray's warning of the White House staff's "mortal blow," Nixon imagines what his spokesman would say: "No one at the White House is involved. Our own investigation is completed. . . ."[16] (Ehrlichman notes that he was not aware of any investigation that could be called "ours.")

On July 8, Nixon and Ehrlichman went swimming in the Pacific and then took a long walk on Red Beach—a strip of coast along the old marine base at Camp Pendleton wonderful for surfers. Although they were later to disagree diametrically over some key parts of this discussion, they agree that Nixon again, as he had already on June 30 with Haldeman, raised the subject of pardons for the Watergate burglars. Now Nixon, according to Ehrlichman, brought up a new issue. Colson had suggested immunity for Hunt in return for his silence; Nixon, displaying close knowledge, asked whether Hunt's lawyer, Bittman, could help. Perhaps they could even enlist Judge Sirica! Ehrlichman, in *Witness to Power,* later claimed that he was appalled; he said he tried reassuring Nixon that Hunt would not blow national secrets. "You simply can't let anyone talk to you about clemency. . . . A conversation like that will bring it into your lap."

Still they talked on. Ehrlichman says the president raised the idea of a reciprocal tit-for-tat pardon after the election; any anti-Nixon protesters convicted for demonstrations—excepting violence or bombings —would be pardoned on one side and the Watergate burglars on the other. Nixon places this discussion later; at this point, no one had even been charged for Watergate, let alone convicted.

One plausible reason for Nixon's admitted and repeated deep concern over Hunt is Ehrlichman's statement, which he relates in his book, that during this beach walk they discussed Hunt's and Liddy's involvement in the Fielding break-in. Nixon has never varied from his insistence that he first learned of the break-in at Ellsberg's psychiatrist's only in March 1973, eighteen months after it occurred. Regarding this discussion with Ehrlichman, his diary states that his advisers warned him that unraveling Watergate "would involve the activities which were perfectly legitimate but which would be hard to explain in investigating the Ellsberg case, the Bay of Pigs, and the other matters where we had an imperative need to get the facts."

But Ehrlichman insists: "From that day forward Nixon knew everything I knew about Howard Hunt's activities"—the attempts to pile more blame on President Kennedy for the failure of the Bay of Pigs and the assassination of President Diem.[17] Apart from charging Nixon with foreknowledge of the Watergate break-in, this is the most serious challenge to the president by one of his two closest advisers.

In his memoirs, Nixon claims that it was only now that he first heard of Magruder's "possible involvement" in the break-in itself. And his diary maintains he strongly urged to Ehrlichman that Magruder volunteer his role and take responsibility. Ehrlichman's note of July 8 catches a different nuance: "I'm not directly involved but as c of staff I bear ult responsibility. I'm resigning," he has Nixon say, in rehearsing a Magruder statement.[18]

Ehrlichman predicts that Magruder will, when questioned, "take the Fifth"; that is, refuse to answer, invoking his constitutional Fifth Amendment right to avoid self-incrimination. Better for Haldeman to tell his protégé Magruder to resign before he is hauled in front of the grand jury, Nixon suggests. Yet Nixon's diary betrays reluctance to see this happen. "Haldeman is naturally very 'tender,' as Ehrlichman pointed out, with regard to Magruder. I feel just as deeply about it as he does." The unstated trouble with Magruder is that no one believes that he is a self-starter, that he alone ordered the break-in. If he goes, there is immediate peril for Mitchell and a line unwinding to Haldeman. And if them, then on to Nixon.

The same problem was consuming the conspirators back at CRP. Magruder told the true story of his, Mitchell's, Strachan's, and Haldeman's involvement to CRP's lawyer, Kenneth Parkinson, with Mardian present. Magruder was willing, if it was so decided, to take the rap. But that course, like Magruder's resignation on "principle," mooted by Nixon, was only briefly contemplated by Mitchell and then quickly overruled. A Magruder confession would merely lead upward.

Parkinson was then told by Mitchell and others that Magruder's true story was in fact an invention. So Parkinson, who now "possessed rough notes of a man who'd given me what I considered to be a false story, which implicated high officials in this government," felt he had a duty to get rid of them, in part, he said, because he didn't have security provisions in his office.[19] He, too, had recourse to the CRP shredder. Through Mitchell's legal gymnastics, Parkinson, as a lawyer and an officer of the court, should not be made party to perjury; so Mitchell made the truth "perjury" and the perjury the "truth."

The orginal cover story, leaving Liddy as the highest CRP officer involved, was clearly the best. It now had to be developed and a second person found to corroborate it.

The conspirators' mood was self-righteous. Their "enemies" were trying to make a mountain out of a molehill. As Magruder later described it, "We were not covering up a burglary; we were safeguarding world peace."[20]

But how to explain away all the money Magruder had authorized for Liddy in his intelligence role? Already the lowly CRP bookkeepers were being brought before the grand jury and talking. And Sloan refused to go along with the lower figure of $40,000 LaRue and Magruder now suggested. He made it $199,000. They again suggested to Sloan that as CRP treasurer he might face personal legal problems. But rather than participate further, and vowing to tell the truth when asked, Sloan resigned. He also retained a lawyer.

Magruder then turned to his assistant Bart Porter, the young man who had arranged the big Hollywood bash the day of the Watergate arrests. Magruder told Porter he was considered a good team player. Would he now help out? Magruder assured him that no one at CRP or the White House had known that Liddy would break in and bug the Watergate. But to protect the president's election, they needed to explain the money.

Porter gave it thought but not for long. He suggested, as he stated in his Senate committee testimony, that he could easily account for

$100,000 in ten annual $10,000 "fictional payments" to people he had engaged to infiltrate possible demonstrations against his "surrogates program." Surrogates were worthies, from the vice president down, who spoke on behalf of the president. They were often the target for demonstrators, and so intelligence was needed for their protection.

Good man, Porter. Attractive and articulate, he was also ambitious. After the election, he would be rewarded. Magruder himself would say that the balance authorized to Liddy was for the same sort of preemptive intelligence, to protect the Republican National Convention. Since two cities were involved, first San Diego (until dropped in the wake of the ITT affair), then Miami Beach, a doubling of costs could be explained. In fact, none of the money given to Liddy had gone on such intelligence, but this was the story now polished up to gull the FBI, grand jury, and prosecutors.

On July 5, the prosecutors made a breakthrough. Al Baldwin had decided to come in from the cold. For turning state's evidence he would be treated not as a defendant but as a witness. On Baldwin's eyewitness account, both Hunt and Liddy could now be tied directly to the Watergate Five in the crime. As the first insider, his evidence was vital—yet strangely there was little investigative follow-up. The FBI did not, after its interview with him on July 10, check the DNC phones Baldwin said he had been listening to. Nor did the prosecutors seek a search warrant for McCord's premises, now that Baldwin had told them he had driven the van there with all the equipment and files. They deemed it too late.

And even more surprising, whenever Baldwin tried to implicate higher-ups, the prosecutors were not interested. Baldwin had worked with Martha, had been to the Mitchells' apartment and spoken to John Mitchell himself. For Baldwin it was a replay of the way CRP's lawyers had treated him. "Whenever I mentioned John Mitchell or made any reference to White House individuals or parties that were connected with the White House, I was constantly being told that it would never reach that far; John Mitchell would never be implicated. . . . It was almost as if they were saying, 'We don't want to hear you say anything about John Mitchell or any other individual. You just tell us about McCord, Liddy, Hunt, and the Cubans, but no one else.' "[21]

If the prosecutors, as they later argued, had to be meticulous about getting admissible evidence rather than hearsay for the trial, then their job at this point was to investigate all the leads. In fact, they saw Baldwin only as a crucial witness to convicting the break-in gang. Politically high-profile people made them nervous, and they showed deference.

Dean was successful in keeping some senior people from facing the grand jury directly. With Henry Petersen's consent, Colson, Krogh, Young, Chapin, and Strachan, and even Colson's secretary, Joan Hall, were allowed to give their sworn testimony to the prosecutors in a Justice Department conference room. The prosecutors' excuse was that undue publicity was avoided. But the effect was to prevent the twenty-three grand jurors who had to decide probable cause of crime from seeing witnesses face-to-face.

When Dean asked Petersen to repeat the courtesy for Maurice Stans, Petersen balked at first, but under heat from Ehrlichman yielded. The grand jurors did insist on seeing Mitchell. By this time, late August, the CRP high command had their story together. Many scheming sessions were held with Dean and LaRue present to assist Mitchell, Magruder, and Porter. Dean coached Magruder for two hours immediately before he went in to be questioned by the grand jury about the money.

The only serious problem was Sloan. He not only testified to the grand jury about the true amounts of cash disbursed to Liddy but also told how Magruder tried to persuade him to commit perjury, a crime in itself.

When Magruder came to testify, he was closely questioned, so the prosecutors claimed, about Sloan's accusation that he had tried suborning his perjury. Magruder had a smooth answer. Sloan had been overwrought about his own potential liabilities under the new and complicated campaign-spending laws. It was a misunderstanding between colleagues. Since it was Magruder's word against Sloan's, the prosecutors did not pursue it. They were more interested in how all the Liddy money had come to be authorized. Magruder was by now word perfect. So was Porter; he was particularly persuasive in corroborating the "surrogates" spending story. Grand jury proceedings are by law supposed to be kept absolutely secret, but Petersen informed Dean. After Magruder's second grand jury appearance on August 18, Petersen told Dean that he had "made it through by the skin of his teeth."[22]

Petersen much later testified that no one believed Magruder's story about the money; and that from the beginning he felt suspicious because "nobody acted innocent." If so, they all benefited uncommonly from the presumption of innocence.

By July 31, according to Ehrlichman—before Magruder's testimony—Kleindienst informed him of a two-hour session with Petersen and Silbert. They were aiming for September 15 as the date for the Watergate indictments and for a trial after the election.[23]

There was one nasty hiccup over the money. It caught the White House by surprise and was the one lead the FBI later admitted it had missed. Kenneth Dahlberg was discovered to have lied about the true source of his $25,000 check, the one that passed through Bernard Barker's bank account. Dahlberg had told the FBI, when Gray had eventually authorized his interview, that the $25,000 was simply made up of Florida contributions to CRP. But the Dade County, Florida, district attorney had started his own investigation into Barker's bank, which had processed the check. Under oath Dahlberg admitted the money was on behalf of Dwayne Andreas, the Hubert Humphrey backer whose contribution CRP had tried keeping secret.

The story now broke on August 25, just as the president had been renominated. It came in *The Washington Post* after a sequence of scoops under a joint byline that was to become familiar: Bob Woodward and Carl Bernstein (sometimes referred to by colleagues as Woodstein).

The federal prosecutors, however, had their eye on Magruder. They were to have a third and last go at him over the entries in his office calendar for January 27 and February 4, which they did not know were the GEMSTONE meetings with Liddy. Mitchell, Dean, and Magruder had considered erasing them, but reckoned the FBI laboratories would soon detect that. (CRP's lawyer, Paul O'Brien, later said this raised his suspicions about Dean, but again he did nothing.) Reportedly out of the presence of their lawyers, Dean, Mitchell, and Magruder concocted another story. The January 27 meeting had been canceled, they would claim; at the second, on February 4, they did nothing but discuss legal problems of the new election law. The presence of Dean as counsel to the president and Liddy as counsel to CRP clothed this version with enough plausibility and the prosecutors swallowed it.

Nixon, aware from his briefings that the White House appeared to be high and dry and that it looked certain that the indictments would be restricted to Liddy, Hunt, and the five arrested, now implemented the bold tactic he had discussed with Ehrlichman in California. Indeed, more than bold, it was, from what we now know, Nixon at his most brazen. On August 29, he told a news conference:

> I can state categorically that no one in the White House staff, no one in this administration, presently employed, was involved in this very bizarre incident. What really hurts in matters of this sort is not the fact that they occur, because overzealous people in campaigns do things that are wrong. What really hurts is if you try to cover it up.

The president further announced that John Dean—the name then meant nothing to the public—had conducted "a complete investigation" and report for him. This was news, especially to Dean, who claims he nearly fell off the edge of the hotel bed from which he was watching the president on TV. From that moment on, Nixon frequently called impatiently for a cosmetic "report" from Dean that would exonerate the White House from involvement in the break-in. If they could somehow preserve the fiction of "no White House involvement" in the break-in, the president appeared to believe, then the cover-up and obstruction of justice somehow did not count.

As Nixon cruised toward election victory, aspects of the Watergate affair that would have damaged a weaker candidate kept surfacing. Considering what we know today, it is ironic how little impact they had. Few in the media, outside notably *The Washington Post* and the *Los Angeles Times,* really paid much attention.

First of all, the Democrats' secret access to Baldwin's guilty knowledge flowered into the full story. On August 5, a DNC lawyer traveled to Connecticut and heard Baldwin's account. They had to be in separate rooms—with Baldwin's lawyer as go-between—to maintain the fiction that Baldwin had not talked to anyone, as required by the prosecutors. But on September 11, Lawrence O'Brien went public with the first flat statement that there had been multiple Watergate break-ins and that DNC phones had been bugged for weeks. *The Washington Post* broke the story of an eighth man, but the *Los Angeles Times* carried off the big scoop with a major first-person story by Baldwin. CBS-TV's

Evening News followed that with a Baldwin interview actually naming Mitchell as involved, but even this produced little reaction in the public at large.

What Nixon successfully labeled as this "bizarre incident" was made stranger still by the September 14 "discovery" of a bug on Spencer Oliver's phone in the DNC offices. The Democrats claimed to have noticed something suspicious. They called in the telephone company, which called in the FBI.

CRP, at the president's furious instruction, brought countersuits against the Democrats and even a libel action by Stans against O'Brien. Apart from the political slanging match, the intrusion of this extra bug caused a secret but intense row among the investigators. The FBI and the telephone company had maintained that, in the initial sweeps after the break-in, no bugs had been found. This was uncomfortable, but the prosecutors could work on the theory that the bugs seized from the burglars had been devices they had removed, and that they had been caught red-handed prior to reinstallation. That theory would not hold in the face of this new bug.

In the end, FBI and prosecutors could not agree. The prosecutors insisted that someone, the telephone company or the FBI, must have missed the September bug the first time around. It could have been a serious matter had any of the defendants contested this evidence at the first trial, but they did not. There have been other theories.[24] Lately it has been speculated that the Democrats themselves discovered it shortly after the break-in, promptly removed it, and then reinstalled it to back up Baldwin's story.

The press coverage of the Mexican and Dahlberg checks and the laundering that accompanied them prompted an investigation by the House Banking and Currency Committee. Democratic Congressman Wright Patman, the chairman, denouncing a massive cover-up, was calling Watergate "the first political espionage case" in U.S. history. Nobody paid much attention but Nixon had anticipated the danger. "All Repubs boycott all committee hearings after the conventions—will hamstring them pass word," Nixon instructed Ehrlichman.[25] It was not an idle threat.

Out front, the government's propaganda machine was readied for the big roll of the dice. On September 15, the indictment was returned by the grand jury and it bore out the president's news conference statement. Only the five arrested inside the DNC plus Hunt and Liddy were indicted on criminal bugging charges. Haldeman noted that their inclusion, as former White House employees, "takes the edge off the whitewash."[26]

There was lavish boasting by Kleindienst of the FBI's investigation being the greatest effort since the assassination of President Kennedy. The attorney general was ready with a mass of statistics of the hundreds of agents involved and the thousands of man hours worked. Yet the FBI, for instance, never once interviewed Haldeman, and, more critically, altogether overlooked Magruder's assistant, Robert Reisner. He had handled Mitchell's GEMSTONE files. Had Reisner been asked he would either have had to lie like the rest or lead the FBI straight to Mitchell. Kleindienst's hollow claims would come back to haunt him and the FBI.

The election campaign had just seven weeks to go. Shortly after the formal indictment, both U.S. District Court Chief Judge John J. Sirica, who had assigned himself the Watergate case, and, in the civil suit brought by the Democrats, U.S. District Court Judge Charles R. Richey, allegedly a friend of the Nixon administration, had ruled that nothing further should be made public in the proceedings until after polling day. The White House had won round one.

CHAPTER 9

Dean Takes Charge

John Dean's first office contact with the president was to witness the signing of the Nixons' wills; he was the in-house lawyer before he was manager of the cover-up. The day the Watergate indictment was handed down was Dean's big day. On Friday evening of September 15, at the end of a busy Watergate week, he was summoned to the Oval Office for only his second meeting with the president—though Nixon had known what Dean was up to from the outset.[1]

This meeting, with Haldeman present, shows that Dean and Nixon were made for each other. It opens in presidential conspiratorial congratulation of his young counsel: "Well, you had quite a day today, didn't you? You got Watergate on the way . . ." Nixon (as he said in his diary) was "enormously impressed" with Dean. "He had the kind of steel and really mean instinct that we needed to clean house after the election."[2]

Dean tells Nixon what he wants to hear. He reviews the first three months of the Watergate investigation and assures the president of clear sailing until polling day:

Dean: I think that I can say that fifty-four days from now that not a thing will come crashing down to our surprise—

Nixon: Say what?

Dean: Nothing is going to come crashing down to our surprise, either—

> *Nixon:* Well, the whole thing is a can of worms, as you know. A lot of that stuff went on . . . but the way you've handled it, it seems to me, has been very skillful because you—putting your fingers in the dikes every time that leaks have sprung here and sprung there [unintelligible] having people straighten the [unintelligible].[3]

Dean counsels the president soberly that "the only problems are human problems . . . human frailties, people getting annoyed and some finger-pointing and false accusations and any internal dissension." And Dean warns of bitterness at CRP between the finance committee staff, who are taking all the flak in the press coverage of the money trail, and Magruder's staff, who are getting away with it. (Dean subsequently arranged a Nixon stroking session for all the finance committee staffers at the White House to counteract their resentment at being ignored when the president visited CRP. The list included Judy Hoback, Stans's "bookkeeper," who at the time was talking to reporter Carl Bernstein.)[4]

Nixon retorts that the CRP staff must understand "this is war," and he tells Dean, "I wouldn't want to be on the other side right now." Together with Haldeman, Nixon fumes about the lawyer for the Democrats and *The Washington Post,* Edward Bennett Williams. "We are going to fix the sonofabitch. Believe me. We are going to. We've got to, because he's a bad man." And here Dean promises, in a reference to the "enemies list," that he has been keeping notes on Williams and many others "who are less than our friends."

There was more to this meeting. Haldeman's notes cover a continuation after the end of the tape transcript. The president looks forward to getting the Justice Department under control and of having the IRS investigate the tax returns of McGovern supporters, although Haldeman cautions against taking risks until after the election. The notes end with Nixon saying, "Anyway, we'll fix 'em."[5]

The House Banking and Currency Committee hearings were looming. Shortly after the Oval Office conversation (in which Dean had commented that "it would be . . . a tragedy to let Patman have a field day up there"), on October 3 the committee met to consider the chairman's request for subpoena power. If granted, it meant witnesses could be compelled to testify on pain of contempt charges. The committee staff had been digging and Patman's subpoena list was revelatory. It named some famous people and many then unknown—Mitchell, Stans, Magruder, and Mardian among the former; Dean, LaRue, Caulfield, and Sloan among the latter.

Surprisingly, a bipartisan majority of the committee voted 20–15 against granting subpoena power. Without it witnesses could defy requests to appear. To this day it is not entirely clear how the "fix" went in. Certainly, the White House used Henry Petersen to write from the Justice Department, pleading that committee hearings would interfere with the Watergate defendants' rights to a fair trial—even though Patman had no plans to call the defendants themselves.

If it is unsurprising that Republicans would vote against, it is odd that so powerful a congressional baron as Patman was not able to line up his own Democrats. Committee members suggest the seventy-nine-year-old Patman was past his best. Some of the southern Democrats were pro-Nixon, anyway, and two other Democrat defectors faced investigations for bribe taking (and much later were convicted). Later one committee member said that White House congressional liaison staff had reminded congressmen of various "past indiscretions."[6]

Patman's last fling before the election was to go ahead with hearings anyway. He summoned Mitchell, Stans, MacGregor, and Dean. All declined to appear and Patman instead had his field day lecturing the empty chairs of the witnesses. Although no one noticed at the time, the Nixonites' arrogant treatment of Congress had its consequences. Patman wrote to Judge Sirica, and his aborted hearings also stimulated an investigation by James Flug, a staff lawyer of Teddy Kennedy's Senate Subcommittee on Administrative Practices, which added much weight to the following year's Senate Watergate investigation. Finally, interfering with Patman was one of the items included in the obstruction of justice Article 1 with which the House Judiciary Committee eventually recommended Nixon for impeachment.

Even as Patman had publicly sought to focus on CRP funds, in secret there had been a crisis over the hush money. Herbert Kalmbach, finding that the demands outstripped the $115,000 he had been given in two installments by Stans and by LaRue, had been asked to go to outside contributors. His concern, he said later in testimony to the

Senate committee, was that he found it distasteful as the president's lawyer to be engaged in "a James Bond scenario."

Kalmbach checked personally with Ehrlichman to ensure that Dean had the authority to direct him and that the fund-raising he was doing was proper. Kalmbach said he reminded Ehrlichman of their wives' and family ties: "I said, 'John, I am looking right into your eyes. I know Jeanne and your family; you know Barbara and my family. You know that my family and my reputation mean everything to me . . .' " Ehrlichman replied that Dean had the authority and that it was proper for Kalmbach to go ahead.

With that Kalmbach picked up $30,000 more in CRP money from LaRue and then turned to Thomas V. Jones, chairman of the Northrop Corporation, an old Nixon political contributor, who had told him he would have funds on hand for "any special need." Jones took a packet containing $75,000 cash from his desk and handed it to Kalmbach. Kalmbach passed it on to Ulasewicz.

But in mid-August, with the next demand for still more, Kalmbach had had enough. The press coverage worried him. And Ulasewicz, at a handover of funds in his car outside the Orange County, California, airport, gave words of caution from an old New York cop. "This is not kosher, Mr. Kalmbach," he said.

On September 21, Kalmbach visited Dean's White House office, with LaRue present, for a reconciliation of the sums. Kalmbach had recorded the sums in miniature handwriting; it was a little short of $200,000, and the records were burned in an ashtray. (Once again, in eminent legal company, evidence was being destroyed.) Now LaRue was to be the moneyman. At this stage there seemed to be enough cash on hand to keep everyone quiet, although secretly there were worries about the continuous demands from Hunt and his wife.

As election day neared, there had been no public mention of hush money, only the odd hint in news stories that "they" were paying legal fees for the accused. Instead, a different kind of fund hit the front pages, and the eventual outcome was not unfavorable to the White House. *The Washington Post* reporter duo of Woodward and Bernstein had a run of scoops over the six weeks beginning mid-September about CRP's "secret" funds. On September 29, the newspaper's lead story was about Mitchell, while attorney general, controlling the fund "used to gather information about the Democrats." Imperishably, it is Mitchell's response about the newspaper's owner's anatomy that has gone into history. Responding to an 11:30 P.M. call by Bernstein, Mitchell expostulated:

> All that crap, you're putting it in the paper? It's all been denied. Katie Graham's gonna get her tit caught in a big fat wringer if that's published. Good Christ! That's the most sickening thing I ever heard.[7]

But on October 25, the White House had its revenge. The reporters alleged that Haldeman also controlled the secret fund for political espionage. Given what we know now, it was not that far off the mark, but the article stated that Sloan had so testified to the grand jury when he had not. That small but critical error gave the White House the opportunity—which it took—to lash back at the *Post.*

What had happened was that Donald Segretti's misdeeds had been uncovered by the *Post* reporters. And the fact of the prankster's secretly being paid by Kalmbach out of campaign funds got garbled and merged with Watergate into one enormous compendium of "political spying and sabotage." The White House issued outraged denials. Nixon even urged Segretti to sue the *Post* for libel.

Even though *The Washington Post* was far nearer the truth than the prosecutors who had swallowed the cover story of Liddy's running Watergate on his own, its editors were now on the defensive. On election eve, the newspaper had seemingly exculpated the mighty Haldeman; it was doubtless the paper's worst moment. Like the rest of the media, it went quiet on Watergate for the last few days of the campaign.

In secret, Dean rapidly established the truth of the White House links to Segretti through Haldeman and his aides Gordon Strachan and Dwight Chapin. Again a new cover story was concocted to place the onus on Segretti and to distance Chapin. Henry Petersen helped out by determining that there was no violation of the election law in the Segretti affair. The FBI was not sure, but on the grounds that its brief was to investigate the Watergate break-in, the Segretti matter was left pending.

As revealed much later in Nixon's diaries, even as he approached his greatest electoral triumph, paranoia was spreading in the White House. "Haldeman spoke rather darkly of the fact that there was a clique in the White House that were out to get him. I trust he is not getting a persecution complex," the president wrote.[8]

Nixon's own practice of concealing from his top advisers what each was saying, of compartmentalizing, hardly helped. The Nixon tapes make clear that he often discussed issues with feigned innocence, pretending not to know something he had just heard from another of his men.

Before George McGovern crashed to defeat, he bought TV time to deliver one last indictment of the Nixon campaign:

> These Republican politicians have fouled the political atmosphere for all of us who see public service as a high calling. They do not seek to defeat the Democratic Party; they seek to destroy it. And in the process, they would deny one of the most precious freedoms of all—your freedom to judge which candidate will better serve your interests and truly reflect your views.[9]

In a memo to Pat Buchanan, Nixon said that this was the "last burp of the Eastern establishment."

It made no difference, of course. The final days of the campaign were dominated by the Vietnam negotiations. Henry Kissinger had imprudently announced on October 26 that "peace is at hand." It was not. While a deal had been struck with Communist North Vietnam, it could not be made palatable to America's ally, President Thieu of South Vietnam. Nixon and his top aides were annoyed with Kissinger for having promised the undeliverable.

But that, too, made no difference. Nixon's own diary for election eve, quoted in his memoirs, suggested that his reelection campaign had received divine assistance—"someone must have been walking with us," he wrote. "The only sour note of the whole thing is Watergate and Segretti."

It seemed accurate to minimize the effect of both affairs. The polls had scarcely closed in California on the night of election day, November 7, before McGovern had conceded. Nixon won by a record margin of forty-nine states to one—the lone McGovern win was not his home state of South Dakota, which he lost, but Massachusetts (the ever-Democratic District of Columbia also went for him). Nixon's share of the popular vote, 60.7 percent, was just short of Lyndon Johnson's all-time record of 61.1 percent. The silent majority was now the new majority. Many traditionally Democratic voters turned their backs on McGovern's radicalism and voted for Nixon. He was the choice, perhaps the hope, of the mass of ordinary Americans.

Nixon now had what he had most desperately fought not to lose—a second term. Both houses of Congress were still in opposition hands, but his personal victory was so sweeping that he believed he could dictate the New American Revolution he was determined to bring about in the structure of government. Yet he was beset with melancholy. He often felt a letdown when the fighting stopped. It would be satisfying to say that it was his foreboding over Watergate that depressed him, but there is more reason to believe he thought that he could get clean away with it.

Nixon's first act was brusque and disconcerting. He ordered Haldeman to summon the entire White House staff, then the Cabinet, and asked for their resignations. Haldeman issued the forms on which they were to write them out.

Although William Safire, the speechwriter, insisted the mood was neither cold nor hostile, Nixon's loyalists were still stunned. Kissinger recalled that the president was grim and remote and his thanks perfunctory, and observed. "It was as if victory was not an occasion for reconciliation but an opportunity to settle the scores of a lifetime."[10]

Had Nixon instead seized the chance to play the political butcher with all those involved in Watergate, he might have saved his presidency. It would have required bloodletting from the top down, but he would have been, as he so often schemed to be later, out front—ahead of the first trial, the Senate investigation, and of any accusations from dismissed associates. But he did not. Few leaders in democracies are good butchers. They try to protect friends, if only to protect themselves, especially when newly reelected.

John Dean had assured Nixon, on September 15, that nothing would come crashing down in the fifty-four days up to the election. He was correct—but once the election was past, the cover-up immediately had a great fall. Try as they might, all the president's men could never put it back together again.

There was no outward sign of disaster. Nixon had removed himself to Camp David for nearly five weeks to work out his plans for restructuring government. His intent was to make the executive branch all-powerful, so that he could virtually ignore Congress. Key sub-Cabinet posts would go only to those superloyal to Nixon. It was breathtaking in conception.

But Congress had other ideas. The Democratic leadership was smarting from the way the election had been fought and unhappy about the drastic reforms they were hearing about. Senate Majority Leader Mike Mansfield, then best known for his opposition to continuing the Vietnam War and his persistent campaign to bring home the 300,000 U.S. servicemen in western Europe, wrote a letter that November to the chairman of the Senate Judiciary Committee. It was kept confidential for many weeks. In it Mansfield suggested they appoint a low-profile senator to be chairman of a "complete and impartial investigation" into the way the election campaign had been fought. His suggestion for the job was Senator Sam J. Ervin, Democrat of North Carolina.[11]

Over in the House of Representatives there had been an unexpected but important change of guard. The Democratic majority leader had been killed in a plane crash and was succeeded by a Kennedy partisan, Thomas P. "Tip" O'Neill of Massachusetts. That change, too, was to be significant before long. O'Neill reckoned that so many bad things had been done by the Nixon men that they simply could not be kept secret indefinitely. Privately, he urged his surprised colleagues in the House leadership to "get ready for impeachment." They wondered whether he was unhinged.[12]

That would have been the general public reaction. At that point, Watergate was virtually invisible. True, the criminal trial was still to come, but it seemed at most a footnote. Nixon seemed utterly secure and the country most interested to see what he would do about everyday issues like school busing, reviving the economy, and ending the Vietnam War.

But paranoia was eating away at all Nixon's top men. Dean, although he had been told his job was protected, already wondered whether he was being set up. Nixon's announcement of a nonexistent "Dean report" and repeated postelection demands for a "Dean statement" spelled trouble.

We know now that within two weeks of his reelection Nixon secretly had decided that Chapin and Strachan, and Colson as well, had to go —Chapin because of the links with Segretti, and Strachan, as Haldeman noted, "because he knows everything." Colson had to go because he was, after Watergate and the Hunt connection, damaged political goods. But Nixon could not face telling Colson, and agreed to keep him into the new year. This might have been because Colson had grave news for the president and his top advisers: The hush money demands from Howard Hunt were beginning to have an ominous ring.

Colson had decided after contacts at one remove (secretaries and wives) to accept, and tape, a telephone call from Hunt in mid-November. The call was both cordial and, with the election over, menacing. The tape transcript is the only one in existence of a conversation with a man directly involved in the Watergate break-in. It vividly conveys the flavor of the commitments the burglars expected, indeed demanded.

Despite Colson's nervous assurances that "everyone's going to come out all right" and repeated "say no more" attempts to fend off incriminating knowledge, Hunt made the president's special counsel listen, aghast.

> *Hunt:* . . . Commitments that were made to all of us at the onset have not been kept. And there's a great deal of unease and concern on the part of the seven defendants, and possibly, well I'm quite sure, me least of all. But there's a great deal of financial expense here that has not been covered and what we've been getting has been coming in very minor dribs and drabs. And Parkinson, who's been the go-between with my attorney, doesn't seem to be very effective and we're now reaching a point at which—
>
> *Colson:* Okay. You've told me, all, all, that, that, don't tell me any more—

Hunt: Okay.
Colson: —cause, I understand that, let me, let me just—
Hunt: —because these people have really got to dig. This is a very long-haul thing but stakes are very, very high—
Colson: [Unintelligible].
Hunt: —and I thought that you would want to know that this thing must not break apart for foolish reasons.
Colson: I agree. Yeah. Oh no, Christ no. . . .[13]

With that hint of the cover-up about to "break apart," Hunt says that "the ready [i.e., cash] is not available" and he sets Colson a deadline—the close of business on November 25—for the "liquidation" of everything outstanding. He makes clear these are promised payments owed since July and August. Hunt says that they can accept delays caused by the election, but now he wants "affirmative action for Christ's sake." And it is more than money they are after. Hunt wants the White House to "get the goddamn thing out of the way once and for all."

To an increasingly distraught Colson, Hunt says that Mitchell has already perjured himself, and he wonders what input Colson has had from Dean about who was responsible for the break-in. Then he unloads:

Hunt: . . . after all, we're protecting the guys who, who were really responsible. But now that's—then, of course, that's a continuing requirement, but at the same time this is a two-way street.
Colson: Uh huh. Uh huh.
Hunt: And, as I said before, we think that now is the time when some moves should be made and surely your cheapest commodity available is money. These lawyers have not been paid.
Colson: Hmm . . .

Hunt obliges Colson by saying that he has always told his lawyer, William Bittman, "that you had absolutely nothing to do with it." But he pushes Colson into agreeing to meet Bittman and discloses that "a memorandum is going to be laid on" CRP's chief lawyer, Kenneth Parkinson. They end with Hunt's saying, and Colson agreeing, "I've had a lifetime of serving my country, and in a sense I'm still doing it." When Colson invokes "we got the president in for four years, and thank God for the country we do," Hunt comments, "Exactly."[14]

According to Dean, Colson could hardly wait to play him the tape, keen for him to hear Hunt say that Colson had known nothing about the break-in. Colson, himself a lawyer, seemed oblivious of the fact that he was now, more than ever, party to the deepening obstruction of justice.

Dean took the tape to Camp David and played it for Haldeman and Ehrlichman (though they denied hearing it). They were busy with high affairs of state. Ehrlichman was to become even more the overlord of all domestic policy. They suggested that Dean see Mitchell and Dean flew the same day to New York. Mitchell was taciturn and had no immediate advice.

Hunt's memorandum to Parkinson, however, went much further than his call to Colson. It was a devastating attack on the handling of the case since the arrests. Hunt, the CIA's clandestine service agent, was particularly embittered at the "failure to quash the investigation while that option was still open." Hunt now made pointed new threats to unravel the whole Plumbers saga. It looked like blackmail.

The memo, noting that congressional elections would take place in two years, said: "The Watergate bugging is only one of a number of highly illegal conspiracies engaged in by one or more of the defendants at the behest of senior White House officials. These as yet undisclosed crimes can be proved. . . . Immunity from prosecution and/or judicial clemency for cooperating defendants is a standing offer."

Hunt was careful to state, "The foregoing should not be interpreted as a threat. It is among other things a reminder that loyalty has always been a two-way street." He extended the deadline to November 27.[15]

It was clear to all the cover-up conspirators that Hunt might blow, and it ought to have been clear what had gone wrong. Although $187,500 had been distributed in hush money by September, only some $20,000 had been paid out between then and the election. This sum had been rustled up by LaRue in the face of grumblings from Mrs. Hunt that they were being let down. Somebody seemed to have forgotten the five-month $450,000 "budget" submitted by Mrs. Hunt in July. No wonder the Hunts were feeling abandoned.

The mood among the defendants awaiting trial was verging on the flaky. The Cubans were in part provided for out of a Miami-based fund and for the rest looked obediently to Hunt. Dorothy Hunt had very much taken charge. At a meeting to discuss Hunt's ultimatum, Liddy says in *Will* she told him that there had "never been a cent for you" in the hush money allocations. The $17,000 she had passed on had come from Hunt's share. Hunt added that since nothing was coming of his approach to Colson, it was now every man for himself. He suggested that he and Liddy write a book, "with the bidding to start at $500,000." (Hunt's memo claimed one media bid of $745,000.) Liddy said he was infuriated that the Hunts should think his loyalty was conditional upon money. "I am not for sale," he said, and left the room.[16]

Dorothy Hunt was suspicious of McCord, the wireman at Watergate, who she thought was a double agent. In fact, as early as July 30, McCord had sent the CIA's Richard Helms a copy of a letter he wrote to his own lawyer. His cover note to Helms read: "From time to time I'll send along things you may be interested in from an info standpoint."

McCord's letter told of an initial attempt by CRP and the prosecutors to lay Watergate at the feet of the CIA, and spelled out an early variant of CRP's cover story. This would pretend that McCord had been bribed by Liddy to take part—apparently based on Baldwin's evidence of seeing Liddy give large cash amounts to McCord. "I will not be patsy to this latest ploy," McCord wrote. It was the first of several McCord letters that were eventually to have convulsive effect.[17]

Hunt's memo to Parkinson did have results. Mitchell now lumbered into action. According to Dean, Mitchell told him to press for a "loan" from the secret $350,000 fund Haldeman had ordered transferred from CRP the previous April. This cash, originally earmarked for Haldeman's private polling, had been kept in a bank safe-deposit box by a friend of Alexander Butterfield's, the Haldeman aide who ran Nixon's office. The hush money linkage into the president's innermost circle was getting tighter.

Haldeman agreed reluctantly to Dean's request, and Gordon Strachan performed a last service before leaving the White House (he was being rewarded with a senior post in the U.S. Information Agency). Strachan had Butterfield drive from the White House to meet his friend at a hotel parking lot to collect $50,000 in a briefcase. Strachan gave it to LaRue, who passed it to Hunt's lawyer, Bittman. But it was not enough. Haldeman told Dean to give LaRue the rest of the $350,000, "the entire damn bundle," but make sure to get a receipt.

Before that transaction, there was a final twist. Some $22,000 of the $350,000 had been disbursed for newspaper advertisements Colson had placed purporting to give Nixon independent support for the Haiphong Harbor mining—but only $7,000-odd had been used. The balance had been returned to Dean's safe; he, in turn, borrowed $4,500-odd to pay for a honeymoon with his second wife, Maureen. Now, in case of awkward questions from investigators, the deficit had to be made up to keep the $350,000 "whole." The ever-obliging CRP finance chief, Maurice Stans, supplied "the ready."

Strachan took the money to LaRue, who was at his Watergate apartment. LaRue donned rubber gloves, which made Strachan realize that his own fingerprints were already on the bills. He asked for the receipt Haldeman had insisted on. LaRue answered, "You'll have to talk to Dean about that." The hush money operation was in business again, or so it seemed.

It was at this point, on December 8, that Mrs. Hunt was killed in an airliner crash while flying to Chicago. Some $10,000 in cash was found with her remains. There was much speculation: It was part of the hush money; she had been assassinated. The FBI and later the National Transportation Safety Board insisted there was no evidence of foul play. Mrs. Hunt had taken out insurance just before takeoff, and $225,000 would now come to the widower. Understandably Hunt, with four children, was shattered; in his own words he was a "destroyed man."

Nixon's attention in December was on the North Vietnamese, who were insisting on the peace deal they had reached with Kissinger before the election and not a jot further compromise. Nixon broke off negotiations and, without announcement, resumed bombing. The president was desperate to force a peace agreement before Congress reassembled and voted to cut off bombing funds. This time he ordered the high-flying B-52s to hit targets in the hitherto off-limits areas around Hanoi and Haiphong.

The so-called Christmas bombing brought world outrage and congressional uproar. United States losses were high, but it worked. The North Vietnamese agreed to some minor changes; President Thieu of South Vietnam was secretly promised that the United States would always come to his aid in extremis, and he was forced to go it alone or come along. He yielded. "Peace with honor" was signed and the biggest prize, the American POWs, were soon on their way home. It was an extraordinary end to America's most unpopular foreign war. It is difficult, twenty years later, to recapture the enormous sense of national and international relief. Kissinger was awarded the Nobel Prize for Peace jointly with his North Vietnamese negotiating counterpart, Le Duc Tho, who did not bother to collect it. Amid all the celebrations over Vietnam, Kissinger's deputy, Alexander Haig, left the White House, catapulted by Nixon over the heads of some two hundred senior officers to be made army vice chief of staff. He would soon be back.

Meanwhile, behind the façade of the Vietnam settlement, Watergate was gnawing away at the foundations of the second Nixon administration. John Dean was at the center of the falling pieces. Besides the hush money strains, there were new chunks falling off all parts of the elaborate cover-up structure. The desperate need to keep the Plumbers under wraps was threatened. Richard Helms, forced out as CIA director, made sure that some embarrassments were cleaned up before escaping as ambassador to Iran. The photos that Hunt had the CIA develop of the 1971 casing of Ellsberg's psychiatrist's offices were handed over by the CIA to the Justice Department. The prosecutors were baffled; Liddy was clearly visible in one, but nobody knew why. Dean tried to get the CIA to take the pictures back, but was rebuffed.

Helms's 1971 deputy, General Cushman, wrote a memo stating that the authority to give Hunt CIA technical help had come from Ehrlichman or Colson or Dean. Ehrlichman was appalled. With Dean's assistance, Cushman was persuaded to withdraw his memo and name no names, but the CIA's deputy executive director, William Colby, had already given Henry Petersen and the prosecutors Ehrlichman's name. They again did not know what to make of it, but the cover-up was getting unmanageable.

Hunt's lawyers in the interim had demanded that the prosecutors make available for his defense the materials taken from his White House safe. After inspecting the FBI's collection, Hunt insisted that two notebooks were missing, which he claimed contained operational details of GEMSTONE. These, he said, would provide him with a defense of acting with due authority. It was Dean's turn to be appalled. Dean took Petersen aside. He confided that only a portion of Hunt's materials had been handed to the FBI agents; the rest, non-Watergate related, had been given to Pat Gray. Petersen was agitated. He asked Gray, who promptly denied ever receiving them. Gray got hold of Dean and warned him to hang tough and stick to saying nothing further. Petersen did nothing.

No one realized that Gray, that Christmas, had destroyed all the Hunt materials he had received, which was another scandal waiting to break. And Dean, moreover, had never handed Hunt's notebooks to Gray. They were still in his own desk and Dean lost no time in putting them through the office shredder.[18]

Word came that even Liddy might be wobbling. It was not true, but the incident showed the widening stresses on the cover-up. Liddy, just before the trial, had been approached for a congressional staff interview in connection with the confirmation hearings of his old Plumbers boss, Egil Krogh, to be undersecretary of commerce, another job reward. Liddy, not wanting his refusal to risk exposing Krogh, telephoned Krogh's office and was told by the secretary that Krogh would be content for Liddy not to make himself available. The next thing Liddy received was his first phone call in months from Dean. "I think you'll recognize my voice," said Dean, careful not to identify himself. The president's counsel explained that Krogh was sorry to be so distant; he wanted to be able to testify he had not spoken to Liddy this past year, but "he's really a good friend of yours."

Then Dean proffered assurances that, with the trial forty-eight hours away, gave Liddy the comforting impression that the White House was taking no chances. Liddy wrote down what Dean said:

1. Living expenses $30,000 per annum
2. Pardon within 2 years
3. Danbury prison
4. Legal fees."

Dean said, "Everyone's going to be taken care of Gordon, everyone." Liddy wanted it understood there was no quid pro quo. "I'll keep quiet no matter what." Dean said he would pass it along.[19]

Dean's version makes no mention of the pardon, but since he claims that Mitchell had authorized that everyone be given the same assurances, there is no reason to doubt Liddy's list. And the offer could have only one source! The action had moved right back to the president. That new year, as the Vietnam climax raged and as the Watergate trial was about to open, Nixon prepared to use the ultimate judicial weapon to hold the cover-up together. Anyone could pay hush money; only he could offer presidential clemency.

After the loss of his wife, Hunt, as he said, was a finished man. He wrote to Colson that his "inability to get any relief from my present situation all contribute to a sense of abandonment by friends on whom I had in good faith relied." There was a limit to his endurance; Hunt insisted that Colson at last fulfill his pledge to meet with his lawyer, Bittman. The implication, after Hunt's savage November memo, was that the time had arrived for a pardon. Colson sent the letter to Dean with a note attached: "Now what do I do?"

With Colson reluctant to act, Dean arranged a meeting with Ehrlichman. Ehrlichman said Colson owed it to Hunt to meet with Bittman; the code was, Colson recalled, that Hunt must be "kept happy" but they all knew they were talking here about an offer of clemency or pardon. Ehrlichman claims he warned Colson that he must never approach the president on the subject; Colson says he heard only that he "need" not.

Colson disobeyed. He met Bittman on January 3, and next day told the lawyer he had spoken to "people" about Hunt's plight. Only the president could deliver on a promise of executive clemency; Colson had to know Nixon's position. Nixon gave Colson his fateful assent. The dire threat Nixon perceived was that Hunt might turn witness for the prosecution:

> Colson told me on Friday that he had tried to do everything he could to keep Hunt in line from turning state's evidence. After what happened to Hunt's wife, etc., I think we have a very good case for showing some clemency.[20]

Despite recording this in his personal diary, Nixon's memoirs attempt to blur the admission. He wrote:

> It now seems clear that I knew Colson was sending messages of reassurance to Hunt through his lawyer—messages that Hunt took to be signals of clemency. I did not believe that any commitments had been made. I cannot even rule out the possibility that I knew similar reassurance was being given the other defendants. I certainly do not remember it, but where Watergate is concerned I have learned not to be categorical.[21]

The tape two days later of Nixon's meeting with Colson is quite categorical:

> *Nixon:* . . . Question of clemency—Hunt's is a simple case. I mean after all, the man's wife is dead, was killed; he's got one child that has—
>
> *Colson:* —brain damage from an automobile accident.
>
> *Nixon:* That's right.
>
> *Colson:* [Unintelligible] one of his kids.
>
> *Nixon:* We'll build, we'll build that sonofabitch up like nobody's business. We'll have [William] Buckley write a column and say, you know, that he, he should have clemency.

The president adds that he would have difficulty with some of the others. And Colson brutally explains that, unlike Hunt and Liddy, "the others didn't know anything direct." The president agrees, "Oh no," when Colson says, "I don't give a damn if they spend five years in jail in the interim."[22]

Clemency, although proffered, had to wait a decent interval until after conviction and sentencing. The same day as the president and Colson spoke, the trial began, and Hunt duly offered to change his not guilty plea, and so not stand trial. But Judge Sirica refused to allow changes of pleas until the prosecution outlined its case on January 10. It would not be the last of the judge's interventions.

It developed that Nixon might have had his eye on the wrong man. Both Colson and Haldeman got the idea that McCord was also changing his plea to guilty, and so informed the president. It wasn't true.[23] In fact, McCord had, in Dean's telling phrase, been "off the reservation" since before Christmas. He was showing signs of a different loyalty.

McCord had from his arrest been resisting any idea of a short jail term followed by clemency. In December, McCord bridled at another attempt by the defense lawyers, led by Hunt's, to argue a "CIA defense." McCord says CRP's lawyers first put forward their CIA theory in July. Since the Watergate Five had been caught red-handed, they had no defense unless they could concoct a plausible motive for having joined in the supposed Liddy-organized burglary. They could not tell the truth. So since Hunt had originally told Barker they were working "above CIA and FBI," it made a sort of sense.

But McCord was adamant. He would not go along with traducing the Company he had served for so long. He sent a fistful of secret letters to his old boss at CIA security, Paul Gaynor. These not only alerted Gaynor to the attempt to implicate the CIA, but also let the CIA know that "those higher up" had been involved. McCord enclosed a list of names: Mitchell, Dean, Magruder, Colson. Gaynor and the CIA did nothing to alert the prosecutors or Judge Sirica—or the White House.[24]

The latter was hardly necessary. McCord had his own line to the White House via Dean's former investigator, Jack Caulfield. Seeing in the ousting of the CIA director a White House plot to blame Helms for Watergate, McCord now activated his link to Caulfield; perhaps "detonated" would be a more suitable term. McCord wrote anonymously:

> Jack—
>
> Sorry to have to write you this letter but felt you had to know.
>
> If Helms goes, and if the WG [Watergate] operation is laid at the CIA's feet, where it does not belong, every tree in the forest will fall. It will be a scorched desert. The whole matter is at the precipice right now. Just pass the message that if they want it to blow, they are on exactly the right course. I'm sorry that you will get hurt in the fallout.

Caulfield, who since leaving CRP had secured himself a plum job in the Treasury's Bureau of Alcohol, Tobacco, and Firearms, now got caught up as the transmission belt between Dean and McCord in a saga of clandestine phone calls and meetings. These usually took place in the second overlook of the George Washington Parkway not far from CIA headquarters.

Dean, claiming he had consulted Ehrlichman, wanted the same assurances that had already been given to Hunt passed on to the rest. McCord was now told in an anonymous call, which Caulfield persuaded Tony Ulasewicz to make for him, that "a year is a long time; no one knows how a judge will go; your family will be provided for. Rehabilitation and job opportunities will be provided for." The time reference was meant to indicate that clemency would come in less than a year. McCord remembered also being told not to accept immunity as an inducement to tell all to the grand jury when called back by the prosecutors to testify after conviction at the trial.

Ulasewicz reported that McCord seemed satisfied, but he was not. On Dean's instruction, Caulfield began a series of meetings in the middle of the trial with the recalcitrant defendant. Some big names were involved, McCord said—Magruder, and Mitchell and Dean as well. McCord was not interested in clemency. He wanted his freedom, now. He then unveiled his plan for getting the charges dropped.

It was ingenious. He had telephoned from his home to the Israeli and Chilean embassies the previous autumn, stating that he was involved in the Watergate scandal and inquiring about visas. McCord maintained that the embassies were subject to national security wiretapping, and he suspected his home phone was tapped as well. A motion made in court to have wiretap evidence against him produced would force the government to dismiss the charges rather than be embarrassed to admit it was bugging embassies.

McCord had already given all this information to the CIA—with a request to Gaynor for assistance. He now gave the dates and times of the calls to Caulfield, who passed them to Dean. The president's counsel told Caulfield to tell McCord he was checking out the wiretaps, but to impress on him the clemency offer came from the "very highest level in the White House." Caulfield took this to mean Ehrlichman, on behalf of the president. McCord claimed that Caulfield told him the president was aware of their meetings and might have a personal message for him.[25] (In fact, this same day Dean reported to Haldeman that

McCord was still off the reservation.[26]) According to Caulfield, Dean told him the scandal was threatening the president and that they were all concerned that McCord was the only defendant "not cooperating with his attorney"—"not following the game plan," as McCord recalled it.

That was true. McCord was in the process of changing lawyers out of disgust at being pressured over the phony "CIA defense." Caulfield delivered Dean's message but McCord would not budge, and he told Caulfield that Magruder, who was then testifying as a government witness at the trial, was perjuring himself. At their last meeting in the third week of January, Caulfield heard for the first time that McCord "was going to make a statement" that would "involve allegations against people in the White House and other high administration officials." Caulfield says he responded with advice. McCord took it as a threat and claims he replied that his will was made out. Caulfield's warning was: "I have worked with these people and I know them to be as tough-minded as you. Don't underestimate them . . ."[27]

But it was the White House that underestimated McCord. Right to the end, they thought his threats were harmless because he had no direct evidence against anyone; what Liddy had told him about Mitchell, Magruder, and Dean was hearsay. On January 8, Dean told Haldeman that McCord was "playing blackmail but he has no hard evidence."

The White House, once they had squared Hunt and minimized the danger from McCord, paid little attention to the trial. In so doing they also disastrously underestimated the judge. John Sirica, a professional boxer in his youth and close friend of heavyweight champ Jack Dempsey, had scraped through law school before practicing with rough-and-tumble cases in Prohibition days. A lifelong Republican who campaigned for Italian American support, he got to the bench in Eisenhower's time and had risen to become U.S. District Court Chief Judge by virtue of his age, sixty-eight. A Conservative who believed in stern law and order, Sirica looked like Nixon's kind of judge. If his only distinction was his dismal record of reversals by the predominantly liberal Court of Appeals, Sirica scoffed that it didn't mean he was wrong. "It just means they've got the last word on you."

Even before the trial of *United States* v. *Liddy et al.* was properly under way, Sirica had suffered two extraordinary Watergate-connected reversals. The first was when he ordered a *Los Angeles Times* journalist to jail for refusing to surrender the tape of the Baldwin interview. The appeals court ordered his release within two hours. The second reversal came when the American Civil Liberties Union intervened as a third party on behalf of Spencer Oliver of the DNC to argue that it would be illegal for the prosecution to make public use in the trial of the contents of his bugged Watergate office conversations. Sirica sided with the prosecutors but suspended proceedings pending appeal and was immediately reversed. The bugged conversations could not be introduced as evidence and to this day their "explicitly intimate" contents may not be publicly divulged.

But Judge Sirica had another judicial propensity: He handed down heavy sentences, the maximum provided by statute, whence the nickname "Maximum John." Unwisely, the Watergate defense lawyers counted too much on his reversal record, hoping he would make so many mistakes that they could overturn the convictions on appeal. In so doing they forgot his way of using draconian sentences as a form of intimidation.

Sirica had indicated before Christmas at a pretrial hearing what he expected. He put the prosecutors on notice they had to get to the bottom of who had hired the men to go into the Watergate. "The jury is going to want to know," Sirica said, rattling off the questions: What did these men go into that headquarters for? Was their sole purpose political espionage? Were they paid? Was there financial gain? Who hired them? Who started this?

As the trial got started, Sirica was dissatisfied with the lack of answers. Jack Anderson had reported pressures on the defendants to get them to change their pleas to guilty. After Hunt's switch, Barker realized that they had no defense; the four Miami men, with misgivings, agreed to plead guilty. Before they could do so, a sensational hush money story broke in *The New York Times*. The Cuban Americans reportedly said they were on "salary"; Sturgis had a book coming; a $900,000 fund at CRP was mentioned; and their chain of command was supposedly Barker-Hunt-Liddy-Colson-Mitchell. This was the biggest cat out of the bag yet. There were flat denials by CRP, Colson, and Mitchell. Sirica listened, frustrated, as one of the prosecutors stated how the defendants had been asked about the news stories and had denied them. When the Miami men pleaded guilty, Sirica sent the jury out and himself questioned them aggressively. He, too, got nowhere. And when Barker told him he had received the serially numbered hundred-dollar bills "in the mail in a blank envelope," Sirica retorted, "I'm sorry. I don't believe you." Nonetheless, the judge had no choice but to accept the changed pleas.

Sirica indicated his growing discontent with the prosecutors. He thought their questioning too soft and occasionally took over. Sirica (wrongly) praised Magruder and (wrongly) berated Sloan as witnesses. But his unusual tactics, which in other circumstances would have raised the hackles of the civil libertarians, eventually contributed to cracking the case. He expressed incredulity when the Cubans, like Hunt, insisted they knew of no one else involved. And on January 30, when the jury found Liddy and McCord guilty, the judge castigated the prosecutors, saying: "I have not been satisfied, and I am still not satisfied that all the pertinent facts that might be available—I say *might* be available—have been produced before an American jury."[28]

The prosecutors, despite basing their whole case on the story that Liddy had been off on his own, have always claimed that they had a strategy to crack the case later. Earl Silbert, the lead prosecutor, explains it this way. No initial offers of leniency in exchange for cooperating with the prosecution had worked. The prosecutors figured, however, that one defendant—McCord—might crack at the prospect of imprisonment and tried getting him to accept a single-count guilty plea. Again rebuffed, their fallback plan was to get convictions and then have the judge compel the burglars to spill all by granting them immunity from further prosecution, on pain of contempt sentences.

There is reason to doubt the strategy would have worked. Liddy, along with the others, was granted immunity but refused to testify either before the grand jury or Congress. He got additional sentences for contempt and stayed in jail until the end without talking. Dean had promised Haldeman that all the defendants would similarly stonewall —"all will sit mute"—and if immunized would continue to do so, despite contempt charges.[29] That McCord eventually cracked was no thanks to Silbert's strategy. The harsh fact was, as Silbert still pleads, that he (and his boss, Petersen) simply could not imagine the obstruction of justice that Mitchell, Dean, and Magruder had pulled off under their noses.[30]

Judge Sirica deliberately let the defendants stew, saying he would weigh his sentences for a few weeks and decide then, based on any indication of cooperation by the convicted with the Senate investigation. Sirica stated:

> Everyone knows that there's going to be a congressional investigation in this case. I would frankly hope, not only as a judge but as a citizen of a great country and one of millions of Americans who are looking for certain answers, I would hope that the Senate committee is granted the power by Congress by a broad enough resolution to try to get to the bottom of what happened in this case.[31]

It was the prospect of the Senate investigation that was Nixon's main Watergate preoccupation in early 1973. The president, as he never tired telling his associates, had made his name as a member of a sensational congressional committee investigating American Communists, most notably Alger Hiss in 1948. Nixon was proud of having caught Hiss in perjury. But discussing Mitchell's Watergate testimony with Colson, Nixon said, "Perjury, that's a damned hard rap to prove."[32] Yet he knew better than most the political and criminal perils of sworn testimony taken before television cameras.

Democrats in Congress were raring for retribution. Already in early January, both House and Senate Democratic caucuses had, as he feared, voted to cut off funds for further military action in Vietnam. The president knew he could expect little mercy and spent hours discussing ways of dealing with the sideshow that could ruin his second term. Yet when the time came, the White House was curiously unprepared. They had counted on their friend, Mississippi Senator James Eastland, chairman of the Senate Judiciary Committee, to keep an eye on the staff investigation being continued by Senator Kennedy's Judiciary subcommittee. On November 22, Ehrlichman noted that any "hearings can make martyrs out of Admin people."[33]

But Eastland had apparently not told Nixon about the letter he got from Senator Mansfield in November proposing a full-scale investigation of Watergate. Mansfield's suggestion of Sam Ervin, a southern Democrat palatable to conservatives, to chair a Select Committee instead of, say, Teddy Kennedy was shrewd. When Mansfield released his letter on January 6, just before the trial, Nixon and Colson immediately saw it as a device for taking "Teddy off the hook."

A month later, all White House efforts to ensure equality in Democrat-Republican membership and in staff numbers on the unstoppable Senate investigation had failed. The Senate voted unanimously 77–0 to set it up on the basis the Democrats wanted—a 4–3 Democratic majority among committee members and even greater Democratic repre sentation on the staff. The Senate Select Committee on Presidential Campaign Activities was formed—forever after known as the Watergate or Ervin Committee, after its chairman.

It was to be three months before public hearings started, but Nixon sensed he had to counterattack to contain the damage. His first move was to order a planning session the weekend following the February Senate vote. Haldeman, Ehrlichman, Dean, and the special counsel to the president, PR adviser Richard Moore, first met in Ehrlichman's office at the San Clemente compound, then moved to Haldeman's rented cottage at Rancho la Costa, a resort complex down the coast and much favored by the Nixon set. Fourteen hours of game planning ensued. The result, Haldeman's notes reveal, was a stratagem more than a strategy: "public posture of full cooperation but privately attempt to restrain." The big effort was aimed at preventing White House witnesses from appearing.

Echoing the president, Ehrlichman asked the bottom-line question: Would the seven defendants remain silent right through the year scheduled for the Senate investigation? Dean reported that, despite continuing payments by LaRue, there were new demands for hush money as the men prepared to go to jail. Dean and LaRue had asked Herbert Kalmbach to get back in the fund-raising business but he had declined. Now they dispatched Moore from La Costa to visit Mitchell in New York to see about raising more. Mitchell's reply, considering the stakes, was surprising. "Tell them to get lost" was the message he gave Moore for Ehrlichman and Haldeman.

The presidential party flew back from California with little settled.

Instead of securing the long-term future of the hush money, they focused on the political repercussions of the Senate hearings, which, characteristically, they saw in public relations terms. The core White House tactic would be to shelter the president's men under the cloak of executive privilege. They would consider answering written interrogatories but they would refuse to appear at hearings, arguing that the traditional confidentiality of the president's dealings with them within the executive branch of government could not be overridden by another branch—not the legislative, in Congress, or the judicial, in the courts. Much would be heard of this doctrine over the next two years.

Nixon turned his attention to securing a scapegoat—a big-name fall guy. Outside the White House, there was really only one candidate: John Mitchell, with Magruder as running mate. In the week of February 13, White House tapes indicate how Nixon was already considering how far big name surgery might have to go. Hunt was linked, through the Plumbers, to Ehrlichman, and Colson; Magruder and Strachan linked Watergate to Haldeman. It was impossible to avoid seeing how close the "problems" were to his own person.

That same week, Charles Colson was leaving the White House to take up his private law practice half a block down Pennsylvania Avenue. Nixon intended Colson to continue to be his hatchet man, and, as Haldeman later explained, he was quickly appointed an unpaid White House consultant so that he, too, was covered by executive privilege and protected from testifying to Congress.[34] "Colson can be more valuable out than in," Nixon is heard saying.

Colson proceeded to advise. The tapes have him telling Nixon that if he believed the Senate hearings would reveal who ordered Watergate, then he should preempt, "let it out" into the public record. Nixon immediately acknowledges that Colson means Mitchell and that Mitchell would perjure himself rather than admit his responsibility, as Magruder has already perjured himself. This is the first evidence, postelection, that Nixon was considering having Mitchell step forward. Ever since June, he had been deeply troubled by Mitchell's culpability, even while admiring his ability to stonewall. But now he conjures with a statement Mitchell might volunteer that the break-in did get authorized at CRP: "This must have occurred. I did not realize it at the time. I was busy at the time." Colson chimes in, "Yeah. John has got one of those marvelous memories that 'I don't know, I don't remember what was said.' "[35] "Great stone face," Nixon commented later.

Though these Nixon-Colson conversations come to no conclusion about what the White House should do, they are revelatory about the president's concerns. Would Hunt crack despite the offer of clemency? Nixon says that if Judge Sirica calls Hunt in, "my view is that he would limit the losses. He wouldn't go all the way" and implicate Mitchell. Nor would he talk of Plumbers matters and so finger Ehrlichman and Colson. Colson omits mentioning his own call to Magruder to get the Liddy plan approved. Finally, attempting to cheer Nixon up, Colson is heard assuring him that the country at large "doesn't give a damn" about Watergate. The POWs have been coming back from North Vietnam to an emotional welcome. Colson tells Nixon, "Everyone I've talked to has said, 'Congratulate the president on the prisoners.' . . . The impact of that is, is the equivalent of a thousand Watergates."[36]

In advance of the Senate hearings, the president, understandably, moved to try to secure the allegiance of the Republican vice chairman of the committee, Senator Howard Baker of Tennessee. The White House intended to have its way with Baker as it had with the FBI's Pat Gray. But Baker, though solidly Republican, was wary of any overt identification with the White House. Before Haldeman and Dean could arrange to have him employ the dour partisan they wanted as the committee's minority staff counsel, Fred Buzhardt (later Nixon's Watergate counsel), Baker had picked his young protégé, Fred Thompson.

Baker managed another rare feat: a completely secret meeting with the president at the White House on February 22. It is unrecorded in the president's supposedly infallible official diary.[37] And no tape of it has been released by the National Archives. What we know about it comes from the tape of a meeting with Ehrlichman next day at which the president gives a rundown. Baker is "on our side—no question about that." Baker feels the way the hearings would "work bad," Nixon says, "would be to call a lot of pipsqueak witnesses, little, little shitasses over periods of weeks to build it up, and then build up the pressure to call" Colson, Haldeman, and Ehrlichman. This, in fact, was the strategy being pursued by Ervin's majority staff.

Baker suggested reversing the order. Call all the big fish in to testify first, as if to say, "What's all this shuffling? The question is whether or not it goes higher." In the president's words, "Prick the boil and then from then on everybody's going to be bored to death."

Nixon is attracted by the idea, except that he worries about getting Haldeman and Colson "in the public domain and going for perjury." He says he suggested that Ervin come down to the White House with the committee counsel and take testimony in private, but Baker would not consider it. If all negotiations over White House witnesses fail, Ehrlichman says, let the big men go and testify, "let it all hang out"—he means brazen it out and "saturate them." Baker would then move to wind up the hearings in a couple of months. Agreeing, the president says, "That's the Baker intent." The problem was, of course, that Baker was in no position to deliver such favors.[38]

While he schemed to defy, deflate, or defeat the Ervin investigation, Nixon fretted over the waiting, and wanted, characteristically, to retaliate first. In February, he unnecessarily pushed a self-destruct button. He had deferred until after the election appointing a permanent successor to the late J. Edgar Hoover. Now he decided after all to nominate Pat Gray for the post of FBI director. For the very first time, the FBI nomination would be subject to Senate confirmation, and therefore, to Senate hearings. Amazingly, Nixon had handed Congress a dagger with which to probe Gray's role in Watergate—months before Ervin and Baker were ready.

The president deliberately chose Gray because, he said, to select someone else would smack of running away. Also, as he told Ehrlichman, he liked the idea of having Gray "get up there and have them beat him over the head about Watergate, and have him say what the hell he's done." Nixon reckoned that Gray could deflect Watergate attention away from the White House to the FBI. But that was not the only reason for the choice.

Nixon picked Gray because he was the complete loyalist. The president did not think he was particularly smart. In fact, Nixon had considered placing him in several other jobs, from the NATO and Bonn ambassadorships to federal appeals court judge. But Gray's loyalty at the heart of the Watergate investigation meant, as Colson suggested in supporting the nomination, that they could fix him up with a couple of assistants to protect the cover-up. "The most important thing over there is to be goddamn sure that the Department [of Justice] and the Bureau understand that we've got enough problems with the Hill without creating any more for ourselves." Says Nixon, "Oh God, I wish we had, I wish we had more of Pat Grays."[39]

Before Nixon calls Gray to the Oval Office, Ehrlichman reminds the president of Gray's Watergate "guilty knowledge." The contents of Hunt's safe had been turned over to him the previous June by Ehrlichman and Dean. Ehrlichman later swore that he never even intimated to Gray that these materials should be destroyed. Yet here, on tape, he can be heard telling Nixon that he had told Gray, "I don't care what you do with it so long as it never appears." Nixon, remembering Hunt's operation against Ellsberg's psychiatrist, worries that these are the incriminating materials: "What is this? Stuff that Hunt did on that case in California?" Ehrlichman says it is other, Colson-related stuff. And when Nixon asserts, "I don't want to get into that" with Gray or, indeed, anyone, Ehrlichman remarks, "I want you to know about it." Never mind deniability, Nixon has got to be given a rundown, perhaps by Dean, on "the kinds of things that are liable to come smoking up," during the Ervin hearings. In view of what Gray knew, John Dean later wrote, "We couldn't afford an angry Pat Gray loose on the streets."[40]

Gray, therefore, needed to be given marching orders. The tape of Nixon's interview with his prospective FBI chief is one of the more chilling records to have come out of the White House. The pliant Gray believes he has done a good job in raising low-level FBI morale, and he flatters himself into thinking he can handle the Congress and the press. He is totally unprepared for the president's harshness. He is now to be more than a loyalist; he is to become the president's tool.

Nixon suddenly demands to know whether Gray has followed through a "directive" to have everyone in the FBI take a lie-detector test over the 1968 bugging of the Nixon campaign plane, which the president claims Hoover told him LBJ ordered. Gray responds that there was no such directive given. "Well, it's given now" retorts Nixon, adding that even a retired number-two man at the FBI, Cartha DeLoach, and his successor, Mark Felt, should also be ordered to take lie-detector tests. It is clearly "off with their heads" time, as Ehrlichman, who is present, chimes in that the White House has tried to set traps for Felt whom they suspect of leaking to *Time* magazine.

To Gray, a sometime Navy submarine captain, Nixon says beguilingly that he wants a relationship with the FBI director like the one he enjoys with the chairman of the Joint Chiefs of Staff. That is, he wants to bypass the Cabinet officer, the nominal superior who should be the intermediary. "With the bureau, it's the president that's the director, not that you have the attorney general as director." They can only have a relationship of trust, however, if Gray restores total discipline in the FBI, which means stopping leaks to the press like those currently plaguing Nixon over Watergate.

Gray must do whatever it takes. "They've got to fear the man at the top. . . . You've got to be brutal," and Nixon adds:

> *Nixon:* If it leaks out of the bureau, then the whole damn place ought to be fired. . . . The Germans, if they went through these towns and then one of their soldiers, a sniper hit one of them, they'd line up the whole goddamned town and say, 'Until you talk you're all getting shot.' I really think that has to be done. I mean, I don't think you can be Mr. Nice Guy over there.

In partisan political matters, Nixon spells out to Gray that he has got to know from him what is going on in a way that is deniable. "I gotta have a relationship here where you go out and do something and deny on a stack of Bibles."

The Senate confirmation hearings are going to be bloody, and if Gray gets confirmed he'll probably be thrown out at the end of Nixon's term. But, meanwhile, "let's do some good for the country. As you know, I would never ask the director of the bureau to do anything that was wrong." But to protect security from this "treasonable" bureaucracy, Nixon says, "we have got to get them, break them."

Then with some imprudence, in light of what was to follow, Nixon concluded his homily to Gray by suggesting at his confirmation hearings, "As far as the Watergate, I'd rather throw it all out there and not be defensive." Gray's parting accolade to the president: "Nixon loyalist . . . you're goddamn right I am."[41]

Only twelve days later, Gray started unintentionally pulling down the pillars of Nixon's temple. Just as John Mitchell had warned they would be, his confirmation hearings were a preview of Watergate. Proud of the FBI's investigation, Gray first basked in the endorsements of his home-state senators from Connecticut. One of them, a member of the Ervin Committee, Lowell Weicker, would later regret gushing that Gray was "a man of absolute integrity."

Gray then astonished the senators by saying they could have access to the FBI Watergate investigation. That offer was promptly countermanded by Attorney General Richard Kleindienst. But Gray, perhaps taking too literally the president's pep talk, unleashed a devastating disclosure. Gray told the Senate Judiciary Committee on February 28 that John Dean had, from the outset, full access to the FBI Watergate investigation; that he (Gray) had frequently discussed the progress of the investigation with the White House; and that he had allowed Dean to sit in on the FBI interviews with Watergate suspects. Overnight, Gray had propelled the almost totally unknown president's counsel into the Watergate limelight.

One of the committee Democrats suggested that Dean be summoned to testify. On March 2, in a press conference, President Nixon said no, invoking what was to become the increasingly controversial doctrine of executive privilege. "No president could ever agree to allow the counsel to the president to go down and testify before a committee."

Earlier and more hastily than they had intended, Nixon was making decisions about just which White House staff might be permitted to testify on Watergate. With Gray's revelations about Dean, Nixon's intended ally on the Ervin Committee, Senator Baker, could no longer hold the earlier line of a quick hearing with the top witnesses. Gray, so avidly instructed in ruthlessness, was secretly abandoned by the president. A few days later, Ehrlichman, in another famous phrase, told Dean, "Let him hang there; let him twist slowly, slowly in the wind." The nomination went on hold; Gray was a political corpse.[42]

Dean himself, who had not met Nixon since a ride on Air Force One in November, was now told to report to the president directly on Watergate without going through Haldeman or Ehrlichman. Nixon at the time was delighted; his diary recorded:

> I am very impressed by him. He has shown enormous strength, great intelligence and great subtlety. . . . I am glad that I am talking to Dean now rather than going through Haldeman or Ehrlichman. I think I have made a mistake in going through others when there is a man with the capability of Dean I can talk to directly.[43]

Within a month Nixon completely reversed that opinion, realizing that his direct line to Dean was a second self-destruct button.

CHAPTER 10

"I'm Not Gonna Let Anybody Go to Jail"

John Dean's new intimacy with the president was Nixon's Ides of March. It was not so quick as Casca's thrust at Caesar but ultimately it was fatal. Because of Dean, the secret of Nixon's tapes was uncovered; because of Dean, the president was publicly and irrevocably tied to Watergate. Dean's word was placed against the president's; and when the cover-up's manager turned informer, his word turned out to be truer and more believed.

Yet Dean was not the instigator of this extraordinary reversal in the president's fortune. Nixon knew, probably better even than Dean, that the roof over the cover-up was rotten; he certainly knew far more than he pretended to know. Dean's distinction was that within a month of starting regular meetings with the president, he had a clearer sense of what was going wrong, and a sharper awareness of the need for self-preservation.

The force that was to break the scandal open in March was the same one that had caused anxiety since Christmas—whether the Watergate team would keep silence. Clemency, pardons, quashing, parole, more money—all had been secretly talked of with the president, and with Haldeman, Ehrlichman, Mitchell, Colson, and Dean. Even Attorney General Kleindienst had been sounded out on leniency.

Nobody, however, had really followed through. Instead, the president had switched his attention to ways of handling the coming Senate investigation. Nixon seemed obsessed only with the question of who could be tied to the initial Watergate break-in; he gave almost no attention to the "post-activities," the subsequent actions by his men in the cover-up, because he knew they were all up to their necks in it. Nixon's tactics consisted of no more than drawing the wagons around the White House, which, of course, meant abandoning those outside to the marauding Indians. The CRP faction led by Mitchell and Magruder would be sacrificed, gently if possible. The White House would be preserved by a cover-up of the cover-up.

Before Pat Gray's feckless revelations to the Senate Judiciary Committee, the president was developing the scenario of having Mitchell step forward. With Ehrlichman, before beginning his meetings with Dean, Nixon continues discussing Mitchell's as well as Colson's and Haldeman's involvement. He admits that "the public . . . gonna believe the worst probably of me, about Bob and maybe about Colson." But there are limits to the sacrifices he will demand of Mitchell and others. Holding out the promise of clemency, Nixon declares, "I'm not gonna let anybody go to jail. That I promise you." He says he has to know whether or not Colson and Haldeman knew about the Watergate bugging—as well as Mitchell—and "then I'll deny that I ever heard it." Nixon makes no mention in his memoirs of these February conversations. Simply in terms of timing, they are highly damaging in view of his insistence that it was only when Dean briefed him that he realized the full extent of the cover-up

Ehrlichman says Mitchell is "going to end up being the fall guy" over the CRP money authorized for Liddy's plan. Mitchell, he tells Nixon, has been saying, " '*You* guys got a problem,' and we're beginning to get to him a little bit. Dean's been hammering away on him to impress on him that *he's* got a problem." He adds: "I think he knew and I think LaRue was sort of his agent and kept him posted. . . . LaRue's in this thing up to his ass."

The talk is of liabilities. Ehrlichman maintains of himself that "I don't have the problém," even with Hunt. But Haldeman has "constructive knowledge of Watergate" through his liaison man with CRP, Gordon Strachan. Ehrlichman suggests Haldeman perhaps never knew that the information Strachan was passing him came from "tapped sources" (which at this time all the president's men believed), but Nixon is well aware of Strachan's function with Haldeman. "Information changer," he calls him on February 23.[1] (In his memoirs, Nixon makes much of being "stunned" on March 13 when Dean tells him Strachan knew about the Watergate bugging.)

As for Colson, while Ehrlichman recognizes that Nixon believes his hatchet man's denials of involvement in the actual bugging, he points out to the president that from his telephone call to Magruder urging the Liddy plan be approved "Colson probably was the sufficient cause of Magruder doing this tap work" at Watergate. What Ehrlichman calls "diligent counsel" could put a circumstantial case together against Colson.[2]

That same day, Nixon had a rare meeting with Attorney General Kleindienst. Nixon suggests that Mitchell has the greatest responsibility, he must have known about "these activities"—the bugging—even though he has denied them. The president's line, the one he had taken with Senator Baker and the one he suggests Kleindienst take, goes like this:

Nixon: John Mitchell's a pure bright guy who would never have done such a thing, that the kids ran away with it. And if John did lie it was simply because he'd forgotten. Now, whether that will wash or not I don't know . . . but I can't have John run the possibility of a charge of perjury. You know. . .

Kleindienst: I couldn't have said it any better. That should get him out of it.

It should be noted that this is a conversation with the nation's chief law officer, the man who would have the final say over a grand jury's decision to bring a charge of perjury. In the same conversation Kleindienst discloses that he knows Ehrlichman has worked with Hunt, and Krogh, on the Pentagon Papers and that "Magruder has the same problem Mitchell has," although Kleindienst does not think Magruder will turn on Haldeman or Mitchell. About the only thing that surprises

Kleindienst is Nixon's story of Hoover's telling him that Johnson had the FBI bug Nixon's 1968 campaign. Kleindienst reckons—mistakenly—that if in public relations terms they can take that story and "really turn it into something . . . it might be the thing, the thing that'll save us."

Nixon believes the thing that might save them is Mitchell, but here he fails in his cardinal request to Kleindienst.

> *Nixon:* I think sometime you've got to talk to Mitchell.
> *Kleindienst:* I've got to talk to Mitchell? You mean about the Watergate business?
> *Nixon:* Well, either that or you talk to Baker, and Baker's gotta talk to him, but—
> *Kleindienst:* Yeah—
> *Nixon:* but—
> *Kleindienst:* I don't think I'd want to talk to him.[3]

Kleindienst was at least wise in this. As a lawyer, he recognized the attempt to make him a direct party to the conspiracy. It did not help him much. Despite agreeing to Nixon's request to stay on as "their" attorney general rather than join John Connally's plush private law firm, Kleindienst would be cruelly used by Nixon only two months later.

There is no evidence that Baker approached Mitchell. Nixon could have done so himself and, as we shall see later, might well have convinced Mitchell to step forward. But Nixon put it off. His more immediate determination was to prevent a "circus" at the Ervin hearings. Nixon knew from his secret February meeting with Baker that however much he huffed, he could not pretend to be cooperating and still resist having his top men testify. His last resort was to demand there be no televising of their appearances: "Three of the president's chief assistants up there like criminals. That's what I'm not going to allow, and that's just final."[4]

The big news story as Nixon began meeting Dean was the leak of one of the dirty secrets from Nixon's first term, the so-called Kissinger taps of the telephones of newsmen and government officials.[5] Someone at the FBI had apparently given the story to *Time* magazine, and Nixon was keen for Dean to discover who. Was it Sullivan—Hoover's former number two who had transferred the wiretap logs to the White House? Not so, said Dean, at this first, February 27, meeting. Was it the present FBI number two, Mark Felt, whom Nixon deeply suspected? Dean relayed Felt's cool denial but agreed he was too close to Pat Gray "for our interests."

But Nixon seemed blithely unaware of the story's impact in making his own scandal cumulative. Instead, he was still determined to have people see how much less wiretapping had been done under his administration, compared to Kennedy's and Johnson's. LBJ even believed Bobby Kennedy bugged him, Nixon says.[6] "We were as limited as hell, I mean, Hoover, good God, we could have used him forever. . . . But Johnson had just apparently used him all the time for this sort of thing . . . used the FBI as his own private patrol." And, of course, Nixon wants Dean to get the dirt on LBJ's supposed 1968 bugging of the Nixon campaign plane.

The most striking aspect of this meeting is how familiar both Nixon and Dean are with each other, and with the material, considering this is their first office meeting in five months. Nixon of course is well aware of how Dean has been the lead man on Watergate; Dean, by turns obsequious and imbued with the Ehrlichman contempt for outsiders, is keen to make a hard-line impression.

Told by Nixon that Mitchell "is the fellow who's going to get hurt most out of this," Dean impresses Nixon with the claim that he has "braced" Kleindienst—a Nixonite term meaning to fix a Congressman, official, or Cabinet member to ensure they put the White House's interest first, and last. Thus Dean claimed to have "braced" the attorney general over the past months on the potential problems to the White House from what the FBI and the prosecutors were doing, and what the trial meant. And, more significantly, he had told Kleindienst that if he saw him "going down the wrong track, I'm going to have tell you why." And Dean commends to Nixon Henry Petersen, Kleindienst's deputy in charge of prosecutions. "Bless his soul; he's a valuable man to us."

The meeting ends with a key point Dean has been trying to sell for months to Haldeman. White House witnesses called before the Ervin committee would, Dean proposes, provide only "written interrogatories," given on oath, somewhat like written depositions. Dean's purpose is to help the president—and, not coincidentally, himself.

As we have seen, Dean had been under intermittent pressure to write a cosmetic report stating there was no White House involvement in Watergate. He had stalled, suspecting that if ever White House involvement was uncovered, the president might produce the report and lament that Dean had misinformed him. Written interrogatories would get Dean off the hook, because those swearing to them—not Dean—would be personally responsible for whatever they said.[7]

For all his self-assurance, Dean—like the president—was clearly caught out the next day by Pat Gray at his confirmation hearings. Dean assures Nixon that "Pat is tough . . . he's ready. He's very comfortable in all of the decisions he has made, and I think he'll be good." Nixon observes sardonically that everyone comments how Gray is his crony yet "I have never seen him socially." To impress Dean, he adds, "Edgar Hoover, on the other hand, I have seen socially at least a hundred times." The thought prompts Dean to reflect how much better off they would have been had Hoover lived. Nixon adds longingly, "He'd have scared them to death, he's got files on everybody, goddamn it." Within hours it is Gray who is scaring the White House.

Dean, unaware of Gray's testimony at this point, discusses Senator Ervin and offers Nixon a surprisingly upbeat assessment of the way the hearings will pan out. They "are going to be hot, and I think they're going to be tough. I think they are going to be gory in some regards." But he is ultimately confident:

Dean: I had thought it was an impossible task, to hold together until after the election until things just—

Nixon: Yeah.

Dean: —started squirting out, but we've made it this far and I'm convinced we're going to make it the whole road and put this thing in, in the funny pages of the history books rather than anything serious. We've got to. It's got to be that way.

Nixon: Would it—it'll be somewhat serious but the main thing, of course, is also the, the isolation of the presidency from this.

Dean: Absolutely.

Nixon: Because it's, because that fortunately is totally true.

Dean: I know that, sir.

Here Dean is as ignorant of how much the president really knows as he is of imminent threats to the cover-up. But this is a good instance of Nixon's creating a record of noninvolvement that might be useful later (much like Colson had done in taping his conversation with Hunt). Repeatedly over the coming weeks, Nixon would be suggesting to his topmost advisers how surprised he was to be learning things they were often aware he already knew.

Suddenly, Nixon remembers Sirica's delay in sentencing "our people," six of whom (except Hunt, who made bond) have been in jail since the end of the trial, and very perceptively asks, "He's trying to work on them to break them, is he?" Nixon tells Dean to "follow these characters to their Gethsemane," and remarks, "I feel for those poor guys . . . particularly Hunt." Told by Dean that "they're hanging in tough right now," Nixon now consults his counsel on clemency. "You couldn't do it, say, in six months?" This—after Haldeman, Ehrlichman, and Colson—is Nixon's fourth substantiated discussion about using his unique presidential power to have the Watergate seven circumvent the wrath of Judge Sirica. Dean clearly is amazed and advises the president to await the outcome of the appeals launched by McCord and Liddy.

Three weeks remained before sentencing, time enough for Nixon and his aides to establish with absolute certainty which of the men was most vulnerable to Sirica's intimidation and to arrange whatever promises and money were required to preserve silence. But with Dean's assurance of "they're hanging in tough," matters were allowed to slide.

Dean reports that Senate investigators are going after the president's personal attorney, Herbert Kalmbach, with a vengeance. They have subpoenaed his records "and he's got records that run all over hell's acre on things for the last few years." Nixon asks nervously, "They can't get his records with regard to his private transactions?" Dean reassures him: "Anything to do with San Clemente and the like" is "out of bounds." Kalmbach is "hunkered down and he's ready to handle it."

As the session concludes with a discussion of Mitchell's vulnerability, Nixon adds that the Ervin Committee is also after his top White House lieutenants. "Or possibly Dean," says his counsel, for the first time adding himself to the Senate's hit list. Nixon, in passing, rejects the very idea. "I think they realize you are the lawyer and they know you didn't have a goddamn thing to do with, with the campaign."[8]

By the next morning, March 1, despite Gray's bombshell testimony naming Dean the previous day, Nixon still seems not to have realized his young counsel's new vulnerability. Dean turns up at 9:18 A.M. to explain: Gray is "giving the little store away," and the president curses, "For Christ's sake, he must be out of his mind . . . is he a little dumb?" Dean agrees, "Little bullheaded." Nixon, the expert poker player, observes: "There's too much bravado there. He's a big strong navy guy, you know; everything's great, boy, let's go, ya ya ya. A guy that has that much outward self-confidence doesn't have that much inward self-confidence." Already he regrets appointing him; within days he is saying he will drop him. Dean agrees contemptuously: "Not that Pat wouldn't want still to play ball, but he may not be able to." Dean follows with as near as one will ever get to the true story behind Gray's complaint to Nixon the previous July that some of his men would "mortally wound" the president. He and Ehrlichman, Dean tells Nixon, "had been leaning on Gray," telling him that instead of making speeches he "ought to sit on top of the investigation and keep an eye on it." So much for the president's claim he wanted Gray to pursue "your aggressive investigation."

Gray, Dean goes on, will retract the offers made to the Senate Judiciary Committee the day before. He will admit not having the authority to invite members of Congress to inspect the FBI's Watergate records. (Nixon: "What the hell, some of those congressmen are damn near under Communist discipline."[9]) Gray's offer to make available the FBI agents who investigated Watergate will also be countermanded.

Dean had made his mark with Nixon. When Kleindienst telephones during the conversation the president tells an assistant to say that he is in a meeting—with Prime Minister Golda Meir of Israel! And the next day, before he had completed his statement that executive privilege prevents White House men from giving congressional testimony in open hearings, the president announced off-the-cuff at a news conference that he would not allow Dean to testify in any congressional forum whatever. As the president's lawyer, Dean had double privilege, Nixon claimed, attorney-client as well as executive privilege.

All this—the Kissinger taps, Gray's revelations, the president's refusal on Dean—reawakened media interest, and the news stories put the White House increasingly into a defensive mode. The next story to break on March 3 was Dean's handling of the materials in Hunt's safe, and the fact that Hunt's notebooks were missing. Even now Dean told no one that he had secretly destroyed the notebooks; indeed, he lied flatly about the matter in a letter he drafted to the Senate Judiciary Committee chairman.

On March 8, *The Washington Post* made huge play of Kalmbach's payments to Segretti, the Nixon saboteur of the Democratic primaries. It was one of the stories the White House had denied the previous October, and it came out thanks to Gray, as did the fact that Gray stated at his hearings that he had passed FBI Watergate documents no fewer than eighty-three times to Dean during the investigation. By March 8, Gray was bringing Ehrlichman's name into the hearings, mentioning five phone calls and two meetings during the same period. Ehrlichman was soon brusquely telephoning Gray—had the senators asked who initiated the phone calls? From the White House point of view, Gray was a walking, talking disaster.

Nixon's response was to suggest they plant questions with Republican senators asking Gray about the FBI's supposed 1968 bugging of his campaign, but Dean, despite having passed them to a Republican trusty, could give no guarantee they would get any press play. Instead, he warned that this week of March 15, when a presidential news conference was scheduled, "will draw more Watergate questions than any other you're likely to see."

In the tape of their March 13 meeting there is a rare if guarded Nixon admission to Dean that he knew about campaign intelligence prior to the Watergate break-in.

Dean: . . . A lot of people around here had knowledge that something was going on over there. They didn't have any knowledge of the details of the specifics of, of the whole thing.

Nixon: You know, that must, must be an indication, though, of the fact that, that they had goddamn poor pickings. Because naturally anybody, either Chuck or Bob, was always reporting to me about what was going on. If they ever got any information they would certainly have told me that we got some information, but they never had a goddamn [laughs] thing to report. What was the matter? Did they never get anything out of the damn thing?

Dean: No, I don't think they ever got anything.

Nixon: It was a dry hole, huh?

Dean: That's right.

Nixon: Jesus Christ.

Dean: Well, they were just really getting started.

Nixon: Yeah, yeah. But Bob one time said something about the fact we got some information about this or that or the other but I, I think, it was about the convention, what they were planning, I said [unintelligible].

Nixon exclaims over the break-in team's lack of a cutout: "To think that Mitchell and Bob would have allowed this kind of an operation to be in the committee." Dean explains that they did not know Liddy would use McCord inside Watergate—and then uncomfortably reminds the president that Dean's own name is being dragged in as the man who originally sent Liddy to CRP.

Nixon and Dean now play out the pros and cons of stonewall versus hang-out, the latter demonstrably not the full disclosure Nixon mythology pretends:

Nixon: I know Ehrlichman always felt that it should be hang-out [unintelligible].

Dean: Well, I think I convinced him why that he wouldn't want to hang out, either. There is a certain domino situation here. If some things start going, a lot of other things are going to start going, and there are going to be a lot of problems if everything starts falling. So there are dangers, Mr. President. I'd be less than candid if I didn't tell you the—there are. There's a reason for us not, not everyone going up and testifying.

Nixon: I see. Oh no, no, no, no no. I didn't mean go up and have them testifying. I meant—

Dean: Well, I mean just, they're just starting to hang out and say, here's our, here's our story—

Nixon: I mean putting the story out to PR buddies somewhere. Here's the story, the true story about Watergate [unintelligible].

Dean: They would never believe it. . . .[10]

But if not hang out, Nixon still wants Dean to produce a "report" or statement that he can offer to the Ervin Committee. Dean clings to his idea of sworn written interrogatories. As a lawyer, he notes, "you can handle written interrogatories where cross-examination is another ball game."

Nixon thinks that Haldeman is the higher-up the Ervin Committee is really after, and Mitchell, too, adds Dean. Dean argues that Haldeman's problem is "circumstantial," purely one of connections to others. He first assures Nixon that Dwight Chapin, the Haldeman man who, while presidential appointments secretary, hired Segretti, knows nothing about the Watergate break-in. Then they come to Gordon Strachan, and at this there is a great Nixon show of surprise. Dean does not know that Nixon had already been told by Ehrlichman, three weeks earlier, that Strachan had transmitted CRP's wiretapped information (as they thought) to Haldeman.

Nixon: He knew about Watergate? Strachan did?
Dean: Uh huh.
Nixon: I'll be damned. Well, that's the problem in Bob's case, isn't it? It's not Chapin, then, but Strachan because Strachan worked for him.

Dean again attempts reassurance, saying that Strachan is ultraloyal to Haldeman and has effectively stonewalled investigators. Nixon answers, "I guess he should, shouldn't he, in the interests of—Why? I suppose we can't call that justice, can you?"[11]

Repeatedly over these first two weeks of March, Dean feeds the president's optimism with foolish predictions. He says he is convinced the White House will make it through the Ervin hearings "with minimal hurt"; there is no reason to think things will "get out of hand"; the Gray hearings will be "turned around"; now "nothing really new is coming out"; the "public cannot take too much more of this stuff."

The men awaiting sentencing, Dean assures Nixon, are "hanging tough"; there is an "outside chance of a mistrial" because of Judge Sirica's conduct of the case. And wrongest of all, Dean tells the president that Sirica is probably going to be "very fair" with Hunt. Unlike Liddy, whose antics in court annoyed Sirica, Hunt has been pathetic and persuasive in his denial that no higher-ups were involved.[12]

In fact, Hunt was close to breaking point. Knowing, as Nixon apparently did not until too late, that sentencing was set for March 23, Hunt wanted his affairs in order. On March 16, Hunt asked CRP's lawyer, Paul O'Brien, to meet him. Hunt was brusque. The "commitments" were not being met. Before he went to jail, Hunt wanted his legal fees of $60,000 settled, plus two years' salary, a further $70,000—$130,000 in all, according to O'Brien. (Apparently, Hunt was anticipating clemency after two years in jail.) Hunt told O'Brien to pass the demand to Dean with the message that unless the funds were supplied by close of business on March 21, he might have to review his options. Hunt mentioned Ehrlichman in saying there were some "seamy" things he had done for the White House. O'Brien suggested that Hunt approach Colson. Hunt recalls O'Brien saying it was time Colson also got his feet wet.

Hunt did pass along a variant of his threat to Colson's law partner David Shapiro. If the commitments were met, no one in his "operation" would blow. Otherwise, after Hunt went to jail, his literary agent would put up for auction his book, to be entitled "Watergate." Hunt listed Mitchell, Krogh, and particularly Dean as among those who ought to be concerned by his potential testimony. Significantly, he told Shapiro that the one weak link among the defendants was McCord, who could well "open up." Hunt felt Colson's partner, who suggested he try an alternative channel via his own lawyer, had brushed him off. But Colson was informed and was deeply alarmed.[13]

There is conflict over when CRP lawyer O'Brien gave the message to Dean, but whenever it occurred, it was explosive.

"You're shitting me," Dean reports saying. "He sent that message to *me* . . . I'm out of the money business. Ever since that three-fifty went over, I'm out of it. And I plan to stay out of it. And Hunt can shove it up his ass!" Dean says he then rattled O'Brien, telling him, "Both of us, as you well know, are up to our teeth in an obstruction of justice." He told him to take Hunt's demand to Mitchell.[14] O'Brien's account backed up the anger, and quotes Dean as saying, "I am going to bust this goddamned thing up."[15]

Dean claims that on March 20 he relented in his refusal, and informed Ehrlichman, who said Hunt's demand was a matter for Mitchell or Colson. Dean phoned Mitchell in New York. Realizing that Martha might pick up an extension, he was indirect. "Is the Greek bearing gifts?" he asked, referring to the Greek American tycoon Tom Pappas who was a big contributor to Nixon campaigns. Mitchell said he would talk further the next day.

But Ehrlichman, while saying little to Dean, reacted sharply to the threat posed by Hunt. He phoned Krogh, then at the Department of Commerce, to warn him of what they perceived to be Hunt's blackmail. Ehrlichman, says Krogh, said that Mitchell was responsible for the "care and feeding" of Hunt.

Krogh came to see Dean. Dean told him the bad news—that the Justice Department had the pictures of Hunt and Liddy outside Ellsberg's psychiatrist's office and that they were bound to surface. According to Dean, when he asked Krogh how much Hunt could reveal about "seamy things," Krogh detonated another bomb. He said he didn't think Ehrlichman had known much beforehand about the Fielding break-in as such, then added: "That one came right out of the Oval Office, John." Dean says he sank back in his chair, and that he and Krogh parted as if they were leaving someone's death bed.[16]

On the evening of March 20, Nixon telephoned Dean at home. Dean, mentioning he had spoken to Ehrlichman that afternoon, says that the president and he must "examine the broadest, broadest implications of this whole thing . . . so that you operate from the same facts that everyone else has . . . the soft spots, the potential problems." When Dean wants time to get his notes together, it is the president who suggests no waiting, but to meet promptly the next morning, alone.

Nixon's personal diary noted that Dean, "according to Ehrlichman, had been a little bit discouraged today," and indicated the president's own growing nervousness. He notes that the Watergate break-in might never have come out but for the retaping being found by the guard: "That's one of the costs of trying to run a campaign and of having some well-intentioned but rather stupid or at least people with very poor judgment working for you." Yet "at the present time we are really caught here without knowing how to handle it."[17]

The tape of the March 21, 1973 meeting is second in importance only to the smoking gun tape of June 23, 1972. It was the first tape that the special Watergate prosecutor was to hear later that year after Nixon was forced to hand it over to Judge Sirica's court. When the prosecutors heard it, they concluded that Nixon was a coconspirator and advised him to retain a criminal lawyer.

The prelude to March 21 had been Nixon's preoccupation with the cosmetic statement on Watergate he wanted prepared by Dean, assisted by Richard Moore, Nixon's confidential adviser who had been sent from La Costa in February on the abortive fund-raising mission to Mitchell. The statement would be for possible release after Sirica's sentencing at the end of the week. The president knew that it would be the thinnest of veils, given what he had just been discussing. Haldeman had explained in detail the transfer of the $350,000 and its use as hush money. And Dean had told Nixon of his own presence at the GEMSTONE meetings with Mitchell, and he claimed to have complained to Haldeman about Liddy's bugging plans. "Well, you won't need to say in your statement the bugging, you could say that they were gonna engage in intelligence operations," Nixon advised.[18]

Nixon had already learned from Dean about the Liddy-Hunt photographs of their pre-Fielding break-in casing, which the CIA had handed over to the Justice Department. Nixon was upset by this, probably hearing about the CIA and the photos for the first time. He later claimed that March 17 was the first time he learned of the Fielding break-in itself—despite Ehrlichman's claim to have told him the previous summer.

Thus on March 21 the president was well aware of the hold Hunt had over the White House when Dean walked in at 10:12 A.M. for a meeting, scheduled for thirty minutes, that was to last almost two hours. It took Dean just over three minutes to get to his point: that the president doesn't know everything Dean knows. (In fact, the president knew all of it, and more, but he did not let on.) The day before, Richard Moore had suggested to Dean that the whole affair sounded like a cancer. Now Dean borrows the analogy, saying the cancer on the presidency is "being compounded."

THE PRESIDENT

Richard Milhous Nixon, the thirty-seventh president of the United States, in a photograph taken in 1969 during his first term in office. (*National Archives*)

THE PRESIDENT'S MEN

Spiro T. Agnew, twice elected vice president, was seen by Nixon as his insurance against impeachment. But Agnew was forced to resign in October 1973 rather than face trial on bribery charges. (*National Archives*)

John M. Mitchell, Nixon's closest political adviser, first attorney general and election campaign manager. Mitchell—as revealed for the first time in this book—offered to plead guilty if the Watergate prosecutors would cease their pursuit of Nixon. (*National Archives*)

In the Oval Office, the president consults with his most senior White House aides, H. R. (Bob) Haldeman (left) and John D. Ehrlichman. Nixon dismissed both men at the height of the Watergate scandal in a vain attempt to save himself. (*National Archives*)

General Alexander Haig (left) responded to Nixon's call to leave the army to replace Haldeman as White House chief of staff. Leonard C. Garment became White House counsel. (*Bettmann Archive*)

J. Fred Buzhardt served as Nixon's counsel during the final year of Watergate. He helped devise the disastrous "Stennis compromise" over access to Nixon's tapes, which led to the "Saturday Night Massacre." Despite suffering a heart attack, he continued with Nixon until the last, and died in 1978. (*National Archives*)

Egil (Bud) Krogh, below, the young Ehrlichman aide propelled into the heart of the Watergate conspiracy as the head of the so-called White House Plumbers. (*National Archives*)

At the time of his nomination to be head of the Federal Bureau of Investigation, L. Patrick Gray (here with his wife) is congratulated by the president. Gray, an ardent Nixon loyalist, unwittingly blew the lid off the Watergate cover-up during his nomination hearings, and had to resign when it was revealed that he had burned evidence entrusted to him. (*National Archives*)

Just before the Watergate arrests, Richard G. Kleindienst—flanked by his wife and the president—is sworn in as attorney general by Chief Justice Warren Burger. His resignation less than a year later was followed by a criminal conviction for failing to testify fully at a congressional hearing. (*National Archives*)

Herbert W. Kalmbach, Nixon's personal lawyer, performing as campaign fund-raiser *extraordinaire*, achieved a record of extracting large contributions from corporate contacts. He was put in charge of the initial hush money operation aimed at keeping the Watergate defendants quiet. (*Bettmann Archive*)

Anthony T. (Tony) Ulasewicz was an ex-NYPD cop whose Runyonesque tales of hush-money drops provided comic relief in the Senate Watergate hearings. Hired to act as Nixon's "private eye," he performed an array of interesting roles, from posing as a newsman after Chappaquiddick to casing burglary targets like the Brookings Institution. (*Bettmann Archive*)

Charles W. Colson, Nixon's political hatchet man, was indicted in both the Ellsberg and Watergate cases. His conversion as a born-again Christian led him to accept a guilty plea, the highest-ranking Nixon adviser to do so. But he never turned against the president. (*National Archives*)

One of the most loyal and toughest members of the Nixon "family" was Rose Mary Woods, his long-time secretary. Here she is seen reenacting her famous stretch, which she claimed "must have" caused the inadvertent erasure of part of the eighteen-minute gap in a key Watergate tape. She was never prosecuted. (*National Archives*)

THE BURGLARY

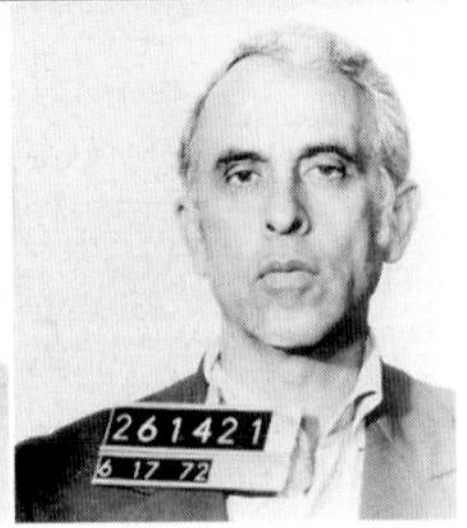

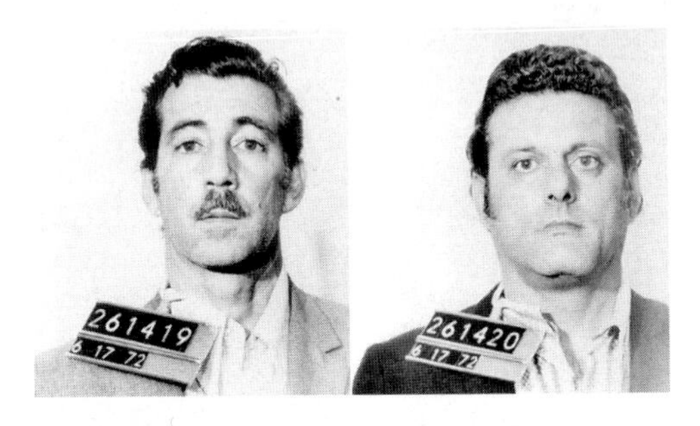

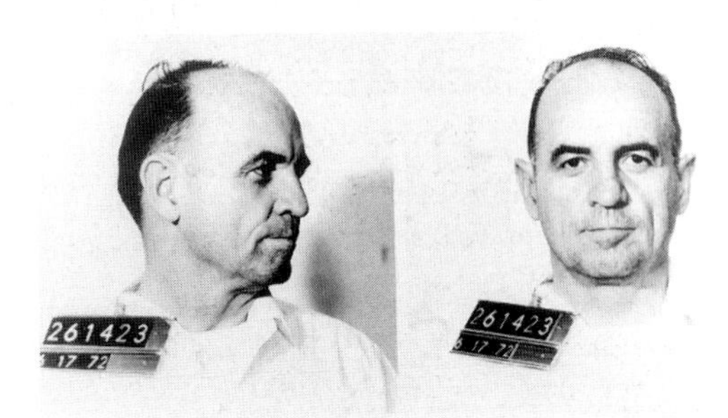

DC police identity shots of the men arrested at the Watergate break-in: top, Bernard Barker and E. Rolando Martinez; left, Virgilio R. Gonzalez and Frank A. Sturgis; left (in 1972) (*FBI Archives*) and below (testifying in 1973) James W. McCord, the ex-CIA man who ripped the cover-up wide open when he wrote a letter to the trial judge charging that higher-ups were involved. (*Bettmann Archive*)

E. Howard Hunt, right (today) (*Brian Lapping Associates*) and below (in 1972), was part of the Plumbers' Ellsberg break-in operation, and recruited the Miami team for Watergate. He had been a veteran CIA clandestine service officer. (*Bettmann Archive*)

G. Gordon Liddy, seen (above right) in 1972 (*Bettmann Archive*) and (above) today, in front of his gun collection, teamed with Hunt in the Plumbers' operations. He planned and led the Watergate break-in while employed as full-time counsel of the Nixon re-election committee, CRP. (*Brian Lapping Associates*)

THE MEN OF CRP

Jeb S. Magruder, in his CRP office (above right) (*National Archives*) and entering jail (above left), (*Bettmann Archive*) was the young Haldeman staffer put in charge of the re-election campaign until John Mitchell (below, with his wife Martha) took over. (*Bettmann Archive*)

Left, Fred LaRue, John Mitchell's closest lieutenant, was in on the cover-up from the outset. He took over distribution of hush money from Kalmbach. (*Bettmann Archive*)

THE INVESTIGATORS

Henry Petersen, as assistant attorney general in charge of prosecutions, decided to restrict the scope of indictments in the first Watergate case to those directly concerned with the break-in. He bitterly resented being taken off the case and replaced by an independent special prosecutor. (*Bettmann Archive*)

Elliot L. Richardson (below) was appointed by Nixon to be attorney general and then dismayed the president by selecting Archibald Cox (below left) to be the Watergate special prosecutor. (*Bettmann Archive*)

Cox's persistence in demanding Nixon's White House tapes infuriated the president, who demanded that Richardson fire him. The result was the so-called Saturday Night Massacre, when Cox, Richardson, and others all left office. (*Bettmann Archive*)

Leon Jaworski (left), the second special prosecutor, proved to be a Nixon nemesis. Jaworski authorized the grand jury to list the president as an "unindicted co-conspirator" and to submit the evidence they had examined to the House impeachment investigation. (*Bettmann Archive*)

Federal Chief Judge John Sirica, although famous for being reversed on appeal, came through in Watergate. His landmark rulings that the president must submit his tapes to the court were upheld by the D.C. Federal Court of Appeals and by the Supreme Court. Sirica also helped bust the cover-up by imposing maximum sentences on the original Watergate Seven, making leniency dependent on their cooperation with the Watergate committee. (*Bettmann Archive*)

ENDGAME

On October 19, 1973, Nixon meets with the leaders of the Senate Watergate committee in an effort to convince them that the "Stennis compromise" on access to the tapes was agreeable to all parties. It was not. From left; Charles Alan Wright, Nixon's constitutional law adviser; Senator Sam Ervin, committee chairman; Nixon; Senator Howard Baker, committee vice chairman; Al Haig, White House chief of staff. (*National Archives*)

John W. Dean (in a contemporary photo, above right) (*Brian Lapping Associates*) with his wife Maureen (above) during his week-long appearance before the Senate Watergate committee in June 1973. Dean's testimony was devastating, and also led directly to the disclosure of Nixon's private taping system. (*Bettmann Archive*)

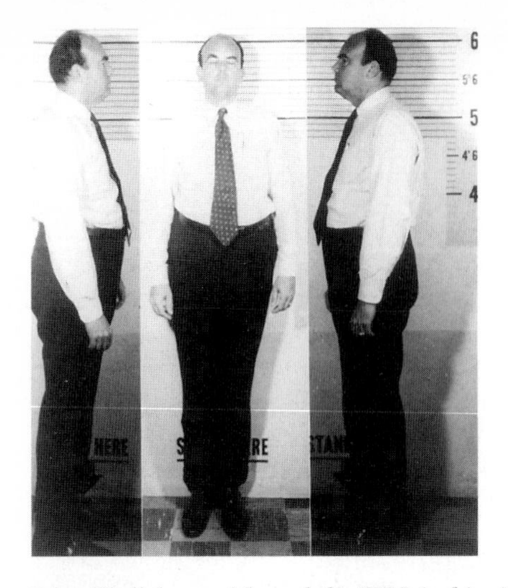

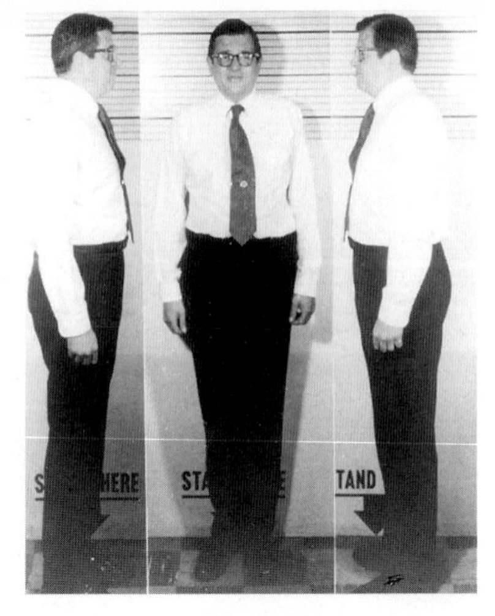

John Ehrlichman (above left) (*FBI Archives*) and Charles Colson (above right) in their FBI identity photos taken at the time of their indictment in 1974. (*FBI Archives*) Right, John Mitchell poses for FBI identity photos after his indictment in 1974 for obstructing justice. (*FBI Archives*)

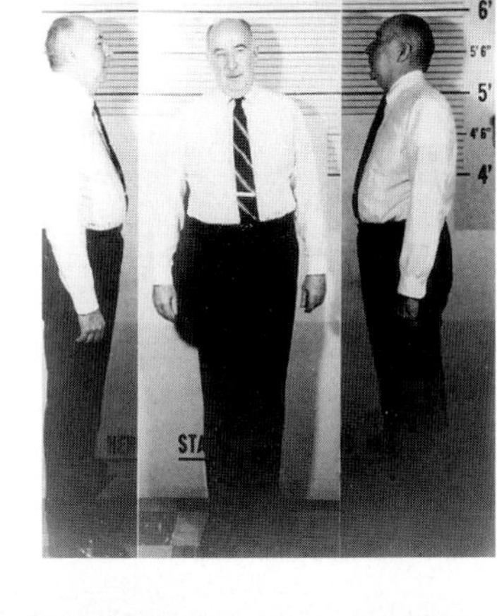

Above left, H. R. Haldeman's FBI identity photos (*FBI Archives*) and above, being interviewed for the BBC/Discovery Watergate television series in 1993, shortly before his death. (*Brian Lapping Associates*)

The chairman of the House Judiciary Committee, Peter Rodino, with John Doar (on the left), chief counsel of the impeachment inquiry. In July 1974 Rodino's committee voted—by bipartisan majorities—to recommend three articles of impeachment against Nixon at a trial by the Senate. (*Dev O'Neill*)

On August 7, 1974, having confirmed to his disbelieving family that he will resign two days later, the president strikes a deceptively happy pose with (from left) son-in-law Ed Cox, Tricia Nixon Cox, First Lady Pat Nixon, Julie Nixon Eisenhower, and her husband David Eisenhower. (*National Archives*)

No longer able to maintain forced smiles for the White House photographer, Julie bursts into tears and Nixon comforts her as Tricia and her husband Ed Cox look on. (*National Archives*)

Dean: Because, one, we're being blackmailed; two, people are going to start perjuring themselves very quickly that have not had to perjure themselves to protect other people and the like. And that is just—there is no assurance—

Nixon: That it won't bust.

Dean: That it won't bust.

As far as Dean is concerned, this is the first time Nixon has been told about anyone being blackmailed, but there is no sound or expression of surprise from the president. He simply agrees that there is no assurance the cover-up won't break open. He shows no surprise when Dean relates Kleindienst's failure to report Liddy's approach at the golf club the day of the break-in. Nixon also calmly states, conspiratorially, that "you're taking care of the witnesses" when Dean spells out how the hush money obstruction of justice involves Ehrlichman, Haldeman, Mitchell—and him.

Although Dean's concern is to lay out the whole story and to get the president to take some action so that "this can be carved away from you," Nixon comes back no fewer than thirteen times to the need to pay off Hunt's blackmail. Nixon's concern is focused on the danger Hunt presents to Ehrlichman and Colson, and if to them, to himself.

Dean recounts how Mitchell has been working on raising the money, feeling "he's one of the ones with the most to lose."

Nixon: How much money do you need?

Dean: I would say these people are going to cost a million dollars over the next two years.

[Pause]

Nixon: We could get that . . . you could get a million dollars. And you could get it in cash. I, I know where it could be gotten—

Dean: Uh-uh.

Nixon: I mean, it's not easy but it could be done.

Dean seems momentarily taken aback, but when the president asks who will handle it, Dean suggests that Mitchell, with LaRue, should be charged with it, although Nixon is very keen to keep going a spurious Cuban exile defense committee as "cover."

Nixon: . . . Our cover there is just going to be the Cuban committee did this for them up through the election.
Dean: Well, yeah. We can put that together. That isn't, of course, quite the way it happened, but—
Nixon: I know, but it's the way it's going to have to happen.

Dean next mentions Krogh's possible perjury over the Plumbers, which brings Nixon back to "your major guy to keep under control":

Nixon: Don't you, just looking at the immediate problem, don't you have to have—handle Hunt's financial situation—
Dean: I, I think that's—
Nixon: —damn soon?
Dean: That is, I talked to Mitchell about that last night—
Nixon: Mitchell . . .
Dean: And, and I told—
Nixon: Might as well, may—have the rule you've got to keep the cap on the bottle that much—
Dean: That's right, that's right.
Nixon: —in order to have any options.
Dean: That's right.
Nixon: Either that or let it all blow right now.

Before getting back to Hunt's money, they detour to discuss the "vulnerabilities." These are the difficulties of partial public disclosure of involvement, like the Segretti dirty tricks that Nixon considers not illegal. But Dean's confidence has waned. For the first time he tells Nixon:

Dean: I am not confident that we can ride through this. I think there are, I think there are soft spots.
Nixon: You used to feel comfortable.

Alas. Dean explains that "everyone is starting to watch out for their own behind." They are getting their own lawyers. And Gray has hampered Dean's ability to deal with his "multitude of people"—Nixon interjects, "Your cover's broken."

This may be the psychological moment when Nixon realizes Dean is expendable, and that Dean senses the new danger to himself.

Nixon: . . . What in the hell, in the hell will you do? Let's suppose that you and Haldeman and Ehrlichman and Mitchell say, "We can't hold this." What, what, then, are you going to say? Are you going to put out a complete disclosure? Isn't that the best plan?

Dean swiftly comes up with his next idea, not yet thought out but ingenious. The attorney general should be told that "this is the first time you're getting all the pieces all together." (Nixon is to cling to that.) A second grand jury should be called with this crucial Dean proviso—that key witnesses be granted immunity from prosecution in return for their testimony. The White House must "avoid criminal liability for countless people," but some would have to go to jail, including Dean. Nixon dismisses the notion. Dean is the president's counsel and, if there is obstruction of justice, that "could be cut off at the pass." Still, "sometimes it's well to give them something and then they don't want the bigger fish."

Dean is not finished on this point. He wants proper coordination, and suggested Henry Petersen be moved from the Justice Department to become White House special counsel—to "tell us how this could be put together, so it did the maximum to carve it away, with a minimum of damage to individuals involved." Nixon warmed to that best of all possible options. It looked like presidential initiative. It gave a reason to send White House men before the grand jury in secret, and to refuse to appear before the Ervin Committee. Also, if they went before a grand jury, told all, and then Hunt blew, so what? Its main attraction for Dean was the central pillar—that despite his mention of jail, there would be immunity for anyone like himself coming forward to tell the prosecutors the truth.

But at that juncture, as Dean spells out his own guilt in handling the blackmail, Nixon's attention snaps back to Hunt. "I wonder if that doesn't have to be continued," he says, meaning hush money. Dean explains how hard it is to continue if clemency cannot be delivered. Nixon accepts that he cannot grant clemency for another year and a half, until after the 1974 midterm elections, if then.

Nixon: Your point is that even then you couldn't do it.
Dean: That's right. It may further involve you in a way you shouldn't be involved in this.
Nixon: No, it's wrong, that's for sure.

A few seconds on, Nixon sighs. "We're all in on it." But it is the phrase "it's wrong" that would come back to haunt him.

They discuss the worst-case hypothesis of indictments against the big fish, and Nixon is now appalled and prophetic:

> *Nixon:* . . . see if we can cut our losses and you say we're going to go down the road, see if we can cut our losses, and no more blackmail and all the rest, and the thing blows and they indict Bob and the rest. Jesus, you'd never recover from that, John.

Nixon prefers to revert to the idea of having Dean come before the Cabinet and pretend that his "investigation" shows no one important involved. No problem with a snow job, says Dean, "We can sell, you know, just about like we were selling Wheaties on our position." But Dean suggests a first-ever thrash-it-out meeting with himself, Mitchell, Haldeman, and Ehrlichman. Nixon avidly agrees: "There must be a four-way talk here of the particular ones we can trust here." Time is of the essence, but not to tell Colson. "I talk to him about many, many political things, but I never talk about this sort of thing because he's, he's very harmful."

Haldeman joined the meeting then and is apparently surprised to learn Hunt is demanding so much money. Nixon again reviews the option to "cut our losses" (meaning to hold the criminal problem to the lowest level)—this time listing those losses to see who can "avoid criminal liability." To the big four he adds Chapin, Strachan, and Magruder.

> *Haldeman:* And Magruder, if you can. But that's the one you pretty much have to give up.
>
> *Nixon:* But Magruder, Magruder, John Dean's point is that if Magruder goes down, he'll pull everybody with him.

Haldeman agrees even though he thinks Magruder wouldn't want to. He observes that "the best leverage" they have over Magruder is that he has to keep his story straight with the White House or else he will be in trouble for perjury. Nixon wants all that sorted out in an urgent meeting with Mitchell. They have a last go-around on the fact they have no choice but to pay Hunt—"would you agree that

that's a buy-time thing, you better damn well get that done, but fast?" instructs Nixon—then at 11:55 A.M. Haldeman leaves to telephone Mitchell.[19]

In his memoirs, Nixon admits that shortly after this meeting he asked his longtime secretary, Rose Mary Woods, if she had any leftover campaign funds. She reported that she had $100,000 on hand. Nixon mentioned it to Haldeman, who, so Nixon says, told him, "You should stay out of this."

But the payoff had to go on. Fred LaRue, having talked to Dean sometime that morning, also phoned Mitchell. He testified that he told Mitchell only of Hunt's demand for money, not the threat. Even then LaRue unilaterally lowered the required sum to $75,000. Mitchell was told it was for Hunt's attorney's fees, and he authorized LaRue to pay it. LaRue took it out of the cash in his filing cabinet that was left over from Haldeman's $350,000.

For a long time afterward, LaRue could not recall precisely which day he paid it, but the drop—in an envelope left in Hunt's lawyer's house mailbox—was later conclusively proven to have taken place the evening of March 21, subsequent to the president's discussion.[20]

Nixon's dictated diary that night states, "As far as the day was concerned it was relatively uneventful except for the talk with Dean." The diary excerpt Nixon selected for his memoirs makes no mention whatever of the Hunt threat and need for payment. Instead, it credits Dean with seeing no choice "but to move to let the facts out" before his men each start "to rat on the other." When the diary Dictabelt was turned over to the prosecutors, they noted that it had a fifty-nine-second gap in it.

That night Nixon also telephoned Colson, who was probably the first man outside the immediate circle to warn about Dean. Colson was circumspect. The president had not taken it kindly when Colson suggested in February that Mitchell ought to step forward. But when Nixon commented what a superb job Dean had done "keeping all the fires out," Colson agreed, with a reservation. More important than the break-in, he said, was the "possibility of somebody charging obstruction of justice." Colson added: "That's where John is—having done all the things that have to be done—that makes him a little more of a participant than you would like." Colson proposed that the president supplant Dean by appointing an outside special counsel. When Dean got wind of this, he recognized he had another enemy in Colson.

The next day was Mitchell's. When he arrived from New York for his White House meeting, three of the participants—Ehrlichman, Haldeman, and Dean—remembered Mitchell saying that Hunt had been taken care of. Ehrlichman even rang his protégé, Krogh, to say that Hunt was "more stable and that his recommendation would be just to hang tough." There was now no need for Krogh to prepare to tell all about the Plumbers before Hunt blew.[21]

But even as Nixon's men breathed a sigh of relief, disaster was approaching. In focusing on Hunt and the genuine threat he posed, they had overlooked the other man "off the reservation," James McCord.

In fact, the president had been rather well briefed on McCord. He knew—by hearing of Dean's reports to Haldeman—about the difficult January meetings at which McCord made clear he was not interested in clemency and insisted the government contrive his mistrial. As Nixon told Haldeman, "McCord did not want to go to jail." McCord's name even came up several times during the cancer conversation, with Dean reminding Nixon that McCord had been spoken to about "commutation."

In his dictated diary of March 20, the president said that McCord "might crack . . . and might say to the judge he is willing to tell all." Certainly, says Nixon, McCord "knows a hell of a lot about Mitchell. Mitchell is the one I am most concerned about."[22]

Nixon might better have been concerned in the first instance about McCord. Unlike Hunt, who following his guilty plea was out on bond, McCord had in fact been briefly jailed following conviction, pending sentencing. He hated it. Gordon Liddy, who for one week shared a cell with him in the foul century-old D.C. jail, wrote that McCord was still smarting from Magruder's being "outside" and bitter about the failure of the government to oblige him with a mistrial over the bugging of his telephone calls to foreign embassies. Liddy reckoned that McCord believed that the whole government was conspiring against him, including his beloved CIA. Because McCord was religious, Liddy speculated that he "jumped at the chance to become once more a good Christian, back on what the conventional wisdom was telling him through the media was the side of the angels."[23]

McCord had decided that the "propitious time" of which he had warned Caulfield had finally come. At about the same period that Hunt was making his "seamy things" threat to the CRP lawyer, McCord was consulting an old CIA acquaintance, Lee Pennington (the man who had helped burn potentially incriminating documents at McCord's home the previous June), about a letter McCord intended writing.[24]

On March 20, McCord turned up in John Sirica's chambers asking to see the judge; failing, he handed over a letter to his law clerk. Sirica's first reaction was that the envelope might contain more hundred-dollar bills. He ordered that McCord take the letter to his probation officer, and in the meantime, Sirica summoned the prosecutors and a court reporter. As Sirica's clerks began explaining about the letter, Earl Silbert, hypercautious to the end, withdrew since McCord had specifically ruled out telling his own lawyer. Sirica read the letter, talked it over with his chief clerk, then resealed it, and decided to sit on it until the sentencing scheduled for March 23. The letter was dated March 19, Sirica's sixty-ninth birthday. "This is the best damned birthday present I've ever gotten." Sirica told his clerk. "This is going to break the case wide open."[25]

The incident with the prosecutors does suggest that Silbert could have passed the news of a McCord letter to superiors at the Justice Department, who might have been expected to alert the White House. Apparently, they did not. One person who was informed was Bob Jackson, a *Los Angeles Times* reporter acquainted with McCord through a parent-teacher association. McCord, in a fail-safe operation, told Jackson that if nothing developed in court, his wife would have a copy of a letter for him at the end of the hearing.

In the end, Sirica scooped both the oblivious men at the White House and the expectant *Los Angeles Times* man at the courthouse. It was one of the great moments of Watergate.

After everyone stood at the summons "All rise" at the judge's entry, and then sat again, it took some time for the fidgeting and whispering to be stilled. Sirica announced that before sentencing he had "a preliminary matter" he wished to put on record. He explained the delivery of

McCord's letter and staged a little show. The judge asked the clerk to unseal the envelope, the letter was taken out and handed up to the bench, and the judge began reading aloud. McCord's style was stilted but the message was unmistakable.

> . . . In the interests of restoring faith in the criminal justice system, which faith has been severely damaged in this case, I will state the following to you at this time which I hope may be of help to you in meting out justice in this case.

McCord's first four points were explosive:

1. There was political pressure applied to the defendants to plead guilty and remain silent.
2. Perjury occurred during the trial of matters highly material to the very structure, orientation, and impact of the government's case, and to the motivation and intent of the defendants.
3. Others involved in the Watergate operation were not identified during the trial, when they could have been by those testifying.
4. The Watergate operation was not a CIA operation. The Cubans may have been misled by others into believing that it was a CIA operation. I know for a fact that it was not . . .

Sirica declared a short recess. The courtroom erupted as reporters sprinted for the phones. McCord had asked to talk privately with the judge in chambers after sentencing. His letter had stated: "Several members of my family have expressed fear for my life" if he disclosed what he knew. He did not "feel confident in talking with an FBI agent, in testifying before a grand jury whose U.S. Attorneys work for the Department of Justice or in talking with other government representatives." Such talk darkened the story further. Liddy, sitting next to McCord, felt he "had gone bad"; McCord told him, "This will help you and others," but Liddy had no use for "an informer."

Back on the bench, the judge stated he would hear McCord under oath before a stenographer, but he made no promises except to postpone his sentencing. Then he turned to the others, Liddy first. Sirica had, as he later wrote, "given up on" the defiant Liddy, who, with counsel Peter Maroulis, made difficulties for the judge throughout the trial. He sentenced him to a firm twenty years and a fine of $40,000, noting he would not be eligible for parole until he had served six years and eight months. Then he handed down the maximum possible terms —forty years each to the Cuban Americans and thirty-five years to Hunt —but made their sentences, unlike Liddy's, "provisional." He would review them after three months, depending on how they cooperated with the Ervin Committee. Sirica, after quoting approvingly another federal judge in a recent trial, made his intentions crystal clear:

> I recommend your full cooperation with the Grand Jury and the Senate Select Committee. You must understand that I hold out no promises or hopes of any kind to you in this matter but I do say that should you decide to speak freely, I would have to weigh that factor in appraising what sentence will be finally imposed in this case. Other factors will of course be considered but I mention this one because it is one over which you have control and I mean each one of the five of you.[26]

The McCord letter and the clear hint he would tell all to the Ervin Committee rather than to the prosecution had cracked the cover-up wide open. It would rapidly unwind all the perjuries and send other coconspirators scrambling for the exit before they were caught out.

McCord had promised in his anonymous note at Christmas that "all the trees in the forest will fall," but the White House seemed unable to believe it. Too quickly, as all the contemporary evidence shows, the president's men comforted themselves with the legalistic view that McCord could not "get" anyone since his evidence would be only hearsay. Even Liddy, promising silence to the end, went to jail claiming that only he had the direct evidence that "could take Watergate any higher." It was not, however, a time for legalisms. McCord had opened the road to havoc.

The president himself sensed it. He had flown to Key Biscayne and there was an immediate flurry of telephone calls. Meeting Haldeman, Nixon was anxious to know "what happened re Hunt?" and to find out "what specifically" Colson had said to Hunt about clemency. The "political pressure" allegation by McCord had touched a sensitive nerve.[27] Nixon was alarmed. He showered Haldeman with instructions of whom to call. Haldeman's notes reveal the urgency: "Dean—did Strachan testify at trial; Kleindienst—has he contacted Baker and Ervin? Get him on finding out what's up at Sirica's; get Moore's judgment, Mitchell's, Dean to ask Kleindienst. 'Our move,' says P, rather than wait.' "[28]

Mitchell is first to call Haldeman, reassuring him that it's all hearsay. McCord "knows nothing except what people told him." Signally, Mitchell advises withholding the planned presidential statement. Nixon "should hunker down" and not do anything to give McCord credence. He should also be aware that defendants' rights could be damaged by any such statement, although Dean, who is being sent to Camp David for the purpose, should continue preparing his report on Watergate.

Dean himself was less confident. He phoned Haldeman to say that McCord might "do a lot of damage," particularly on "post-June 17"—the cover-up—and expressed worries that the White House was "one step behind."[29] Dean telephoned Haldeman even as he was trying to escape journalists besieging his home for reaction to Gray's continuing revelations. Though left twisting in the wind by Ehrlichman, Gray was still rattling on before his Senate hearings. His latest gaffe was that Dean "probably lied" to FBI agents questioning him the previous June about Hunt's White House office.

Damage control of an ineffectual kind exercised the White House. Ehrlichman telephoned the president, who noted in his diary, "lets find out where the bodies are buried." McCord's revelations, Nixon observed, "may go more the Mitchell-Magruder route than the White House route. . . ." Ehrlichman's note has the president wanting to counter McCord. In his diary, Nixon says he told Ehrlichman, "Let's prick the boil early and get it over . . . the more I lean to the idea that we should be calling for a grand jury."[30] But Judge Sirica had another forum in mind.

Unknown to the White House, two days before sentencing, another lawyer had been invited by Sirica to be present in court to hear the judge admonish the defendants to cooperate with the Ervin Committee. He was Sam Dash, a law professor at Georgetown University, who had unexpectedly become chief counsel to the Senate Watergate investigation.[31]

There was an irony about his position. Dash had only recently, as a losing defense counsel, argued that a trial judge acted improperly in promising to review a severe sentence in return for a prisoner's cooperation. But although he avers he still disapproved of the practice, Dash had drawn that precedent to Sirica's attention, hoping that his Senate investigation would be the beneficiary. Until McCord came along, the Senate investigation had not been getting very far.

Sirica's pressure worked. Before the day was over, McCord had initiated a meeting with Dash and began unloading what he knew. Dash was electrified and asked McCord to name names. McCord wanted to proceed slowly, putting most of it in writing, but plainly the wall of silence had cracked. At their second meeting on Saturday, McCord produced a memo that indicated precisely where in the trial transcript Magruder had committed perjury. More important, it went on to state that Magruder was "involved in the Watergate operation sequence" and that Magruder knew the names of others involved, one of them John Dean.

Dash was impressed. For the first time the Senate investigation had more than suspicion to go on. McCord insisted on strict confidentiality until he could testify on oath before Dash's masters, the senators on the committee, but surprisingly McCord's lawyer suggested that the fact of Dash's meetings be made public. McCord had a new lawyer, Bernard Fensterwald, who had helped McCord raise bond to get out of jail only a short time after the trial and was looking on the case as a crusade. Fensterwald was wealthy, a noted supporter of radical causes, and also an advocate of further investigation into the Kennedy and Martin Luther King assassinations. Too late the Nixon men sensed danger from Fensterwald, even though he had once been heard to say that he didn't give a damn about McCord, but was after Nixon. Mitchell urged that they plant FBI information with newspapers to smear him with his Kennedy links, but nobody got around to it.[32]

Fensterwald understood publicity better, and what followed that weekend deepened the disaster for Nixon. On Sunday, with the president in Florida and Dean at Camp David struggling to write his "report," Sam Dash obtained Senator Ervin's authorization to put out a press release.

It was a bare-bones statement saying only that McCord had begun giving Dash names of others involved, but naïve in the ways of the

Senate and the media, Dash allowed himself to be drawn into further comment. When reporters arrived to pick up the release, he was immediately beset with a storm of questions. Television crews demanded he do it again for them. Dash fended off demands for the names but obliged with a rash answer: "I was impressed with McCord's sincerity and earnestness . . . I believe that McCord is trying to tell us the truth." The White House, when they heard it, were incensed, and typically moved to counterattack Dash personally.[33]

But there was more going on that Sunday than either the White House or Dash was aware of. At McCord's home, reporter Bob Jackson was trying to make up for the McCord letter scoop he had lost to Sirica. For some months Jackson had been working with McCord on the big story McCord would tell in the newspaper under his own name, much the way Al Baldwin had done the previous autumn. It had been heavy going.

As Jackson was leaving he happened to overhear McCord taking a phone call from a reporter. From the answers, he gathered McCord was declining to reveal the names of the higher-ups he had named at his meetings with Dash. It was *Washington Post* reporter Bob Woodward on the line, following up the Dash news conference. Jackson had not even heard about the Dash meetings with McCord. So he asked and at last got the break that Woodward missed: McCord told Jackson he had named Magruder and Dean.

Even before the story hit the streets, the *Los Angeles Times* had its reporter with the presidential party at Key Biscayne follow up Jackson's story. White House Press Secretary Ron Ziegler, after checking, came to find the reporter with a dire message. If the *Los Angeles Times* went ahead with Jackson's McCord story, John Dean would sue for libel. The *Los Angeles Times* never even blinked, but John Dean had. He had for the first time consulted an outside lawyer about his own problems. The fat was in the fire.

CHAPTER 11

A Modified Limited Hangout

McCord's fingering of Magruder, Dean, and, eventually, Mitchell sensationally reopened the case. It was a bombshell. At the time, no one outside the conspiracy believed the White House would have been so stupid as to have left traces of involvement. There were lots of suspicions, particularly about CRP. But the charge of interference in the FBI investigation by Dean, the president's counsel, the allegation that he had lied, and now, in the *Los Angeles Times* the accusation that he had prior knowledge of the bugging—these added up to an enormity. Dean, though little known, was the man Nixon said had investigated and reported to him that no one in the White House was involved.

McCord's actions reopened the case for the media, who were forced to pay attention after only half-interested coverage of Pat Gray's gaffes. They reopened the case for the embarrassed prosecutors, who had conducted the trial on the premise that no one above Liddy was involved. Now McCord said they were wrong. United States attorneys Earl Silbert and Seymour Glanzer were frustrated in their attempts to get McCord to testify to the grand jury. Making an exception, Judge Sirica ruled that McCord must first go to Ervin Committee investigators, but the prosecutors would go after the others he had named.

The most severe damage to the president was sustained in secret. McCord was blowing two cover-ups: He was not merely fingering those involved in the planning and execution of the Watergate break-in; he was also ripping open the hush money and clemency conspiracy to obstruct justice. And he was doing so just at the moment when the president had been planning to get out in front of the developing scandal. That strategy was in ruins; now the original Watergate cover-up had to be covered up, an even more desperate venture.

Prior to McCord's revelations, Nixon's men had tried to square the circle—partially exposing those involved at CRP and at the White House while limiting their criminal liability and at the same time appearing to give the president credit for cracking the case. The scheme quickly went through several variants. Nixon liked Dean's proposal for a second grand jury, especially because grand jury testimony was always kept secret. What Dean liked about it was the prospect of immunity from prosecution to those cooperating, like himself. With immunity they would not have to go to jail whatever else happened. When Ehrlichman objected on the grounds it would stink of a continuing cover-up, the ever-ingenious Dean had an alternative. The president would refer the key witnesses to a panel of top Justice Department appointees (eventually he proposed a presidential commission), but always with the proviso that the guilty not be prosecuted. Instead, they would be required by the president to resign. This time it is Haldeman who sees that this, too, smacks of further cover-up.

Ehrlichman pushes very strongly for Dean to write a phony report. It would be the president's insurance policy. If a disastrous development occurs, the president can defend himself, saying he had known nothing of it, he had relied on the previous report from Dean, his counsel. Ehrlichman seems oblivious to the panic he is creating, probably unwittingly, in Dean. The president's counsel sees such language as setting him up as the future fall guy. When Nixon toys on March 21 with sending a "Dean report" to the Justice Department, Ehrlichman, alarmed, realizes the implications: "Christ, I don't know where it stops."[1]

At this stage, Colson proposes a special counsel, new to the case, to advise the president of the growing criminal problems. Haldeman on March 22 also thinks it not a bad idea to go thus far: Have Magruder indicted, and then have the White House "control the prosecution" so that he could be acquitted. Haldeman, the former advertising agency executive, was not a lawyer, but he showed here a nice eye for the abuse of office.[2]

Finally, with Mitchell down from New York to join what Nixon's memoirs first termed these "inefficient minuets" around the options, they reach a conclusion: Instead of executive privilege for all White House men before the Ervin Committee, it will now be executive session—meaning all (excepting Dean, who would use double privilege as the president's lawyer) will agree to testify, but only behind closed doors. This is a huge retreat from the original Nixon refusal to allow any former or present White House staff person to testify, but it would, at least in Nixon's view, avoid the circus of televised hearings.

They also agreed to send to Ervin a "report" or "statement" addressed by Dean to the president. This document would, the president makes clear, not be specific but would exculpate all White House personnel from the narrow issue of involvement in the planning and execution of the Watergate break-in, and to hell with what came after. Dean, saying he's already drafted part B on the Segretti sabotage, has now to tackle Watergate. He asks that they wait to see how it turns out before deciding how to use it. Mitchell, too, is wary about Ehrlichman's enthusiasm for publishing the Dean statement. "That introduces the problem for us," he says.

The tape of this meeting ends with a marvelous passage of black humor about the decision reached:

> *Nixon:* . . . You think we want to, want to go this route now? And the—let it hang out, so to speak?
> *Dean:* Well, it's, it isn't really that—
> *Haldeman:* It's a limited hangout.
> *Dean:* It's a limited hangout.
> *Ehrlichman:* It's a modified limited hang out.
> *Nixon:* Well, it's only the questions of the thing hanging out publicly or privately.
> *Dean:* What it's doing, Mr. President, is getting you up above and away from it. And that's the most important thing.
> *Nixon:* Oh, I know, but I suggested that the other day and we all came down on, remember we came down on, on the negative on it. Now what's changed our mind?
> *Dean:* The lack of alternatives, or a body [laughter].

Ehrlichman: We, we went down every alley [laughter]. Let it go over.

Nixon: Well, I feel that at, I feel that this is, that, I feel that at the very minimum we've got to have the statement, and let's look at it, whatever the hell it is. If, if it opens up doors, it opens up doors, you know.

Ehrlichman: John says he's sorry he sent those burglars in there, and that helps a lot.

Nixon: That's right.

Mitchell: You are very welcome, sir [laughter].

Haldeman: Just glad the others didn't get caught.

Nixon: Yeah, the ones we sent to Muskie and all the rest, Jackson and Hubert and uh [unintelligible with tape noise].

Ehrlichman: I get a little chill sitting over there in that part of the table there.[3]

The jokes were premature; the little chill at the end might have been foreboding: Within twelve hours, McCord had spilled the beans. But there was a last twist to the meeting. At the end of the nearly two-hour session, the president is left alone with his old friend and adviser John Mitchell. The conversation is remarkable for what is *not* said. Since February 13, if not earlier, Nixon has at least contemplated having Mitchell step forward and shoulder the blame. Now he cannot bring himself to raise the matter directly. He does not ask Mitchell whether he did in fact authorize the Watergate operation, nor what he did about hush money and Hunt's threat of the day before. True, Nixon knew the tape recorders were rolling, but enough criminal talk had taken place before the hidden microphones for that not to have been an issue. Perhaps they had discussed the matter elsewhere. Probably it was simply too painful for Nixon to mention what he was about to inflict on Mitchell.

Instead, he suddenly lurched into a line totally contrary to the one he had just been pursuing. Recalling Sherman Adams, President Eisenhower's aide who was fired for accepting the gift of a vicuña coat, Nixon says he did not want that to happen with Watergate.

Nixon: . . . I don't give a shit what happens. I want you all to stonewall it, let them plead the Fifth Amendment, cover-up, or anything else, if it'll save it, save the plan. That's the whole point. On the other hand, I would prefer, as I said to you, that you do it the

> other way. And I would particularly prefer to do it that other way if it's going to come out that way anyway. And that my view that with the number of jackass people they [Ervin Committee] are going to—the story they get out through leaks, charges and so forth and innuendos will be a hell of a lot worse than the story they're going to get out by just letting it out there.

Nixon's memoirs claim that this was "an oblique way" of having Mitchell understand they had to "take a chance" and make a painful shift in Watergate strategy. Mitchell himself says he took it to mean nothing more than dropping executive privilege. Yet having used the Adams parallel, Nixon must have known he could hardly expect his old friend to step forward. It might keep recurring as an option, but Nixon understood better than anyone that if Mitchell admitted blame for Watergate, it was beyond belief that Nixon had not known as well. As Nixon had put it: "The President's campaign manager, that's pretty goddamned bad. That's damn near as bad as it is out there."[4]

In any case, McCord was about to get Mitchell. Dean knew it as soon as he saw that the *Los Angeles Times* had gone ahead with its story. It was all over *The Washington Post,* too.[5] Dean was well into the drafting of the Watergate section of his report, but he knew it was hopeless. To keep claiming innocence for White House people was to pile lies on top of lies, compounding the conspiracy rather than "carving it away" from the president, as he had tried advising.

Over the weekend, Dean had revived, in phone calls to Haldeman, the idea that he alone go to the grand jury—with immunity, of course. He suggested doing it before McCord testified in closed session to the Ervin Committee later that week. Dean explained, as Haldeman's note shows, his testifying "wld go no further . . . Dean feels higher loyalty than M[itchell]—and concerned re own a[ss]. so go for informal immunity."[6] Dean advocates gushingly to Haldeman he is the ideal witness from the White House viewpoint; he would take the affair no higher because he "has no knowledge of what Mitchell knows or did, nor does he re Jeb [Magruder], also doesn't know full extent of G S[trachan] knowledge."[7]

By Monday, March 26, Nixon, after he "continued [his] soul-searching" with Haldeman, had decided that Dean would *not* have immunity, but neglects to tell him. Neither was Dean told that Nixon had considered suspending him as counsel following the McCord story. To his diary Nixon confided that he had told Haldeman of the necessity of getting "this whole thing cleaned up" by going before the grand jury.

> I said that we simply wouldn't be able to govern, we couldn't do the job we could do for the country if we allowed it to go on. I said that each man had to go up there and I said that when a man was charged he probably had to take a leave of absence.[8]

This seems to have been the first mention of dropping key people. Nixon said he meant Magruder, who had in the meantime been rewarded with a good job at the Commerce Department. But it was soon to apply to the topmost echelon of the White House staff. Haldeman caught the inference. As Nixon put it in his diary:

> . . . what happens if someone in the White House is charged? Haldeman immediately reacted and said "well that's exactly of course what they want. To drive somebody in the top command out of office and indicate that the whole White House is shot through with corruption." And he's right. We have to find a way to cut this thing off at the pass before it reaches that point. Because there's no question in my mind that neither Haldeman or Ehrlichman are guilty. The Colson matter is something else again . . .[9]

On Sunday at Key Biscayne—there is no doubt that McCord's letter to Sirica spoiled their weekend—Nixon worries about how to counter McCord's prospective testimony to the Ervin Committee. He falls back on an old chestnut: Declassify old secrets to "open up Kennedy stuff" and "get out Diem." This was the attempt, left dormant since the end of 1971, to exploit the "State Department" cables Hunt had faked in order to smear the Kennedys and "prove" their involvement in the murder of Diem, a Roman Catholic. Again, nothing came of the idea except the eventual backfire against Nixon.[10]

Nothing came either of the one piece of sane advice they got over the weekend. Nixon had Haldeman call up William Rogers. The president had stood by while Henry Kissinger undermined Rogers as secretary of state, but Rogers had been Eisenhower's attorney general, and Nixon respected him as a lawyer. He now contemplated getting him as an inside adviser.

Rogers's immediate advice goes to the heart of the matter. McCord's break is "very significant just in itself"; the Gray-Dean business has put a cloud over the FBI investigation; Kleindienst's closeness to Mitchell undermines trust in the Justice Department; and Judge Sirica has now switched attention from the political aspect to an issue of integrity. Rogers recommends that a special prosecutor be appointed, though at the same time warning that this, as Haldeman notes, "breaks china, can't put back together."[11]

Rogers further cuts through the White House cant. The idea of a Dean report is incredible, he insists. And for a very simple reason of logic the White House seems to have forgotten. If, as Nixon wishes, Dean reports that no one in the White House is involved, then "why cover up if we don't know the real story; just isn't believable; the attempts to cover up make the basic alibi of noninvolvement inconceivable." Whatever the consequences and whoever is involved, steps must now be taken, advises Rogers. If Mitchell turns out to be in it, then for the president it will "really be tough," but they have no choice but to "take the lumps."[12] Nixon agrees to see Rogers but is clearly not ready to accept his advice.

That same day, March 26, in response to the *Los Angeles Times*, Nixon had Ron Ziegler issue a statement saying Nixon telephoned Dean to reaffirm his confidence in him. Nixon also told Ziegler "to avoid statements on Magruder." The distinction was noted by the press.[13]

At Camp David, Dean began, at Haldeman's suggestion, he says, his own taping of telephone calls. He telephoned Magruder and got him to agree that the McCord accusation of Dean's knowing about the break-in was wrong—it was a "bum rap." Obviously, the call was designed, like Colson's taping of Hunt, to obtain an exculpation to be produced in evidence. (Dean also tried that week to get a statement from Liddy exonerating the White House counsel but the strong man declined to make an exception to his total silence, arguing that it would give him problems with assertion of his rights as a defendant.)

What, of course, the conversation with Magruder revealed was Dean's total complicity in the cover-up. Magruder predicts that McCord will name Mitchell, and probably Strachan and Colson, too, when he testifies before the Ervin Committee, even though his knowledge is only hearsay. He quickly and anxiously moves off the *Los Angeles Times* story to remind the president's counsel how important it is to his and Mitchell's position that Dean stick with the lies he, Magruder, has already told to the grand jury. "I am going to have to rely on you," he says. Dean responds with a lie: "I don't plan to go out and talk in any forum." (He has just told Haldeman he wants to go to the grand jury.)

In this conversation, Magruder made Dean realize that he, too, might have to perjure himself if called to testify under oath. And Dean made Magruder realize that he had better get his own lawyer, in addition to being represented by CRP's counsel.[14] The thoughts were to be mutually destructive within days.

For in truth, both Magruder and Dean were now wobbling. The men around the president focused on Magruder and took their eyes off Dean, because they knew the former was deeply incriminated in the break-in and the perjury of the "cover" story told at the trial. Dean, they persuaded themselves, was indeed being unfairly accused of having had prior knowledge of the Watergate bugging. Dangerously, the president's close circle kept relying on Dean as its source for what was happening.

Still sojourning at Camp David, Dean was spending a good deal of time on the phone to CRP's lawyer, Paul O'Brien. Since his conversation with Dean about Hunt's threat, O'Brien had become nervous about his own possible involvement in obstruction of justice, and he wanted out. But getting out was no simple matter, and this led to yet another curious permutation of accusation and guilt. It boiled down to this. Magruder, having panicked, had consulted CRP's lawyers about McCord's revelations. He had then, O'Brien told Dean, laid out yet another version of how the whole Watergate intelligence plan had come about. The White House, he said, not CRP, originated it. "Dean had cooked the whole thing up at Haldeman's instructions." It was an "accomplished fact" by the time Dean had sent Liddy to CRP, and then Colson, Haldeman, and even the president had pushed for its implementation. Magruder and Mitchell had been afraid that if they did not go ahead with the Liddy plan, Colson might take over the operation, and so GEMSTONE had been authorized.

Interestingly, Dean makes no mention of all this in his later Senate testimony nor in his own memoirs. But there are three contemporary sources—Haldeman's notes of Dean's phone calls, Nixon's dictated diary (which was not always accurate), and one Nixon tape—that point to the existence of such a scenario. In all three, we can see how the unexpected twist of switching the onus from Mitchell back to the White House was received with alarm.

On Monday, March 26, Dean had already mentioned to Haldeman O'Brien's idea that if Mitchell stepped forward it would solve a lot. However, the "real q is why M going to such great lengths to keep it quiet—only basis cd be if it goes higher than M."[15] That was a dangerous thought indeed. By Tuesday, it is clear why it did go "higher."

Jeb Magruder was telling O'Brien, apparently for the first time, about the White House's instigation of the Liddy plan. Mitchell, said Magruder, had merely "signed off on" the Watergate break-in. Dean's explanation for Magruder's new version, according to Haldeman, was that Mitchell and Magruder had "their ass in a sling" and were "mixing apples and oranges for their own protection." And Dean reports an intriguing offer from O'Brien. If the president wants to force it to a head, the CRP lawyers could waive their retainer and lawyers' privilege with their clients and report to Nixon on all the facts—a clear indication that Parkinson and O'Brien were now running scared.[16]

And so, by now, were Nixon's men. This is how they received Haldeman's report of what Magruder had reportedly told O'Brien:

> *Haldeman:* Then the final step was—all of this was rattling around in January [1972]—the final step was when Gordon Strachan called Magruder and said Haldeman told him to get this going. "The president wants it done and there's to be no more arguing about it." This meaning the intelligence activity, the Liddy program. Magruder told Mitchell this, that Strachan had ordered him to get it going on the president's orders and Mitchell signed off on it. He said, "Okay if they say to do it, go ahead."
> *Nixon:* Uh, was that, this is the bugging?
> *Haldeman:* The whole thing including the bugging.
> *Nixon:* Shit.[17]

After much discussion, Haldeman comes up with an idea to turn the tables on Mitchell, the "big enchilada," in Ehrlichman's phrase. Magruder, he says, should confess he lied and, to avoid going to jail, seek immunity. The U.S. attorney would grant it if he thought Magruder was going to get Mitchell. "The interesting thing," muses Haldeman, "would be to watch Mitchell's face at the time I, I recommend to Magruder that he go down and ask for immunity and confess . . ."[18]

By one of those coincidences that would be jeered in the theater, a few moments later Haldeman telephones Mitchell in New York to ask him to come down for another urgent meeting only to discover that Magruder is sitting in Mitchell's office. We have on the Nixon tape just Haldeman's side of the conversation, but his surprise is patent.

> *Haldeman:* . . . Did he tell you that Jeb wants to meet with you? . . . Oh he is? Okay. That's the—I thought, well, the last I heard he wanted to get together with the two of us . . .

The Magruder development has clearly gnawed at Nixon. He suddenly asks:

> *Nixon:* Bob, how do you analyze Magruder tossing it off to you rather than to Mitchell? That startled you, didn't it?
> *Haldeman:* Well, he hits Mitchell, too. He is just trying to wrap me because he wants to get you in. I think my view is that what Magruder was doing here was firing a threat to the president.[19]

The president, anything but reluctant to encourage subornation of perjury, wonders whether there is any way Magruder might "stick to his story," the "old story" as it is termed by Ehrlichman, who lucidly explains why not:

> *Ehrlichman:* I tell you I am to the point now where I don't think this thing is going to hold together, and my hunch is that anybody who tries to stick with a story that is not susceptible to corroboration is going to be in serious difficulty.

Nixon fastens on the possibility of using Magruder against Mitchell. He toys with having at last the one-on-one meeting on Watergate with Mitchell that he says he has been avoiding. He would confront Mitchell with Magruder's new version, "and Mitchell says 'Yes. I did it.' Then what do we say?" He flounders. Haldeman insists that "it's greater knowledge than we possess right now—if he would only confess." But, of course, Nixon knew Mitchell would not.

> *Nixon:* Mitchell, you see, is never, never going to go in and admit perjury. I mean you can talk about immunity and all the rest, but he's never going to do that.
> *Haldeman:* They won't give him immunity anyway, I wouldn't think, unless they figure they could get you . . .[20]

That, as we shall see, was an extraordinarily prophetic remark. But in this preoccupied group it quickly passed. There was no Nixon-Mitchell meeting. Nixon's memoirs claim that "before we were able even to reach a decision" on Mitchell, they had to deal with a recalcitrant John Dean. The claim is a non sequitur. The very fact of Dean's recalcitrance (which they had known of since Monday) made it imperative that Nixon see Mitchell. In fact, Nixon shrank from the confrontation, probably because he knew that his only option was to sacrifice Mitchell and preserve Haldeman.

There is one further possible reason for Nixon's reluctance. The next day, March 28, information came to the White House that "Mitchell is on [the] verge of breaking—suicide." First Martha, now John. The comment sits there in Haldeman's notes, attributed to Mitchell's closest friend, Fred LaRue. LaRue's ultimate credibility is one reason for believing it.[21]

It is not the only mention of suicide in Watergate. Magruder said he contemplated killing himself at this period. Dean says he worried that his wife, Maureen, might do so. Ehrlichman discloses that he briefly fantasized, when in the cockpit of Air Force One, seizing the controls and crashing, ending it for everyone. By the end of April, Nixon was hoping he would not wake up in the morning.

Before they got that news about Mitchell, Nixon urged on Haldeman first thing on March 28 "the need to decide what to do if events overrun us." Nixon was desperate to get out a statement affirming that he had ordered his staff to cooperate with the investigation. The question was which forum? He instructed Haldeman to raise with Mitchell his notion of having everyone appear before the grand jury, and also the new suggestion from Colson that the president once again insist that all present and former White House staff members were covered by executive privilege. Colson, unaware he was being dragged in so forcefully by Magruder, rings Haldeman to harp on the point that everybody else does face an obstruction of justice problem and warns that the greatest danger is a special prosecutor with a runaway grand jury. "Dean's in the soup," he says, but don't overreact.[22]

Haldeman, judging by his notes, was mainly interested in finding out firsthand what Mitchell and Magruder were trying to put off on the White House. He did, and it was alarming. They were saying the plan was "hatched here." Quoting Magruder, Mitchell told Haldeman that Colson had called not once but twice from the White House "to get going on this thing" and, specifically, to get information on Lawrence O'Brien.[23] Magruder's story about Haldeman's liaison to CRP, Gordon Strachan, was every bit as disturbing as Dean had reported to them the previous day. Strachan, Mitchell told Haldeman, had assured Magruder that Haldeman had approved the plan; moreover, Strachan had been given copies of the bugging obtained from the DNC phones for the White House. Haldeman, taking notes as he listened to Mitchell describe what Magruder had told him, even drew a little diagram of people at the White House who supposedly had "full knowledge" of the plan, adding the name of Colson aide Richard Howard to the growing list.

Mitchell then gave Haldeman the rundown of the problem emerging with Dean. (Haldeman had heard it daily from Dean that week.) It was that Dean no longer wished to stick with the false version of the GEMSTONE meetings and the money "cover story" to which Mitchell, Magruder, and his assistant Bart Porter had already falsely testified.

Haldeman calls Magruder into the Mitchell meeting. It was, by Nixon's later account, traumatic. Magruder was pathetic, Nixon wrote. He had been one of Haldeman's bright boys, and he had no wish to harm his powerful mentor, who was also his passport to freedom. He pleaded for help with money and hinted at clemency to cut short his time if he had to go to jail—although Haldeman was careful not to include that hint in his notes. What the notes do show, unmistakably, is Magruder pointing the finger at Dean.

Magruder obviously got wind of Dean's reluctance to stick by him from their Monday phone call. Now Magruder confesses to Haldeman that he has perjured himself in testifying there was only one GEMSTONE meeting, and claiming that intelligence was never discussed with Liddy. Haldeman permits himself a rare comment in his notes ("this cld be the little thing that does it"). Magruder complains that since the false testimony was Dean's idea, Dean "cannot now say there was" more than one meeting and reveal discussion by Liddy of intelligence. Further, it was Dean who suggested destroying Magruder's desk diary, although CRP's lawyers had forestalled that.[24]

Haldeman summoned Dean from Camp David to sort this conflict out with Mitchell and Magruder that afternoon. Dean protested but came, and when he arrived at the White House, it was, he says, to a different Haldeman. Gone was the warmth of their past contacts. He told Dean to work the matter out with Mitchell and Magruder—"I'm not involved in this and I don't want to be involved." Dean said he recognized that Haldeman, too, was beginning to protect his flank; and he later wrote, "Now he had detached himself from me."[25] Haldeman sent Dean to meet his two coconspirators just down from the Oval Office. In answer to Magruder's pleading, Dean replied that the issue was moot; he was not considering testifying anywhere. But he then maddened Magruder by refusing to commit himself as to what he would testify to, when and if he was called.

Mitchell, says Dean, calmly asked him what he did remember. The young counsel explained that he remembered both meetings vividly, and had learned only afterward that Magruder had testified falsely. Dean says he was struck by Mitchell's "hapless calm" compared with Magruder's desperate aggression. When he ventured that he could "only speculate" on what had happened to get GEMSTONE authorized, however, Mitchell startled him by telling him to go ahead and speculate.

Dean had not expected to be challenged. He blurted out that he suspected that Colson and Haldeman had piled on the pressure and "you finally said 'what the hell' and approved it to get them off your back. My theory is that you just threw the dice on it." In his book, Dean describes Mitchell's response:

> "Your theory is right," he said quietly, "except we thought it would be one or two times removed from the committee."[26]

Dean's published version, which is far more colorful and personalized than his original testimony before the Ervin Committee, has him shattered by Mitchell's admission. (Mitchell later denied the exchange.) But Dean says he realized that if he told the truth, as he was preparing to do, he would have to betray this secret too. By telling him, Mitchell was playing his best card, counting on Dean's filial feelings for him. Dean claims, "*Now* I felt the razor edge between the squealer and the perjurer. I had never felt more squalid."[27]

Dean concealed his feelings well in reporting to Haldeman. He tells Haldeman that Mitchell and Magruder "both said they both signed off on this"—news that Nixon's top men would cherish. The bad news was that Dean himself could see no way to do what they wanted him to —corroborate their false testimony. Yet Dean tells Haldeman the more he looks at the "post-June activity"—the cover-up—"the more he thinks we can work it out." For some days, Dean and Colson have been insisting, separately, that the president needs to have legal advice from a top criminal lawyer to see precisely what the liabilities are. Now Haldeman apparently acquiesces—that "Dean hire one"—and Dean mentions Charlie Shaffer of Rockville.[28] Little does Haldeman or Nixon realize what Dean has in mind.

The president is the next to talk on the phone with Haldeman. His concern is that Dean use his executive and attorney-client privileges to avoid testifying at all about the two 1972 Mitchell-Liddy meetings he attended. Clearly, Haldeman and the president are still treating Dean as if he were one of them. Haldeman's faith in swallowing Dean's line about consulting a lawyer for them all is quite arresting in its naïveté for Dean was now off the reservation.

The investigations were gathering pace. The prosecutors, badly embarrassed by the McCord letter, had cut off their supply of secret information to Dean, which in itself unsettled the conspirators. But in truth Earl Silbert and his prosecution team were not making much headway. They hauled Liddy in before the grand jury and he took the Fifth more than twenty times. In vain did they get him immunized; his refusal to talk got him further sentences for contempt, but he did not break.

The prosecutors also immunized the Cuban Americans but, since they did not know much, got little from them. Hunt was also given immunity, but the previous week's payoff proved a good investment. There was a bit of a wobble reported by his lawyers. Hunt was jealous of McCord's apparently getting off and there was some talk of its being his "turn." But Dean soon reported to Haldeman that all was well. Hunt was supposedly providing the grand jury with a written statement and claiming his Fifth Amendment rights on all else. The slippery and distracting nature of Hunt's testimony was later noted by Silbert; he complained that "Hunt has lied a great deal before the grand jury in his six appearances."[29]

The prosecutors' greatest frustration was not being able to get their hands on McCord until after he had cooperated with the Ervin Committee. And Sam Dash, the committee counsel, was having his own problems. When, on March 26, Dash turned up to see McCord, together with Fred Thompson, the Republican minority counsel appointed by Senator Baker, McCord refused to speak to them, demanding to appear under oath before the senators themselves. Dash reluctantly agreed to put his request to Ervin.

To Dash's chagrin, Ervin okayed a closed session under Baker's chairmanship; Ervin had to absent himself because of a family funeral. Dash thought the session a disaster. With Baker in charge, the senators declined to grant McCord immunity from prosecution; indeed, they tended to treat him as a suspect rather than as a cooperating witness. In the end, however, it didn't matter. What he had to say was too electrifying and could not be kept secret. The maverick junior Republican senator from Connecticut, Lowell Weicker, who had unsuccessfully demanded that the hearings be public, was identified as the main "non-attributable" briefer to reporters.[30]

There were huge headlines. Mitchell and Colson—as well as Magruder and Dean—were now named as having knowledge of the bugging. Senior Republicans were appalled. Vice President Agnew, then still publicly untainted, was quickly telephoning Haldeman urging presidential counteraction; so was Republican National Committee Chairman George Bush. So, too, was the party elder, Senator Barry Goldwater. He told Nixon it was probably past time to make statements to clear up what Goldwater knew to be lies and misstatement. From such a loyalist that was ominous stuff.[31]

One totally new puzzle piece McCord provided the Senate investigators was Robert Reisner, Magruder's administrative assistant at CRP. Dash's staff subpoenaed him on March 29. When news of that subpoena appeared the next day in *The Washington Post,* Magruder realized the game was up. Reisner was to be that "little matter" Haldeman had earlier noted.

That Reisner had totally escaped questioning until now was a blunder by both the FBI and the prosecutors. Reisner not only knew that Magruder had attended all three GEMSTONE meetings with Mitchell but had himself been materially involved. He had arranged for an easel to be obtained for Liddy's famous charts at the show-and-tell presentation. Crucially, Reisner had been told by Magruder to inform Liddy that the plan had been approved after the March meeting. He had also handled the dictated logs of the Watergate buggings, putting them in the "Mitchell files," which Magruder kept. And on the day after the break-in, he had taken care of Magruder's files, even putting one through the shredder.

Reisner, who had been rewarded with a better job in the administration, went straight to the White House counsel's office, where he met Fred Fielding, Dean's number two. Fielding, he says, told him there was a lot of fast and loose play going on, and that in the end all you have is your integrity.[32]

Magruder made a few ineffectual defensive moves. He telephoned Reisner to offer him a lift to work, but Reisner declined. They agreed to meet with the CRP lawyer later but Reisner never showed up. Magruder telephoned Reisner demanding that he forget about the easel; he added, "Everybody else is cooperating . . . If this gets out of hand, they're going to impeach the president."[33] Reisner said he was sorry; he would have to tell the truth. That evening Magruder called again and was altogether calmer and apologized for being overly anxious.

The next day, Magruder flew to Bermuda to meet a lawyer he had been advised to engage. The lawyer was at a bar association convention, but they had urgent business. The way things were going, Magruder, although neither he nor anyone else in the conspiracy knew it, was running a few critical days behind Dean.

Nixon, though immersed in Watergate, had to attend to the presidency. On March 29, he made a TV address announcing price controls on meat, and in the same broadcast he gave warning to North Vietnam against violations of the cease-fire in Indochina. He had wanted to make his statement on Watergate at the same time, but had been persuaded to keep matters separate.

That night Haldeman got a dire warning from Mitchell about Dean. Everyone, according to Mitchell, is saying Dean is not making proper judgments. Haldeman is the only one Dean trusts, says Mitchell, and he should maintain close contact with him. At this point, however, the president's entourage made one of its regular shifts to the West Coast, leaving Dean behind.

On March 30 came Nixon's first real public concession that Watergate could not be ignored. The statement released by Ron Ziegler marked a profound change from Nixon's earlier position that present and former White House staff members would be prevented from testifying under executive privilege. The president now acknowledged that they would offer to appear "informally" before the Ervin Committee, under an arrangement to be worked out that safeguarded the separation of powers between the branches of government. All White House staff would, "at the direction of the president," appear before the grand jury. This last was gratuitous: They had no choice. If the grand jury summoned them, they had to appear on pain of contempt. Still, to embattled Republicans, it seemed that the president was at last taking some action to "get out front."[34]

In fact, in these last days of March, Nixon, although he did not know it, was about to undergo the slow torment of his betrayal by John Dean. This Friday the president's counsel went to meet Charles Shaffer at an apartment near his suburban office in Rockville, Maryland. The meeting had nothing to do with seeking criminal expertise for the White House. Dean wanted a lawyer. He was scrambling to save his own skin.

CHAPTER 12

The Linchpin

Nixon lost valuable time in April before realizing that John Dean had defected. By then he had effectively lost control of the situation, with Dean outwitting him.

John Ehrlichman had taken steps to nail Dean, if necessary, even as the presidential party left for San Clemente at the end of March. He was the new overseer of the cover-up, having first secured a letter of appointment establishing "attorney-client privilege" with the president. At Nixon's instruction, Ehrlichman had spoken to (and taped) Kleindienst, assuring him of the president's belief in the innocence of his top White House echelon (CRP was left unmentioned). But if anything to the contrary turned up, Ehrlichman told the attorney general, the president was counting on him for advance warning. Kleindienst could not help but note that at their last meeting Nixon had told him that his White House Watergate contact was Dean, and only Dean.

Colson, too, had been warning Nixon of Dean's big problems. Now someone tipped off Ehrlichman about the skeleton in Dean's professional closet: the conflict of interest dispute responsible for his leaving his original Washington law firm. Ehrlichman asked that Dean's White House personnel file be sent to San Clemente. Dean got the message, and it probably added to his eagerness to unburden himself.

Nixon thought that his March 30 statement had created a breathing space. Instead, it gave Dean the space to live a double life: by day still the president's counsel: by night the ultimate stool pigeon. A more sinister White House would have had him shadowed. But Dean's secret meetings with lawyer Charles Shaffer at the D.C. boundary with Maryland in a Friendship Heights apartment went undetected.

Shaffer, a courtly man from Tennessee, might have been a political problem for Dean. He was yet another of the Robert Kennedy Justice Department prosecutors who crop up throughout the Watergate story. He had been part of the so-called Hoffa team, which prosecuted the Teamsters Union leader. But Dean was not worried about Shaffer's politics; what he needed was expertise in criminal law. Beginning with a five-hour session on March 30, the two men spent much of that weekend talking. Dean wanted Shaffer to explain how to approach the prosecutors before they came after him, as they surely would based on the McCord charges. Shaffer wanted the whole story first.[1]

Dean says that for the first week or so he held off mentioning the president and national security issues, but he spilled all the rest: the GEMSTONE meetings, the cover-up, hush money, Hunt's safe. Shaffer told him he had, as he already knew, grave problems with obstruction of justice. At least by coming to him, he had quit the conspiracy. Shaffer says he was not particularly shocked by the revelations, but that he was impressed with the scale of the problem he was up against and the caliber of the people with whom Dean was tangling. Shaffer's first advice was that Dean minimize contacts with his fellow conspirators and make no further move to complete or transmit the "Dean report," which had by now run into many pages.

Late one night, Shaffer recommended that Dean not rush into meeting the prosecutors; they would haul him before the grand jury and hang him with charges before he had a chance to explain. Dean had big information to bargain with here. Although it was past midnight, Shaffer suggested that he call the member of Earl Silbert's prosecution team he knew best, Seymour Glanzer. Dean was appalled; he knew the way it worked. They would report to their boss, Henry Petersen, and the word would be back with Nixon in a flash. Shaffer insisted that if he were to represent Dean he had to do it his way; there were webs of informality that clever counsel could spin to protect both clients and information. As Dean watched, Shaffer telephoned: "Brother Glanzer," he said, "You need to talk with me. You don't know how badly you need to talk to me . . . put some coffee on."[2]

Shaffer negotiated an informal arrangement, not uncommon in

American legal practice, pending a final "plea bargain." Dean would offer information and the prosecutors provisionally agreed not to use it; they would not even take notes when meeting Dean and Shaffer. Most important of all, the prosecutors agreed to keep the entire Dean matter secret from their Justice Department superiors. Silbert and Glanzer pulled the head FBI agent, Angelo Lano, into their plot. If he wanted to keep abreast, he, too, had to vow not to tell his superiors. After learning about the way Acting FBI Director Gray spilled all his team's work to Dean, Lano could not resist the temptation to break discipline and be in on what was going on. This secret cocoon was absolutely vital to Dean's tactics.

Shaffer, before he delivered Dean to them in person, soon realized that Silbert and Glanzer, like Nixon, were transfixed with the planning and execution of the Watergate break-in. Despite McCord's naming names, they still did not understand the immensity of the cover-up and obstruction of justice that had been perpetrated. Shaffer was ready to show them but it was tough going, partly because Dean had so much detail to unravel for them.

Shaffer was primarily intent, of course, on securing the best deal for John Dean—the immunity from prosecution that Dean had been harrying Haldeman and the president for in the weeks before. That was difficult, too. The more he heard, the more Silbert was persuaded he could not allow Dean to have immunity; he was the linchpin of the conspiracy and he had hoodwinked Silbert. In any case, the question would have had to be referred to Silbert's boss, Petersen, and that would break the secrecy deal.

Dean, watching his back, was careful to inform Haldeman and other coconspirators that he was meeting with his lawyers. By April 4 he had telephoned Haldeman with the news that the lawyers were meeting with the U.S. attorneys. It is odd that Nixon and Ehrlichman, as lawyers themselves, did not immediately grasp what Dean was up to. The problem for historians with this key week is that there was no taping system installed in San Clemente. We have Haldeman's and Ehrlichman's notes and Nixon's diary reflections, but the account is necessarily more incomplete than the rest.

On the first Monday in April, Mitchell was worried about Dean and again phoned Haldeman, saying if Dean "does what he suggests, he will unravel the whole thing." Mitchell urges: "Only salvation is for me to talk to him," Haldeman notes. But it is Dean who calls Haldeman reporting crisply that his lawyer advises that he break off contact with Mitchell and Magruder and cease writing the "Dean report." Dean agrees—using the White House Situation Room—to transmit its first anodyne section on the Segretti sabotage. He tries some reassurance on Haldeman. If it comes down to an impossible situation, he would "rather take contempt or Fifth than cause anyone a prob," but that opens the way for him to be indicted.[3]

By this time Nixon is considering whether to "cross the bridge on Dean," seeing his counsel as part of the problem obstructing his second term. The president complains to Haldeman and Ehrlichman that the first three months—what was supposed to be his New American Revolution—"was all wasted." In vain, Nixon asks to be isolated from the Watergate discussions. He plans now to drop Kleindienst as attorney general, as well as dropping Gray from the FBI. But as far as the White House top staff is concerned, he orders that "there be no falling out amongst our own people . . . can't get every man for himself; all on the team—no one's going to flush you."[4] As for himself, he wants to counter Watergate by going out to the country—"get P on TV not wearing horns."[5]

The horns at that moment had been placed on Haldeman's head by none other than the junior Republican on the Ervin Committee, Senator Weicker. Ever since McCord had testified, Weicker had been publicly suggesting that Haldeman must have known about all the White House political espionage, and now he called for Haldeman's resignation. Senators Ervin and Baker promptly dissociated the committee, stating that it "has received no evidence of any nature connecting Haldeman to any illegal activities," but still Nixon foamed. He suggested asking Senator Goldwater to demand that Weicker disqualify himself, "like a judge who has a prejudice in advance."[6]

Dean, of course, had the evidence against Haldeman and everyone else, and was intending to give it to the prosecutors. But first he lulled the president's men on the West Coast into thinking the contrary. On the Wednesday of this fatal week, Dean sedulously reported to Haldeman a version of what his lawyers had found out from the prosecutors at their first meeting the previous night.

Dean explained that he would be called the following week before the grand jury. He was not a "target" of the grand jury (i.e., a potential defendant), nor was Haldeman; indeed, Haldeman might not be called at all, unless to corroborate other statements. Silbert had lied to Dean's lawyer—as one of his own hardball ruses—that Liddy was telling all to the prosecutors and had "freed the WH"; Dean swallowed it and passed it on to a no doubt startled Haldeman. Finally, Dean noted, in another variation on his theme, that his lawyer believed he might be given "practical immunity" concerning "technical violations" in the cover-up. Dean slyly added that he still thought that Magruder was the most serious problem, and that Magruder, too, now had his own lawyer.[7]

Haldeman's notes record a welter of Watergate discussion that week in California. Nixon is plainly terrified of having to drop Haldeman; his chief of staff is essential to him, not least in "the K situation—can handle the rest but not that," meaning the prickly Henry Kissinger. But the call for Haldeman to walk the plank is coming not from Kissinger but from John Connally, the former leader of Democrats for Nixon who has recently turned Republican. Connally, whom the president wants to promote as his successor, unsettled Nixon on Haldeman but fascinates him with the suggestion that Watergate is the opportunity to win the White House–Congress confrontation once and for all.[8]

Dean, meanwhile, keeps up the flow of unnerving news. Gordon Strachan has been to see Henry Petersen. Dean thinks that it is only about Segretti but speculates that the prosecutors have to be aware, from Hunt, Liddy, and the Cubans, that Liddy's White House contact was Strachan. Indeed, the prosecutors are onto Strachan. He, too, is subpoenaed for the following week by the grand jury. Dean also reports that secretaries are being interviewed. McCord has already put the Ervin Committee onto Liddy's secretary, but Dean tells them Mardian's has also been summoned. They are key witnesses: They typed the memos and kept the office calendars, which are to incriminate a number of important people. Dean pops in his daily call that he is meeting, as Haldeman notes, with "lawyers tonite."[9]

At the Western White House, the president and his men step deeper into the quagmire, Ehrlichman in the lead. He has a surreal meeting with CRP lawyer Paul O'Brien, who has been worrying about his own involvement in obstruction of justice and who travels all the way to the West Coast wanting, he says, to let the president know what's going on. O'Brien does not realize how much they already know, and Ehrlichman does not let on. For two hours Ehrlichman listens.

O'Brien's point was that Dean was the "key problem," especially because of the hush money. And Ehrlichman was probably jolted to learn that O'Brien was going to see Kalmbach, Nixon's personal lawyer and hush money fund-raiser, in nearby Long Beach.[10] Immediately after seeing O'Brien, Ehrlichman, with Haldeman, spent two and a quarter hours with the president.

Later that day, April 5, Nixon has Ehrlichman meet with a new candidate for FBI director. The president, without telling him, had firmly decided over a week earlier that Gray would have to go. Attorney General Kleindienst has recommended Federal District Judge Matt Byrne to take Gray's place but has insisted that Ehrlichman observe jurisdictional proprieties and delay approaching him. Byrne, at that moment, is presiding over the retrial in Los Angeles of Daniel Ellsberg on charges of theft and the 1971 release of the Pentagon Papers. Undeterred, and on Nixon's instructions, Ehrlichman had Byrne in, and even arranged for the president to shake hands with him. In his diary Nixon said of Byrne, "I was impressed by his real steel-like handshake. He has good tough cold eyes and is the right age, 42 years. Unfortunately his case isn't over for a month."[11]

The hapless Gray was to stay acting FBI director, twisting slowly in the wind, for three more weeks until he, too, was consumed in the conflagration. Nixon had Haldeman call Gray, ordering him to request his nomination be withdrawn—"tell him we're with him. No one felt worse than we did"[12]—and Gray promptly called Nixon back. It was a difficult call, Nixon confided to his diary; ultraloyal Gray obviously did not feel he had done anything wrong and did not want to go. But Gray was now expendable, in Nixon's view, for foolishly and unnecessarily reviving Watergate and tarnishing John Dean.

Finally, Ehrlichman, too, held a clandestine meeting. At least it was intended to be secret, but his secretary logged the location in his diary, the San Clemente Bank of America branch parking lot. Ehrlichman was catching up with another of his deep concerns—the president's private lawyer, Herbert Kalmbach. The problem, which O'Brien had raised with Kalmbach, was the hush money. Kalmbach faced appearances before the grand jury and the Ervin Committee and was disturbed to learn from a telephone call with Dean that he had retained Shaffer and that they should no longer talk. Ehrlichman now wished it to be forgotten that he had given the original okay for Kalmbach to raise hush money, and he hoped Kalmbach would lay it all on Dean.

As ever there is conflict between the accounts of the two, with Kalmbach's version much fuller. Ehrlichman, he says, surprised him with the news that Haldeman (who would also have been surprised) was leaving the White House soon and that he, Ehrlichman, would be taking over his duties. Kalmbach reported Ehrlichman saying: " 'Now, Herb, you make sure that you tell that John Dean directed you in this activity,' meaning the payments to the defendants, and I remember . . . turning to him and I said, 'And you, too, John.' And he looked at me and he nodded."[13]

As the presidential party prepared to leave the West Coast, they got the news from Dean that the prosecutors for the first time wanted to meet with Dean himself. The meeting was to be the next day, a Sunday. It would be off-the-record, with no action taken, Haldeman notes. In Dean's lulling version, the prosecutors want "what happened pre not interested in post—can of worms." ("Pre" the break-in, because they want Dean for his knowledge of the Liddy planning meetings.) Further reassurance is that the grand jury scope "is not broad."[14]

Thus, in contrast to his later Senate testimony, in which he claimed that on April 8 Haldeman told him not to meet the prosecutors, Dean in fact made no secret to Haldeman on April 7 that he would be meeting them. Haldeman's notes make clear the White House took this in its stride. It is difficult to reconcile this fact with Dean's later claim that Haldeman, in advising him on April 8 not to meet the prosecutors, made his imperishable remark: "Once the toothpaste is out of the tube its going to be very hard to get it back in."[15]

Nixon did not seem unduly disturbed. Haldeman's note of the conversation on the flight back has the president in a philosophical mood, reversing himself on Mitchell yet again. "Make clear to him P stands firm w[ith] him; P has gone over this whole thing have to hang together" Haldeman is told.[16] Yet even before the presidential plane had landed in Washington, Dean had gone to meet the prosecutors. At last Silbert and Glanzer came face-to-face with their tormentor. Silbert knew him from his Justice Department days, and by their account they were not very impressed. The enormity of Mitchell's betrayal of office hit them, but Dean lost them with the detail; his account was not very coherent. He, of course, knew far more than they did. They suggested he go back to his files, cross-check with newspapers, and try to pin down the evidence for his allegations. While Dean was talking to them in secret at Shaffer's Rockville office, the telephone rang with a call for him. It was the White House switchboard, with whom Dean had left Shaffer's number, "patching" in a call from the Spirit of '76, as Air Force One was renamed. He was to be in Ehrlichman's office at 4 P.M.

The best evidence for what was said at this meeting is Ehrlichman's phone call with Nixon later that evening, which was taped. The only version available of it is one of Nixon's edited transcripts (which have often proved to be inaccurate). It is apparent, however, that Dean withheld the fact that he had already been in discussions with the prosecutors. Nixon is left with the impression that Dean is meeting the prosecutors late on Sunday night merely to make an appointment to see them informally on Monday. And he is to testify to the grand jury only about events prior to the break-in and "not testify to anything after the fact," i.e., the cover-up. This is an extraordinary fantasy. Nixon makes it clear that he is counting on Dean to confine his incrimination to Magruder, and not get to Mitchell. "He'll be damn careful, he's protective about it . . . We don't want, Mitchell, you know popping off." In Nixon's vocabulary that meant sounding off against him in public.

Ehrlichman says that Dean is, first, to discuss the matter with Mitchell. Nixon says: "Mitchell must say—'Go in and hard-line it.' " But the president is concerned about what will happen after Dean "pulls the plug on Magruder." He reckons that Magruder is going "to pull it on Mitchell rather than on Haldeman." The president and his chief domestic adviser decide that Magruder, as Nixon puts it, "had better plead the Fifth Amendment. I don't think he's got any other choice."[17]

Nixon could not have been more ill informed. With Shaffer's upping the ante in pursuit of immunity for his client, Dean was now way past Mitchell and well into the cover-up. He was beginning to lay out the deep-six evidence against Ehrlichman and the hush money and $350,000 case against Haldeman. As for Magruder, he was beyond the option of staying silent under his Fifth Amendment rights and was about to corroborate Dean and take down Mitchell, as well as his friend Bart Porter, who had lied for him.

The reason Nixon, Ehrlichman, and Haldeman remained so ill informed for another week was the secrecy Dean had imposed on the prosecutors. Attorney General Kleindienst was in no position to keep the White House posted; Silbert and Glanzer had not disclosed a whisper of their contacts with Dean to him or anyone else. So with great cunning, Dean could tell his coconspirators that he was seeing the prosecutors, and at the same time serve as the sole source of what he was telling them. And, as we have seen, he lulled them.

It would be a few more days before Nixon caught up, and everything exploded in his face. He had to deal with another awful problem. He had been told in California that Vice President Agnew, following his calls to Haldeman, was offering to speak out in support of the president —on one condition: that the president see him first. Nixon put him off; presidents never have time for their vice presidents. It was not for another week, on April 10, that it became evident why Agnew was trying to see Nixon.

The vice president called Haldeman to his office for help with a problem. George Beall, the U.S. attorney in Baltimore, was investigating construction industry payoffs, campaign contributions, and tax evasion among associates of the former Maryland governor, now vice president, Spiro Agnew.[18] Agnew protested his innocence but explained to Haldeman that there might be potential for embarrassment. Could the White House talk to Republican Senator J. Glenn Beall, the prosecutor's brother, and ensure Agnew's name did not come up? Nixon's memoirs claim that he did not see how he could do anything to help. But Haldeman's note of his report to Nixon has him instructed to talk to "G. Beall" and say they were aware of the case. Indeed, the note states that Nixon was aware that the publicity will "finish the VP" because those under investigation were so close to him for so long.[19] (Only seven days later, Agnew remarked to Kissinger that "Nixon would be lucky to save himself.")[20]

The prospect of ousting a vice president was hair-raising, and it remained unknown to the public for another four months. As the Watergate scandal tightened around the president, with another scandal engulfing his potential successor, Nixon began, over the next few months, to regard Agnew as his "insurance against impeachment"—his assumption being that the Democrat-controlled Congress would never stomach Agnew to succeed a Nixon forced from office.

Watergate now moved to a crescendo. Also on April 10, Haldeman notes that they began scouting for top lawyers for himself and Ehrlichman in case they are "brought in tangentially." And for a new presidential counsel to supplant Dean, Nixon turned to one of his old law partners who had been serving at the White House since 1969, Leonard Garment. Appalled at what he learns, Garment calls for Nixon to clean house and—rather late in the day—place himself at the head of a "movement of reform."[21]

Ehrlichman's exercise in damage control began with an attempt to negotiate an arrangement for White House staff to appear at the approaching Ervin Committee hearings. It proved awkward. Senator Ervin had already ruled out Nixon's offer of informal appearances; "they're not royalty," he had said. Nixon's final card was to allow his people to testify provided the hearings weren't televised. He lost that bid, too. Clearly, he had very little clout left.

On April 10, Magruder gave in to pressure from his lawyers to come clean with the whole story. Once they heard it, they realized they had to get him to the prosecutors before they got to him. It was now a race to see who could tell the most, thereby gaining maximum consideration from the prosecutors.

That same day, Dean had his final meeting with John Mitchell. Dean's memo, produced at the instruction of his lawyer, and dated two days later, is the most contemporary source. In giving permission for the meeting, the prosecutors suggested Dean go wired, but he says he indignantly refused. This meeting took place in Mitchell's law office, just down the hall from his old CRP office. Mitchell once again explored the possibility of Dean's not testifying at all. Dean regretted that there was no way around it. "I said I appreciate that my testimony could cause him problems, and because of my personal feeling toward him I found this a dreaded situation." At least Dean told Mitchell what was coming, which is more than he did for Nixon.

Dean's memo has him saying that the whole thing was extremely damaging to the president and had to end. He hoped his testimony "would not start some sort of pissing match" between CRP people and the White House. He had "always been the man in the middle of this nightmare," meant nobody any harm, but now had to protect himself "from becoming everybody's scapegoat." Somewhat in conflict with his later story that he had "speculated" for Mitchell how Watergate got approved, Dean's memo stated, "I reminded him that I have never asked he [*sic*] or Jeb—flat out—to explain their involvement . . ."

Mitchell, Dean says, told him he planned to stonewall charges against him and inquired whether Dean would pass on to him whatever he told the grand jury—to which Dean replied that he should get a lawyer. Mitchell again sought to impress on Dean the fact that his testimony could be very embarrassing for the president and he should consider this carefully. Significantly, Dean says he left Mitchell with the impression that "the options of my not appearing were still under consideration—but not much consideration."[22]

The next day, that thought was still on Mitchell's and Nixon's minds. Mitchell told Haldeman that Dean was "the one thing that really unscrambles the operation"; they should try to get Dean not to appear before the grand jury. That point worried Nixon, too: "Is that the linchpin?" he asked Haldeman to put to Ehrlichman.[23]

Ehrlichman was working on a dodge to make things difficult for Dean and Magruder. The president could not stop the grand jury appearances; any interference at this stage would have caused an uproar. So they tried a different tack. Ehrlichman's idea involved cutting off the prosecutors' option of granting immunity from prosecution to any White House witnesses willing to cooperate with them. He telephoned Kleindienst. The attorney general passed on Ehrlichman's request to Henry Petersen, who, as head of the Justice Department's criminal division, had the sole statutory power over immunity. Petersen later said it did not make much sense to him at the time. It suddenly made more sense a few days later when Petersen learned that Dean had been secretly talking to the prosecutors. The White House was trying to frighten the squealers.

It was at this point that Charles Colson got back into the act and eventually touched a nerve with Nixon. Colson's own concerns at being incriminated had been reignited in early April. A lawyer friend of his had also been in Bermuda for the bar association convention and reported meeting Magruder and his lawyer at the drinks bar. According to Colson's friend, Magruder had "made sweeping charges about everyone in the White House being involved," including Colson. On April 4, Colson arranged to have himself put on a lie detector; he passed the test with his answer that he had no prior knowledge or involvement in Watergate.[24] On April 8, the polygraph story was front page in *The New York Times,* much to the scorn of Ehrlichman and others.

Nixon, however, was impressed. He interpreted what Colson told him about the Magruder Bermuda exchange as Colson's "evidence" that Mitchell might be trying to set up Haldeman as a scapegoat. On April 12, Nixon called Colson in Massachusetts and the tape of this conversation is remarkable for what it says about Nixon's despairing mood. Colson tries to buck up Nixon's spirits—to act on Watergate so that the country can be aware of the "extraordinary accomplishments" of his years in office. Nixon says some of his closest advisers believe that Watergate is "going to destroy the presidency" but Colson won't hear of it. It's a catchy name, "they'll remember the goddamn Watergate," Colson says, but it won't destroy the presidency, not if the president acts fast.

Nixon, despite a month's agonizing, sounds helpless. Of his closest people, he says, "What the hell we do about them I don't know." How to bring it to a conclusion, he says "nobody knows." He is worried about "everybody going off in his own direction. That's not good." Colson, who earlier had been approached by Ehrlichman for what Nixon calls a written "précis" of how he sees Watergate unfolding, reminds Nixon of what he has been suggesting since January: Mitchell ought to step forward and take the blame. That was his recommendation then; now he omits names but Nixon gets his point, except he says, "That's pretty tough" to take action. Colson promises to put his recommendations in writing the next day.[25]

On Friday, April 13, Colson returns, both with his recommendations and with startling news that sends Nixon and his men into a frenzy of weekend action chasing the wrong hare. It is that Hunt is about to blow and will tell all to the grand jury by Monday. It means that they have only until then to preempt him with action that can be depicted as the president "breaking" the case.[26]

So many events in Watergate happened over weekends—the break-ins, Mitchell's resignation, Nixon's reactions to McCord, Dean's going to his lawyer. But the long weekend from Friday, April 13, to Monday, April 16, was a climacteric. Despite frenzied press coverage, the real events took place largely in secret and the action proceeded on two tracks. The president and his men were reacting to a major perceived threat from Hunt, and quickly lined Mitchell up to be the fall guy. But suddenly they were ambushed: The prosecutors finally decided they had to report to their superiors what they had been hearing from Dean.

Colson had set all the panic buttons ringing on Friday when he told Ehrlichman the story about Magruder in Bermuda and added that Magruder had been talking to journalists. Ehrlichman explodes and Haldeman has Larry Higby telephone Magruder three times that Friday, taping him, which had by now become second nature among colleagues at the White House. They are gut-wrenching conversations, and in the course of them Magruder says something electrifying: that his testimony will give Mitchell, Dean, and Strachan as well as himself problems. "They want big fish . . . and they're going to get . . . me and Mitchell."[27]

Tantalizingly, Magruder claims that he still has not decided whether to stay silent or to tell the whole story. In fact, that very Friday Magruder's lawyers were preparing to take him into a meeting with the prosecutors to try bargaining a lesser sentence in return for his cooperation. The prosecutors for the first time, although the White House does not yet know it, are obtaining crucial corroboration for what Dean has been telling them.[28]

Ehrlichman, when he reviews the Higby tapes, realizes that the White House now possesses firsthand evidence with which to confront Mitchell. But he is also preoccupied by Colson's Hunt story—if Hunt blows, not only Mitchell but also Ehrlichman, for his role in the Ellsberg affair, is in jeopardy. Colson has it both from government sources and Hunt's lawyer, Bittman, that the hush money details are "all coming out." Hunt would also say he had opposed the second break-in, but had gone ahead because Liddy said that Mitchell had ordered it. Colson, says Ehrlichman, also reported a rumor that Mitchell had given a "blood oath" to Liddy that he would get a presidential pardon.[29]

The planning—or plotting—reached a frantic pace. Colson and his law partner, David Shapiro, had developed a scheme involving Liddy: He would be called by the president and told that he would now get clemency, but *only* if he told the truth. Liddy would "get" Mitchell. The centerpiece of the Colson-Shapiro plan was an announcement that a presidential investigation by Ehrlichman had been turned over to the prosecutors. This would "steal march on Hunt, break the case. P. comes out on top."[30]

Meanwhile, Colson recommended, Dean should be dropped and, crucially, Mitchell, the "key to Watergate, be persuaded by the president to step forward." Shapiro added the bizarre recommendation that Mitchell plead insanity; Shapiro wanted to be defense counsel with such a plea. When this was reported to Nixon, he thought it an "absurd idea," but the rest of it caught his fancy. Nixon told Haldeman he really felt for Mitchell but "M should say I take respon; maybe Moore shld talk to him; nothing we can do to save them."[31] Colson's idea that Dean be replaced is rather rashly communicated by Ehrlichman to Dean, who understandably takes this as more evidence he is being abandoned. Still Nixon's closest advisers do not know that either Dean or Magruder has actually talked to the prosecutors in person. They are focused on the following week and so plan to use the weekend to work out how to get the president out in front.

Of all the Watergate tapes those of Saturday, April 14, are the most redolent of an underworld cabal. The admissions made, even by Haldeman and the president, who alone knew that the secret tape machines were running, are breathtaking. For example, in their first meeting that morning Nixon discloses to his two paladins that he *did* imply clemency for Hunt in his January discussion with Colson; he even has a note of Colson's handling of it. And Nixon further discusses how "the clemency issue" has to be handled with Magruder and even Mitchell. They are to be given expressions of deep affection from the president. That should do it. Nixon acknowledges, too, that like the rest of them he knew that Dean was deep in the payments to defendants—"I knew it, I knew it," he says, before correcting himself for the tape. "I knew, I must say, I didn't know it, but I must have assumed it . . ." Finally, Nixon admits to hearing from someone about the March 21 payoff to Hunt's blackmail threat, three weeks earlier, that "Mitchell then said it was taken care of—am I correct?"

When the president's impeachment was recommended by the House of Representatives, this tape transcript was not yet released; it emerged only later in court after Nixon had left office. It leaves very little to the imagination.

The plotters' main purpose, after the weeks of minuets, is to have Mitchell fall on his sword. He is to be told by Ehrlichman, based on their tape of Magruder's talking to Higby, that allegations have come to the president's attention and the president must act. Either Mitchell moves first by going to the U.S. attorneys or he faces the music when the president turns all his "new" information over to the attorney general. The idea is to make it look as though Ehrlichman has investigated the affair, found out the truth for the first time, and made it possible for the president to crack the case. They even contemplate using the previous day's date as the moment when the president first heard; later they would change that, equally falsely, to March 21, when Dean gave the "cancer on the presidency" briefing. It was audacious and might just have worked had they initially covered all the bases. But they had not.

Their first meeting that day lasted nearly two and a half hours. As the tape shows, they relied both on Magruder's statements (as taped by Higby) and on what Colson and Shapiro were telling them (though Nixon worries, "Is Colson a liar?"). Their principal concern is Hunt. Ehrlichman reports Colson's belief that the next forty-eight hours are the last chance to get out front; "once Hunt goes on, then that's the ball game." Nixon wonders whether Hunt is preparing to talk on "other activities . . . what Colson meant about the door to the Oval Office" (meaning the break-in at Ellsberg's psychiatrist, which was a constant Nixon worry). Ehrlichman says he could not talk about it with Shapiro present—implying a national security matter.

They discuss Magruder, and Ehrlichman opines that having the Higby tape in their possession "beats the socks off him if he ever gets off the reservation." Nixon comments that "that tape is invaluable, is it not?" and moves to Mitchell. Ehrlichman explains that the purpose of having Mitchell called in is to say "the jig is up." Ehrlichman mentions a postmidnight telephone call from Dean recommending something similar—with a startling difference. When Mitchell stonewalls, Dean suggests the president would call the U.S. attorney and ask to appear before the grand jury himself. (Dean now says it was Shaffer's idea to jolt them.) At the time Nixon responded, "I won't even comment on that."

Haldeman, understandably less worried now about his own vulnerability with Magruder's having exculpated him on the Higby tape, objects to trying to get Mitchell head-on. He suggests reverting to his old idea of getting Mitchell by a different route, "for Magruder to come voluntarily and nail Mitchell." That way, Haldeman would repay Magruder's loyalty. Asking an innocent man to carry the blame wouldn't do; they needed to have a rationale for sacrificing Mitchell. Thus they come as near as they ever do, on any tape, to acknowledging how Watergate started. Haldeman says he accepts the "scenario that Dean spun out to Mitchell" where Mitchell said the bugging was supposed to "be three or four times removed" from CRP.

Mitchell, he says, was not "specifically aware of the Watergate bugging at the time it was instituted," but he authorized the Liddy plan. When Nixon first released his own edited transcript of this tape, the following passage was deleted and one can see why. Haldeman says of the Liddy plan, "He had okayed that." Nixon interrupts with "He knows very well." Nixon goes on to explain that only a month earlier, Mitchell had told Nixon's friend Bebe Rebozo, "In the ITT thing, I may have perjured myself but I sure didn't on this goddamn thing."

With that key point, it is possible to understand the explanation that follows. Ehrlichman has had Mitchell's previous sworn testimony reviewed by a staffer. So they believe that Mitchell authorized Liddy's intelligence plan, didn't know precisely about the plan to go back into

Watergate, but has somehow managed not to commit perjury about it all, as he assured Rebozo. Says Ehrlichman, "He was never asked the right questions." There follows a classic game plan sequence where Ehrlichman recites a hypothetical newsmagazine lead and Nixon leaps at it:

Ehrlichman: ". . . these efforts resulted in Mitchell going to the U.S. attorney's office on Monday morning at 9 o'clock, asking to testify before the grand jury. Charges of cover-up by the White House were materially dispelled by the diligent efforts of the president and his aides in moving on evidence which came to their hands in the closing days of the previous week."
Nixon: I, I'd buy that.

At one point, Nixon announces he has decided that Dean has to go: "give 'em an hors d'oeuvre and maybe they won't come back for the main course. Go out, John Dean." But Nixon quickly understands Ehrlichman's argument that he is more valuable on the inside than loose on the outside. And Nixon starkly agrees when Ehrlichman explains the hush money involvements:

Ehrlichman: . . . If the wrongdoing which justifies Dean's dismissal is his knowledge that the operation is going on—
Nixon: Yeah.
Ehrlichman: —then you can't stop with him. You've got to go through the whole place wholesale.
Nixon: Fire the whole staff.

They run through the names of people who should speak to Mitchell before Nixon suddenly says to Ehrlichman, "John, go see Mitchell." Haldeman laughs. They know Mitchell cannot stand Ehrlichman. But Nixon says "the message to Garcia has got to be carried"—a heroic exhortation, familiar to most Americans, from a classic Spanish American War morality tale. Ehrlichman will take on the mission; he is the lawyer, he has "investigated" Watergate. Haldeman, though, will telephone Mitchell to invite him down, so that he does not think he is being shafted "unilaterally" by Ehrlichman. They rehearse what he will say to Mitchell.

Ehrlichman, as a lawyer, realizes that they are in possession of incriminating information that they have to be able to say they turned over to the authorities. They have to "make" a record. Ehrlichman says to Nixon: "It is not what Mitchell says that matters today. It is the fact that you have acted on information today." He proposes getting in touch himself with the prosecutors on Sunday.

Nixon responds that it "is a pain for me to do anything. The Mitchell thing is goddamn painful." He instructs Ehrlichman how to explain Nixon's absence. "You've got to say: 'This is the toughest decision he's made. It's tougher than Cambodia, May eighth and December eighteenth [both 1972], put together. And that he just can't bring himself to talk to you about it. Just can't do it . . .' " Ehrlichman says he will appeal to Mitchell with "today is probably the last day you can take that action, if you're ever going to take it. Do the president a bit of good." Says Nixon, not for the last time, "We're going to prick this boil and take the heat. Am I overstating?"[32]

From here the president went to a delayed appointment on Vietnam cease-fire violations with his new vice chief of army staff, General Alexander Haig, and Henry Kissinger. Kissinger notes that Nixon was absolutely shattered.

He soon found out why. Len Garment filled him in: Watergate was about to blow and make turmoil over Vietnam seem trivial. Garment did not know the full dimensions, but he predicted, said Kissinger, that "the outcome of the recent election might well be reversed; there was likely to be a battle to death." Only a wholesale purge of the White House could save things.[33]

Kissinger said he realized they were now faced with stagnation in foreign policy and a rearguard struggle to prevent everything from unraveling. Kissinger says he got Garment to let him pass the word at a meeting he called for Sunday of the administration's leading policy figures—George Shultz, the treasury secretary, and Arthur Burns, the chairman of the Federal Reserve Board, the U.S. central bank.[34]

How much of Kissinger's account is amplified with hindsight is unclear. Nixon says of the morning session with Kissinger and Haig that he went beyond his "good meeting" on Vietnam. His dictated diary says he told Kissinger that "we really had to draw the wagons up around Haldeman." What he did not yet tell Kissinger was that this very morning with Ehrlichman and Haldeman, he had decided that because of Watergate, Kissinger's move to succeed William Rogers as secretary of state must be delayed. They needed the appearance of stability.[35]

But there was not much time left. As Mitchell flew down posthaste from New York, Haldeman telephoned Magruder, tracking him down with difficulty through his lawyers. At last Haldeman (also taping him) discovered that Magruder had decided to tell all to the prosecutors. Even then Magruder did not confess he had already met the prosecutors the day before. But the substance was clear: "It's gone now," Magruder said, he was pleading guilty and not standing trial. The prosecutors have "got witnesses on witnesses on witnesses now" and "there's no reason for me to be quiet because they don't, they've got everything anyhow." Haldeman mouthed his nonknowledge for the tape so as not to implicate himself.[36] But afterward he recounted Magruder's story to Nixon, hyping it a little, "You got to understand, Bob, is that this whole thing is going down the drain," Haldeman quotes Magruder saying, "everybody is gonna crumble."

> *Nixon:* . . . what about the White House spot?
> *Haldeman:* Jeb says unfortunately, "I will to a degree implicate John Dean and to, possibly to some degree, Gordon and I hate to do it," but he said, "Where I am now there's nothing. I, I can't pull any punches."
> *Nixon:* Shit.

Nixon can see that this "does it." Yet because Magruder is pleading guilty and not standing trial, they delude themselves that his evidence will remain secret. Just as Dean is keeping them in the dark about his actions, so Nixon does nothing here to alert Dean to the danger looming from Magruder. He is more immediately concerned to help reinforce Gordon Strachan, who is still part of the stonewall.[37]

Ehrlichman has listened on an extension to the Magruder-Haldeman telephone call just before Mitchell arrived at the White House. Knowing that Mitchell was still ignorant of Magruder's defection, however, he did not let on. The two men sat in Ehrlichman's office at his desk rather than the coffee table; Mitchell noted him fidgeting. He said later it occurred to him the changed location might have been because he was being taped, and he was right. Neither liked nor trusted the other. Ehrlichman had fancied being attorney general when Mitchell stepped down, and fretted when Mitchell got Nixon to put in his friend Kleindienst instead. The meeting was a classic circling of wrestlers failing to come to grips.

For a hard man, Ehrlichman turned limp. He did not "take the message to Garcia," or anything like it. Nixon had said he did not want Rogers to talk to Mitchell because Mitchell would wind him around his finger. Whether Ehrlichman simply funked it or thought he could be more subtle, he did no better. Not only did he not follow his own suggestion of saying "The jig is up," but he also completely failed to deliver the president's message that Mitchell should take the opportunity to go down to the U.S. attorney or else face the prospect of the president's incriminating him with the authorities.

Instead, Ehrlichman said, "I wouldn't attempt to tell you what to do" and then came up with a confabulation that Nixon had certainly not discussed in their preparatory meeting that morning:

> *Ehrlichman:* The thing that was lurking in the, in the president's mind and that I could not disabuse him of was, "is—you think John thinks that he ought to hold back for me?" . . .
>
> *Mitchell:* Hold back from the president?
>
> *Ehrlichman:* Hold back—no, no, no, no. Hold back from coming forward on account of the president. In other words, if you were to think I shouldn't really—even say to yourself, "I shouldn't come forward on this because I would hurt the president," or something of that kind. He said: "Well, somebody's got to talk to him and say: 'Don't, don't hold back on account of the presidency.' "
>
> *Mitchell:* . . . well, what you're saying is that he's leaving the options to me.
>
> *Ehrlichman:* Totally.

In fact, Ehrlichman was supposed to say Mitchell's options had run out. With that it is hardly surprising that Mitchell declines to see the president, saying he did not wish to embarrass him, and departs stating he is staying exactly where he is—stonewalling it. What possibly pushed

Ehrlichman off his stride is that Mitchell planted some barbs of his own, reminding Ehrlichman that the Mitchell faction had been covering up for the White House other things that were worse than Watergate. At different times in the meeting, Mitchell mentions the $350,000 fund, Colson's call to Magruder, and the genesis of the whole intelligence plan at the White House.

When Ehrlichman tries getting near the point that time to "put pluses on the side of the presidency is rapidly running out," Mitchell bluntly asks him what "brother Dick" is proposing to do. The message carrier falters and suggests it comes down to giving the president's "Ehrlichman report" to the authorities. Mitchell instantly emphasizes that nothing must be done "to impinge upon anybody's rights." He is against any statement being rushed out. Indeed, he suggests the president get a top lawyer in—Chapman Rose, one of their old New York law partners, in fact—and let him talk to the attorney general first.

The nearest Mitchell comes to admitting liability is that he cannot now change his position, "because I'm too far, far out." Regarding his involvement, he says, in another classic phrase: "I got euchred into this thing, when I say, by not paying attention to what these bastards were doing. . . . I really don't have a guilty conscience. I didn't authorize those bastards to go ahead." In other words, it happened behind his back.

Ehrlichman warns Mitchell, without disclosing that the evidence has come from Magruder, that the prosecutors have "got you made here." He adds the false story Dean's lawyer got from Silbert that "Liddy has been talking," and that Hunt has been saying that Liddy told how they had to go back into Watergate for the second break-in because "Mitchell personally insists on it." Mitchell is disbelieving. He says, "That's about as far from the facts as you can possibly get." And he states, despite the impossibility of getting a fair trial with all the publicity, his final refusal: "With all of this there's certainly no possibility that I would ever turn around and say, 'Yes, I was part and parcel of this' "[38]

Mitchell left the White House, never to return. A CBS-TV crew filmed him on the way back to New York. He gave them the brush-off and stayed loyal to Nixon, as he did to the end, even as his close friend had decided to cast him adrift. Despite Ehrlichman's promises to keep Mitchell abreast of secret developments with the prosecutors, no one made any effort to do so.

The only real tip-off to a friend came from Magruder to Bart Porter, his young former assistant. Porter, believing Magruder innocent, had agreed to lie about the CRP money allocated to Liddy and had been a vital crutch for the previous September's cover story. Porter was now appalled. He came to Washington from New York and consulted Magruder's lawyers. They promised to alert him when Magruder went to the prosecutors, but promptly deceived Porter by ensuring Magruder got in first. Magruder bumped into Porter on Saturday outside the White House, and he apologized; he told him that he had preempted him. Porter belatedly contacted the prosecutors and eventually went to jail for perjury.

After meeting with Mitchell, Ehrlichman felt they were on top of the story. But they still had no idea about Dean, who was, in fact, well ahead of them. He came around from his own White House office to meet Ehrlichman and Haldeman alone for the last time. He says he wanted to rattle their cage a bit. That morning with Shaffer, he had worked up a list of who might be in jeopardy, which he read out in Ehrlichman's office. It had fifteen names on it. There were only three, predictable, names for the "pre" break-in activities. But heading the "post," or cover-up, list were: Haldeman, Ehrlichman, Dean, LaRue, O'Brien, Kalmbach, and Ulasewicz, with question marks by Stans, Parkinson, Colson, and Bittman. He had all the "post" names listed for potential obstruction of justice, with the statute sections noted plus the penalties: five years jail and, respectively, $10,000 and $5,000 fines.[39]

Dean says he further added the explosive news—in contrast to all the assurances he had been given them until now—that the list was based on what Shaffer had learned from the prosecutors. He said that Ehrlichman and Haldeman were targets of the grand jury investigation, and so were all the rest on the list. Ehrlichman protested that he had talked to Kleindienst and been told that the prosecutors were investigating only the break-in. Haldeman said, "Keep the damn list to yourself."[40] But Dean also showed it to Richard Moore at the White House and went through the reasons why it made sense. Moore, he said, was shaken and said that if it was true, it would be a tragedy for the country.

Ehrlichman and Haldeman did not grasp the seriousness of Dean's list. Ehrlichman was in a hurry to brief the president on Mitchell, and he laughed when he raised the subject of the list with Nixon. Haldeman said it was a worst-case scenario, and then seemed to mock Dean. Haldeman said Dean had suggested that maybe everybody on the list should plead guilty and get immediate clemency from the president.

Haldeman: That shows you the somewhat unclear state [laughs] of John Dean's analytical thinking.
Ehrlichman: No way.
Nixon: It's a shame. There could be clemency in this case and at the proper time, having in mind the extraordinary sentences of Magruder . . .

Magruder, of course, has not been anywhere near sentencing yet, but Nixon has just been told by Haldeman that, with cumulative sentences, given the counts against him, he could face up to 135 years in jail.

Nixon is more interested in Ehrlichman's report about Mitchell. Told that he "lobbed mud balls at the White House at every opportunity," Nixon is furious: "Throwing it off on the White House isn't going to help one damn bit." But he concedes, "It's a hell of a problem for us." Nixon is not really surprised that Mitchell refused to step forward. He still thinks Mitchell will never go to prison but he is aghast at the prospective developments. "Does a trial of the former attorney general of the United States bug you? This goddamn case . . ."[41]

It was a frantic Saturday at the White House. The president and Haldeman were also trying to put together a Haldeman public statement covering his supposedly tangential involvement in the Segretti affair, which Nixon dismissed as mere dirty tricks. But first Ehrlichman had to complete his "investigation" by meeting Magruder and his lawyers. When they told him what Magruder had now revealed to the prosecutors, Ehrlichman realized that his proposed "report" added nothing to what the authorities already had. Still, to substantiate the spurious claim that the president had been active in uncovering the cover-up, he had to complete the report and submit it. Dean had advised him to stay clear of Silbert for fear of being hauled before the grand jury himself. So Ehrlichman telephoned his favorite law enforcement officer, Richard Kleindienst.

The attorney general was not amused. His own prosecutors have kept him in the dark; it is clear from the tape of Ehrlichman's phone call that Kleindienst does not even know they have talked to Magruder. Now as Ehrlichman tells him Magruder had implicated the CRP high command, including Mitchell, it is Kleindienst's turn to caution Ehrlichman. He tells him he is perilously close to information on the commission of a crime: "Yours is a very goddamn delicate line as to what you do to get information to give to the president and what you can do in giving information to the Department of Justice." Kleindienst reminds Ehrlichman that he has always suggested a special prosecutor for the Watergate investigation.[42]

When Ehrlichman rejoins the president and Haldeman, Nixon for the first time gets into serious discussion about whether Haldeman will have to resign over his Segretti statement. Republican leaders are bound to call for it. The issue has been festering since Connally put it to Nixon two weeks back. Haldeman makes it absolutely clear that he has no wish to resign but acknowledges that for Nixon it is a "crunchy thing." Dean would have to go, too, he remarks. Nixon impatiently concentrates on suborning Dean's evidence. "I wish we could keep him away from that," he says regarding Dean's insistence that the hush money was a conspiracy to obstruct justice—even though Ehrlichman recalls to Nixon's face that the defendants were paid for "the purpose of keeping them on the reservation."

In frustration at the end of these daylong conversations, Nixon says that what concerns him is "the dragging it out and being, having it the only issue in town." He declares:

> The thing to do now is have the sonofabitch done—indict Mitchell and all the rest and there'll be a horrible two weeks—a terrible terrible scandal . . .[43]

Apart from the nagging Haldeman issue, Nixon's view is that the wagons can be drawn around himself and at least Haldeman and Ehrlichman. That evening before going out, Nixon lamented his lost Watergate opportunities in what he says was to be his last "full diary dictation" for more than a year.

> It's too bad we were unable to do something about it. I suppose during the election campaign there was a feeling we couldn't do anything for fear of risking the election. Yet that was a mistake, as it turned out, because we were just postponing the day that we would have to face up to it. Immediately after the election, of course, would have been the time to move on it frontally, and yet we did not move then for reasons that I probably will understand later. I just wasn't watching it closely then and nobody was really minding the store. We were leaving too much to Dean, Mitchell, et al.[44]

Their evening is spent, of all places, at the White House correspondents annual dinner. Nixon, viscerally, hates the occasion. This year two tiresome cub reporters from *The Washington Post*—Woodward and Bernstein—are getting awards. And the emcee will cause much merriment with mock introductions between the top White House men present and a man they may be getting to know better—Judge Sirica.

Later that evening, Nixon was on the telephone again to Haldeman. He could not let the issue go, but was bracing himself to get his side of the story out. He now yields to his top men testifying on TV at the Ervin hearings, partly because Haldeman predicts that once the story breaks the networks will no longer wish to cover the "stale" hearings. Nixon confides that Bebe Rebozo is staying overnight and he has filled him in on Mitchell—yet his other friend, Mitchell, remains unfilled in. Nixon wants a "line" established by all involved that they had no intent to buy silence with the payments to the defendants. That way, "It's the word of the felons against the word of the men who raised the money." Prematurely, Nixon says to Haldeman:

> Now we pretty much know what the worst is. I, I do, I don't know what the hell else they could have that's any worse.[45]

The president telephones Ehrlichman. He wants Colson forewarned of Magruder's blabbing; "we owe it to Chuck" to help him not commit perjury. Ehrlichman agrees that such a tip-off gets around Kleindienst's admonition to him against passing on criminal information. But still there's to be no warning to Mitchell. Ehrlichman coldly reckons there's "not one chance in fifty" Mitchell won't be indicted, and that his best chance is to get a change of venue for the trial and stall it for months.

The hush money is still on Nixon's mind and so is Dean. The president bares his teeth and tells Ehrlichman what Dean has to understand about who holds the keys to his future.

> *Nixon:* Look, he's got to look down the road to, to one point that there's only one man that could restore him to the ability to practice law in, the, case things still go wrong.
> *Ehrlichman:* Uh-uh.
> *Nixon:* Now that, he's got to have that in the back of his mind . . . don't tell him, but you and I know that.
> *Ehrlichman:* Yeah.
> *Nixon:* With him and Mitchell there isn't going to be a goddamn question . . .[46]

That is the single starkest reference on the tapes to the extortionate abuse of presidential power. Others have been told of the promise of "so-called clemency" and pardons: Here with Dean, Nixon is suggesting that he can withhold a pardon if Dean goes off the rails, for he emphasizes that only a president, by pardoning a criminal, could restore his license to practice at the bar.

Nixon discusses further how they will work on Sunday to prepare statements to forestall Hunt's "blowing"—and then bids Ehrlichman get a good night's sleep. It was probably the last for any of them. Ehrlichman notes he has an urgent call in from Kleindienst, which he will leave until the morrow. Another procrastination too far.

CHAPTER 13

A Procrastination Too Far

Sunday, April 15, was the watershed of Watergate. It was the day Nixon finally learned he had been deceived by Dean. From then on, he was certain Haldeman and Ehrlichman would be incriminated. And although he hated the thought, he realized that they, like Mitchell, would have to be sacrificed if he himself were to survive.

It was a day that overloaded even the normally efficient White House. There were so many comings and goings that the president's daily diary, which is a bible of record, got in a mess. And because of the overload and because it was Sunday, the secret presidential recording system ran out of tape at one key location, or so Nixon later said.

Attorney General Kleindienst, unlike the president, had stayed on after the White House correspondents dinner, calling at the hospitality suites hosted at the hotel by leading newspapers and magazines. As he was leaving, he received an urgent telephone call. It was Henry Petersen; his prosecutors had broken the Watergate case. They had to come around to Kleindienst's house right away, in spite of the fact that it was 1 A.M.[1]

Earlier that Saturday evening, Petersen had been forced to go back to his office. The U.S. attorneys Silbert and Glanzer felt they could no longer keep their dealings with Dean secret from their superiors. Magruder had furnished them with corroboration of Dean's account of the

GEMSTONE planning meetings and the initial cover story, and Dean had gone way beyond Magruder to implicate Haldeman and Ehrlichman in the hush money. The prosecutors had been made a gift of the massive obstruction of justice case at the heart of government, and it was still going on.

Petersen, when Silbert and Glanzer arrived, concealed whatever irritation he felt at his subordinates for withholding such vital information from him. His world had fallen in. Mitchell had been his boss, given him his chance and his unprecedented promotion to deputy attorney general; he had trusted Dean, but he and Mitchell had duped him.

The prosecutors explained how Dean was bargaining for immunity and that they were inclined not to give it. They also challenged Petersen's own cozy relationship with Dean, which was about to turn nasty. They then told him that Dean had a tale of Ehrlichman's agreeing that documents from Hunt's safe be given to Pat Gray, and that Dean had told Petersen about it. If that was true, why had Petersen not told his prosecutors? It was an embarrassing moment.

Even though Dean had not yet so much as whispered to Silbert and Glanzer about his dealings with Nixon, Petersen saw the implication. According to Glanzer, he got to his feet, paced around his office, and after several violent expletives said, " 'The president is going to be impeached.' And that was very startling to us. And he said, 'It doesn't make any difference whether he's involved in complicity in this matter or whether he's just plain incompetent. Either way they will say he should be impeached.' "[2]

Petersen said they had to report to Kleindienst, and he brushed aside their objections that they had promised Dean to keep their dealings secret. Glanzer reached Shaffer, who in turn reached Dean; hearing this in the middle of the night, Dean was frantic. He pleaded for Shaffer to go back and have Petersen allow him to tell the president of his dealings with Silbert before the prosecutors did. It was too late. With Dean at least, Petersen was dealing no longer.

Kleindienst was still in his dinner clothes when Petersen arrived with Silbert and Glanzer. He had been weeping, he told them, ever since Petersen's call—although, of course, Kleindienst had known since Ehrlichman's telephone call earlier that evening that Magruder had implicated Mitchell. They went over the case until 5 A.M. and agreed that Kleindienst had to brief the president first thing that morning.

Kleindienst says he wept again. He could see that Mitchell, his mentor, was going to jail. He had, of course, feared as much since the approach by Liddy at the Burning Tree golf club on the day of the Watergate break-in, but had turned a blind eye. Now it stared him in the face. He decided, since there was apparent conflict of interest, that he would have to recuse himself from the case and have Petersen take over. He snatched a couple of hours' sleep before trying to reach the president.

Dean says he slept uneasily, and on awakening got in touch with Shaffer again. They decided they had to up the ante further still if they were to have any chance of getting immunity before the ax fell. They would meet again with Silbert and Glanzer that Sunday and Dean would have further disclosures for them.

When Kleindienst called the White House, the president was still asleep. Nixon did not breakfast until 9:45 A.M. Kleindienst called back at 10:13 and found the president unsuspecting. He assumed his attorney general was calling him about Magruder and Kleindienst's pet proposal for a special prosecutor to take over from the Justice Department, a plan that Nixon had firmly decided the night before to reject. Kleindienst managed to leave him none the wiser about what had happened overnight; the two-minute call never got to the nub. Despite Kleindienst's request for an urgent meeting, Nixon scheduled it to follow an hour-long reception after a Palm Sunday service in the East Room. In between, Nixon managed time for a forty-minute meeting with Ehrlichman.

In light of what is to come, their talk has an air of bizarre nonchalance. Nixon anticipates the indictment of Mitchell and Magruder: "Well, Christ almighty, that's the fish, the big fish. Goddamn it, what more do they want?" He comments that Kleindienst "hasn't been very helpful throughout this thing," and mulls over what Hunt's testimony on Monday will do to Colson. Ehrlichman says they are hoping that Colson is having "surreptitious contact with Hunt." Then Ehrlichman spins a wonderful new scenario not heard before on the tapes.

Say, Ehrlichman suggests, that the hush money had a "benign motive" if it was to protect Nixon's election campaign; a corrupt motive if protecting culpability of those involved pre-Watergate, like Mitchell and Magruder. The two motives get intermingled. Nixon latches on. "Take Dean as a case in point. This says something that Dean was not, we could get him out of it, he could weasel out . . ."

Ehrlichman now adds his fantasy. Since Hunt had written forty books, he might have written another, an insider exposé of how he broke into the Watergate at the request of CRP. The White House would pretend that it did not care what Hunt said to the prosecutor in secret, but a Hunt book would have been politically damaging. So, says Ehrlichman, the choice of forestalling publication by arranging family support payments was "pretty easy." (Having dreamed this up, Ehrlichman was later to testify under oath that this had been his noncriminal motive throughout.)

Both men profess ignorance of what Kleindienst wants to see Nixon about. Perhaps, says the president, he might have "other information." Ehrlichman reckons that "he will this morning have, I think, as much knowledge about this thing as we have."[3]

Nixon goes off to his service, comforted by his 60–33 percent approval rating in the most recent Gallup poll; Ehrlichman goes back to a long meeting he had interrupted with Gordon Strachan, despite Kleindienst's warning that he should no longer be dealing with criminal evidence. Strachan is supposed to get his story straight so that he won't incriminate Haldeman when he testifies. But Ehrlichman's notes show that Strachan clearly stated that he had sent Haldeman the famous political matters memo reporting the approval of the Liddy plan and that after the break-in, he had showed it to Haldeman. Strachan also explained that at one stage in the Magruder-Liddy feud, he had suggested that Mardian take over intelligence from Liddy, but that Haldeman told Strachan to let Dean handle it. These latter tidbits implicating Haldeman further were probably news to Ehrlichman.

After 1:12 P.M. they mattered little. Kleindienst had fretted during the long reception following the worship service. He had never before been to the president's hideaway office in the Executive Office Building, and he was waiting in the outer reception area when Nixon finally arrived. Kleindienst plunged straight in.

He mentions "what has been transpiring for a week with John Dean and his attorneys," but Nixon interrupts, sidetracking into other issues and impressing Kleindienst with his knowledge of the Magruder and Dean "information." It takes Kleindienst quite a time to get through to Nixon. But he gets his attention with the real news: Dean, Strachan, and Magruder might testify to Haldeman's and Ehrlichman's knowledge, and conduct, either before or after the break-in. "Both?" exclaims Nixon, betraying his surprise that Ehrlichman, too, will be brought in. There's no proof yet, but there is circumstantial evidence that could be "a very serious question with regard to both of them," Kleindienst says. That is why he is disturbing the president this Sunday afternoon.

Even though Nixon learns that Dean is the source of some cover-up allegations against Ehrlichman, he still does not seem to register the scale of Dean's betrayal. He immediately protests that Haldeman and Ehrlichman have given him absolute denials. He suggests that Kleindienst and the prosecutors have got to "live with" Dean's and Mitchell's claim that they said no to Liddy at the second GEMSTONE meeting. Kleindienst tries to get across the fact that the "serious question" is the obstruction of justice, but Nixon, instead, argues with him over motives in paying defendants, eventually agreeing that it is criminal to offer convicted defendants money to stay quiet—precisely Hunt's case, of which Nixon is thoroughly, if secretly, aware.

Kleindienst throws in a further worry. There is a "possible case on Colson," too, albeit a weak one. Unaware of the president's secret involvement, Kleindienst suggests they have to "keep this general story off the streets," which, with Judge Sirica, will be difficult. Mitchell, he says, will of course be indicted but he suggests that his case might, with appeals and lawyer's motions, take ten years. And Kleindienst raises the hope that with a clever lawyer, Mitchell might beat conviction at trial.

Nixon asks his attorney general for his recommendation, but before Kleindienst can answer steamrollers him:

Nixon: . . . It's embarrassing and all the rest but it'll pass. We've got to, we've got to just ride it through, Dick. . . . We don't run to the hills on this. . . . The main thing is to handle it right.

They reflect on the way the first investigation was handled. Kleindienst notes that the conduct of the White House last summer "really created great suspicions in the minds of Silbert and Petersen." Kleindienst's own conduct in turning a blind eye is indirectly touched upon:

Kleindienst: . . . Everybody was just scared to death. They didn't know where the damn thing was going to end.
Nixon: They thought there was an election, you know. Let's face it, that's why John—
Kleindienst: Why sure, I understand, I understand. . . . I determined that I was going to have the broadest kind of overview . . .

It has all rather taken them away from the main point. Now, twenty-five minutes in, to the president's astonishment, Kleindienst reveals how Dean has implicated Ehrlichman. He has informed the prosecutors that Ehrlichman told him to deep-six the contents of Hunt's White House safe, that they were instead given to Acting FBI Director Gray, and that Ehrlichman initially ordered that Hunt was to leave the country. Manifestly, Nixon is staggered. Four times he queries Kleindienst to confirm that it is Dean himself who has revealed this information. Then he tries to steer Kleindienst away from Hunt's safe. That's national security, "not the Watergate." But now the president at last knows what Dean has been up to.

Unsurprisingly, Nixon seems distracted, and at first finds it hard to follow Kleindienst's convoluted explanation of Dean's bargaining process: the fact that Dean's statements are "conditional"; that if the prosecutors do not conclude a "deal" with him, "then Dean presumably wouldn't testify this way with respect to Ehrlichman . . ." Anyway, Dean won't be offered immunity, Kleindienst insists. Nixon is perplexed, but the thought percolates. If denying Dean immunity meant that Dean would not testify . . . and if Dean does not testify about Hunt's safe or about getting Hunt out of the country, then "they have no one else who can say that." Ehrlichman would be off the hook.

They go on to Haldeman. Kleindienst mentions the transmittal of documents, via Strachan, with the budgetary approval for Liddy's "sophisticated intelligence operation" and, as Nixon's own notes show, "indicating Liddy was in eavesdropping." Then there's the $350,000 fund given to LaRue, also via Strachan. Nixon affects no surprise. Kleindienst, unaware of the depth of Nixon's involvement, now presents the only two options he sees for safeguarding the presidency. One is that Nixon, before the story gets out, ask his top men to take leaves of absence until the issue of their being indicted is resolved. The other is to suspend them after their alleged involvement is disclosed.

Nixon expresses his unhappiness at the idea of removing anyone who is "innocent"; removing them too soon "indicates that maybe I know something." But he recognizes that he has to appear to Kleindienst to be willing to act without fear or favor. "The Justice Department and the presidency are going to come out clean because I don't tolerate this kind of stuff," Nixon says. "But my point is, Dick, I can't let an innocent man down . . ."

Liddy, Kleindienst assures him, is not talking after all (in that, if nothing else, the prosecutors had tricked Dean). Nixon again cannot mask his astonishment; he asks Kleindienst to check. And what about Hunt? They have been panicking all weekend because Hunt is supposed to be blowing the next day. "Hunt doesn't know anything," says Kleindienst. Surely, the president says, Hunt knows about the obstruction of justice. "Isn't that the one where Mrs. Hunt or somebody . . ." —realizing, perhaps, that he is saying more than he should, Nixon adds—"I don't know what that is . . . don't want to get so deeply involved."

Kleindienst repeats that they have "got to do something quick before this gets out of hand." And Nixon, before the attorney general can mention it, remarks that Kleindienst will have to disqualify himself from the case because of his association with Mitchell. But Nixon wants Silbert to remain the lead prosecutor under the nominal oversight of Henry Petersen. Kleindienst objects that Petersen is also a Nixon appointee and vulnerable to attack.

Ever since Watergate began, Kleindienst has lobbied for an outside special prosecutor, not to take the case over from the U.S. attorneys but merely to give it an impartial look. The special prosecutor would be on hand to substitute for the attorney general in making final prosecution decisions. Nixon rejects the idea (only to find himself forced to accept something far worse a little later), and Kleindienst goes off to fetch Petersen,[4] the man Dean has told Nixon was a "good soldier."

Nixon summoned Ehrlichman immediately to his office. There is no tape of this meeting; Nixon later claimed the spool had run out during his meeting with Kleindienst and nobody was on duty on Sunday to replace it. Ehrlichman's notes show no realization that Dean had done them in. They indicate only that Nixon told him Dean's lawyers—not Dean himself—had been meeting with the prosecutors for a week. But beyond Dean's implicating Ehrlichman in the order to "deep-six" and have Hunt leave the country, Nixon tells him that Kleindienst does not believe either he or Haldeman are indictable—"tangential stuff," Ehrlichman notes.[5]

Nixon's memoirs glide over this hour-long meeting. His office diary shows that Haldeman was not telephoned for another hour. And the transcript from that call—phones were on different tape machines—again omits mention of Dean's squealing. Haldeman's note of a subsequent conversation with Secretary of State Rogers indicates that Kleindienst had outlined the case against himself and Ehrlichman but there is still no mention of Dean. One may conclude that Nixon did not rush to inform his two closest aides what awaited them.[6]

By the time that afternoon was over, however, Nixon had certainly heard enough to realize the threat to them all was grave indeed. Kleindienst located Petersen working on his boat and rushed him as he was, in a grubby T-shirt, jeans, and sneakers, to his first direct meeting with Nixon. Kleindienst gave Petersen written delegation to act as attorney general in the Watergate case, then accompanied him to fill in the president fully on what Dean was disclosing.

Dean, Petersen reported, had spent all day Saturday talking with the prosecutors in Shaffer's office. They had told him they would do the best they could for him, and offer him their good offices if he cooperated.[7] Dean had, Petersen went on, made a prima facie case against both Haldeman and Ehrlichman on obstruction of justice. As for planning Watergate, Petersen said a key factor in the information brought against Haldeman by Dean was that the White House chief of staff had failed to take action when Dean informed him of the second GEMSTONE meeting. Nixon, until this time, had been telling himself that this was in Dean's favor; now it implied criminal inaction by his top man. Petersen noted that he was amazed how calmly Nixon took the allegations of Haldeman's and Ehrlichman's involvement. It was possible, Petersen said, that Magruder might plead guilty the next day and put out a statement implicating himself and perhaps Mitchell.[8]

Petersen, like Kleindienst, believed that dire action was needed. He flatly recommended that Haldeman and Ehrlichman resign. According to Nixon, Petersen said:

> The question isn't whether or not there is a criminal case that can be made against them that will stand up in court, Mr. President. What you have to realize is that these two men have not served you well. They already have, and in the future will, cause[d] you embarrassment, and embarrassment to the presidency.

Nixon reiterated that he had to have proof of their guilt before he could fire them. Petersen replied, "What you have just said, Mr. President, speaks very well of you as a man. It does not speak well of you as a president."[9] Nixon suggested that Petersen talk to both his top men to get their side of the story but Petersen did not fall for that one. First, he said, he wanted to build the case—and would the next day put to the president what he had on them in writing.

Petersen testified later that in those few hours Nixon faced, "in my judgment, the last chance for the administration to demonstrate its integrity."[10] At the time, they agreed the president should deal directly with Petersen on Watergate matters. Unobjectionable on the face of it, this arrangement for the first time gave Nixon a direct line into the way the prosecution was developing.

Instead of communicating the worsening news to Ehrlichman and Haldeman, Nixon decided on an excursion. He went off with Bebe Rebozo for a two-hour cruise on the presidential yacht *Sequoia.* Nixon says that he gave Rebozo an account of the case against his top aides. He says that he wanted them helped with their legal expenses and Rebozo volunteered that he and another of the president's close friends, Bob Abplanalp, would raise up to $300,000. It would be given them in cash, "because he [Rebozo] would not be able to do the same thing for the others."

Further support for the suspicion that Nixon had delayed fully briefing his top assistants about Dean is to be found in a note in Nixon's memoirs: "I dreaded having to go to the White House and face the bleak choices I knew were waiting . . ."[11]

It was 7:45 P.M. Sunday and both Ehrlichman and Haldeman were waiting. They had been talking to William Rogers, the secretary of state, about their rapidly shrinking options. Rogers now advised that none of the president's men should step aside until charges were brought. Anyone indicted should take a leave of absence; only those admitting to crime should submit resignations. To Nixon, the latter meant Dean, and eventually Magruder and Strachan, who had been given high administration posts outside the White House.[12]

Haldeman's notes of the Sunday night meeting with Nixon convey a whiff of the fast-moving drama. It seems quite clear that Haldeman is hearing for the first time the full story of Dean's treachery. In a rare comment Haldeman records "P obviously very awkward." The combination of Dean and Magruder means that Haldeman and Ehrlichman are going to be called before the grand jury in short order—although it "troubled" the president that Petersen did not wish to have them both before the grand jury until he had heard all the others. "Petersen is crusading," Nixon says.

What to do? For instance, "What will LaRue say he got the $350,000 for?" To which Ehrlichman replies that LaRue is going "to open up completely." Ehrlichman mentions having a call in to Dean asking him to come to the office. The president says Dean owes it to him to come in and explain what he thinks he is doing. Nixon telephones Petersen to check whether there is anything further to report and immediately discovers that Dean is again one jump ahead of them. Petersen reports that Dean's lawyer has already informed them of Ehrlichman's call, and he says that he has advised against such a meeting. However, Dean has proposed sending a message to the president, and Petersen says he sees no objection to a meeting between Dean and Nixon. Petersen's other news is that Mitchell has met Liddy this Sunday, and that, in Petersen's view, a signal from the president would get him to talk. Nixon agrees and calls back a few minutes later telling Petersen to call Liddy's lawyer that evening.

Almost immediately there is another call. It is "Haldeman's Haldeman," Larry Higby, with a phone message that Dean wants Haldeman to pass on to the president. Dean, who has been telling the prosecutors even more than Petersen knows, has realized that Ehrlichman's call means Nixon has finally heard of his turning state's evidence. Dean's message to Nixon read:

1. I hope you understand my actions are motivated totally out of loyalty to you, the President. And if it's not clear now it will become clear.
2. Ehrlichman requested to meet tonight but I feel it inappropriate at this time. I am ready and willing to meet with you, meaning the President, at any time to discuss these matters.
3. I think you, meaning the President, should take your counsel from Henry Petersen who I assure you does not want the presidency hurt.[13]

At Nixon's instruction, Haldeman asks the White House operator to get Dean at home and instruct him to come in immediately to meet the president. Dean arrived at 9:20 P.M.

Dean and Nixon had not met for three weeks. Dean, admitting later he felt shaken at meeting the president after having taken it upon himself to end the cover-up, testified in his first version that the president was friendly. By the time he got to his book, Dean has the president disheveled, with alcohol on his breath. Dean says he began by trying to explain why his going to the prosecutors had been out of loyalty. However, he had difficulty deciding whether Nixon was intent on breaking with the cover-up or on continuing it—something not noted in his Senate testimony.

Nixon's memoirs give only three paragraphs to the meeting, and he noted that whenever Dean spoke of Ehrlichman his voice had "a vindictive edge." Nixon's first contemporary handwritten note reads "totally privileged"—reflecting that Nixon had quickly sought assurance from Dean that he would never mention his conversations with the president to the prosecutors. Nixon also noted that Dean mentioned the wiretapping of news columnist Joseph Kraft and "other newsmen." It was another piece of Dean blackmail, deftly placed. In *Blind Ambition,* Dean turned it into a Nixon injunction that he was not to talk about national security matters. At this time, only the 1969 Kraft tap, done at Nixon's instruction by freelance operatives, was still not public knowledge.

Nixon had ready a list of questions—the first, interestingly, was "how deep was Petersen in this." Now that he was to be dealing with Petersen directly, Nixon needed to catch up on all Dean's insider trading and on a man Dean had repeatedly described as "invaluable." One of Dean's answers was that Petersen had provided Dean a daily report on the original grand jury investigation and that there was nothing "improper" in this.[14]

At Dean's suggestion and in his presence, Nixon telephones Petersen —claiming that Dean has left the room—to refine his earlier orders that Liddy should now break silence. Liddy's lawyer should be brought into the Oval Office to hear the message straight from the president. It has always seemed a bizarre incident, especially as Liddy never broke silence. But it gained a totally different complexion when years later a Nixon tape of the following day was released. It turns out that Dean suggested to Nixon that Liddy knew about the illegal wiretaps and that that's why Nixon should call him in.

As there is no tape of this Nixon-Dean meeting (the empty reel had still not been replaced that Sunday night), we must depend on the two men's own accounts and on what Haldeman noted Nixon saying afterward. Both Nixon and Dean recall they discussed the matter of Hunt's blackmail, his threat, and clemency on two occasions. According to Dean, Nixon made light of it; Nixon's March 21 suggestion that he could get a million dollars had only been a joke, the president said. And near the end of their talk, Nixon had stood up from his desk (where the microphones were) and moved away in a manner Dean thought significant. Nixon "went behind his chair to the corner of the Executive Office Building office and in a nearly inaudible voice said to me he was probably foolish to have discussed Hunt's clemency with Colson." That remark, Dean later testified, suggested that Nixon had been trying to avoid being recorded on any tape recorder placed there to set up Dean. (Dean was not among the handful of Nixon's staff who knew about the automatic taping system.)[15]

In this same conversation, Nixon caught something from Dean that he *did* want on tape. It was the discussion of Dean's negotiations with the prosecutors. Nixon said Dean seemed very cocky and he got the distinct impression that Dean was saying he expected to get immunity from prosecution. That made Nixon seethe.

As for obstruction of justice, "Dean briefed Haldeman and Ehrlichman every inch of the way"; they are involved, regardless of motive, says Dean. Obstruction of justice is "as broad as the imagination of man." It's a conspiracy of circumstances.[16] Nixon's memoirs omit it, but Haldeman's notes show that Dean thought the evidence against them so overwhelming that it would require them both to take leaves of absence.

In *Blind Ambition*, Dean says that when Nixon asked him if he would resign, too, Dean replied that he was not happy about it but that he would oblige whenever the president asked. Obviously, at this point Dean knew that he hardly had a choice in the matter, but the comment brought from Nixon the rash remark that Haldeman and Ehrlichman also stood ready to go. That was an extraordinary thing to say, and it put them on an equal level of "guilt" with Dean. The president's counsel was to use Nixon's gaffe with supreme cunning against them, and Nixon, in the days to come.

Dean claims, but Nixon makes no mention of, a spectacular farewell. "I told the President that I hoped my going to the prosecutors and telling the truth would not result in the impeachment of the President. He jokingly said, 'I certainly hope so also,' and he said it would be handled properly."[17]

Ehrlichman and Haldeman were immediately called back in. There was one further item not in Nixon's or Dean's version, but which Nixon told them Dean had said. It was about the contents of Hunt's safe. "D thks Gray may have destroyed it," Haldeman's notes have Nixon telling them. This was a very explosive matter. Conspiracy in criminal destruction of evidence is something no high official wishes to admit. Dean later claimed that it was in January that Gray first told him he had destroyed the Hunt material and that he had told Ehrlichman then. Gray had no such recollection.

According to Haldeman's notes, what happened next was that Ehrlichman, in Nixon's presence, telephoned Gray at home. "G said he'd say knew nothing about it," Haldeman records. After a further twenty-minute conversation with Nixon and Haldeman—of which we know nothing—Ehrlichman calls Gray a second time. Now Haldeman's notes read: "must tell truth—state the facts don't get crosswise on this. G says he didn't know where the papers came from, didn't open it—destroyed it."[18] (The next day Gray, when asked by Petersen, was still denying that he had received any documents.)

In early March, Gray and Ehrlichman had had one conversation about these files in which Gray suggested that Dean "stand awful tight."[19] Gray's own testimony as to these late Sunday night calls does not support Ehrlichman. In the first one, Gray says, Ehrlichman simply informed him that Dean had been talking to the prosecutors for some time, "and we think you ought to know about it." He did not remember volunteering that he would say he knew nothing, which Haldeman noted down at the time. Of the second call, Gray said Ehrlichman bluntly told him, "You better check your hole card," to which Gray replied, "I destroyed them long ago."

Gray was interrogated at length by the grand jury for his interpretation of the term "hole card." He testified that Ehrlichman had neither replied "God, what have you done?" nor "I'm glad you destroyed them, that's following my orders." Gray could only remember "hole card" and he took it to mean "look to your defenses." (In stud poker, a hole card is the one dealt facedown on the table; only you can look at it, and it might be regarded as your hidden resource.) Gray took it to mean the files that had been given to him, and so straightaway he answered he had destroyed them.[20]

This night in Nixon's office the conspirators are not seeking information; they are in desperation trying to rerig new versions to explain their actions. Nixon and Haldeman, who witnessed Ehrlichman's side of the conversations, later supported Ehrlichman's claim that the telephone call to Gray was the first time he had heard of the documents' destruction. Nixon, writing about only one of the calls, says, "We watched the blood drain from his face as he listened to the reply." Nixon quoted Ehrlichman as saying, "There goes my license to practice law."[21] It was a true prediction. Ehrlichman was to go to jail denying that he had ever intimated to Gray that the documents be destroyed. But both he and Nixon had overlooked their taped February 14 conversation in which Ehrlichman revealed to Nixon that he had told Gray, "I don't care what you do with it so long as it never appears." Only two weeks later, when the story broke in the newspapers, did Nixon accept that Gray had to resign.

Poor Henry Petersen. Having been up all the previous night and having said good night to the president twice already this evening, he received yet another call from Nixon near midnight to report a little of his conversation with Dean. Nixon omits, significantly, the fact that Gray has confessed to the destruction of the documents. Nixon claims that he had asked Dean, "Now when do you want to resign?" and Petersen, who later claimed he was exasperated, retorts that it is premature. After all, Dean, he says, is "the first one who has really come in." Nixon blusters:

> We must not have any questions now on this. You know I am in charge of this thing. You are and I am. Above everything else, and I am following it every inch of the way [a phrase Dean just gave him], and I don't want any question that's of the fact that I am way ahead of the game. You know I want to stay one step ahead of the curve.[22]

Nixon claims to Petersen that Haldeman and Ehrlichman are ready to resign (something omitted from his memoirs). But the president is clearly pumping Petersen for information. He repeats his request for "a little sheet of paper" from Petersen listing what he feels their vulnerabilities are. Nixon says he has told Dean to wait—again a stretch of the facts—and he says he will hold off on Dean's resignation until he hears from Petersen. This, again, is something he has no intention of doing. Nixon is soon on the telephone again to Haldeman, arranging to have the president "cracking the case" story planted by Press Secretary Ron Ziegler.

Haldeman has already talked to Ziegler about Dean's being relieved of his Watergate assignment. Now they are to put out "re P on top of case—Petersen and Dean talked to—break in case—P ahead of Justice Dept, pushing Liddy etc." Nixon confides what Petersen has told him about the obstruction of justice allegation: "It's [a] tough case to prove but *looks* bad E & H only involved as not actors just exposed to it . . . this is where need lawyer."[23]

So this catastrophic day ends on a characteristic fantasy of PR, of good advice for Haldeman and Ehrlichman to get a lawyer, and of persisting ignorance about Dean. Nixon continued to be indecisive about his young counsel; he did not want to throw Dean to the wolves for fear he would himself be dragged down. But it was already too late.

That Sunday afternoon, before meeting the prosecutors, Dean claims he showed his lawyer copies of the ultrasecret Huston plan, which he had removed, illegally, from his office. The Huston plan, it will be remembered, dealt with Nixon's proposals to free the intelligence agencies from legal restraints on bugging and break-ins against domestic dissenters. Dean's lawyer was appalled. The documents were placed in a safe-deposit box and the key eventually handed to Judge Sirica.

The incident indicated that Dean was ready to play hardball in his negotiations for immunity. That afternoon he disclosed to Silbert and Glanzer that the Watergate burglars had earlier conducted a break-in at Ellsberg's psychiatrist's and that the photographs were sitting in Justice Department files. What Nixon, Ehrlichman, and Krogh—and Mitchell, indirectly—had believed was worth paying Hunt blackmail to keep silent about had almost casually been revealed by Dean.

The prosecutors were stunned. This on top of the massive obstruction of justice! They did not quite see where the matter fit, but they took with deadly seriousness the fact that Dean had just given them knowledge of a new crime. Moreover, its target, Daniel Ellsberg, was himself on trial at that very moment. They realized, Silbert says, a disclosure had to be made to the court. They did not wake up Petersen but decided to sleep on it and inform him on Monday.

CHAPTER 14

Crack-up

As this Palm Sunday ended, Nixon could not help but feel he was on the way to his own Calvary. Secretly, he knew that the jig was up, not just for Mitchell but for them all. Haldeman and Ehrlichman would have to go, too, yet he had to be certain that in going they would not turn on him. By Tuesday, he was confiding to Haldeman that he had to try to save "what was left of the presidency," and the next morning, still bleaker, was requesting of his chief of staff that "if this goes the way it might, wants me [Haldeman] to take all the office material and hold it for the library." It was only three months since Nixon's second inauguration.[1]

The Nixon who prided himself on being tough in poker and politics, playing a mean hand and facing down foreign and domestic opponents, now had poor cards, but his play was weaker still. Most un-Nixon-like, he complained that week, "I've trapped myself."[2] They were now, as Dean put it succinctly on March 21, in "a domino situation."

As most politicians discover, it is tougher to deal with friends than enemies, and Dean, so recently counted as one of the inner circle, was a friend turned unpredictable enemy. Nixon knew better than Haldeman and Ehrlichman what hostages he had given to Dean in their many hours of discussion in March. The one that most tormented Nixon and to which he kept returning was the Hunt payoff. As Haldeman's notes reflect, "P should have turned it to US Attorney" when Dean told him of Hunt's threat. "Real prob. give it hard thot."[3]

The interests of the top conspirators were diverging; they all sensed that. On the evidence of the tapes, Nixon and Ehrlichman, particularly, started to assume new attitudes toward their past knowledge. The classic Nixon whopper, whatever his motive, was to say to both his closest men that he had never been told that Hunt was threatening Ehrlichman with his "seamy things" message. "I didn't know," Nixon tells them twice on April 16. Yet the March 21 tape carried the exchange with Dean he had forgotten or wanted buried:

> *Dean:* Hunt now has this direct threat against Ehrlichman. . . . He says, "I will bring John Ehrlichman down to his knees and put him in jail. I have done enough seamy things for he [*sic*] and Krogh that they'll never survive it."
>
> *Nixon:* What's that, on Ellsberg?
>
> *Dean:* Ellsberg and apparently some other things I don't know the full extent of it.
>
> *Nixon:* I don't know about anything else.[4]

Nixon's dilemma was horrible. Apart from covering up his own criminal knowledge, even from his closest associates, he had been made the possessor of official knowledge of prima facie criminal allegations against the senior White House staff—not to speak of close associates outside. He absolutely had to take action, to "get out front," before the system did. Not to act risked further cover-up, yet to act might cause further defections damaging to himself. The dilemma was never resolved, because it was probably unresolvable.

This Holy Week 1973 was the beginning of the period that people then old enough to be aware remember from Watergate, when seemingly never-ending revelations broke daily in the press and on television screens, each one more amazing than the last. It started quietly. As late as April 17, Haldeman could observe with satisfaction, "You know where the Watergate story is in *The Washington Post* today? Page nineteen."[5] But that same day, Watergate was front page again in the *Los Angeles Times* with a story claiming that a major White House Watergate initiative was imminent and that one or more high-level officials would be named as having acted without the president's approval. This, though Nixon never admitted it, was the result of the leak he and Haldeman had arranged on Sunday night, and it pointed at Dean.

What to do about Dean remained the central quandary. He still occupied his EOB office—"an asp in our bosom," Colson warned—in spite of the fact that, as Ehrlichman put it, he and the president were now in an adversary situation. But Nixon, not wishing to turn on Dean lest Dean turn on him, found it impossible to move decisively.

On what was to be his final day of meetings with Dean, Nixon first tried getting him to sign a letter offering to resign, "as a result of my involvement in the Watergate matter," or to request a leave of absence for the same reason; Dean declined. He would go only if Haldeman and Ehrlichman went, too. Nixon backed down. Then Dean held out the possibility of his not testifying after all. The prosecutors might simply find that the cases against White House people were merely technical violations and "chuck them all out."[6]

It was as if Dean had mesmerized him. Nixon had been told by Kleindienst and Petersen that unless Dean pulled off a bargain with the prosecutors, all the charges he had secretly made against everyone would not be used in evidence. One way to obstruct the bargaining was to deny Dean immunity. That way instead of being a cooperating witness he would become a defendant. Maybe that would work. Colson, for his own reasons, agreed. "Let's get it clearly understood that that sonofabitch doesn't get immunity. I want to nail him."[7]

But Dean was, as usual, ahead of them. On April 16, Petersen gave the president alarming news of the tough line Dean's lawyer, Shaffer, was now taking in his negotiations with the prosecutors. It was that if Dean was not given a deal but instead made to stand trial, then Dean and Shaffer would "try" the whole administration. Dean had been only an "agent" of higher-ups.

Petersen: His counsel says he wants a deal. This man was an agent. This man didn't do anything but what Hald—

Nixon: Haldeman and Ehrlichman told him to do.

Petersen: —and Mitchell, and if you insist on trying him we, in defense, are going to try Ehrlichman, Haldeman, Nixon, and this administration. That's going to be our defense.

Nixon: He'd try it. The president too?

Petersen: It's a goddamned poker game. Yessir.[8]

That was the first time Nixon heard what he took as an explicit threat against himself. It now seemed clear that he was damned if Dean did get immunity and testify as a witness and damned if Dean, without immunity, was cornered as a defendant. But since Petersen volunteered that the prosecutors would grant Dean immunity only as a last resort, Nixon decided to take a chance. A denial of immunity certainly offered the opportunity to delay Dean's testimony. By this time, Nixon had convinced himself that once criminal charges were brought, the Ervin hearings—where he could no longer prevent Dean from testifying—would be postponed so as not to prejudice the trials. In addition to delay, announcing that there would be no immunity might make Dean think again, and it had the added bonus of making Nixon look good. Nixon's memoirs disclose his underlying reason: "The final part was my calculation that, without immunity, Dean would be less likely to turn against me in hope that I would grant him an eventual pardon."[9]

Timing was critical. Petersen promised Nixon twelve hours' notice of Magruder's appearing in court, with Haldeman and Ehrlichman possibly listed by the prosecutors among the coconspirators, albeit unindicted at this stage. But the *Los Angeles Times* story suggested that the news might break in the press first. On April 17, in the middle of an official visit by Italian Prime Minister Giulio Andreotti, Nixon decided to get out front of Watergate.

He had imagined simply announcing "I can say that the Watergate case has been broken," but had not dared. He knew the prosecutors believed they had done it, and still Dean's phrase echoed from the day before. To Nixon's "We triggered it," Dean had had the nerve to respond: "When history is written . . . you'll see why it happened. It's because I triggered it. I, I put everybody's feet to the fire because it just had to stop."[10]

The president decided to make a brief statement in the White House newsroom before reporters and TV cameras, but to take no questions.

There was incredible tension. The press had been on standby since 3 P.M. It was now 4:42 P.M. Nixon said he had two announcements to make. One reporter noticed that his hands were shaking. The first announcement was of a surprise agreement with the Ervin Committee. Because the separation of powers between the executive and legislative branches was, Nixon claimed, being preserved in a new arrangement, White House witnesses would, after all, agree to appear, but executive privilege was "expressly reserved" and might be asserted in a refusal to answer "any question." Nixon made clear he was making this exception to his standard practice only because "wrongdoing has been charged." It was less of a concession than it appeared.

The second announcement was his first personal statement on the Watergate case since the previous October. There had been, he declared, unspecified "major developments." On March 21, he stated, he had begun "intensive new inquiries" and the previous Sunday he had reviewed "the facts which had come to me in my investigation," as well as the prosecutors' case, with Kleindienst and Petersen.

Nixon then said that anyone in the executive branch who was indicted would be suspended from his post, and anyone convicted would be discharged. This was fairly obvious. But then he made a gratuitous statement. He felt it made the White House look good, though it mattered little and had even less impact on the public. The wording had to be hedged so as not to infringe the statutory right of the prosecutors. But it went straight to the heart of Dean's situation, and Dean knew it:

> I have expressed to the appropriate authorities my view that no individual holding, in the past or present, a position of major importance in the administration, should be given immunity from prosecution.

Nixon ended, as he was to end so many more public statements: "I condemn any attempts to cover up, no matter who is involved." With that he left the briefing room. Press Secretary Ziegler was engulfed in a storm of questions. One exchange, now a classic, came out of this briefing. Ziegler, who had been told much more about the collapse of the cover-up than he has ever let on, had rehearsed with Nixon and Ehrlichman beforehand how he should describe Nixon's statement. It was, Ziegler was told, "the operative statement." When in the turmoil of questioning he used the phrase, R. W. Apple, Jr., of *The New York Times* asked if that meant all previous statements had been "inoperative." Yes, said the hapless Ziegler.

The president's announcement on immunity, Dean and Shaffer recognized, had stymied them. They continued escalating their negotiations. Once the prosecutors made it clear that Dean, like Magruder, would have to plead guilty, albeit to lesser chargers if he cooperated, Shaffer told them they were not the only show in town. He would turn elsewhere for immunity—to the Ervin Committee. And in return for immunity, he would trade the whole story, the president and all. That, however, was still some weeks away.

First, Dean and his associates counterattacked through the press. After the coverage in the April 18 newspapers of Nixon's statement, Ziegler reported Dean telling him, "I can't take this rap" and threatened to "call in some friendly reporters." Nixon was alarmed. He said that Ziegler, by knocking Dean, was missing the point: The president did not wish to express publicly any loss of confidence in his counsel. He deputized Ziegler to tell Dean that they were "not throwing anyone to wolves." (The very day before, of course, Nixon had told Haldeman, "We're not throwing you to the wolves with Dean.")[11]

A short while later, Ziegler was back with a response. "Dean said the president *is* out front . . ." but he added: "keep in mind [that] the Dean report also involved 21st [March] discussion with the President." Nixon understood only too well the sound of blackmail. He instructed Ziegler not to leave any impression with reporters that the "Dean Report" was false.[12] But countering impressions was by now too late.

Nixon, desperate to change his sleep pattern, took Ehrlichman and Haldeman for an overnight stay at Camp David on April 18. It turned out to be one of their most miserable evenings. They could not escape the exploding press coverage. Frantic telephone calls flooded in; Woodward and Bernstein had a sensational story for the next day's *Washington Post.* It was the whole Magruder story, with an inaccuracy right at the beginning.

Woodward and Bernstein later blamed *Post* editor Ben Bradlee for personally rewriting the offending lead:

> Former Attorney General John Mitchell and White House Counsel John W. Dean III approved and helped plan the Watergate bugging operation according to . . . Magruder.

Among the sources listed was the White House. Not even Dean's enemies at the time were saying he had approved and planned Watergate, but when the story appeared, Dean instantly suspected he was being set up. He went menacingly public. Instead of going through Ziegler, Dean had his secretary call—in a trembling voice, reporters noted—the major news organizations to read his statement. ". . . Some may hope or think that I will become a scapegoat in the Watergate case. Anyone who believes this does not know me . . ." That was fuel to the flames.

Still transfixed, Nixon dared not call for Dean's resignation. He felt trapped because he had rashly told Dean that Haldeman and Ehrlichman stood ready to resign. Dean had neatly incorporated this into a resignation letter he drafted, tying his departure to theirs. Obviously, Nixon could not accept it. That day Nixon had a discreet check made with his Secret Service detachment to inquire whether Dean might have found out about the president's secret taping system. They thought not.

Overanxious about Dean's immunity, Nixon blundered in another direction. While at Camp David that April 18, having heard, wrongly, that Dean was being granted immunity, Nixon angrily telephoned Petersen. Petersen denied it but to humor Nixon said he would check. When he had done so, according to Petersen, Nixon insisted: "I've got it on tape, if you want to hear it."[13] At the time, mention of tape did not sound unusual to Petersen; heads of state taped conversations. But that little Nixon slip started a legal pursuit that was to dog him to the end. Petersen's subordinate, Silbert, was the first prosecutor to ask Nixon to hand over all tapes, among other evidence. Only later would they mean anything, but the story started here.

The president was also wrestling with what to do about Haldeman and Ehrlichman. Petersen, intending to name them as unindicted co-conspirators, told Nixon they had to go for the sake of the presidency. So said Len Garment and John Connally; so, too, said William Rogers at one stage, although he saw timing as the determining factor. Only Henry Kissinger in this period was heard arguing that it would be an injustice to ditch Haldeman.

At Nixon's request for a "piece of paper," Petersen had on April 16 given him an initial outline of evidence against the president's two top men. When Ehrlichman was shown it by Nixon, he made an admission of something he has ever since denied. Petersen's paper read ". . . that

Ehrlichman through Dean informed Liddy that Hunt should leave the country." Ehrlichman now said:

> *Ehrlichman:* Well, that's interesting that, that Dean would take that remark and go out and act on it . . .
> *Nixon:* Told [unintelligible].
> *Ehrlichman:* Hunt, yeah, that it came through Dean.
> *Nixon:* But, but apparently they didn't leave—in other words, you were discussing it. I told, I tried to tell Petersen, "Well, look, I can imagine them having a discussion—" he said, "he ought to leave the country . . ."[14]

Ehrlichman here is accepting that he made the "remark" to get Hunt out of the country and that Dean acted on it, and then later it got countermanded. Ever afterward, however, Ehrlichman claimed this was a false charge by Dean. He relied on Colson's claim that he, not Ehrlichman, revoked it. At the time, Nixon was told by Petersen the countermanding hardly mattered; if the story ever came out, it would have damaging impact on Nixon.

Petersen's point about Haldeman's inaction was equally damaging. His paper noted that after Dean reported to Haldeman about the second GEMSTONE meeting in Mitchell's office in February 1972, "no one issued any instructions that this surveillance program was to be discontinued."[15] That, Petersen told the president, was "misprision [concealment] of a felony." Petersen said he was sorry to say it: Both men had to resign for the sake of the office of the president.

By the evening of April 16, Petersen was reporting yet more potential criminality by Ehrlichman and Haldeman about which Nixon pretended to be surprised. First was the fact that two days after the break-in, Dean had reported to Ehrlichman about Liddy's "confession"—"terribly important," said Petersen because neither of them disclosed this to the authorities. In Haldeman's case, he, too, had okayed Dean's approach to Herbert Kalmbach to raise money for the defendants.[16] Haldeman's intended defense—that he didn't know what the money was for—had been discussed with Nixon, but was becoming untenable before he had even tried it out.

This evidence was only the beginning. On April 17, Petersen told Nixon that he had confronted Pat Gray, who now recanted his earlier denials and confessed that he had burned the documents given him by Ehrlichman and Dean from Hunt's safe. Petersen asked Gray, " 'Why did you do it?' He said, 'Well, I suppose because I took them at their word.' "[17] That implied that Gray believed he had been ordered to destroy the material; this was another nail in Ehrlichman's coffin. Shortly afterward, Dean passed a lie-detector test on the issue of Gray being told to destroy the Hunt documents while Gray declined the prosecutors' request to do the same.

As for Haldeman, Petersen told Nixon that Fred LaRue had "broken down and wept like a baby" before the grand jury.[18] LaRue was a fatal link to Haldeman and the $350,000 fund used to pay hush money. Haldeman urged Nixon that he be allowed to resign or take a leave of absence and go public with a statement as soon as possible. He still wanted to say that he believed the money was only for defendants' legal fees and family support, even though he guessed the public would never believe it.

Then on April 18, Petersen finally dropped the other shoe. They had dreaded this but rather hoped it might have gone away when Hunt did not, as feared, "blow." Dean must have wondered when it would come out. He even flirted with the topic in a conversation with the president on April 16, reassuring Nixon while all the time concealing his newest betrayal. That same day Silbert committed the charge to paper. He notified Petersen that he had been told "that at a date unspecified Gordon Liddy and Howard Hunt burglarized the offices of a psychiatrist of Daniel Ellsberg . . ."[19]

Petersen duly advised the deputy assistant attorney general supervising the prosecution at the Ellsberg trial, then under way in Los Angeles, to check their evidence files. Nothing was found that could be linked to such a break-in. However, a check with the FBI's famous "indices" revealed that a Dr. Fielding had been approached by agents about Ellsberg, but had declined to be interviewed. This led Petersen and Silbert finally to understand the meaning of the photos of Liddy and Hunt in a parking space labeled "Fielding"—the break-in casing photos—which had been a mystery ever since the Justice Department had received them from the CIA.

All that took another day. As Petersen, taking his call from Nixon at Camp David, tells it, Nixon said, " 'What else is new?' And then I dropped the next bombshell. It was that Dean had informed Silbert that Liddy and Hunt and company had burglarized Dr. Fielding's office, who was Ellsberg's psychiatrist. The president said, 'I know about that. That's a national security matter. Your mandate is Watergate. You stay out of that.' "[20]

Petersen remembered the president's anger. Ehrlichman was in the room with Nixon and recalls the president saying after hanging up, "That should keep them out of it. There is no reason for them to get into it. What those fellows did was no crime; they ought to get a medal for going after Ellsberg."[21]

Once back from Camp David, Nixon met Petersen and elaborated his national security argument, telling how he had to act on his own in the Ellsberg affair when FBI Director Hoover supposedly refused. On the tape Nixon is heard saying, "Nothing in terms of break-ins or anything was approved." But he understands what Hunt was doing and would have approved at the time.

Petersen asks, "Is there any other national security stuff that we could inadvertently get into through Hunt?" He asks in order to be able to "stay away from" it. Nixon says there are other things and mentions that Hunt was involved in "bugging, apparently." He says (possibly thinking of what else Dean can unload) that columnist Joseph Kraft was bugged. He manages to tell someone, at last, that Hoover "bugged our plane" during the 1968 campaign. And he completes this little tour with the spurious claim that "I have never used the word [*sic*] 'national security' unless it is."[22]

Petersen passed along to Silbert the president's order to stay away from the Fielding break-in and "he was kind of upset about it." The official in charge of the Ellsberg prosecution was told to "forget it."[23] Petersen sat on his knowledge of the break-in for nine days. He later testified that his position was legally sustainable. Investigation showed that there was nothing in the prosecution file "producible" to the Ellsberg defense on this burglary.[24] But Petersen worried about the situation nonetheless. What he did not then know was that a petty criminal had already pleaded guilty to the Fielding break-in in order to have it taken into consideration with other offenses!

There was another more important reason for Petersen's eventual change of heart. He and his prosecutors realized that Dean had told about the break-in purely as part of his relentless bargaining, and the longer they delayed disclosure of it the longer Dean held a threat of blackmail over the prosecutors' heads. On April 25, Petersen decided the break-in had to be disclosed at least to the Ellsberg trial judge. Petersen went to Kleindienst and told him that "you're out of Watergate but you are not out of Ellsberg. I need some help." The attorney general would have to brave the president's wrath and persuade him to relent. They both agreed they would resign if Nixon refused.[25]

Kleindienst made the same point to Nixon as Petersen had to him: If they did not disclose to the court, Dean would hold it over their heads. To Kleindienst's surprise, Nixon agreed that the judge should be notified. Petersen reassured Nixon, wrongly, that this step "won't affect the Ellsberg case." He described it as an attempt by Dean to "blackmail the prosecutors."[26]

Nixon knew better whom Dean was blackmailing—himself. He asked Haldeman to warn Ehrlichman that another roof was about to fall in. Dean might be called to testify before the Ellsberg judge and bring the whole mess into the open. When Ehrlichman called back anxiously, Nixon explained he had asked Kleindienst to urge that the U.S. attorney in Los Angeles do everything "to see that this is not something that comes out publicly." He pondered whether he could "stomp" and say "Look, this is national security" but suggested to the stricken Ehrlichman that after his fruitless April 18 order from Camp David, "that's about as far as I can go on that."[27]

At this stage the Justice Department had agreed only that the materials related to the Fielding break-in be filed with the judge in camera for his inspection alone. The hope was that he would not disclose it publicly. The judge was the same W. Matthew Byrne whom Ehrlichman had approached about becoming the new FBI director, and who had said he was interested in the job. Byrne was now appalled. Even though Kleindienst told Nixon on April 26 he believed "nothing would be done tomorrow,"[28] Byrne sent the jury out and that day held an open court session with both prosecutors and defense counsel. He refused to accept the materials in camera. "If the government is going to turn this information over to the defendants, it should do so promptly," he said, and gave the U.S. attorney until the next morning to check with Washington.[29]

It is clear that there was no way to resist. "Let's get the goddamned thing hung out there," Nixon tells Kleindienst on April 26. Turning to Haldeman, he says, "Comes down to bust the Ellsberg case. That ain't all bad, is it?" Haldeman is dismayed; after all the emotional and political commitment they have made, "it'd be nice if, if they could convict [Ellsberg] . . . Otherwise, it'd be too bad."[30]

On April 27, Kleindienst instructed the U.S. attorney to tell Judge Byrne they still did not want the break-in material turned over to the Ellsberg defense and to request the court to keep it. Impatient over the possible taint to the case, the judge instead ordered that it be passed to the defense and then he commanded a full-scale government investigation to report to him forthwith on all aspects of the break-in.

When this second Liddy-Hunt break-in was disclosed, it was a bombshell. Ellsberg's lawyers demanded a mistrial but the case was left hanging, pending the new investigation. There was still more disgrace to come. The FBI rapidly got back into the case and began checking anew on the Kissinger taps to see if there were any wiretaps on Ellsberg. That same day, the FBI interviewed Ehrlichman, who could "not recall" who specifically reported to him about the break-in. A few moments later, Ehrlichman made rapid calls in an attempt to line up his subordinates who had directed the Plumbers: Egil Krogh and David Young. The final cave-in could not be long delayed.

Once Nixon realized, on April 25, that it was Dean who had betrayed the secret of the Plumbers to the prosecutors, the departure of Ehrlichman and Haldeman was a foregone conclusion. There was no real surprise; as early as the week before, they were all gloomily mulling over such possibilities. Nixon suggested that if it came to trial and they were acquitted, "it washes away" and they could come back to government. He even offered them money—for legal fees—up to $300,000 was available in a secret fund of contributions managed by Bebe Rebozo. When they demurred, Nixon replied, "No strain; doesn't come out of me."[31] On April 18, both aides secretly agreed with Nixon to step aside from their official duties—with deputies taking over—and work with lawyers on their defense and possible counterattacking public statements. On April 19, Nixon himself held a meeting with their lawyers.

There was surprisingly little concern for John Mitchell's fate. Nixon expostulated in one late-night phone call, as Haldeman noted: "The tragedy is Mitchell—why doesn't he step up? is going to get it without question; don't think he can stall it out; should assume resp."[32]

But even Mitchell had at last acted to defend himself. He had admitted to reporters off the record, so Haldeman's lawyer said, that, together with Haldeman, he had engineered the cover-up. Nixon scoffed, "Mitchell's drinking."[33] Then on Good Friday, outside the federal courthouse in Washington, after being hauled in for a reportedly bruising reencounter with the grand jury he had impressed the previous autumn, Mitchell now had his "operative" statement. For the first time, he publicly acknowledged attending the GEMSTONE meetings. But far from fulfilling Nixon's longing that he take responsibility, Mitchell insisted he had rejected Liddy's plans. "I'd like to know who it was that kept bringing it back and back," he said to reporters. That was his dig at the White House.

The Easter weekend passed with Nixon separated from Haldeman and Ehrlichman. The president went to Florida intending to get a week's rest; Ehrlichman, in particular, was worried about Nixon's overwrought state. His aides stayed behind to concentrate on working with their lawyers, with Nixon encouraging them and their wives to go to Camp David. On this trip, as now increasingly, Nixon was accompanied by Ron Ziegler, who was to become his close adviser. There were huge press stories that weekend.

After spending Easter Sunday at Robert Abplanalp's private island in the Bahamas, the president came back to a six-hour session with speechwriter Patrick Buchanan and Chapman Rose, his and Mitchell's former law partner brought in to give advice. Nixon resolved that both Haldeman and Ehrlichman could not simply take leaves of absence but must resign and fight their case—and his—from the outside. Ziegler conveyed the decision by phone to Haldeman, who noted: "Lv is not a viable choice."[34]

Ehrlichman was especially outraged and fought for a reprieve. Nixon cuts short his Florida stay. Two days later, on April 25, the president conceals his horror when Ehrlichman discusses what Dean might yet do.

> *Ehrlichman:* I think it's entirely conceivable that if Dean is totally out of control and if matters are not handled [unintelligible] that you could get a resolution of impeachment—
> *Nixon:* That's right.
> *Ehrlichman:* —on the ground that you committed a crime.
> *Nixon:* Right.
> *Ehrlichman:* —and that there is no other legal process available to the United States people . . .

Ehrlichman suggests that before they take action, Nixon must listen to his tapes. "You better damn sure know what your hole card is," he says, repeating that famous phrase.[35] (Ehrlichman has always maintained he never knew of the secret taping system and that when he mentioned "tapes," he was referring to tapes he assumed everyone, like himself, was making during the cover-up's collapse.)

Nixon is, in fact, so worried about the March 21 conversation that he says he might, after all, have to grant Dean immunity if only to prevent him from testifying about it. Ehrlichman disagrees; they should make sure that Dean is prosecuted in order to destroy his credibility.

Listening to tapes was the first step in Nixon's only real defense strategy: to use his tapes, however selectively, to disprove whatever charges Dean might level against him. That day Haldeman withdrew twenty-two tapes from the ultrasecret storeroom and began to listen. The president was interested in March 21, first and foremost.

The talk of tapes, moreover, suggests to Nixon the horrifying possibility that Dean has taped *him.* Can they check? he asks Haldeman, absurdly. They discuss shoulder-holster recorders and other phantasmagoria. Nixon was now frightening himself. For instance, he passes on the gloomy news that Strachan, their trusty, has failed a lie-detector test administered by the prosecutors, whereas Magruder passed his. Almost unnoticed, the next day Magruder resigned from his post at the Commerce Department.

On that next day, April 26, Haldeman listens to the March 21 tape, makes a full note, and goes back to Nixon with good news. There are some dicey things here, but if Dean ever testified about the Hunt payoff, Haldeman would testify that Nixon had said "but that would be wrong." Never mind that Nixon had not said this, at least not in regard to the payoff; he had said "it would be wrong" about eventual clemency, as Nixon well knew, and as Haldeman's own notes of the tape faithfully record.[36]

Before they can celebrate, there is a rush of disastrous news. Reporters have the story of Gray's being "ordered" to destroy the Hunt documents. Nixon is angered. It is now clear from the tape, released much later, that he promptly tried to force Gray into yet another cover-up. He telephoned Kleindienst, ordering him to tell Gray that he must not say that Ehrlichman and Dean told him to destroy the documents, and that if he does, the president will say Gray lies.

In fact, the full story is already running in the New York *Daily News*, following a leak from Senator Weicker to whom Gray had partially confessed the day before. But Nixon is still seeking to reverse the tide.

Haldeman listens as Nixon goes through three telephone calls with Kleindienst. Finally, Nixon gets Kleindienst to agree that Gray will "tough it out," telling his story only in the secrecy of the grand jury. There Gray will say he mistakenly "gathered" that the documents should be destroyed, and that he is guilty only of "bad judgment."

Nixon, to Kleindienst's amazement—and doubtless Gray's—says finally, "I'm not suggesting that Gray will go. We don't have to do that to him first thing . . . he's got a right to have his day in court." Besides, the president adds, "I don't have a substitute, not yet." Turning to Haldeman, who has been listening, Nixon says, "I just don't think we can have Gray resign. I don't want Gray's statement of resignation to come out tomorrow in direct conflict with Ehrlichman."[37]

But the hapless Gray, sleeping on it, decides that it would "take too long" to explain his conduct to the FBI, and at last he does the decent thing.[38] The next day, he cuts himself down from further twisting in the wind, but he also obliges Nixon. His public statement does not say he was ordered to destroy the materials. It states, as instructed, merely that "allegations" have become public, and that he is resigning to preserve the "image" of the FBI. Gray left believing himself a much wronged loyalist. He was disgraced, but never prosecuted, and in this might have been the most fortunate of those involved in Watergate. His FBI subordinates were nearly speechless with rage at his deceit. Not only had the top cop destroyed evidence, but in his safe after he left they also found all the Watergate documents the CIA had given to him and which he had failed to pass on to his agents.

That day Nixon took a day trip to Mississippi, then spectacularly and destructively flooded. He had decided, with the Gray story all over the front pages, that Haldeman and Ehrlichman should take leaves of absence the next day, Saturday. He would fire Dean the following week, before Congress reconvened. His principal speechwriter Ray Price was ordered to prepare a TV address.

Haldeman's and Ehrlichman's lawyers were deeply concerned for their clients if they lost the protective mantle of the White House. They both had appointments the following Thursday to meet the prosecutors and Ervin Committee counsel, Sam Dash.

By now, Nixon had other preoccupations. Reporters were checking out a story that Dean had given the prosecutors evidence against "Mr. P." Nixon was beside himself. He telephoned Petersen, then summoned him. Petersen denied that there was anything in it. He tried explaining that his prosecutors themselves were uneasy over his own contacts with the president. But at Nixon's instruction, and telephoning from the Cabinet room, Petersen reached Silbert, who confirmed that Dean had said nothing to them about the president at this stage. Shaffer, however, had threatened, "we will bring the president in"—but in non-Watergate areas. Petersen said Silbert regarded it only as an elaboration of Shaffer's earlier threat to "try the administration." At this Nixon acts as if relieved, and he orders the story "totally knocked down."[39]

But Petersen was himself getting deeply restless. He later testified that he had told the president that "if I reach the point where I think you are involved, I have got to resign. If I come up with evidence of you, I am just going to waltz it over to the House of Representatives."[40] Nixon had told Haldeman two days earlier, "Dean may become totally intractable and if he does, you're going to have one hell of a pissing contest. . . . I don't see the Senate starting an impeachment of the president based on the word of John Dean."[41] Yet he had heard the echo of impeachment from Dean, Ehrlichman, and now Petersen.

Nor was that the end of it. Growing skeptical, Petersen told the president he could not supply the promised memorandum of the prosecution case against Haldeman and Ehrlichman because it trespassed on grand jury matters. He also told Nixon that he could no longer ask him to wait on Dean's negotiations; the president was free to act. For Nixon that was only freedom to cut his tormentor loose: "Question is how mad do we make Dean?" Haldeman noted.[42]

Nixon departed for Camp David, moaning that he had no one to help him work on his speech and leaving his aides with the comforting conviction that their lot was to be leaves of absence rather than resignation. Haldeman and Ehrlichman would preempt Dean by announcing they had asked for leave, and then Dean would be told the president was peremptorily placing him on leave.

While at Camp David, Nixon reversed himself again. Leaves of absence were ridiculous. They gained him nothing over resignations. If he were to appear to be cleaning house, he had to bite the bullet. Haldeman was not told until Saturday evening in a telephone call from Ziegler. Ehrlichman was appalled; so were their lawyers. They saw the perils of being lumped together with Dean. Whatever Nixon said to the contrary, resignation implied that he had no further confidence in them. Ehrlichman, without telling Haldeman, telephoned Nixon and said the president himself should resign. According to Nixon, Ehrlichman was cordial but blunt. He pointed out that Nixon had himself committed illegal acts—he mentioned the fake Diem cable, which had again been in the newspapers as part of the Gray story—and said, according to the president, "all the illegal acts ultimately derived from me."[43] It left Nixon shaken.

Just after midday Sunday, Nixon at last called Haldeman to say the die was cast. He asked him to tell Ehrlichman and bring him to Camp David to hear personally that they had to do "what is right for the presidency." He would see Haldeman first. Ziegler reinforced the call, saying the decision had, in fact, been made the week before in Florida. Their letters should say that they considered leave but decided themselves to volunteer their resignations. It "will work," says Ziegler. The president would "definitely separate Dean totally out."[44]

Ehrlichman says he was barely civil when he joined Haldeman on the helicopter to Camp David. He learned that Nixon had spent the previous day with William Rogers and imagined that Nixon had asked Rogers—as he had asked Ehrlichman in the past—to do the dirty work. Nixon's memoirs reveal that Rogers did argue strongly that leaves of absence were no longer viable, that Nixon had come to the same conclusion, and had, indeed, asked Rogers to convey the message. Rogers declined; Haldeman and Ehrlichman had been involved in forcing his resignation as secretary of state (temporarily deferred), and the irony was lost on none of them.

However, Nixon's memoirs reveal another powerful influence. He had been surprised that Saturday morning to find his elder daughter, Tricia, waiting for him. She had been talking all night with the family, and they wanted him to know they all agreed there was no choice but to have Haldeman and Ehrlichman resign. Even though Tricia did not feel that both men served the president well in the way they handled people, there was nothing personal in their recommendation. "I am speaking for Julie, David, and Mama as well," she said. Whatever he did, "just remember we will support you and we love you very much." And with that Tricia left Nixon to his ruminations.[45]

Arriving at Camp David, Haldeman cycled over to Aspen Lodge ("an unusual way to ride to political doom," he reflected later). There were banks of tulips out all down the slope. Haldeman was shaken when Nixon said that last night "I prayed that I wouldn't wake up." Haldeman said he told Nixon that he could not indulge himself; he had to go on.[46]

Haldeman also said that although he opposed the president's decision, he would abide by it. But he emphasized that his lawyers wanted his and Ehrlichman's resignations separated from Dean's. In the end, to Haldeman's chagrin, they were announced simultaneously, despite Ziegler's express commitment.

Ehrlichman's account is even more emotional. Nixon sobbed uncontrollably. "It's like cutting off my arms," Nixon said, and he repeated his offer of money. "That would just make things worse," Ehrlichman said he replied. Near tears himself, he asked only that Nixon "explain all this to my kids."[47]

Nixon's account has him saying that he "almost prayed" he wouldn't wake up. Ehrlichman, he said, had put his arms around him, saying, "Don't *think* that way."[48] Nixon says he told Haldeman he felt enormous guilt and that the responsibility and much of the blame rested with him. He had put Mitchell in charge of the campaign and "Colson's activities were in many cases prompted by my prodding." He remembers Haldeman "proud and secure," insisting that nothing had changed Nixon's mandate. Nixon remembers Ehrlichman saying he would live to regret this decision, adding, "I still feel I have done nothing without your implied or direct approval."[49]

Haldeman's notes, written immediately afterward, throw some additional light. Nixon evidently went on to discuss his own resignation. Haldeman notes that he gave Nixon his own argument: "you can't resign—he thks E feels he shld (phone last nite) E tld him he had evid. re P knew about fake cable re Diem." The notes further disclose that immediately after Nixon's meeting with Ehrlichman, Haldeman was called back in to review it. The president was concerned, "cause thks E wants him to admit he ordered illegal acts."[50] Nixon wrote in his memoirs that in asking them to resign he had done what was necessary, not what he believed was right. "I had sacrificed, for myself, two people to whom I owed so much."

Next to Camp David, and entirely unaware of what awaited him, was Attorney General Kleindienst. He had decided on the day that the Gray and Ellsberg fiascoes dominated the news that he, too, must now resign. He would tell the president rather than wait until Monday. But Nixon said he wanted him to go at the same time as Haldeman, Ehrlichman, and Dean. Kleindienst was horrified. Why at the same time? He pleaded to be allowed a decent separation. Nixon asked him to do him this one last service, and Kleindienst yielded. His successor, recommended by Rogers, the then defense secretary Elliot Richardson, overheard their conversation. As he rode back in the helicopter to Washington, he told Kleindienst "I wouldn't have done what you just did for anybody."[51] Richardson meant it.

Richardson says that he asked Nixon point-blank whether he was involved in Watergate and got an absolute denial. Before he left, in Haldeman's and Ehrlichman's presence, Nixon impressed upon his new attorney general that the Ellsberg matter was still in the "national security area."[52]

One of the other casualties of this fortnight, although he stayed in office, was Henry Petersen. He had been flattered to be brought in; he knew the president wanted the investigation turned off but had trusted Nixon. Basically, he believed that no president would stoop so low. Yet the president, in furtherance of the cover-up, abused him by, among other things, passing on to his top aides secret grand jury information that Petersen supplied him. After Watergate, Petersen's hitherto fine reputation as an incorruptible long-serving career civil servant was tarnished. He was, understandably, embittered.

Nixon, deeply dejected, remained in Camp David working on his speech. He says he told Ray Price that if he felt he should resign, then he should include that in the final draft. Price replied saying that Nixon had a duty to complete the job he had been elected to do.

It is possible that Nixon might have saved what was left of his presidency had he now come out and said, Sorry, my fault. But Price wrote the speech he was told to, showing Nixon as the great investigator who had been wronged and who would now be fearless in putting things right. The speech had the president accepting responsibility but no blame. At the time it did not ring true to many who heard it.

It was a Monday evening when Nixon spoke. The resignations had already been released to the press. His main message in the broadcast was that "we must maintain the integrity of the White House, and the integrity must be real not transparent. There can be no whitewash at the White House." As Nixon was to say so many times, vainly, it was time to move on to the nation's real business of peace and jobs. He ended by asking for the people's prayers and for their help, and said, "God bless each and every one." He wanted the 1,361 days remaining in his second term "to be the best days in America's history."

The effect of this first broadcast to the nation about Watergate was simply immense shock. If, as Nixon insisted, Ehrlichman and Haldeman were "two of the finest public servants it has been my privilege to know," why were they resigning? What more was there?

CHAPTER 15

Testimony

After the April 30 amputations of his right and left arms, as Nixon described Haldeman and Ehrlichman, one opposition fantasy was that Nixon's pursuers had him surrounded and that it remained only to get him to come out. It was more difficult than that. Certainly, most Democrats would have been appalled had he resigned and allowed Agnew to succeed. At this point, however, the scandal that was to sweep away the vice president was still months away.

The removal of Nixon's top aides did not stanch the wound. Within ten days, the Kissinger taps affair revived when the government admitted that Ellsberg had, despite all previous denials, been overheard. Judge Byrne had had enough. The cumulative effect of government misconduct—the Fielding break-in, the publicized offers to him of the top FBI post, and now the wiretaps for which records could not be found—offended, he said, a sense of justice. He not only declared a mistrial, he also dismissed all charges. Nixon's great enemy, Daniel Ellsberg, was a free man while Nixon's own men now saw jail looming ahead of them.

The general public only at this stage began to take more interest. One reaction was that if the president was prepared to rid himself of his closest aides and his White House counsel, plus two attorneys general—for Kleindienst was lumped in with Mitchell—then something was rotten indeed. On the other hand, the president *had* acted.

He said he had learned about the cover-up only on March 21, just five weeks before. Those sympathetic to Nixon could conclude that he was making a resolute attempt to get to the bottom of Watergate. Nixon's memoirs admit, belatedly, that this "attempt" to get out front was dishonest, inept, and a failure. In any case, by May 10, his standing in the polls had declined precipitously to a 44–45 percent negative rating. It was the first time he had fallen behind.[1]

There was a newcomer to the scene of battle. Alexander Haig, the man who had risen from colonel to four-star general and army vice chief of staff on the strength of his White House service, was now brought back, at Haldeman's suggestion, to be his successor as Nixon's chief of staff. Haig was inexorably drawn into the crisis management of Nixon's Watergate siege. A political conservative, he fed Nixon's hard-line instincts and avidly promoted the apocalyptic notion that the Watergate challenge to Nixon was an attempt to reverse the result of the presidential election. One of those who worked close to Haig in Nixon's first term saw him as driven only by his personal advancement; his role over the next fifteen months would be deeply ambivalent.[2]

Two political and legal processes now began. The Ervin Committee would go for as much Watergate proof as it could get and seek to inform, indeed educate, the public by its televised hearings. It would not be put off by appeals that publicity would prejudice fair trials for the growing list of defendants. And, the criminal justice system would pursue prosecutions in an unconventional way. The demand for a special prosecutor, with authority independent of the Justice Department, was now irresistible. On May 1, at Republican initiative, the Senate unanimously voted a resolution calling for such an appointment to be made. On May 7, the new attorney general, Elliot Richardson, announced he would do so. Two days later, before Richardson's choice had been made, Nixon publicly pledged that the man appointed would have "the total cooperation of the executive branch."

It was the Watergate special prosecutor who was to become Nixon's nemesis. This need not have happened as it did. There had been a time when Nixon could have had a special prosecutor of his own choosing, if only he had made a move. Kleindienst had from the outset been recommending one, though possibly with some sense of personal concern after the approach to him on the golf course by Liddy the day of the break-in. But Nixon would not hear of it. He did not want to appear to be undermining his own Justice Department prosecutors, and he sensed inherent danger in the investigatory independence that would have to be granted.

In any event, Nixon got the worst of all worlds. By waiting too long, he lost control of the choice. Changing attorney generals was a tactical blunder; there was no public demand for Kleindienst's head and had he been kept on, he could have seen to it that the chosen special prosecutor was not hostile. Instead, Nixon gave his opponents their opening. There had to be Senate hearings to confirm Richardson as the new attorney general. And the Democrats extracted as price for the confirmation, an extraordinary and unprecedented degree of independence for the special prosecutor. Too late Nixon realized he had gone too far in stating on April 30 that he was giving Richardson "absolute authority to make all decisions bearing upon the prosecution of the Watergate case and related matters." Nixon's memoirs recalled that he had "put the survival of my administration in his hands."

Not that Nixon was unprepared to rely on him. Elliot Richardson was like Charles Colson, a successful Boston Republican, also Nixon's Harvard man. He had served faithfully, first as number two in the State Department, then in the Cabinet as secretary of health, education, and welfare; when he got his second-term promotion to the Pentagon as defense secretary, Richardson saw himself on a par with Kissinger. He looked good and sounded judicious. Above all, he had never stepped out of line.

But now Richardson astounded Nixon. After going through a list of one hundred names and then a short list of thirteen, Richardson appointed someone not even on it to become the Watergate special prosecutor: a Harvard Law School professor named Archibald Cox, who had been President Kennedy's solicitor general. Cox imprudently, and he still says unthinkingly, had Teddy Kennedy among his friends attending his swearing-in ceremony. The symbol of Kennedyesque revenge escaped Cox but angered Nixon. "If Richardson had searched specifically for the man whom I would have least trusted," wrote Nixon in *RN*, "he could have hardly have done better." Cox much later asked Richardson how he got Nixon to agree to his appointment. "I never asked him," replied Richardson.[3]

Richardson then compounded the disaster for Nixon by giving Cox carte blanche. Richardson's charter with Cox, agreed to under Senate pressure, delegated the attorney general's "full authority" to Cox to investigate not just Watergate but

> . . . all offenses arising out of the 1972 presidential election for which the Special Prosecutor deems it necessary and appropriate to assume responsibility, allegations involving the President, members of the White House staff or presidential appointees.

Cox could be dismissed only by the attorney general, and then only for "extraordinary improprieties." At the last minute he asked Richardson for two more key commitments to strengthen his "charter": to be free to speak publicly whenever he wished and to decide "whether and to what extent he will inform or consult with the attorney general"—to be free, in other words, from the responsibility of reporting immediately any startling development to Richardson, or Nixon. Such complete independence for an official serving at the discretion of the president was extraordinary.[4]

Nixon publicly mouthed "full support" for Richardson, but privately protested. Cox's authority was too broad. Richardson blithely assured him that the offending subclause about allegations involving the president and his men referred only to the 1972 election, but Nixon knew better. It was the first of several disastrously differing textual interpretations.

Cox's appointment and his recruitment of a whole team to the Watergate Special Prosecution Force, as it was called, had the effect of delaying the criminal cases. This naturally infuriated Earl Silbert and his original team of much misled prosecutors, who claimed that they now had the case 85 percent complete. Yet though they had nothing until McCord cracked, even at the hand-over to Cox, Silbert still knew nothing of the crucial Colson involvement in clemency for Hunt. Colson, even at this late stage, was being treated as a witness rather than as a defendant.[5]

More important for Nixon, delay in issuing indictments meant that there was now less reason for trying to postpone the Ervin hearings. The president briefly had an ally in Cox, who went to court to try to stop Dean and Magruder from being given special immunity to testify. But Judge Sirica, having demanded everyone cooperate with Ervin in the first place, was having none of it.

Not that there ever was any chance that Ervin would have agreed to be put off. By mid-May his committee was the only show in town, and he and his staff made the most of it. Dean made a beeline for them. Having failed to impress the prosecutors with his accusations against the president—which he began only after being dismissed by Nixon—Dean and his lawyer were now dealing with Sam Dash, the Ervin Committee chief counsel.

Dash had been under secret pressure from Senator Howard Baker and the Republican Senate leadership to cut short both his preparations and the hearings themselves. But after Dash's initial fiasco with McCord's closed session in late March, the investigation staff had been making better progress. They had been getting corroboration from the smaller CRP witnesses, like Robert Reisner and secretaries. They had cooperation from Kalmbach on the payments to defendants. And they got Ervin's agreement to go for a gradual buildup of the whole story, rather than rush on, as Baker had secretly agreed with Nixon, the big White House witnesses.

Baker was playing a subtle game. As a Republican and one who had nominated Nixon at the convention, he wanted to give his president and the White House what advantage he could. He went to his secret February meeting with Nixon as a friend, but he later said he came away uneasy, telling himself, "Baker, you better steer a center course here. You better not become the agent of the White House."[6] At first, he succeeded brilliantly. For instance, each time he was outvoted in closed committee session on key issues, such as the order of witnesses and granting of immunity, he would subsequently move to make the vote unanimous. This concealed any partisan maneuvering from the public.

In dealing with Dash, Dean and his lawyer insisted that he keep the explosive information they were intending to supply away from Baker lest he funnel it straight back to the White House. Dean did trust one Republican, the maverick Lowell Weicker, and secretly approached him with a headline version of his story, intending to enlist him. It worked. Weicker went to Dash in great excitement. Ervin, too, was excited at the prospect of having Dean as star witness. The committee chairman privately authorized Dash to meet alone with Dean and Shaffer and develop the evidence Dean would present.

A succession of late-night meetings, either in Shaffer's office in Rockville, Maryland, or at Dean's Alexandria, Virginia, home, persuaded Dash that Dean's evidence against the president was credible, and devastating, and that the committee had to give Dean immunity. It could not be total immunity, the so-called transactional immunity that Dean wanted. It would be "use immunity," meaning that Dean could not be prosecuted solely on the basis of information he gave at the Senate hearings. The prospect of Dean's slipping away to the Ervin Committee impelled the prosecutors to assemble a dossier of their evidence on Dean, legally sealing it before he testified. In this way they could still be in a position to prosecute, but that was still ahead.

Ervin now approached Baker and the committee's one all-out Nixon loyalist, Senator Edward J. Gurney of Florida, with Dash's immunity proposal. They were incensed. "I don't want to let him off the hook," Baker said. Gurney was even more severe: "Dean's just trying to use this committee to escape punishment for the crimes he committed." The two senators voted against, but with Weicker's vote and his own four Democrats, Ervin had the two thirds necessary to grant immunity.[7]

The Ervin hearings, televised live, began on May 17, 1973. The setting was the Senate caucus room with its grand pillars, chandeliers, and mahogany paneling. The hearings were a bigger media success than anyone imagined. In those pre-cable days, such intrusion into daytime TV fare was at first an uncertain venture. Advertisers complained, and the networks rotated the live coverage among them. Only Public Broadcasting Service television was live, gavel-to-gavel.

That soon changed. In the first week McCord's testimony, which dealt with the January clemency offers, was even more explosive than expected. Jack Caulfield was then called to confirm McCord's story. At this point, the senators were falling over themselves to caution the viewing audience that what they were hearing was only hearsay and that such testimony would be inadmissible in court. But it was sensational and constituted the first open implication of the president. The president alone had the power to grant executive clemency.

It was also riveting viewing, with comic relief from Bernard Barker, Al Baldwin, and, above all, Tony Ulasewicz with his Runyonesque tales. Chairman Sam Ervin was an instant TV hit with his mixture of homeliness and admonition, his quotations from the Bible, Shakespeare, and folk wisdom. (Some people underestimated him; Ervin was also a graduate of Harvard Law School.)

In the middle of McCord's damaging testimony, on May 22 the President put out his second major statement in a month. He would not resign. But the statement—which Haldeman said later was meant to be the whole story—contained more lies, and would become a benchmark against which subsequent revelations would be measured. Indeed, six of Nixon's first seven points intending to rebut or preempt allegations against him were also subsequently shown to be false. One of them, perhaps the most notable was this: "At no time did I attempt, or did I authorize others to attempt, to implicate the CIA in the Watergate matter."

At that time, this item passed unnoticed in the mass of the things Nixon did admit to. He acknowledged the "national security" wiretaps, the Huston plan (although not all its details) and the Plumbers unit. He even acknowledged that he had not wanted the Watergate investigation to uncover the Plumbers so-called "national security" activities, and while he "assumed responsibility" he denied he had at any time authorized illegal actions. This May 22 statement aroused the suspicions of prosecutors Silbert and Glanzer and was one of the reasons they secretly recommended to Cox that Nixon would now have to be questioned like any other witness.

The president also changed his ground on the subject of executive privilege. Regarding present or past White House staff, he said, the privilege "will not be invoked as to any testimony." The last word turned out to be the operative one; it would soon be clear that privilege would continue to prevent access to any documents or tape recordings.

As for resignation, two days after his statement and following a White House reception for Vietnam POWs and their wives, Nixon had this exchange with his daughters: "Do you think I should resign?" Tricia recorded him saying "with a seriousness that produced a wave of exclamation such as 'Don't you dare.' " When Julie later told reporters that the family had talked him out of resigning, the White House press office ungallantly said the president had never seriously considered it. Yet in his memoirs Nixon reveals that he also asked Haig on June 3 if he should resign.[8]

The second week of Ervin's hearings was even more damaging. Hugh Sloan and Maurice Stans, though in some disagreement, made clear it was well understood that CRP money for Liddy had been authorized by Mitchell. It now seemed incredible that the prosecutors had not believed Sloan when he testified to Magruder's suggestion he commit perjury.

Then came the newly repentant Magruder, a star at the end of that second week. His was the first public eyewitness account of the GEMSTONE meetings. Magruder did not damage the president and was careful not to implicate Haldeman directly. But the others were sent reeling—Mitchell, Mardian, LaRue, Colson, Strachan, and Dean.

Everyone now waited for Dean. There was no longer any question, from Dean's own guerrilla warfare of press leaks, that he was going to be the ultimate stool pigeon in incriminating the president. Nixon himself desperately prepared in private by listening for hours on end between June 4 and June 11 to his still-secret tapes.

The transcripts of Nixon's comments in the intervals between listening are predictably damning stuff. He is trying to find a way of countering Dean with selective versions from the conversations they had held. A widening circle was now becoming aware of the secret tapes: Haig; the newly appointed White House counsel, Len Garment and Fred Buzhardt; Stephen Bull, a young aide who has taken over as tapes custodian; and Ron Ziegler.

Nixon still worries that Dean might have taped his end of some telephone calls: for instance, Nixon calls to Dean from Key Biscayne the day Sirica read out McCord's letter. Nixon frets that he might have checked that day with Dean that Hunt had been taken care of. Buzhardt reports that Dean's files are empty. Either he had nothing or he has taken it with him.

Dean, like all the Ervin witnesses, had first to appear in executive, or closed, session. His lawyer had resisted this because he didn't want Republican "spies" reporting back to Nixon. Dash had informed Ervin alone from his secret meetings that Dean was going to incriminate the president. But to placate the Republicans, an executive session was scheduled for June 16, a Saturday.

Baker was the only senator present and, after the legal preliminaries compelling Dean to testify in return for immunity, the vice chairman made to depart, leaving the proceedings in the hands of committee counsel. He resumed his seat, however, when Dean coolly said, "Senator, I have one point . . . Your name does come up in my testimony and I didn't want you to be caught off guard." Dean then deftly recounted Baker's secret meeting with Nixon and the senator's own staff's contacts with the White House. "The White House may have . . . felt there was going to be cooperation and possible assistance," said Dean.

According to Dash, Baker was obviously disturbed. The senator replied that his recollection of the possibly twenty-minute-long meeting with Nixon was that "virtually all" of it was concerned with his effort to persuade the president to waive executive privilege. Dean smarmily agreed that he was not suggesting any impropriety on Baker's part.[9] The next morning, on a TV interview program, Baker made a point of disclosing his own version of the meeting with Nixon. Again according to Dash, Dean's tactics worked: "Baker went out of his way to handle Dean with kid gloves" in the public sessions that followed.[10] Baker now says only that he detested Dean's attempt to intimidate him.

Dean was scheduled to appear in public session on Monday. That weekend, however, Soviet President Leonid Brezhnev flew in for a long-scheduled summit meeting. Out of deference to America's international image, the committee agreed—over Weicker's objection—to delay the hearings for a week.

The presence of the Kremlin leadership did not stop the jockeying. At a June 18 news conference (the day Brezhnev was received at the White House), Special Prosecutor Cox told a questioner that he was studying whether he might seek a court subpoena against the president and whether a president could be indicted before being impeached, the latter, of course, purely academic. Cox's remarks brought a quick complaint from White House Chief of Staff Haig. Nixon, he told Richardson, wanted Cox to lay off.

Dean and his lawyers were also concerned about the postponement of the public session. It meant that the Republican side could have another whole week to work over Dean behind closed doors. They could leak and rip his story to pieces before he ever appeared in public. The next day, June 19, timed to perfection, such a leak of Dean's previous Saturday testimony occurred. It was a small point—Dean had admitted borrowing some of the CRP cash in his White House safe for his honeymoon—but damaging to him. Shaffer demanded to see Ervin, whom he told that Dean would decline to appear in any more closed sessions. If Ervin cited him for contempt, Dean was willing to sit out the time in whatever cell the Senate had for such offenders. Ervin bowed; he had no wish for his star witness to be cut up. Over Baker's protests, Ervin agreed that Dean would not be questioned again before he appeared in public session. Baker says he suspects Dean's side leaked the honeymoon money story.

Dean finally appeared on June 25, almost exactly a year after he had plunged into the Watergate cover-up. Just behind him sat his wife, Maureen, a striking young woman in demure dress and with platinum hair severely drawn back. Dean, his spectacles selected to convey studiousness, carefully read his statement for two whole sessions that first day; he was then questioned for four more days. He was never really shaken. The Huston plan for domestic intelligence and the political "enemies list," both hitherto undisclosed, caused a big stir. But his accusations against the president were what the public noticed. And what Nixon noticed was that in worrying about March 21 he had been concentrating on the wrong tape.

Senator Baker coined the imperishable phrase in questioning Dean: "What did the president know and when did he know it?" He evidently meant to exculpate Nixon from prior knowledge of the break-in but Dean ambushed him and neither Baker nor Nixon liked the answer. Dean was able to trace the president's involvement in the cover-up to his own first real meeting with Nixon on September 15, 1972. It was the earliest that anyone had alleged a Nixon involvement, and it referred to a conversation the tape of which Nixon had not even bothered to have checked. Dean also charged that Nixon had been involved both in executive clemency discussions and in the payoff of Hunt's blackmail; and that he continued the cover-up after he, Dean, warned him to cut out "the cancer." All these were items Nixon had explicitly denied in advance.

Most crucially, Dean urged investigators to test his credibility by going after Nixon's tape of the April 15 meeting. It was the first public mention that such tapes might exist; Dean disclosed that Nixon himself had offered a tape to the prosecutors. Dean claimed that the April 15 tape would corroborate his version of events. Ironically, this particular tape is one that does not exist because, as we saw, according to Nixon the reel ran out.

John Dean's testimony was a virtuoso performance; it was his word against the president's. Nixon acknowledges that at the time he did not see the true import of Dean's accusations but in his memoirs he had got it. "It no longer made any difference that not all of Dean's testimony was accurate. It only mattered if *any* of his testimony was accurate. And Dean's account of the crucial March 21 meeting was more accurate than my own."[11]

Although he got some dates mixed up, most of what Dean said was later confirmed. To the public he was no hero, but a man who had squealed to save his own skin. In his column Joseph Alsop went so far as to call him "a bottom-dwelling slug." After Dean testified, there was a July Fourth holiday recess and a curious lull as the country pondered the enormity of what it had heard.

The Nixon counterattack was not long in coming. First was John Mitchell. The president's closest adviser was expected to be the most important rebuttal witness of the whole investigation. It had not helped Mitchell, however, that on June 27 his own close adviser, Fred LaRue, had pleaded guilty to charges of obstruction of justice, the first conspirator to do so.

Appearing over a period of two and a half days, Mitchell's terse dictum entered the language instantly: "We sure as hell weren't volunteering anything." The former attorney general and Nixon campaign chief made no opening statement and kept his answers short. The contempt in his voice and his recalcitrant challenges, not to mention his glaring silences, make it imperative to view his testimony rather than simply read it. Mitchell denied that he had approved the break-in and wiretapping of the DNC. However, he acknowledged playing a role in the cover-up (without calling it that) but had not informed Nixon on the grounds that it might have crippled his reelection chances. Mitchell's testimony—that at all three GEMSTONE meetings he had rejected Liddy's plans—directly contradicted Magruder's and Dean's. "In hindsight I not only should have thrown him out of the office; I should have thrown him out of the window," he said of Liddy.

In some respects Mitchell's tale was true enough. What had gone on before Watergate was far more important than the break-in itself. But his picture of Nixon was harder for the Ervin Committee to take—and, doubtless, the national audience, too. Had the president been informed of the cover-up, Mitchell maintained, he would have "lowered the boom" on his aides and a whole catalog of White House horrors would have been revealed that could have cost him the election. Mitchell said that he meant the Ellsberg break-in, the removing from Washington of ITT lobbyist Dita Beard, the forging of the State Department Diem "cables," and the plot to firebomb The Brookings Institution. "The best thing to do was to keep the lid on." Mitchell was adamant: "I still believe," he said, "that the most important thing to this country was the reelection of Richard Nixon. And I was not about to countenance anything that would stand in the way of that reelection."

It was different after the election. Mitchell later conceded that it might have been better for the country had he revealed to Nixon what he knew as the second term got under way. He refused to accept the term "cover-up." Nixon had never discussed Watergate with him, he said, and he never raised it.

Asked what could have given Magruder the idea GEMSTONE had been approved, Mitchell said, "I assume others were interested in implementing the plan." But how could he explain Magruder's direct testimony? "I can't explain anyone's testimony but my own," he retorted. Why, then, would Magruder have told Reisner it was approved and told Sloan that a budget of $250,000 had been approved? Mitchell said he could not account for others, adding, "It was either a misunderstanding or a contravention of my orders." It was a "palpable damnable lie" that Magruder had shown him any wiretap logs, Mitchell said.

He admitted, however, knowing in advance that Magruder would be perjuring himself. But he denied, in spite of Dean's testimony, that he had suggested getting Kalmbach to raise money, along with much else, including the fact that he had told Dean that his theory of the break-in "was not far wrong." In a remark that drew a gasp in the caucus room, Mitchell told Ervin that, in hindsight, "It might even have been better, Senator, as you say, to take them out on the White House lawn; it'd have been simpler to have shot them all."

Mitchell also implicated Ehrlichman and Haldeman in the cover-up: "I would say they had a very active concern, just as I had. He referred to his own role as being part of a consensus. For people who liked a man's man, Mitchell's appearance, yielding nothing, standing by the president, was a tonic after the squealing of Magruder and Dean. But any relief was temporary.

Two days after Mitchell completed his defense of the president, Nixon was found by Haig in bed coughing up blood. Nixon made light of it but by midday his doctors had diagnosed viral pneumonia and ordered him moved to Bethesda Naval Hospital. Just before he left, Senator Ervin telephoned him. Nixon was still in bed. Ervin was in the middle of a committee meeting, about to vote to demand that Nixon supply the committee with documents. Nixon was refusing on the grounds that his waiver of executive privilege applied only to testimony not documents. A snarling match ensued in which Nixon blurted out "There's no question who you're out to get."[12] Ervin was distressed and depressed. It was plain that despite the severity of Dean's accusations, the committee had to have corroboration, but Ervin could not see where it might come from. The answer was not long in arriving.

The Ervin investigators had the task of building up a complete picture of the president's working day and style. Presidential counsel Len Garment had coached White House staff not to volunteer anything but, if asked direct questions, not to lie, even about Nixon's secret taping system.

On Friday, July 13, the witness being given a preliminary background interview was the man who had run the president's daily schedule during the first term, Alexander Butterfield. He had gained promotion to chief of the Federal Aviation Administration and was about to leave on a trip to Moscow. As was committee practice in such closed session interviews, the Democrats' investigator, Scott Armstrong, began the questioning. He showed Butterfield memos that Nixon's counsel Fred Buzhardt had supplied the Ervin Committee, which included segments of what looked like verbatim conversation between Nixon and Dean. He was asked where they could have come from. Butterfield observed that memos were routinely dictated after conversations with Nixon, but he could not explain the extensive quotes. The questioning moved to other areas.

For the Republican minority staff, Don Sanders got his turn after the first three hours of fencing. Sanders, who had been in the FBI, where it was common knowledge that the late Director Hoover had taped all discussions, wanted to get back to the Buzhardt memos. They looked like transcripts to him, and then there was Dean's suggestion that the president had taped him on April 15. He asked Butterfield whether to his knowledge any of the presidential conversations were taped.

Butterfield says he remembers replying that, since they had already interviewed Haldeman and Higby, he assumed that they already knew about the taping system.

The investigators certainly did not. They listened tensely as Butterfield revealed to them that virtually everything in Nixon's presence was taped. Then they rushed off with their fantastic news.

Ervin and Dash immediately understood the immense significance of this breakthrough—and the advantage of having the Republicans make it. Butterfield says that he called Baker, told him what he had revealed, and received his assurance that he would not have to testify in public. Baker remembered differently. He said he told Butterfield to tell the president and to remain on standby to be called before the committee.[13]

Dash took the precaution that Saturday of testing the revelation's impact on the one man it could make or break—John Dean. One of Dash's assistant counsels, James Hamilton, remembers standing by the fireplace at Dean's home so as to gauge his reaction when Dash told him. "I never will forget it. John broke into this huge smile. This beaming smile because he knew after all the work he'd done and his testimony and all the thought he'd given to what he had to say that he was right and he was convinced that the, the tapes would bear him out."[14]

At the White House, they remained oblivious. Nothing was done until Garment returned on Sunday evening from a weekend trip and had an urgent conclave with Haig and Ziegler. Still nothing was done. The president was ill but not incommunicado.

Nixon's memoirs disclose it was not until Monday morning did Haig tell him what had happened. He said he was shocked and certainly seems to have forgotten that he had waived executive privilege for spoken testimony. He wrote: "I thought that at least executive privilege would have been raised by any staff member before verifying" the existence of the taping system. He says he raised with Haig whether or not to destroy the tapes. Haig said that he would discuss it with the lawyers. Nothing was done.[15]

On Monday morning, Butterfield was still apparently under the impression that someone else, like Haldeman, would be lead witness about the tapes. He was having his hair cut when he was reached by an Ervin Committee counsel and told that he would be required to testify in public that afternoon. He refused. Butterfield then watched on the barber's TV as a young man approached Ervin, then left the caucus room. The telephone rang again. The message was that Ervin had said that if Butterfield did not comply with the order to appear, the Senate sergeant at arms would arrest him on the street.

Butterfield was inserted as a surprise "mystery" witness into the afternoon schedule. He testified for only half an hour, but it was thirty minutes that ensnared Nixon. The news was utterly sensational. In a story replete with bugging, it now emerged that the president had bugged himself. And the revelation suggested a resolution of many mysteries.

Butterfield said twice in his testimony—and was not questioned about what he meant—that the tapes "were the substance on which the president plans to present his defense." He added:

> I only hope that I have not by my openness and by my adherence to all instructions received to date given away something which the president planned to use at a later date in support of his position.

At the touch of a button, as I reported that night to *The Times* of London, John Dean could now be contradicted by the president—or corroborated.

After making sure that none of those involved with installing and operating the taping system would be permitted to testify, Haig ordered the system closed down. All the tapes were transferred from the Secret Service to a special room under the "president's own safekeeping"—meaning that Haig had the combination.[16]

Haig convened a war council at Nixon's hospital bedside. Buzhardt was in favor of destroying the tapes and so, says Nixon, were Vice President Agnew, John Connally, Nelson Rockefeller, and Henry Kissinger. Mrs. Nixon, too, had she been consulted, would have urged they be destroyed forthwith.[17] Garment argued that the tapes were evidence and he strongly opposed destroying them. Haig suggested that destroying them would, in the public mind, be like a display of guilt. Garment says he also raised the technical question of how such a large quantity of tapes could be destroyed—there were more than five thousand hours' worth. But his main argument, he says, was that destruction would be the first Article of Impeachment to remove the president from office. Haig's book, *Inner Circles,* recalls only Garment threatening to resign if the tapes were burned, as does Nixon.

Haldeman, though no longer part of the White House, was asked and was against destroying them. Never release them, he said; retention could be accomplished under the cloak of executive privilege. But the tapes were "our best defense."[18] Indeed, Haldeman had already been rehearsing what he would testify to, when called before the Ervin Committee, about the September 15 tape as well as the March 21 tape.

There was an added calculation that was obvious. If Nixon could get a half-million-dollar tax deduction for donating his vice presidential papers, then these tapes were worth literally millions. They could be used to write the greatest memoirs ever.

There was yet another reason that was not so obvious. Haig states that Nixon kept the tapes to protect himself not only from Dean but also from others. As Nixon said in his memoirs, "I was prepared to believe that others, even people close to me, would turn against me just as Dean had done, and in that case the tapes would give me at least some protection."[19] Nixon had not forgotten how Ehrlichman had, prior to resigning, accused him of being involved in illegal actions. But it was all too late.

On Tuesday, July 17, the Ervin Committee wrote to the president asking to hear the relevant tapes. Now there was no question about the tapes' legal standing. The next day, Special Prosecutor Cox followed with a similar letter, coldly specific, with dates and times gleaned from meeting and phone logs the White House had supplied. He asked for tapes of eight conversations.

On July 23, in a letter to Ervin, Nixon refused, citing executive privilege, and gave a further reason. He had recently listened to some, he admitted. While they are "entirely consistent with what I . . . have stated to be the truth . . . they contain comments that persons with different perspectives and motivations would inevitably interpret in different ways." He added that, therefore, "the tapes would not finally settle the central issues" in the Watergate inquiry. Faced with Nixon's refusal, the committee promptly voted to subpoena the tapes.

Nixon's refusal had also contained the phrase "none will be" made public, but that was an untruth. Just one week later, Haldeman appeared at the Ervin hearings after Ehrlichman had put in a combative performance defending Nixon. The long-feared ex-chief of staff, by contrast, was all smooth charm, belying the image of the "Berlin Wall" he had supposedly erected around Nixon. He came equipped with what Ervin called a phony defense, declining on grounds of executive privilege to testify about Nixon's tapes. But once that had been overruled, Haldeman whipped out a long prepared statement, based on a key tape.

It was of the March 21 meeting, massaged as agreed with Nixon. The most impressive contradiction of Dean's version of discussing money for Hunt was that Nixon had indeed talked about raising the million dollars, yet had immediately stated "but it would be wrong." Alas for Haldeman. Mention of his listening to the tape met with incredulity from Senator Ervin and most of the committee. Why should he, a disgraced ordinary citizen, be allowed to take twenty-two White House tapes home overnight when a duly constituted committee of a coequal branch of the U.S. government was refused the chance to check whether his version was accurate?

Haldeman was nevertheless confident that he could get away with misquoting the tape, under oath, because he was confident that it would never be released. But even as Haldeman and Nixon were listening to the tapes and plotting back in June, the process that was eventually to force their disclosure was moving inexorably forward. It was to put Nixon on a direct collision course with Special Prosecutor Cox.

Within days of assuming office, Cox had been sending letters to White House counsel Fred Buzhardt, requesting assurance that the files were secure. Although Buzhardt did not know it, David Young, of the Plumbers, had already told the prosecutors that Ehrlichman had been moving incriminating documents from his own files into the protection of the presidential papers. On June 11, Cox renewed Silbert's request for the tape of Nixon's April 15 conversation with Dean—the one in which Nixon believed Dean claimed he had been given immunity.

Buzhardt replied that this was not a tape of their conversation but a tape of Nixon dictating his account of the meeting. (The reason was, of course, that at the time Nixon offered to let Petersen hear a tape, he did not realize the reel had run out. In addition, neither Nixon nor Buzhardt, who had recently been informed of it, wished to reveal the then still secret White House taping system.) Even so, Buzhardt declined to supply Cox even with the Dictabelt—which of course did not exist.

Cox's response on June 20 was crisp and carried the ominous hint of a legal summons against the president, a subpoena, if necessary. It was not long after this that Haig, at Nixon's behest, made his telephone call to Attorney General Richardson warning Cox off.

For a few days, Nixon thought he had Cox cold. While the president was at the Western White House, the *Los Angeles Times* ran a story saying that the special prosecutor was investigating the deals that had enabled Nixon to purchase his property in San Clemente. Based on a conversation between Cox's spokesman and some of the newspaper's reporters, it seemed, however, that the story had gone too far. Cox, in fact, was asking only for news clippings about the property deals; he was not yet investigating. But Nixon was incandescent.

Haig telephoned Richardson, who called Cox, and then called Haig back to explain the misunderstanding. Haig thought that Cox ought to put out a denial. According to Richardson, "Haig said that he was not sure the president was not going to move on this to discharge Mr. Cox." The statement Cox put out Nixon found inadequate. "At this point the president broke in on the conversation. The president said he wanted a statement by Mr. Cox making it clear that Mr. Cox was not investigating San Clemente, and he wanted it by two o'clock."[20] Nixon was left fuming.

The first Monday after Butterfield disclosed the tapes, July 23, saw the hostilities between Cox and Nixon go public. Behind the scenes, Haig telephoned Richardson again, complaining that the "boss was very uptight about Cox." This time Cox's assistants had been writing to the tax investigators of the Internal Revenue Service. Richardson was told that " 'If we have to have a confrontation we will have it.' General Haig said that the president wanted 'a tight line drawn with no further mistakes' and that 'if Cox does not agree we will get rid of Cox.' "[21] Poor Richardson, the man in between.

That same day a letter went off to Cox refusing him the tapes he had asked for on July 18. The president's newly recruited constitutional adviser, University of Texas law professor Charles Alan Wright, wrote that the president had "inherent" power to withhold material from the courts—even if it were to lead to failure of prosecutions—and he had now decided to do so. Furthermore, Wright introduced a whiff of grapeshot, warning Cox that he was subject to instructions from superiors, including the president. He could have access to presidential evidence only as and if the president saw fit. The stage was now set for a battle royal.

Cox doubtless had his reply drafted in advance of the Wright letter. No sooner had he received it than he was in Judge Sirica's court obtaining his first subpoena *duces tecum,* a "bring with you" summons, telling Nixon, or any subordinate officer, to attend court with the tapes listed—now nine—plus documents. At 6:20 P.M., taking with him a federal marshal, who had to leave his gun at the door, Philip Lacovara, counsel to Cox, served the subpoena on Buzhardt at his White House office.

Two days later, Nixon, "with the utmost respect for the court," declined to obey the subpoena's command. It was, he wrote, inconsistent with the constitutional position of the presidency. The president "is not subject to compulsory process from the courts." Judge Sirica was unimpressed and the next day issued an order to Nixon to show cause why the tapes should not be produced as evidence. Thomas Jefferson had been the only other president served with a subpoena. In this case, Nixon had not only been served; it was the first time in U.S. history that a judge had ordered a subpoena *enforced* upon a president. The occasion was sufficiently momentous for both Cox and Sirica, particularly, to make sure that they were seen to be standing on solid rock. As Cox later wrote, they had to keep in mind an awesome question: If Nixon refused, "how can compliance be achieved?"[22]

The answer was to have an unchallengeable position grounded in public common sense. They staged an extraordinary demonstration of the common people's will by bringing the Watergate grand jury into an unusual open court session. Cox had already informally polled the twenty-three grand jurors to make certain of their position on enforcing the subpoena. Sirica wanted them to act in public.

As Archibald Cox recently retold the story:

> It was a marvelously symbolic scene. . . . There were the people of the United States calling on the highest official in the United States to do his share to contribute to the administration of justice. . . . The judge recounted the procedure and then asked them, one at a time, did they want the order to show cause to issue? And while one was nervous as to whether in all this drama they would say yes, when the first two or three said yes, by then one could relax and know that the others were going to follow on, but I think it was one of the one or two most dramatic scenes in all Watergate.[23]

The first of Nixon's two great contests with the courts had begun.

John Ehrlichman was also about to enter the first of his many entanglements with the courts. In August, a Los Angeles County grand jury indicted him and the Plumbers for the 1971 Fielding break-in. The

California state court had been asked to hold off while Cox considered federal proceedings in the case. But the state authorities were impatient and indignant. What tipped it was Ehrlichman's blanket defense of the Fielding break-in before the Ervin Committee.

If Haldeman had belied his stern reputation by soft-soaping the senators, then Ehrlichman before the Ervin Committee lived fully up to his as the contemptuous autocrat. He might have been only a Seattle "land use" lawyer who gained power through being an effective Nixon campaign advance man, but beginning on July 24 Ehrlichman put on a confrontational performance that made gripping television by any standards.

His position on presidential power was absolute. He argued that there were inherent powers for a president to act outside the law "to protect national security information against foreign intelligence activities." But it was an awkward situation. Ehrlichman was maintaining that although the president did not authorize the break-in against Ellsberg's psychiatrist, he could have done so had he wanted to. Since the FBI reported to the White House the Pentagon Papers had also been supplied to the Soviet Union, there were national security reasons for examining Ellsberg's psychiatric files for possible motive, emotional or ideological.

Senator Ervin was having none of it:

> *Ervin:* Foreign intelligence activities had nothing to do with the opinion of Ellsberg's psychiatrist about his intellectual or emotional or psychological state.
>
> *Ehrlichman:* How do you know that, Mr. Chairman?
>
> *Ervin:* Because I can understand the English language. It's my mother tongue [applause].

Ehrlichman was caught trying to defend the indefensible. Of course, it was acknowledged there were many ways to "acquire" information covertly. But just because insurance investigators, say, might bend the spirit of the law, this hardly allowed the law to be crucified in the name of the president. Part of Ehrlichman's problem was the existence of the "covert operation" authorization memo he had initialed, noting: "If done under your assurance that it is not traceable."

Ehrlichman's testimony before the Ervin Committee that he had *not* authorized a break-in, only a covert operation, under which a nurse or another doctor might somehow have been persuaded to facilitate access to Ellsberg's psychiatric file, was never shaken. Not until many years later did a taped conversation with Nixon emerge in which Ehrlichman is heard saying:

> *Ehrlichman:* I've been going through my old files up there. The way that project was finally represented to me was that it was a covert look at some files, which could be read to be that they walked in when the nurse wasn't looking and they flipped through the file.[24]

The "could be read to be" is the giveaway. The guilty knowledge in the Plumbers entourage that they'd broken the law had been continuous. In December 1972, as he later admitted at Ehrlichman's trial, David Young had tampered with this memo, removing key parts from the original. Then in March, when they feared Hunt "blowing," Ehrlichman had Young bring him the key files from which he removed an envelope marked SENSITIVE, containing the critical authorization memos. Ehrlichman, according to Young, remarked, "I think I better keep those memoranda because they're a little too sensitive and show too much forethought."[25] Unfortunately for Ehrlichman, there were other copies.

After, as Nixon delicately put it, the shit hit the fan in the Ellsberg trial, Ehrlichman consulted with the Plumbers' codirectors, Krogh and Young, to keep their stories in line. Krogh was going to accept responsibility, but maintain the national security line. But Young was bothered. When he complained that Ehrlichman had not told the FBI agents interviewing him that he had given the operation prior approval, Ehrlichman had replied, "They didn't ask me."[26] In May, Young was given immunity from prosecution, and, although listed as an unindicted coconspirator, turned witness against Ehrlichman and began testifying before the second Watergate federal grand jury in August.

The Plumbers' actions prompted the first and abortive move in Congress to discuss Nixon's impeachment—and by a Republican at that. Congressman Paul McCloskey, who had had the temerity to challenge Nixon in the 1972 Republican primaries, gave notice of a debate in the House of Representatives on June 6. But he was thwarted by lack of a quorum, brought about by Nixon loyalists. Such are the quirks of Congress that McCloskey's full speech was printed in the *Congressional Record*. With hindsight, his connection of the Fielding break-in to the Watergate cover-up made pretty good sense.

Less viable was the first actual impeachment resolution, introduced into the House. Massachusetts Congressman Robert Drinan, a Roman Catholic Jesuit priest and former law school dean as well as liberal Democrat, moved it on July 31 principally on the grounds of the secret bombing of Cambodia. He also listed Nixon's secret taping and the Plumbers among other alleged "high crimes and misdemeanors." The House Democratic leader, Tip O'Neill, who had a strong, if still publicly undisclosed, interest in a proper Nixon impeachment, told Drinan, as he had earlier Democratic movers, that it was "premature." But since the resolution was on the floor, he had to ensure that the Democrats were not ambushed by a White House-inspired call to vote in which a defeat would have discredited the very notion of impeachment. O'Neill had unsuspecting assistance from the Republican minority leader, Gerald Ford. Ford checked with the White House; Nixon had no interest in a vote, Ford told O'Neill, who relaxed.[27] Ford little suspected that turbulent events were about to end his long congressional career for higher things.

CHAPTER 16

Sirica Rules

August 1973 was as astonishing a month as any in Watergate. As Nixon pondered how to get rid of Special Prosecutor Cox, and so evade the threatened court disclosure of his incriminating tapes, further perils beset his administration. Watergate was now seeping out far beyond the cover-up like an unstoppable stain. August also saw a loss of presidential power. On August 15, the bombing of Cambodia was ordered ended by Congress, which also required its own prior approval for any further U.S. military action in Indochina. It was the beginning of the end for South Vietnam.[1]

At home a new battlefront opened in *The Washington Post* over Nixon's income tax deductions. Then came confirmation that the amount of taxpayers' money spent on security and improvements at Nixon's Florida and California homes had snowballed from the initially admitted $25,000 to $17 million. The tax and homes affairs eventually did huge damage to Nixon, probably far more than the early distaste over the cover-up.

Finally, the secret investigation of Maryland bribery involving former governor, now vice president, Agnew, erupted into public view with a story in *The Wall Street Journal.* It was quickly followed up with allegations that Agnew had continued taking bribes, in plain envelopes, in his White House office in the Executive Office Building. Agnew, until then the one major administration figure to have escaped taint in the

Watergate scandal, issued furious denials and settled in to battle for his political life.

The threat to government was well expressed as a nightmare. If Nixon was to be impeached, which was being increasingly talked of, even if still unlikely, a crook would succeed him into office. The theoretical possibilities were preposterous: They might face a double impeachment. Certainly, that was the view of Attorney General Richardson, dealing with the Agnew case.

One man thought he could see a way out, or at least explore it. It has never been revealed until now, in interviews conducted for the 1994 Watergate TV series, that John Mitchell actually took steps that August to preserve Nixon by himself pleading guilty. The move failed, partly because the deal Mitchell wanted—an agreement with the special prosecutor to drop the pursuit of the president in return for Mitchell's guilty plea—simply was unattainable, and partly because it was simply too late. But a secret meeting was initiated by Mitchell with James Neal, the top trial lawyer in Cox's Special Watergate Prosecution Force, to discuss what Mitchell had to offer. Though by now the court battle for the tapes was under way, Neal especially had a sneaking worry that they might fail to corroborate Dean after all. Breaking Mitchell was an exciting prospect, but it didn't work out. In the end Mitchell balked.*

Nixon's memoirs are silent on this episode, but they note that Mitchell informed him that Agnew believed Richardson was out to get him. There can be little doubt that it would have powerfully reinforced Nixon's conviction that Cox was out to get the president. Hard information to that effect from Mitchell, that Cox's men were not interested in laying off the president in return for Mitchell's head, would have convinced Nixon that they must have Cox's head. "I felt that he was trying to get me personally. I wanted him out," Nixon wrote.[2]

Nixon chose that August to stage his long-awaited public counterattack on Dean and all the other allegations that were mounting. He issued a second statement and made a second televised address, on August 15, dealing almost entirely with Watergate. The broadcast contained his one apology, brief as it was. Looking straight at the camera he said, "I regret that these events took place." He was surprisingly

* It is described in detail in Appendix I.

polite about the Ervin Committee: "I do not question the right of a Senate committee to investigate charges made against the president," he avowed.

Nixon's main thrust was that he should be allowed to keep his tapes private; he suggested that the privilege he claimed for his conversations with his aides was comparable to that between husband and wife. He claimed, as his counsel had before the courts, that to make his tapes public would "destroy" the principle of presidential confidentiality. The president's "supplementary" statement, issued that day, at least corrected his unsustainable earlier position that he had first heard about the Fielding break-in on April 18; he now made it March 17—a date that Ehrlichman would forever contest.

The next day, now almost unnoticed under the onrush of events, Jeb Magruder entered his guilty plea in court. He was the one man, after the initial Watergate Seven, to go down for bugging the DNC. He pleaded to a one-count compendium of felony charges: unlawful conspiracy to intercept wire and oral communications, to obstruct justice, and to defraud the United States.

At Nixon's first televised news conference in fourteen months, held on August 22 in San Clemente, his opening statement was that Henry Kissinger had at last been made successor to William Rogers as secretary of state. All the questions, however, were about Watergate. Nixon told reporters that he was confident Haldeman and Ehrlichman would be exonerated; he confirmed for the first time the account of his discussion with Dean over the million-dollar payoff. And he affirmed that Haldeman's distorted account of the March 21 tape had been "accurate." Once again the fabrications uttered were to become benchmarks against which Nixon's later disclosures would be judged.

The court battle over the tapes did not at the time seem especially urgent. The public, indeed the lawyers involved, all assumed that the issue would have to go all the way to the Supreme Court, taking perhaps until 1974. The president, said a spokesman, would abide by a "definitive" decision of the Supreme Court, but Nixon declined to define what that meant.

In court there were some ominous signs, more obvious perhaps with hindsight. The man drafting all the Nixon briefs and arguing his case, Professor Charles Alan Wright, essentially held that enforcing the court process on Nixon would destroy the presidency itself. But on August 17, he argued that if the president chose to defy a court order, "the only power in the court is to dismiss the prosecution." In other words, all that was left for the court in such an event was to order the prosecution's case dismissed. Spotting this for the "backdoor" ultimate power of the president to dismiss the prosecutor himself, Archibald Cox responded in oral argument that what the president could not dismiss or terminate was the grand jury. The grand jury represented the people, and the people had a right to every man's evidence.[3]

It was no surprise, but of enormous moment, that Judge Sirica ruled against Nixon. But the judge chose what he called the "middle ground" —that the president supply the tapes, not to Cox and the grand jury, but in the first instance to the judge himself. Sitting in chambers, he would listen and rule on Nixon's claims for privilege, and where he found conversations on the tapes not privileged but relevant to the investigation, he would turn them over to the grand jury.

Nixon appealed and so did Cox. On September 13, the U.S. Court of Appeals came up with a compromise proposal to avert a constitutional clash. It suggested excluding the judiciary and have the tapes listened to by a group consisting of Nixon or his representative, plus Wright and Cox. Cox and Buzhardt met three times but a week later advised the appeals court that "these sincere efforts were not fruitful." Wright had filed a final brief with this explosive broadside: "To tear down the office of the American presidency is too high a price to pay even for Watergate."[4]

Leonard Garment's diary of September 20 notes, "Think Cox was willing to go along, perhaps even eager, but WH position had probably been decided upon previously with Haig and the President." In their negotiations, Buzhardt offered "written summaries" of the tapes that would be mostly in the third person. Cox responded that courts would never accept such material as final trial evidence. But Cox had toyed, reluctantly, with the idea of accepting, for the pretrial grand jury phase, verbatim transcripts vetted for accuracy by a court-appointed "third party verifier," who alone would listen to the tapes. Cox sent a six-page document spelling this out, but the president's lawyers took only forty-five minutes to call back: "The answer is 'No,' " said Buzhardt.[5] The plan would come back to haunt Cox.

From then on events moved inexorably, although public attention was focused not on Nixon and Cox but on Agnew. Agnew had been vociferously denouncing the charges against him, but Nixon had been careful not to say too much. Asked directly at his August 22 news conference, Nixon expressed confidence in Agnew's integrity and courage but said it would be improper to comment on the charges.

Agnew was believed to have a large right-wing chunk of silent majority support, which Nixon didn't want to alienate. Still, the affair faced him with multiple dilemmas. While the Democrats could not stomach Agnew succeeding him—the vice president was thus his "impeachment insurance"—Nixon could not afford the taint of corruption. His stance as the great investigator of the Watergate cover-up meant that Agnew had to be rigorously pursued. But how?

The man who helped was a Justice Department newcomer, Robert Bork. A conservative law professor who attracted Nixon's eye, he was appointed solicitor general, but had taken time to wind up his university tasks before coming on board that summer. Almost immediately, Haig attempted to recruit Bork as the president's chief counsel. To appeal to Bork's patriotism, Haig told him about the Moorer-Radford affair, involving the chairman of the joint chiefs' "spy" at the White House.[6] Then he told him that the White House counsel's office was in such chaos that he, Haig, had been unaware that Butterfield had been going to reveal Nixon's tapes. And Haig told Bork about the investigation of the vice president.

After twenty-four hours' reflection, Bork decided he would rather not be the president's counsel. As Nixon's lawyer, he said, he would have to listen to the tapes. Haig's reply, referring to Nixon, was that "if anybody forces him to give up those tapes he will burn them first and then resign."[7] Bork stayed solicitor general, number three at the Justice Department, the government's lawyer at the Supreme Court, a job he had always wanted.

As the Baltimore federal prosecutors' evidence of old-fashioned bribery piled up against Agnew, Richardson and Bork agreed that the vice president had to be made to resign. The way to do so was to convince him that he faced indictment as a common criminal. Vice presidents, contended Bork, were different from presidents, against whom the only remedy was impeachment.

Both Buzhardt and Haig favored resignation but opposed indictment —and fiercely argued with Richardson and Bork that Nixon did, too. But in a meeting, which Bork recalled in a recent interview, Nixon surprisingly reversed himself. He had other worries.

> We'd just, we'd finished the argument about Agnew and he'd agreed [to] the indictment. And then he turned to me and said, "Once the impeachment starts they go very fast, don't they, or once the process starts?" And I said, "Not necessarily." I went over the [1868] case of Andrew Johnson and how long it took to get the impeachment rolling against him. But he was clearly thinking about it quite seriously.[8]

But, in truth, the route Nixon took with Agnew was arguably a tactical mistake. An Agnew impeachment might not have been the swift affair Nixon and Bork had assumed, but have been so dragged out as to leave the Congress with no stomach for a second impeachment, of Nixon.

Buzhardt and Haig duly passed Nixon's decision to Agnew and secret plea bargaining started. Agnew made clear that whatever happened, he would not go to prison. Near the end of September, Richardson was prepared to offer this quid pro quo: resign and be let off with a simple guilty, or "no contest," plea to a charge of income tax evasion though admitting to the bribes.

Agnew complained to Nixon, who admits intervening. Richardson, he said, must not insist on "unreasonably tough terms."[9] Richardson stood firm, and Nixon preferred not to risk his resignation. Then, when *The Washington Post* disclosed the plea bargaining, and CBS quoted Henry Petersen telling associates "we've got the evidence; we've got it cold," Agnew attempted his end run.

The vice president visited Carl Albert, Speaker of the House of Representatives, to demand that Congress investigate the charges against him—a preliminary to the dreaded word "impeachment." Albert and the chairman of the House Judiciary Committee, Congressman Peter Rodino, were ready to agree before reportedly being talked out of it by Democratic majority leader Tip O'Neill. O'Neill had only one impeachment in mind.[10] They told Agnew no; it was a matter for the courts.

Agnew had a couple of final throws. He mounted a public campaign and brought audiences to their feet, cheering his defiant "I will not resign if indicted." He denounced the Justice Department for vindictiveness, suggesting that Petersen, the top Justice Department prosecutor, was out to recoup his reputation after failing at Watergate. This was embarrassing to Nixon; he had to defend Petersen while pleading with the press not to convict Agnew in advance.

Agnew also filed briefs attempting to stall the grand jury, but Bork counterfiled. Finally, in secret, Agnew capitulated. He now accepted essentially the same bargain he had turned down before. Richardson settled in the end for "somewhat less than we wanted."[11] But he got an even more complete—and damning—summary of the evidence into the record. The commitment to keep Agnew out of prison would be granted by the judge only on a recommendation of leniency from the attorney general.

On October 10, Agnew made a dramatic appearance in the federal district courtroom in Baltimore and pleaded nolo contendere, no contest, to the charge of income tax evasion. Invoking Richardson's recommendation for leniency, the judge said he would except Agnew from his usual practice of sending tax evaders to jail, and imposed a three-years' suspended sentence plus a ten-thousand-dollar fine. By this time Agnew was the ex–vice president, having resigned in a one-sentence letter to the new secretary of state, Henry Kissinger.

Two days later Nixon announced Agnew's replacement. Haig claims Nixon also offered him the post. But the president's first choice had been John Connally until the Democratic congressional leaders informed him that the turncoat onetime "Nixon Democrat" would never be confirmed by the Senate. Indeed, such was Nixon's plight that he was also told that the only man likely to be confirmed was one of

Congress's own, a man who had never contemplated higher office, the Republican House minority leader, Gerald Ford. Nixon was later quoted by Nelson Rockefeller (who became Ford's vice president) as saying, "Can you imagine Jerry Ford sitting in this chair?"[12] Clearly, Nixon thought that Ford, generally seen as a genial but limited Republican journeyman, was also good impeachment insurance.

As it turned out, the Agnew affair was truly double-edged for Nixon. It had called attention to the notion of impeachment; on October 9, Chairman Rodino sent to the government printer 718 pages of research material his Judiciary Committee counsel had marshaled on the subject.[13] And with Agnew only the second vice president in history to depart in this manner, the affair greased the skids of high-level resignation.

As the Agnew scandal concluded, Nixon's thoughts were elsewhere. "Now that we have disposed of that matter, we can go ahead and get rid of Cox," he told Richardson.[14]

CHAPTER 17

Massacre

In one weekend in October, Nixon made his big play. It was the kind of unpredictable and bold action that had served him well in foreign crises. His aim was to end his torment over the tapes, rid himself of Archibald Cox, and put Watergate behind him. Instead, he smashed his administration beyond repair and ensured that his own impeachment proceedings became inevitable. And, in a final volte-face, he felt compelled to hand over a batch of his tapes he had gone to such lengths to keep secret.

Nixon had been projecting plausible ways of firing Cox long before the conclusion of the Agnew affair. As his memoirs record, Nixon considered Cox a "parasite . . . the partisan viper we had planted in our bosom."[1] Now, as the court battle for the tapes neared its climax, Nixon was emboldened by Yale constitutional law professor Alexander Bickel, who published an article saying that since Cox was an employee of the executive branch, he could simply be fired and the tapes case "mooted." Bickel's was a classic example of legalistic argumentation that wise politicians ignore.

On October 11, Haig says, he told Connally that "we are probably going to fire Cox within a week or ten days."[2] To the White House's consternation, Cox had just indicted Egil "Bud" Krogh in the new federal case against the Plumbers' break-in at Ellsberg's psychiatrist. Haig was instructed by Nixon to tell Richardson that Cox had exceeded his charter by venturing into territory involving national security. Cox's response was that national security might be none of his business but perjury was. Krogh was indicted for lying to the earlier grand jury.

Nixon had taken the tapes listed in the first court subpoena to Camp David on the weekend of September 29, and his secretary, Rose Mary Woods, had begun the work of getting "the gist" typed out.[3] Nixon now says he had begun to believe that the appeals court would rule against him. Rather than go to the Supreme Court, he said he contemplated submitting written summaries to Judge Sirica, with matters irrelevant to Watergate omitted.

It was the same approach Buzhardt had tried and failed to sell to Cox in the "compromise" negotiations suggested by the appeals court a week earlier. That Nixon persisted with it was completely unknown at the time and demonstrates that Nixon did not wish to risk an adverse ruling from the Supreme Court, which he knew he could not have flouted.

Several things emerged about the tapes that weekend at Camp David. They all made the prospect of handing them over to a judge even more unthinkable. First, Nixon discovered, according to his aide Steve Bull, whose task was to cue the tapes for Woods, that two of the nine tapes listed in the subpoena did not exist. No one would believe they had not simply been destroyed, particularly considering which ones they were. One covered Nixon's first phone call with Mitchell after the break-in; the other covered Dean's late-night meeting with Nixon on April 15. Their nonexistence was to be kept secret.

Rose Mary Woods also had difficulty making out what was on the first tape she tackled, which recorded Nixon's initial meetings back in the White House after the break-in with Ehrlichman, then Haldeman. The poor acoustics of his EOB office were responsible and resulted in many "unintelligible" notations in the later transcripts. Nixon listened to the three of them talking, so Woods says, and ran the Sony recorder back and forth himself. They were working with the originals, not copies. After twenty-nine hours' work, Woods still had not finished the first conversation.

Back in Washington, on Monday, October 1, she came to the president in some panic. She thought she might have caused a small gap in the Haldeman part of the tape. She had been on the telephone while using the foot pedal of a Uher machine supplied that morning for faster working. There was now a buzzing sound while she had been on the phone for four or five minutes. The gap was another reason the tapes themselves could not be submitted to the judge—no one would believe this accidental wipeout story.

On October 6, the Yom Kippur War began. Israel had been caught by surprise with attacks from Egypt and Syria. By October 12, with Soviet and U.S. airlifts to the combatants, it was heading toward a superpower crisis. That same evening Nixon appeared at a televised ceremony with his replacement vice president, and the U.S. Court of Appeals issued its ruling: Nixon must hand over the tapes for Sirica's inspection. Nixon had a week to lodge an appeal with the Supreme Court.

Whether or not it was because Nixon reveled in crisis management, having the day before intervened forcefully to end an American bureaucratic deadlock and order the Pentagon to accelerate the airlift to Israel, he now became commander in chief of the tapes situation. Certainly, Len Garment believes that the president's decisiveness in the Middle East made him "exhilarated," free at last to cut resolutely through his wretched tapes entanglement.[4]

Nixon credits Buzhardt with the idea that now emerged. Buzhardt, who as Pentagon chief counsel had a good working relationship with the Senate Armed Services Committee chairman, John Stennis, now recommended this Mississippi Democrat (and Nixon backer) as the ideal outsider to "verify" the written summaries against the tapes. Stennis, of course, though respected as a man of integrity was not the sort of court-appointed third party Cox had once had in mind.,

On Sunday, October 14, Nixon attended church for the first time in six months. He invited Stennis to the White House worship service, and raised the matter of listening to the tapes. Stennis said he reckoned he could handle it.

In the incredibly complex negotiations that now ensued, if Nixon had dealt directly with Elliot Richardson instead of going through Haig, a great deal of destructive confusion might have been avoided. On

October 15, Haig called Richardson. Having been involved with Middle East policy as number two under Rogers at the State Department in Nixon's first term, Richardson imagined he was being asked for advice in the crisis. Haig obliged him with an account of the worsening fighting, but only as a curtain-raiser. He then told Richardson straight out that Nixon was going to fire Cox and submit his own verified written summaries of the tapes to Judge Sirica. He even had a draft letter from Nixon, dated the day before, ordering Richardson to relieve Cox of his duties, effective at 9 A.M. that very day.[5] "It he does that," Richardson says he told Haig, "I will have to resign."[6]

From here on versions part company at crucial points. Richardson says it was only later that he realized that the Nixon game plan all along had been to force Cox to quit or to put him enough in the wrong to justify firing him. And, as a prerequisite, "induce Richardson to go along."[7] Whether or not this is so, the fact is that they could not afford the resignation of Richardson, the recognized Mr. Integrity in the administration who had just masterminded Agnew's departure. Haig wanted to know what the alternatives might be. Buzhardt, joining this meeting, reminded them that the previous month Cox had given consideration to having a third party verify transcripts of the tapes. To Richardson that seemed viable enough to pursue but he returned worried to his office. "We've got a problem that may be worse than Agnew," he told Deputy Attorney General William Ruckelshaus.[8]

However, Nixon says that later that Monday he and Haig agreed a change of plan. Richardson would be told that they no longer insisted on firing Cox but that the White House would proceed with submitting written summaries of the tapes to the court, and that they had decided that Senator Stennis should be the neutral verifier.

With Buzhardt, Haig called on Stennis. The senator did not quite remember the conversation with Nixon the way the president had, when Stennis was supposed to have said that he could "handle it." Haig says Stennis was worried about his health (he was recovering still from a street shooting earlier that year). He wanted to sleep on it, conditioning his agreement on acceptance of the plan by senators Ervin and Baker. And, being a former judge, Stennis asked Haig what Cox's reaction to the idea was.[9]

According to Richardson, Haig called him that afternoon, saying that only with the greatest difficulty had he sold the compromise to the president. Cox would not be fired. But Nixon had angrily said "This is it," meaning that after getting these written tape summaries verified by Stennis, Cox would have no further access to presidential materials. Such a ban was, of course, a critical and impermissible infringement of the special prosecutor's independence.

Richardson says he advised against such "foreclosure." Indeed, Richardson's first written draft spelled out that the Stennis arrangement applied just to the nine subpoenaed tapes and that any future Cox requests would be the subject of renewed negotiations with the White House. It was Buzhardt, according to Richardson, who urged that this passage be dropped altogether in the final draft on the grounds that it was "redundant," because the contents of the nine tapes was all that was currently at issue.[10] Richardson's reasoning was that if the Stennis method proved acceptable to Cox for the first nine tapes, it could be applied to any further requests that arose. Or so he thought.

Richardson agrees he told Haig that he thought the Stennis plan "reasonable enough" to warrant trying to persuade Cox.[11] Nixon says he was told by Haig that Richardson went further: If Cox refused to accept, Richardson would support Nixon in the controversy that was bound to ensue, but Richardson, said Haig, anticipated no problem with Cox.

As Richardson explained it, however, Cox deemed the first suggestion unacceptable; indeed, it was a rehash of what he had declined in the negotiations ordered by the appeals court. Cox did not doubt Stennis's honesty but, he says, Buzhardt as counsel to the president was certain to prepare the summaries, written in the third person, in a fashion favorable to Nixon, and Stennis, a Nixon admirer, "under the best of circumstances would tend to rely upon Buzhardt who had previously worked for him."[12]

Cox, who a few days before had reminded Richardson that the president could not fire him, "only you can," agreed they had to avert a constitutional crisis if at all possible.[13] He asked the attorney general to put the Stennis compromise in writing, which was done on Wednesday; the proposal, following Buzhardt's urging, referred only to the "subpoenaed tapes," omitting all reference to further access or more subpoenas. Richardson, in his initial discussion with Cox, had proposed that the question of future access simply be deferred.

Cox replied on Thursday, offering to work out a solution, but seeking major amendments. One sought an undertaking that, if at the eventual criminal trials the court required the actual tapes, they would be supplied; this was important. Transcripts or summaries might be submitted to grand juries but they would simply not be admissible evidence at trial when everyone knew the full tapes existed. Another amendment was Cox's sticking point, about future access: The narrow scope of Richardson's proposal was a "grave defect." Cox insisted that the prosecutor continue to have "entitlement to other evidence." He wanted this spelled out.[14]

Nixon says Haig reported the difficulty but claims that even Richardson thought it was unreasonable for Cox to want access to additional tapes and documents. "More than ever I wanted Cox fired," Nixon wrote.[15] Not mentioned in the memoirs explicitly but one added goad, surely, was that Nixon heard at this moment from Bebe Rebozo that Cox's prosecution team was behind an IRS investigation of Rebozo's and Nixon's finances, including the secret Howard Hughes contributions. Haig telephoned Richardson on October 18 to complain that investigating Rebozo was outside Cox's charter.

On Thursday evening, Richardson, unaware of the Rebozo development, attended a meeting with Haig, Buzhardt, and Garment, the latter hearing about the Stennis proposal for the first time. His clear recollection today is that all, including Richardson, agreed that if Cox would not accept the compromise, he must go—preferably resigning, but, if not, Richardson would do the necessary. Charles Alan Wright also joined the meeting, speaking so glowingly of the wisdom and generosity of the Stennis compromise that Richardson urged him to try his hand persuading Cox. The others, excluding himself, says Richardson, agreed that if Wright did not succeed, Cox should be fired. Richardson says he went home expecting that he himself would have to resign.

This was clearly a crunch moment in the imbroglio which, like all serious ventures, was touching farce. Wright reached Cox at dinner at his brother's house. He now gave Cox an ultimatum: No actual portions of tapes would ever be provided, and also—this for the first time—Cox must agree not to subpoena anything further from Nixon. Cox says he knew the terms were unacceptable but rather than break off, he urged Wright to put them in writing, to which he promised a reply.

That Thursday evening it was Nixon, Haig's memoirs maintain, who was adamant. "No more tapes, no more documents, nothing more! I want an order from me to Elliot to Cox to that effect now."[16] One other source places Buzhardt at this meeting, too. Buzhardt is said to have exhorted Nixon to leave the issue open, realizing that Nixon's order blew all negotiating room away. Nixon's account omits all this.

Friday, October 19, was the deadline for filing Nixon's appeal with the Supreme Court. This was why Wright had come back from Texas; he had even made out the hundred-dollar check for the filing fee. His initial job, however, was to put the ultimatum to Cox in writing. His first letter answered Cox's written amendments and made clear that Nixon "could not accede . . . in any form" to Cox's objections, in particular "the prosecutor's entitlement to other evidence" from the president. Wright said that if Cox thought there was any purpose in further talk, he stood ready. "If not, we will have to follow the course of action we think in the best interest of the country."[17] Cox replied, putting on record Wright's ultimatum of the night before, which Wright had left vague. Cox said that he wanted to avoid confrontation but could not break his promise to the Senate on which his and the attorney general's appointments had been based.

Wright responded that further discussions would be futile. He defined the restriction sought on Cox as referring only to "private presidential papers and meetings"—a category that covered the tapes as well as all the conspirators' documents that were then being transferred into presidential files—and went on to describe the proposal as "unprecedentedly generous."[18]

Richardson, intent on resignation, notified Haig on Friday that he wanted to see the president, but instead was called to another meeting in Haig's office. Richardson says that Haig now came up with a further variation. Obviously, the threat of Richardson's resignation had caused a rethink. The Stennis summaries, Richardson later wrote, "would be submitted *to the court* and *the court* would be told that this was as far as the president would go, but Cox would *not* be fired."[19] This, as Nixon put it, would "bypass Cox." Richardson says, "My need to resign had again evaporated." He then noticed, reviewing the Wright-Cox correspondence, the proposed restriction on future access. That, he pointed out, had never been part of his proposal. He told them he thought Cox would resign if such restrictions were insisted upon. But that was exactly what they wanted to hear.

Richardson now joined the discussion about how to give a flat order restricting Cox. He claims they did not reach a decision, though "when I left the White House that Friday morning, the idea of restricting Cox's right to pursue other tapes and documents was still alive." Richardson's version insists he never gave clear indication of his own attitude.[20] And he had said nothing further on his own intentions. That all rather suggests the Brahmin Richardson was being impenetrable and could have confused Haig.

Haig's version—not published until twenty years later—is in total opposition. He claims that Nixon, enraged on the Thursday, wanted an order issued to Cox to desist. Certainly, Wright's telephone call to Cox and follow-up letters bear that out, but Richardson was the only one who could issue that order. Haig claims that Richardson suggested a cease and desist order, but then backed down.[21] Nixon's memoirs say that Haig told him Richardson was suggesting "parameters" be placed around Cox that would include the order to forbid further pursuit of the tapes.

After lunch with his associates—and after a chat with Cox—Richardson says that on Friday afternoon he telephoned Haig and Buzhardt to report that he had changed his view. He now felt Cox would not resign. Richardson also says that he argued that the Stennis proposal should definitely not be linked with the future access restriction. The White House should try to sell the Stennis proposal direct to Judge Sirica and leave the other issue in abeyance. He claims that Haig promised there would be further consultation before any decision.

Len Garment recently concluded: "It was in the failure to really confront that little bump in the road in the discussions on Friday that all of the miscalculations took place, if they were miscalculations, and I think they were. So the subsequent Saturday night catastrophe occurred."[22]

According to Nixon, Haig brought him word of the bump, a "tepid" complaint from Richardson, he calls it, "about some of the terms of our plan for dealing with Cox" but added, " 'It's no big deal.' "[23] That same afternoon, Nixon had a private meeting with Rebozo, who had flown up urgently from Miami. The story of Cox investigating the $100,000 Hughes contributions was all over the *Miami Herald*, confirmed by Cox's press spokesman.

That Friday afternoon, apparently unbeknownst to Richardson or Cox, Haig was secretly arranging flights to Washington for senators Ervin and Baker, then on out-of-town visits, to come see Nixon. Two days earlier, the Ervin Committee's subpoena and lawsuit for tapes had been turned down in Sirica's court on the grounds the courts had no jurisdiction between Congress and the executive. Now Nixon personally offered the senators the fruits of the Stennis compromise. Without checking, and apparently given the impression that Cox and Richardson had agreed to it, they agreed, too.

On this of all days, Cox had been in court to produce another guilty plea to obstruction of justice by the biggest fish yet. It was John Dean. He had not, after all, been able to bargain immunity. Trial prosecutor James Neal's sealed evidence was enough to persuade Dean's lawyer that they could go no further. In return for limiting his conviction to a single felony of conspiracy to obstruct justice, Dean would pledge his complete cooperation with the prosecution, but he would still go to jail. Neal, aware of the drama engulfing Cox, suggested to Shaffer on the way that they could think again and come back the following week. Shaffer decided to press on. Dean appeared before Sirica.

Dean's plea was an additional shock to the White House. Cox publicly reserved the right to prosecute Dean for any future perjury. That meant, and was intended to signal, that the special prosecutor believed what Dean had testified to so far. As *The New York Times* noted on Saturday morning, Dean "is the key witness in any potential proceeding against the President." The titanic struggle for the tapes was precisely over Dean's word against the president's.

The next thing Richardson knew, so he says, was from a 7 P.M. telephone call from Haig. The president would not buy the attorney general's latest idea to defer the issue of Cox's future access. Haig's version is that when he passed this news along by reading aloud a letter the president was sending him, the attorney general made no objection. Richardson disagrees, insisting, with his staff, that he was "angry and upset."[24] He only understood much later how it had never been intended for him to know, until the last possible moment, that restricting Cox's future access was an integral part of the plan.

Richardson called Cox to read him the letter's key presidential instruction. It directed Cox "to make no further attempts by judicial process to obtain tapes, notes or memoranda of presidential conversations." Richardson emphasized he had no intention of carrying out the instruction and, Cox says, told him he would try to get the president to rescind it. Cox was even more surprised to hear Richardson say that Senator Ervin was supporting the Stennis compromise.

Richardson, telephoned by mistake by another presidential counselor, commented, "I've been shabbily treated."[25] Whereupon Haig called him in consternation. What passed between them is disputed. Nixon's memoirs later reported that Haig told him Richardson had apologized; he had had a drink and things looked better now. (Haig was subsequently involved in telling senators that Richardson's drinking was part of the problem.) Richardson says that he then prepared his own resignation in earnest.

Cox, however, took action that put him, rather than Nixon, out front in the crisis. Through James Doyle, a *Washington Star* journalist he had recruited as his press spokesman, Cox secured a copy of the lengthy Stennis announcement being issued by the White House press office. Toward the end, Nixon noted that Cox had rejected the compromise. The announcement then said, in classic Nixonese: "Though I have not wished to intrude on the independence of the Special Prosecutor, I have felt it necessary to direct him, as an employee of the Executive Branch . . ."

Doyle advised Cox that their time was short. It was past 9 P.M., newspaper deadlines were imminent, and they had to move fast to ensure that Cox's reply got equal prominence with Nixon's announcement. Cox's formulation was crisp: "It is my judgment the President is refusing to comply with the court," and he would so advise the judge and abide by his decision. Nixon's order to desist was "in violation of the promises which the Attorney General made to the Senate . . . I shall not violate my promise."

Cox also made the telling new point to the public that the restrictions on "best evidence" might enable "wrongdoers who abused high government office" to go free, because judges would be unable to order production of material needed for fair trials. He mentioned the pending prosecutions of John Mitchell and Maurice Stans, adding, "I cannot be party to such an arrangement."

Richardson had prepared his own tortured press release stating that while he agreed with the Stennis compromise, the attempt to restrict Cox's "hypothetical" future access was inconsistent with the special prosecutor's independence. That had not been part of his proposal. But Richardson did not release his statement because the White House announcement carried no mention of Nixon's sending a letter to the attorney general. Nixon simply stated that he himself directed Cox to desist, period.

Unlikely as it seems, next morning Richardson was still trying either to retain his position or yet again use a threat of resignation as a bargaining chip to reverse the situation.

Cox's "defiance" was front-page news that Saturday—ahead of the Stennis compromise in the final edition of *The Times* of London as well as in *The New York Times*. Yet Charles Wright was euphoric, claiming as he checked out of his hotel to go back to Texas that the American people would give a tremendous sigh of relief that the constitutional crisis was over. Had nobody moved—not Cox, not Nixon—and all instead trooped into court on Tuesday as scheduled, the cataclysm might have been averted. If the White House still clung to its calculation that Cox would resign, however, it was soon disabused.

The special prosecutor called a news conference for 1 P.M., and two of the networks prepared to carry it live. Cox recalls he was anything but defiant. "I was in tears, complaining to my wife, Phyllis, 'I can't fight the president of the United States. I was brought up to honor and respect the president . . .' " Mrs. Cox helped him pull himself together, and he went to his office, where he told his staff that if he was dismissed they must stay on the job no matter what the president might seek to do.[26]

That morning, Senator Ervin, whom Haig had arranged to be flown back to North Carolina late by a special air force plane, finally got in touch with a desperate Sam Dash, his committee's chief counsel. Dash had spoken to Senator Baker, who was exuberant. Dash could not understand how Ervin could have accepted the compromise, particularly as Nixon's statement claimed that not only had Ervin and Baker agreed, but also that it was "at their request and mine" that Stennis had consented to authenticate the summaries. According to Dash, Ervin exploded. He had agreed to accept only whole verbatim transcripts for the committee; Nixon had said nothing about Cox. At Dash's suggestion, Ervin agreed to issue a statement contradicting Nixon, and Dash informed Cox. Later Ervin would agree that he and Baker had been "zonked" by Nixon.

Senator Stennis claimed that he, too, had never agreed to Nixon's plan. He understood that he would be authenticating whole transcripts, not summaries, and that "there was never any mention" of suggesting a court accept his material; as a former judge, he knew that to be unacceptable.[27]

On Saturday morning, Richardson had sent Nixon a last-gasp letter making quite clear that he was no longer "on board." He reminded Nixon that Cox's charter specified that the attorney general "will not countermand, nor interfere with the special prosecutor's decisions." The presidential instruction itself, Richardson wrote, "gives me serious difficulty." He did not believe that the "price of access to the tapes" in the Stennis compromise should be the "renunciation" by Cox of further court action. Richardson expressed the hope that they could all seek some further accommodation, and he set out yet more refinements of the proposal. Haig, intercepting the letter, told him that it was pointless.

Richardson, however, caught Cox on the telephone as he was about to begin his National Press Club news conference, and he read him the key parts of his letter to Nixon. It was at least apparent that they would have to find another attorney general to fire him. That was a powerful solace to Cox, and he made telling use of it.

Nixon's memoirs record that Cox adopted the air of "a modest and even befuddled professor." In fact, Cox showed humility but was not befuddled. His statement was like a civics lecture for the plain man or woman at home that Saturday. "I am certainly not out to get the president of the United States. I am even worried, to put it in colloquial terms, that I am getting too big for my britches, that what I see as principle could be vanity. I hope not. In the end I decided that I had to try to stick by what I thought was right . . ."

Cox was careful not to attack the Stennis proposal head-on; he suggested that he and Richardson had been negotiating a compromise in good faith. But he made it crystal clear that third-person written summaries were no substitute for listening to the tapes. And he doubted that they could be accepted as evidence at trials. Nixon's direction to him to desist irreparably damaged his independence to pursue the case wherever it led. It was not he but the president who was in "noncompliance," he said, and he would draw that to the court's attention. Cox emphasized that it was institutions that mattered. He would abide by what the judge said.

In answer to questions, Cox suggested that only Richardson, who had hired him, could fire him. With Richardson's telephone call in his ear, Cox could rattle Nixon one last time by recalling that President Andrew Jackson had to fire a succession of Treasury secretaries before getting one willing to follow orders. Cox added, though, that a president "can always work his will."

Nixon, in the throes of a Middle East crisis with the Soviet Union, says he could not allow President Brezhnev to watch him be openly defied by a subordinate, but that was secondary. Cox, by defying a presidential order on live television, was giving Nixon the justification —which he, Haig, Buzhardt, and Wright had so assiduously worked for—to fire him.

As soon as Cox's news conference was over, Len Garment telephoned Richardson to ask whether, because of the Middle East crisis, the attorney general would first dismiss Cox, then resign later on, giving the country breathing space. Richardson refused. Obviously, receipt of Richardson's letter at the White House had made clear they were about to face a possible string of resignations. When Garment told Nixon, the president's response was, "I'm not surprised that that pious bastard cares more for his ass than his country."[28]

It was not long before Haig telephoned Richardson with a brusquer order: Fire Cox. The attorney general asked for an appointment to see Nixon.

What became known as the Saturday Night Massacre was now launched. Richardson, while awaiting the summons, had discussed the situation with his deputy, Bill Ruckelshaus, whom Nixon had personally dubbed Mr. Clean when he temporarily took over from Gray as acting FBI director. Ruckelshaus said that he was bound by the same pledges to the Senate over Cox as Richardson. He, too, would resign.

Richardson turned to Robert Bork, the solicitor general. Bork had fretted at not being part of the Stennis negotiations. He says he would certainly have challenged Haig and his associates early on about their assumption that Cox would resign; that had been wishful thinking. Since he had been appointed solicitor general well before Cox came on the scene, however, he felt that he was not party to his superiors' pledges. Furthermore, he agreed with his friend Alex Bickel that it was within the president's power simply to fire Cox. He would do what had to be done, "but I don't want to stay on and be perceived as an apparatchik." So he would fire Cox, then resign himself. At this Richardson and Ruckelshaus remonstrated; someone had to stay on and mind the shop at the Justice Department.[29]

Richardson, summoned to see Nixon, was first met by Haig, who appealed to him not to rock the boat during the Middle East crisis. Richardson was unmoved. At 4:30 P.M., he entered the Oval Office. Nixon appealed to him. What would Brezhnev think? Kissinger was at that moment negotiating in the Kremlin. Nixon asked him to delay his resignation for a few days at least. "I'm sorry," Nixon said, "that you insist on putting your personal commitments ahead of the public interest." Richardson says he replied, with the blood rushing to his head, "I can only say that I believe my resignation *is* in the public interest." Their perceptions differed, Nixon agreed unhappily, noting that it was "an emotional meeting." Richardson, the ultimate team player and Nixon loyalist, had answered to a higher loyalty.[30]

Haig next telephoned Ruckelshaus. If the Middle East was so critical, Ruckelshaus asked, why not delay sacking Cox for a week? Haig famously replied: "Your commander in chief has given you an order. You have no alternative." Ruckelshaus chipped in, "Except to resign." Bork is your man, he told Haig.[31] Nixon's memoirs note that Ruckelshaus resigned, but the White House stated that night he had been "discharged." Haig later disclosed that Nixon had said of Ruckelshaus, "We don't owe him anything but a good kick in the ass. Ruckelshaus has to be fired. I don't want him to go back to Indiana and run for the Senate."[32]

Garment and Buzhardt were sent in a black limousine to collect Bork who, seeing one White House lawyer next to the driver, the other in the back, thought "they looked like a couple of mafiosi."[33] Obviously, they could not afford for him to have second thoughts: After Bork there was, literally, no one else, by statute, in line to become acting attorney general. A letter of appointment was waiting at the White House ordering him to "discharge Mr. Cox immediately." But there was much more in that letter for which Bork blithely assumed responsibility. In the same breath as it ordered him to dismiss Cox, the letter ordered Bork "to take all steps necessary to return to the Department of Justice the functions now being performed by the Watergate Special Prosecution Force." In one burst of fire Nixon had shot the sheriff and scattered the posse of deputies—and although Haig was to confess publicly three days later that this act was "not too well visualized," that was precisely how the country would see it.

For the moment, Bork simply signed another letter to Cox "discharging you, effective at once." He was shown in to see Nixon, who said, "You've got guts." Nixon even asked Bork if he would like to be attorney general. It sounded like a job offer, and Bork replied, "That would not be appropriate."[34]

The federal district court later found that the manner of Cox's dismissal violated Justice Department guidelines but the appeals court later ruled the case moot. At least in part for wielding the ax, however, Bork was years later to be denied confirmation to the Supreme Court.

Richardson called Cox to commiserate, quoting a passage from *The Iliad* that federal judge Learned Hand—for whom they had both clerked—had once inscribed in Greek on a photograph given to Richardson: "Now, though numberless fates of death beset us which no mortal can escape or avoid, let us go forward together, and either we shall give honor to one another, or another to us."

Cox dictated a memorable last brief comment to be given by James Doyle: "Whether we shall continue to be a government of laws and not of men is for Congress and ultimately the American people" to decide.

A brief sense of euphoria gripped the White House. Action at last.

Garment remembers the mood. They believed they had cleared the air. If so, it was the onrush preceding a tornado.

At 8:25 P.M., Ron Ziegler announced the massacre, unnecessarily aggravating matters for Nixon by going whole hog and saying that "the office of the Watergate Special Prosecution Force has been abolished as of approximately 8 P.M. tonight." Its functions would be transferred back to the Justice Department to the very officials who had been deemed too compromised to continue in April. Haig then compounded matters by ordering FBI agents to seal the Cox headquarters and the offices of Richardson and Ruckelshaus. By then network TV was crackling with bulletins and instant specials were preempting the Saturday night schedules. If Haig had deliberately tried to stage something looking like a coup for the cameras, he could hardly have done it better.

It was as if the country had been plugged in. Between then and the time Congress returned to business on Tuesday after Veterans Day, there was the greatest outpouring of electronic protest ever seen. Western Union alone, which was used to transmitting three thousand telegrams a day, was up to thirty thousand by Sunday morning, and in all carried more than three hundred thousand. Its computers, crude by comparison with today's, had to be reconfigured to go faster, and still the lines were clogged. The White House itself, which usually only discloses favorable reactions, admitted having four thousand favorable to seven thousand unfavorable responses over four days. Elliot Richardson, for one, believes three million messages rained down on Congress.

This was the firestorm. And the scenes at the special prosecutor's offices on K Street late Saturday fed the blaze. Haig later claimed he had sent in the FBI because there had been reports of people taking out files. What it looked like, however, was the reverse: that he had sent in the FBI to make sure nothing more on Watergate ever got out—the ultimate cover-up.

In fact, ever since Friday, Cox's staff people had been busy "protecting" their files. They first rented a bank safe-deposit box to store their correspondence with the White House. Then the various task forces Cox had established for different cases went about making copies of their prosecution memoranda to take home for safekeeping.[35] So Haig's excuse had a basis in fact.

The FBI man ordered to seal the offices was, ironically, the same agent who had been working closely with the prosecutors since the Watergate break-in, Angelo Lano. Called that Saturday evening, he was told that the new FBI director, Clarence Kelley, wanted Cox's office secured—"nothing in or out; the people can come and go, but not outsiders."[36] Lano was horrified. The prosecutors were his friends. Many of them were recent graduates who had managed to get deferment from Vietnam service and who deeply mistrusted a military man like Haig who they knew had repeatedly tried to interfere with their work. That evening, rushing in from home, they found Lano and his agents at the office. They treated them as turncoats.

Henry Ruth, as Cox's deputy and now acting special prosecutor, soon arrived and defused some of the tension, but everyone was on edge. Ruth tried to establish the status of the office. No one seemed to know. There had been no official notice or departmental letter to implement Ziegler's announcement. Acting Attorney General Bork had gone home.

At around 10 P.M., Ruth called the journalists milling around into the office library. Visibly upset, he described how guards had tried to prevent his entering the office and how the Watergate Special Prosecution Force had simply been abolished by White House fiat. "One thinks in a democracy maybe this would not happen. . . . I was thinking in the car coming in that perhaps it was not *Seven Days in May*. Maybe this is *One Day in October*." The reference was to a novel supposing a U.S. military coup. Someone asked James Doyle what his plans were and he said, "I'm going home to read about the Reichstag fire."

I vividly remember the scene. As I wrote for *The Times* of London the following Monday, "There was a whiff of the Gestapo in the chill October air." Some in London thought this excessive, but I later talked to another man who originally thought Watergate of no consequence but who that evening had the same reaction. His name was Leon Jaworski, and, sooner than anyone thought possible, he would move from being a top Texas lawyer to become Cox's replacement.

The White House was beginning to realize it had a bigger problem than anticipated. Kissinger telephoned from the Kremlin to complain about a pressing matter. He felt that his diplomacy had been undercut by a letter Nixon sent directly to Brezhnev. He had unusual trouble getting through to the White House switchboard. What on earth could be happening in Washington late on a Saturday night? "Will you get off my back? I have troubles of my own," Haig told him.[37]

The wider world had troubles of its own, too. The previous Friday, Nixon had sent Congress a message asking for $2.2 billion for military aid to Israel. Saudi Arabia retaliated. On Saturday, along with other Arab oil producers, it announced a boycott of oil sales to the United States. A few days later, for the first time OPEC tested its strength by rapidly quadrupling oil prices. Supply fell, and shortages were followed by a severe economic slump. The "oil shock" cannot be attributed to Watergate alone, but Nixon's perceived political weakness certainly contributed to the crisis. And the oil crisis without question contributed to the decline in Nixon's political fortunes at home.

On Sunday there were predictable reactions from Democrats like senators Kennedy and Muskie but the Republican voices were the danger signal. John Anderson, chairman of the Republican conference in the House, predicted, correctly, that "impeachment resolutions are going to be raining down like hailstones." Outside the White House, a lone demonstrator held up a sign—HONK FOR IMPEACHMENT—and for the next two weeks, there was such cacophony that the president spent even more time at Camp David than usual.

That Sunday at the prosecutors' office Doyle did his best to keep the story boiling. He insisted on allowing the press in past the FBI agents (replaced late that afternoon by U.S. marshals). A telephone call from the Justice Department informed him that Henry Petersen was upset about his Reichstag remark. Petersen was raring to crack down on Cox's whippersnappers, who had stolen "his" investigation. Doyle told the press that the prosecutors would continue their work providing the Justice Department allowed it; that made front-page news. But it did not change the fact that the White House meant to abolish the entire Cox apparatus and staff. On Monday, Bork announced that Petersen was taking charge of Watergate again—apparently unaware that the special prosecutor, because of Dean's testimony, planned to call Petersen as a witness in the main obstruction of justice trial.

At the White House on Monday, hubris reigned. Patrick Buchanan, by now a close Nixon adviser, acknowledged the uproar to the author, saying "it's as unpopular as hell when it first breaks" but predicted a Nixon rebound. William Safire, the White House speechwriter turned columnist, likewise hailed the president's "big play." That Nixon, Haig, and Buzhardt had also learned nothing is found in their response to the court. Now that the Friday midnight deadline for appeals to the Supreme Court had expired, the president's lawyers were required to file their response to Judge Sirica's order for the tapes. And so they did, but by yet again offering the third-person summaries of the Stennis compromise.

Sirica was "plain damned angry." He had watched Saturday's events on TV and thought the president had lost touch with reality. To him the order to the FBI looked like some Latin American coup. When on Monday he read Nixon's lawyers' filed response, he decided that should they continue their defiance in open court on Tuesday and refuse to produce the tapes, he would take on the president. Sirica drafted an order directing the president to show cause why he should not be cited for contempt, and he prepared to fine him between $25,000 and $50,000 for every day the tapes were not turned over. Sirica said he hardly slept that night for anxiety.[38] None of this was public.

Despite the Veterans Day holiday, the leadership of the House of Representatives, Democrats all, now met privately to confront the issue Tip O'Neill had secretly put to them the previous January. Carl Albert, the speaker, with no vice president in office, at this time uneasily stood next in line to succeed should Nixon go. Albert now agreed that the time had come. On Congress's return on Tuesday, he would announce a House Judiciary Committee investigation to establish whether grounds existed for an impeachment.

Elsewhere in the country, reaction ran strongly against the administration. Labor leaders at the AFL-CIO convention passed a unanimous motion urging Congress to impeach Nixon if he would not resign. Only the year before, the same unions had withheld their traditional endorsement from Democratic presidential candidate McGovern in a move that benefited Nixon's reelection.

From a less expected quarter came a similar demand. The president of the American Bar Association said that the weekend actions were attempts "to abort the established processes of justice" and publicly called on Congress to take appropriate action. Impeachment was about to become a household word.

When Congress reconvened on Tuesday morning, the motions for impeachment began, as predicted, raining down. Speaker Albert referred them to the Judiciary Committee and its chairman, Peter Rodino, announced that for only the second time in American history and the first since President Andrew Johnson in 1868, "formal preparations for impeachment proceedings" against the president had begun. For the first forty-five minutes of the session not a single Republican member rose to support Nixon. And when finally one did, it was Gerald Ford, still minority leader though vice president–designate, who said they agreed to the referral to committee. The private message to the White House from Republicans was even blunter: If the president did not yield the tapes, then Republican congressmen would "not go to the wall" for him over impeachment.[39]

That morning 80 percent of representatives surveyed said that they believed Nixon's actions would delay the consideration of Ford's vice presidential nomination. Speaker Albert, however, had made it clear there was no linkage between impeachment and the Ford nomination. Indeed, one member of the Michigan delegation (a Democrat) had raised cheers in the House chamber when he suggested speedy confirmation for the vice president so that Nixon could resign and Ford take over.

But Haig, as he stated at a news conference that afternoon, worried that "there would be a turnover of the government" to the party that lost the election, if Nixon were removed, and Albert succeeded him in office. It was also John Connally's view. Connally, who felt he had just been deprived of the vice presidential nomination, wanted a White House counterattack on the Democrats: "Someone should accuse them of stealing the presidency." Connally said that if Nixon could only stand up to the situation for two or three more weeks the American people would understand. "I agreed," says Haig.[40]

Representatives of the people, in the form of the forty-six members of the two federal grand juries—the original Watergate grand jury and the newly formed one investigating other abuses—were at that same moment called from their statutorily secret deliberations to a public occasion in Sirica's courtroom. This time the judge, an image of sternness, wanted to reassure the jurors that nobody fooled around with the judiciary; their work was sacrosanct. He read their oaths again. The grand juries "remain operative and intact," he said. "You are not dismissed and will not be dismissed except by this court as provided by law." He did not say the phrase "despite the president" but it could be so inferred. He called the special prosecutor's lawyers into chambers and told them that "the law can take care of this situation." He urged them to continue their work while he prepared for his encounter that afternoon.

It was a busy Tuesday morning. Elliot Richardson held a farewell press conference, carried live on TV from the Justice Department auditorium. The White House hoped that after a stroking session with Nixon on Monday, the attorney general, having resigned, would go peacefully. It started well enough with Richardson giving an account of events that seemed designed to be easy on the White House. At the end, however, the bleakness showed through. He said he would have done what Cox had done, hoped that there would be another special prosecutor, and, when asked whether he thought Nixon should be impeached, declined to answer. It was a "question for the American people," he said. Pointedly, he added, "I have no reason to believe the president would defy a court order."

(Haig to this day blames Richardson for "reneging" and says that urging Nixon not to fire Cox, but to try instead for the Stennis compromise was "the greatest mistake I made as Nixon's chief of staff."[41] How Nixon would have averted an identical outcome by a straightforward firing of Cox, Haig does not explain.)

That morning Charles Wright, still untouched by the firestorm, had come back from Texas to present the Stennis compromise to Judge Sirica. But he, too, now was disabused. He joined a crisis meeting of Haig and Buzhardt that was looking at the political shambles they had created. Haig, chastened by the Cox debacle, made no attempt to urge John Connally's ideas of counterattack, but rather went along when all the lawyers advised, and Nixon agreed, to reverse course. The president would, after all, turn the actual tapes over to Sirica, and so inform the judge in court that afternoon.

This, the greatest of Nixon's reversals, is dealt with skimpily in his memoirs. Nixon does not embrace the Connally-Haig line about the Democrats' "stealing" the presidency. His first consideration was the "risk" of an impeachment resolution "being raced through"; then he notes the hints that Ford's confirmation as vice president could be conditioned on his surrendering the tapes. Finally, claims Nixon, there was need to relieve the domestic crisis—which he had created—to reduce the Soviets' temptation to take advantage during the still tense endgame of the Yom Kippur War. "It was a wrenching decision for me," he writes. Indeed, Nixon knew what those tapes would expose.[42]

The news came as another bombshell when it was disclosed in court that afternoon. The room was packed. There were eleven of Cox's assistants at the prosecution table, including Henry Ruth. Charles Wright waited calmly with Leonard Garment; only they knew what was about to happen. Sirica was eight minutes late. Then for eight minutes he read aloud portions of the appeals court decision, which affirmed, with slight modification, his order to the president to hand over the tapes. He turned to Wright. "Are counsel for the president prepared at this time to file with the court the response of the president to the modified order of the court?"

Wright walked to the podium, less arrogantly, one observer thought, than on his earlier appearances. It was, in fact, his last and possibly worst moment in the case. "Mr. Chief Judge, may it please the court," he said, "I am not prepared at this time to file a response. I am, however, authorized to say that the president of the United States will comply in all respects with the order of August twenty-nine as modified by the Court of Appeals."

There was silence, then gasps, then shuffling as reporters tried tip-toeing out to file this new sensation. Judge Sirica waved them back to their seats and, as if disbelieving, asked Wright: "You will follow the decisions or statements delineated by me?" "In all respects," Wright replied. He tried a last encomium of the Stennis compromise but admitted that after the events of the weekend, "there would have been those who would have said the president is defying the law. This president does not defy the law." Sirica replied, "Mr. Wright, the court is very happy." But the judge remembered to discuss with Wright the need for a timetable, an index, and an analysis. The White House now had to identify for Sirica's inspection in camera what it claimed to be privileged on the tapes. But the incriminating evidence was now on its way into the criminal justice system. Instead of a big play, it was a shot in the foot from which Nixon would never recover.

That same afternoon Acting Attorney General Bork at last got around to abolishing the Watergate Special Prosecution Force, re-creating it as an office of the Justice Department with Henry Petersen in charge. The Cox prosecutions nevertheless continued unimpeded, and within two days, in the face of strong demands from his own Republicans, Nixon had little choice but to appoint a new special prosecutor. The choice, which came on October 31, was Leon Jaworski, a Texas Democrat for Nixon, but an eminent lawyer. Jaworski ended up with greater independence than Cox, and he was the prosecutor who would hear the tapes.

CHAPTER 18

The Missing Tapes

Nixon had been under enormous strain for months. His advisers thought he had returned to work far too quickly after his pneumonia in July. That was followed by the Agnew affair, his war with Cox, and then defeat on the tapes. Richardson, now the third attorney general to have departed, was worried about Nixon's stability, and Tip O'Neill noticed some odd behavior by Nixon at a briefing for congressional leaders on the Yom Kippur War.

Two days after Nixon surrendered his tapes, the American people and the rest of the world woke up to the news that, in response to Soviet troop movements, U.S. forces worldwide had been put on nuclear alert. The immediate reaction in much of the media was to wonder whether the president was mad.

From Kissinger's and Haig's memoirs and other sources now available, it is clear that while Nixon was not mad (he did not even attend the National Security Council meeting at which the "increased alert status" decision was taken; Haig thought him too distraught), his psychological state during this period was deeply unsettled. Watergate, Kissinger reports him saying the night of the alert, was being pursued by his opponents "because of their desire to kill the president. I may physically die."[1] He tended sometimes to defer decisions to Haig and at other times blustered, maintaining at one news conference that "when I have to face an international crisis, I have what it takes."

There was no question that the alert was linked to Watergate. Kissinger believed, although he did not say so at the time, that the Kremlin leadership had acted the way it had because of the president's weakness. Haig believed so, too. But what they were faced with publicly at the time was the opposite accusation—that Nixon might have engineered the crisis to show that he was both in control and personally irreplaceable in the superpower relationship. Kissinger was openly incensed. At a news conference called to explain the alert, he was beset with Watergate questions, and he berated reporters for creating a crisis of confidence in foreign policy as well.

On October 26, Nixon held a tense news conference of his own during which he unleashed a broadside against the media, saying he had "never heard or seen such outrageous, vicious reporting in twenty-seven years of public life." He added: "When people are pounded night after night with that kind of frantic, hysterical reporting, it naturally shakes their confidence. And yet I should point out that even in this week when many thought that the president was shell-shocked, unable to act, the president acted decisively in the interest of peace, in the interest of the country, and I can assure you that whatever shocks gentlemen of the press may have or others, political people, these shocks will not affect me in doing my job."

Whether or not he was fully in control of foreign policy, Nixon had now lost control of the evidence that would eventually damn him at home. In conceding on October 26 that a new special prosecutor would be appointed, he stated with bravado, "I do not anticipate that we will come to the time when he would consider it necessary to take the president to court." But his nightmare was worse even than that. Even before Leon Jaworski got properly into the job, much of Nixon's White House top echelon was dragged into court. The reason was that in agreeing to hand over the nine subpoenaed tapes, the president had omitted to point out that two of them did not exist. Now the court had to be told.

First a crestfallen Buzhardt found out what Nixon, his aide Steve Bull, Rose Mary Woods, and Haig had known since at least September 29: that apparently neither the June 20, 1972, telephone call with

Mitchell nor the late-night meeting with Dean on April 15, 1973, had been recorded. On October 30, only a week after the judge had said how happy he was that Nixon was complying with his order, Sirica was told the bad news by Buzhardt in chambers. Buzhardt said that, as regards April 15, a timer had malfunctioned and the reel had run out. Jaworski's prosecutors wanted an open court hearing, but Buzhardt tried to fend them off by offering for interview the Secret Service agents in charge of the taping system.

When the Secret Service expert stated he had never heard of any malfunction, the prosecutors persuaded the judge to hold public hearings to subject the White House witnesses to cross-examination. What followed was the first courtroom confrontation between lawyers from the White House staff and the prosecutors they detested. There was no jury because it was not a trial, just an investigation. But, in fact, Nixon's last vestiges of credibility were on trial, with the press present in force to report the testimony.

This initial session had Buzhardt fumbling and altering his explanations. The reason the April 15 meeting had not been recorded now had nothing to do with a malfunction, but was because there were so many meetings that Sunday that the six-hour tape had been used up long before Dean arrived after 9 P.M. It also emerged that the custody of the tapes was something less than impressive. The Secret Service logs looked like fragments of brown paper bags. They disclosed that someone like Haldeman could take away original tapes with no documentation showing what was done with them before they were returned.

Steve Bull was given a tough time. He told about the transcribing sessions with Rose Mary Woods at Camp David and added a new detail —that the tapes had been taken to Florida as well. He also revealed that he and Nixon had spent up to twelve hours listening to tapes the previous June, before Butterfield disclosed the existence of the system. The White House instantly refused to make available this June tape of Nixon listening to tapes, the so-called tape of tapes. It now became horribly clear that Nixon, at the time he proposed the Stennis compromise, was well aware the full complement of tapes no longer existed and that he had intended pushing through Buzhardt's written summaries without revealing this fact.

Haig's memoirs affirm that the nonexistent tapes issue did not cause any serious anxiety in the White House. Haig would have us believe of Nixon that "at this point he had not begun to understand the degree to which his own word was suspect."[2] If so, both men soon learned the opposite.

The missing tapes led to a flood of editorial calls for Nixon's resignation. Included were such staunch pro-Nixon newspapers as the *Detroit Free Press,* which on November 4 stated "Enough is enough." Contrary to the Haig-Connally vision of Speaker Albert's stealing the presidency for the Democrats, the paper equably suggested that once Ford was confirmed as vice president, Nixon should step down. *Time* magazine, in its first editorial in fifty years, said, on November 12 "Richard Nixon and the nation have passed a tragic point of no return." It went on: "A President's big decisions cannot be put into a compartment separate from his other actions, his total behavior . . . the nightmare certainly must be ended."

Joining this chorus was the first Republican senator to call for the president's resignation, Edward Brooke of Massachusetts. Another very senior Republican, Senator George D. Aiken of Vermont, said the House should "either impeach him or get off his back." And Senator Barry Goldwater, who had come to be regarded as the Republican elder, said that Nixon's credibility "had reached an all-time low from which he may not be able to recover." Even obedient Jerry Ford, the vice president-in-waiting, stated that he thought Nixon ought now to produce all documents necessary to clear things up.

But, of course, he could not. And Buzhardt, Garment, and even Haig were now to find out why—although they kept the secret to themselves. Haig states that one reason Buzhardt did not panic over the missing tapes was that Nixon had told him, as he had earlier written to Cox, that for the April 15 conversation there was a Dictabelt of Nixon's recollection of the meeting. Buzhardt was supposed to find that and hand it over to the judge. But after being made a fool of in court and after searching through the president's and Rose Mary Woods's files, Buzhardt could not find the Dictabelt. When on November 5 he reported this to Nixon he got a shocking response. According to Garment, Buzhardt came to tell him of their exchange: "Fred said, 'Well, that's a bit of a problem,' and the president at that point said, 'Well, we—why don't we just—I have my notes; we'll make a Dictabelt.' . . . We were ground down . . . but this was really very alarming."[3]

Garment says he told Buzhardt that he would have to go back to court and reveal that the president was proposing to manufacture evidence. They decided they had to see Nixon, and although Haig saw little point, insisted on flying to Key Biscayne to confront him.

Haig, as ever, has a different version. Before Buzhardt and Garment arrived, Haig claims, it was he who discussed the missing Dictabelt with Nixon. Nixon was at a loss, says Haig, and apparently Nixon did not feel able to disclose to Haig the story that appears in his memoirs: that he had ceased recording Dictabelts the night before his meeting with Dean, on April 14.

Haig writes:

> "You know, Al," he said, "as far as the Dictabelt is concerned, all we have to do is to create another one."
>
> It took me a long moment to respond to this statement. Nixon's words shocked me, in the literal sense that I felt something like a tingle of an electric current along my scalp.
>
> "Mr. President, that cannot be done," I said. "It would be wrong, it would be illegal; it would be totally unacceptable. It's just impossible."

Haig says he never sought an explanation, it was never discussed with the president again, and it was "the only time he ever suggested an impropriety to me."

Haig says he told Buzhardt and Garment on their arrival in Florida what the president had just said about the Dictabelt.[4] Garment, of course, says *they* told *him*. Yet why had Nixon told anybody? He could simply have done the job secretly himself, saying, "Look, I've found the Dictabelt." Nixon's memoirs make no mention of this suggested fabrication of evidence, attributed to him by his closest supporters. Indeed, they imply that at this point the absence of the Dictabelt had not been "finally confirmed."[5]

Haig writes that if Garment and Buzhardt were agitated before, now they were beside themselves. Buzhardt, particularly, had been put in a position of making a false statement to Cox. He could be indicted or even disbarred.

Once again versions part company very significantly here. Garment insists that when he and Buzhardt went to Key Biscayne, they clearly agreed on one major step:

> What Fred said, and what we said communally, was that, it was, it looked like it might only be a matter of time before everything was going to fall in and that the president should start thinking about the possibility of when and how he would terminate the presidency.[6]

Buzhardt, who later admitted being concerned at the time about the consequences to Nixon of cash being inappropriately handled for him, told prosecutors that for their Key Biscayne meeting, "Also on the agenda was a recommendation that the president resign."[7] Uncharitably, Haig concedes only that "it may be so" they had come to urge Nixon to depart. But Haig does remember the lawyers' talk of their own resignations. Once again, Haig sees the specter of the Democrats stealing the presidency resulting from the publicity over such high-profile resignations.

Haig tells them that if they resign, Ford may never be confirmed. Nixon has the right to due process. "If you won't defend him knowing more about the case than anyone else, who will? If he fails to get due process this will grievously wound the country and bring down consequences no one can measure or foresee. You may think you can desert him but you can't desert him without deserting the country."[8]

Haig adamantly refused to let them meet Nixon. On that they are all agreed. Garment says it was "nonsense" to think Congress might not confirm one of their own in Jerry Ford. Furthermore, he and Buzhardt did not want to resign; they just wanted other lawyers to take the strain of the president's case.

Nixon's memoirs have it that Haig told him that Garment and Buzhardt "had had it," but say nothing of Haig's telling him they wanted him to resign. He did get a new lawyer, even as Buzhardt and Garment soldiered on.

While Buzhardt was squirming in the witness-box during the tapes hearing, Nixon at least partially admitted responsibility. In a long statement on November 12, he insisted that the tapes were not missing but, instead, never recorded. The public was now informed that a third tape did not exist—the supposed April 15 Dictabelt. Nixon said that a search of his files found only his handwritten notes, "but not a dictation belt." Nixon gave his agreement to a court-appointed panel of experts to examine "all tapes in question" for any evidence of alteration.

Nixon's response to the suggestion by Buzhardt and Garment that he consider resigning was to begin yet another counteroffensive. He repeatedly issued statements saying he would not resign. And he started meetings with Republican congressmen, eventually talking to all 234. He met also with a select group of southern Democrats. There were mixed reviews. It did not escape notice that Nixon was wooing his likely jurors; the members of the House were going to have to be his grand jury, deciding whether he should face impeachment.

The White House had dubbed his offensive "Operation Candor," although Nixon insisted the title was a press creation. Nixon remembers being asked on November 15, during one meeting with congressmen, whether there was another shoe to drop. He answered: "As to the guilt of the president? No," adding, "If the shoes fall, I will be there to catch them."[9]

That afternoon, deep in the White House, Buzhardt had made another depressing discovery. The gap Rose Mary Woods thought she had made in the June 20 tape was not five minutes long, but eighteen and a half minutes. He summoned Haig but there was worse news still. Buzhardt now realized he had been wrong in assuring Haig on October 1 that the gap was on a tape not under subpoena. He explained it was indeed one of those covered and would have to be delivered to the judge, "gap or no gap." That meant another public hearing. Haig was irritated. Nixon, he says, erupted.[10]

Even when Buzhardt's misreading of Cox's subpoena was explained to him, Nixon persisted in asking "if we could still argue that it wasn't covered by a subpoena."[11] When he had calmed the president down, Buzhardt suggested, says Haig, that he locate Haldeman's notes for the section of obliterated tape. Incredibly, Haldeman still controlled the combination lock to his office files. When he gave his assent Nixon inevitably found that the notes were all about Watergate. Haig says that

Nixon immediately suggested getting electronic experts to try reconstituting the tape gap. A man from the top secret communications establishment, the National Security Agency, was called in. No luck. Buzhardt at the same time tried re-creating the humming noises on the tape with the tape recorder.

Meanwhile, Operation Candor was rudely interrupted when someone in the Internal Revenue Service passed details to Providence, Rhode Island, newspapers of Nixon's income tax returns. They showed that for 1970 the president had paid only $792 and, in 1971, $878 tax on income of more than $400,000. This revelation and Nixon's response on live television probably did him more damage among ordinary people than any of the charges of obstruction of justice. "People have got to know whether or not their president is a crook. Well, I am not a crook," Nixon said on November 17, offering to pay extra tax if the IRS found against him.

In none of his public appearances did Nixon mention the tape gap problem. On November 20, he even told a meeting of Republican governors in Memphis, Tennessee, that all the crucial tapes were intact. When asked if other bombs were about to explode, Nixon responded, according to the governor of Tennessee, "If there are, I am not aware of them."

The very next day, the eve of Thanksgiving, as the headlines proclaimed NO MORE BOMBSHELLS, another detonation roared through Sirica's court. The hapless Buzhardt, together with Garment, paid their first visit to the special Watergate prosecutor's office and told the new incumbent, Leon Jaworski, of the tape gap Nixon and Haig had been sitting on since October 1.

Buzhardt had also tried and failed to reproduce the hum. He told Jaworski that he could see no way that it had been accidental, saying of Rose Mary Woods, "she has no defense."[12] Jaworski suggested telling Sirica; Buzhardt pleaded to wait until after the holiday, even as Jaworski stolidly telephoned. The judge called them into chambers privately and heard Buzhardt say that Woods was to blame, but that he needed a few more days to investigate. Sirica, sensing another cover-up, suggested a public hearing. Buzhardt again pleaded for time; Sirica gave him one hour and a half. And once again the president's counsel was in court. He restricted himself to stating there was an eighteen-minute "audible tone" obliterating conversation, and, in a lawyer's sophistry, said that the president had been told of the defect in "subpoenaed tapes" only the week before.

Again, it was utterly sensational news. First, the missing tapes, now an eighteen-minute gap. And it was a gap in the very first Watergate discussion Nixon had at the White House with Haldeman. Sirica now ordered the tapes turned over to him, "not because the court doesn't trust the White House and the president. The court is just interested in seeing that nothing else happens."

Rose Mary Woods, the president's secretary for twenty-five years, was humiliated. At her first court appearance, when there had not been a whisper of any eighteen-minute gap, Woods had protested too much. Questioned about precautions she took while working with original tapes, she said:

> *Woods:* Everybody said be terribly careful. I mean I don't think . . . I don't want this to sound like I am bragging but I don't believe I am so stupid that they had to go over it and over it. I was told if you push that button it will erase and I do know even on a small machine you can dictate over something and that removes it and I think I used every possible precaution to not do that.
>
> *Prosecutor Volner:* What precautions did you specifically take to avoid . . . recording over it, thereby getting rid of what was there?
>
> *Woods:* What precautions? I used my head. It is the only one I had to use.

Judge Sirica ordered this testimony reread out loud. Woods was the only witness at this hearing to have her constitutional rights against self-incrimination read to her. She insisted she had been told the damaged tape was not on the subpoena list; that was why she had made no mention of the gap in her prior testimony. "All I can say is that I am just dreadfully sorry."

Her questioning stretched over three days. She now had her own lawyer with her in court since Garment and Buzhardt had said they could no longer represent her. Her new counsel hardly helped matters for Nixon by suggesting that Woods was being made a scapegoat.

Miss Woods's most celebrated moment came when Prosecutor Jill Volner asked her to demonstrate in court how she made the gap in the manner she suggested might have happened. She had to re-create receiving a telephone call while transcribing. It involved removing earphones, stretching with her left hand backward to the main desk telephone, lifting the receiver, then, with her right hand, pressing the "record" instead of the "stop" button, all the while keeping the pedal depressed with her left foot on its left "forward play" side. This was said to be the only combination that kept the tape moving while recording over what had been on it.

As Woods attempted this contortion, Volner observed, "You just picked your foot up off the pedal." Retorted Woods, "That is now because I don't happen to be doing anything." At Volner's suggestion, the judge agreed that the lawyers could inspect Woods's White House office and produce photographs. The official White House photographer's black-and-white pictures of the "Rose Mary Woods stretch" made the front pages the next day and appeared in color on the cover of *Newsweek* with the title ROSE MARY'S BOO-BOO.

The 150-odd people who heard the tape gap played in court, this writer included, are unlikely to forget the eerie experience of sitting listening to the eighteen-minute oscillating hum. In line with Woods's testimony that the gap she "must have" caused lasted a maximum of five minutes was the fact that the principal "white noise," the oscillating hum, at that point shifted to what I reported to my newspaper as a "background whir," then picked up strongly at the end just before Nixon's voice broke in once more.

The prosecutors next called Haig to testify. As the president's chief of staff, he was the highest-ranking active White House official to have been called to the court, and he made no effort to conceal his distaste. No one, he declared to reporters during a recess, was interested beyond the press "and D.C. residents." But he was to outdo himself in the witness-box. Haig claimed that when he first heard that the damaged tape was subpoenaed after all, he did not dare tell the president until a day and a half later. Most shocking to him, he said, was Buzhardt's inability to make the tape recorder duplicate the hum by itself.

This led Haig to introduce what he called "a devil theory." On December 6, he was asked under oath if he ever suspected anyone other than Rose Mary Woods was involved. To general surprise, he answered in the affirmative. He said when Buzhardt told him of the change that occurred to the tape's tone after five minutes, he had suggested "some sinister force" had added the rest. There was nervous laughter. The judge asked, "Has anyone ever suggested who that sinister force might be?" Haig answered that the most vital thing was to identify who had access to the tapes. "Precisely," muttered Sirica.

Outside the courtroom Haig offhandedly told reporters that Woods might well have been responsible for the whole gap. "I've known women that think they've talked for five minutes and have talked an hour," he said. Haig's memoirs claim that his remark about a sinister force was only a joke. At the time Sirica did not think it funny.

Haig testified that only Nixon, Woods, and Steve Bull had access to the tapes. Nixon's memoirs state, "I also know that the only explanations that would be readily accepted are that I erased the tape myself or that Rose Mary Woods deliberately did so, either on her own initiative or at my direct or indirect request." But Nixon insists he did not do it and that he completely believes Woods when she says she did not. His conclusion, or best guess, is that a faulty machine was the villain.[13] Haldeman suggests that Nixon himself made the gap—as a first desperate attempt to erase all the Watergate discussion. Sirica agreed, writing later that Haig's description "probably fitted the President, as well as anyone."[14]

The court-appointed panel of experts eventually reported the eighteen-minute gap had been erased by "hand operation" of the controls, not by foot pedal. The prosecutors considered charges of destruction of evidence, but acknowledged that proving criminal intent would be difficult. Jaworski in late 1974 advised Woods's lawyer that no action would be taken. Nixon still relies on a later explanation by the manufacturer that the Uher recorder could have malfunctioned. But at the beginning of 1974, it was what was on the tapes rather than what might be missing that was to cause the trap to close around Nixon.

CHAPTER 19

Nixon's "Enemy Within"

At the turn of Nixon's final year, the shortages brought about by the Arab oil embargo began to bite and the energy crisis for the first time became a household word. Nixon tried some token gestures, flying by regular airline instead of Air Force One to California to save fuel. Haig could at last stop worrying about the Democrats "stealing" the presidency; Gerald Ford was sworn in as vice president on December 6. For many, it was now clear there was a replacement for an impeachable president.

Also in December one Nixon nemesis, John Sirica, was named *Time* magazine's Man of the Year. Another, John Doar, was appointed special counsel to the House Judiciary Committee for the impeachment investigation. Doar's long and incredibly painstaking review of the evidence began. And Special Prosecutor Leon Jaworski secretly told Haig that the president had better get a criminal lawyer.

The reason was starkly obvious. Jaworski had now heard a tape. The subpoenaed tapes had been handed over to Sirica on November 26. In regard to only four of the seven did Nixon claim executive privilege over what he said was non-Watergate material; the three others went intact to the grand jury, which meant they were handed straight on to the special prosecutors. They listened, first, to the Dean-Nixon "cancer" conversation of March 21, 1973.

It was a rare moment of truth. Dean had testified from memory about the conversation. The president had said that the tape would bear out his claim that Dean had lied. Nixon was still maintaining that he had only heard about the cover-up for the first time on March 21, and had begun his own new investigation. At the touch of a button, the prosecutors would find out who was telling the truth.

Prosecutor Richard Ben-Veniste wrote later that they were stunned. Dean had been right. "It was like hearing a fifteen-minute summary of our case. The crimes came spilling out, one on top of another." And when Haldeman joined the conversation there was no "but it would be wrong" to pay hush money, as Haldeman and the president had repeatedly claimed.

The prosecutors also learned that Hunt's final demand for hush money had not been satisfied by the time of this conversation; indeed Hunt's threat was plainly the main reason Dean had sought the meeting. Until then, all the available testimony had suggested that the $75,000 had been delivered the night before, on March 20. Now the prosecution faced for the first time the possibility that the president had himself been involved in the payoff. Turning off the tape, "We knew that we had turned the corner on Watergate. We knew how important it was that we kept the investigation alive to get this evidence, and why Nixon fought so bitterly over it."[1]

Jaworski, stunned by the tape, later reflected that "I had known it was going to be tough and rough and that I was going to be faced with a whole lot of difficult decisions but none that I thought affected the president." Now it was different. "I for the first time realized that President Nixon was involved and culpably involved."[2]

On reviewing the tape, Jaworski was apparently less shocked by the discussion of the million-dollar payoff than by an exchange among the conspirators about how to avoid self-incrimination when testifying under oath. Nixon had said to Haldeman, "Just be damned sure you say 'I don't remember; I can't recall; I can't give any honest, an answer to that that I can recall.' "[3]

According to his press aide, "Jaworski reddened. 'Can you imagine that?' he said. 'The President of the United States sitting in his office telling his staff how to commit perjury.' Jaworski spoke of this exchange many times over the next months."[4] Like many of his staff, he simply could not understand why Nixon had taped such self-incrimination, even less why he had turned it over.

Jaworski's staff prosecutors, whom he inherited from Cox, worried about their new boss's closeness with the White House. They knew that Haig was out to get them, Ben-Veniste in particular, but it was a needless worry. Jaworski, though an establishment man, was also a straight lawyer.

Haig did, however, work on Jaworski. The lawyer had been a military prosecutor at the Nuremberg Nazi war crimes trials and was still known to his staff as "Colonel." As an acquaintance of LBJ and part of John Connally's set, Jaworski could be assumed to be well disposed toward presidents and their special problems. Haig told him the situation in Washington was "revolutionary," Jaworski remembered. Haig confided in him his view of the great dangers facing the republic from the threat to the presidency. He told Jaworski—as he had earlier told Bork—of the dark secret of the chairman of the joint chiefs's "spy" at the White House, the then still undisclosed Moorer-Radford affair. Jaworski later said, "Haig at one point said, 'Now I'm going to put the patriotic monkey on your back' just like that. He said, 'I think that you've had to answer the call of your country before.' "[5]

Jaworski, however, shrewdly exploited his position extracting from Haig cast-iron guarantees of independence that Archibald Cox could never have hoped to get. Not only could Jaworski continue suing in court for tapes and evidence, but he was also protected from dismissal without the assent of a bipartisan leadership group in Congress. Nixon had never wanted another special prosecutor, but Haig assured him that Jaworski would "bring in his own people" (he never did) and "see to it that the staff limited its activity to relevant and proper areas." If true, once again Haig had miscalculated.[6]

Immediately there were ominous signs that Haig's optimism was unwarranted. Nixon's and Ehrlichman's protégé Egil Krogh, awaiting trial in the Fielding break-in, had persisted with Nixon's line of a "national security" justification. But after talking to Jaworski, he changed ground dramatically. To Nixon's dismay, Krogh now stated, "I cannot in conscience assert 'national security' as a defense," and pleaded guilty to violating the civil rights of Dr. Fielding. Krogh's defection was second only to Dean's in the damage it inflicted on Nixon's cause. Jaworski had quoted the Nuremberg precedent to him, pointing out that "following orders is not enough."

On December 21, Jaworski had a legal lesson for Haig. In the middle of a genial meeting in the warm glow of the White House map room, the special prosecutor brought up the March 21 tape. Haig's memoirs make no direct mention of this meeting. Jaworski says Haig assured him that the president's lawyers were satisfied that there was no criminal case against Nixon. Jaworski, who unlike Haig had listened to the tape, told him he was wrong. Jaworski said, "in my judgment the President was criminally involved and [I] told him that he'd better get the finest criminal lawyers he could find in the country." The thing to do, said Jaworski, was to make sure the president knew.[7]

Nixon was his own lawyer as well as a suspect. Evidently after talking to him, Haig telephoned Jaworski back, in excitement: "There was no overt act that followed the meeting" of the twenty-first, he said.[8] An overt action is needed to turn a conspiracy into a crime, and the White House seemed to believe that Nixon's words on tape alone could not convict him. Once again, whoever briefed Haig on conspiracy law was wrong. But Nixon, who knew more than anyone about the peril he faced from the March 21 tape, had already secretly tried to establish just when that "overt act"—the final payment to Hunt via an envelope left in his lawyer, Bittman's, mailbox—had been made.

It was only later that Charles Colson revealed he had been instrumental in obtaining from Bittman the beguiling assurance that the payoff occurred *before* March 21. Unfortunately for Nixon, the prosecutors were to establish that Bittman was wrong; they had got, as we have already seen, hard proof the payoff occurred *after* the conversation on March 21.

Nixon was aware of another peril on a tape not yet surrendered. Telephoning Colson, ostensibly to discuss his religious experience (Colson had been "born again" not long before), Nixon asked whether Colson was sure they had never discussed clemency for Hunt. No, said Colson, and subsequently testified so under oath, despite his religious rebirth, until a tape of a discussion with Nixon revealed the contrary. This tape, however, proved one of the toughest to locate. Buzhardt denied its existence, and it was produced only after Nixon had resigned and left office.

That Christmas, Nixon at least took Jaworski's practical advice: the president engaged James St. Clair, a prominent Boston trial lawyer, to become head of his Watergate defense.

Those defenses were now sagging across a wide front in spite of Nixon's efforts to shore them up. He had released a financial statement to try to clear up the government expenditure on his houses. He had asked the Joint Congressional Committee on Taxation to review his income tax returns—and promised to abide by any recommendations it might make for back taxes. (In April, finding improper deductions, principally those for his "vice presidential" papers, the committee presented him with the bill. Nixon agreed to pay $432,787.13, which the White House said almost wiped out his savings.)

Nixon issued statements on the ITT affair and the connection between milk price increases and campaign contributions. In the milk case, Nixon was particularly annoyed that the special prosecutor was dangling immunity to encourage a witness to testify against his (and Jaworski's) friend John Connally. In an extraordinary episode that showed how little they had learned from the Saturday Night Massacre, both Haig and Nixon bombarded the deputy attorney general with imperious telephone commands. Nixon even demanded that Henry Petersen, the man he had so abused in the cover-up, must go. But it worked no better than it had in the previous October. The Justice Department turned aside Haig and the president.[9]

In January the long-kept secret of the Moorer-Radford affair finally broke. Senator Baker ventured that it might redound to the president's credit. Small hope. Rather than a great national security matter that had to be kept secret for the country's good, it looked more like a bizarre scandal involving the top military spying on Henry Kissinger. Senate hearings were held. Admiral Moorer denied absolutely any suggestion he had spied on Kissinger. Yeoman Radford, who had been banished and wiretapped but never punished, stood up well under some tough questioning. Clearly, somebody was lying. Senator Stennis obliged the president—Kissinger was called but not Haig—by effectively quashing the Moorer-Radford investigation before it was complete. The big question of why Nixon had taken no action against the military's spying was left hanging. It, too, damaged Nixon's image as a tough president.

The real dangers for Nixon, however, were still secret, in his tape recordings. Having planned to use them in his defense, he now saw them as his "enemy within." He had moved from one disastrous expedient to another, first saying "no more" to further releases, then giving way in order to survive. Now, in January 1974, he writes, "I even talked about destroying the tapes." But again he dared not. Nixon quotes from Tricia's diary, which he was shown only later, as a reminder of how much better she understood the outcome than he did.

> Something Daddy said makes me feel absolutely hopeless about the outcome. He has since the Butterfield revelation repeatedly stated that the tapes can be taken either way. He has cautioned us that there is nothing damaging on the tapes; he has cautioned us that he might be impeached because of their content. Because he has said the latter, knowing Daddy, the latter is the way he really feels.[10]

Nixon acknowledges that at this time he discussed resignation with family, friends, Haig, and Ziegler, but that he decided to fight on because although his "case" was flawed, the "cause" of his presidency was noble. He claims to have argued that resignation would eventually undermine the whole form of American government. His son-in-law David Eisenhower went further; in February he told a news conference that Nixon would not resign even if impeached.

Nixon publicly stated that he did not believe himself guilty of any "legally impeachable offense." At the time, he emphasized the "criminal" requirement for impeachment and said he did not believe the House of Representatives would vote to send him before the Senate for an impeachment trial.

But one man was certain of it. It is now known that Jaworski felt Nixon would save the country a lot of agonizing if he would simply resign and let Ford be president. As special prosecutor he had to get on with the Watergate criminal trials. He did so in the conviction that he had a criminal case against the sitting president. Yet Jaworski believed it was no part of his job to get entangled in the politico-judicial thicket of impeachment, which might possibly wreck the obstruction of justice trials. Jaworski's wrestling with his Nixon evidence dilemma provoked a rebellion, which was kept completely secret at the time, by the younger members of the staff. While Jaworski worked it through, he set in motion further actions that were eventually to lead to Nixon's downfall.

He kept the heat on for more evidence. On January 22, Jaworski met the president's new lawyer, James St. Clair, and requested twenty-two more tapes. St. Clair stalled and then, as Nixon said in his State of the Union message, "One year of Watergate is enough," passed Jaworski a blank refusal.

The surrender of the original tapes to the prosecutors, however, accelerated completion of the indictments against Nixon's coconspirators. The tapes themselves were played in the secrecy of the grand jury room. The jurors, too, were astounded, particularly at the amounts of money Nixon and Dean bandied about.

Before going along with the major indictments, these same twenty-three citizens who had been assessing Watergate evidence since the outset wanted to hear testimony from Nixon himself. The grand jury foreman wrote to him. The president would not be required to come to the secret hearing room in the courthouse, but could meet the grand jury wherever he deemed appropriate. St. Clair suggested the grand jury submit written questions, but when they refused, the president's lawyer turned them down flat. None of this byplay was made public until a little later when Nixon revealed his refusal to testify.

Prosecutor Ben-Veniste, then in daily supervision of the Watergate grand jury, was toying with various ways of tackling Nixon's role. In theory, the grand jury might have named Nixon in a formal proceeding; if the prosecutor refused to do so, the jurors could make a "presentment," an incriminating statement, directly to the judge. Ben-Veniste and his colleagues were trying to figure out how to get their Nixon evidence from the grand jury into the hands of the House Judiciary Committee impeachment investigation. Then they suddenly found out, inside their own office, that Jaworski had, after his own secret legal research, decided not to proceed against Nixon at all. A battle royal ensued to get him to change his mind.

Jaworski's first concession was to agree simply to pass the tapes on to the Judiciary Committee. But the young Turks of "Cox's Army" wanted the grand jury to name Nixon at least as an "unindicted coconspirator"; they argued this was crucial. Otherwise, if he was not named, the evidence of his tape conversations might be ruled inadmissible in the criminal trials to come.

Jaworski was adamant. He even cited Cox's view that such a tactic would be unfair. But it says much for Jaworski's willingness to consider argument that additional concessions were wrung from him. His staff people contended that any Nixon evidence, including the tapes, which they might ask the court to send to the impeachment investigation, ought to be properly indexed, analyzed, and signposted to make it comprehensible. Jaworski agreed, provided that nothing accusatory was stated, and finally he consented to a neutral "road map," a succinct itemizing of the evidence with cross-references. It turned out to be a model for John Doar's Judiciary Committee impeachment inquiry.

There remained, however, the matter of naming Nixon. Ben-Veniste came up with an ingenious compromise. He drafted a few sentences by which the grand jury would vote to name Nixon an unindicted coconspirator and record it in the secret minutes but not in the indictment, which would be made public. That would be fair to Nixon; it would also safeguard the tapes as evidence at trial. Nixon's name would not have to be revealed until the moment came for the trial defendants to be entitled to know all those on the list.

Without commenting either way, Jaworski adopted the idea as his own, and on February 25, he addressed the grand jury. The jurors put many tough questions to him but they finally agreed, and secretly voted 19–0, with one abstention. The deed, and the deal, was done. The event was formally recorded in the minutes:

> . . . [the] Grand Jury, by a vote of 19 to zero, determined that there is probable cause to believe that Richard M. Nixon (among others) was a member of the conspiracy to defraud the United States and to obstruct justice charged in Count One of the instant indictment, and the Grand Jury authorized the Special Prosecutor to identify Richard M. Nixon (among others) as an unindicted co-conspirator.[11]

The public and Nixon knew nothing of it, even when a very strange scene occurred in Sirica's court on March 1. Warned as usual by spokesman Doyle that there would be a "proceeding," a large press contingent was on hand. With twenty-one of the grand jurors present, Jaworski rose to tell Judge Sirica that the grand jury had "material to be delivered." Vladimir Pregelj, the foreman, handed up two envelopes. One contained the indictment; the second what Pregelj described as a "sealed report." Judge Sirica, who had received only a few minutes forewarning, read silently the two-page "Report and Recommendation." It stated that the grand jury had heard, and listed, evidence it regarded as material to Nixon's impeachment proceedings and then declared:

> It is the grand jury's recommendation to the court that the evidence referred to above be made available to the House Judiciary Committee for such use as is appropriate in the impeachment proceedings . . .[12]

Ben-Veniste rose and produced from under the table a bulging brown briefcase that he asked be handed up. "This is the material made reference to in the document," he said. Nobody in the public section was any the wiser, but the transmittal of the Nixon tapes, White House documents, and road map had just been made from the executive branch to the judiciary; the request was that it now be handed to the third, legislative branch, Congress, which was preparing to sit in judgment on the president.

The press scrambled for the indictment. It was long-anticipated news but still it struck with immense force. In the case to be known as *United States* v. *Mitchell et al.*, Mitchell, Haldeman, Ehrlichman, Colson—only the year before some of the most powerful men in government—along with Mardian, Strachan, and CRP lawyer, Kenneth Parkinson, were charged with conspiracy to obstruct justice, and a list of other crimes. One of the counts of perjury against Haldeman alleged that his account of Nixon's saying on March 21 that raising a million dollars "would be wrong" was false. Nixon, of course, had supplied the evidence to damn his loyal lieutenant.

One particular count alarmed Nixon. It alleged that the March 21 payoff for Hunt had occurred *after* Nixon's discussion with Dean. Nixon promptly telephoned Colson, in part to commiserate over his being indicted but also to check how Hunt's lawyer, Bittman, could now retract his earlier assurance the payoff had come *before* March 21.[13]

The indictment was a long document listing all the alleged crimes in the Watergate cover-up, and it carried a pregnant phrase, little noticed at the time, linking those indicted "with persons known and unknown."[14]

The prosecutors had protected their secret about the naming of Nixon but almost immediately there was a flap over another story. It was that in a straw poll the grand jury had unanimously actually voted to indict Nixon. The prosecutors worried that this might unlatch the true story of Nixon's being named as an *un*indicted coconspirator, and they issued furious denials. But the story was, in fact, true. Whether it was out of the presence of the prosecutors or, as one grand juror, George Gross, claims, in the presence of Ben-Veniste, nineteen grand jurors present had lightheartedly raised both hands for a 38–0 straw poll vote to test whether they really wanted to indict Nixon.[15]

At the time, all attention was focused on the mystery briefcase handed up to the judge in court. Judge Sirica, though by now (as he later wrote) disgusted by the tapes and convinced of Nixon's guilt, deferred his ruling. Oddly, St. Clair, on Nixon's behalf, offered no objection to its transferral to the impeachment inquiry. Haldeman and Strachan did, though they lost on appeal. On March 26, the "bulging briefcase" was turned over to the House Judiciary Committee. Now the effective "grand jury" for the president had the evidence.

And still the quest for tapes went on. Jaworski's team was on the way to court again, but heavier demands were coming from the Judiciary Committee. It insisted it had an absolute right to evidence in impeachment cases, and on April 11, with key Republicans defecting from Nixon, issued its own subpoena for more than forty Nixon tapes. If the president did not comply, he was warned, the first Article of Impeachment against him might be contempt of Congress.

Nixon tried one last ploy. Recalling his agonies before Christmas with the Dictabelt and the tape gap, he had said to Ziegler, "We will take some desperate strong measure."[16] What he contemplated was like an extended replay of the Stennis compromise. He wanted again to release summaries, not full transcripts. To begin with, speechwriter Pat Buchanan was put in charge. Haig claims being told nothing about it and was clearly not amused when, through a press leak, he discovered Nixon's secret operation right under his nose. Reading the typescript —which he surprisingly claimed "contained nothing that could reasonably be interpreted as expressing criminal intent or action"—he sensed the possibility of a dangerous backlash. This naked record might "turn his supporters against him." Haig, saying Nixon "will never survive this," went to the president, who, in "real anger," agreed to give up the project. Haig says he had the transcripts destroyed.[17]

In April, Nixon revived the idea, this time with the advice of his lawyers overriding Haig. Faced with a subpoena from the impeachment inquiry for forty-two conversations and another subpoena from Jaworski for sixty-four more tapes, Nixon decided on his "desperate move." Doing the final edit himself, Nixon deleted from the transcripts what he considered irrelevant and removed even the mildest of "hells" and "damns," among other expletives. According to Haig, Nixon said, "My mother would turn over in her grave if she knew I used such language."[18]

On April 28, Haig sent a military aircraft to fetch Jaworski, who was resting at his Texas ranch, for a secret rendezvous at the White House. According to one account, Haig was full of bluster against the young prosecutors. But his main purpose was to give Jaworski a preview of the fifty-page statement the president intended issuing with his edited tape transcripts, and to ask him to comment on it. Jaworski agreed to read anything offered, declined to make comments, and was returned to Texas unimpressed with what he had perceived to be threats.

The next day, Nixon announced in a television address that he was making public his version of forty-six taped conversations. With the transcripts bound in volumes to make the bulk look far bigger than it was (though it was more than twelve hundred pages), Nixon claimed that his edited transcripts "will at last, once and for all, show that what I knew and I did in regard to the Watergate break-in and cover-up were just as I have described them to you from the beginning."

Haig, twenty years on, still writes—despite what we know of his conversation with Jaworski about the damning March 21 conversation—that "I knew this to be true." But he also claims that the "rational part of his being" told him Nixon was finished. Haig admits the public reaction to the transcripts was even worse than he had anticipated, and he now admits to wishing the tapes had gone up in smoke the previous summer.[19]

The transcripts went on sale as a blue book the size of a telephone directory. Pages and pages were excerpted in newspapers. Two paperback books of the transcripts appeared within a week and were bestsellers. "Expletive deleted" went into the language. The unvarnished quality of the conversations was what shocked the public quite as much as the incriminating substance of what was said. There was a sordid feel, as if a group of small-time crooks was scheming its way out of a mess, rather than the popularly imagined majesty of the Oval Office. Probably no president could withstand having his raw conversations published; certainly no president under suspicion. As it was, what Nixon edited out only made matters worse. People tended to believe that the deleted expletives were far worse than they were, and the notation "material unrelated to presidential action deleted" only heightened suspicion that these portions covered even worse wrongdoing.

The reaction was a second firestorm. Politicians vied with each other in denunciation. Senator Hugh Scott, the Republican minority leader, who had all along been calling for the publication of the transcripts as a means to exculpate the president, now delivered the wrath he had threatened if he was deceived. Scott called them "shabby, disgusting, immoral."

The *Chicago Tribune,* one of the most conservative newspapers in the country, on May 9 called outright for Nixon's impeachment: "We saw the public man in his first administration and we were impressed. Now in about 300,000 words we have seen the private man and we are appalled."

Even loyal Jerry Ford, trying to keep his head, admitted publicly the Nixon of the transcripts was not his friend of twenty-five years; he was "a little disappointed" by them.

It was indeed a desperate throw. Nixon had argued that executive privilege protected these confidential conversations absolutely and had bitterly surrendered the first seven only to the secrecy of the grand jury. Now he threw more than twelve hundred pages to the wild winds of public opinion. The effect was predictable. The House Judiciary Committee demanded the actual tapes themselves to test Nixon's version—and, indeed, Nixon's edited transcripts were promptly found sorely wanting.

The battle for more tapes had become triangular again when Jaworski obtained his first court subpoena. He had sought cooperation by nonjudicial means. But after he informed Haig of his belief in the president's guilt at their December meeting, it was hardly surprising that Nixon, despite protestations to the contrary, had slammed the door in his face. Jaworski wanted sixty-four more tapes; at the last minute his staff had almost casually added the date of June 23, 1972, the day Nixon discussed using the CIA to stall the FBI. That was the tape to be called the "smoking gun."

St. Clair, on behalf of Nixon, moved on May 2 to quash the subpoena, arguing that the prosecutors had all the tapes they needed for the trials of those indicted. Nixon once again invoked executive privilege. Most significantly, St. Clair argued that some of the tapes would, at trial, be "inadmissible hearsay" since the parties to the conversation, Dean and the president, were not "named parties."

While Sirica considered the motion, the prosecutors approached Jaworski. They argued that St. Clair had outmaneuvered himself. Now they could use their trump card. They could disclose that the grand jury had secretly authorized naming Nixon as an unindicted coconspirator. Only Jaworski could make that decision. He was very cautious and did not wish to get ahead of public opinion as far as the president was concerned.

It did not take him long to agree, but he thought it only fair to warn the president first and to try a final compromise. Jaworski arranged a meeting for the next day, Sunday, with Haig and St. Clair, taking several of his deputies with him, including the one who got up Haig's nose, Richard Ben-Veniste. Only that lunchtime Haig had been interviewed on one of the Sunday TV shows, ABC's *Issues and Answers*, and asked rhetorically: "At what point in the review of wrongdoing does the review itself involve injustice, excesses, and distortions, which, in effect, result in the cure being worse than the illness itself?"

Ben-Veniste now showed St. Clair the minutes of the grand jury proceedings. "As St. Clair read it his face and neck flushed with color," says Ben-Veniste. St. Clair seemed to think the grand jury had actually indicted Nixon.[20] Jaworski explained to Haig and St. Clair a compromise he wanted the president to consider. He produced a list of twenty key tapes out of the sixty-four subpoenaed. If the president would hand them over, the prosecutors would delay the naming of Nixon until the last minute.

Haig quotes Jaworski as offering a "regular old horse trade." Haig says he answered that if he were a lawyer "I'd suspect that you were trying to blackmail me and the President." Jaworski replied, Haig says, "There's blackmail and there's blackmail."

Haig says he urged Nixon to listen to these tapes. There could be nothing on them as bad as being named in court as an unindicted coconspirator, Haig says he reasoned. Haig says Nixon began listening to the tapes on Monday, May 6 (the log records he began immediately, that Sunday[21]), but after a while he called Haig in. "There's no need for me to go on listening. . . . No one is to listen to these tapes. . . . No one—understand, Al. No one. Not the lawyers. No one. Lock 'em up."[22]

Haig, full of foreboding, met Jaworski to tell him of the president's refusal. He says Jaworski was incredulous. "This is no way to save the president," Jaworski supposedly said, to which Haig claims he replied, "I'm not trying to save the president, Leon. I'm trying to save the presidency." Jaworski says he replied, "You may be destroying the presidency." Not long after this Jaworski's friend John Connally passed on to Nixon something the special prosecutor had told him. It was that "the president has no friends in the White House."[23]

Twenty years later, Haig explains his remark by saying he was trying to prevent Nixon's future from being decided by any means other than due process of law. That was why, he says, he opposed resignation until the final moment. As so often with Haig, this is a logical non sequitur; impeachment, in the president's case, was the only due process of law. Instead of taking up its challenge Haig fought to avoid it, falling back like a retreating sniper until there were no more positions left.

What had happened after Jaworski's offer, says Nixon, was that he spent a day and a half listening to the tapes until he got to the June 23, 1972 conversation. Nixon claims that the tape that was to be the "smoking gun" was not "my primary reason" for refusing Jaworski access. But with hindsight, he wishes he had put it into the public domain immediately rather than wait for it to be forced out of him. What Nixon does not say is that such a release would have required him to admit that he had been publicly lying since his first statement on the issue almost a year before. The June 23 conversation continued to gnaw at him for the next three months.

Nixon decided that neither the special prosecutor nor the impeachment inquiry would get any more tapes. "Perhaps this is Armageddon," Nixon tells Ziegler privately, "but I would rather leave fighting for principle."[24] Publicly, Ziegler was issuing repeated denials that Nixon would resign. "He is up for the battle, he intends to fight it, and he feels he has a personal and constitutional duty to do so."

Jaworski now, like Cox before him, went to court to ask that the subpoena for the sixty-four extra tapes be enforced. The secret of the president's being named an unindicted coconspirator went undivulged for another month, despite being disclosed to lawyers for Mitchell and his codefendants. Then it broke on June 6, in the *Los Angeles Times*. The revelation damaged Nixon the more because his own edited transcripts had just educated the public in the meaning of "unindicted coconspirator." Henry Petersen, explaining on April 17, 1973 what was then planned against Haldeman and Ehrlichman, had told Nixon, "For example, I am indicted. You're an unindicted coconspirator. You are just as guilty as I am . . ."

It was widely and correctly assumed at the time that Jaworski had advised the grand jury that Nixon's actual guilt was for the impeachment proceeding rather than the grand jury to decide. St. Clair regretted the grand jury's action and pointed out that being named did not *prove* someone a conspirator.

One of Nixon's principal coconspirators that same week stunned both the White House and the country by pleading guilty. Charles Colson, on March 7, had with Ehrlichman and the Plumbers been indicted a second time for the break-in at Ellsberg's psychiatrist's office. Now, after lengthy bargaining with the prosecutors and an intense prayer meeting the night before his court appearance, Colson pleaded guilty to obstructing justice by attempting to defame Daniel Ellsberg. In return, all charges against him were dropped, both in this case and in the main Watergate cover-up case. Colson was required to be a witness against his codefendants, but he had not abandoned Nixon. St. Clair insisted that he believed Colson's testimony in the impeachment inquiry would be "highly supportive of the president," and he was right in this, if little else.

The effect of Colson's guilty plea was, however, symbolic. He was the first of the president's inner circle to have accepted that what he had done in Nixon's service was illegal, and it tightened the political noose.

Another "deal" at this time was the first guilty plea in American history by a former attorney general. Richard Kleindienst, after negotiations with Jaworski's office, pleaded guilty to a misdemeanor for not having testified fully to a congressional committee. It was in relation to the ITT matter. Had he testified truthfully at the time, when asked if Nixon had ever interfered in the antitrust suit, it is likely he would not have been confirmed as attorney general. Now Kleindienst was disgraced. But he had the extreme good fortune to come before Judge George Hart, who suspended both the one-month sentence and the fine. The man who had been attorney general throughout the Watergate cover-up escaped going to jail. Jaworski argued that Kleindienst was due "some consideration" because he had volunteered his self-incrimination to the special prosecutor in the first place. Three of Jaworski's staff resigned in protest.

Jaworski's eye was on Nixon, however, and he had one further surprise. When Judge Sirica ordered enforcement of the subpoena for the sixty-four tapes, Jaworski did not sit back and wait. The same day that the White House filed with the U.S. Court of Appeals, Jaworski leapfrogged them by going to the top, asking that the Supreme Court decide the issue on an accelerated basis. The White House could no longer play for time. On May 31, the United States' highest court agreed to consider the issue and entered the Watergate case. It set the hearing for July 8. Only later did one of the associate justices jolt Jaworski with word of how close the vote to permit leapfrogging had been.[25]

As the courts moved to the unique showdown in the case of *United States of America* v. *Richard M. Nixon, President,* Nixon's fate was being decided in the House Judiciary Committee. It was clear that publication of Nixon's transcripts had torn the heart out of the swing congressmen crucial for his survival.

CHAPTER 20

Only One Chance to Impeach

By the time Nixon left in early June on his penultimate foreign trip as president—a Middle East journey that drew vast cheering crowds—the process of recommending his removal from office by impeachment was all but settled. Impeachment has two stages, however. First, the House of Representatives has to recommend it and specify the charges; then the Senate conducts a trial.

Since the first stage of the process was, like grand jury proceedings, taking place behind closed doors, the public did not fully understand the approaching certainty, nor did Nixon himself. The president still thought he had a fighting chance, especially if it came to the second stage of the Senate trial where he could escape conviction and removal from office with as few as thirty-four of the one hundred votes.

It seemed to many foreign governments incredible that it had come to this. They had counted too heavily on their relations with Kissinger and the unfailingly reassuring Al Haig. Yet in the year since first Dean and then, most forcefully, Ehrlichman had advised Nixon that impeachment was a possible outcome, the president's actions had been an incremental series of self-destruct moves.

Americans inherited impeachment from the English, but there it was used only for the king's advisers and was dropped altogether when it became possible to vote down or ease out undesirables by parliamentary means.

Americans prefer a written process to guarantee the separation of powers. According to the Constitution, a president may be impeached for—in a phrase borrowed straight from the English—"treason, bribery or other high crimes and misdemeanors." That last category was deliberately left vague, allowing the Congress to decide as necessary what an impeachable offense is. But the emphasis is on the word "high" rather than "crimes"—with the understanding it has to be an abuse of power that damages the state. This ultimate reckoning of a president's accountability had been used only once, in 1868, when the impeachment of President Andrew Johnson narrowly failed because the Senate vote fell one short of a two-thirds majority.

From the formal start of the Nixon impeachment process, provoked by the sacking of Archibald Cox the previous October, the focus of battle had been on the issue of partisanship. Certainly, most Democrats wanted Nixon out, but they sensed well enough that the country would never accept his removal if it looked politically partisan. The Democratic leadership knew it had to get irrefutable evidence that would convince enough Republicans to desert Nixon's camp and vote him out.

From Nixon's viewpoint, the best way to ensure survival was to paint the whole exercise as no more than a "Kennedy-backed" revenge exercise, a partisan settling of scores. He was looking to a combination of unbendingly loyal Republicans and die-hard Democratic conservatives to defeat an impeachment resolution in the House, or, if need be, to provide the "blocking third" that would ensure acquittal in the Senate.

Unfortunately for Nixon, he had never been comfortable with either wing of the Republican party, nor they with him. He went with allies where he found them, usually western conservatives or southern Democrat reactionaries. He had not looked after the interests of Republicans in either house of Congress. And most Republicans, seeing themselves as representatives of the party of rectitude and law and order, were more easily shocked by malfeasance at a Republican White House than were Democratic congressmen shocked by the doings of a Democratic president. That double standard was one of Nixon's abiding grievances.

Still, Nixon tended to judge the process in political terms, calculating that impeachment would cut Republicans both ways. He believed that in spite of the fact that a Watergate-ridden president might impair their chances in the 1974 midterm elections, Republican activists and ordinary Nixonite voters would still be outraged if their congressmen dared impeach him without clear cause. That was another miscalculation.

When the impeachment inquiry began in the autumn of 1973, Nixon was always running from behind. The Democratic leadership, Tip O'Neill especially, was determined to keep him at a disadvantage, but it equally wanted to make sure that there were no mistakes. You get only one chance to impeach a president.

The congressman who succeeded to the chair of the House Judiciary Committee (following the defeat of Nixon's old friend Emmanuel Celler) was Peter Rodino of New Jersey. It fell to him to lead the impeachment inquiry. Rodino, like Judge Sirica of Italian American descent, was the very personification of a cautious man. It took him until December to pick another cautious and thorough man as committee counsel. This was John Doar, a former Justice Department prosecutor. Doar gradually built up a staff of more than forty lawyers to analyze all the existing evidence. It included Bernard Nussbaum, now the Clinton White House counsel, and, among the younger lawyers, a twenty-six-year-old just out of Yale Law School named Hillary Rodham.

It took Doar until May 9 to have the evidence all sifted and laid out ready to present to his thirty-eight committee members, lawyers all. He then proceeded to drive them to distraction as he stolidly read his way through the multivolume Statements of Information over a period of six weeks.

Doar saw his job not as one of investigation but of analysis. The prosecutors who informally briefed him got irritated when he did not pick up their excitement at specific offenses. Having heard the tapes themselves, for instance, they were desperate for Doar to ask for the March 21 "cancer" conversation, which the prosecutors thought made an open-and-shut case against Nixon. Doar, however, was more interested in the whole pattern of Nixon's behavior at the White House. He did not think Congress would impeach solely on the basis of the March 21 tape, however incriminating they and he found it. So he built up a phenomenally painstaking record from all available sources. They had the Ervin Committee records, which included much excellent investigation. They had the testimony from the civil suits. Above all, as a committee with near absolute power to command the evidence, Doar had access to secret grand jury testimony.

By April, Doar and his staff possessed the material contained in the bulging briefcase transferred to them by Judge Sirica. It included the road map of the special prosecutor's investigation and the tapes he had obtained. Once these were played in secret before the House Judiciary Committee in late May—and were leaked—Nixon's stock fell lower still, and dramatically worsened when Doar had new transcripts made that restored much more damaging material that Nixon had edited out of his transcripts. The Judiciary Committee made its own demands, eventually asking for 147 further presidential conversations; Nixon defied the committee to the end.

Nixon's "grand jury" in the House Judiciary Committee consisted of twenty-one Democrats and seventeen Republicans. If all the Republicans stayed firm he needed only two defections from the Democrats and he would be home free on a tied vote. There were three southern Democrats whose districts had all voted heavily for Nixon in the 1972 presidential election. Walter Flowers (Alabama), James Mann (South Carolina), and Ray Thornton (Arkansas) were all seen as potential swing votes for Nixon. However, he could not count on the Republicans staying solid. Nixon's team set its sights on bracing wobbly moderate Republicans, but the danger to Nixon was that he was already losing support among key conservatives. Senator Goldwater, the leading right-wing voice, was seen as most important. His public statements were erratic although he was clearly warning Nixon that he had to pull something out of the hat to save himself.

Far more serious was the defection in March of Senator James Buckley. The senator, brother of the right-wing columnist William F. Buckley, Jr., whom Nixon had supposed would write articles boosting Hunt for clemency (he interviewed him on TV instead), had been elected as part of Nixon's "new majority" only in 1970. He ran on the conservative ticket in New York. But in March, Senator Buckley concluded that Nixon had lost his mandate to carry out the policies of the radical right, and so publicly urged him to resign, before he suffered "death by a thousand cuts." Neatly reversing Nixon's and Haig's rationale, Buckley urged that Nixon resign to *save* the presidency.

Nixon pooh-poohed it publicly, but right-wing erosion was what he feared most. On the House Judiciary Committee there was an approximate equivalent to Buckley. He was M. Caldwell Butler of Virginia. Ever since the Civil War, Virginia had been barren ground for Republicans. But with the backlash against the permissive sixties there had been a swing, and Butler was a neoconservative Republican.

By March 23, Butler foresaw an explosion in the committee's Republican ranks. By April 3, he answered to the tag "persuadable" on impeachment and on April 11 was the first Republican to join the Democrats in voting to subpoena the president's tapes. By May 1, Butler identified three Republicans and two southern Democrats "who are going to wind up making the decision and it worries the hell out of me."[1] At the time he kept these thoughts from publication.

Butler, to everyone who asked him which way he was inclining, said he was weighing the evidence. So, indeed, did Republican moderates anguished by the prospect of turning their own president out of office. In the secret committee sessions, Butler began noticing the nuances of skepticism among his newer Republican and southern Democrat colleagues. He discovered he was not alone. The Democratic leadership bided its time. It sensed there were the beginnings here of the much-sought-after bipartisanship. What was eventually known as the unholy alliance or the fragile coalition was beginning to form.

The second serious defection by a committee Republican came on May 1 when William Cohen, then a noted liberal freshman representative from Maine, voted with the Democrats. He joined in authorizing Chairman Rodino to write tersely to Nixon that his edited transcripts failed to comply with the committee subpoena for the actual tapes. That marked Cohen as a traitor to the Republican leadership—and to some of his constituents. Cohen was the first committee member that summer to receive letters containing silver coins, as if for Judas, or small stones, with the message "He that is without sin . . ."

Yet there were more ominous messages for Nixon. Cohen's own little-noticed motion for a more polite letter than Rodino's requesting access to the tapes was defeated, but it picked up bipartisan votes, including two southern Democrats (Mann and Flowers) and two moderate Republicans (Thomas Railsback of Illinois and Hamilton Fish of New York), plus, again, Caldwell Butler.

By the end of May, Flowers was publicly stating that he supported "negative inferences" being drawn from Nixon's refusal to supply the evidence demanded by the committee. The public, however, was still in the dark about the way the committee judgments were forming, even though there was a torrent of anti-Nixon leaks from the committee's left-wing Democrats.

For much of June there was an interlude while Nixon was on tour overseas doing what he did best, first in the Middle East and then shortly after in Moscow. On the trip to Moscow, however, the magic had deserted him. There were no more breakthrough agreements on nuclear weapons. Instead, there were reports implying a lack of stability in his insistence on following a punishing schedule in the Soviet Union despite being stricken with phlebitis, a dangerous inflammation of the veins. Stories even ran suggesting that he was trying to kill himself to avert impeachment.

A damper had been put on the Middle East trip by Secretary of State Kissinger's dramatic public threat to resign. The Kissinger taps of officials and newsmen were now sticking like a tar baby to the impeachment inquiry. A committee leak suggested Kissinger had, contrary to his own confirmation testimony, been an originator of the tapping. Kissinger called a news conference in Vienna to demand that he be cleared or he would resign. It was grand theater. Nixon eventually wrote to the Senate Foreign Relations Committee that the wiretaps had been done under his presidential authority; Kissinger's role had been to help choose the targets. Kissinger never resigned but he always complained of the impossibility of proving negatives. Some of these wiretaps were deemed illegal by the House Judiciary Committee and were later cited as part of its recommendation for Nixon's impeachment.

The trial of Ehrlichman and the Plumbers' team for the infringement of Ellsberg's psychiatrist's civil rights in the Fielding break-in made big headlines in June before ending swiftly with convictions. Nixon lamented privately, but was unhelpful publicly, refusing Ehrlichman support from White House files. At the trial, both Egil Krogh and David Young testified for the prosecution that Ehrlichman had authorized the operation, knowing that it implied "entry." Young also admitted under cross-examination that he had tampered with the Plumbers'

White House files in December 1972, deleting and removing incriminating items. He had escaped prosecution by having secured a grant of immunity in return for his cooperation.

On June 30, the Ervin Committee ended its trailblazing life and quickly issued its damning final report on the president. Senator Baker released, as his own minority opinion, a special report on the CIA's involvement in Watergate. It offered no conclusions, but documented how the CIA might have known in advance of both the Fielding and Watergate break-ins. And it pointed to many instances in which the CIA had covered up its own involvements and awareness of the cover-up, including the deliberate destruction by Richard Helms of the CIA's own in-house tape recordings in January 1973.

The CIA was also at the center of some new allegations by Charles Colson. The former White House special counsel, who had started serving his prison sentence in June, revealed to a journalist that in January 1974 Nixon had wanted to dismiss CIA Director William Colby because of suspicions the agency was deeply involved in Watergate. According to Colson, Nixon had been dissuaded by Kissinger and Haig. Colson also testified similarly to the House Judiciary Committee. He said that Nixon had told him in January that he had received a lot of information about the CIA's involvement that was very peculiar. However, Colson said Haig had invited him to his home one Sunday to continue the discussion and concluded by saying, "Chuck, we may go down and be impeached but we simply can't drag the government of the United States with us."[2]

It all went unexplored at the time. There is a whisper of it in Nixon's memoirs: The CIA was good cover. Haldeman buys the theory of a CIA plot in his book. But Colson, who claims to have been shown the CIA Watergate file by Buzhardt, today has switched from suspecting the CIA to a belief that the Watergate break-in was inspired by feuding factions of the Hughes empire! It is all extraordinary stuff and is best explored by conspiracy theorists.[3]

Shortly after Nixon got back from the Soviet Union on July 3, the House Judiciary Committee entered its final phase. A good indication of how close to their chests swing members had kept their cards was the falsely optimistic readings given to Nixon. His congressional liaison staff told him he would have at least one of the southern Democrats. *Time* magazine editors, one of their columnists told Kissinger, were now convinced Nixon would weather impeachment. Jerry Ford, a man of the House of Representatives, told Nixon, "You've got this beat," but Nixon was more gloomy. His own diary records only that "I am convinced that we can see it through to the end—however the end comes out." Nixon recognized that the next two weeks were the crux.[4] What his memoirs do not harp on, of course, is that he alone among his men had listened to the tapes he dared not surrender. And, of course, the members of the Judiciary Committee were among the few who had heard the first damning batch of tapes he had been forced to yield.

The committee now released some four thousand pages of evidence, the first batch of the more than seven thousand pages it had gone through in six weeks of closed session. It also released its own transcripts of the eight surrendered Nixon tapes, and pointed out the discrepancies between them and the versions in Nixon's April 30 blue book. The impression that Nixon had deliberately left out the worst bits was irresistible, even though in some cases what the committee managed to recover from behind the notations "[unintelligible]" in the blue book was in Nixon's favor.

What completely escaped the attention of Nixon and the Republican leadership, however, was the secret defection of enough Republicans to make impeachment sufficiently bipartisan to carry the whole House. The pressure had been growing for weeks on men like Butler and Cohen. The breach in the Republican façade opened at a caucus, a private meeting of their committee members, on July 11, the same day that John Dean impressed them with his testimony in closed session. The senior Republican on the committee, Edward Hutchinson of Michigan, challenged his colleagues to a show of hands. Whatever the evidence, he seemed to be saying, "Republicans can't vote to impeach a Republican president."[5]

The fat was now in the fire. Cohen felt his leader was trying to isolate him, and he reacted angrily, protesting that he was not ready to decide anything. To Cohen it seemed as partisan as anything the Republicans had accused the Democrats of. Before the row boiled over, Thomas Railsback, a respected moderate, intervened to say that he, too, was not ready to decide. The president's key defender, Charles Wiggins of California, sensing the danger in forcing the issue, agreed it was unwise to have votes or a show of hands at this stage.

But "on the fence" was a polite way of saying that some Republicans were leaning to impeach. By July 18, the day that presidential lawyer James St. Clair gave his final speech in closed session, it was being publicly suggested by leading Republicans that four to five of their committee members were prepared to vote against Nixon. Yet they had to have something to vote on. And it was here, at the end of all these months of weighing the evidence against Nixon, that the process nearly broke down. The draft articles recommending impeachment were produced on July 19 by counsel John Doar. To the swing votes they appeared too scattershot and unsustainable. They ranged all the way from the secret bombing of Cambodia to the alleged fraud of Nixon's tax payments. At least one Republican, Harold Froehlich of Wisconsin, tended toward solving his political dilemma by allowing the Democrats to draft such hopeless articles that he could easily vote against them.

With the committee debates scheduled to go live in TV prime time the following Wednesday evening, some quick and powerful drafting had to be done. The gravity of the evidence had to be put across to the public in such a way as to make plain what a "high crime" was—and to show why it would be necessary to recommend a president's removal from office.

Rodino and the Democratic leadership knew, moreover, that the language had to be acceptable to the swing votes, and the chairman seems to have allowed the redrafting process to develop that weekend almost organically. Flowers began drafting; so did Butler and Thornton. From the Judiciary Committee's own minority staff, Railsback had one of the expert counsel, Tom Mooney, called in to assist. In close contact with Rodino and John Doar was Mann, a transmission belt for the exchange of drafts.

By Monday, with two days to go before the TV debates, there still had been no group meeting. But that day Flowers approached Railsback and suggested that they each get "some guys together."[6] Without offering an explanation, Railsback invited members individually to his office the next morning, with Mooney the sole noncongressman. It is not unusual for Democrats and Republicans to meet in this way to transact legislative business; but on so sensitive a matter, this was exceptional. Most were surprised to see who was there. They started running through the charges against Nixon, throwing out the ones they agreed were not going to make it, finally narrowing them down to the abuse of power and obstruction of justice.

Railsback wondered whether they should not try to censure Nixon rather than impeach him, but it was clear their consensus was for impeachment. What they needed to illustrate were Nixon's "high crimes." Obstruction of justice was the cover-up of the Watergate affair (which Thornton, a former state attorney general, held was still continuing). The abuse of power article, they felt, went wider than Watergate and should include the Kissinger taps, the Fielding break-in, and misuse of federal agencies—the FBI, the CIA, even the Internal Revenue Service.

After a long meeting, there were twenty-four hours left before the TV debates. The swing members jokingly referred to themselves as the "magnificent seven" rather than the unholy alliance. The Democrats came back with more suggestions from their own caucus, and the bipartisan group drafted and redrafted, refining the language. There were no real objections from the Democratic leadership. Chairman Rodino had always stated publicly that "impeachment had to come out of the middle."

On Tuesday, to everyone's surprise, one of the conservative Republicans on the committee nobody had considered, Lawrence Hogan of Maryland, announced that he had decided to vote to impeach. There was fury in the Republican establishment; Hogan was attacked for attempting to perk up his faltering campaign for governor. Yet if so, that meant impeachment was politically attractive, even for a conservative Republican, a dire prospect for Nixon.

Conservative Democrats were also falling away from the president. Nixon's congressional liaison reported that all three committee southern Democrats were lost. Nixon says he was stunned. He had steeled himself to lose possibly two, but losing all three meant his impeachment was a certainty. He accepted the political arithmetic that losing one committee southerner was equivalent to losing five southerners on the House floor. In a last-ditch effort to get one back, he approached Alabama governor George Wallace, hoping he would put heat on Congressman Flowers. It was fruitless; Wallace refused. Nixon says he turned to Haig, saying, "Well, Al, there goes the presidency."[7] Twenty years later, Haig views the breaking of the Wallace connection as the moment when the question became not whether Nixon would resign but "how to arrange this event while remaining true to the Constitution."[8] The skids under Nixon were at least being looked at inside the White House, if not yet greased.

Nixon recalls a subsequent conversation with Congressman Joe Waggonner, a total Nixon last-ditcher from Louisiana. He left Nixon convinced that the House was lost, and he faced an impeachment trial in the Senate unless he resigned first. In his memoirs, Nixon admits considering the "personal" factors—the years of lawsuits costing millions that would follow resignation, and, although Nixon does not mention it, there was the personal consideration that conviction in the Senate would strip him of his ex-presidential emoluments for life. That night in his notes Nixon wrote, "Lowest point in the presidency, and Supreme Court still to come."[9]

The arrival of the tapes case in the Supreme Court had been of high constitutional moment, as well as grand theater, beginning with the day of the oral argument on July 8. After the absolute guarantees of independence that he had received from Haig and Nixon, and which Bork had written into legal regulations, Leon Jaworski had been angered by St. Clair's defense tactics. In a replay of the argument against Cox, the president's lawyer claimed that the court had no jurisdiction whatever since the disputants, Jaworski and Nixon, were both members of the same executive branch of government. Jaworski decisively answered this gambit, arguing he represented the "sovereign authority of the United States" in such a prosecution.

St. Clair went on to claim that the grand jury's naming Nixon as an unindicted coconspirator was a "nullity" and prejudiced the president's case in the impeachment hearing. During the questioning by the associate justices that enlivens these oral arguments, Jaworski surprised them—and St. Clair—with his disclosure that there had been no mention of Nixon's being named as a coconspirator in the "bulging briefcase" material passed to the House Judiciary Committee. Nothing accusatory had been transmitted, only neutral evidence. As for the grand jury naming Nixon, this was part and parcel of the admissibility of evidence for the criminal trial of *Mitchell et al.* for which he needed the sixty-four extra tapes.

That was the nub of the case. Could executive privilege be invoked by a president to decide, on his own, to withhold evidence from both prosecution and defense in a criminal trial? In its ruling, before getting to this principal issue, the court dismissed St. Clair's argument against jurisdiction on the basis of the "intra-branch" nature of the litigation. Then it refused to accept the president's concern about prejudice on the grounds of his being named an unindicted coconspirator.

Finally, the court ruled that executive privilege could indeed obtain, as Nixon had long claimed was the presidential prerogative. But the victory was Pyrrhic, because in this case it would not apply. The claim to withhold evidence on the grounds of "the generalized interest in confidentiality" could "not prevail over the fundamental demands of due process of law in the fair administration of criminal justice." The president could not place himself above the law.

Nixon, the court said, must hand over the sixty-four subpoenaed tapes to Judge Sirica for his in camera inspection, and the judge would then decide what to excise on privilege grounds. Included, of course, was the fatal June 23, 1972 "smoking gun" conversation. Only two days before the Supreme Court decision, Nixon says, he had noted in his diary that "how we handle the 23rd tape is a very difficult call because I don't know how it could be excerpted properly." This suggests that Nixon was still hoping he might "abide by the court's ruling without actually complying with it"—recycling the Stennis solution yet again.[10]

The Supreme Court decision, delivered the very day the impeachment debates began on TV, destroyed what hope Nixon had. At San Clemente, Haig waited to wake him with the bad news from Washington. The vote was 8–0 (Associate Justice Rehnquist recused himself) to uphold the Jaworski subpoena. Nixon, who had appointed four of the nine justices, had hoped there would be some "air," as he put it, some split that would allow him to claim that the ruling was not definitive and hence need not be obeyed. Eight to zero could hardly have been more definitive.

Nixon says he had counted on the Supreme Court's making "at least some provision for exempting national security materials"—a clear reference to his hope that he could still keep a national security blanket over the attempt to stall the FBI with the CIA.[11] But the opinion, written by Chief Justice Warren Burger, made plain that Sirica would decide. Nixon then made the country spend another eight hours wondering whether he would comply or "abide by" or defy the Supreme Court.

The potential constitutional confrontation was grave. What could the judiciary do if the president defied its orders? It could cite him for contempt but it could hardly send a federal marshal to arrest him. The question would come back to Congress. Congress would have to decide if defiance, too, was an impeachable offense, and doubtless it would have done so had Nixon chosen to defy. But some members of the impeachment committee admitted afterward that they had no answer to the question of what would happen if the president refused to comply. If the president as commander in chief ordered the armed forces to surround the Congress, what then?

A similar thought seems to have crossed the mind of Defense Secretary James Schlesinger, who instructed the joint chiefs that any orders to the military from the White House were first to be referred to him. The joint chiefs were reported irritated and privately complained that this was redundant. And when Haig later found out what Schlesinger had said, he was angry. He still is, mostly at the very suggestion the American military would have been thought capable of such dereliction.

However, Kissinger discloses that on August 2, Haig mentioned to him, "as an idea being canvassed," that "it might be necessary to put the 82nd Airborne Division around the White House to protect the President." Kissinger says Haig agreed when he protested that the presidency could not be conducted from a White House ringed with bayonets.[12] It was, thankfully, in the end all the stuff of nightmares.

Just in time for the evening news on the East Coast, eight hours after the Supreme Court ruling on July 24, St. Clair appeared before cameras and reporters at San Clemente to read Nixon's response. He did not disclose—as Nixon did much later—that they had been considering not complying. While disappointed, Nixon stated that "I respect and accept the court's decision." As soon as the news bulletins finished, the programs switched live to the impeachment debate in the House Judiciary Committee. No Hollywood scriptwriter or TV scheduler could have managed such an extraordinary juxtaposition.

CHAPTER 21

Endgame

The televised impeachment debates in the House Judiciary Committee stretched over six days. Unlike the Senate's Ervin Committee's hearings the previous summer—lively affairs with witnesses, knockabout, and grandstanding—they consisted of sober parliamentary speechmaking and debate on the most serious of matters. Yet those who saw them will remember these debates as not merely absorbing television but also as extraordinarily responsible, high quality, and often deeply emotional argument. They were not all one-sided, either; the president's defenders had one very good day in court.

In the end, the committee reached its powerful bipartisan verdict without benefit of what was already being called a "smoking pistol."[1] The tape of June 23, 1972 was still to come. It was the rest of the evidence that convinced them. And if it was clear from the beginning which way sentiment was moving, it was still for many viewers at home a chill moment when the final "Aye" was uttered, like a lamenting gasp, in the vote on Article I. That came in TV prime time on July 27, a Saturday evening. Dealing with the obstruction of justice in the cover-up, it concluded thunderously:

> In all of this, Richard M. Nixon has acted in a manner contrary to his trust as President and subversive of constitutional government, to the great prejudice of the cause of law and justice and to the manifest injury of the people of the United States.

> Wherefore Richard M. Nixon, by such conduct, warrants impeachment and trial, and removal from office.

In reaching this point, the "fragile coalition" of Republicans and southern Democrats needed to create the committee's central majority, had sturdily survived some alarms. The drafting and redrafting had gone on tirelessly to ensure that the high crimes being described would not only find acceptance among the maximum number of committee members but also be comprehensible to the country at large. And beyond that, to be sustainable in proceedings before the whole House and Nixon's subsequent trial in the Senate.

The articles were still in working draft form when the televising of the debate—which had required the House to vote a rules change—began on July 24. Chairman Rodino watching for the cue from television producers, opened the session with a homily to the United States' good fortune to have endured through two hundred years under the rule of law. He then focused on the oath of office, taken at each inauguration and often barely listened to, in which the president swears to take care that the laws be faithfully executed. The charge that Nixon had violated his oath was the leitmotif of all that followed.

The senior Republican, Edward Hutchinson, wryly dissented from Rodino's view, stating that "ours is more of a political than a judicial function after all." He remarked that, even as they opened debate, "the committee has not resolved just what an impeachable offense is."

It was a dangerous phrase. To general surprise, the next most senior Republican, Robert McClory of Illinois, suggested impeachment was the proper remedy for a president, and he admitted to being disturbed by the evidence of abuse of power. McClory, who generally supported Nixon, had already alarmed the president's camp on July 19 when he suggested the full House would vote to impeach. This first evening, when proceedings were interrupted once by a bomb threat, the only member of the fragile coalition to speak was the Illinois Republican Thomas Railsback. He had been so involved in the drafting that he had not had time to prepare a speech. So he spoke extempore, and with extraordinary emotion. He declared himself an anguished friend of Richard Nixon. He spoke not of principles but of the disturbing evidence. The Democrats were transfixed: Railsback was making the case against Nixon. He came to the end of his allotted time, but a Democrat yielded him two minutes of his time to continue. The clear tenor of Railsback's remarks, reverberating as the televised session ended, was that Republicans would impeach a Republican president.

On the second day, it was eight hours more before all the opening personal statements were concluded. Yet another midwestern Republican, Harold Froehlich of Wisconsin, unhappily confessed to being troubled over the obstruction of justice. The number of Republican defections looked like rising to seven, possibly eight of their total seventeen members. It was devastating news for Nixon. Nor could he take much comfort in the tone of some of the remarks.

Among the best remembered were those of black Congresswoman Barbara Jordan, who remarked sonorously that she and her race had not been included in the original "We the people" of the Constitution. But now as a full-fledged inquisitor, the former Texas state judge declared: "My faith in the Constitution is whole, it is complete, it is total, and I am not going to sit here and be an idle spectator to the diminution, the subversion, the destruction of the Constitution."

Making perhaps an even greater impact among their pro-Nixon constituents were the statements from the conservative members of the fragile coalition. Alabama's Walter Flowers, flag pin in his lapel, asked, "What if we fail to impeach? Do we ingrain forever in the very fabric of our Constitution a standard of conduct in our highest office that in the least is deplorable and at worst is impeachable?" Butler of Virginia bit the bullet of party loyalty. "For years we Republicans have campaigned against corruption and misconduct in the administration of the government of the United States by the other party," he said, "but Watergate is our shame."

By the third day of debate, the first two draft articles, after frantic reworking, were more or less phrased as the majority wanted them. But so much effort had gone into this enhancing that the job of refining the myriad charges against Nixon into usable specific form had been skimped.

On this ground the president's defenders counterattacked. Their battle cry was "specificity"—where were the specifics? Introducing the latest draft, Paul Sarbanes, Democrat of Maryland and former Rhodes scholar, was asked to explain the allegation in it that Nixon "made it his policy" to obstruct justice. Charles Wiggins, representing Nixon's old California district and the most able of the president's defenders, asked artfully to be told "exactly when the policy was declared . . . and if I get an answer to that, I would like to know in what manner it was declared." Sarbanes stumbled. He had been given the new articles by a coalition member only moments before the debate.

Another Nixon defender, Charles Sandman of New Jersey, weighed in like a battering ram. "Do you not believe that under the due process clause of the Constitution that every individual, including the president, is entitled to due notice of what he is charged for?" Again Sarbanes stumbled, arguing that since Nixon's lawyer, James St. Clair, had been present throughout, due notice had been given.

A lunch recess was rather promptly called to allow the majority to regroup. They had been caught off-balance. The Doar staff was preparing a background report containing all the specifics, but it had been scheduled to be delivered later to the full House and was not ready. Meanwhile, on national television the Nixon defenders appeared to be winning this particular argument.

After lunch Sarbanes tried to recoup by setting out a narrative of the facts against Nixon. He knew the case inside out and did well. But in dealing with a "course of conduct," Sarbanes admitted that "there is not one isolated incident that rests behind each of these allegations." He was vulnerable to Sandman's complaint that this was a "rehash," not specifics.

Still, the Nixonites had the day. Wiggins insisted: "Wouldn't it be a damning indictment, Mr. Chairman, of this committee if, after all this time and all this money, we were unable to state with specificity what all this was about?"

The coalition's James Mann, the courtly conservative Democrat from South Carolina who had also secretly taken the lead in redrafting, spoke to the point. "In my judgment," he insisted, "the charges that are included in Article I notify him of what he is charged with. And they set out something extra, the means by which he is alleged to have committed the offense . . . Let us be reasonable."

But Sandman, a brilliant TV demagogue, was not to be stopped. He sneered: "Isn't it amazing they have so much but they are unwilling to say so little? Isn't it amazing? They are willing to do anything except make these articles specific." Delbert Latta of Ohio, a total supporter of Nixon, chimed in: "A common jaywalker charged with jaywalking anyplace in the United States is entitled to know when and where the alleged offense is supposed to have occurred. Is the president of the United States entitled to less?"

In a state of some disarray, six of the coalition members got together during the evening dinner recess. They acknowledged that the "specificators," as Flowers called Wiggins and Sandman, had momentarily got them licked. Cohen for one knew the case inside out and insisted they counterattack with the specifics they had. They were worn out from the intensive week's business. But at the evening session, again in prime time TV, the process of pouring details of the evidence into the record before a national audience began in earnest.

Sandman's tactic of delaying the main vote and using the debate time to demolish the impeachment case was now turned against him. Sandman had used the parliamentary motion to "strike," or delete, charge after charge from Article I. Now Railsback, for the coalition, shrewdly launched the countertactic of spelling out the detail, "specifically," of Nixon's own involvement in each charge, agreeing when they adjourned near 11 P.M. to continue doing so the next day.

On Saturday, when they reconvened just before 1 P.M., the process was clear. Article I itself had been made more specific. It substituted the wording "course of conduct or plan" for the original "policy"—it seemed apt since Nixon had used "plan" on his tapes as his word for the cover-up. It was Flowers who now moved to strike, and clause by clause, section by section, the coalition members rose to make the specific case. Some of them, like Cohen and Butler, prefaced every sentence with "specifically." Soon Sandman cried enough, but the coalition wanted all the facts out in public and kept right on until 7 P.M.

Now it was prime time TV again. Rodino let Flowers have almost the last word to make clear, after the parliamentary maneuvering, that he, too, was voting, painfully, for impeachment. Flowers spoke to the liberal Democrats, saying, "Let's face it, it is less difficult for some than others"; he hoped that, as Democrats, they would never have to face impeaching a president of their own party. And suddenly the debate on

Article I was over. The vote, technically, was on the Sarbanes substitute as amended, but it was the real thing. There was a chorus of ayes and noes, with Rodino averring that "the ayes appear to have it" before deferring to the traditional demand for roll call, which takes place right in the committee room, in this case room 2141 of the Rayburn House Office Building. Apart from the clicking of press cameras, there was tense stillness as the clerk called the names, Democrats first. The article had achieved its majority even before the first Republican, Hutchinson, voted no. Then a little later came Railsback with the first Republican aye, followed by five more until Rodino, as chairman, came last, almost sighing his croaked affirmation.

On July 29, McClory increased the number of defecting Republicans to seven—out of seventeen—when his aye made the vote 38–10 for Article II: abuse of power. In that debate another memorable Watergate phrase went into the language when James Mann said that if presidents were not held accountable, "the next time there may be no watchman in the night."

Article III, charging Nixon with contempt of Congress for refusing to comply with the committee subpoena for tapes, passed 21–17, with Flowers and Mann joining most Republicans voting against while McClory and Hogan joined the Democrats. Two more bitterly argued articles—on the secret bombing of Cambodia and on evading income tax and benefiting from government-funded home improvements—failed 12–26. The latter debate, which made particular sense to ordinary voters, was deliberately scheduled in prime time by the Democrats and did untold further damage to Nixon, especially since new disclosures of fraud charges by the IRS were made.

The air of government corruption thickened with the news that day that Nixon's favorite, former Treasury Secretary John Connally, had been formally charged with bribery, among other offenses, in connection with the 1971 "milk fund" scandal. Connally went to trial and gained a rare acquittal at the hands of a District of Columbia jury. However, this undoubtedly damaged his presidential chances, if not his pretensions.

Nixon, still at San Clemente, says he refused to watch any of the televised impeachment proceedings. He had been swimming in the Pacific at the time of the vote on Article I and was getting dressed in the beach trailer when he heard by telephone that he had become the first president in 106 years to be recommended for impeachment. Kissinger watched and, though sickened, said later he, too, would have voted with the majority for impeachment.[2] Nixon says he was alternating between optimism and fear. He places the "last time there was any real hope" when he went to a dinner party with old California friends on July 21. His daughter Tricia, who went with him, noted that the guests were in high spirits, as if it were "a million light-years away from the turmoil." But for her it was "the eye of the hurricane." She, too, did not know about the June 23, 1972 tape, which Nixon noted was "like a slow-fused dynamite waiting to explode."[3]

As soon as Nixon had received the Supreme Court's command to surrender the sixty-four tapes, he asked Buzhardt in Washington to listen to the June 23 conversations. Buzhardt's verdict was devastating. Politically, it was the "smoking gun," he told Haig, though legally not necessarily fatal. Haig says he told him to listen again and discuss it with St. Clair. (Buzhardt later said he had a confrontation with the president, who then refused to speak to him for a week[4]). St. Clair, claims Haig, having only discussed the tape on the phone with Buzhardt and still not having heard it—or indeed any other—ventured that the key conversation was "ambiguous," that it could be handled.

Haig, Buzhardt, and St. Clair have always maintained that only at this point did they become aware of the contents of the June 23 tapes. However, Nixon's diary notes, "The 23rd tape we have talked over time and time again."[5] That would suggest they all knew what they were talking about. (Indeed, Jaworski was to remind Haig that the previous May when he had tried his abortive "horse trade," the chief of staff had told him he "couldn't see why I wanted those tapes because there was not anything of value in them." On being reminded, Haig had said "That's right! And that's what I believed!"[6] In any case, in his memoirs Nixon says that Haig, after talking to St. Clair, gave his opinion that Buzhardt was being alarmist and that the situation was "not completely unmanageable."

By the weekend, reflecting on the impeachment vote, Nixon's diary reckons differently. Referring to St. Clair and Haig, Nixon writes:

"They will listen to the tapes and my guess is that they might well come in to me and say 'we just don't think this is manageable.' "[7]

On July 26, St. Clair had a very uncomfortable time in Sirica's court. He came pleading for time in handing over the tapes. The judge reminded him that two months earlier he had been ordered to produce the tapes, along with indexes. Sirica wanted no more delay. If a prompt timetable could not be agreed for the following week, he would set it himself. Sirica then quietly asked St. Clair if he had not listened to these tapes in preparation for the impeachment. The lawyer repeated his insistence that he did not himself listen to tapes. Over St. Clair's objections, Sirica instructed him to listen to them personally; he wanted the president's lawyer answerable to the court. St. Clair wearily agreed. "All right, now we're getting somewhere," said Sirica. St. Clair—and Buzhardt and even Haig—had now been put under notice that withholding their knowledge of evidence might place them in jeopardy.[8]

Now for the first time Nixon's diary starkly contemplates "whether I decide to bite the bullet" of immediate resignation or to wait for the full House vote and then to resign, to spare the country six months of an impeachment trial. The diary also contemplates for the first time the predicament of his personal finances. It does not say so, but the implication is that Nixon knows impeachment would strip him of his $60,000 annual pension, plus lifetime expenses to run an office. Nixon's end days were upon him.[9]

Nixon's prediction about what would happen when St. Clair finally heard the June 23 tape proved accurate. St. Clair not only agreed with Buzhardt but he also asserted that it so contradicted the defense he had made before the House Judiciary Committee that unless it was made public he, too, would be party to obstruction of justice.

That night Nixon could not sleep and sat up rationalizing his choices on his yellow legal pad. They were few. Resign now; resign in a month; or fight through the Senate. Until nearly 7 A.M. he listed the pros of resigning and the cons, which included putting the country through the torment of a Senate trial with the outcome, final conviction and removal from office, "all but settled." But, Nixon says, his natural instincts welled up and he ended up writing "end career as fighter."[10]

When Nixon got up that day, the news was that John Ehrlichman had been sentenced to jail, minimum twenty months, in the case of the 1971 Plumbers' break-in at Ellsberg's psychiatrist. He got concurrent sentences for each of four charges, conspiracy to violate the psychiatrist's rights, and three counts of perjury. Outside court on bail Ehrlichman, defiant as ever, maintained that the judge had been wrong to disallow his national security defense, which would be the grounds for his appeal. Nixon's promise that no one would go to jail—made originally to Ehrlichman—was looking distinctly hollow.

That same morning Patrick Buchanan breakfasted with reporters and floated the idea of rushing impeachment through the House, as a foregone conclusion, to get to a prompt Senate trial. His idea was to stanch the hemorrhage, and perhaps to avoid conviction. Buchanan said he had not discussed it with Nixon, but the young speechwriter, one of the president's last remaining political advisers, was certainly in tune with Nixon's thinking and the White House did not disown the notion.

Nixon now faced the final defection, led by his chief of staff. Although Haig omits it, Kissinger says that the previous Friday, July 26, he went to Haig, broke an unspoken rule they had about not mentioning Nixon's resignation, and told him the end should occur as soon as possible. Kissinger says, "Haig and I had a special responsibility to end the agony if that was in our power and to bring about a smooth transition." Kissinger claims Haig agreed completely.[11]

Haig's version is that he had read the June 23, 1972 transcript two days before his Wednesday July 31 meeting with Nixon, and he now believed it would "establish his guilt in the public mind and also in his trial before the Senate." Nixon's memoirs claim clearly that Haig read the transcripts for the first time on the Wednesday, and imply he read them in his presence. But there is no conflict about Haig's opinion. Nixon says Haig told him that "I just don't see how we can survive this one." Haig says he added that the Cabinet wouldn't hold, nor the party nor the staff. "Once this tape gets out, it's over."[12]

By afternoon, Ron Ziegler had listened to the tape and Nixon could tell he, too, felt the situation was all but hopeless. So Nixon's decision to "end career as fighter" lasted less than twenty-four hours. He says he told Haig on August 1 that he had decided to resign.

Even before Nixon told him, Haig says that he had consulted again with Kissinger. The secretary of state was "the agent of transition," the most senior Cabinet officer to whom the president would deliver his resignation. According to Kissinger, this was not just contingency planning. Haig told him the "smoking gun" had been found, and Kissinger says he told Haig that their role now was "to ease Nixon's decision to resign."[13]

Haig protests endlessly that he never suggested resigning to anyone, least of all Nixon. Yet Haig's own account is that he told Kissinger: "The situation is terminal, Henry. One way or another Nixon's presidency is over. He needs our help." Oddly, Kissinger reports Haig telling him that the June 23 tape had been turned over to Sirica the previous day (it had not) and, odder still, Haig did not show Kissinger the transcript. Haig did, however, show it to other senior White House staffers. They, "with tears in their eyes," agreed the president could hold no longer. Unstated is the fact that they all realized their defense of Nixon now rested on sixteen months of straight lies.[14]

Haig, who at one moment argues so fiercely that the president must have due process, now says he believed, as did Kissinger, that it was dangerous for the country to go through the one due process offered a president: an impeachment trial. Haig makes clear he favored resignation, but would not advise Nixon so, or so he claims.

When Nixon told Haig on the Thursday of his decision to resign—making the move the following Monday—Haig did suggest resigning, immediately. It would be better to be gone, because the June 23 tape was due to be given to Sirica on Friday, August 2. If the president waited until Monday, it would be right in the middle of the uproar over the tape. If he left straightaway, Haig advised, by Monday all the attention would be on Ford as the new president.

Haig says Nixon demurred. He needed to take the family to Camp David to explain, adding that he didn't want delegations of Republicans coming telling him what to do. Nixon's version, however, is that he agreed to think about Haig's suggestion of a quick exit, and that only later that afternoon, after hearing Ziegler argue against it, did he decide it would be Monday. Nixon claims that he wanted his friends to have the chance to react to the June 23 tape and get off the hook.

Where both Haig and the president agree is that he asked Haig to brief Ford to be ready to succeed within days, but not told precisely when, and that total secrecy must be kept.

Nixon went off for a brief river cruise with his close friend Bebe Rebozo, who was stricken, Nixon says, when told he would resign; he told Nixon "you just don't know how many people are still for you." In fact, the effect of the televised impeachment debates was dramatic. On August 2 the Louis Harris poll showed 66–27 percent favoring impeachment—a 13 percent increase from the week before.

Nixon says he extracted a promise from Rebozo to help him persuade the Nixon women, provided, Rebozo said, he make one last try to mount a defense. Nixon agreed, even though he says he recognized it was hopeless. It was Thursday evening. Nixon had turned around again.

Haig's imbroglio with Ford was about to begin, a bizarre but possibly crucial subplot within the final act. Before meeting Ford as instructed, Haig had taken the precaution of consulting Buzhardt for what he calls "legal guidance" on the options unfolding. Buzhardt supplied him with a written list of alternatives to the president's simple resignation.

Haig and Ford's chief of staff, Robert T. Hartmann, did not get along well, to put it mildly. When Haig discovered, on arriving at the vice president's office next door to the White House, that Hartmann was staying for the meeting, he decided neither to give Ford the president's message nor to go through Buzhardt's options. Instead, he told Ford only about the tape, the staff's view that the president's impeachment was now certain, and that Ford should hold himself in readiness. Ford remembers Haig saying that he had not himself seen the tape transcripts—which is odd if he had seen them the previous Monday—but that the contents would show the president had deceived them all. Ford says he was angry and the hurt was deep.

At noon Haig rang Ford back and asked for a second meeting, this time alone. That afternoon he told him Nixon intended to resign. What Haig did next shook the vice president. Ford says Haig asked what his recommendations for Nixon were, and Ford says he told Haig that it would be improper for him to respond. Haig laid out for Ford the list of options, saying only that they had been drawn up, Ford remembers, by unnamed "knowledgeable people on the White House staff."[16]

The first three options were unexceptionable, if odd: that Nixon might temporarily step aside until impeachment was settled; that he might just stay on in office; and that he might try to persuade the House to vote censure rather than impeachment. But the final three were deeply compromising and all contained variations of the word "pardon." They were: the president could pardon himself and then resign; he could add all the Watergate defendants to his own pardon and then resign; and, finally, he could resign and hope that his successor would pardon him. According to Ford, Haig specified that "Nixon could agree to leave in return for an agreement that the new president—Gerald Ford—would pardon him." Ford, twenty years later, uses similar words; that it was "resigning in return for me as President granting him a pardon."[17]

Haig claims that he neither presumed to instruct Ford nor to tell him that he, Haig, believed (as he admits he did) that Nixon deserved to be pardoned. But in such sensitive dealings between men of the world there need be nothing explicit. It is enough for the issue to be raised for the message to be passed. The whole interlude makes sense only if Haig had wanted to be assured, in his own mind, that Ford understood what was required.

Haig furiously denounces those who suggested later this is where the allegation of a "trade" of resignation for a pardon originated, notwithstanding the Ford memoirs' phrase "in return for an agreement." Haig even claims that Nixon had no choice in the matter, denying the evidence of his own options list. Had, for instance, Ford indicated he was not inclined to pardon, then Nixon still had time to exercise the option of pardoning himself. That, however, would cost Nixon the dignity Haig admits he was so keen to preserve, but it was certainly a choice Nixon had. Ford maintains that the whole episode weighed heavily on him. He told Haig he wanted time to think about it, to talk to his wife, and, he says, he also wanted St. Clair's "legal assessment of Nixon's problems"—a clear reference to the pardon.[18]

When Hartmann was told what Haig had been up to, he exploded. Hartmann, Ford says, was suspicious of everybody, and he now speculated that Haig would instantly have reported to Nixon that the vice president was "not uncomfortable with" a pardon. Hartmann went further: He told Ford he ought to have thrown Haig out of his office for this "monstrous impropriety" and called a news conference to say why. Ford, saying Hartmann was making a mountain out of a molehill, had no time for a deeper discussion with his aide until the next morning.[19]

Ford says that his wife, Betty, learning only around midnight of the upheaval that was to change their lives, insisted that he not make recommendations about Nixon to anyone. At around 1:30 A.M., Ford claims that Haig rang him to say that nothing had changed. Ford says he responded that he had talked to Betty, and said, "We can't get involved in the White House decision making."[20]

Who called whom and said what was, as we shall see shortly, a matter of disturbing contradiction at the time. Haig's latest version, characteristically, muddles matters further by suggesting that he had telephoned Ford the night *before* Nixon told him he was resigning.[21]

The next morning there was a reckoning of sorts. St. Clair, called in by Ford to discuss Haig's option list, commented only that he had not been the source of any such legal advice. That set the stage for a collision between Ford on the one hand and Hartmann and other Ford staffers on the other who were brought in to warn the future president of the peril they thought he had been placed in by Haig. According to Hartmann, Ford told them he, not Haig, had initiated the middle of the night call. And in complete contradiction with the later Ford memoirs' version, that Ford and his wife had decided "this just has to stop; it's tearing the country to pieces." Ford had telephoned Haig, saying, "They should do whatever they decided to do; it was all right with me."[22]

Faced with their contradictions, Ford accepts that "recollections differ." Hartmann stands by his own "vivid recollections." His principal ground is that had Haig already been told "we can't get involved," as Ford's memoirs version claims, there would have been no need for the rearguard action Hartmann and other senior staff now made the vice president undertake on August 2. To persuade Ford, Hartmann recruited Nixon adviser Bryce Harlow, who agreed that it was "inconceivable" that Haig was not carrying out a mission for Nixon, and the chief of staff must now be disabused. In the presence of Harlow and Hartmann and others—Ford says he wanted witnesses—the vice president wrote some notes in longhand and telephoned Haig. Ford told Haig that "nothing we talked about yesterday afternoon should be given any consideration in what decision the president may wish to make."[23]

Haig says it sounded like Ford was reading from a text, and he guessed that the vice president had been got at by his staff. He says he was baffled but he absolutely denies the Harlow idea that he was on a mission from Nixon. Hartmann himself has never stated there was a deal. He reckons that the message was simply and—for Ford—damagingly passed. Bafflingly, Haig also now writes that there could be only one reason for pardoning Nixon "and that was for the good of the country, to spare it from a trial in the Senate."[24] Yet it was resignation that spared the country a trial in the Senate while a pardon spared Nixon a trial in *court.*

Even though he omitted giving Ford a transcript of the June 23 tape, Haig acted to fill in other Nixon defenders who had been deceived. On August 2, the day the tapes were handed over to Sirica, Haig called in Congressman Charles Wiggins, who was gearing up to lead Nixon's defense in the whole House. Just before the committee's vote on Article I, Wiggins had focused on the June 23 meeting. Observing that Nixon admitted giving instructions that the FBI not be allowed to expose CIA activities, Wiggins went out on a limb in the public debate. "I would think that the weight, if not the preponderance of the evidence in favor of the president, is that he acted in the public interest as distinguished from corruptly."

Wiggins then twice read the transcript and saw that he had been gulled. "Essentially what it was," Wiggins said recently, "was that the president of the United States had consensually agreed to join a conspiracy. Stating it in lawyer language, to hide relevant information from the FBI." Wiggins told Haig he had to tell the rest of the committee, but the chief of staff begged him to wait until Monday, when Nixon would make an announcement about the June 23 tape. Wiggins agreed, but was deflated.

That same Friday, as if Shakespeare were tidying up before the dénouement, John Dean was hauled into court by Judge Sirica and given the heaviest sentence so far of those who had bargained their guilty pleas—a minimum of one year in jail. In a husky voice, Dean asked for compassion. He admitted he had done wrong but added to "say I'm sorry is not enough." He said he would continue trying "to right the wrongs"—a reference to the requirement he testify fully as a prosecution witness at the coming trials. Charles Shaffer, his lawyer, in a final vain motion to defer sentence, insisted that the single most important thing Dean had done was to have tried "in his way to end the cover-up" before McCord's letter broke. Sirica, who believed it was only after that letter that Dean jumped ship, was having none of it.[25] He told Dean consideration had already been shown when he was allowed to plead guilty to a single charge when fifty might have been preferred. Dean looked shaken.

That night Nixon confronted the fact that he would have to tell his wife and daughters he had lied to them, too. His memoirs do not quite put it so; he says he had to tell them about the June 23 tape and prepare them for the impact on his attempts to cling to office. Julie later disclosed that "we never sat down as a family to talk about Watergate."[26] Not surprisingly, the family was now even more loyal than Rebozo.

Nixon's memoirs quote poignantly again from Tricia's diary. She flew down immediately from New York on being telephoned by her sister. It is clear that Nixon, the day before, had told Julie, but not his wife, of his "tentative" decision to resign. None of them had yet heard about Nixon's agreement with Rebozo to mount one last defense; even Rebozo, meeting Tricia, mentions only the resigning, and urges her to pretend she knows nothing when she sees her father.

Tricia says she countered Nixon's argument that he must resign for the country's sake: "I told him for the good of the country he must stay in office." Noting that her emotions are "usually completely controllable externally," Tricia bursts into tears. "When Daddy said, 'I hope I have not let you down,' the tragedy of his ghastly position shattered me."[27]

Nixon's questing tentative phase was to recur with his friends throughout the final week. It was perhaps his way of saying he was sorry.

Yet the Nixon daughters had steel and were not to be put off by "bothersome words," as Tricia described the June 23 transcript. With Mrs. Nixon present at a family conference, after the two young couples had read it, Tricia and her husband, Edward, agreed the words could be taken two ways, and, with Julie, came out strongly against resignation. Julie's husband, David Eisenhower, was less sure. Tricia writes that Nixon told them of the disaster to the country for a president to be impeached. "What would the Soviets not dare . . . Look at what they had already attempted in the last Mideast dispute."

They left Nixon staring into the fire in the Lincoln sitting room. In order to have the log fires he loved despite the ninety-degree temperature outside, Nixon ran the air-conditioning high. Joining Mrs. Nixon —who, Nixon says, had insisted her husband fight to the finish—both young couples now broke down. The key thing Tricia notes is that "we left feeling he still might not resign."[28]

She was right. That Friday night, Nixon decided on the option Rebozo had raised, as he put it, "to yield to my desire to fight." He would not resign on Monday but instead release the June 23 tape and test the reaction. If bad, Nixon could "resume the countdown towards resignation"; if less bad, then he could examine one last time the forlorn option of a Senate trial. He called a startled Haig to reverse engines. Ray Price should cease working on a resignation speech; rather, they should work up a speech or statement on the June 23 tape.[29] It was quite late, Haig recalls, and he did nothing more that night.

At what was to be his final sojourn at Camp David, Nixon says he was bolstered by his young family urging him at every opportunity to fight on. It happened in the swimming pool and in the sauna. Over dinner on Saturday, all agreed he would postpone any decision until after the tape transcript's release on Monday. Nixon coined an odd jingle for them: "It's fight or flight by Monday night."[30]

As if to prove the instability of Nixon's position, on Saturday the president received a letter from a key senator, Republican whip Robert Griffin of Michigan, reportedly a member of Jerry Ford's home state cabal. Unless the president resigned, Griffin wrote, impeachment was certain, and unless he turned over the sixty-four tapes as ordered by the Supreme Court, he, Griffin, would vote to convict him at a Senate trial. For Haig and Nixon, it was a possible signal that Ford's friends were going public to force the president's resignation.

On Sunday, amid great tension and rumor in Washington of imminent developments, Nixon had Haig, St. Clair, Ziegler, Buchanan, Price, and others fly to Camp David. Haig, sensing it might be the last time, took his wife along. It was decided that a written statement was better than a speech about the June 23 tape. Nixon saw that his advisers had shifted the emphasis from the tape's contents to "my failure to inform them of its existence."

Nixon handed Haig a page of handwritten notes that he wanted central in the statement. It was the final defense that Rebozo and his daughters had urged him to attempt, the final bid to explain away the meaning of the words on the wretched June 23 tape.

Nixon decided to make use of Pat Gray one last time. His conversation with the acting FBI director on July 6, 1972, in which Gray had warned the president that his staff was trying to "mortally wound you," had, Nixon wanted it argued, ended with the president urging that the FBI investigation go forward. Nixon's ingenious new position was:

> From this time when I was informed that there were no national security interests involved or would be jeopardized by the investigation, the investigation fully proceeded without regard to any political or other considerations.[31]

It had not, of course. Saying so was a lie on top of all the others. Haig quickly said the argument was no use. He told Nixon that St. Clair and the other lawyers were going to jump ship if changes were made in their draft—though Haig says he questioned their insistence that Nixon admit to an offense no one had up to then accused him of, namely, not informing his lawyers he had known of the June 23 tape's true contents three months earlier.

"The hell with it," Nixon responded. "It doesn't matter. Let them put out anything they want." It was, after all, reaction to the tape that Nixon was supposedly testing. For Haig, though, it was a sad moment. His commander in chief could not even command the words to be issued in his own name.[32] His own defenders, Haig included, were covering themselves.

On Monday morning, Kissinger met Nixon. There was no word about Watergate, nor of the imminent release of the tape. The president encouraged his secretary of state to pursue foreign policy briefings with southern Democrats. Ford could help arrange it. To Kissinger, Nixon appeared to be living in a surrealistic world.[33] Not so Haig, for whom things were becoming menacingly real. He and St. Clair were on the line together to Jaworski, alerting the special prosecutor that the June 23 transcript would be released that afternoon. "Both of them were just repeating over and over again to me" that they had not known the contents, says Jaworski.[34] In fact, both men had read the transcript as much as a week earlier.

In Jaworski's view, "Haig still wanted to hold an umbrella over the president," saying apropos the June 23 conversation, "I believe the president didn't focus on the matter." Jaworski reminded Haig and St. Clair, and they agreed they had known the simple fact, that Nixon had listened to these tapes back in May. Now all Jaworski wanted was to have that "false impression removed."[35] Jaworski then gave his own staff instructions that no comment whatever be made in reaction by the special prosecutor's office.*

All afternoon long, the White House kept putting off the press briefing. Finally, at 4 P.M., the partial "raw" White House transcripts were put out along with a statement. It caused Nixon's third and final firestorm. The reaction was instantaneous, first from Charles Wiggins. As the deceived Nixon defender, his words were almost more powerful than

* It was one of the final ironies of Watergate that the June 23, 1972 tapes were not included in the first draft of the special prosecutor's subpoena but only added at the last moment. The prosecutors even worried initially that the episode of Nixon's using the CIA to stymie the FBI investigation might both confuse the jury and help the defendants in the main cover-up trial. But a young prosecutor, Jerry Goldman, suggested the only way they would ever *disprove* Nixon's, and Haldeman's and Ehrlichman's, claim of national security for the CIA-FBI episode was to get the tapes. The subpoena had to be retyped.[36]

any others. Nixon should resign, and if not, he said, "I am prepared to conclude that the magnificent career of public service of Richard Nixon must be terminated involuntarily." Wiggins now said he would vote for Article I; within a few hours, all ten Republicans who had defended Nixon at the House Judiciary Committee had gone over to the other side. Tip O'Neill, trying not to relish the moment, said that while confession was good for the soul, "it doesn't save the body." He reckoned Nixon's support in the 435-member House was down to 75.

Ever-loyal Jerry Ford announced that while he stood by his belief that Nixon was not guilty of an impeachable offense, he would now, as a party to the outcome, cease saying so in public. He stated he had not been informed of the tape's contents until the president's statement—true, to the extent that a member of Ford's staff had to filch from Haig's office a White House press office transcript for the vice president.

The gist of the new revelation, as we have seen, was that Nixon used the CIA to cover up Watergate for explicitly political, not national security, reasons. Nixon did so, moreover, nine months before the time he had previously claimed to have first heard of any cover-up. That was the lie he had lived with publicly and privately since the outset. Senator Howard Baker's question—"What did the president know and when did he know it?"—had been answered in spades.

Not much attention was paid finally to Nixon's accompanying statement, but it showed that the cover-up was continuing. There was no longer any mention of national security, but it still clung to the fiction that Gray, at the president's instruction, had pressed ahead with the FBI's supposedly "vigorous" investigation. The statement claimed—as Nixon's memoirs admit was false—that when he listened to the tapes the previous May, he "did not realize the extent of the implications," but he now agreed they were "at variance" with his prior statements. His false May 22, 1973 statement, he explained, had been "based on my recollection at that time."

Above all, Nixon could not let go of the main thrust of his "modified limited hangout." Perhaps he had even come to believe it. Baldly, in spite of everything, Nixon insisted that "the basic truth remains that when all the facts were brought to my attention, I insisted on a full investigation and prosecution of those guilty." It was breathtaking that Haig and his lawyers had allowed him to state such a falsehood. But

Nixon had after all exonerated them by including an apology for "the serious act of omission" of not having informed them, as well as the congressmen, about his own knowledge of the June 23 conversations.

Nixon insulated himself from the immediate uproar by taking his family for a dinner cruise on the presidential yacht. He said they talked about everything except what was on their minds. Yet Mrs. Nixon, he learned weeks later, the next morning began to organize the packing for the move from the White House.

Nixon had Rose Mary Woods call Haig from the boat to find out what the reaction had been to the transcript's release. He says he anticipated that "few, if any, would want to be found standing with me." Woods came back to report it was "about the way we expected." His hard core were in "back of him but concerned"; Goldwater would stay quiet; and House Republican leader Rhodes said it was "very bad." The Cabinet was reported "solid," which Nixon doubted.

Nixon says he recognized "the inevitability of resignation" but until plans were complete for the announcement, he intended to play the role of president to the hilt. He was determined not to appear to have resigned "because of a consensus of staff or Cabinet opinion or because of public pressure. It had to be seen as something that I had decided completely on my own."[37]

This was almost true. The decision *was* Nixon's. What clinched it, though, was the certainty that not only had he "lost" the congressional support of his own party and his natural allies among conservative Democrats, but also that they would actually convict him at trial and remove him from office. The president read the political arithmetic better than most, and he could read, even if he shut his ears to the broadcast media, all the demands of friends that he resign.

Alexander Haig has made, and still makes, too much of his claim that his role during this final stage was to protect the president from what he insists on calling banana republic pressure—lest Nixon presumably change his mind and decide to fight on. Yet what actually happened over the next three days culminated in the very thing Haig professes to have averted: Republican leaders trooping to the White House to discuss the numbers with the president. This confirmed the very pressure that led Nixon to decide as he did. The image of a man resigning under congressional pressure—rather than fleeing before he was thrown out—was exactly what was being expertly stage-managed in Nixon's behalf.

This is the reality of the background to the final days. Nixon, having decided to resign, had to pretend he had not. He asked Haig to summon a Cabinet meeting for Tuesday and proceeded to tell this funereal group that he had considered resigning but would not. To do so, he pretended further, would set a precedent of taking America down the road to a parliamentary-type government, where the executive is dependent on a confidence vote in the legislature. If he became involved in a Senate trial, he wanted the Cabinet members to think of themselves as "the functioning trustees of the president and the government." He asked them to do their jobs; Nixon said his problems were his own responsibility.[38]

The response was active doubt. Jerry Ford spoke up and claims to have stated that had he known what he then knew from the June 23 tape, he would not have made the statements he had over the previous two years. He announced that he expected to continue to support the administrations's foreign policy, but he would remain silent on the president's fate.

Nixon wanted to talk of inflation and economic policy, but at this point the dam broke and there is some confusion as to the order in which the members spoke. William Saxbe, a blunt senator whom Nixon had appointed attorney general in place of Richardson, broke in to ask whether he would have sufficient leadership power. Perhaps they should wait and see before taking economic initiatives. At this point, the chairman of the Republican National Committee, who had been invited to attend, spoke up. He thought resignation should be talked about. This was George Bush. Haig, whose opinion of Bush was not high, was glad when Kissinger overrode him with a Delphic utterance. "We are not here to give the president excuses. We are here to do the nation's business." The meeting continued in desultory fashion for more than an hour and a half, and the word went out to an amazed public, and Congress, that Nixon was not resigning.[39]

Nixon then called Kissinger into the Oval Office to say that he *was* resigning. Kissinger claims that he, in fact, took the opportunity to tell the president that he *had* to resign (again the very thing Haig says he worked so hard to avert). An impeachment trial would paralyze foreign policy and be too dangerous for the country. Nixon should "leave in a manner that appeared as an act of his choice." Nixon replied simply that he would take seriously what Kissinger said and be in touch, leaving Kissinger, so he claims, uncertain about Nixon's intent.[40]

Nixon's congressional liaison chief reported that Nixon's support was down to seven out of one hundred senators. Senator Goldwater had been asked by the Republican congressional leaders to convey to the president their assessment of how hopeless the situation was. Ford had lunch with them and reports Goldwater saying, "We can be lied to only so many times."[41] Nixon arranged for the Senate and House Republican leaders to come in with Goldwater the next afternoon.

Haig then told the president that Haldeman had called, asking that if Nixon resigned, he first should pardon all the Watergate defendants, balancing the act with amnesty for all Vietnam War draft dodgers. Haig says Nixon barely listened. But Nixon claims he called Haldeman back, heard him out, and did not give an immediate answer. The president heard that Ehrlichman had made a similar plea for pardon via Rose Mary Woods. Haldeman even had his lawyers send Nixon a piece of text dealing with the blanket pardon to be inserted in his resignation speech. Finally, Nixon instructed Buzhardt to pass the word: no. His resignation was, Nixon insisted, to be a "healing action" for the country and a blanket Watergate pardon would defeat the purpose. So much for Nixon's promises that his men would never go to jail.[42]

That left the family to deal with. Nixon had promised one last fight. He asked the faithful Rose Mary Woods, whom his daughters called "Aunt Rose," for her help in telling the family he was, after all, going to resign. He says he asked her to tell them that his support was so low he could no longer govern. "Tell them the whole bunch is deserting now and we have no way to lobby them or keep them," he says he told her.

That same Tuesday, he took out a pad and marked it "resignation speech," called Haig and Ziegler in and told them he had decided to resign Friday and announce it Thursday night. "Well, I screwed it up real good, didn't I?" he commented. He said Haig answered that he would make an exit "as worthy as my opponents were unworthy."[43]

Haig's memoirs give far more space than Nixon's to this afternoon meeting, which Haig reports was a rambling affair lasting two hours. He says it was not clear which way Nixon would go as the meeting developed. In characteristic fashion, Nixon himself considered all the options, the outrageous and the rational. Haig says Nixon even imagined he might "just run it out" to a criminal trial and jail following impeachment and removal from office, "but go out with my head high." Haig was spellbound at the performance. At last Nixon announced that he would, on Friday, be "over Chicago as Jerry Ford takes the oath at noon."

Haig reports one final chilling moment when Nixon despairingly said: " 'You know, Al, you soldiers have the best way of dealing with a situation like this . . . You just leave a man alone in a room with a loaded pistol. . . .' 'You just have to go on, Mr. President,' " Haig says he replied.[44]

Kissinger was not yet told. He received a call from Nixon that evening with no word about resignation. Instead, Nixon told him he would cut off all military deliveries to Israel until its government agreed to a comprehensive peace; he regretted not having done it before. Kissinger wondered if this was "retaliation" for his earlier urging Nixon to resign. He prepared the decision papers on Israel but they were never signed.[45]

"A day for tears," Tricia's diary records, as Rose Mary Woods did Nixon's bidding with the family, telling them his decision was irrevocable and that they could help most now by not challenging it. The anguish Pat Nixon went through can only be imagined; a private, gentle person, she still stood fiercely by her man. Tricia wrote, "We must not collapse in the face of this ordeal. We must not let him down." They did not. In public they were movingly stoical to the last second. That evening Julie was away from the White House, but she left a note of defiance on Nixon's pillow. It pleaded with him to wait; "go through the fire just a little bit longer . . . millions support you." Nixon wrote that if anything could have changed his mind this was it, but it was past changing now; it was best for the country to go. By Wednesday, his very last countdown had begun.[46]

Publicly, Washington was in a ferment all that week. Crowds, mostly silent, gathered outside the White House, including a dwindling number of hard-core Nixon supporters. Of them none has been more quoted than Earl Landgrebe, a Republican congressman from Indiana.

"Don't confuse me with the facts. . . . I won't vote impeachment . . . not even if they take me outside and shoot me," he said on TV.

Congress, repeatedly swept by rumor and more factual reports, went ahead with impeachment planning. Press tickets for Nixon's trial were printed. Nixon's remarks to his Cabinet notwithstanding, the newspapers were unimpressed; *The Washington Post* lead story said resignation was only a matter of timing. The *Providence Journal Bulletin*, which had broken the story of Nixon's tax returns the previous year, reported flatly that Nixon had made an "irrevocable" decision to resign. The White House spokesman, no longer bothering to deny the story, merely stated he could not confirm it.

On Wednesday, in a flurry of preparations, Haig briefed the vice president on the handover—although according to Ford, Haig said Nixon's decision still was not final—and went ahead with staff arrangements. But, in fact, this Wednesday was the culmination of Haig's banana republic fixation—at any rate, so he recounts. The term had been used the day before by reactionary Republican Senator Carl Curtis, who was among those in Nixon's final bunker.

What the world saw was Senator Goldwater, Senator Hugh Scott, and Representative Rhodes early that evening coming out of the White House to speak to the press and television cameras. They made no bones about the fact they had told the president that the outlook was "gloomy." They were old party friends calling on their leader. They had not needed to tell him to resign. Goldwater and Rhodes (it was only later learned) had told him that they personally would vote to impeach.

Kissinger for one saw nothing amiss in duly elected people bringing Nixon to the realization that to resign was in the national interest. Kissinger, though unelected, says "privately I would steer him towards resignation." He even punctures Nixon's own claim to the Cabinet that resigning under pressure might turn the American system toward a parliamentary vote of no confidence. "That was, of course, hardly the issue." Impeachment was just not a simple vote of no confidence.[47]

Earlier that day, having heard that Goldwater was being pressured to join the call for resignation, Haig had panicked and scheduled a secret lunch with the senator at which he once again presented his arguments against this "trespass on the Constitution." He reports saying to Goldwater:

> "Senator, you simply cannot let this happen. This is a banana republic solution." I went on to say that, in the United States of America, delegations from Congress do not give a President his marching orders. Once that tawdry precedent is established, everything changes forever. Separation of powers goes out the window, the sovereignty of the people is compromised. . . . I concluded: "Things are bad enough already; the Constitution is under enough stress. If the President goes, he must go on his own terms, by due process of law, as the result of his own uncoerced decision.)[48]

It seems doubtful that Goldwater needed any lectures from the unelected Haig; he humored him. He knew the message to put across and had already done so by telling Ford, after the tape's release, that Nixon's friends were fed up with being lied to. "The best thing he can do for the country is to get the hell out of the White House, and get out this afternoon."[49]

Haig says he did not tell Nixon of his conversation with Goldwater. But even before the delegation arrived, Nixon had written in his draft resignation speech the fact that he had met them and they had "unanimously advised" that he did "not have support in Congress for difficult decisions affecting peace abroad and our fight against inflation at home," which, in fact, they never discussed.

Nixon notes that "they were here to narrow my choices." Goldwater led off. Nixon had a maximum of eighteen of the hundred senators left with him; Scott thought it only fifteen. "It's pretty grim," he said. Goldwater reckoned Nixon might beat articles I and III in the whole House, but even he was leaning toward convicting Nixon for Article II —abuse of power. The day before, Rhodes had announced he would impeach on two articles. Nixon, glancing at the presidential seal in the ceiling, said, "I don't have many alternatives, do I?"

Nixon says Rhodes misunderstood this comment and replied that he didn't want to tell reporters outside that they had discussed any specific alternative. "Never mind," Nixon said. "There'll be no tears from me." It was bravado. Outside, it was not what the leaders said afterward, but seeing them on the White House lawn before TV cameras that carried the unmistakable message to the nation that Congress had given Nixon the word. After the meeting, Nixon says he asked to have the family told that "a final check of my dwindling support in Congress" confirmed his resignation. Rhodes, Goldwater, Scott—and, fell blow, even Senator John Stennis—would be voting for his removal. Nixon's decision was irrevocable. He didn't want it discussed anymore at dinner.[50]

Nixon cannot have been unaware of congressional suggestions that he somehow be granted immunity from prosecution if he resigned. On August 6, a senior Democrat in the Senate leadership said he would oppose amnesty, but on August 7, Chairman Rodino asked a Republican colleague to pass the word he had no interest in pursuing criminal action if Nixon resigned.[51] Nixon might have been heartened by this, but he makes no mention of it in his memoirs.

Nixon summoned Kissinger to tell him that his decision to resign was definite. "He could save our foreign policy only by avoiding a constitutional crisis," Kissinger reports Nixon telling him. Kissinger responded that history would treat the president more kindly than his contemporaries. Nixon's response to such statements: "It depends who writes the history." Kissinger says he felt a great tenderness for Nixon.[52]

That evening's session with the family is captured more poignantly in pictures than words. Nixon wanted the official photographer, Ollie Atkins, on hand. Nixon says he thought bravado was the only way to get through the occasion, so he started arranging the photo lineup. But it was too much for daughter Julie. She sobbed and threw her arms around her father. That picture speaks volumes.

The photo session was followed by another meeting with Kissinger, who was summoned to the White House from a dinner party. The secretary of state spent three hours with Nixon, including thirty minutes in the Lincoln bedroom in which, at Nixon's invitation, they prayed together.

Kissinger's account belies several others at the time for which it had been assumed he was at least partly the source. Kissinger says beating against the carpet and railing against fate was not what he remembered. But Nixon was distraught, and "he bared his soul." He wanted to know what history would say of him, and Kissinger kept trying to assure him it would remember his famous achievements. They discussed the unbearability of a criminal trial and Kissinger told Nixon that if it happened he would resign—adding in his memoirs, "And I believe I would have." Shortly after he left at midnight, Kissinger says Nixon called to ask him not to remember their encounter as one of weakness: He would rather have him remember the times he had been strong. Kissinger says he answered that if he ever spoke of the occasion, it would be with respect.[53]

That night, according to Nixon, it was Ron Ziegler who had the last word. "It's the right decision," he said. "You've had a great presidency, sir."

Both Haig and Kissinger speak of Nixon's last full day in office as attempting a note of routine. Haig and the president ran through the checklist of the move to San Clemente. On it was "RN financial condition," but Haig now says he does not remember discussing it. But Haig does remember planning the shipment of all the tapes and Nixon documents to California and talking over which of the White House staff should go with him.

The press was in a ferment of anticipation. At midday Ziegler announced only that "the president"—without naming him—would meet the congressional leaders that evening before making a TV speech. Tip O'Neill gave the first hard information. He let it be known that Ford was going to be sworn in at noon on Friday, but the White House was saying nothing.[54] The press was also told officially that Nixon had met Vice President Ford for more than an hour that morning. It was assumed it was the handover.

Nixon's memoirs say that he thought Ford would "measure up" to the job—conveniently overlooking his earlier scorn. In any case, the meeting gave the two men an opportunity to have whatever exchanges they needed about Haig's approach to Ford the week before. Nixon was clearly resigning without pardoning himself or anyone else. Ford has always maintained he had absolutely no exchanges with Nixon or his representatives about a pardon until a month later, when he decided to grant it.

Haig, meanwhile, had asked Jaworski to lunch at his home. The shrewd special prosecutor, forewarned by an anxious staff, immediately opened by saying, "I think we should have a clear understanding, Al, that we're not going to reach any kind of agreements about the president." Haig countered with his announcement that the president was taking his tapes to California and assured Jaworski there would be "no hanky-panky" with them. Jaworski says that Haig admitted to him for the first time that "I haven't the slightest doubt that the tapes were screwed with. The ones with gaps and other problems." Jaworski says he warned Haig that they must remain available to the prosecutors: "Any failure along that line will mean court hearings."

Jaworski gathered from Haig that the president was deteriorating physically and mentally. One of his most difficult problems, Haig told Jaworski, was in convincing the Nixon family that he had to resign. Haig stated that there would be no pardons before Nixon left office, and he gave Jaworski his view that Nixon would take the Fifth Amendment against self-incrimination rather than testify in John Mitchell's trial or anywhere else. Jaworski says it was he who raised the crunch issue of criminal prosecution. A resigning president, bereft of his constitutional powers, would certainly face indictment. "I asked Haig if congressional supporters of the president were going to pass a resolution that would, in effect, tell me not to move against him." It may be wondered what inferences Haig drew from such a question. Replied Haig: "Oh, yes, I think it will be passed within a day or two." This answer was astonishing, given the hostility in Congress.[55]

Haig's version omits the damaging remarks about "screwed tapes," as well as the possible congressional resolution exempting Nixon from prosecution (which by that time had shrunk to a token nonbinding sense of Senate resolution). He also omits Jaworski's opening statement and claims that it was he who raised the "main purpose of the meeting," which was that the president was asking for nothing and that Haig wanted Jaworski to issue a statement saying that "there was no deal between the president and the special prosecutor." Jaworski did oblige with such a statement.

Nixon, although Haig is silent on it, got the message. When Haig came back from lunch, Nixon says he told him he would take his chances. "Some of the best writing in history has been done from prison." Nixon adds that Haig told him that "from their conversation he got the impression that I had nothing further to fear from the special prosecutor." This hardly accords with Haig's version of the conversation with Jaworski, and Nixon, who disliked Jaworski intensely, had his doubts anyway. "I said that considering the way his office acted in the past, I had little reason to feel reassured."[56]

Jaworski's own assistants were relieved by his account of the Haig meeting but not totally reassured. "Would Nixon really leave office without making any provision for protecting himself from the criminal process?" Relief came only when they heard the speech and realized that it was true.[57]

Nixon was right to be skeptical of Haig's reassurance about Jaworski. The special prosecutor says that "there was no question" but what he would have gone back to the grand jury and let it decide to indict Nixon: He delayed only because he wanted the Mitchell trial jury selected, and sequestered, so that the huge publicity of charging the ex-president not prejudice the cover-up trial.[58] In the end, the pardon Ford later gave Nixon explicitly anticipated his criminal trial and voided it.

Nixon worked with Ray Price on the final draft of his very cleverly crafted resignation speech. Price and Haig remember him cursing the impossibility of squaring his instinct to stay and fight with his decision to go. The non sequitur went into the speech: "I'm not a quitter," he said, and quit.

Preparing for his TV address, Nixon wore the same suit and tie he had worn on TV in Moscow in May 1972—the moment of the first undetected Watergate break-in. He began taking his formal farewells. First were the congressional leaders, Democrats, mostly men with whom there was no burying the hatchet. Carl Albert, the House Speaker, who the previous October had been haplessly next in line of succession until Ford was confirmed vice president, blurted out to Nixon, "I have nothing to do with this whole resignation business." Senate leader Mike Mansfield, who had surprisingly stated in public that impeachment proceedings should be pursued even after resignation, now said nothing. There were incongruities: "I'll miss our breakfasts," Nixon said.

More congenial, yet dreadfully painful, was the final gathering in the Cabinet room with friends who had not deserted, a conservative bipartisan congressional group down to forty-six. They crowded around closely as Nixon, sitting in the central chair at the Cabinet table, celebrated their past triumphs, and then told them how he hated what he was about to announce. Now, he said, they had to give their allegiance to Ford. Nixon's friends, openly weeping, caused the president to burst into tears himself, choking out his words, "I hope I haven't let you down."[59]

Haig, who had witnessed the scene, was desperately worried that Nixon might not be able to get through his broadcast, less than half an hour away. But Nixon, who had vetoed his family's suggestion of backing him up in the Oval Office while he spoke, rapidly recovered his composure. As the custodian of his own image, Nixon was not going to muff his exit. This final speech was a good performance, the delivery firm, the eyes glittering in the lights as he spoke directly to the camera. The message was difficult to credit. Nixon was actually giving up what he most prized. The instant after-analysis by TV commentators was, for once, not unfavorable. Dignity was emphasized.

What Nixon said, however, was graceless. It was less an explanation, owed to the millions who had elected him, of why he was departing less than halfway through his second term than it was a first building block for a new reputation. Indeed, the speech cleverly implied that the American separation of powers doctrine, which he had so long used as a defense, was actually irrelevant. He wanted to continue, but could no longer, because—as if he were governing within some scorned parliamentary system—his political base in Congress had disappeared. Not only that. Nixon then gave being forced to quit the dignity of formal precedent: ". . . with the disappearance of that base, I now believe that the constitutional process has been served, and there is no longer a need for the process to be prolonged." The word "impeachment" was never mentioned. Nixon simply claimed he was putting the country ahead of his fight for "personal vindication." He got in his beloved quote from Theodore Roosevelt about the man in the arena, "who, at the worst, if he fails, at least fails daring greatly."

It might have been impossible for a man of Nixon's pride and complexity to explain what he had done to bring it to this pass. He said he wanted his departure to hasten the "process of healing." There were a few words of contrition. He deeply regretted "any injuries that may have been done" and that "if some of my judgments were wrong, and some were wrong," then they were made in what he believed were the best interests of the nation.

After watching this Nixon recital of his achievements, Leon Jaworski thought of Haig's confidence that Congress would act to block any proceeding against him. "Not after this speech, Al, I thought. He hasn't given Congress even a crumb of remorse to chew on." The special prosecutor, who knew the case against Nixon better than anyone, later observed that it would have been a good speech for a president resigning because of illness or over policy disagreements. It was not the speech of a man who had violated his presidential oath ". . . by transforming the Oval Office into a mean den where perjury and low scheming became a way of life."[60]

Kissinger, as was his custom after major speeches, walked back with Nixon to the residence. Nixon remembers him saying that "historically this would rank as one of the great speeches." Courtier to the last, what other comfort could Kissinger think of? "By now we had uttered all the words possible," he writes.[61]

When Nixon got back to his family, they embraced in a "tender huddle." Nixon began to shake violently and Tricia noticed that her father had perspired "clear through your coat." In a minute, the fit passed. What Nixon calls a tragicomic scene then ensued. Mrs. Nixon, hearing chants outside, wanted to pull her husband to the window, thinking they were supporters. In fact, as Tricia noted, it was a crowd singing "Jail to the Chief," and she and her husband, Ed, tried talking loudly to drown it out. It was in vain. Nixon had already heard the shouts and understood them.[62]

Haig, who says he remained after the family had gone, finally left Nixon sitting alone in the dark. He assumed Nixon had stayed there all night and that is the story that subsequently gained wide credence.

Nixon's own version is that he had bacon and eggs and placed telephone calls to supporters until around 1:30 A.M.; "I told each that I hoped I had not let him down." Finally, he had his valet, Manolo, turn all the lights out, and he walked the corridors. "I was not afraid of knocking into anything in the dark," he recalled, in evident rebuttal to the stories that had him wandering talking to the pictures.[63]

The next morning, Nixon's 2,027th and final day in the presidency, Haig had him sign a letter to the secretary of state that would be delivered around 11:35. It said, "I hereby resign the Office of President of the United States." Nixon's mind was now on his farewell address to his staff and Cabinet, scheduled for 9:30 in the grand setting of the East Room. He was marking books for quotations, including, again, a biography of Teddy Roosevelt.

He caught up with his family. His stoic wife, Pat, was wearing dark glasses to hide, Nixon says, two sleepless nights and "the tears that Julie said had finally come that morning." To the horror of his wife and Tricia, however, they discovered there were going to be television cameras at what they thought was a private occasion. "It was too much," they said, "that after all the agony television had caused us its prying eye should not be allowed to intrude . . ." But it was. "That's the way it has to be," Nixon said. He said they owed it to the people, their people.[64]

Nixon also knew that television, not books, makes the popular record for posterity. He was preparing one last command performance. For the first time in public he would wear reading glasses, as if a mask had slipped. Dutifully, Mrs. Nixon took her dark glasses off and marched in with him to the last playing of "Hail to the Chief" to find her place marker behind him on the platform. She maintained her composure throughout this ordeal but as I reported in *The Times* next day, "the faces of the Nixon women told it all."

According to Tricia, "At last the 'real' Nixon was being revealed as only he could reveal himself. By speaking from the heart people finally know Daddy." Kissinger saw it very differently. "It was as if having kept himself in check all these years he had to put on display all the demons and dreams that had driven him. . . . It was horrifying and heartbreaking . . ." Haig found it rambling, "sentimental and noble, scholarly and corny, self-conscious and magisterial, and above all unabashedly old-fashioned and American."[65]

It was certainly an intensely emotional and often distressing occasion. Most of those present cried and Nixon himself was on the verge of breaking down at least a couple of times. It has to be said, however, that the speech reads better than it sounded. True, there were uncomfortable jokes about his taxes, about the country needing "good plumbers." There was a snarl when he said of his administration that "no man or no woman ever profited at the public expense or the public till. That tells something about you. Mistakes yes, but for personal gain never." This from a man whose assets tripled during his first term.

He once again paid disjointed tributes to his father and mother, a "saint," he called her, though many felt that could have been applied to his wife, too. Julie later wrote that much of the regret Nixon felt yet left unspoken was "that he had let his family down."[66]

His central message was, however, compelling in its defiance. You can get Nixon out, it said, but down never. He says in his memoirs he wanted to inspire his people to go on, but the message was also to himself. He read haltingly from the young Theodore Roosevelt's diary about the death of TR's young wife: that "the light went from my life forever," and then, looking up, misty eyed, Nixon recalled that TR went on not only as president "but as an ex-president." This was the example Nixon wanted remembered.

And finally something that, had he said it or even digested it fourteen months earlier, might have made a difference. Whether or not this most complex of men truly believed it, it was to become a sort of epitaph.

> Never be petty. Always remember others may hate you but those who hate you don't win unless you hate them, and then you destroy yourself.

Self-destruction, Nixon's tragedy, was complete. "Good luck, Mr. President," Nixon says he told his successor, soon to be sworn in as the thirty-eighth president. Ford and his wife went arm in arm with the Nixons past the diplomatic reception room, across the lawn where the military had laid a red carpet. There was no more "Hail to the Chief," only the clattering of Marine One, the presidential helicopter. With Pat going ahead, Nixon turned and waved with a grimace, then a smile as he produced his two-handed V signs. On the flight to Andrews Air Force Base where they would board the renamed Spirit of '76 for the last time, Nixon says he leaned back and closed his eyes. He heard Pat saying, to no one in particular, "It's so sad, it's so sad."[67]

Ford's inaugural speech is remembered for the phrase—which he had wanted Hartmann, his speechwriter and chief of staff, to leave out—"our long national nightmare is over."

On August 20, by a vote of 412–3, the House of Representatives formally endorsed the Judiciary Committee's impeachment report.

On September 8, President Gerald Ford granted Nixon the full pardon he had been unwilling to extend to his accomplices. This action in fact put a merciful end to Nixon's and the country's agony over Watergate, even as it inflicted a wound on the new president and the Republican Party.

Ford's proclamation specified the pardon was for "all offenses against the United States which he, Richard Nixon, has committed, or may have committed" during his term of office. Accepting it, which Ford said was tantamount to admission of guilt, Nixon said:

> That the way I tried to deal with Watergate was the wrong way is a burden I shall bear for every day of the life that is left to me.

APPENDIX 1

John Mitchell's Plea

In August 1973, at the height of the Watergate crisis, the specter appeared of a "double impeachment," with both Vice President Agnew and Nixon threatened with removal from office. As the president's White House defenders acted to produce Agnew's resignation, one man thought he could see a way out for Richard Nixon. It has never been revealed until now, in interviews conducted in 1993 for this summer's BBC-TV/Discovery Channel *Watergate* TV series,[1] that John Mitchell actually took steps to try preserving Nixon by himself pleading guilty. He was ready to be the fall guy.

The move failed, partly because the deal Mitchell wanted—an agreement by the Watergate special prosecutor to drop the pursuit of the president in return for Mitchell's guilty plea—was unattainable and partly because it was simply too late. But Mitchell's ploy did go so far as a secret bargaining meeting between him and James Neal, the top trial lawyer in Archibald Cox's Watergate Special Prosecution Force, to discuss what Mitchell had to offer. Though by then the court battle for the White House tapes was under way, none had yet been handed over by Nixon. The prosecutors—Neal especially—had no assurance that the tapes would corroborate what Dean had been testifying to that summer. Corroboration of any kind by Mitchell could be invaluable.

It began with a call from Mitchell's lawyer, Bill Hundley, to Neal. They, like so many other lawyers in Watergate cases, had been buddies in the "Hoffa team," prosecuting the Teamsters Union boss in Robert Kennedy's Justice Department. They agreed to meet secretly.

Neal: We arranged to take different paths, and, and we went and met in the basement of the Supreme Court, and it, and, it was a cloak-and-dagger clandestine sort of thing, and we got up, sure enough Bill, Bill Hundley said that "Mr. Mitchell wants to discuss a plea bargain and cooperation." Now that meant a certain thing to me: that we were going to discuss the disposition of his situation, and he was going to give us testimony about others, including the president. We finally, I said, "We're interested in that."

Hundley: Mitchell's single concern, apart from himself, of course, his single concern was President Nixon that, you know, he had intense loyalty to Nixon and he believed that Nixon was a great president and if, if there was one thing that Mitchell wanted to stop or wanted to see not happen as a result of Watergate would be bringing down the presidency. And as Watergate kept building up and building up and building up, of course things got worse and worse for Nixon. Somewhere in that period, as the public demand was building up for the impeachment of Nixon and Mitchell having this view that he would be willing to do almost anything to stop that, he was always very fatalistic about himself. He was going to be indicted; he was going to be convicted, probably go to jail. And he, he wasn't going to be a fink and he wasn't going to get born again and he wasn't going to write any books. Quite frankly, some of that is quite admirable, at least I viewed it that way, not being a fink and things like that. Somewhere in that period of time he came up with the idea to me that he would be willing to plead guilty.

Neal was gripped with intense excitement. He sensed a break in the case. Unlike the other members of Cox's staff who were chafing at the bit in court, Neal had been deeply suspicious of the July bombshell disclosure by Alexander Butterfield of Nixon's tapes, and he had been cautioning Cox to tread carefully:

Neal: Well, the first thing that went through my mind is that this is some sort of a trick. That we would jump on the president, we would demand the tapes, he would resist for a while, and then he'd turn over the tapes and say, "Look you, you, you have harassed me, you're Democrats, you're Bob Kennedy crowd," that

> he was always talking about we were part of the, just an extension of the old Kennedy administration, and that he would say, "Here are the tapes," and they would be nothing like what Dean had talked about, and we would be trapped, and embarrassed, and fall on our face. . . . The president was now revealed to be innocent, and we'd be out of business.

To Neal, Hundley did not disclose his hand at the outset:

> *Hundley:* I think I left it a little vague when I got in touch with him. I think what I did, as a matter of fact I'm sure what I did is I said would you be interested in talking about a plea bargain. And that, of course, connotes possible quid pro quo and what not, yes? I did not say, look, he wants to testify or he wants to be a government witness but I did say I'd like to talk to you about a possible plea bargain here. Yes.

Neal went back to Cox and said, " 'Archie, we've had an enormous, enormous breakthrough. Mitchell is going to seek a plea bargain and cooperate,' and I don't know whether we'd set the next meeting at that time or not, but, but Mr. Cox was as satisfied as I was." The special prosecutor agreed that if they could get Mitchell's testimony in return for a guilty plea, they would almost hardly need the tapes they were pressing Nixon to surrender.

They agreed on a formal meeting with Mitchell at his suite in the Woodley Park Hotel. It was in August and although neither man can now recall the date, it lasted all day. Until this time, Hundley now relates, Mitchell had no defense strategy but to count on error on the part of the eventual trial judge they might face. If it was John Sirica, they thought they might have a chance and so reverse any conviction on appeal. Mitchell, Hundley said, had never made any protestation of innocence, even privately. He was resigned to his fate.

But Hundley said Mitchell was absolutely protective of the president. When Hundley tried arguing they had to use the tapes to show the White House had been out to get him, Mitchell simply said, "Bill, there are things you just don't understand." He attributed hostility to his position not to Nixon but to Haldeman and Ehrlichman, who were trying to cover themselves, and above all to Colson, whom he hated.

It is not known what discussions Mitchell had with Nixon at this period, or with the White House lawyers. Certainly, before Mitchell testified at the Ervin committee, there was a noticeable White House effort to accommodate him. The memo sent by the White House counsel, J. Fred Buzhardt, to the Ervin Committee hearings to try embarrassing Dean had also directly incriminated Mitchell. Now the White House stated that this was only a Buzhardt hypothesis, not the President's position, and that was some balm for Mitchell.

At the meeting with Neal, there was joking for a bit and some anecdotes. Hundley is a very amusing man. Neal was a former marine who had knocked about a bit. Even as tough a prosecutor as Neal does not every day get to discuss a possible guilty plea with a former attorney general.

> *Hundley:* It was up in Mitchell's hotel room and I don't think the two of them had ever met before. As, as I say, the private John Mitchell could be quite personable. He had a dry sense of humor, witty and, you know, Jim Neal was very outgoing, expansive, and they, they got along pretty well. And, you know, they bandied back and forth. Jim, of course, was, you know, doing the very best he could to see if he couldn't line up, you know, John Mitchell as a witness. I think Mitchell made it abundantly clear right in the beginning that as far as he was concerned Nixon was the greatest president that ever lived and knew nothing about him and would never, never ever say anthing bad about Nixon because there was never anything bad to say about him. . . . And Jim, being a very smart prosecutor, reminded Mitchell of that, you know, that how about Haldeman and Ehrlichman and their reference to get you to be the fall guy, and Mitchell sucked on his pipe a little bit and said something to the effect that, "well, you don't know everything, Jim," and by then I think it was Jim and John, you know. And "I would never, ever testify against Haldeman or Ehrlichman." And then I believe that Jim probably knew that Mitchell had this tremendous feeling about Colson and, you know, he said something, "Well, John, you know, how about Chuck Colson?" And Mitchell looked at him and said, "I would love to give him up, you know." And it went back and forth like that.

But as the discussion wore on, it became clear that Mitchell had in mind a different bargain from that envisaged by the prosecutors.

Hundley: Mitchell's idea was, look, he'd be willing to plead guilty, bite the bullet, but he would not testify and he in turn wanted the prosecutors to agree in return for his plea of guilty that they would stop and leave Nixon . . .

Neal: I started to question him, and he would say "Huh huh," smoking his pipe, "well, that's not exactly the way that happened," and "huh huh" and we went on and on, and finally it, I don't know if, in retrospect, I don't, why it took this long, but it seems to me in my recollection it was a couple of hours before it suddenly came to me: Wait. This man is not prepared to cooperate.

So I take Bill out in the adjoining—it was a suite—I take Bill Hundley out in the adjoining bedroom and I say, "Bill, what's going on?" and Bill Hundley says, you know, "I don't know." I, he said, "I came here with, expecting, I can't tell you, Jim, that we've had a lot of conversation about this, but in my experience I thought that what we were coming over here for was for John Mitchell and me to give you a proffer and talk about a plea bargain, and I was expecting that he would: cooperation. I, I don't know. I'm, I'm surprised as you are." Now that's where we stood.

Hundley: I knew, I knew that Mitchell, there was one thing John Mitchell would never be is a fink. He didn't have a fink bone in his body, you know. And it aborted; that was the end of that. Jim was not prepared to run up the American flag for Nixon and Mitchell was not prepared to be a fink, so nothing came out of it basically.

Neal: We probed it some more, and finally we had the dénouement and, and it turns out that John Mitchell had come there with the idea that he would accept responsibility for everything, and he would enter a plea to whatever we wanted provided we would give up the pursuit of—he didn't care about Haldeman or Ehrlichman so much—but we'd give up the pursuit of the president. And so when we learned that, we, you know, we said, "Well, thank you very much. That's not what we are interested in. We're interested in you cooperating, you telling us what you know, and for that you will get some consideration." And when we realized that what he wanted to do was to be the fall guy and save the president, that ended the day.

Hundley: I am sure that I told Mitchell that I didn't think it would work but, you know, if you want me to try I'll try. I didn't think there was a snowball's chance in hell that, that Neal or Archie Cox were going to lay off Nixon. At that time I thought they were determined to indict him, yes, but that I was willing to try.

Neal: . . . We didn't, we didn't say, "You've got to give us Nixon." What we were looking for is truthful information from, from John Mitchell. Now, if he'd, he'd come in, if he'd come in and said Nixon was no more, longer, was not involved in this in any way, he'd have a difficult time convincing [us] of this, because by this time even I had been, was beginning to become convinced that Dean was telling the truth, by virtue of what others, identified by Dean, had told us . . .

Nixon's memoirs are silent on this episode. Given the continual contact Hundley said that Mitchell had had with Nixon, it seems inconceivable that Nixon was unaware of his friend's dealings with the prosecutors. At this period the memoirs note that Mitchell told Nixon about Agnew's belief that Richardson was out to get him. Hard information from Mitchell that Cox's men were not interested in going easy on the president, even in return for Mitchell's head, would have been powerful reinforcement for Nixon. He was increasingly annoyed by the way Cox was allowing his young prosecution staff free rein to go after himself and his personal friends. "I felt that he was trying to get me personally. I wanted him out," Nixon wrote.[2]

Nixon gave a party for Mitchell when finally, after serving nineteen months for conspiracy to obstruct justice and perjury, he got out of jail. The unconfirmable story is told by close Mitchell friends of a woman going up to him and saying, "Oh Mr. Mitchell, I'm so sorry." To which Mitchell is said to have replied, "No more than I deserved, my dear." That he was unable to be the salvation of his close friend at the time of his deepest trial was a secret regret he took to the grave in 1988.

Neal secured Mitchell's conviction at the trial, along with Haldeman's and Ehrlichman's. The former attorney general was to serve nineteen months for conspiracy to obstruct justice and perjury. Before he went to jail, however, Mitchell gave Neal a present. It was an autographed copy of Bernstein and Woodward's *All the President's Men*, with an inscription reading: "To one of the nicest guys I know unfortunately cast in the wrong spot at the wrong time."

APPENDIX 2

The Tape Transcripts

The story of Nixon's tapes and the transcripts made from them is long and complicated. The first "transcripts" to be made public, on April 30, 1974, were Nixon's own edited versions, and they quickly proved to be seriously incomplete. Even so, they undoubtedly got the widest circulation. They were sold first by the U.S. Printing Office as a telephone-directory size blue book and then issued in paperback editions produced by *The New York Times* and *The Washington Post*.

Even though Nixon's edited versions surprised and shocked the public (and put the phrase "expletive deleted" into the language), they were undermined severely by improved and drastically different transcripts of eight key tapes produced by the House Judiciary Committee impeachment investigation. These went on sale in July 1974.

The next transcript to be made public was the "smoking gun" conversation. Released by the White House Press Office on August 5, 1974, it was one of three conversations transcribed of June 23, 1972 (six days after the Watergate break-in). Incomplete but still devastating, parts were later published in the Judiciary Committee's report recommending impeachment.

Ever since Nixon left office he has fought tenaciously through the courts to prevent further disclosure of his tapes, which run to more than four thousand hours. He himself, meanwhile, has had transcripts made of every conversation he deemed relevant to Waterate, but has not made them public.

The public has had to be satisfied, over twenty years, with a very slow drip of release. In October 1974, the Watergate special prosecutor played portions of tapes at the main cover-up trial, and those portions became public through newspapers. Not until May 28, 1980 were those few tapes made available for public listening, with transcripts, at the National Archives.

On June 4, 1991, all seventy-odd tapes acquired by the special prosecutor for use in his investigations were finally made available for listening, with transcripts. By this time the tapes had been banished from easy tourist access in the heart of the capital to the National Archives' relatively remote Nixon Project, on South Pickett Street in the suburbs of Alexandria, Virginia.

Since that date, no further transcripts have been provided, although beginning on May 17, 1993, the Nixon Project has been making more "abuse of power" tapes available for listening. The first batch, for May and June 1972, purport to be, according to the National Archives, "all previously unreleased tape segments relating to Watergate" for those two months. Parts of these contain new damaging material and have been used in this book as transcripts made by the TV series researchers.

These latest tapes have also been digitally enhanced for better audibility, but are still extremely difficult to make out. What is worse, the National Archives has added what is termed a "distinctive tone," lasting several seconds, indicating both withheld "restricted information" and whole segments deemed too unintelligible to be reviewed by the National Archives staff responsible for clearances. As a listening aid, however, the National Archives publishes the log its staff made of each tape. The logs include the archivist's notes, listing the contents, and make clear that there is more on these tapes than the untrained ear can hear.

Bibliography

Aitken, Jonathan. *Nixon: A Life.* London: Weidenfeld & Nicholson, 1993.

Ambrose, Stephen E. *Nixon, Volume II: The Triumph of a Politician 1962–1972.* New York: Simon & Schuster, 1989.

———. *Nixon, Volume III: Ruin and Recovery 1973–1990.* New York: Simon & Schuster, 1991.

Anderson, Jack. *The Anderson Papers.* New York: Random House, 1973.

Ben-Veniste, Richard, and George Frampton, Jr. *Stonewall: The Real Story of the Watergate Prosecution.* New York: Simon & Schuster, 1977.

Bernstein, Carl, and Bob Woodward. *All the President's Men.* New York: Simon & Schuster, 1974.

Breslin, Jimmy. *How the Good Guys Finally Won: Notes from an Impeachment Summer.* New York: Viking, 1975.

Chester, Lewis, et al. *Watergate: The Full Inside Story.* New York: Ballantine, 1973.

Colodny, Len, and Robert Gettlin. *Silent Coup: The Removal of Richard Nixon.* New York: St. Martin's, 1991.

Colson, Charles W. *Born Again.* Old Tappan, N.J.: Spire Books, Fleming H. Revell Co., 1977.

———. *Life Sentence.* Lincoln, Va.: Chosen Books, 1979.

Congressional Quarterly, Inc. *Watergate: Chronology of a Crisis.* Wayne Kelley, exec. ed., Washington, D.C.: 1975.

Cox, Archibald. *Courts and the Constitution.* Boston: Houghton Mifflin, 1987.

Dash, Samuel. *Chief Counsel: Inside the Ervin Committee.* New York: Random House, 1976.

Dean, John W., III. *Blind Ambition: The White House Years.* New York: Simon & Schuster, 1976.

———. *Lost Honor.* Los Angeles: Stratford Press, 1982.

Doyle, James. *Not Above the Law: The Battles of Watergate Prosecutors Cox and Jaworski: a Behind-the-Scenes Account.* New York: Morrow, 1977.
Drew, Elizabeth. *Washington Journal: the Events of 1973–74.* New York: Random House, 1975.
Ehrlichman, John. *Witness to Power.* New York: Simon & Schuster, 1982.
Eisenhower, Julie Nixon. *Pat Nixon.* New York: Simon & Schuster, 1986; Zebra 1986.
Ervin, Sam J., Jr. *The Whole Truth.* New York: Random House, 1980.
Felt, W. Mark. *The FBI Pyramid, From the Inside.* New York: G. P. Putnam's Sons, 1979.
Ford, Gerald R. *A Time to Heal.* New York: Harper & Row, 1979.
Garza, Hedda. *The Watergate Investigation Index: Senate Select Committee Hearings and Reports on Presidential Campaign Activities.* Wilmington, Del.: Scholarly Resources, 1982.
———. *House Judiciary Committee Hearings and Report on Impeachment.* Wilmington, Del: Scholarly Resources, 1985.
Griswold, Erwin N. *Ould Fields, New Corne: the Personal Memoirs of a Twentieth Century Lawyer.* St. Paul, Minn.: West Publishing Co., 1992.
Haig, Alexander M., Jr. *Caveat.* New York: Macmillan, 1984.
———, and Charles McCarry. *Inner Circles: How America Changed the World: A Memoir.* New York: Warner Books, 1992.
Haldeman, H.R. *The Ends of Power.* New York: Times Books, 1978.
Hartmann, Robert T. *Palace Politics: An Inside Account of the Ford Years.* New York: McGraw-Hill, 1980.
Hougan, Jim. *Secret Agenda: Watergate, Deep Throat and the CIA.* New York: Random House, 1984.
Hunt, E. Howard. *Undercover: Memoirs of an American Secret Agent.* New York: Berkley, 1974.
Jaworski, Leon. *The Right and the Power: The Prosecution of Watergate.* New York: Reader's Digest, 1976.
Kissinger, Henry. *The White House Years.* Boston: Little, Brown, 1979.
———. *Years of Upheaval.* Boston: Little, Brown, 1982.
Kleindienst, Richard. *Justice.* Ottawa, Ill.: Jameson Books, 1985.
Kutler, Stanley I. *The Wars of Watergate: The Last Crisis of Richard Nixon.* New York: Knopf, 1990.
Liddy, G. Gordon. *Will.* New York: St. Martin's, 1980.
Lukas, J. Anthony. *Nightmare: The Underside of the Nixon Years.* New York: Viking, 1976; Penguin Books, 1988.
McCord, James W., Jr. *A Piece of Tape: The Watergate Story: Fact and Fiction.* Rockville, Md.: Washington Media Services, Ltd., 1974.
McLendon, Winzola. *Martha.* New York: Random House, 1979.
Magruder, Jeb Stuart. *An American Life.* New York: Atheneum, 1974.
Nixon, Richard M. *Six Crises.* Garden City, N.Y.: Doubleday, 1962, 1969.
———. *RN: The Memoirs of Richard Nixon.* New York: Grosset & Dunlap, 1975.
———. *In the Arena.* New York: Simon & Schuster, 1990.

Oudes, Bruce, ed. *From: The President: Richard Nixon's Secret Files*. New York: Harper & Row, 1989.
Price, Raymond. *With Nixon*. New York: Viking, 1977.
Richardson, Elliot. *The Creative Balance: Government, Politics, and the Individual in America's Third Century*. New York: Rinehart & Winston, 1976.
Safire, William. *Before the Fall: An Inside View of the Pre-Watergate White House*. Garden City, N.Y.: Doubleday, 1975.
Sirica, John J. *To Set the Record Straight: The Break-in, the Tapes, the Conspirators, the Pardon*. New York: Norton, 1979.
Staff of *The Washington Post*. *The Presidential Transcripts*. New York: Dell, 1974.
Ulasewicz, Tony, with Stuart A. McKeever. *The President's Private Eye: The Journey of Detective Tony U. from N.Y.P.D. to the Nixon White House*. Westport, Conn.: MACSAM Publishing Co., 1990.
U.S. Department of Justice. Watergate Special Prosecution Force. *Report*. Washington, D.C.: 1975.
U.S. House of Representatives. Committee on the Judiciary. *Statement of Information, Hearings, Report*. 93d Congress, 2d session, 1973–1974.
U.S. Senate Select Committee on Presidential Campaign Activities. *Hearings, The Final Report*. 93d Congress, 2d session, 1973–74.
Walters, Vernon A. *Silent Missions*. New York: Doubleday, 1978.
White, Theodore H. *The Making of the President 1968*. New York: Atheneum, 1969.
———. *The Making of the President 1972*. New York: Atheneum, 1973.
———. *Breach of Faith: The Fall of Richard Nixon*. New York: Atheneum, 1975.
Woodward, Bob, and Carl Bernstein. *The Final Days*. New York: Simon & Schuster, 1976.
Young, David R. *The Presidential Conduct of American Foreign Policy 1969–1973*. Deposited thesis, Bodleian Library, Oxford University, released 1989.

Notes

The following abbreviations are used throughout the notes section:

CWC	Colson papers, with box numbers whenever available
FBI	Federal Bureau of Investigation archive
HJC	House Judiciary Committee impeachment investigation
SI	Statement of Information, followed by book number
NSI	Nixon Statement of Information, followed by book number
TW	Testimony of Witnesses, followed by book number
HRH	Haldeman papers, with box numbers whenever available
JDE	Ehrlichman papers, with box numbers whenever available
NA	National Archives
NP	Nixon Presidential Materials Project
NT	Nixon tape transcript (Nixon tape means NP tapes released for listening only)
PPF	President's personal file
SJC	Senate Judiciary Committee
SSC	Senate Select Committee on Presidential Campaign Activities (Ervin Committee)
WHT	White House-edited transcript
WSPF	Watergate Special Prosecution Force

Chapter 1: Breakthrough and Break-in

1. Haldeman notes, June 16, 1972, HRH box 45, NP. Nixon, while in the Soviet Union, stopped dictating his diary for fear of being bugged; he had also ordered Haldeman to procure a powder puff and pancake makeup so as not to be exposed to a Soviet TV makeup artist: Nixon, *Memoirs*, p. 618; Haldeman notes, May 24, 1972, HRH box 45, NP.

2. Nixon, *Memoirs,* p. 607.
3. Reinaldo Pico testimony, SSC executive session, November 20, 1973, pp. 30–34, NA.
4. Nixon memo to Haldeman, January 8, 1969, HRH box 229, NP; withdrawn at Nixon's request, published in Oudes, *From: The President,* p. 1.
5. Nixon, *Memoirs,* p. 357.
6. Ehrlichman, *Witness to Power,* p. 52.
7. Nixon, *Memoirs,* p. 226.
8. Haldeman, *The Ends of Power,* p. 117.
9. Kissinger, *The White House Years,* p. 244.
10. Nixon, *Memoirs,* p. 334.
11. White, *The Making of the President 1972,* p. 363.
12. Nixon, *Memoirs,* p. 358.
13. Safire, *Before the Fall,* p. 166.
14. HJC SI book VII, 1: pp. 142–45.
15. Ibid.
16. HJC SI book VI, 1: p. 207.
17. Young, *Foreign Policy,* p. 263*fn.*
18. John Caulfield testimony, SSC executive session, March 16, 1974, p. 31; published HJC SI book VII, 1: p. 509.
19. Young, *Foreign Policy,* p. 247.
20. Nixon, *Memoirs,* p. 496.
21. Haldeman memo to Lawrence Higby, February 19, 1970; Nixon memo to Haldeman, March 2, 1970; Haldeman memo to Egil Krogh, March 4, 1970; HRH boxes 57, 70, 164, NP. In Oudes, *From: The President,* pp. 98, 103–4, 106.
22. Nixon, *Memoirs,* p. 457; Kissinger, *The White House Years,* p. 514.
23. Nixon, *Memoirs,* p. 460; Nixon memo to Haldeman, May 13, 1970, HRH box 229, NP; in Oudes, *From: The President* p. 127.
24. May 9, 1970, *Washington Star.*
25. Nixon memos to Haldeman, May 13, 1970; in Oudes, *From: The President,* pp. 127–35.

Chapter 2: "Dirty Tricks"

1. Tom Huston memo to Haldeman, August 12, 1969, HRH box 51, NP: published in Oudes, *From: The President,* p. 38.
2. Huston memo to Haldeman, July 16, 1970, HRH box 70, published in Oudes, *From: The President,* p. 147.
3. Huston testimony summary, executive session Senate Armed Services Committee, May 21, 1973; published HJC SI book VII, 1: pp. 376 et seq.
4. Haldeman, *The Ends of Power,* p. 152.
5. Huston memo to Haldeman, June 8, 1970, HRH box 70, NP; published in Oudes, *From: The President,* p. 141.

6. Huston plan memos, HJC SI book VII, 1: pp. 384 et seq.; Huston memo to Haldeman, July 10, 1970, HRH box 70, NP; published in Oudes, op. cit., p. 145.
7. Huston memo, first week of July 1970, supplied May 15, 1973 to executive session Senate Armed Services Committee; first published by John Dean SSC 3 Hearings: p. 1319.
8. Nixon, *Memoirs,* p. 474.
9. HJC SI book VII, 1: pp. 454–61.
10. Huston memo to Haldeman, July 11, 1970, HRH box 70, NP; published in Oudes, *From: The President,* p. 148.
11. Huston memo, August 5, 1970, SSC 3 Hearings: pp. 1325–29.
12. Huston memo to Colson staffer George Bell, January 25, 1971, CWC box 38, NP; published in Oudes, *From: The President,* p. 208.
13. John Dean, *Blind Ambition,* p. 9.
14. Lawrence Higby memo to Dean, August 10, 1970, HRH box 70, NP; published in Oudes, *From: The President,* p. 151.
15. Safire memo to Haldeman, August 4, 1970, SSC 21 Hearings: p. 9738.
16. Colson memo to Nixon, November 6, 1970, PPF box 6, NP; published in Oudes, *From: The President,* pp. 166–70.
17. Nixon, *Memoirs,* p. 496.
18. Nixon memo to Haldeman, January 14, 1971, HRH box 140, PPF box 3, NP.
19. Colson *Watergate* TV series interview, 1993.
20. Nixon, *Memoirs,* p. 677.
21. Ibid., p. 501.
22. Aitken, *Nixon: a Life,* p. 497.
23. May 5, 1971 NT, 9:55 A.M.–, p. 12, NP.
24. Speechwriter Bill Safire at the time was convinced that Nixon was more realistic about the press than he seemed, but later confessed, "I was wrong about that." When Nixon said that "the press is the enemy" he meant just that. Nixon wanted the media to be "hated and beaten," Safire wrote, and in devoting "his most combative instincts against what he saw to be an unelected unrepresentative elite, lay Nixon's greatest personal political weakness and the cause of his downfall" (Safire, *Before the Fall,* p. 343).
25. Nixon memo to Haldeman, May 9, 1971, HRH box 164, NP; published in Oudes, op. cit., pp. 250–54.
26. June 13–28, 1971, *The New York Times.*

Chapter 3: The Pentagon Papers

1. Nixon memo to Haldeman, June 15, 1971, PPF box 3, NP; in Oudes, *From: The President,* p. 270.
2. Nixon, *Memoirs,* p. 509.
3. Haldeman Action Paper, June 15, 1971, HRH box 112, NP; in Oudes, *From: The President,* p. 271.
4. Nixon, *Memoirs,* p. 510.

5. Griswold, *Ould Fields, New Corne,* p. 304; he misspells Gayler's name.
6. Ibid., p. 310.
7. Kissinger, *The White House Years,* p. 730.
8. Haldeman, *The Ends of Power,* pp. 154–55.
9. William C. Sullivan memo to William D. Ruckelshaus, May 11, 1973, HJC SI book VII, 2: pp. 692–96.
10. July 6, 1971 NT, 11:47 A.M.–12:45 P.M., p. 8, NP.
11. FBI interview of Mardian, May 10, 1973, HJC SI book VII, 2: p. 757.
12. October 8, 1971 NT, 10:04–10:06 A.M., p. 1, NP.
13. Nixon, *Memoirs,* p. 597.
14. Ibid., p. 513.
15. Ibid., p. 512.
16. Colson *Watergate* TV series interview, 1993; Caulfield SCC 22 Hearings: p. 10356; WSPF security files, NA; Dean, *Blind Ambition,* p. 38.
17. Colson affidavit, April 29, 1974, HJC NSI book IV: p. 49.
18. Colson notes, June 29, 1971, CWC box 18, NP; in Oudes, *From: The President,* p. 286.
19. Haldeman, *The Ends of Power,* p. 156.
20. Colson memo to Haldeman, June 25, 1971, CWC box 14, NP; in Oudes, *From: The President,* p. 283.
21. Haldeman memo, June 22, 1971, HRH box 112, NP; published in Oudes, *From: The President,* p. 278.
22. Patrick Buchanan memo to Ehrlichman, July 8, 1971, HJC book VII, 2: pp. 708–11.
23. Colson tape transcript, SSC 9 Hearings: pp. 3878–80.
24. Colson memo to Ehrlichman, July 6, 1971, HJC SI book VII, 2: pp. 706–7.
25. Hunt SSC 9 Hearings: p. 3662.
26. Hunt, *Undercover,* p. 148.
27. Cushman tape transcript, July 7, 1971, HJC SI book VII, 2: p. 728.
28. Hunt SSC 8 Hearings: pp. 3383–89.
29. CIA employee affidavit, May 18, 1973, HJC SI book VII, 2: p. 854.
30. SSC 9 Hearings: p. 3677; Hunt, *Undercover,* p. 178.
31. Ehrlichman affidavit, April 26, 1974, HJC SI book VII, 2: p. 805.
32. Ehrlichman, *Witness to Power,* p. 265.
33. Haldeman, *The Ends of Power,* p. 157.
34. Dr. Lewis J. Fielding affidavit, April 29, 1973, HJC SI book VII, 2: p. 975.
35. Young memo, July 21, 1971, HJC NSI book IV: p. 105.
36. Young memo, July 28, 1971, HJC NSI book IV: p. 122.
37. Donald Santarelli *Watergate* TV series interview, 1992.
38. Liddy, *Will,* pp. 203–4.
39. Colson memo to Ehrlichman, July 22, 1971, CWC box 15, NP; in Oudes, *From: The President,* p. 299 (marking indicates Nixon was briefed on memo's contents).
40. Liddy, *Will,* p. 203.
41. CIA Director of Security Howard Osborne affidavit, May 9, 1973, HJC SI book VII, 2: pp. 900–4.

42. Ibid.; Helms testimony, Senate Foreign Relations Committee, in HJC SI book VII, 2: p. 898.
43. J. Edgar Hoover letter to Krogh, August 3, 1971, SSC 6 Hearings: p. 2655.
44. Hunt grand jury testimony, June 6, 1973, HJC SI book VII, 2: p. 979.
45. Hunt memo to Colson, July 28, 1971, SSC 9 Hearings: p. 3886.
46. Krogh and Young memo to Colson, August 3, 1971, SSC 9 Hearings: p. 3893.
47. Krogh grand jury testimony, January 30, 1974, HJC SI book VII, 2: pp. 983–84; Young grand jury testimony, August 22, 1973, HJC SI book VII, 2: p. 987.
48. Ehrlichman SSC 6 Hearings: p. 2548.
49. April 18, 1973 NT, 3:05–3:23 P.M., p. 9, NP.
50. Ehrlichman affidavit, April 30, 1974, HJC NSI book IV: p. 63.
51. SSC 1 Hearings: p. 372.
52. Haldeman, *The Ends of Power*, p. 195; Hougan, *Secret Agenda*, p. 29.
53. Hunt, *Undercover*, p. 167. Hunt's book contains so many inaccuracies that caution is advised.
54. Hunt testimony, SSC 9 Hearings: p. 3711.
55. Liddy, *Will*, p. 226.
56. Ibid., p. 227.
57. Young memo to Ehrlichman, August 26 1971; Ehrlichman memo to Colson, August 27, 1971, HJC SI book VII, 2: pp. 1215–20.
58. Liddy *Watergate* TV series interview, 1993.
59. Liddy, *Will*, p. 229.
60. Had the raid really failed? Although Krogh and Young were told they got nothing on Ellsberg, there was later testimony that the team did find his files. Dr. Fielding, alerted the next evening by the police to the break-in, rushed to his office. The police form records that Dr. Fielding reported nothing missing. But he later filed an affidavit claiming that Ellsberg's files had been "thoroughly rummaged through," and testified that sheets were outside the envelopes he had left them in and "had been fingered over."

    Certainly the CIA's second and more detailed psychological profile on Ellsberg contained the CIA psychiatrist's suggestive observation on "the highly competent kind of analysis with which it can be said with certainty that he was treated . . ." (Fielding affidavit, HJC SI book VII, 2: p. 97; CIA assessment of Ellsberg, HJC SI book VII, 3: pp. 1415–20.)
61. Krogh grand jury testimony, January 30, 1974, HJC SI book VII, 3: p. 1313.
62. HJC SI book VII, 3: pp. 1315–16.
63. Ehrlichman grand jury testimony, June 8, 1973, HJC SI book VII, 3: p. 1327.
64. Colson interview WSPF, August 16, 1973; WSPF security files, NA.
65. HJC SI book VII, 3: p. 1330.
66. CIA assessment, HJC SI book VII, 3: pp. 1415–20.
67. HJC SI book VII, 2: p. 1129.
68. SSC 9 Hearings: p. 3672; Hunt, *Undercover*, p. 179.
69. Ehrlichman note, September 18, 1971, HJC SI Appendix III: p. 197.
70. Ibid.: p. 209.

71. Lukas, *Nightmare*, p. 115.
72. HJC SI Appendix III: p. 209.
73. One other person read Hunt's fabricated dispatch, believed it, and was sickened. L. Patrick Gray, speaking after he had been disgraced and reduced to seeming Nixon's fool, as acting FBI director, testified, "I was ashamed of what I read in that dispatch to believe that my government would be involved in that kind of effort to assassinate the president of another nation." Gray was a Roman Catholic; it was the anti-Kennedy effect Nixon intended (SSC 9 Hearings: p. 3485).

Chapter 4: From SANDWEDGE to GEMSTONE

1. SSC The Final Report: p. 240.
2. Ibid.: p. 248.
3. Liddy, *Will*, p. 251.
4. Gordon Strachan general political matters memo to Haldeman, July 1, 1971, HJC SI Appendix IV: p. 21.
5. Strachan memo to Haldeman, September 18, 1971, HJC SI Appendix IV: p. 9.
6. Strachan memo to Haldeman, October 7, 1971, HJC SI Appendix IV: pp. 20–21.
7. Strachan memo to Haldeman, October 11, 1971; Higby memo to Dean, October 19, 1971; Strachan memo to Higby, October 20, 1971, HRH, NP.
8. Strachan talking paper for Haldeman's October 28, 1971 meeting with Mitchell, HJC Appendix IV: p. 45.
9. Dean memo to Mitchell, January 12, 1972, SSC 3 Hearings: p. 1149.
10. Liddy, *Will*, p. 237.
11. October 8, 1971 NT, 10:40–10:46 A.M. pp. 1–2, NP. Incidentally, Ehrlichman on this tape terms the Kissinger taps "illegal"—so much for Nixon's public insistence they were "lawful."
12. Ibid., p. 4, NP.
13. October 25, 1971 NT, 12:35–2:05 P.M., p. 2, NP.
14. Liddy, *Will*, pp. 251–52.
15. Ibid., p. 253.
16. Ibid., p. 254.
17. Krogh *Watergate* TV series interview, 1993.
18. December 14, 1971, *The Washington Post*.
19. May 18, 1977, *The Washington Post*.
20. Ehrlichman tape transcript, December 22, 1971, published in Colodny and Gettlin, *Silent Coup*, p. 445.
21. Ehrlichman SSC 6 Hearings: p. 2533.
22. Haldeman note, December 22, 1971, HRH, NP.
23. Ehrlichman note, December 23, 1971, HJC SI Appendix III: p. 214; Haldeman note, December 31, 1971, HRH, NP; Ehrlichman, *Witness to Power*, p. 281.

24. Young, *Foreign Policy*, p. 289.
25. Kissinger, *Years of Upheaval*, p. 808.
26. Young, *Foreign Policy*, p. 20.
27. Liddy, *Will*, pp. 268–69.
28. Ibid., pp. 266–67.
29. Hunt, *Undercover*, p. 186; Magruder SSC 2 Hearings: p. 793.
30. Liddy, *Will*, p. 260; Magruder, *An American Life*, p. 203.
31. Liddy, *Will*, p. 262.
32. Ibid., p. 165.
33. Liddy *Watergate* TV series interview, 1993.
34. Liddy, *Will*, p. 265.
35. Buchanan memo to Mitchell and Haldeman, January 11, 1972, HRH Buchanan file, NP.
36. Liddy, *Will*, p. 265.
37. Ibid., p. 273.
38. Ibid.
39. Dean SSC 3 Hearings: p. 930.
40. Mitchell SSC 4 Hearings: p. 1610.
41. Liddy, *Will*, p. 276.
42. McCord, *A Piece of Tape*, p. 17.
43. McCord interview with the author, November 1993.
44. Liddy, *Will*, p. 280.
45. Ibid., p. 281.
46. Magruder SSC 2 Hearings: p. 839.
47. Dean SSC 3 Hearings: pp. 930–31. (In late February, Liddy did again approach Dean at the White House, but Dean claimed he cut him short.)
48. Ibid., p. 930.
49. Colodny and Gettlin, *Silent Coup*, make much of Haldeman's desk diary showing him in Key Biscayne on February 4, 1972, but he wasn't: Haldeman notes and Nixon's phone log of February 4, 1972, NP.
50. SSC The Final Report: pp. 160–61.
51. SSC The Final Report: p. 192; Haldeman note, June 13, 1972, HRH box 45, NP.
52. April 14, 1973 NT, 8:55–11:31 A.M., p. 18, NP.
53. Liddy, *Will*, p. 291.
54. Dr. Edward M. Gunn interview by WSPF, filed October 21, 1975, WSPF security files, NA.
55. Liddy, *Will*, p. 289.
56. Ibid., pp. 289–91.
57. Liddy *Watergate* TV series interview, 1993.
58. Liddy, *Will*, p. 293.
59. Magruder, *An American Life*, p. 227.
60. Liddy, *Will*, pp. 291–92.
61. Ibid., p. 292.
62. Hunt SSC 9 Hearings: p. 3684.

63. Strachan political matters memo to Haldeman, February 16, 1972, HJC SI Appendix IV: p. 92.
64. Magruder SSC 2 Hearings: p. 793; Magruder, *An American Life*, p. 213.
65. Colson memo to Mitchell, February 28, 1972, CWC box 131, NP; in Oudes, *From: The President*, p. 371.
66. April 21, 1971 NT, 4:18–6:13 P.M., p. 2, NP.
67. Magruder testimony, 1974 trial of *United States* v. *Mitchell et al.;* court transcript, p. 4517.
68. Mitchell SSC 4 Hearings: p. 1614.
69. LaRue SSC 6 Hearings: p. 2281.
70. Strachan SSC 6 Hearings: p. 2453.
71. Ibid.: p. 2454.
72. Strachan talking paper for Haldeman's meeting with Mitchell, April 4, 1972, HRH J. Dean file, NP.
73. Haldeman SSC 8 Hearings: pp. 3036–37.

Chapter 5: The Money Trail

1. Haldeman note, April 5, 1972, HRH box 45, NP.
2. Haldeman note, April 29, 1972, HRH box 45, NP.
3. Robert A. Reisner SSC 2 Hearings: p. 493.
4. Magruder, *An American Life*. p. 234.
5. Hunt, *Undercover*, p. 197.
6. Hugh W. Sloan, Jr., SSC 2 Hearings: pp. 540–41.
7. Maurice H. Stans SSC 2 Hearings: p. 697.
8. SSC The Final Report. pp. 446, 581, 870, 905 et seq.
9. In vain does Nixon still deny ever "selling ambassadorships." The very day in 1974 he announced his denial, Kalmbach pleaded guilty to doing so and got immunity on all other charges. He was hardly acting in his own behalf.
10. The case of seeking but not asking for the London embassy is even odder. Walter Annenberg, the kindly wealthy Nixon backer who had been ambassador to Britain since 1969, gave $254,000 more to the 1972 Nixon campaign, and stayed on. He might not have known that another Nixon close friend coveted the post. W. Clement Stone, a Chicago insurance multimillionaire, pledged Kalmbach $3 million for the 1972 campaign. Stone's son-in-law saw Colson at the White House in early April 1972, Colson reported in an EYES ONLY memo to Mitchell:

    > He mentioned that Clem very much wants to be our Ambassador to Great Britain after the election . . . obviously Clem should make his desires known to you and Maury Stans . . . I gather he simply expects that he will be picked as the best man available in the country and therefore he needn't ask. I am therefore simply advising you that he very much wants it but will not ask for it.

    Watergate intervened. Annenberg's eventual successor was Elliot Richardson (Colson memo to Mitchell, April 24, 1972, CWC box 48, NP; in Oudes, *From: The President*, pp. 426–27).

11. Liddy, *Will*, p. 297.
12. Hougan, *Secret Agenda,* p. 12 et seq.; McCord interview with the author, 1993.
13. McCord interview with the author, November 1993.
14. McCord interview with the author. A still mysterious blunder, involving Liddy, McCord, and New York Republican advertising men calling themselves the November Group, at this point nearly blew the plan to bug the DNC. Both Jack Anderson and the Democrats themselves got wind of the plan. But the story got garbled, and in the end no action was taken. Anderson never ran it, and the Democrats decided to take no countermeasures.
15. McCord SSC 1 Hearings: p. 164.
16. October 25, 1971 NT, 12:35–2:05 P.M.; p. 4, NP.
17. Haldeman note of phone call from Kleindienst, May 2, 1972, HRH box 45, NP.
18. It later emerged that Hoover's aides had narrowly interpreted Kleindienst's order and sealed solely the actual office; the supporting office suite, open to his staff, contained 104 linear feet of files marked "personal and confidential" and "official and confidential." Miss Helen Gandy, Hoover's secretary since World War I, later testified to a congressional committee that she had gone through them and destroyed those she thought not pertinent. The inquiry never established exactly what happened, although there were many suspicions (Hougan, *Secret Agenda,* p. 133; inquiry into the destruction of Former FBI Director J. Edgar Hoover's files and FBI record keeping, 94th Congress, 1st session, 1975; Harvard *Crimson,* November 10, 1973).
19. Liddy *Watergate* TV series interview, 1993.
20. Lukas, *Nightmare,* p. 203.
21. Colson oral history interview, June 15 and 21, 1988, by Fred J. Graboske, a NARA staff member who listened to and indexed all the Nixon tapes, NP.
22. Colson *Watergate* TV series interview, 1993.
23. Handwritten Colson note, May 15, 1972; memo for the record, May 16, 1972, CWC, NP; oral history interview, 1988, NP.
24. Liddy, *Will,* p. 313.
25. Hougan, *Secret Agenda,* p. 155. McCord, having sat through Baldwin's subsequent testimony without challenge, now suggests his colleague was mistaken—no bugging was listened to until the following week, McCord claims (1993 interview with the author).
26. Hougan, *Secret Agenda,* effectively explodes the version of the first break-in told at the time. It was never properly investigated, mainly because the FBI, federal prosecutors, and eventually congressional committees became, understandably, more interested in political responsibilities than in forensic detail. Hougan's is the most thorough exposé of all the break-in anomalies. His revisionist version raises perhaps more questions than it answers and Hougan honestly admits ending up in many a cul-de-sac. But it is troubling that after twenty years some of the simpler questions about the break-in remain unanswered.
27. Liddy, *Will,* p. 313. Even though McCord (agreeing with Hougan) now says

that he knew nothing about an alarm, the point is that all concerned seemed to believe there was one, acted accordingly, and were stymied.

28. Liddy, *Will*, p. 319.
29. McCord interview with the author, 1993. McCord added that since the team had made so much noise getting the main door off he did not wish to risk more noise in picking the lock on O'Brien's office. He had not said this in 1973.
30. Barker *Watergate* TV series interview, 1993.
31. Haldeman note, June 13, 1972, HRH box 45, NP. Buchanan/[K.] Khachigian "assault strategy" memo to Haldeman, June 8, 1972, HRH box 137, NP; in Oudes, *From The President*, p. 463.
32. McCord interview with the author, 1993.
33. Liddy, *Will*, p. 325.
34. Ibid. O'Brien, who died in 1990, remained skeptical of the Magruder scenario. He said he had not known about Hughes's secret contributions to Nixon via Rebozo. "If I had, you wouldn't have had to break into my office to get it. I would have told the whole world," J. Anthony Lukas reported him saying, in the introduction to his 1988 Penguin edition of *Nightmare*.
35. Hougan, *Secret Agenda*, also traces a conspiracy involving the suspicious movements on June 16–17 of what he calls Watergate's "sixth man," Louis Russell. Russell, coincidentally associated with Congressman Richard Nixon in the 1948 House of Representatives Un-American Activities Committee investigation of Alger Hiss, had fallen on hard times. He was a drinker involved with call girls. He was also a part-time informant for Jack Anderson, a recent employee of the security firm guarding Watergate, and at this point being paid a retainer by McCord Associates! Hougan claims that Russell was McCord's aide in deliberately sabotaging the Watergate break-in. It was sabotaged, Hougan speculates, to protect from discovery the bugging of a call girl operation McCord and Russell were conducting against the Columbia Plaza apartments—in line of sight from both the DNC and the Howard Johnson's. That bugging, Hougan theorizes, was being conducted by the CIA and/or other intelligence agencies.

    The sabotage was of course not meant to include the arrest of McCord; that was a mistake. Russell confirmed his presence at the Howard Johnson's on the evening of June 16 in an otherwise inconclusive interview with the FBI (WSPF security files, NA). He died of a heart attack the day he was summoned to appear at the Senate Watergate Committee in July 1973. McCord told the author in 1993 that he had used Russell for "personnel" background checks, which he was good at.

    See also Colodny and Gettlin, *Silent Coup*, to whom a file on the federal call girl case was passed by associates of John Mitchell (Jerris Leonard *Watergate* TV series interview, 1992).
36. Magruder SSC 2 Hearings: p. 797.
37. Reisner SSC 2 Hearings: p. 494.
38. Colson *Watergate* TV series interview, 1993. In impeachment inquiry testimony in July 1974 (HJC TW book III: pp. 255–56), Colson claimed Mitchell

said it jokingly, but by the main cover-up trial in late 1974 he testified it was why he believed that Mitchell had been responsible for the Watergate bugging.

39. Liddy, *Will*, p. 327.
40. Hunt, *Undercover*, p. 233.
41. Ibid., p. 237.
42. Report of the Inquiry into the Alleged Involvement of the Central Intelligence Agency in the Watergate and Ellsberg Matters, 94th Congress, 1st session ("Nedzi Report"), quoted in Hougan, *Secret Agenda*, p. 267*n*.
43. Anderson, *The Anderson Papers*, p. 128.
44. McCord, *A Piece of Tape*, p. 29.
45. Liddy, *Will*, p. 333.
46. Martinez *Watergate* TV series interview, 1993.
47. In his 1993 *Watergate* TV series interview McCord stated on camera that he *did* retape the doors! Given his extraordinary exertions to deny it twenty years earlier and his admission only that he failed to remove someone else's retaping, this casual new admission is a real test for his Christian veracity. When the author reminded him of his earlier version, McCord suggested he would have to consult his 1973 book; even so, he stuck with his new admission when videotaped the next day.
48. McCord, *A Piece of Tape*, p. 30.
49. Leeper SSC 1 Hearings: p. 114.
50. Liddy, *Will*, p. 336.
51. Baldwin SSC 1 Hearings: p. 406.

Chapter 6: The Lost Weekend

1. Hunt, *Undercover*, p. 249.
2. Liddy, *Will*, p. 340.
3. Ibid., p. 341; Sloan SSC 2 Hearings: p. 577.
4. Liddy, *Will*, p. 343; Magruder, *An American Life*, p. 250.
5. Liddy, *Will*, p. 344.
6. Seymour Glanzer notes of interviews with Magruder, April 13–14, 1973, WSPF files box 72, NA; SCC 2 Hearings: p. 798.
7. Magruder, *An American Life*, p. 254.
8. Reisner *Watergate* TV series interview, 1993.
9. Colodny and Gettlin, *Silent Coup*, p. 168; Magruder *Watergate* TV series interview, 1993. (The Rev. Magruder, a Presbyterian minister, insisted that the TV interview be taped with him wearing vestments and sitting in front of the altar of his church in Lexington, Ky.)
10. Liddy, *Will*, p. 346.
11. Kleindienst testified that he telephoned Petersen saying that those arrested at Watergate "should be given no treatment different than anybody who might have been arrested in circumstances of that kind." Petersen testified he "thought it a little odd that he should make that statement because I did not know any other way to treat them" (SSC 9 Hearings: p. 3613). But Petersen's

prosecutors never knew. Assistant U.S. Attorney Silbert stated, "Neither Mr. Kleindienst not Mr. Moore ever conveyed the fact of this meeting to this office until Mr. Moore did so in early April 1973. Had either done so the results of the first investigation may have been completely different" (Silbert memo to Archibald Cox, June 7, 1973, WSPF, p. 21, NA).

The *FBI Watergate Investigation*, the analysis of the FBI's Office of Planning and Evaluation (FBI Archive), read at pp. 54–55:

> It is difficult not to find fault with the failure of Kleindienst to immediately advise the Bureau of Liddy's contact with him which occurred just a few hours after the DNCH break-in. Had he done so there is no doubt our investigative direction at CRP would have been vastly different. First we would not have had to conduct an exhaustive investigation to identify Liddy as we had to. Secondly, it is easy to speculate that the successful cover-up would have never gotten off the ground since we would have had reason to zero in on Mitchell and Liddy rather than waste our time checking into McCord's security set-up and security co-workers at CRP. That investigation did not lead to involvement of any other security people and in effect a waste of time.

12. Kleindienst *Watergate* TV series interview, 1993.
13. Nixon, *Memoirs*, p. 627.
14. Aitken, *Nixon: a Life*, pp. 496–97.
15. FBI Airtel, June 17, 1972, no. 139-4089-9, p. 9 FBI.
16. Ibid., p. 6 FBI.
17. Bernstein and Woodward, *All the President's Men*, p. 18.
18. Helms *Watergate* TV series interview, 1993.
19. FBI Airtel, June 17, 1972, no. 139-4089-10, FBI.
20. Mardian *Watergate* TV series interview, 1993.
21. LaRue, *Watergate* TV series interview, 1993. For the first time, LaRue disclosed his terrible foreboding that day. His wife noticed: "Fred, what's wrong with you?" She said, "You look strange. You look like you're really upset about something. I said, "I just can't talk about it right now but something has occurred that could very well bring down this administration."
22. Magruder, *An American Life*, p. 260.
23. Hunt, *Undercover*, p. 251.
24. Nixon, *Memoirs*, p. 626.
25. Colson *Watergate* TV series interview, 1993.
26. Haldeman, *The Ends of Power*, p. 31.
27. Ibid., p. 34.
28. LaRue *Watergate* TV series interview, 1993.
29. Hunt, *Undercover*, p. 253.
30. *FBI Watergate Investigation*, p. 29, FBI.
31. Baldwin *Watergate* TV series interview, 1993.
32. Walter Pincus, June 17, 1992, *The Washington Post*.
33. Dean *Watergate* TV series interview, 1993.

Chapter 7: Instant Cover-up

1. Haldeman note, June 19, 1972, HRH box 45, NP.
2. Magruder, *An American Life,* p. 265.
3. Ehrlichman, *Witness to Power,* p. 317.
4. Hunt, *Undercover,* p. 255.
5. Liddy, *Will,* p. 357.
6. Ehrlichman *Watergate* TV series interview, 1993.
7. Robert Bennett in a deposition, April 19, 1973 (cited HJC SI book II: pp. 220–21) said that Liddy phoned him 3:30–4 P.M. to tell Hunt the signals had changed.
8. Dean, *Blind Ambition,* p. 95.
9. Dean, HJC TW book II: p. 329.
10. Dean, *Blind Ambition,* p. 96.
11. Nixon, *Memoirs,* p. 627.
12. Magruder, *An American Life,* p. 267.
13. Ibid., p. 268.
14. Earl J. Silbert memo to Archibald Cox, June 7, 1973, WSPF files, NA.
15. Angelo Lano *Watergate* TV series interview, 1993.
16. C. W. Bates's "running" FBI headquarters memorandum of investigation: June 21, 1972 reference to Kunkel theory. In 1992, Kunkel was added to the long list of those asserted to be the mysterious source Deep Throat. It is possible, yet problematic. Woodward and Bernstein have now stated that when Deep Throat dies they will reveal his identity; Kunkel died in 1992 and they are silent.
17. Haldeman note, June 19, 1972, HRH box 45, NP.
18. Haldeman telephone notes, June 20, 1972, HRH boxes 29–30, NP.
19. Kleindienst, *Justice,* pp. 148–50; Ehrlichman's office log records that from 9:55–10:30 A.M. the meeting was "joined by Kleindienst." Kleindienst's memory is not infallible, however. His book also states that the Watergate trial ended well before the 1972 election—it only began two months afterward!
20. Dean SSC 3 Hearings: pp. 937–38; *Blind Ambition,* pp. 109–10, 180–81.
21. Ehrlichman, *Witness to Power,* p. 318.
22. Strachan SSC 6 Hearings: p. 2458.
23. Haldeman, *The Ends of Power,* p. 44.
24. Haldeman notes, June 20, 1972. HRH box 45, NP.
25. *NBC Nightly News,* June 20, 1972, quoting Democratic sources.
26. Haldeman note, June 20, 1972, HRH box 45, NP.
27. June 20, 1972 Nixon tape, 4:35 P.M. NP; partial transcript by *Watergate* TV series. The quality of the tape is very poor, as were most of the recordings done in Nixon's EOB office. Coincidentally, this tape includes discussion of how "extremely good" is the quality of the Oval Office taping—"super secure," says Nixon.
28. FBI teletype, June 17, 1972, no. 139-4089-9, p. 6, FBI.
29. Mardian SSC 6 Hearings: p. 2362.

30. LaRue *Watergate* TV series interview, 1993.
31. November 6, 1973 draft of statement to Judge Sirica and in Nixon, *Memoirs*, p. 634, although *Memoirs* omits the first sentence and adds the elision marks. Also unmentioned in *Memoirs* is that when the Dictabelt was handed to Sirica, the prosecutors discovered a twenty-five-second "live" pause following that dictation, as if the president was holding back.
32. Haldeman note, June 20, 1972, HRH box 45, NP. Wrongly, Haldeman states in his book that because Nixon called from the residence there is no tape. But in the president's daily diary the call is logged from the president's EOB office; assuming the tape had not—again—run out, it is unexplained why the National Archives did not in 1993 release it along with the others of that period.
33. Haldeman *Watergate* TV series interview, 1993.
34. June 21, 1972 Nixon tape, 9:30–10:38 A.M., segment 1–4, released for listening only May 1993, NP; partial transcript by *Watergate* TV series.
35. *FBI Watergate Investigation,* p. 11, FBI.
36. Kleindienst SSC 9 Hearings: p. 3564.
37. Mirto *Watergate* TV series interview, 1993.
38. Baldwin *Watergate* TV series interview, 1993.
39. June 22, 1972 Nixon tape, 9:40 A.M., released May 1993, NP; Partial transcript by *Watergate* TV series.
40. Mitchell's telephone logs are not complete. Frequently, important home phone calls were not logged at Mitchell's end—like the president's call on June 20, 1972.
41. June 23, 1972 NT, 10:04–11:39 A.M., p. 3, NP.
42. Ibid., p. 7, NP. The conversation ranged wide, including the fact that the British government had floated the pound, to which Nixon replied, "I don't care about it. Nothing we can do about it." And when told of speculation against the Italian currency, he replied, "I don't give a shit about the lira."
43. Nixon's obsession with the Bay of Pigs needs explaining. First, he had been vice president when the operation to overthrow Castro had been planned. As a presidential candidate in 1960, he had been infuriated when the Democratic candidate, Kennedy, had been given a top CIA briefing. He was even more infuriated when Kennedy exploited this briefing in a TV debate, coming out for action against Castro when Nixon felt inhibited by secrecy from responding.

    That was part of the background. More recently, Nixon had been infuriated by Helms. The previous autumn, in 1971, as part of Nixon's post–Pentagon Papers vendetta against the Democrats, he had demanded that Helms hand over to Ehrlichman the files on the Bay of Pigs, "or else," as Ehrlichman's notes recorded.

    Nixon's clear hope was to find something even more humiliating against the Kennedys and the Democrats—as if the public debacle of the CIA-supported invasion was not enough. Although Helms was told that the president must have all the facts to be able to deal with questions, the CIA director declined to hand the files to Ehrlichman and asked to see Nixon.

The meeting was held on October 8, with Ehrlichman present for part of the time. Ehrlichman's notes show the pressure Helms was exposed to; the president had to know the full facts for his upcoming summits in China and Moscow. Nixon vowed he would neither hurt the CIA nor attack his predecessor, President Johnson. Helms replied that there was only one president at a time and he worked only for Nixon. Helms allowed that he had found a document, but it was only fragments. The president, saying that Ehrlichman was his lawyer (actually, it was Dean at this time), wanted Helms "to deal with Ehrlichman as you would with me." Ehrlichman said, "I'll be making additional requests," to which Helms had replied, "Okay, anything."

But it was not to be. When Ehrlichman read the materials, he found they were indeed fragmentary, incomplete, and according to Nixon's memoirs the full file was never supplied. "The CIA was closed like a safe and we could find no one who would give us the combination . . ." So now Nixon again wanted to play on Helms's nerves over the Bay of Pigs and get his fingers dirty in Watergate.

In *Memoirs,* p. 641, Nixon gives a different but revealing rationale for the June 23 meeting: "If the CIA would deflect the FBI from Hunt, they would thereby protect us from the only White House vulnerability involving Watergate that I was worried about exposing—not the break-in, but the political activities Hunt had undertaken for Colson." He did not explain.

44. Haldeman, *The Ends of Power,* p. 67.
45. Ehrlichman, *Witness to Power,* p. 315.
46. Helms memo to Walters, June 28, 1972. HJC SI book II: p. 459.

Chapter 8: Payoffs and Perjury

1. June 30, 1972 Nixon tape, 3:28 P.M., segment 4, released for listening 1993, NP; partial transcript by *Watergate* TV series.
2. June 30, 1972 Nixon tape, 3:28 P.M., segment 2, released 1993, NP; partial transcript by *Watergate* TV series.
3. Haldeman had reported to Nixon on June 24, as revealed in the first Nixon tape ever released from a Camp David telephone, that Walters, after delivering Friday's message to Gray, said that there was no problem with the director (presumably Helms); June 24, 1972, 2:29 P.M., released 1993, NP; partial transcript *Watergate* TV series.
4. Vernon A. Walters SSC 9 Hearings: p. 3409.
5. O'Brien later claimed that he believed, initially, that the money was coming from the CIA. O'Brien also said that Bittman, at a July 6 conference on the case, told Mardian that Hunt was saying that Liddy had CRP "superiors" in the operation. O'Brien did nothing at the time but later testified at the House Judiciary Committee impeachment hearings that he took it to be an implied threat by Hunt.
6. SSC 9 Hearings: p. 3898.
7. June 28, 1972 Nixon tape, 11:16 A.M., released 1993, NP; partial transcript by *Watergate* TV series.

8. Nixon, *Memoirs,* p. 649.
9. June 28, 1972 Nixon tape, 11:16 A.M., released 1993, partial transcript by *Watergate* TV series.
10. June 30, 1972 NT, 12:57–2:10 P.M., pp. 1–2, NP. HJC SI book II: pp. 514–6 has a different version.
11. June 30, 1972 Nixon tape, 3:28 P.M., released 1993, NP. The attribution of the quote was difficult to establish by the *Watergate* TV series transcriber, but it is affirmed in the National Archives log of the conversation.
12. June 30, 1972 Nixon tape, 4:30–6:19 P.M., released 1993, NP; partial transcript by *Watergate* TV series.
13. Bates FBI "running" memo, reference June 28, 1972, p. 6, FBI.
14. Nixon, *Memoirs,* p. 651.
15. Ibid., p. 1062.
16. Ehrlichman notes, July 8, 1972, JDE box 6–7, NP.
17. Ehrlichman, *Witness to Power,* p. 325; to buttress this 1982 account is Ehrlichman's contemporary note of May 1973. [Nixon]: "Did I know about it sooner? (Nod by E—no sound) . . . if so it made no impression" (HJC SI Appendix III: p. 263).
18. Ehrlichman notes, July 8, 1972. JDE box 6–7, NP.
19. Parkinson examination, trial *United States* v. *Mitchell et al.,* 1974.
20. Magruder, *An American Life,* p. 272.
21. Baldwin *Watergate* TV series interview, 1993.
22. Dean SSC 3 Hearings: p. 952.
23. Ehrlichman notes, July 31, 1972, JDE box 6–7, NP.
24. Hougan, *Secret Agenda,* speculating that McCord was bugging phones connected to the DNC but not inside the Watergate, suggests that the "September bug" was crudely planted by the Democrats.
25. Ehrlichman note, July 8, 1972, JDE box 6–7, NP.
26. September 15, 1972 NT, 5:27–6:17 P.M., p. 1, NP.

Chapter 9: Dean Takes Charge

1. June 26, 1972 Nixon tape, 9:50–10:45 A.M., segment 1, released 1993, NP; partial transcript by *Watergate* TV series.
2. Nixon, *Memoirs,* p. 682.
3. September 15, 1972 NT, 5:27–6:17 P.M., p. 11, NP.
4. Dean memo to Dwight Chapin, September 8/9(?), 1972; meeting arranged for September 25, HRH box 45–47, NP.
5. Haldeman notes made in July 1973 after listening to September 15, 1972 tape; obtained from grand jury in HJC SI book II: p. 639.
6. June 3, 1973 *Frankfort State Journal,* in Stanley I. Kutler, *The Wars of Watergate,* p. 233.
7. Bernstein and Woodward, *All the President's Men,* p. 105.
8. Nixon, *Memoirs,* p. 711.
9. October 25, 1972 George McGovern TV address.

10. Kissinger, *The White House Years,* p. 1407.
11. January 7, 1973, *Washington Star.*
12. Breslin, *How the Good Guys Finally Won,* p. 11.
13. November 13 or 14, 1972 transcript of Dictabelt recording by Colson of phone conversation with Hunt; exhibit 35A in trial of *United States* v. *Mitchell et al.,* NARA; also published in SSC 9 Hearings: pp. 3888–91.
14. Ibid.
15. November 14, 1972, memo by Hunt and his wife. Full text in Congressional Quarterly's *Watergate: Chronology of a Crisis,* p. 99-A. Both Hunt and his lawyer Bittman swore it did not exist until Hunt, on October 28, 1974, confessed on the witness stand during the Watergate cover-up trial that he had indeed given it to Bittman two years earlier. Bittman's law partners in Hogan and Hartson had concurred in suppressing it, but in early November it was produced before an enraged Judge Sirica, who gave Bittman an uncomfortable time in court. (See Doyle, *Not Above the Law,* pp. 382–386.)
16. Liddy, *Will,* p. 376.
17. SSC 9 Hearings: pp. 3841–42.
18. Dean did not disclose his criminal destruction of evidence during five days of testimony to the Senate Watergate Committee, nor did he, during six months of dealings, tell the prosecutors; only after he had bargained his guilty plea to lesser charges in October 1973 did he confess.
19. Liddy, *Will,* pp. 379–80.
20. Nixon, *Memoirs,* p. 745.
21. Ibid., pp. 745–46.
22. January 8, 1973 NT, 4:05–5:34 P.M., p. 5, NP.
23. Haldeman note, January 9, 1973, HRH box 45–47, NP.
24. SSC 9 Hearings: pp. 3834–39.
25. McCord SSC 1 Hearings: p. 132.
26. Haldeman note, January 13, 1973, HRH box 45–47, NP.
27. Caulfield SSC 1 Hearings: p. 254.
28. Sirica, *To Set the Record Straight,* p. 88.
29. Haldeman note of conversation with Dean, January 8, 1973, marked "P," meaning drawn to the president's attention, HRH box 45–47, NP.
30. Silbert *Watergate* TV series interview, 1993.
31. Judge Sirica statement at bail hearing, February 2, 1973; in Dash, *Chief Counsel,* p. 5.
32. January 8, 1973 NT, 4:05–5:34 P.M., p. 11, NP.
33. Ehrlichman note, November 22, 1972, JDE box 6–7, NP.
34. March 13, 1973 NT, 12:42–2 P.M., p. 1, NP.
35. February 13, 1973 NT, 9:48–10:52 A.M., p. 7, NP.
36. February 14, 1973 NT, 10:15–10:49 A.M., p. 18, NP.
37. Dean memo to Nixon, February 20 or 21, 1973, SSC 3 Hearings: p. 1245; also, with the Nixon handwritten notation "file John Dean," PPF box 7, NP; in (with incorrectly surmised dates) Oudes, *From: The President,* pp. 585–86.

38. February 23, 1972 NT, 9:36–10:05 A.M., p. 14, NP.
39. February 13, 1973 NT, 9:48–10:52 A.M., p. 3, NP.
40. Dean *Blind Ambition*, p. 182.
41. February 16, 1973 NT, 9:08–9:38 A.M., p. 26, NP.
42. Ehrlichman tape of telephone call with Dean, March 7 or 8, 1973, SSC 7 Hearings: pp. 2950–51.
43. Nixon, *Memoirs*, p. 779.

Chapter 10: "I'm Not Gonna Let Anybody Go to Jail"

1. February 23, 1972 NT, 9:36–10:05 A.M., p. 8, NP.
2. Ibid., p. 9, NP.
3. February 23, 1973 NT, 10:08–10:52 A.M., p. 30, NP.
4. Ibid.
5. *Time* magazine had the scoop and it led to a demonstrable lie by Mitchell. The story had the detail that Mitchell, when attorney general, authorized the taps, which was true. Kleindienst first learned of the secret taps from *Time* and decided to issue a press release. Initially he checked with his old boss and buddy, Mitchell, and, based upon his response, issued the following statement:

   > I state further that I have the strongest personal assurance from Mr. Mitchell that he never authorized or was asked to authorize the implementation of such devices against reporters on White House orders.

   Years later Kleindienst asked Mitchell why he "misinformed me." Secrecy, came the answer. "That explanation did not satisfy me then, and it does not now" (Kleindienst, *Justice*, p. 233).
6. February 28, 1973 NT, 9:12–10:23 A.M., p. 25, NP.
7. The tape of February 27, 1973 was not among Nixon's edited versions of his Watergate conversations released in 1974. He made it seem as if he only began meeting Dean the next day, February 28.
8. February 28, 1973 NT, 9:12–10:23 A.M., p. 48, NP.
9. March 1, 1973 NT, 9:18–9:46 A.M., p. 15, NP.
10. March 13, 1973 NT, 12:42–2 P.M., p. 66, NP.
11. Ibid., p. 59, NP.
12. Ibid., p. 53, NP.
13. David Shapiro memo for the file, March 16, 1973, HJC TW book III: p. 328.
14. Dean, *Blind Ambition*, p. 192.
15. Paul L. O'Brien HJC TW book I: p. 128.
16. Dean, *Blind Ambition*, p. 198.
17. Nixon, *Memoirs*, pp. 790–91.
18. March 17, 1973 NT, 1:25–2:10 P.M., p. 6, NP.
19. March 21, 1973 NT, 10:12–11:55 A.M., NP.
20. The Watergate special prosecutor established proof in returning indictments

in *United States* v. *Mitchell et al.*—which proof was passed to the House Judiciary Committee. LaRue knew he had arranged the "drop" after giving a dinner party. One of his guests from Cincinnati could prove by airline tickets and lodging receipts from a Washington club that the date indeed was March 21. After dinner, LaRue gave another dinner guest an envelope containing the $75,000 and he made the drop.

21. Krogh grand jury testimony, HJC SI book III, 2: p. 1278.
22. Nixon, *Memoirs,* p. 790.
23. Liddy, *Will,* p. 399; In a 1993 interview with the author McCord says he saw the true Christian light again as soon as he was arrested in June 1972. When it was remarked that he had subsequently left jail to burn incriminating evidence, he smiled and claimed that he had still kept making mistakes. "The Holy Spirit was talking to me but I was not listening," he said, but he was by March 1973.
24. McCord interview with special prosecutors, February 27, 1974, WSPF security files, NA.
25. Sirica, *To Set the Record Straight,* p. 97.
26. *United States* v. *Liddy et al.,* transcript of proceedings, March 23, 1973: pp. 39–40; also in HJC SI book IV, 1: pp 232–33.
27. Nixon, *Memoirs,* p. 803.
28. Haldeman notes, March 23, 1973, HRH box 47, NP.
29. Ibid.
30. Nixon, *Memoirs,* p. 803.
31. Dash, *Chief Counsel,* p. 27.
32. Haldeman notes, March 27, 1973, HRH box 47, NP. Haldeman records Mitchell passing on a tip he had received from the senior partner of the law firm that first represented McCord. F. Lee Bailey, Mitchell says, told him how Fensterwald telephoned to say, "We don't give damn re McC we're after R. Nixon."
33. Haldeman note, March 26, 1973, HRH box 47, NP.

Chapter 11: A Modified Limited Hangout

1. March 21, 1973 NT, 5:20–6:01 P.M., p. 17, NP.
2. March 22, 1973 NT, 9:11–10:35 A.M., p. 38, NP.
3. March 22, 1973 NT, 1:57–3:43 P.M., pp. 59–60, NP.
4. March 20, 1973 NT, 6:00–7:10 P.M., p. 11, NP.
5. *The Washington Post,* under Woodward's byline, lifted it from its joint syndication wire with only passing credit to Jackson's scoop.
6. Haldeman note, March 24, 1973, HRH box 47, NP.
7. Haldeman note, March 25, 1973, HRH box 47, NP.
8. Nixon, *Memoirs,* pp. 804–5.
9. Ibid., p. 805.
10. Haldeman note, March 25, 1973, HRH box 47, NP.
11. Haldeman note, March 24, 1973, HRH box 47, NP.

12. Haldeman notes, March 26, 1973, HRH box 47, NP.
13. Nixon, *Memoirs,* p. 806. Nixon omits saying that the call never happened. Ziegler's statement, however, went uncorrected until the press secretary eventually ventured it was he who had embellished it. But Haldeman's notes of the president's instructions to Ziegler include "I called Dean" (March 26, 1972, HRH box 47, NP).
14. Transcript of Dean's recording of conversation with Magruder, March 26, 1973, SSC 3 Hearings: p. 1258.
15. Haldeman note of Dean phone call, March 26, 1973, HRH box 47, NP.
16. Haldeman note, March 27, 1973, HRH box 47, NP.
17. March 27, 1973 NT, 11:10 A.M.–1:30 P.M., p. 15, NP.
18. Ibid., p. 51, NP.
19. March 27, 1973 WHT, 11:10 A.M.–1:30 P.M., *The Presidential Transcripts,* p. 209.
20. March 27, 1993 NT, 11:10 A.M.–1:30 P.M., p. 46, NP.
21. Haldeman note, March 28, 1973, HRH box 47, NP. Only the worry over Mitchell's suicide, however, has never been elaborated. Of all the books, it is mentioned only in Dean, *Blind Ambition,* attributed, two weeks later, to LaRue.
22. Haldeman note, March 27, 1973, HRH box 47, NP.
23. Haldeman note, March 28, 1973, HRH box 47, NP. The note has Mitchell quoting Colson "specifically L. O'Brien info re Fla dlgs." (Whether those were Florida dealings undertaken by DNC Chairman Lawrence O'Brien or info that O'Brien had on Nixon's has never been explained—although O'Brien denied ever knowing about the Hughes contributions held in Florida by Rebozo.)
24. Haldeman note, March 28, 1973, HRH box 47, NP.
25. Dean, *Blind Ambition,* p. 222.
26. Ibid., p. 224; cf Dean SSC 3 Hearings: p. 1007.
27. Dean, *Blind Ambition,* p. 224.
28. Haldeman note, March 28, 1973, HRH box 47, NP.
29. Silbert memo to Cox, June 7, 1973, NA.
30. Haldeman note of phone call from Agnew, March 29, 1973, HRH box 47, NP.
31. Ehrlichman note, March 30, 1973, JDE box 6–7, NP.
32. Reisner *Watergate* TV series interview, 1993.
33. Magruder, *An American Life,* p. 344. The "impeach" quote was not in Reisner's 1973 Senate testimony, though in the 1993 *Watergate* TV series interview he affirmed it.
34. Haldeman note of phone call from Agnew, March 31, 1973, HRH box 47, NP.

Chapter 12: The Linchpin

1. Dean HJC TW book II: p. 254.
2. Dean, *Blind Ambition,* p. 229.

3. Haldeman note, April 2, 1973, HRH box 47, NP.
4. Ibid.
5. Haldeman note, April 4, 1973, HRH box 47, NP.
6. Ibid.
7. Ibid.
8. Haldeman note, April 5, 1973, HRH box 47, NP.
9. Ibid.
10. Ehrlichman's notes of this meeting—and past examples show his notes to be less full than Haldeman's—contain a rare written identification of the "commitments" so much talked of and never queried, if Watergate testimony is to be believed. The note reads, "L commitment ¬EK; H ditto ¬CC"; Ehrlichman translated "Liddy had a commitment from Krogh . . . Hunt had a commitment from Colson, and these commitments, I took it, related to executive clemency." Ehrlichman makes clear he has it at third hand; O'Brien, relating to him what Magruder said, stated that a check with Krogh did not bear out the claim (SSC 7 Hearings: pp. 2922–32).
11. Nixon, *Memoirs,* pp. 813–14, Haldeman's film, *Watergate* TV series, 1994.
12. Haldeman note, April 5, 1973, HRH box 47, NP.
13. HJC TW book III: p. 564.
14. Haldeman note of phone call with Dean, April 7, 1973, HRH box 47, NP.
15. Dean SSC 3 Hearings: p. 1010. Oddly, although Haldeman made no note of such a remark, before he died he accepted he had made it! (*Watergate* TV series interview 1993.)
16. Haldeman note, April 8, 1973, HRH box 47, NP.
17. April 8, 1973 WHT, 7:33 P.M.; *The Presidential Transcripts,* p. 230. This version incorrectly times it at 7:33 *A.M.* when they were still in California and there was no taping system.
18. Nixon, *Memoirs,* p. 823. Nixon's view was that this was common practice for state governors. "I said facetiously to Haldeman when he told me about it, 'Thank God I was never elected governor of California.' "
19. Haldeman notes, April 10, 1973, HRH box 47, NP.
20. Kissinger, *Years of Upheaval,* p. 90.
21. Ibid., p. 76.
22. SSC 3 Hearings: p. 1308.
23. Haldeman note, April 11, 1973, HRH box 47, NP.
24. Colson HJC TW book III: p. 434.
25. April 12, 1973 NT, 7:31–7:48 P.M., p. 13, NP.
26. Curiously, Haldeman in his 1977 book, *The Ends of Power,* pins this panic about Hunt on Dean, saying it was disinformation from the prosecutors. But there in Haldeman's notes of April 13, 1973 (HRH box 47, NP) it was definitely Colson, as it was again when he and Ehrlichman discussed it with Nixon the next day (April 14, 1973 NT, 8:55–11:31 A.M., p. 2, NP).
27. Transcript of Higby calls to Magruder, April 13, 1973, HJC SI book IV, 2: p. 654.
28. HJC SI book IV, 2: p. 612.
29. Ehrlichman notes of meeting with Colson and David Shapiro, April 13, 1973;

SSC 7: p. 2933. The "blood oath" is indistinct at the foot of the page, but in his testimony Ehrlichman went over the notes, clearly explaining (SSC 7 Hearings: p. 2801).

30. Haldeman note, April 13, 1973, HRH box 47, NP.
31. Ibid.
32. April 14, 1973 NT, 8:55–11:31 A.M., NP.
33. Kissinger, *Years of Upheaval,* p. 75. (Kissinger and Haig, especially, were to make this "theft" of the election a piece of recurrent special pleading.)
34. Ibid., pp. 78–79.
35. Nixon, *Memoirs,* p. 822.
36. Haldeman tape of Magruder, April 14, 1973, HJC SI book IV, 2: p. 714.
37. April 14, 1973 NT, 1:55–3:55 P.M., pp. 6–7, NP.
38. Transcript of Ehrlichman tape of meeting with Mitchell, April 14, 1973, HJC SI book IV, 2: pp. 725–68.
39. SSC 3 Hearings: p. 1312.
40. Dean, *Blind Ambition,* p. 253.
41. April 14, 1973 NT, 2:24–3:55 P.M., NP.
42. April 14, 1973 WHT, approximately 6 P.M.; *The Presidential Transcripts,* pp. 340–45.
43. April 14, 1973 NT, 5:15–6:45 P.M., NP.
44. Nixon, *Memoirs,* p. 822.
45. April 14, 1973 NT, 11:02–11:16 P.M., pp. 3–4, NP.
46. April 14, 1973 NT, 11:22–11:53 P.M., pp. 21–22, NP.

Chapter 13: A Procrastination Too Far

1. Kleindienst, *Justice,* p. 160. Curiously, at his earlier Ervin testimony, Kleindienst claimed he had gone home early.
2. Glanzer *Watergate* TV series interview, 1993.
3. April 15, 1973 NT, 10:35–11:15 A.M., p. 12, NP. Ehrlichman accurately characterizes the timid state of press coverage at this stage with virtually everything, despite McCord, still secret, but Nixon is not deluded:

   Ehrlichman: We are at a kind of ebb tide right now in this whole thing, in terms of the media as I see it. They are all a little afraid to get too far out on a limb on this because they think something's going on with the committee negotiations, and there's no news breaking, and so they are kind of—

   Nixon: waiting . . . They'll get a full tide when they get to the grand jury . . . (WHT, *The Presidential Transcripts,* p. 375).
4. April 15, 1973 WHT, 1:12–2:22 P.M.; *The Presidential Transcripts,* pp. 376–402. Nixon's handwritten note of the meeting, HJC SI book IV, 2: p. 929.
5. Ehrlichman note, April 15, 1973, JDE box 8, NP.
6. Ehrlichman's *Witness to Power* is no help. He says, for instance, that only after 9 P.M. did Nixon tell him "he'd just been told by Henry Petersen about

the contents of Hunt's safe." This is obviously incorrect, as his own notes prove. A Haldeman note of an evening meeting, which included Ehrlichman, places this at 7:45 P.M. Interestingly, Nixon's own notes of both his 2:20 P.M. meeting with Kleindienst and his 4 P.M. meeting with Petersen record a mention of "Gray's documents," meaning that he had already twice discussed Hunt's safe beforehand.

But Haldeman's account in *The Ends of Power* of how Nixon first told him about Dean's treachery is even more illuminating. He places Nixon being shocked about Dean at the president's meeting with Petersen—whereas the Kleindienst tape shows he had told Nixon one and a third hours earlier. What is clear from Haldeman's notes of the 7:45 P.M. meeting is that Nixon there recounts details about Dean he learned at both the two afternoon meetings. So this evidence suggests strongly that Haldeman and Ehrlichman were not promptly apprised of the dire threat Dean posed to them—either Nixon did not have the heart to tell them or the president wanted to ponder how it affected his own fate.

7. Silbert later contradicted Petersen; the previous day Glanzer had met Shaffer (not Dean) and told him the prosecutors were thinking of insisting on a guilty plea (Silbert memo to Cox, May 31, 1973, WSPF files, p. 4, NA).
8. Haldeman note, April 15, 1973, HRH box 47, NP.
9. Nixon, *Memoirs,* p. 827.
10. HJC TW book III: p. 82.
11. Nixon, *Memoirs,* p. 827.
12. That same evening, Kissinger arranged his secret meeting over in the main White House offices with George Shultz and Arthur Burns. Having learned from Ehrlichman that Mitchell had the major responsibility for the crisis, Kissinger now implies that he believed Nixon, too, was involved. "It simply was not credible . . . that Nixon's paladins had acted totally on their own." Shultz and Burns, he says, were at first unbelieving at the storm about to break. They agreed to keep in touch and try saving the republic. "Presumptuous as it may seem, we thought a duty had fallen on us to preserve as much moral substance for the national government as could be salvaged" (Kissinger, *Years of Upheaval,* p. 80).
13. Haldeman notes, April 15, 1973, HRH box 47, NP. This version, taken down at the time, differs slightly from the version given by Dean SSC 3 Hearings: p. 1313, and on WHT, *The Presidential Transcripts,* pp. 410–11.
14. Nixon's handwritten notes, HJC SI book IV, 2: pp. 1047–48. The "not improper" reference is in Haldeman's note of debriefing Nixon, immediately Dean had left (April 15, 1973, HRH box 47, NP).
15. SSC 3 Hearings: p. 1017.
16. Nixon's handwritten notes, HJC SI book IV, 2: p. 1048.
17. SSC 3 Hearings: p. 1046.
18. Haldeman notes, April 15, 1973, HRH box 47, NP.
19. Ehrlichman tape of conversation with Gray, March 7 or 8, 1973, SSC 7 Hearings: p. 2950.

20. Gray grand jury testimony, July 20, 1973, HJC SI book IV, 2: pp. 1074–75.
21. Nixon, *Memoirs,* p. 829.
22. April 15, 1973 WHT, 11:45–11:53 P.M.; *The Presidential Transcripts,* pp. 416–17.
23. Haldeman notes of midnight phone call from Nixon, April 15, 1973, HRH box 47, NP.

Chapter 14: Crack-up

1. Haldeman notes, April 17 and 18, 1973, HRH box 47, NP.
2. Haldeman note, April 17, 1973, HRH box 47, NP.
3. Ibid.
4. March 21, 1973 NT, 10:12–11:25 A.M., p. 29, NP.
5. Haldeman note, April 17, 1973, HRH box 47, NP.
6. April 16, 1973 NT, 10:00–10:40 A.M., p. 39, NP.
7. Ehrlichman tape of conversation with Colson, April 17, 1973, HJC SI book IV, 3: p. 1330.
8. April 16, 1973 WHT, 1:39–3:25 P.M.; *The Presidential Transcripts,* p. 474.
9. Nixon, *Memoirs,* p. 831.
10. April 16, 1973 NT, 10:00–10:40 A.M., p. 24, NP.
11. April 17, 1973 NT, 3:50–4:35 P.M., p. 21, NP.
12. Haldeman notes, April 18, 1973, HRH box 47, NP.
13. HJC TW book III: p. 97. (This is the fullest account Petersen gave.)
14. April 16, 1973 WHT, 3:27–4:04 P.M.; *The Presidential Transcripts,* p. 502; NT, p. 5, NP. The latter transcript of the same tape, produced by WSPF, has "unintelligible" where the Nixon-edited transcript puts the word "Hunt" in Ehrlichman's mouth.
15. SSC 9 Hearings: pp. 3875–76.
16. April 16, 1973 WHT, 8:58–9:14 P.M.; *The Presidential Transcripts,* p. 519.
17. April 17, 1973 WHT, 2:46–3:19 P.M.; *The Presidential Transcripts,* p. 588.
18. Ibid., p. 586.
19. HJC SI book VII, 4: p. 1930.
20. Petersen grand jury testimony, HJC SI book VII, 4: p. 1966.
21. Ehrlichman, *Witness to Power,* p. 371.
22. April 19, 1973 NT, 10:12–11:07 A.M., pp. 1, 5, NP.
23. HJC SI book VII, 4: p. 1966.
24. SSC 9 Hearings: p. 3631.
25. Ibid.: p. 3644.
26. Haldeman note, April 25, 1973, HRH box 47, NP.
27. April 25, 1973 NT, 7:25–7:39 P.M., pp. 1, 11, NP.
28. Haldeman note, April 26, 1973, HRH box 47, NP.
29. Transcript of *United States* v. *Russo* in HJC SI book VII, 4: pp. 1999–2004.
30. April 26, 1973 NT, 3:59–9:03 P.M., p. 33, NP.
31. April 17, 1973 NT, 5:20–7:14 P.M., pp. 49, 52, NP.
32. Haldeman note, April 17, 1973, HRH box 47, NP.

33. April 26, 1973 NT, 3:59–9:03 P.M., pp. 67–68, NP.
34. Haldeman note, April 23, 1973, HRH box 47, NP.
35. April 25, 1973 NT, 11:06 A.M.–1:56 P.M., p. 28, NP.
36. Haldeman notes, April 26, 1973, at tape counter number 367, HRH box 47, NP. Haldeman testified to the opposite in SSC 7 Hearings: p. 2897.
37. April 26, 1973 NT, 3:59–9:03 P.M., pp. 33–123 and 147–48, NP.
38. SSC 9 Hearings: p. 3492.
39. April 27, 1973 WHT, 5:37–5:43 P.M.; *The Presidential Transcripts,* pp. 667–70.
40. SSC 9 Hearings: p. 3632.
41. April 25, 1973 NT, 6:57–7:14 P.M., p. 11, NP.
42. Haldeman note, April 27, 1973, HRH box 47, NP.
43. Nixon, *Memoirs,* p. 846.
44. Haldeman note, April 29, 1973, HRH box 47, NP.
45. Nixon, *Memoirs,* pp. 845–46.
46. Haldeman, *The Ends of Power,* pp. 374–75.
47. Ehrlichman, *Witness to Power,* p. 357.
48. Haldeman said he was hurt when he learned from a Nixon TV interview in 1977 that he had used the same speech with Ehrlichman. At the time he had felt kinship with Nixon; after the TV admission it was just a conversational ploy (Haldeman, *The Ends of Power,* p. 375). Nixon never did explain to Ehrlichman's children.
49. Nixon, *Memoirs,* pp. 847–48.
50. Haldeman notes, April 29, 1973, HRH box 47, NP.
51. Kleindienst, *Justice,* p. 168.
52. Richardson *Watergate* TV series interview 1993.

Chapter 15: Testimony

1. Nixon, *Memoirs,* pp. 850–51.
2. Young, *Foreign Policy,* pp. 312 et seq.
3. Cox *Watergate* TV series interview, 1993.
4. Order establishing Office of WSPF, *Federal Register,* June 4, 1973, p. 14688.
5. Silbert memo to Cox, June 7, 1973, WSPF files, NA.
6. Baker *Watergate* TV series interview, 1993.
7. Dash, *Chief Counsel,* p. 118.
8. Nixon, *Memoirs,* pp. 868, 874.
9. Dean SSC Executive Session, June 16, 1973. Unpublished but declassified September 17, 1992, Legislative Archive, NA.
10. Dash, *Chief Counsel,* p. 155.
11. Nixon, *Memoirs,* p. 893.
12. Ibid., p. 899.
13. Baker *Watergate* TV series interview, 1993.
14. Hamilton *Watergate* TV series interview, 1993.
15. Nixon, *Memoirs,* p. 900.

16. Haig testimony, court hearing, December 5, 1973, in HJC SI book IX, 1: pp. 385–87.
17. Eisenhower, *Pat Nixon,* p. 627. Patrick Buchanan also advised Nixon to destroy the tapes.
18. Nixon, *Memoirs,* p. 901.
19. Ibid., p. 903.
20. Richardson affidavit, HJC SI book IX, 1: p. 405.
21. Ibid.
22. Cox, *Courts and the Constitution,* p. 10.
23. Cox *Watergate* TV series interview, 1993.
24. April 18, 1973 NT, 3:05–3:23 P.M., p. 9, NP.
25. Young grand jury testimony, August 23, 1973, HJC SI book VII, 4: p. 1846.
26. Young memo of meeting with Ehrlichman, April 30, 1973, originally produced in SSC executive session; in HJC SI book VII, 4: p. 2037.
27. Breslin, *How the Good Guys Finally Won,* pp. 41–43.

Chapter 16: Sirica Rules

1. Haig still wishes Nixon had defied Congress on Vietnam and Cambodia and fought on to the end, risking impeachment on the war issue on which Haig reckons—unlike Watergate—he might have carried the day (Haig, *Inner Circles* p. 314).
2. Nixon, *Memoirs,* p. 932.
3. Nixon's reply brief, August 17, 1973, U.S. District Court, District of Columbia; Cox's argument, August 22, 1973, at court hearing (Congressional Quarterly, *Watergate,* pp. 293–94).
4. Letters September 20, 1973 by Wright and Cox to U.S. Court of Appeals for the District of Columbia (Congressional Quarterly, *Watergate,* p. 317). Nixon reply brief to U.S. Court of Appeals, September 19, 1973 (Congressional Quarterly, *Watergate,* p. 317).
5. Doyle, *Not Above the Law,* p. 122.
6. Bork *Watergate* TV series interview, 1993. The secret of the Moorer-Radford scandal had also at the same time been conveyed to the Watergate Committee senators and staff. Amazingly, even though mention was repeatedly made of "another national security matter," they all kept the secret.
7. Bork *Watergate* TV series interview 1993.
8. Ibid.
9. Nixon, *Memoirs,* p. 916.
10. Breslin, *How the Good Guys Finally Won,* pp. 60–61.
11. Richardson, *The Creative Balance,* p. 103.
12. *Newsweek* magazine in the spring of 1974; quoted here by Hartmann, *Palace Politics,* p. 117.
13. October 10, 1973 published as House Document No. 93-7; *Impeachment, Selected Materials.*

14. Richardson affidavit to impeachment inquiry, June 17, 1974, HJC SI book IX, 1: p. 332.

Chapter 17: Massacre

1. Nixon, *Memoirs,* p. 929.
2. Haig, *Inner Circles,* p. 368.
3. Nixon, *Memoirs,* p. 918.
4. Leonard Garment. Neither Garment's nor Haig's 1992 account were, of course, available for the otherwise excellent and exhaustive case history *The Saturday Night Massacre,* published by The Kennedy School of Government, Harvard University, 1977 (revised 1983).
5. Haig, *Inner Circles,* p. 394.
6. Richardson, *The Creative Balance,* p. 40.
7. Ibid., pp. 39–40.
8. Doyle, *Not Above the Law,* p. 143.
9. Haig, *Inner Circles,* p. 395.
10. Richardson letter to Senator Charles Mathias, November 30, 1973, SJC Saxbe nomination Hearings: pp. 77–79.
11. Richardson, *The Creative Balance,* p. 40.
12. Cox, *Courts and the Constitution,* p. 19.
13. Ibid., p. 17.
14. Cox's comments on Richardson's proposal, October 18, 1973, SJC 1 Special Prosecutor Hearings: p. 9.
15. Nixon, *Memoirs,* p. 931.
16. Haig, *Inner Circles,* p. 399.
17. SJC 1 Special Prosecutor Hearings: p. 9.
18. Supplied by WSPF to HJC SI book IX, 2: pp. 795–96.
19. Richardson, *The Creative Balance,* p. 41 (italics in original).
20. Lukas, *Nightmare,* p. 587.
21. Haig, *Inner Circles,* pp. 399–400.
22. Garment *Watergate* TV series interview, 1993.
23. Nixon, *Memoirs,* p. 932.
24. Richardson, *The Creative Balance,* p. 42.
25. The remark was first published by Aaron Latham, "Seven Days in October," April 29, 1974, *New York* magazine.
26. Cox, *Courts and the Constitution,* p. 23.
27. December 5, 1973, *The Washington Post.*
28. Garment *Watergate* TV series interview, 1993.
29. Latham, "Seven Days in October."
30. Richardson, *The Creative Balance,* p. 44; Nixon, *Memoirs,* p. 934.
31. Latham, "Seven Days in October."
32. Haig, *Inner Circles,* p. 419.
33. Bork *Watergate* TV series interview, 1993.

34. Doyle, *Not Above the Law,* p. 193.
35. Ibid., p. 171.
36. Ibid., p. 194.
37. Kissinger, *Years of Upheaval,* p. 552.
38. Sirica, *To Set the Record Straight,* pp. 167–80.
39. Haig, *Inner Circles,* p. 419.
40. Ibid., p. 420.
41. Ibid., p. 407.
42. Nixon, *Memoirs,* p. 937. See Nixon, *In the Arena,* pp. 40–1, on learning of Democrats' contingency plan.

Chapter 18: The Missing Tapes

1. Kissinger, *Years of Upheaval,* p. 581.
2. Haig, *Inner Circles,* p. 423.
3. Garment *Watergate* TV series interview, 1993.
4. Haig, *Inner Circles,* pp. 425–28.
5. Nixon, *Memoirs,* p. 946.
6. Garment *Watergate* TV series interview, 1993.
7. WSPF interview of J. Fred Buzhardt, February 28, 1975, WSPF security files, NA.
8. Haig, *Inner Circles,* p. 428.
9. Nixon, *Memoirs,* p. 948.
10. Haig, *Inner Circles,* pp. 431–32.
11. Nixon, *Memoirs,* p. 949.
12. Doyle, *Not Above the Law,* p. 254.
13. Nixon, *Memoirs,* pp. 950–51.
14. Sirica, *To Set the Record Straight,* p. 198.

Chapter 19: Nixon's "Enemy Within"

1. Ben-Veniste and Frampton, *Stonewall,* pp. 201–5.
2. Jaworski oral history, Baylor University, Texas, vol. II, p. 551; vol. IV, p. 1080.
3. March 21, 1973 NT, 10:12–11:55 A.M., p. 89, NP.
4. Doyle, *Not Above the Law,* p. 265.
5. Jaworski oral history, vol. II, p. 514.
6. Nixon, *Memoirs,* p. 944.
7. Jaworski oral history, vol. II, p. 554.
8. Jaworski, *The Right and the Power,* p. 54.
9. Silberman memo of phone calls, April 30, 1974, WSPF security file, NA.
10. Nixon, *Memoirs,* p. 976.
11. Doyle, *Not Above the Law,* p. 328 (Government brief May 10, 1974 in *United States* v. *Mitchell et al.*, filed in camera.).
12. Doyle, *Not Above the Law,* p. 310.

13. Colson HJC TW book III: p. 363.
14. HJC SI book III, 1: pp. 354–56.
15. George Gross *Watergate* TV series interview, 1993.
16. Nixon, *Memoirs,* p. 946.
17. Haig, *Inner Circles,* pp. 446–47.
18. Ibid., p. 452.
19. Ibid., pp. 452–53.
20. Ben-Veniste and Frampton, *Stonewall,* p. 278. Haig especially resented Jaworski bringing Ben-Veniste along. In *Inner Circles,* he recounts his interrogation by the young prosecutor before the grand jury on February 25.
21. Ibid., p. 294; Haig interview with WSPF, July 3, 1975, WSPF security files, NA.
22. Haig, *Inner Circles,* pp. 454–55.
23. Nixon, *Memoirs,* p. 1001.
24. Ibid.
25. Jaworski oral history, vol. II, pp. 660–61.

Chapter 20: Only One Chance to Impeach

1. July 27, 1975 *Roanoke Times* article by Wayne Woodlief from transcripts of contemporaneous 1974 tape-recorded Butler interviews.
2. Colson HJC TW book III: p. 362.
3. The best treatment is in Hougan, *Secret Agenda.*
4. Nixon, *Memoirs,* p. 1042.
5. Unpublished interviews with coalition members taped by Father Don Shea and Tom Mooney, 1975.
6. O'Shea and Mooney interviews.
7. Nixon, *Memoirs,* p. 1050.
8. Haig, *Inner Circles,* p. 472.
9. Nixon, *Memoirs,* p. 1051.
10. Ibid., p. 1043.
11. Ibid., p. 1052.
12. Kissinger, *Years of Upheaval,* p. 1199.

Chapter 21: Endgame

1. Jack Germond, *The Washington Star,* cited in Nixon, *Memoirs,* p. 1040.
2. Kissinger, *Years of Upheaval,* p. 1198.
3. Nixon, *Memoirs,* pp. 1049, 1053.
4. Buzhardt interview with WSPF, February 28, 1975, WSPF security files, NA.
5. Nixon, *Memoirs,* p. 1052.
6. Jaworski, *The Right and the Power,* p. 208.
7. Nixon, *Memoirs,* p. 1053.
8. Doyle, *Not Above the Law,* p. 342.
9. Nixon, *Memoirs,* pp. 1053–54.

10. Ibid., pp. 1056–57.
11. Kissinger, *Years of Upheaval,* p. 1196.
12. Haig, *Inner Circles,* pp. 476–77; Nixon, *Memoirs,* p. 1057.
13. Kissinger, *Years of Upheaval,* p. 1198.
14. Haig, *Inner Circles,* pp. 477–78. Also on p. 517, fn, Haig confusingly quotes Jaworski saying of his (Haig's) efforts "he had a goal, to keep his President in office, and he tried."
15. Nixon, *Memoirs,* p. 1058.
16. Ford, *A Time to Heal,* p. 3.
17. Ibid., p. 4; Ford *Watergate* TV series interview, 1993.
18. Ford, *A Time to Heal,* p. 4.
19. Ibid., p. 6; Hartmann, *Palace Politics,* p. 131.
20. Ford, *A Time to Heal,* p. 9.
21. Haig, *Inner Circles,* p. 485.
22. Hartmann, *Palace Politics,* p. 135.
23. Ford *Watergate* TV series interview, 1993; Hartmann, *Palace Politics,* pp. 135–37; Ford, *A Time to Heal,* p. 13.
24. Haig, *Inner Circles,* pp. 483, 485–86.
25. Sirica, *To Set the Record Straight,* p. 271.
26. Eisenhower, *Pat Nixon,* p. 625.
27. Nixon, *Memoirs,* p. 1060.
28. Ibid., pp. 1060–61.
29. Ibid., p. 1061.
30. Ibid., p. 1062.
31. Ibid.
32. Haig, *Inner Circles,* p. 491.
33. Kissinger, *Years of Upheaval,* p. 1200.
34. Jaworski oral history, vol. IV, p. 1139.
35. Jaworski, *The Right and the Power,* p. 207.
36. January 16, 1974 WSPF memo, NA; Ben-Veniste and Frampton, *Stonewall,* p. 269.
37. Nixon, *Memoirs,* p. 1064. Out of this is born the myth, which Haig also nurtures, that nothing should be, or was, done to pressure Nixon. Certainly, no one can deny that recording the dubious "first" in American history of resigning the presidency was, literally, an awesome and agonizing decision. And no one can take away from Nixon that it was in the end done swiftly and uneventfully.

    Haig was certainly not loath to accept the great acclaim at the time for whatever he did to ease the final exit. He says himself he was asked to do things that no White House chief of staff has ever been asked. Kissinger, in saying that Haig's role "could not be filled by choirboys," pays him an enormous tribute in his *Years of Upheaval.* Without Haig's sustaining Nixon while moving him toward resignation, Kissinger says he doubted a "catastrophe" could have been avoided. Yet Kissinger totally disagrees with Haig's analysis.

Haig, a proud man of vaulting ambition, has not, even twenty years on, in his *Inner Circles,* done a very lucid job of explaining what he was about. He starts from the insistence that nothing was to be done to deny the president "due process" and that nothing damage the American system. He argues that it would be like a "banana republic" to have Republican congressional leaders go in to tell Nixon to resign. He finally states that it would substitute a British-type parliamentary system for the American separation of powers for Congress to be able to oust an elected president by withdrawing its support.

Kissinger, in *Years of Upheaval,* wrote that "impeaching the president was not the same as a parliamentary vote of no confidence . . ." Nixon had to resign "because his own judgment of the national interest dictated it. Or else he should be brought to this realization by elected officials." And Kissinger goes further: He credits Haig with doing the very thing Haig denies—"He was encouraging old friends of the President who had stood by him in difficult times to tell him frankly about the prospects in Congress" (p. 1205).

38. Nixon, *Memoirs,* p. 1066.
39. Ibid. Kissinger, *Years of Upheaval,* p. 1204, has it differently: "We are not here to offer excuses for what we cannot do. We are here to do the nation's business," he claims to have said, seeking to draw the painful proceedings to a close and preserve Nixon's self-respect.
40. Kissinger, *Years of Upheaval,* p. 1205.
41. Ford, *A Time to Heal,* p. 22.
42. Nixon, *Memoirs,* p. 1080.
43. Ibid., pp. 1067–68.
44. Haig, *Inner Circles,* pp. 495–96.
45. Kissinger, *Years of Upheaval,* p. 1205.
46. Nixon, *Memoirs,* pp. 1068–70.
47. Kissinger, *Years of Upheaval,* p. 1203.
48. Haig, *Inner Circles,* p. 498.
49. Ford, *A Time to Heal,* p. 22.
50. Nixon, *Memoirs,* pp. 1072–73.
51. Kutler, *The Wars of Watergate,* p. 545.
52. Kissinger, *Years of Upheaval,* pp. 1206–7, 1209.
53. Ibid., pp. 1207–10.
54. As bureau chief of *The Times* of London, the author's problem was the time difference, London being five hours ahead and first edition deadline around 3 P.M. Washington time. Top Republican congressional sources confirmed to me the O'Neill story. My first edition story was hard, it had all the details and led, "President Nixon is set to announce his resignation tonight." Still, the London office was not satisfied. An assistant editor wanted assurance so that the paper could carry that night a special supplement on the Nixon years. I replied that I was a reporter, not a prophet, but I tried to get more. Good White House sources I had developed were not returning calls.

    I thought of a young staffer I had met, who was genial and an Anglophile. He also worked in the virtually defunct White House Office of Communications, then as now. I called David Gergen. I explained my problem. I didn't want to quote him, but I wanted to help London with their decision on the special supplement. Gergen wouldn't be quoted but said, "Fred, there are moving vans in Executive Drive." The point was that the press at the White House was that afternoon rigorously confined inside the press room; from there you could see nothing. Gergen's was the confirmation we needed; the special, not unsympathetic to Nixon's achievements, ran from the first edition, 4:35 P.M. Washington time, four hours ahead of Nixon's broadcast.

55. Jaworski, *The Right and the Power*, pp. 217–19.
56. Nixon, *Memoirs*, p. 1080, Haig, *Inner Circles*, p. 501.
57. Ben-Veniste and Frampton, *Stonewall*, p. 296.
58. Jaworski oral history, vol. II, p. 675.
59. Nixon, *Memoirs*, pp. 1081–82.
60. Jaworski, *The Right and the Power*, p. 220.
61. Nixon, *Memoirs*, p. 1084; Kissinger, *Years of Upheaval*, p. 1212.
62. Nixon, *Memoirs*, pp. 1084–85.
63. Ibid., p. 1085.
64. Ibid., p. 1087.
65. Ibid., p. 1088; Kissinger, *Years of Upheaval*, p. 1213; Haig, *Inner Circles*, p. 505.
66. Eisenhower, *Pat Nixon*, p. 656.
67. Nixon, *Memoirs*, p. 1090.

Appendix I: John Mitchell's Plea

1. Conducted by Paul Mitchell, of Brian Lapping Associates, the production company making the *Watergate* TV series.
2. Nixon, *Memoirs*, p. 932.

Index

INDEX

INDEX

INDEX

INDEX

INDEX

INDEX

INDEX